Growing Perennials in Cold Climates

Also Published by the University of Minnesota Press

Gardening with Prairie Plants: How to Create Beautiful Native Landscapes
Sally Wasowski
Photography by Andy Wasowski

Trees and Shrubs of Minnesota
Welby R. Smith

Growing Fruit in the Upper Midwest
Don Gordon

Flowers for Northern Gardens
Leon C. Snyder Jr.

Gardening in the Upper Midwest
Leon C. Snyder Jr.

Trees and Shrubs for Northern Gardens
Leon C. Snyder Jr.
Photography by John Gregor

Wildflowers of the Northern Great Plains
F. R. Vance, J. R. Jowsey, J. S. McLean, and F. A. Switzer

Northland Wildflowers: The Comprehensive Guide to the Minnesota Region
John B. Moyle and Evelyn W. Moyle
Photography by John Gregor

Growing Perennials in Cold Climates

Mike Heger
Debbie Lonnee
and John Whitman

Revised and Updated Edition

University of Minnesota Press
Minneapolis
London

All photographs by John Whitman, with exception of the following:

Photographs by Mike Heger: *Aconitum* 'Spark's Variety' (page 12); *Cimicifuga* 'Atropurea' (page 77); *Dianthus superbus* (page 120); *Rudbeckia* 'Gold Drop' (page 326); *Sedum reflexum* (page 341).

Photographs by Debbie Lonnee: *Dicentra* 'Gold Heart' (page 124); *Echinacea* 'Coconut Lime' (page 130) and 'Sunrise' (page 134).

Photographs of these plants were furnished by the Netherlands Flower Bulb Information Center: *Narcissus* 'Acropolis,' 'Actaea,' 'Geranium' (page 280); *Tulipa* 'Angelique,' 'Fantasy,' 'General De Wet,' 'Groenland,' 'Juan,' 'Lilac Wonder,' 'Lustige Witwe,' 'Peach Blossom,' 'Queen of Bartignons,' 'Red Riding Hood,' 'Shakespeare,' 'Union Jack,' 'West Point' (pages 365–67).

Photographs by Donna Whitman: Grasses (page 172) and all photographs of John Whitman.

Page v: *Phlox divaricata* 'Chattahoochee,' *Hemerocallis* 'Satin Silk.' Page vi: *Clematis* 'Dr. Ruppel,' *Dicentra* 'Gold Heart.' Page vii: *Heliopsis helianthoides* 'Karat,' *Phlox* 'The King.' Page 1: *Iris* 'Lorilee.' Page 381: *Lilium* 'Connecticut King.'

Originally published in 1998 by Contemporary Books, a division of NTC/Contemporary Publishing Group, Inc.

First University of Minnesota Press edition, 2011

Published by the University of Minnesota Press
111 Third Avenue South, Suite 290
Minneapolis, MN 55401-2520
http://www.upress.umn.edu

Library of Congress Cataloging-in-Publication Data

Heger, Mike.
    Growing perennials in cold climates / Mike Heger, Debbie Lonnee, and John Whitman. — Rev. and updated ed.
       p.   cm.
    Originally published: Lincolnwood, Ill. : Contemporary Books, c1998.
    ISBN 978-0-8166-7588-3 (pb : alk. paper)
    1. Perennials—Snowbelt States. 2. Perennials—Canada. I. Lonnee, Debbie. II. Whitman, John, 1944–
III. Title.
    SB434.H425 2011
    635.9'32—dc22

                                2010047847

Printed in China on acid-free paper

The University of Minnesota is an equal-opportunity educator and employer.

18 17 16 15 14 13 12 11   10 9 8 7 6 5 4 3 2 1

CONTENTS

The Perennials
  by Common Name   VII

Acknowledgments   IX

Introduction   XI

Major Perennial Groups   XII

Part I. The Most Popular
        Perennials   I

1. Individual Listings   3

Achillea   5

Aconitum   12

Actaea   74

Alchemilla   18

Aquilegia   23

Artemisia   30

Asclepias   36

Aster   41

Astilbe   50

Baptisia   58

Campanula   63

Chelone   70

Chrysanthemum coccineum   344

Chrysanthemum corymbosum   344

Chrysanthemum × morifolium   104

Chrysanthemum–Rubellum Group   111

Chrysanthemum × superbum   234

Chrysanthemum weyrichii   111

Cimicifuga   74

Clematis   79

Coreopsis   91

Delphinium   97

Dendranthema × grandiflora   104

Dendranthema species   111

Dianthus   115

Dicentra   124

Doellingeria   41

Echinacea   130

Euphorbia   136

Eurybia   41

Ferns   141

Filipendula   153

Geranium   158

Grasses   167

Heliopsis helianthoides   180

Hemerocallis   184

Heuchera   193

Hosta   200

Hylotelephium   336

Iris (Bearded)   210

Iris (Siberian)   222

Lamium maculatum   229

Leucanthemum–Superbum Group   234

Liatris   240

Lilium   246

Lysimachia   261

Monarda 266
Narcissus 272
Nepeta 284
Oenothera 289
Paeonia 294
Phlox 304
Platycodon grandiflorus 315
Pulmonaria 320
Rudbeckia 326
Salvia 331
Sedum 336
Symphyotrichum 41
Tanacetum 344
Thermopsis 349
Tradescantia 354
Tulipa 359
Veronica 373

PART II. THE BASICS OF GROWING PERENNIALS 381

2. Understanding Perennials 383

How Perennials Grow 383
Buying Perennials 383

3. Selecting and Preparing a Site 385

Soil and Light 385
Soil and Moisture 386
Spacing 389
Companion Planting and Good Design 389

4. Planting Perennials 393

Buying Bare Root Plants 393
Planting Bare Root Perennials 393
Buying Potted Perennials 394
Planting Potted Perennials in the Garden 395
Planting Potted Perennials in Large Pots 396
Transplanting 396

5. Caring for Perennials 398

Water 398
Mulch (Summer) 399
Fertilizing 401
Weeding 403
Staking 404
Deadheading 405
Pruning 406
Winter Protection 407

6. Solving Perennial-Growing Problems 409

Diseases and Insects 409
Marauders 413

7. Propagating Perennials 415

Sexual Propagation 415
Asexual or Vegetative Propagation 416

8. Special Uses for Perennials 419

Cut Flowers and Foliage 419
Dried Flowers, Foliage, and Seed Heads 420
Perennials as Food 421

9. Tools and Supplies 422

Glossary 424

The Perennials by Common Name

Balloon Flower (see *Platycodon grandiflorus*)   315
Bearded Iris (see *Iris*, Bearded)   210
Bee Balm (see *Monarda*)   266
Bellflower (see *Campanula*)   63
Bleeding Heart (see *Dicentra*)   124
Bugbane (see *Cimicifuga*)   74
Catmint (see *Nepeta*)   284
Caucasian Daisy (see *Tanacetum*)   344
Columbine (see *Aquilegia*)   23
Coneflower (see *Rudbeckia*)   326
Coral Bells (see *Heuchera*)   193
Cranesbill (see *Geranium*)   158
Creeping Phlox (see *Phlox*)   304
Daffodil (see *Narcissus*)   272
Daylily (see *Hemerocallis*)   184
Dead Nettle (see *Lamium maculatum*)   229
Evening Primrose (see *Oenothera*)   289
False Indigo (see *Baptisia*)   58
False Lupine (see *Thermopsis*)   349
False Spirea (see *Astilbe*)   50
Garden Mum
    (see *Chrysanthemum* × *morifolium*)   104
Garden Phlox (see *Phlox*)   304
Gayfeather (see *Liatris*)   240
Hardy Mum (see *Chrysanthemum* species)   111
Lady's Mantle (see *Alchemilla*)   18
Larkspur (see *Delphinium*)   97
Lily (see *Lilium*)   246
Loosestrife (see *Lysimachia*)   261
Lungwort (see *Pulmonaria*)   320
Meadowsweet (see *Filipendula*)   153

Milkweed (see *Asclepias*)   36
Monkshood (see *Aconitum*)   12
Oxeye (see *Heliopsis helianthoides*)   180
Painted Daisy (see *Tanacetum*)   344
Peony (see *Paeonia*)   294
Pinks (see *Dianthus*)   115
Purple Coneflower (see *Echinacea*)   130
Sage (see *Salvia*)   331
Shasta Daisy (see *Leucanthemum*)   234
Siberian Iris (see *Iris*, Siberian)   222
Snow Daisy (see *Tanacetum*)   344
Speedwell (see *Veronica*)   373
Spiderwort (see *Tradescantia*)   354
Spurge (see *Euphorbia*)   136
Stonecrop (see *Sedum*)   336
Sundrops (see *Oenothera*)   289
Tickseed (see *Coreopsis*)   91
Tulip (see *Tulipa*)   359
Turtlehead (see *Chelone*)   70
Woodland Phlox (see *Phlox*)   304
Wormwood (see *Artemisia*)   30
Yarrow (see *Achillea*)   5

ACKNOWLEDGMENTS

Our special thanks to Mary Frances Maguire Lerman, who helped in the initial stages of preparing the manuscript for the first edition of this growing guide. Her degree in horticultural science led her into a multifaceted career, which included working extensively with perennials in the Minneapolis park system and in her own yard. For six years she wrote for the *Minneapolis Tribune*. She also contributed to the *Minnesota Horticulturist* magazine and numerous booklets sponsored by the Minneapolis Park and Recreation Board.

Thanks to these wonderful people for their help along the way: Rob Amell, Jodi Molnau Anderson, Julia Anderson, Lloyd Bachman, Kim Bartko, Monica Baziuk, Ardith Beveridge, Arla Carmichael, George Cleveland, Cy DeCosse, Dana Draxten, Laverne Dunsmore, Dennis Edwards, Sally Ferguson, Kristen Gilbertson, Ben and Hideko Gowen, Jean Heger, Don Hollingsworth, Michael Hunst, Linda Hundstad, Bonnie Johnson, Bill Jones, Pamela Juárez, Steve Kelley, Greta Kessenich, Anne Knudsen, Phil Kobbe, Margaret Kromer, Betsy Kulak, Patty Leasure, Dr. Ben Lockhart, Elizabeth Marshall, John Nolan, Deborah Orenstein, Todd Orjala, Duane Otto, Barb Pederson, Todd Peterson, Paulette Rickard, Kurt Schroeder, Judy Sloate, David Smith, Twyla Sporre, Lynn Steiner, Karen Stever, Norton Stillman, Dale Sullivan, Terry Stone, Rob Taylor, Kristian Tvedten, Bob and Carol Voyles, Julius Wadekamper, Jeanne Weigum, Regina Wells, Donna Whitman, Kathy Wilhoite, Rob Wilson, Jack Worel, and Landon Winchester.

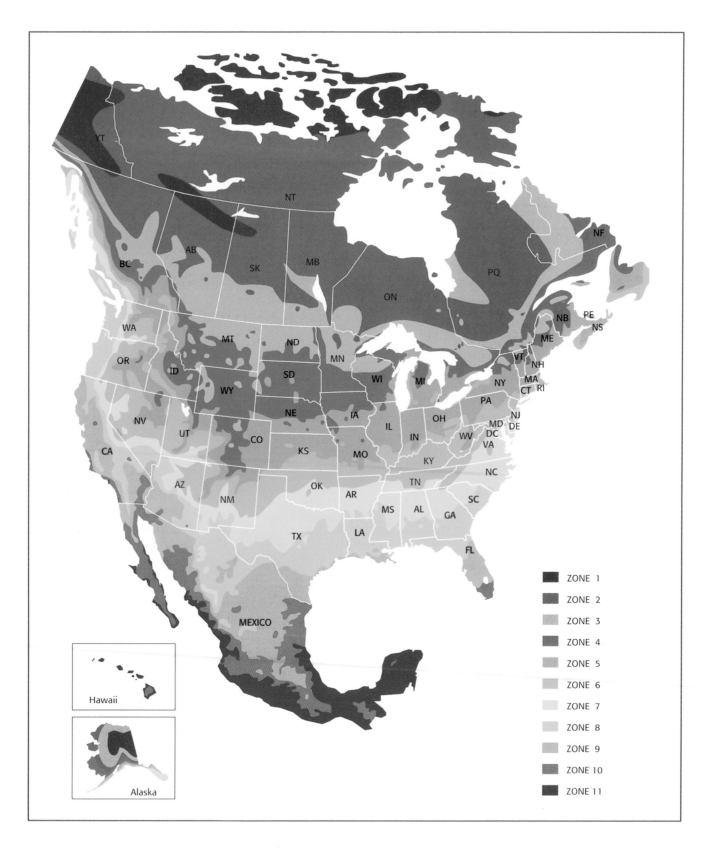

ZONE 1
ZONE 2
ZONE 3
ZONE 4
ZONE 5
ZONE 6
ZONE 7
ZONE 8
ZONE 9
ZONE 10
ZONE 11

Hawaii

Alaska

Growing Perennials in Cold Climates is aimed primarily at gardeners living in Zones 1–5. It will also be helpful to gardeners in portions of Zone 6. A cold climate is characterized by temperatures that can dip below –20°F (–29°C), as well as by snow during the winter.

INTRODUCTION

If you live in a region in which winter temperatures can dip below –20°F (–29°C), then—no matter how hot your summers are—you live in what gardeners consider to be a cold climate. Living in a cold climate means that the perennials you choose and the ways in which you grow them require special attention.

A number of years ago, we began searching for a book that would help us grow perennials in cold-climate conditions. To our surprise and frustration, though we searched long and hard and asked a number of gardeners, bookstores, and nurseries for advice, we could find nothing that really met our needs. Some books included bits and pieces of helpful information, but none served as a true cold-climate growing guide. Our discovery led to a collaboration that lasted for nearly ten years—a decade of research, field-testing, and writing that led to the first edition of *Growing Perennials in Cold Climates*.

The goal of this completely revised new edition is to provide updated growing information on the most popular perennials proven to thrive in cold climates. In this process we have been helped by some of the finest perennial growers, both amateur and professional. Combining their advice and expertise with our personal experience with growing hundreds upon hundreds of perennials, we have selected what we consider to be the finest perennials from the many

thousands available to gardeners today and included them in this guide.

We limited the book to the fifty most popular perennial groups. Within those groups we chose approximately 2,000 wild and cultivated varieties best suited to cold climates. We then awarded a five-star rating to just over 500 to identify them as the choicest plants among an already select group. We wanted to give every gardener, from the novice to the most advanced perennial grower, an incredible range of colors, forms, sizes, textures, and scents from which to work.

As you look through *Growing Perennials in Cold Climates*, you will quickly discover that the information on each variety is unlike the quick sketches so typical of other perennial gardening books. There are in-depth profiles of every plant group, each a valuable mini-booklet on cold-climate growing conditions. Descriptions and specific growing details on each variety within the group provide the gardener with everything needed to grow flowers successfully. The concentration of material in one place is unique. Unlike other perennial gardening books, there is no need to flip back and forth to find succinct, plant-specific information on topics as wide-ranging as companion planting and propagation.

You will also find as you read that we say things in simple, everyday language so that anyone can understand even the more sophisticated aspects of growing perennials. The lists of varieties in each plant group are laid out in clear, concise, and easy-to-use charts. Part II, "The Basics of Growing Perennials," provides everything you need to know to buy, grow, and nurture cold-hardy plants. Even more advanced gardeners may find a few fresh ideas here.

Growing Perennials in Cold Climates is the book we would have liked to own at the beginning of our gardening careers. It would have saved us so much wasted money, time, and energy—not to mention disappointment—as we sadly watched plants we had carefully selected and nurtured die off before their prime. In its depth and presentation of hard-to-find information, we believe this book was and continues to be the only one of its kind. It is our hope the book helps you to grow beautiful perennials that always thrive in cold-climate conditions.

We have worked very hard to make this the very best book possible on cold-climate perennial gardening, but we realize that there is always something to be learned. If you have any tips or gardening secrets you would like to share with us, or if you would like to criticize, correct, or add information, please write to us at P.O. Box 212, Long Lake, MN 55356. Please include a stamped, self-addressed envelope if you would like a reply.

—*Mike Heger, Debbie Lonnee, and John Whitman*

MAJOR PERENNIAL GROUPS

Name	Bloom Time	Expected Longevity	Maintenance	Years to Bloom	Preferred Light
Achillea (Yarrow)	Early summer to late summer	10 to 15 years	High	From seed: 1 to 3 years From potted plant: 1 year	Full sun
Aconitum (Monkshood)	Summer to early fall	25+ years	Low	From seed: 3 years From potted plant: 1 year	Light shade
Alchemilla (Lady's Mantle)	Late spring to early summer	25+ years	Low	From seed: 2 years From potted plant: 1 year	Light shade to full sun
Aquilegia (Columbine)	Spring to early summer	3 years	Medium	From seed: 2 years From potted plant: 1 year	Light shade
Artemisia (Wormwood)	Not generally applicable	25+ years	Medium	From seed: 2 to 3 years From potted plant: 1 year	Full sun
Asclepias (Milkweed)	Mid- to late summer	25+ years	Low	From seed: 2 to 3 years From potted plant: 1 year	Full sun
Aster (Aster)	Summer to late fall	5 to 15 years	Medium	From seed: 2 years From potted plant: 1 year	Full sun
Astilbe (False Spirea)	Early to late summer	15+ years	Medium	From seed: 2 to 3 years From potted plant: 1 year	Light to medium shade
Baptisia (False Indigo)	Spring to early summer	25+ years	Low	From seed: 3 years From potted plant: 1 to 2 years	Full sun
Campanula (Bellflower)	Late spring to late summer	2 to 20 years	Medium	From seed: 2 years From potted plant: 1 year	Full sun to light shade
Chelone (Turtlehead)	Late summer to early fall	25+ years	Low	From seed: 2 to 3 years From potted plant: 1 year	Light shade to full sun
Cimicifuga/Actaea (Bugbane)	Summer to late fall	25+ years	Low	From seed: 3 years From potted plant: 1 year	Light to medium shade
Clematis (Clematis)	Early summer to fall	25+ years	High	From seed: 3 years From potted plant: 2 years	Full sun to light shade

Name	Bloom Time	Expected Longevity	Maintenance	Years to Bloom	Preferred Light
Coreopsis (Tickseed)	Late spring to late summer	5 to 10 years	Medium	From seed: 1 to 2 years From potted plant: 1 year	Full sun
Chrysanthemum × morifolium (Garden Mum)	Late summer to late fall	5+ years	High	From seed: Not applicable From potted plant: 1 year	Full sun
Chrysanthemum species (Hardy Mum)	Late summer to late fall	10+ years	Medium	From seed: 2 years From potted plant: 1 year	Full sun
Delphinium (Larkspur)	Late spring to summer	3 to 5 years	High	From seed: 1 to 2 years From potted plant: 1 year	Full sun
Dianthus (Pinks)	Spring to summer	2 to 10+ years	Medium	From seed: 1 to 2 years From potted plant: 1 year	Full sun
Dicentra (Bleeding Heart)	Spring to summer	3 to 10+ years	Medium	From seed: 2 years From potted plant: 1 year	Light to full shade
Echinacea (Purple Coneflower)	Early summer to fall	15+ years	Low	From seed: 1 to 2 years From potted plant: 1 year	Full sun
Euphorbia (Spurge)	Spring to summer	10+ years	Low	From seed: 2 years From potted plant: 1 year	Full sun
Ferns	Not applicable	25+ years	Low	From spores: 2 to 7 years From potted plant: 2 years	Light to full shade
Filipendula (Meadowsweet)	Early to midsummer	15+ years	Low	From seed: 2 to 3 years From potted plant: 1 year	Full sun to light shade
Geranium (Cranesbill)	Spring to late summer	15 to 20+ years	Low	From seed: 2 to 3 years From potted plant: 1 year	Full sun to light shade
Grasses	Spring to fall	25+ years	Low	From seed: 3 to 5 years From potted plant: 2 years	Variable
Heliopsis helianthoides (Oxeye)	Summer to early fall	10+ years	Low	From seed: 2 years From potted plant: 1 year	Full sun to light shade
Hemerocallis (Daylily)	Spring to late summer	25+ years	Low	From seed: 3 years From potted plant: 1 year	Full sun to light shade
Heuchera (Coral Bells)	Summer	5 to 10 years	Low	From seed: 2 years From potted plant: 1 year	Full sun to light shade
Hosta (Hosta)	Early summer to late fall	25+ years	Low	From seed: 4 years From potted plant: 2 years	Light to medium shade
Iris (Bearded Iris)	Spring to early summer	10+ years	High	From seed: 4 years From potted plant: 1 year	Full sun
Iris (Siberian Iris)	Late spring to early summer	25+ years	Low	From seed: 3 years From potted plant: 2 years	Full sun
Lamium maculatum (Spotted Dead Nettle)	Late spring to early summer	5 to 10+ years	Low	From seed: 1 to 2 years From potted plant: 1 year	Light shade
Leucanthemum–Superbum Group (Shasta Daisy)	Summer to late summer	3 to 5 years	Medium	From seed: 1 to 2 years From potted plant: 1 year	Full sun to light shade
Liatris (Gayfeather)	Midsummer to early fall	15 years	Low	From seed: 2 years From potted plant: 1 year	Full sun
Lilium (Lily)	Early summer to early fall	10 to 15+ years	Medium	From seed: 3 to 4 years From potted plant: 1 year	Variable
Lysimachia (Loosestrife)	Summer to late summer	25+ years	Medium	From seed: 2 years From potted plant: 1 year	Full sun to light shade
Monarda (Bee Balm)	Summer	20 years	High	From seed: 2 years From potted plant: 1 year	Full sun

Name	Bloom Time	Expected Longevity	Maintenance	Years to Bloom	Preferred Light
Narcissus (Daffodil)	Spring	5 to 25 years	Medium	From seed: 3 to 6 years From bulb: 1 year	Full sun
Nepeta (Catmint)	Summer	15+ years	Low	From seed: 2 years From potted plant: 1 year	Full sun to light shade
Oenothera (Evening Primrose, Sundrops)	Spring to summer	25 years	Medium	From seed: 2 years From potted plant: 1 year	Full sun
Paeonia (Peony)	Late spring to early summer	25+ years	Low	From seed: 5 to 7 years From potted plant: 2 to 3 years	Full sun
Phlox (Creeping Phlox, Garden Phlox, Woodland Phlox)	Spring to fall	10+ years	Low to medium	From seed: 2 years From potted plant: 1 year	Variable
Platycodon grandiflorus (Balloon Flower)	Midsummer to late summer	25+ years	Low	From seed: 2 years From potted plant: 1 year	Full sun
Pulmonaria (Lungwort)	Early spring	25 years	Low	From seed: 2 years From potted plant: 1 year	Light to medium shade
Rudbeckia (Coneflower)	Late summer to early fall	25+ years	Low	From seed: 2 years From potted plant: 1 year	Full sun
Salvia (Sage)	Early summer to late summer	10 to 15 years	Low	From seed: 2 years From potted plant: 1 year	Full sun
Sedum (Stonecrop)	Spring to fall	25+ years	Low	From seed: 2 to 3 years From potted plant: 1 year	Full sun
Tanacetum (Caucasian Daisy, Painted Daisy, Snow Daisy)	Early summer	10+ years	Medium	From seed: 2 years From potted plant: 1 year	Full sun
Thermopsis (False Lupine)	Early summer	25 years	Low	From seed: 2 years From potted plant: 1 year	Full sun
Tradescantia (Spiderwort)	Early summer to early fall	5 years	Medium	From seed: 2 years From potted plant: 1 year	Light shade to full sun
Tulipa (Tulip)	Early to late spring	5 to 15 years	High	From seed: 5 to 7 years From bulb: 1 year	Full sun
Veronica (Speedwell)	Late spring to fall	20 years	Low	From seed: 2 years From potted plant: 1 year	Full sun

The Five-Star System

We have awarded five stars to those perennials we believe are among the finest you can possibly buy. When you see five asterisks (*****) behind a plant name, you know it's one of the very best plants available on the market. We are constantly evaluating new plants, some of which will receive the coveted five stars in future editions.

PART I

The Most Popular Perennials

The following sections give you detailed information on growing the most popular perennials. The information is customized for growing plants in cold climates. The plants listed in each section represent an excellent cross section of cold-hardy perennials. These selections come from decades of hands-on experience and years of personal field testing. With more than 2,000 plants to choose from, you will find those that meet your personal needs and preferences. All of these plants are affordable and available through local nurseries or mail-order sources.

CHAPTER I

INDIVIDUAL LISTINGS

Each section on a specific plant group gives you full information on everything from the most simple to the more technical aspects of growing. Match the information to your needs and preferred method of gardening. While the sections follow the same general format, the varying information under each heading is specific to that section and can make a big difference in your success.

Whether you are just beginning to grow perennials or have been doing so for years, each section will guide you in simple, clear, concise language to your dream: stunning plants with bountiful bloom for a minimal amount of wasted effort, money, and time. For many, the ultimate purpose of perennial gardening is a sense of peace, serenity, and joy. Perennial gardening is a process and, to many, a passion. Having good information is just one step along this wonderful journey.

Varieties

You will find more than 2,000 varieties of perennials listed in the sections that follow. Some have been rated with five stars to show that they are among the best plants available on the market today. The varieties have been listed as much as possible according to guidelines recently agreed upon by members of the Perennial Plant Association. Read through the entire listing of varieties to avoid missing a plant that may be described under a different heading in catalogs or other gardening guides. You don't have to be able to pronounce the Latin names. Just write them down if you're buying plants locally, or make sure they are submitted correctly when using mail-order sources.

The Listings Here's a brief explanation of the way plants are named and listed. The name of each section represents a group of plants (genus), such as *Aquilegia* for Columbine. We'll use this plant as an example of how the book is laid out. The plants placed under the heading *Aquilegia* are there because they share many similarities. In the plant listing at the end of the section, some plants are in italics. These are wild (species) Columbines, such as *Aquilegia alpina*. These plants occur naturally in the wild. When a new plant is created by a breeder, it is known as either a cultivated variety (cultivar) or a strain and given a name of the breeder's choice. A cultivar will appear with single quotation marks, such as 'Corbett.' Cultivars are genetically identical. Occasionally, you may see a plant name without any single quotation marks, as with Songbird Series. This indicates a strain, a group of plants that can be grown from seed. The plants will be similar, but not necessarily identical, to their parents once mature. Some sections end with a list of named varieties and/or hybrids. These are crosses between previously described plants.

Sources

In each section is a list of mail-order sources for bare root plants. In a few cases, you will also find possible seed sources. When ordering, keep these tips in mind:

- Order by Latin name. Good online sites and catalogs will list both Latin and common names. You can often place orders online.
- Printed catalogs are expensive to produce, and a number of companies no longer offer them. If they do, there is usually a charge, often applied to your first purchase. Availability of these and their cost is usually posted online.
- Phone numbers are listed for those who do not have internet access. Call to ask about information on catalogs and their cost. You can also ask about the availability of specific plants. If you order by phone, get the name of the person you talk to, and keep it on file.
- You can also write a company to ask about catalogs. Whenever doing this, always include a stamped, self-addressed envelope. Companies will reply with information or simply send you a catalog.
- If you order plants by mail, fill out the form completely, and don't forget to include the charge for shipping, handling, and state tax when required.
- Companies will frequently offer "substitutions" for plants that are sold out. Whether you are willing to accept these is strictly a personal decision. Avoid the need to substitute by ordering plants early.
- Specify the date you would like to receive your shipment. Plants mailed in extreme cold often die, and even if they don't, they may require special handling to keep them alive until planted outside.
- Ask what kind of guarantee the company offers. The longer, the better. Most companies will guarantee their plants for at least one year. However, some plants do not bloom the first year. In that case, it's reasonable to ask for an extension of the guarantee.
- When plants arrive, check them immediately to make sure they are not dried out, damaged, diseased, or dead. With some bare root plants, it's quite hard to tell. Plant and care for them as advised. If they don't spring to life, immediately ask for a replacement or refund.
- Keep records and label all plants. If a plant turns out to be an "imposter," ask for a replacement or refund.
- For additional information on sources go to www. plantinfo.umn.edu. This site lists sources for thousands of plants. Individual sources usually have their own web sites, often with plant photos and descriptions. Additional information on any given plant is generally available online.
- Finally, the availability of plants does vary by year. We have listed 2,000 varieties; a few of these may go out of favor for a while or may not be available in a certain year if production cannot keep up with demand. Always let a company know if you want a specific plant that is out of stock. They may know of a source for that plant or inform you when it will be available once again.

Using the Growing Guide

Please read the chapters in Part II if you are not an experienced perennial gardener *before* delving into individual plant sections in Part I. The chapters in Part II do contain some specific tips not found in the rest of the book.

While we have tried to keep the language simple and easy to understand throughout this book, you may run into unfamiliar words. Read the glossary in advance to understand their meaning.

The material in individual sections of Part I may appear to be repetitive. However, you will find subtle differences in the text. It is these seemingly small points that lead to success with each perennial. There is an advantage to having all of the growing information in each section: You will not be frustrated by having to flip back and forth to get specific facts that vary by plant.

The lists of plants at the end of each section in Part I contain many terrific perennials. Please note that mail-order catalogs may differ in how these plants are categorized. If you order the plants as listed in this book, the mail-order companies will understand what you're after. And that's what really counts.

'Heidi'

ACHILLEA

(ah-KILL-ee-ah)

YARROW

Bloom Time	Expected Longevity	Maintenance	Years to Bloom	Preferred Light
Early summer to late summer	10 to 15 years	High	From seed: 1 to 3 years From potted plant: 1 year	Full Sun

Yarrows brighten the garden from June to September. They are versatile, easy to propagate, and capable of withstanding quite dry conditions once mature. Yarrows are available in a wide range of colors and heights. Their attractive foliage looks good throughout the season and is often aromatic. Yarrows are a must for anyone trying to establish plantings that will attract butterflies. Some of them, particularly the taller forms, are excellent for use in fresh and dried flower arrangements. Though most make good garden plants, *Achillea millefolium* (Common Yarrow), which is a common roadside native, can be invasive and is best planted in natural settings.

How Yarrows Grow

Yarrows have fibrous roots and form mounds of green or gray green foliage. The leaves are usually fernlike in appearance. The numerous small flowers are tightly packed into flat clusters, or *corymbs*, that sit atop fairly strong stems. Yarrows grow rapidly. As they mature, they form a spreading crown with many shoots and flowers. If spent flowers are not removed, Yarrows will produce a heavy seed crop and will often self-sow. However, many named varieties will not come true from seed.

Where to Plant

Site and Light Yarrows thrive in open, sunny areas. They form fewer flowers when grown in light shade, and taller varieties may require staking.

Soil and Moisture Yarrows prefer soils that drain freely. Excessively fertile soils may cause plants to get leggy or floppy. If your soil is compacted, replace it with good soil, or mix in as much organic matter as necessary to loosen it up. Good materials include peat moss, compost, and rotted manures. Soils that retain too much moisture, especially in winter, often lead to root rot and death.

Spacing Space plants approximately 12 to 18 inches (30 to 45 cm) apart. Most varieties expand quickly to fill any allotted space.

Companions

The low-growing types of Yarrow, planted as edging or rock garden plants, are splendid in combination with *Dianthus* (Pinks) and *Campanula* (Bellflower). 'Moonshine' is stunning combined with *Nepeta racemosa* 'Blue Wonder' (Raceme Catmint) and *Dianthus*–Plumarius Group 'Mrs. Sinkins'/'Aqua' (Hardy Garden Pink). Plant it as well with *Artemisia abrotanum* (Southernwood) and *Veronica spicata* ssp. *incana* (Spike Speedwell). Especially impressive are groupings involving *Hemerocallis* (Daylily), *Leucanthemum*–Superbum Group (Shasta Daisy), *Phlox* (Garden Phlox), and early-flowering ornamental **Grasses**.

Planting

Bare Root Plant bare root stock as soon as you can work the ground in spring. Remove the plants from their shipping package immediately. Snip off broken or damaged root tips. Soak plants in room-temperature water overnight. Place a small amount of superphosphate in the base of the planting hole. Fill the hole with soil. Place the crown 1 inch (2.5 cm) below soil level. Fill in with soil, firm with your fingers, and water well. Dissolve ½ cup (about 114 g) of 10-10-10 fertilizer in 1 gallon (about 4 liters) of water. Pour ½ cup (about 120 ml) of this starter solution around the base of each plant. If you prefer organic fertilizer, use fish emulsion instead.

Potted Plants Plant potted Yarrow after all danger of frost has passed in spring. If the soil in the container is dry, soak it thoroughly and let it drain overnight before planting. Carefully remove the plant from the pot to avoid shattering the root ball. Plant it at the same depth as in the pot, after preparing the hole in a similar manner to that for a bare root plant. Fill in with well-prepared soil, press firmly to get rid of all air pockets, and water immediately. Pour ½ cup (about 120 ml) of starter solution around the base of each plant.

How to Care for Yarrows

Water Water young plants consistently until they're growing vigorously. Mature plants tolerate dry conditions but prefer regular watering. Always saturate the soil thoroughly with each watering.

Mulch Place a 1-inch (2.5-cm) layer of organic mulch around the base of each plant as soon as the soil warms up in spring. Good mulches include dried grass clippings, shredded leaves, and pine needles. The main purpose of the mulch is to inhibit the growth of annual weeds.

Fertilizing Avoid too much nitrogen, as this leads to the growth of weak, floppy stems requiring staking. A light application of 5-10-10 fertilizer each spring is enough for a full season's growth. Sprinkle a tablespoon (14 g) around the base of each plant as new growth emerges in spring, and water it immediately to dissolve the granules and carry nutrients to the root zone. If stems still flop over, don't fertilize at all the following season.

If you prefer organic fertilizers, use alfalfa meal (rabbit pellets), blood meal, bonemeal, compost, cow manure, fish emulsion, Milorganite, or rotted horse manure. Bonemeal must be added to the soil at planting time to be effective.

Weeding Yarrows are very shallow-rooted and easily damaged by hoeing. Control weeds with a light organic mulch and regular hand weeding.

Staking In moist, overly fertile soils and windy locations, the taller varieties of Yarrow may require staking. *Achillea millefolium* (Common Yarrow), *Achillea filipendulina* (Fernleaf Yarrow), and *Achillea ptarmica* (Sneezewort) commonly need staking, but varieties such as 'Coronation Gold' and 'Moonshine' normally stand up well on their own. Begin staking when the shoots are just 2 to 3 inches (5 to 7.5 cm) tall. Pea stakes work well.

Deadheading Removing spent flowers prevents Yarrows from spreading by seed and encourages additional bloom. *Achillea millefolium* (Common Yarrow) and *Achillea ptarmica* (Sneezewort) can be invasive if not deadheaded. When the flowers fade, cut the stem off just above a leaf or a location where you see new buds forming. This will encourage the formation of a new flowering shoot.

Winter Protection Mature Yarrows rarely require any winter protection other than normal snowfall. If by early December there is no snow, protect the plants with a 3- to 4-inch (7.5- to 10-cm) layer of marsh hay, whole leaves, pine needles, or clean straw. Remove this mulch as soon as it starts to warm up in early spring. If you leave it on too long, the plants may mildew or rot.

Problems

Insects Yarrows rarely suffer insect damage.

Disease Yarrows are susceptible to root rot if planted in very poorly drained soils. Proper site selection and soil preparation will ward off any potential problems. In very wet seasons, the foliage may turn brown as the plant nears the end of its bloom period. Simply cut the plant back to the ground, and allow it to grow a fresh mound of foliage. The new plant should be vigorous and healthy. High humidity in late summer and fall can also lead to outbreaks of powdery mildew, but this is mainly an aesthetic concern. Cut off all foliage and clean up the area after a severe frost in fall.

Propagation

Division Most Yarrows benefit from being divided every 1 to 3 years. Do this in early spring just as new growth emerges from the soil. Dig up the clump with a spade or garden fork, and shake off as much soil as you can. Separate the clump into smaller pieces by cutting or pulling it apart. Discard the central, woody core. Large plants yield numerous divisions. Plant these as you would bare root plants, making sure that the divisions are not allowed to dry out before they are replanted.

Cuttings Yarrows are easily propagated by basal or stem cuttings taken from mature plants. Cut off the tips of the stems in spring before the plant sets flower buds or in summer after flowering. Take cuttings with three sets of leaves in the early morning when plants are under minimal stress. Each cutting should have several sets of leaves. Cut about ¼ inch (6 mm) below a leaf node, and remove all but the top set of leaves. Plant it immediately in moist rooting medium. Keep humidity high but not excessive. Stem cuttings usually root in about 4 to 6 weeks. Transplant the young plants into pots or a protected garden location as soon as they have formed an adequate root ball. Water frequently until plants are well established.

Seed Seed of the species Yarrows produces plants essentially the same as the parents. Seed of 'Debutante,' 'Parker's Variety,' and 'Summer Pastels' also produces plants resembling the parents. However, many other named varieties do not. Increase stock of these by division or cuttings.

Start seeds indoors 12 weeks before the last expected frost. Seeds germinate in 10 to 20 days at 65°F to 70°F (18°C to 21°C). Dropping the temperature by 10°F (6°C) at night often speeds up germination. The seed is very small and requires light for germination. Simply press it into the surface of a moist germination medium. Enclose the seed tray in a polyethylene bag to keep humidity high and encourage rapid germination. Remove the bag as soon as seeds begin to sprout. When seedlings have developed their first set of true leaves, plant them in individual pots. Harden them off for 14 days before planting them outdoors after all danger of frost in spring. You can also sow seed directly into a cold frame or a specially prepared seedbed in fall. Be sure to keep the soil evenly moist at all times until it freezes up and again in spring until germination occurs. First-year bloom will be highly unlikely with this method, since the seeds will sprout in late spring.

Special Uses

Cut Flowers Many varieties of Yarrow produce lovely, long-lasting cut flowers. The bold heads make excellent focal points. The double-flowering forms of *Achillea ptarmica* (Sneezewort) are popular for fresh flower arrangements and are often used as filler material in similar fashion to *Gypsophila* (Common Baby's Breath). Cut stems when the flowers just begin to show full color. The pollen should be visible at the time of cutting, or vase life will be short. Cut long stems, and strip off the lower leaves. Harvest a few stems from several plants so that you can enjoy both indoor and outdoor bloom. Some gardeners grow extra plants just for cut flowers.

Dried Flowers Yarrows produce superb dried flowers. Varieties of *Achillea filipendulina* (Fernleaf Yarrow) stand out. Cut the stems in bloom but before the pollen sheds. If you wait until later, the flowers may turn brown instead of retaining their natural color. Strip off all lower leaves, bunch the stems together, and secure them with a rubber band. Hang these upside down in a dark, dry, well-ventilated area. Keep the humidity low with a dehumidifier if necessary. Let the flowers cure until they're thoroughly dry. If you have space and enough time, hang the stems individually to avoid distorting flower heads when they're bunched together. An alternative method is to dip the heads in powdered borax, set the stems in water, and let them dry slowly over a long period of time. You may even get better color if you dry flowers quickly in intense heat and extremely bright light. The faster they dry, the better the color. It sounds odd, but the easiest way to do this is in the back of your car hanging from a rope. However, a few of the Yarrows, such as 'Debutante,' don't dry well in the air. They are best dried in sand, silica gel, or cat litter.

Sources

Ambergate Gardens, 8730 County Rd. 43, Chaska, MN 55318, (877) 211-9769

Bluestone Perennials, 7211 Middle Ridge Rd., Madison, OH 44057, (800) 852-5243

Busse Gardens, 17160 245th Ave., Big Lake, MN 55309, (800) 544-3192

Earthly Pursuits, 2901 Kuntz Rd., Windsor Mill, MD 21244, (410) 496-2523

Fieldstone Gardens, Inc., 55 Quaker Lane, Vassalboro, ME 04989, (207) 923-3836

ForestFarm, 990 Tetherow Rd., Williams, OR 97544, (541) 846-7269

Goodwin Creek Gardens, P.O. Box 83, Williams, OR 97544, (800) 846-7359

VARIETIES

VARIETY	COLOR	HEIGHT	HARDINESS
Achillea filipendulina			
(Fernleaf Yarrow)	Golden yellow	40″	−40°F
'Cloth of Gold'	Deep gold	40″	−40°F
'Gold Plate'	Deep gold	40″	−40°F
'Parker's Variety'	Buttery gold	40″	−40°F

The flowers of these selections are large and ideal for cutting. The plants may need staking if grown in rich soils or partial shade.

VARIETY	COLOR	HEIGHT	HARDINESS
Achillea millefolium			
(Common Yarrow)			
'Appleblossom' ('Apfelbute')	Bright pink	30″	−40°F
'Cerise Queen'	Deep to shell pink	24″	−40°F
'Fanal' ('The Beacon')	Cherry red	24″	−40°F
'Fire King'	Red	24″	−40°F
'Great Expectations' ('Hoffnung') ('Hope')	Pale amber yellow	24″	−40°F
'Heidi' ('Heide')	Pale rose	24″	−40°F
'Lilac Beauty'	Pale lilac pink	24″	−40°F
'Oertel's Rose'*****	Pink aging to white	26″	−40°F
'Paprika'	Rose red	24″	−40°F
'Red Beauty'	Rose red	24″	−40°F
'Red Velvet'	Dark rose red	24″	−40°F
'Royal Tapestry'*****	Purple/white center	24″	−40°F
'Salmon Beauty' ('Lachsshönheit')	Salmon pink	36″	−40°F
'Sawa Sawa'*****	Light magenta	36″	−40°F
'Snow Sport'	White	18″	−40°F
'Summerwine'	Wine red	24″	−40°F
'White Beauty'	White	24″	−40°F

The flowers of plants in this group tend to fade as the blooms mature. Stems often require staking to support blooms. Frequent division is highly recommended to keep plants manageable. All Yarrows in this group blend beautifully into borders and many make excellent cut flowers.

VARIETY	COLOR	HEIGHT	HARDINESS
Achillea ptarmica			
(Sneezewort)	White	24″	−40°F
'Angel's Breath'	White (D)	24″	−40°F
'Ballerina'	White (D)	12″	−40°F
'Snowball' ('Boule de Neige')	White (D)	18″	−40°F
'The Pearl'	White (D)	24″	−40°F

These Yarrows can be invasive but are excellent cut flowers, often taking the place of *Gypsophila* (Baby's breath) in bouquets. Seed for the named varieties is available, but rarely produces double (D) flowers. Propagate all doubles by cuttings or division.

Achillea ptarmica

Anthea

'Fire King'

'Moonshine'

VARIETY	COLOR	HEIGHT	HARDINESS
Achillea sibirica			
(Siberian Yarrow)			
'Kamtschaticum'	Pastel pink	18″	−30°F
'Love Parade'	Soft pink	24″	−30°F
'Stephanie Cohen'	Pale pink/darker center	24″	−30°F

This Yarrow has leathery, bright green foliage. It blooms from midsummer into early fall.

VARIETY	COLOR	HEIGHT	HARDINESS
Achillea tomentosa			
(Woolly Yarrow)	Bright yellow	6″	−40°F
'Maynard's Gold' ('Aurea')	Golden yellow	8″	−40°F

These plants form a dense mat of silvery, aromatic foliage and make great ground covers or rock garden plants.

VARIETY	COLOR	HEIGHT	HARDINESS
Achillea (Named varieties and hybrids)			
'Angelique'*****	Dark red	24″	−40°F
Anthea*****	Pale yellow	36″	−40°F
'Apricot Delight'	Apricot to rose pink	16″	−40°F
'Coronation Gold'	Bright yellow gold	36″	−40°F
'Credo'	Soft yellow	36″	−40°F
'Debutante'	Mix (seed)	24″	−40°F
'Fireland' ('Feuerland')	Red orange	30″	−40°F
'Fiesta'	Purple and white	24″	−40°F
'Froelich'	Rich rose	18″	−40°F
'Gloria Jean'	Rose pink	24″	−40°F
'Jungfrau'	Soft yellow	24″	−40°F
'Moonshine'*****	Lemon yellow	24″	−40°F
'Orange Queen'	Salmon	30″	−40°F
'Pomegranate'	Dark red	26″	−40°F
'Pretty Belinda'*****	Lilac pink	20″	−40°F
'Richard Nelson'	Wine pink	24″	−40°F
'Rodney's Choice'	Deep magenta	24″	−40°F
'Saucy Seduction'	Rose pink	24″	−40°F
'Schwellenburg'*****	Gold	24″	−40°F
'Strawberry Seduction'	Velvety red	18″	−40°F
'Summer Berries'	Mix (seed)	30″	−40°F
'Summer Pastels'	Mix (seed)	18″	−40°F
'Sunny Seduction'	Mid yellow	26″	−40°F
'Terra Cotta'	Peach yellow to copper	30″	−40°F
'Walter Funcke'	Copper red to caramel	20″	−40°F
'Wonderful Wampee'	Pinkish white	18″	−40°F

'Angelique' has rich red flowers. Anthea is more upright with lighter blossoms than 'Moonshine,' perhaps the best landscape Yarrow. Sturdy 'Pretty Belinda' has richly colored, flat flowers. 'Schwellenburg' combines the silvery foliage of 'Moonshine' with the gold flowers of 'Coronation Gold.' Chose 'Terra Cotta' and 'Walter Funcke' for unique bloom colors.

'Spark's Variety'

ACONITUM

(ack-oh-NEYE-tum)

MONKSHOOD

Bloom Time	Expected Longevity	Maintenance	Years to Bloom	Preferred Light
Summer to early fall	25+ years	Low	From seed: 3 years From potted plant: 1 year	Light shade

Monkshoods, with their attractive foliage and flowers, are choice mid- to late-season, vertical accent plants. Both their flowers and foliage are lovely. The bloom time for different varieties extends for many weeks from summer into fall. These perennials are long-lived and relatively maintenance free. All parts of the plants are poisonous, but, without a doubt, the roots are potentially the most lethal. In fact, Native Americans used juice from Monkshood root as a poison on the tips of their arrows. Gardeners with very young children may decide not to have this perennial in the garden. Wear gloves when working with Monkshoods to prevent sap from coming in contact with open sores, your eyes, or your mouth.

How Monkshoods Grow

Monkshoods form small tuberous roots similar in appearance to turnips. Glossy, dark green leaves, reminiscent of those of Delphiniums, clothe the sturdy, upright stems. The flower heads form at the top of these stems. Common names such as Monkshood and Helmet Flower refer to the shape of the blooms. If spent flowers are not removed, capsules form which split open to expose numerous seeds.

Where to Plant

Site and Light Monkshoods are medium-light plants that prefer light shade. However, in cold climates, they grow well in full sun if the soil remains consistently moist throughout the growing season. Choose the planting site carefully, as these perennials do not like to be disturbed. Avoid hot, dry, and windy sites. Most Monkshoods are tall plants that do well placed in the back of the garden.

Soil and Moisture Monkshoods prefer a fertile, evenly moist soil that drains freely. Good drainage is critical in preventing disease. Add lots of organic matter to the soil. Good amendments are compost, leaf mold, or rotted manures. A better amendment is peat moss, since most Monkshoods prefer a slightly acidic soil with a pH of 5.5 to 6.5.

Spacing Plants look best in groups of three or more, but a single plant can make a lovely specimen. Plant Monkshoods in a triangular pattern 15 to 18 inches (37.5 to 45 cm) apart.

Companions

Plant early-flowering, blue types with varieties of tall, late *Astilbe* (False Spirea). Fall bloomers look great with the Asiatic forms of *Cimicifuga* (Bugbane). If you're growing the plant in full sun, combine the unusual white-flowered types with purple *Phlox* (Garden Phlox) or blue-flowered varieties with yellow *Achillea* (Yarrow) or *Rudbeckia laciniata* 'Autumn Sun'/'Herbstsonne' (Cutleaf Coneflower). *Aconitum carmichaelii* (Azure Monkshood) is attractive with *Sedum* 'Autumn Joy'/'Herbstfreude' (Stonecrop) and warm-season **Grasses**. *Aconitum henryi* 'Spark's Variety' (Autumn Monkshood) often blooms along

with *Phlox*–Paniculata Group and *Hemerocallis* (Daylily).

Planting

Bare Root Plant bare root stock as soon as you can work the ground in spring. Remove plants from their shipping package immediately. Snip off broken or damaged root tips. Soak plants in room-temperature water overnight. Place a small amount of superphosphate in the base of the planting hole. Fill the hole with soil. Place the crown of each plant just under the soil surface. Firm soil around the roots, and water well. Dissolve ½ cup (about 114 g) of 10-10-10 fertilizer in a gallon (about 4 liters) of water. Pour ½ cup (about 120 ml) of this starter solution around the base of each plant. If you prefer organic fertilizer, use fish emulsion instead.

Potted Plants Plant potted Monkshoods after all danger of frost has passed in spring. If the soil in the container is dry, soak it and let the pot drain overnight before planting. Tap the plant from the pot without breaking the root ball. Plant it at the same depth as in the pot, after preparing the hole in a similar manner to that for a bare root plant. Fill the hole with soil, firm with your fingers, and water immediately. Use ½ cup (about 120 ml) of starter solution around the base of the plant.

How to Care for Monkshoods

Water Keeping the soil evenly moist is key to long-term success with Monkshoods. Check the soil frequently, and if it starts to dry out, water immediately. Always saturate the soil deeply with each watering.

Mulch Apply a 2-inch (5-cm) layer of mulch around Monkshoods to keep the soil moist and cool. Apply it as soon as the soil warms up in late spring or early summer. Good mulches include dried grass clippings, shredded leaves, and pine needles. Mulch also inhibits the growth of weeds that compete with the plants for water and nutrients.

Fertilizing Fertilize every spring with 1 tablespoon (14 g) of 10-10-10 fertilizer per plant. Sprinkle granules around the base of each plant just as growth emerges, and water immediately to move the fertilizer into the root zone. Follow up with another feeding several weeks later. Foliar feeding throughout the season results in stronger plants and more bloom.

If you prefer organic fertilizers, use alfalfa meal (rabbit pellets), blood meal, bonemeal, compost, fish emulsion, Milorganite, or rotted manures. Bonemeal must be added to the soil at planting time to be effective.

Weeding It is easy to damage the tuberous roots during cultivation with a hoe. Pull weeds up by hand around the base of the plant. Mulch keeps most annual weeds in check and makes hand-pulling weeds much easier.

Staking Staking tall Monkshoods may be necessary. You can use pea stakes placed early in the season to support the plants. As the foliage grows, it will hide the stakes. A second method is to stake individual stems. Put stakes in the ground when the plant is just beginning to sprout in spring. As the stem grows taller, tie the plant to the stakes at regular intervals with loose, figure-eight knots.

Deadheading Remove faded flowers unless you want to collect seed. Removing spent blossoms rarely results in additional bloom. Deadheading simply stops seed formation and directs all of the plant's energy into forming a healthier plant for the following season.

Winter Protection After a killing frost, cut stems to the ground. When the ground freezes to a depth of 2 inches (5 cm), cover new plantings with 4 to 6 inches (10 to 15 cm) of marsh hay, whole leaves, clean straw, or pine needles. Mature Monkshoods survive well with normal snow cover. If there is no snow by early December, apply winter mulch. Remove mulch in early spring, since these perennials begin growth very early and are susceptible to crown rot if the mulch remains on too long.

Problems

Insects Aphids can be a problem if Monkshoods are planted in a dry, sunny area without consistent watering. Wash the insects off with water, or use insecticidal soap if they form a large colony. Cyclamen mites can result in distorted leaves and dried-up flower buds. Plants infected with mites should be removed and destroyed. Other known insect pests include four-lined plant bugs and leaf miners. While unsightly, their damage rarely results in permanent injury to the plant.

Diseases Monkshoods are susceptible to stem and crown rots, rust, verticillium wilt, powdery mildew, and bacterial blight. Leaves infected by bacterial blight or leaf spot should be removed immediately and destroyed. Most of these diseases occur on plants stressed by lack of water.

Propagation

Division Monkshoods grow slowly and resent division. If you want to increase your stock, divide the tuberous roots in early spring. It will take 2 or 3 years for the plants to mature.

Seed Growing Monkshoods from seed is for the patient gardener who enjoys a challenge, as the seed develops a dormancy upon ripening. In addition, these perennials grown from seed may take 3 years or longer to flower. Furthermore, seedlings from named varieties may not produce plants identical to the parent plant. The seeds can be extremely erratic in germination, taking anywhere from 7 to 300 days to sprout. Fresh seed gives the best results, and, in fact, seed older than 1 year may not germinate at all. Collect the seed as soon as it ripens, and sow it over moist medium. Seal the seed tray in a polyethylene bag, and keep it at 60°F to 65°F (16°C to 18°C) for 3 weeks. Then place the tray in the crisper of your refrigerator for 6 weeks. Check the tray regularly, and remove it from the cold if you see any seeds sprouting. If no germination has occurred by the end of 6 weeks, remove the tray, and place it in a spot where the temperature will remain at 60°F to 65°F (16°C to 18°C). If the seeds do not sprout within 2 to 3 weeks, place the tray back in the refrigerator for another cold treatment of 6 weeks. Check it regularly for germination. If nothing has happened by the end of 6 weeks, remove the seed tray and keep it moist and cool. Be patient, as it may take a long time for these seeds to sprout. Transplant young seedlings to pots as they get their first set of true leaves.

Some growers prefer sowing fresh or purchased seed outdoors in the fall in a cold frame or seedbed. The chill of winter helps break the seeds' dormancy, and some young plants should emerge the next spring. Be patient; some of the seed may not germinate until a year later. Keep the germination medium evenly moist at all times.

Special Uses

Cut Flowers Harvest Monkshoods in full bud for nice, long-lasting cut flowers. Remember that all plant parts are poisonous. Wear gloves when working with them, and keep them away from children. Place stems in warm water up to the base of the flowers, and let them sit in this bath overnight in a cool, dark place. Strip off lower leaves that will be submerged in the final arrangement. 'Arendsii' may be the best selection for cut flower use.

Dried Flowers and Seed Heads Cut spikes when the first blooms just begin to open. Hang them upside down in a dark, dry, well-ventilated area. Though difficult to dry, they may form an interesting combination of flowers and buds. The seed heads, however, do dry very well.

Sources

Ambergate Gardens, 8730 County Rd. 43, Chaska, MN 55318, (877) 211-9769

Busse Gardens, 17160 245th Ave., Big Lake, MN 55309, (800) 544-3192

Fieldstone Gardens, Inc., 55 Quaker Lane, Vassalboro, ME 04989, (207) 923-3836

Fraser's Thimble Farms, 175 Arbutus Rd., Salt Spring Island, BC V8K 1A3 Canada, (250) 537-5788

Joy Creek Nursery, 20300 NW Watson Rd., Scappoose, OR 97056, (503) 543-7474

Roots and Rhizomes, P.O. Box A, Randolph, WI 53956, (800) 374-5035

Van Bourgondien Dutch Bulbs, P.O. Box 2000, Virginia Beach, VA 23450, (800) 622-9959

Aconitum carmichaelii

VARIETIES

The nomenclature of Monkshoods is quite mixed up in commercial trade. Plants are often listed under different headings in different catalogs. What really counts are the following characteristics: flower and foliage color, bloom time, height, and hardiness. These plants are poisonous so be careful when working with them (wear gloves). Keep children away from them. The plants demand rich, moist soil to thrive! The following varieties are among the best for cold climates and worth seeking out.

VARIETY	COLOR	HEIGHT	HARDINESS
Aconitum × cammarum			
(Monkshood)			
'Bicolor'	White/blue	48"	−40°F
'Blue Sceptre'	White/purple blue	36"	−40°F
'Bressingham Spire'*****	Deep violet blue	36"	−40°F
'Newry Blue'	Navy blue	48"	−40°F
'Pink Sensation'*****	Lilac pink/white	48"	−40°F

The flowers of these Monkshoods are stunning combined with the glossy dark green foliage below. They bloom in late summer. With the exception of 'Bressingham Spire,' their stems may need staking.

Aconitum carmichaelii			
(Azure Monkshood)	Purple blue	36"	−40°F
'Arendsii'*****	Dark blue	36"	−40°F
'Barker's Variety'	Violet blue	60"	−40°F
'Spatlese'	Soft purple blue	60"	−40°F

This species and its forms have lustrous leathery foliage and a long bloom period. They bloom in mid to late summer.

Aconitum fischeri (see *Aconitum carmichaelii*)

Aconitum henryi			
(Autumn Monkshood)			
'Spark's Variety'	Dark blue	60"	−40°F

The species is rarely sold. Look for 'Spark's Variety' with its intensely colored flowers and dark green foliage. The stems will need to be staked. It blooms in late summer.

Aconitum lamarckii			
(Pyrenees Monkshood)	Pale yellow green	36"	−40°F

This European species offers a color not commonly encountered in Monkshoods. Stems are weak and may require staking. It blooms in mid to late summer.

Aconitum napellus			
(Garden Monkshood)	Indigo blue	48"	−40°F
'Album' (var. *albidum*)	Gray white	40"	−40°F
'Blue Valley'*****	Clear blue	40"	−40°F

VARIETY	COLOR	HEIGHT	HARDINESS
'Carneum'	Light salmon pink	40″	−40°F
'Rubellum' (var. *roseum*)	Pale pink	40″	−40°F

These Monkshoods are readily available, although plant parts are extremely toxic. Still, they remain choice garden plants for their lovely blossoms and glossy rich green foliage. Flowers bloom in mid to late summer and even on occasion into fall. The pink-flowered forms require cool night temperatures for the development of good color. 'Blue Valley' has very large blooms.

Aconitum pyrenaicum (see *Aconitum lamarckii*)

Aconitum septentrionale
(Wolfsbane)

VARIETY	COLOR	HEIGHT	HARDINESS
'Ivorine'	Ivory white	36″	−30°F

The species can be hard to find, so look instead for 'Ivorine.' The plant grows into a lovely, upright perennial with summer bloom.

Aconitum (Named varieties and hybrids)

VARIETY	COLOR	HEIGHT	HARDINESS
'Blue Lagoon'	Violet blue	12″	−40°F
'Cloudy'*****	Blue tinged white	24″	−40°F
'Eleonora' ('Eleanor')*****	White/violet tips	40″	−40°F
'Stainless Steel'*****	Metallic blue	40″	−40°F

'Blue Lagoon' is heavily branched, giving a very full appearance. 'Cloudy' is perhaps the most floriferous and longest blooming Monkshood available today. Its individual blooms are quite large and its sturdy stems remain upright without being staked. 'Eleonora' is similar to *Aconitum × cammarum* 'Bicolor' but is actually a better garden plant. It has loosely-branched spikes of flowers that are more informal looking than most common forms of Monkshood. 'Stainless Steel' is an excellent variety with deeply divided, glossy, gray green foliage and loosely-branched spikes of flowers. It blooms in midsummer on sturdy stems.

Alchemilla mollis

ALCHEMILLA

(al-kuh-MILL-uh)

LADY'S MANTLE

Bloom Time	Expected Longevity	Maintenance	Years to Bloom	Preferred Light
Late spring to early summer	25+ years	Low	From seed: 2 years From potted plant: 1 year	Light shade to full sun

Lady's Mantles are low-growing plants with scallop-edged, fan- or kidney-shaped leaves providing season-long interest. They are especially attractive after a rain shower or when coated with dew. The leaves are covered with small hairs which trap water droplets with a reflecting air bubble under each one. This creates fascinating patterns in any light. Delicate sprays of flowers wave in a chartreuse to yellow glow when in full bloom. If spent flowers are not removed, most varieties self-seed quite readily, making these perennials especially valuable as ground covers. All varieties produce lovely leaves and flowers, both of which are prized in floral arrangements.

How Lady's Mantles Grow

Lady's Mantles grow close to the ground from fibrous roots and form rounded leaves, which have an interesting vein pattern and a shape reminiscent of a human hand. Spikes of chartreuse flowers pop above the leaves and are showy from late spring to early summer, depending on the variety. Since this perennial can form seed without pollination, it may produce lots of seed. If allowed to fall to the ground, the seed often germinates freely to increase the size of the original grouping. Individual plants will form multiple crowns and become quite large over the years.

Where to Plant

Site and Light Lady's Mantles are medium- to high-light plants. They need some shade in areas with hot, prolonged summers. Basically, the plants like it cool and moist, so avoid hot, dry spots in full sun. These perennials grow well under trees as long as they get some light and lots of moisture.

Soil and Moisture Lady's Mantles prefer evenly moist soils that drain freely. Avoid boggy areas, as these will spell certain death. Drought stresses these plants severely and will cause the leaves to become unattractive. They turn brown on the edges. Add lots of organic matter to the soil to help it stay cool and moist. Highly recommended are compost, leaf mold, peat, or rotted manures.

Spacing Plant Lady's Mantles in groups of three to five plants for best effect. Space dwarf types about 8 inches (20 cm) apart and larger varieties about 12 to 15 inches (30 to 37.5 cm) apart.

Companions

Alchemilla (Lady's Mantle), with its unique texture and flowers, is a wonderful edging or ground cover perennial. Use it with woody plants such as *Cotinus* (Purple Smokebush) or *Berberis thunbergii* 'Atropurpurea Nana' (Crimson Pygmy Japanese Barberry) to paint dramatic garden pictures, or plant it as a carpet under *Rosa* (Hardy Roses). It is elegant in combination with *Astilbe* (False Spirea), blue- or purple-flowered varieties of *Geranium* (Cranesbill), *Campanula* (Bellflower), *Salvia* (Sage), *Heuchera micrantha* 'Palace Purple' (Small-Flowered Alumroot), blue-foliaged *Hosta* (Hosta), and *Iris* (Siberian Iris). Try it with white- or yellow-flowered plants, in combination with silver-leaved perennials, or with fine-textured plants such as **Ferns**.

Planting

Bare Root Plant bare root stock as soon as you can work the ground in spring. Remove the plants from their shipping package as soon as they arrive. Snip off broken or damaged root tips. Soak plants in room-temperature water overnight. Place a small amount of superphosphate in the base of the planting hole. Fill the hole with soil. Plant the crown just under the soil surface. Fill in with soil, firm with your hands, and water well. Dissolve ½ cup (about 114 g) of 10-10-10 fertilizer in 1 gallon (about 4 liters) of water, and pour ½ cup (about 120 ml) of this starter solution around the base of the plant. If you prefer organic fertilizer, use fish emulsion instead.

Potted Plants Plant potted plants after all danger of frost has passed in spring. If the soil in the pot is dry, soak it and let it stand overnight before planting. Tap the plant out of the pot without breaking the root ball. Plant it at the same depth as in the pot, after preparing the hole in a similar manner to that for a bare root plant. Fill the hole with well-prepared soil, firm with your fingers, and water immediately. Use ½ cup (about 120 ml) starter solution around the base of each plant.

How to Care for Lady's Mantles

Water Lady's Mantles thrive in cool, moist conditions and cannot tolerate hot dry sites. During extended heat waves, water the plant frequently. Saturate the soil thoroughly each time you water.

Mulch Place a 2-inch (5-cm) layer of mulch around the base of each plant as soon as the ground warms up in spring. Dried grass clippings, shredded leaves, and pine needles work well. These also inhibit weeds, which use up available moisture and nutrients.

Fertilizing Early in spring when the young plants are showing signs of initial growth, sprinkle a tablespoon (14 g) of 10-10-10 fertilizer around the base of each plant. Water immediately to dissolve the granules and move nutrients into the root zone. Additional feeding through the spring and summer will encourage stronger, healthier plants.

If you prefer organic fertilizers, use alfalfa meal (rabbit pellets), blood meal, bonemeal, compost, cow manure, fish emulsion, Milorganite, or rotted horse manure. Bonemeal must be mixed into the soil at planting time to be effective.

Staking Staking is not necessary.

Weeding Adding summer mulch around the base of young plants inhibits the growth of most annual weeds. Any that do pop up are easily pulled by hand. Mature plants form such thick canopies of foliage that weeds generally sprout only on the outer edges.

Deadheading Flower scapes often flop down and look messy as they age. Use pruning shears to cut off the old flower stems if you don't like their look or if you do not want the plant to form seed.

Winter Protection Mature plants do not require winter protection other than natural snowfall. Protect young plants with a 6-inch (15-cm) cover of marsh hay, straw, whole leaves, or pine needles the first year. Remove the mulch as soon as the weather starts to warm up in early spring.

Problems

Insects There are no regular insect problems with Lady's Mantles.

Disease Diseases, likewise, are of very minor concern with this plant.

Propagation

Division Lady's Mantles can remain undisturbed for 6 to 10 years before division is recommended. Dig a plant up in early spring just as new growth begins. Cut the crown into sections with a sharp spade or knife, making sure that each division has a strong root system. Plant these new divisions immediately as you would a bare root plant.

Cuttings Lady's Mantles can be propagated by cuttings taken off new growth in spring. Timing is critical, as the stem tissue must be neither too soft nor too hard. Early in the day cut off the top couple of inches (5 cm) of a stem ¼ inch (6 mm) under a leaf node. Remove the lower leaves, and dip the bottom portion of the cutting in rooting hormone. Tap the cutting lightly to remove excess hormone, and stick it immediately into moist rooting medium. Provide high humidity around cuttings during the rooting process. As soon as a cutting has formed a strong mass of roots, pot it up or plant it in a protected spot in the garden. Keep rooted cuttings evenly moist at all times.

Seed If you're starting seeds indoors, sow them about 12 weeks before the last expected frost in spring. Sow seeds no deeper than ⅛ inch (3 mm) in moist germination medium. Keep humidity high by enveloping the tray in plastic. Kept at 70°F to 72°F (21°C to 22°C), fresh seed should germinate within 1 to 3 weeks. As soon as seedlings emerge, remove the plastic. Transplant seedlings to individual pots once they have their first set of true leaves, and grow them indoors until all danger of frost has passed. Harden plants off for 14 days before planting them in the garden.

If your seed doesn't sprout using the first method, it may be old and require special treatment.

Old seed often needs a moist chilling period, called *stratification*, to overcome dormancy. Sow the seed over moist germination medium. Place the seed tray in a plastic bag and put it in the refrigerator for 6 weeks prior to following the steps outlined in the preceding paragraph. Or, hold the seed tray at 70°F (21°C) for 3 weeks, then place the tray in your freezer for 5 weeks. After that, keep the seed tray at 40°F to 50°F (4°C to 10°C) to induce germination.

You may have to vary or combine these methods to get seed to germinate. Be patient.

Probably the simplest germination method is to sow old seed in a moist growing medium outdoors just before the ground freezes. The moist chill of winter will overcome dormancy. Keep the medium evenly moist at all times until it freezes for the winter. Seedlings emerge late the following spring.

As mentioned, Lady's Mantles often self-sow with little help from gardeners. If you want seedlings in your garden, avoid the use of preemergent herbicides and the use of chemical fertilizers around the parent plant, as these products often kill germinating seedlings. Small amounts of organic fertilizers should cause no problems.

Special Uses

Cut Flowers *Alchemilla mollis* (Lady's Mantle) is a choice cut flower. Its stems may last up to 14 days in water. When it's placed in clear glass, its lovely leaves and delicate flowers are breathtaking. Though some arrangers strip off the leaves to use the flowers in combination with other plants, the leaves of all varieties are handsome in floral arrangements.

Dried Flowers Cut stems just before full bloom. Cut flower stems several days apart to ensure getting at least one at just the right stage. Once past prime bloom, the flowers dry poorly. Bunch the stems and hang them upside down in a dark, warm, well-ventilated location. Use a dehumidifier if necessary to keep the moisture level low. Dried flowers generally retain a soft green coloration.

Sources

Ambergate Gardens, 8730 County Rd. 43, Chaska, MN 55318, (877) 211-9769

Bluestone Perennials, 7211 Middle Ridge Rd., Madison, OH 44057, (800) 852-5243

Busse Gardens, 17160 245th Ave., Big Lake, MN 55309, (800) 544-3192

Digging Dog Nursery, P.O. Box 471, Albion, CA 95410, (707) 937-1130

Fieldstone Gardens, Inc., 55 Quaker Lane, Vassalboro, ME 04989, (207) 923-3836

Goodwin Creek Gardens, P.O. Box 83, Williams, OR 97544, (800) 846-7359

Greer Gardens, 1280 Goodpasture Island Rd., Eugene, OR 97401, (800) 548-0111

Joy Creek Nursery, 20300 NW Watson Rd., Scappoose, OR 97056, (503) 543-7474

Venero Gardens, 5985 Seamans Dr., Shorewood, MN 55331, (952) 474-8550

Alchemilla mollis

VARIETIES

VARIETY	COLOR	HEIGHT	HARDINESS

Alchemilla alpina

(Mountain Mantle)	Lime green	8″	−40°F

This species is best suited for partially shaded rock gardens or walls. Keep it moist, as it is not as heat tolerant as other members of this group. It has wonderful silver edges on its leaves that look like open palms.

Alchemilla erythropoda*****

(Dwarf Lady's Mantle)	Citron yellow	10″	−40°F

This may be the most commonly sold dwarf form. It has attractive bluish-green serrated foliage, and the dainty blooms take on striking reddish tones as they age. It is ideal for rock gardens and grows best in partial shade.

Alchemilla glaucescens

(Dwarf Lady's Mantle)	Chartreuse	10″	−40°F

Attractive, kidney-shaped leaves with silvery undersides along with its dwarf stature set this species apart from other Lady's Mantles.

Alchemilla mollis*****

(Lady's Mantle)	Chartreuse	24″	−40°F
'Auslese'	Greenish yellow	12″	−40°F
'Thriller'	Bright greenish yellow	18″	−40°F

This is the best all-around landscape plant among the Lady's Mantles. It has tiny, star-like clusters of flowers and grayish green foliage that delights floral arrangers. This perennial makes an excellent ground cover because of its rapid growth. It is a choice plant for garden design in that it blends well with so many other plants.

Alchemilla pubescens (see *Alchemilla glaucescens*)

Alchemilla subsericea (see *Alchemilla alpina*)

Alchemilla vulgaris

(Common Lady's Mantle)	Yellow green	18″	−40°F

Most plants sold in this country as *Alchemilla vulgaris* (Common Lady's Mantle) are probably *Alchemilla mollis* (Lady's Mantle). The true Common Lady's Mantle is slightly smaller, has fewer delicate hairs (pubescence) on its leaves, and bears greener flowers.

Mrs. Scott Elliot Hybrids

AQUILEGIA

(ack-wuh-LEE-gee-uh)

COLUMBINE

Bloom Time	Expected Longevity	Maintenance	Years to Bloom	Preferred Light
Spring to early summer	3 years	Medium	From seed: 2 years From potted plant: 1 year	Light shade

Columbines have been favorite perennial flowers for many decades. Their dancing blooms with their sweet nectar attract hummingbirds and bumblebees. The flowers come in myriad colors and varied forms. The flowers bloom for long periods, often as long as a month. Some are quite fragrant. The leaves, in groups of three, sway gently in the breeze, giving the plant an open, airy feel.

How Columbines Grow

Columbines grow from long, fleshy roots into graceful plants with stiff, leafy stems. In spring or early summer, the stems are topped with numerous delicate blooms. If left on the plant, these mature into crispy brown, fingerlike seed capsules which break open on top. As the stems sway in the breeze, the seeds are scattered around the mother plant. Numerous seedlings germinate the following season. Columbines cross-pollinate so freely that self-sown seedlings may not look like their parents.

Where to Plant

Site and Light Columbines are medium-light plants that prefer cool conditions. Partial shade will prolong flowering and produce better coloration. If planted in full sun, they must have consistently moist soil. Avoid planting tall varieties in very windy sites where they may need staking.

Soil and Moisture Columbines like rich, moist soils that drain freely. Plants commonly die out in compacted soils. Add lots of organic matter. Good soil amendments are compost, leaf mold, peat moss, and rotted manure. This organic matter keeps the soil loose and moist. If you have heavy clay soil, replace it or a build a raised bed.

Spacing Space Columbines according to their potential size. Smaller plants should be about 6 to 12 inches (15 to 30 cm) apart, while larger ones can stand about 18 inches (45 cm) apart. Columbines look best in groups of at least three to five plants.

Companions

Depending on the variety, Columbines are good in rock gardens or mixed borders, or massed in natural settings. They combine well in the border with *Baptisia* (False Indigo), *Delphinium* (Larkspur), *Geranium* (Cranesbill), *Iris* (Bearded Iris), *Nepeta* (Catmint), *Oenothera* (Evening Primrose), and *Paeonia* (Peony). In the woodland garden, combine *Aquilegia canadensis* 'Corbett' (Canadian Columbine) with *Phlox stolonifera* (Creeping Phlox) selections such as 'Blue Ridge' or 'Sherwood Purple.'

Planting

Bare Root Plant bare root stock as soon as you can work the ground in spring. Remove the plants from their shipping package immediately. Snip off broken or damaged root tips. Soak plants in room-temperature water overnight. Place a small amount of superphosphate in the base of the planting hole. Fill the hole with soil. Place the crown just below the soil surface. Fill the hole, firm the soil, and water immediately. Dissolve ½ cup (about 114 g) 10-10-10 fertilizer in 1 gallon (about 4 liters) of water. Pour ½ cup (about 120 ml) of this starter solution around the base of each plant. If you prefer organic fertilizer, use fish emulsion instead.

Potted Plants Plant potted Columbines after all danger of frost in spring. If the soil in the pot is dry, soak it and let the plant stand overnight. Tap the plant from the pot, keeping the root ball intact. Plant it at the same depth as in the pot, after preparing the hole in a similar manner to that for a bare root plant. Fill in with soil, firm with your fingers, and soak immediately. Pour ½ cup (about 120 ml) of starter solution around the base of the plant.

How to Care for Columbines

Water Keep the soil evenly moist at all times throughout the growing season. During very hot dry weather, check the soil regularly. When you do water, saturate the soil to a depth of 8 to 10 inches (20 to 25 cm) each time.

Mulch Place a 2-inch (5-cm) layer of organic mulch around each plant after the soil has warmed up in spring. Good materials include dried grass clippings, shredded leaves, and pine needles. Mulch keeps the soil moist and cool while inhibiting the growth of annual weeds. The regular use of mulch may minimize leaf miner damage on the foliage. However, if you want plants to self-seed, don't mulch early in the season.

Fertilizing Columbines are heavy feeders. Give the plants a boost each spring just as growth emerges by sprinkling 10-10-10 fertilizer around the clumps. Water immediately to dissolve the granules and move nutrients into the root zone. Give them a second feeding just as the buds are forming. Columbines also respond well to biweekly foliar feedings with a water-soluble fertilizer.

If you prefer organic fertilizers, use alfalfa meal (rabbit pellets), blood meal, bonemeal, compost, cow manure, fish emulsion, Milorganite, or rotted horse manure. Bonemeal must be mixed into the soil at planting time to be effective.

Weeding Mulches reduce weeding but may also stop Columbines from self-seeding. Cultivating around the plants will also kill numerous seedlings. Control weeds by gently pulling them up by hand. Once Columbine seedlings have emerged, you can place mulch around them and the mother plant.

Staking Staking is not necessary for most varieties. Tall-growing types may require staking in windy areas. Tie individual stems to bamboo or plastic stakes in loose figure-eight knots.

Deadheading Remove all spent flowers if you do not want Columbines to self-sow. Removal of all spent flowers may prolong a plant's life. If you want the plant to self-sow but remain healthy, remove most of the flowers, letting just a few form seed.

Pruning Consider cutting Columbines back after bloom. Cutting tall varieties to a height of 4 inches (10 cm) encourages bushy growth at their bases and may result in longer life for individual plants. However, there is no universal agreement on this practice, and its effectiveness may vary among varieties. It is a very good practice if plants are heavily infested with leaf miners.

Winter Protection With normal snowfall, mature Columbines are hardy. However, if there is no snow cover by early December, mulch plants with a 4- to 6-inch (10- to 15-cm) layer of marsh hay, clean straw, whole leaves, or pine needles. Remove the mulch as soon as the weather starts to warm up in early spring to prevent rot.

Problems

Insects Leaf miners that leave white winding trails in the leaf tissue, red spider mites that cause leaf discoloration, and stem borers that feed in the plant crown can be a problem and may kill some plants. If leaf miners are a serious problem, cut the entire plant to its base and destroy the leaves. Usually, the plant will grow a fresh mound of clean, healthy foliage. Red spider mites are most common in hot, dry weather. Mist the foliage and keep the plants moist during periods like this to discourage their presence. Borers are very difficult to control and often destroy selected plants. The regular use of chemicals on these perennials is not recommended. It may be preferable to accept less than perfect foliage. Starting seedlings yearly will provide a constant source of new plants to replace any lost to insect damage.

Disease If your soil is heavy and compacted, crown rot may kill plants during the late winter or early spring. Avoid rot by planting your Columbines in soils that drain freely. Fungal diseases such as leaf spot and powdery mildew occasionally infect plants as well. Leaf spot causes blotching on the leaves, while powdery mildew shows up as white, powdery film on the leaves. Providing good air circulation around the plants is perhaps the most important step in preventing fungal diseases. Remove and destroy any infected leaves. Wilts caused by incurable viral infections can also be a minor problem. Dig up and destroy severely infected plants to stop the spread of this disease. Do not confuse wilt disease with stress caused by underwatering. Wilts show up in individual plants of a group. If a whole group of plants looks wilted, chances are they need a good watering.

Propagation

Division Dividing Columbine plants is not easy, but it can be done. The fingerlike roots are long and quite fleshy. In certain situations, division can serve as a way of rejuvenating an older plant and extending its short life. Dig the plant up in spring just as it shows signs of new growth. Dig deeply to get all of its fleshy, tapering roots. Cut the plant apart with a sharp knife, making sure each division has a healthy portion of crown with roots attached. Plant these immediately as you would a bare root plant.

Seed Columbines are easy plants to start from seed and will often bloom within 2 years of germination. Many fine seed-grown strains are available, but they are generally short-lived. Starting new plants from seed each year assures a constant supply of flowering-sized Columbines.

There are numerous ways to grow these perennials from seed. If you have plants growing in your garden, let them form seed. Do not fertilize heavily with chemical fertilizers or use herbicides once the seeds have fallen to the ground. Once seeds have germinated, dig the seedlings up along with a small amount of soil and plant them wherever you want. Do this when they are just 2 to 3 inches (5 to 7.5 cm) tall, as older plants resent being moved. If you are growing different varieties close to each other, seedlings will often end up with characteristics of each.

You can also collect seed as it matures and plant it immediately in sterile germination medium in a cold frame. Keep the medium evenly moist at all times until it freezes for the winter. The moist chilling period (or stratification) will encourage rapid germination the following spring. Transplant the seedlings to pots or a protected garden location once they have developed their first set of true leaves.

Seed, either collected from your plants or purchased, can also be started indoors. Sow seeds over moist germination medium, barely covering them, as seeds need some light to germinate. Insert the tray into a plastic bag, and place it in the crisper of your refrigerator for 3 to 6 weeks. Remove the tray after this period or as soon as any seeds start to germinate. Keep the growing medium at a temperature of 70°F to 75°F (21°C to 24°C) and evenly moist at all times until seedlings emerge. Germination is irregular and may take 30 days or longer. Be extremely patient, as it may even take months, especially if the seed is old. As soon as seedlings begin to emerge, remove the

plastic, and drop the temperature to 60°F to 65°F (16°C to 18°C). When plants develop their first set of true leaves, plant them in individual pots. Harden the plants off for 14 days before planting them outdoors after all danger of frost in spring.

Special Uses

The flowers of *Aquilegia canadensis* (Canadian Columbine) were once used by Native Americans as a tranquilizer. The tips of the spurs of most Columbines contain a sweet nectar. This is often sucked out by young children and has given rise to the common name Honeysuckle.

Cut Flowers Columbines produce stunning cut flowers. Cut stems as long as necessary for the arrangement when the flowers are just opening. Soak the stems in warm water all the way up to the buds for about an hour. Remove any leaves that would be underwater in the final arrangement before placing stems in your vase. Using a floral treatment in the water will help prolong vase life. Some arrangers believe that rubbing salt on the base of the stem before placing it in water may also help extend the life of the flowers. 'Nora Barlow' and McKana Hybrids are excellent for cutting. *Aquilegia caerulea* (Rocky Mountain Columbine) is one of the best wild Columbines for cutting.

Dried Flowers Columbine flowers do not dry well. However, if you let the seed pods form and dry on the stems, they are excellent in dried arrangements. You can also cut stems as soon as seed heads form and hang them upside down to dry them in a more controlled fashion at the stage you most prefer.

Sources

Arrowhead Alpines, P.O. Box 857, Fowlerville, MI 48836, (517) 223-3581
Bluestone Perennials, 7211 Middle Ridge Rd., Madison, OH 44057, (800) 852-5243
Earthly Pursuits, 2901 Kuntz Rd., Windsor Mill, MD 21244, (410) 496-2523

Elk Mountain Nursery, P.O. Box 599, Asheville, NC 28802, (828) 683-9330

Evermay Nursery, 84 Beechwood Ave., Old Town, Maine 04468, (207) 827-0522

Fieldstone Gardens, Inc., 55 Quaker Lane, Vassalboro, ME 04989, (207) 923-3836

ForestFarm, 990 Tetherow Rd., Williams, OR 97544, (541) 846-7269

Fraser's Thimble Farms, 175 Arbutus Rd., Salt Spring Island, BC V8K 1A3 Canada, (250) 537-5788

Joy Creek Nursery, 20300 NW Watson Rd., Scappoose, OR 97056, (503) 543-7474

Niche Gardens, 1111 Dawson Rd., Chapel Hill, NC 27516, (919) 967-0078

Siskiyou Rare Plant Nursery, 2115 Talent Ave., Talent, OR 97540, (541) 535-7103

Streambank Gardens, 22481 Burton Rd., Milton, DE 19968, (302) 684-8918

Sunlight Gardens, 174 Golden Lane, Andersonville, TN 37705, (800) 272-7396

White Flower Farm, P.O. Box 50, Litchfield, CT 06759, (800) 503-9624

McKana Hybrids

Songbird Series

VARIETIES

Choose varieties by height; flower color, shape, and size; spur size; and foliage color. In most situations, the native species like *Aquilegia caerulea*, *Aquilegia canadensis*, and *Aquilegia chrysantha* are longer lived than named varieties and hybrids. Select an assortment of varieties to extend the bloom season from early spring to midsummer. These plants crossbreed easily so don't expect seedlings to be identical to their parents if a variety of Columbines is grown in the same garden.

VARIETY	COLOR	HEIGHT	HARDINESS
Aquilegia akitensis (see *Aquilegia flabellata*)			
Aquilegia alpina			
(Alpine Columbine)	Medium blue/white	24″	–40°F

This species has green stems that emerge from a mound of blue-green, finely divided foliage to produce nodding flowers from mid spring to early summer.

Aquilegia bertolonii			
(Alpine Rock Columbine)	Blue/white	6″	–40°F

Bluish green foliage, short green stems tinged reddish purple at the base, and delicate buds that unfurl into nodding blue-white flowers make this very early blooming plant delightful.

Aquilegia caerulea			
(Rocky Mountain Columbine)	Light blue/white	24″	–40°F

This wildflower, a parent to many fine hybrids, is popular for long-spurred flowers that typically face upward on stems rising from a base of light green foliage. The plant blooms in late spring to early summer and will self-sow.

Aquilegia canadensis			
(Canadian Columbine)	Brilliant red/yellow	36″	–40°F
'Corbett'	Pale yellow	24″	–40°F
'Little Lanterns'	Red/yellow	18″	–40°F

Most people refer to this fine native plant as Wild Honeysuckle. The nodding flowers have short spurs filled with nectar. It is one of the first of the taller Columbines to flower each year. The plant self-sows. 'Corbett' and 'Little Lanterns' are very showy with delicate lanterns dangling from stems above a mound of mid-green foliage.

Aquilegia chrysantha			
(Golden Columbine)	Yellow	30″	–40°F
'Yellow Queen'	Lemon yellow	30″	–40°F

The species and the fragrant 'Yellow Queen' are knockouts in the garden with their large flowers that have extra long spurs. The plants display deep green foliage and flower in late spring.

Aquilegia discolor	Blue/cream	6″	–40°F

This tough plant blooms early in the season and is ideal in the rock garden. Its tidy foliage is grayish green.

Aquilegia flabellata			
(Fan Columbine)	Blue/white	18″	–40°F
'Alba'*****	White	10″	–40°F
'Black Currant Ice'	Purple/creamy yellow	12″	–40°F
Cameo Series	Rose/white	8″	–40°F
'Mini Star'	Blue/white	6″	–40°F

VARIETY	COLOR	HEIGHT	HARDINESS
var. *pumila*	Blue/white	8″	−40°F

Fan Columbine is noted for its heavy, bluish green foliage; compact growth; and show of nodding, waxy flowers in late spring. It tends to live longer than other Columbines, self-sows, and is very easy to grow from seed.

Aquilegia formosa			
(Formosa Columbine)	Red/yellow	42″	−40°F

A number of Columbines have flowers similar to jester caps. This is one of the best examples with its short red spurs, yellow-orange sepals, and yellow pistils. This makes a charming display combined with the gray-green foliage below.

Aquilegia longissima			
(Longspur Columbine)	Pale yellow	36″	−30°F

Although a short-lived species, this makes a fine specimen plant noted for its attractive green foliage and upright flowers with extremely long spurs and subtle fragrance. Longspur Columbine blooms in late spring to early summer.

Aquilegia viridiflora			
(Green-flowered Columbine)			
'Chocolate Soldier'	Chocolate purple/green	12″	−40°F

The species has greenish flowers and somewhat hairy stems. Its offspring displays unusual foliage and floral coloration.

Aquilegia (Named varieties and hybrids)			
'Biedermeier'	Mix	12″	−40°F
'Black Barlow'	Purplish black (D)	30″	−40°F
'Blue Butterflies'	Deep blue white	10″	−40°F
Clementine Series*****	Mix (D)	18″	−40°F
'Crimson Star'	Crimson/white	24″	−40°F
'Dorothy Rose'	Light rose pink (D)	24″	−40°F
Dragonfly Hybrids	Mix	24″	−40°F
'Kristall'	White	24″	−40°F
'Leprechaun Gold'*****	Violet	24″	−40°F
'Lime Sorbet'	Lime green to white (D)	40″	−40°F
McKana Hybrids	Mix	24″	−40°F
Mrs. Scott Elliot Hybrids	Mix	30″	−40°F
Music Series*****	Mix	18″	−40°F
'Nora Barlow'	Rose pink/white (D)	30″	−40°F
'Rose Barlow'	Rose pink (D)	30″	−40°F
'Ruby Port'*****	Dark red (D)	24″	−40°F
'Snow Queen'	Pure white	30″	−40°F
Songbird Series*****	Mix	24″	−40°F
Tower Series	Mix	24″	−40°F
'William Guinness'	Deep purple/white	24″	−40°F
Winky Series	Mix	18″	−40°F
'Woodside'	Mix	24″	−40°F

These are all choice plants for cold-climate gardeners. The Clementine selections have upward facing double (D) blooms. All of the Columbines with double flowers are particularly striking. 'Leprechaun Gold' and 'Woodside' have variegated foliage. The Songbird Series includes excellent Columbines, each named after a bird. Seed mixes produce Columbines in a wide color range. Although these plants often self-sow, the offspring may not resemble the parent plant.

'Valerie Finnis'

ARTEMISIA

(ar-tuh-MEEJ-ee-uh)

WORMWOOD

Bloom Time	Expected Longevity	Maintenance	Years to Bloom	Preferred Light
Not generally applicable	25+ years	Medium	From seed: 2 to 3 years From potted plant: 1 year	Full sun

The varied textures and colors of Wormwoods make them one of the most popular foliage plants. Depending on the variety, they have either gray to silver or green foliage. The gray to silver Wormwoods come in a wide range of heights and provide excellent contrast to other perennials, often softening the transition from one plant to the next. Although the gray to silver types do produce tiny flowers, they are generally insignificant. Most of the gray- to silver-foliaged Wormwoods also exude an interesting, somewhat medicinal aroma. The green-foliaged types produce handsome foliage and more notable flowers.

How Wormwoods Grow

Wormwoods grow from fibrous roots into attractive foliage plants. Some form delicate, ferny foliage while others grow narrow, indented leaves. Only a handful produce flowers of any importance. The overall shape of the plant varies greatly by variety. Some form a lovely mound of foliage, while others have more upright growth. Some Wormwoods produce underground stems, or stolons, and will spread into larger clumps, making them effective ground covers in sunny, dry locations.

Where to Plant

Site and Light Most Wormwoods thrive in hot, sunny sites. In shade, they often become lanky and sparse. The green-leaved varieties prefer it slightly cooler.

Soil and Moisture Wormwoods like loose, airy soils that drain freely. Sandy, quick-draining soils are ideal for the gray- to silver-leaved types. If soils stay wet during the dormant period, the roots and crowns may rot. Most of the Wormwoods grow well in poor soils with limited nutrients. If you have heavy clay soil, replace it with good soil or build a raised bed. The green-leaved varieties prefer more evenly moist soils and slightly higher fertility.

Spacing Space according to the potential size of the plant. Avoid crowding Wormwoods, as this often limits air circulation and may lead to disease. Place shorter plants 12 to 15 inches (30 to 37.5 cm) apart, while the spreading and taller forms do well 18 to 24 inches (45 to 60 cm) apart.

Companions

The silver to gray or green foliage coloration and variation of form make the different varieties of *Artemisia* (Wormwood) extremely valuable in combinations with other perennials and shrubs. They are especially attractive near blue, lavender, pink, or yellow flowers. They also harmonize or tone down harsh color combinations. Combine *Artemisia ludoviciana* 'Valerie Finnis' (White Sage) with *Achillea* 'Heidi' (Yarrow), *Aconitum carmichaelii* (Azure Monkshood), and *Coreopsis* 'Full Moon' (Tickseed). *Artemisia abrota-*

num (Southernwood) is pleasing next to fine-textured **Grasses** and *Sedum* 'Autumn Joy'/'Herbstfreude' (Stonecrop).

Planting

Bare Root Plant bare root stock as soon as you can work the ground in spring. Remove plants from their shipping package immediately. Snip off broken or damaged root tips. Soak plants overnight in room-temperature water. Place a small amount of super-phosphate in the base of the planting hole. Fill the hole with soil. Place the crown of the plant just below the soil surface. Fill in with soil, firm with your fingers, and water immediately. Dissolve ½ cup (about 114 g) 10-10-10 fertilizer in 1 gallon (about 4 liters) of water. Pour ½ cup (about 120 ml) of this starter solution around the base of each plant. If you prefer organic fertilizer, use fish emulsion instead.

Potted Plants Plant potted Wormwoods after all danger of frost has passed in spring. If the soil in the pot is dry, water and let stand overnight before planting. Tap the plant out of the pot, keeping the root ball intact. Plant it at the same depth as in the pot, after preparing the hole in a similar manner to that for a bare root plant. Firm the soil around the base of the plant, and water immediately. Pour ½ cup (about 120 ml) starter solution around the base of the plant.

How to Care for Wormwoods

Water All Wormwoods need plenty of water until mature. The gray- to silver-leaved varieties need little moisture once they are older and growing vigorously. They are drought-tolerant, not drought-proof, so they may require some water during extended dry periods. If overwatered, the gray to silver varieties tend to get floppy or lanky. If this happens, prune and shape them to the desired size, and cut back on watering. The green-leaved varieties don't like it dry. Keep them moist throughout the growing season for better foliage coloration and flowering. Whenever you do water, saturate the ground thoroughly.

Mulch Since mulches keep soil moist and cool, avoid them around mature gray- to silver-foliaged Wormwoods. However, a light mulch is helpful for varieties with green foliage. Keep it away from the crown of the plant to avoid causing rot. Good mulches include dried grass clippings, shredded leaves, and pine needles. The use of a mulch will inhibit the growth of weeds.

Fertilizing Wormwoods with gray to silver foliage need little or no fertilizer. High amounts of nitrogen can cause lanky, sparse growth. Wormwoods with green foliage respond well to either chemical or organic fertilizers applied in early spring and just before flowering. A chemical fertilizer such as 5-10-10 or 10-10-10 is fine.

For organic fertilizers, mix bonemeal into the soil at planting time and sprinkle alfalfa meal (rabbit pellets), blood meal, compost, fish emulsion, Milorganite, or rotted manures on the soil surface for additional nutrients. Always water immediately after application of fertilizer.

Weeding Wormwoods grow vigorously and compete well with weeds. Any weeds that do pop up are usually on the outside edges of the clumps, and these are easily pulled by hand, especially if the soil is moist. Avoid the use of tools, which can damage the root system.

Staking *Artemisia lactiflora* (White Mugwort) may need staking, especially if planted in a windy area. The simplest support is pea stakes stuck into the ground early in the spring. As the plant grows, the stakes are covered and are not visible at all.

Deadheading With the exception of *Artemisia lactiflora* (White Mugwort), these plants are grown for foliage only. Most of the flowers are inconspicuous and not worth worrying about.

Pruning Some of the gray- to silver-foliaged varieties may get bare in the center as the season progresses. If this happens, cut the plants partially back, and you will get an abundance of growth from the side buds. This results in a nice full look for the balance of the growing season. The following year, you may want to divide the plant and remove the central area.

Winter Protection Most Wormwoods are very hardy and do not require winter protection. Gardeners in the far North should mulch *Artemisia lactiflora* (White Mugwort) with 6 inches (15 cm) of marsh hay, clean straw, or whole leaves if there is no snow cover by early December. Since most of these perennials are extremely sensitive to overly wet soils, remove winter mulch promptly in early spring to avoid rot.

Problems

Insects Wormwoods produce oils that seem to deter insects, so they are rarely bothered at all.

Disease The gray- to silver-colored Wormwoods may rot out in poorly drained soils. Drainage is especially important during the dormant season. If plants are covered with a winter mulch, remove it immediately when the weather warms up in spring.

Propagation

Division Plants sometimes become sparse in the center as they mature. This is an indication that it is time to divide them. This is best done in early spring just as they begin growth. Dig up the clump and divide it into pieces with a spade. Discard the weak central crown. Plant healthy divisions from the outside of the plant as you would bare root plants. Keep the soil moist at all times until the plants are growing vigorously. Regular division is important to the plants' health and is also key in keeping the more aggressive spreaders from overtaking portions of the garden.

Cuttings Cuttings taken in spring from the base of the plant will root easily within weeks. Stem cuttings taken up to midsummer may also root well. Take cuttings with three sets of leaves, making the cuts ¼ inch (6 mm) below a leaf node. Remove all but the top leaves, and dip the bottom of the stem in rooting hormone. Plant immediately in a rooting medium. Keep moist at all times until plants take root and begin new growth. Excessive humidity during rooting can cause disease. Transplant to pots or a permanent location after a strong root system has formed.

Seed Plants are not commonly started from seed, but it can be done. Plant seed indoors 14 weeks before the last expected spring frost. Press seed into the surface of a sterile, moist germination medium. Avoid covering the seeds, since they need light to germinate. Keep them evenly moist at 60°F to 65°F (16°C to 18°C) until germination begins. Normally, seeds begin to sprout within 30 days. Once seedlings have their first set of true leaves, plant them in individual pots. Harden them off for 14 days, and plant outside after all danger of frost in spring.

Special Uses

Cut Foliage Wormwoods often wilt after being cut if not properly handled and conditioned. As you cut stems, place them in water immediately, and keep them out of the sun. Once indoors, put cut stems in water that is 110°F (43°C). Some people place the lower inch (2.5 cm) of the stems in boiling water for a few seconds before doing this. Others lightly hammer the bottom of the stems of woodier varieties to encourage uptake of water. Let the stems rest in water overnight, and arrange them the following day with other cut flowers. Use floral preservatives in the water. *Artemisia ludoviciana* (White Sage) and its varieties are among the best for cutting. Cut stems before the flowers show any grayish white flower color, as you'll get a cleaner and lighter look. *Artemisia absinthium* 'Lambrook Silver' (Common Wormwood) with its soft feathery form is another favorite of flower arrangers. *Artemisia lactiflora* (White Mugwort) is favored by arrangers for its deep green foliage and creamy white plumes of flowers.

Dried Foliage The foliage of the taller gray- to silver-foliaged Wormwood varieties is good for drying. Cut and bundle stems, removing any unattractive lower leaves. Hang the bundles upside down in a dark, warm, dry place with good ventilation. Don't touch the stems or leaves until they're thoroughly dry. The stems become extremely brittle and must be handled carefully. Dried leaves are often used as a component of potpourri.

Artemisia ludoviciana 'Silver King' (White Sage) is commonly used for making wreaths.

Sources

Ambergate Gardens, 8730 County Rd. 43, Chaska, MN 55318, (877) 211-9769

Bluestone Perennials, 7211 Middle Ridge Rd., Madison, OH 44057, (800) 852-5243

Digging Dog Nursery, P.O. Box 471, Albion, CA 95410, (707) 937-1130

Earthly Pursuits, 2901 Kuntz Rd., Windsor Mill, MD 21244, (410) 496-2523

Fieldstone Gardens, Inc., 55 Quaker Lane, Vassalboro, ME 04989, (207) 923-3836

Richter's Herbs, 357 Hwy 47, Goodwood, ON L0C 1A0 Canada, (905) 640-6677

Sandy Mush Herb Nursery, 316 Surrett Cove Rd., Leicester, NC 28748, (828) 683-2014

Well-Sweep Herb Farm, 205 Mount Bethel Rd., Port Murray, NJ 07865, (908) 852-5390

Artemisia lactiflora　　　　　　　　　　　'Silver Mound'/'Nana'

VARIETIES

The following varieties are choice selections for cold-climate gardening. Many others are available, but they simply are not hardy enough to be included in this book.

VARIETY	COLOR	HEIGHT	HARDINESS
Artemisia abrotanum			
(Southernwood)	Gray green	36″	−30°F

This species is grown for its finely-divided, aromatic, gray-green leaves. Though often planted in herb gardens, it is, unfortunately, not used as often as it could be. It is lovely planted next to a pathway, at the edge of a shrub border, or in combination with other foliage perennials. Cut back hard in early spring if you want a dense, tight form. The leaves are sometimes used as moth repellent.

VARIETY	COLOR	HEIGHT	HARDINESS
Artemisia absinthium			
(Common Wormwood)			
'Lambrook Mist'*****	Gray	30″	−40°F
'Lambrook Silver'	Gray	36″	−40°F

Common Wormwood was once used to flavor absinthe, a powerful drink now banned throughout Europe. This plant produces tiny grayish flowers and tends to become somewhat woody with age. Its foliage has limited fragrance, and these named varieties were selected for their more silvery leaves. Prune back as necessary to keep plants bushy.

VARIETY	COLOR	HEIGHT	HARDINESS
Artemisia lactiflora*****			
(White Mugwort)	Green	60″	−30°F
'Guizhou'	Blackish green	60″	−30°F

White Mugwort is valued for its vertical growth and plumes of creamy white flowers in late summer. The flower stems are useful for arrangements and hold up quite nicely. Its broad leaves are dark green with a silvery coloration beneath. 'Guizhou' has blackish green foliage and purple stems. White Mugwort is unusual in that it prefers a moist soil.

Artemisia ludoviciana			
(White Sage)			
'Silver Frost'	Silver gray	18″	−40°F
'Silver King'	Silver gray	36″	−40°F
'Silver Queen'	Silver gray	36″	−40°F
'Valerie Finnis'*****	Silver white	24″	−40°F

These are lovely perennials with slightly aromatic, silver-gray foliage. The plants spread rapidly, forming large clumps and must be placed with this in mind. 'Valerie Finnis' is less aggressive than the others, making it a better garden plant. Inconspicuous grayish white flowers bloom in late summer. 'Silver Frost' has finely cut leaves while 'Silver King,' 'Silver Queen,' and 'Valerie Finnis' have much broader foliage. Pinching taller varieties early in the season results in more dense, compact growth.

Artemisia procera (see *Artemisia abrotanum*)

Artemisia purshiana (see *Artemisia ludoviciana*)

Artemisia schmidtiana			
'Silver Mound' ('Nana')*****	Silver	8″	−40°F

This is a lovely, mounded plant with silvery scented foliage. The center becomes sparse on large mature plants, so regular division is often necessary to maintain the neat rounded form. This is one of the most popular Wormwoods in cold climates.

Artemisia stelleriana			
(Beach Wormwood)	Silver white	16″	−30°F
'Silver Brocade' ('Boughton Silver') ('Mori's Form')	Silver white	10″	−30°F

Perhaps the best of this group for use as a ground cover, this plant thrives in poor dry soils and even tolerates salt. It does bear tiny yellow flowers, but they are of little value. The plant is more desirable for its tight dense form.

Asclepias tuberosa

ASCLEPIAS

(uh-SKLEE-pee-us)

MILKWEED

Bloom Time	Expected Longevity	Maintenance	Years to Bloom	Preferred Light
Mid- to late summer	25+ years	Low	From seed: 2 to 3 years From potted plant: 1 year	Full sun

Certain varieties of Milkweed make wonderful additions to the perennial garden. Their flowers are rich and brilliant in color, cover the plants for a long period of time during the summer months, and turn into attractive pods that can be used in dried flower arrangements. The blooms are extremely attractive to butterflies (especially monarchs) and bees. These can be long-lived plants and are nearly maintenance free. They are rarely bothered by insects or diseases.

How Milkweeds Grow

Asclepias tuberosa (Butterfly Milkweed), the most commonly grown variety, emerges late in spring and develops multiple stems with bluish green, willowy leaves. The sword-shaped leaves spiral up the stem. The plant's taproot is very long, and it should not be disturbed once mature. Its tightly clustered flowers are usually vibrant orange. As its bloom season ends, the plant forms narrow pods that open at maturity to scatter silky seeds into the wind. *Asclepias incarnata* (Swamp Milkweed) is much taller, with waxy, lilac-pink or occasionally white flowers. All Milk-weeds exude a milky sap from damaged leaves and stems.

Where to Plant

Site and Light *Asclepias tuberosa* (Butterfly Milkweed) demands full sun and relishes dry, hot sites. *Asclepias incarnata* (Swamp Milkweed) prefers full sun but will grow fairly well in very light shade. Milkweeds are good choices for the flower garden or for more natural settings.

Soil and Moisture *Asclepias tuberosa* (Butterfly Milkweed) does best in lighter soils that drain freely. It does not need a fertile soil to do well. Replace heavy clay soils with good soil. Amend all soils with organic matter, or build a raised bed to ensure good drainage.

    Asclepias incarnata (Swamp Milkweed) needs an evenly moist soil and will grow right down to the edge of a pond. Soils should contain generous amounts of organic matter such as peat moss, compost, leaf mold, and rotted manure. In the case of this plant, acidic peat moss is most highly recommended, since Swamp Milkweed prefers a slightly lower pH (6.5 or less).

Spacing Space plants 18 to 24 inches (45 to 60 cm) apart. Carefully place *Asclepias tuberosa* (Butterfly Milkweed) in a permanent location, since it does not like to be transplanted once mature.

Companions

Choose companion plants carefully, as the two species have dramatically different cultural needs. *Asclepias incarnata* (Swamp Milkweed) combines nicely with **Chelone** (Turtlehead), **Monarda** (Bee Balm), and moisture-loving **Grasses**. *Asclepias tuberosa* (Butterfly Milkweed), on the other hand, grows well with plants preferring dry soils. These include *Schizachyrium scoparium* (Little Bluestem Grass), **Artemisia** (Wormwood), **Coreopsis** (Tickseed), *Echi-nacea* (Purple Coneflower), **Oenothera macrocarpa** (Ozark Sundrop), and **Salvia** (Sage).

Planting

Bare Root Plant bare root stock as soon as you can work the ground in spring. Remove plants from their packaging immediately. Snip off broken or damaged root tips. Soak plants overnight in room-temperature water. Place a small amount of superphosphate in the base of the planting hole. Fill the hole with soil. Place the crown 1 inch (2.5 cm) below the soil surface. Fill in with soil, firm with your fingers, and water well. Dissolve ½ cup (about 114 g) 10-10-10 fertilizer in 1 gallon (about 4 liters) water. Pour ½ cup (about 120 ml) of this starter solution around the base of each plant. If you prefer organic fertilizer, use fish emulsion instead.

Potted Plants Plant potted plants after all danger of frost. If soil in the pot is dry, soak it overnight before planting. Tap the plant out of the pot without breaking the root ball. Plant at the same depth as in the pot, after preparing the hole in a similar manner to that for a bare root plant. Fill in with soil, firm with your fingers, and water immediately. Pour ½ cup (about 120 ml) starter solution around the base of the plant.

How to Care for Milkweeds

Water *Asclepias incarnata* (Swamp Milkweed) thrives in soil that is consistently moist throughout the season. *Asclepias tuberosa* (Butterfly Milkweed) tolerates dry conditions but does very well if watered regularly. Never let it dry out during droughts. Whenever you water, saturate the soil thoroughly.

Mulch Mulch keeps the soil moist and cool and is particularly important for *Asclepias incarnata* (Swamp Milkweed). Plants of *Asclepias tuberosa* (Butterfly Milkweed) grown in heavy soils are best left unmulched. Good organic mulches include dried grass clippings, compost, pine needles, and shredded leaves. Avoid placing mulch against stems, since this can lead to disease. Add additional mulch as it decomposes.

Fertilizing Sprinkle a little 10-10-10 fertilizer around the base of each plant just as growth emerges in spring. Water immediately to dissolve the granules and carry nutrients into the root zone. You can repeat this step as needed several weeks later, but, generally these are not plants requiring high fertilization.

If you prefer organic fertilizers, use bonemeal in the soil at planting time. Scratch blood meal, cow manure, fish emulsion, Milorganite, or rotted horse manure into the soil surface early in the season for additional nutrients.

Weeding Since these plants may emerge late in spring, you should mark their location with a durable label to avoid damaging them while weeding early in the season. Weed by hand around the crown of Milkweeds to avoid damaging eyes or new growth in spring. The use of a summer mulch around *Asclepias incarnata* (Swamp Milkweed) helps keep annual weeds in check.

Staking *Asclepias incarnata* (Swamp Milkweed) may need staking if planted in a very open, windy area. Place stakes in the ground when the plant is 3 inches (7.5 centimeters) tall. Tie the plant to the stake at regular intervals as it grows taller. Use a soft material or twine tied in a loose figure-eight pattern to secure the stem to the support.

Deadheading If not removed, the flower heads form interesting seed pods. As the pods ripen and burst open, the silky seeds gradually drift away in the breeze, but even the empty seed pods add interest in the landscape.

Winter Protection Winter protection is not normally necessary on established plants, as these Milkweeds are native to the colder regions of the United States.

Problems

Insects There are no major problems with insects if Milkweeds are grown properly.

Disease *Asclepias tuberosa* (Butterfly Milkweed) will not tolerate compacted, clay soils. In poor soil, the plant may die over the winter from root rot. If you have loamy soil, this should not be a problem. Leaf spots and rust do occur but are relatively rare.

Propagation

Division Division of *Asclepias tuberosa* (Butterfly Milkweed) is not generally recommended, but it can be done. Use a spade or fork to dig up the plant. Digging the plant is somewhat like trying to remove long carrots from the vegetable garden without breaking them. Work slowly and carefully in a circular motion around the clump. Cut the crown apart with a sharp knife, being certain that each division includes a section of healthy root tissue. Plant immediately as you would a bare root plant.

Root Cuttings It is possible, although difficult, to propagate *Asclepias tuberosa* (Butterfly Milkweed) from root cuttings. Lift a mature plant as soon as you can dig in the garden in spring. Cut roots into 3- to 4-inch (7.5- to 10-cm) sections, and plant each one vertically in a moist, well-drained medium. Place the end of the cutting that was nearer the crown up when planting. Firm the medium around the cuttings, and keep it evenly moist until new growth emerges. Transplant the cuttings to pots or a garden location once they've established a strong root system and begun to grow foliage.

If you want to preserve the parent plant, dig to one side and remove just one root. Cut this into sections, and plant each one as outlined here.

Seed Milkweeds often take 2 to 3 years to flower from seed, especially if not sown until spring. There are a number of methods of growing Milkweeds from seed.

If you collect mature seed and plant it immediately in moist germination medium, it will often sprout in less than 30 days. The problem in cold climates is that these young seedlings must be protected during the first winter. Transfer them indoors, and grow them under lights.

You can also collect seed and store it until the late fall. Before the ground permanently freezes for the winter, plant the seed in a cold frame or protected area. Just press the seed into moist growing medium and keep it moist until it freezes. The winter's cold will break the dried seed's natural dormancy, and seedlings will emerge in spring. Transplant the seedlings to pots or a permanent location when they're 2 to 3 inches (5 to 7.5 cm) tall.

Collected or purchased seed can also be started indoors. Fill a seed tray with moist germination medium, and press the seed into the surface of the medium. The seed can be lightly covered or left exposed during germination. Place the tray in a plastic bag, then put it in the crisper of your refrigerator for 3 to 6 weeks. After that time, take it out and keep it at 65°F to 70°F (18°C to 21°C). If, after a couple months, seed hasn't germinated, put the seed tray back in the refrigerator for another 3 to 6 weeks of cool treatment. Always check the tray regularly when it's in the crisper. If any seeds start to sprout, remove it immediately. After germination, lower the growing temperature to 55°F to 60°F (13°C to 16°C). Plant in individual pots when plants are 3 inches (7.5 cm) tall. Harden them off for 14 days, and transplant outside after all danger of frost.

Special Uses

Cut Flowers Milkweeds produce stunning cut flowers that are not only attractive but also long lasting. Sear the end of the cut stem with a flame right after harvest to prevent the milky sap from coming out. Place flowers into water immediately. You should be able to enjoy them for a number of days. Adding 2 tablespoons (28 g) of sugar per quart (liter) of water is highly recommended for prolonging vase life. When working with Milkweeds, it is best to wear rubber gloves, as the sap can be a skin irritant to certain individuals.

Dried Flowers You may want to experiment with drying these flower heads in the bud stage, rather than in full bloom. Hang them upside down in a dark, dry, well-ventilated location.

All Milkweeds have interesting seed pods that are decorative in dried arrangements. Collect them as they mature at the stage that most appeals to your taste. Of course, if you wait too long they split open, revealing the silky seeds inside. They will dry well hanging upside down or standing upright.

Sources

Deer-resistant Landscape Nursery, 3200 Sunstone Ct., Clare, MI 48617, (800) 595-3650

The Fragrant Path, P.O. Box 328, Fort Calhoun, NE 68023, (no phone listed)

Fraser's Thimble Farms, 175 Arbutus Rd., Salt Spring Island, BC V8K 1A3 Canada, (250) 537-5788

Park Seed Company, 1 Parkton Ave., Greenwood, SC 29649, (800) 213-0076

Prairie Moon Nursery, 32115 Prairie Lane, Winona, MN 55987, (866) 417-8156

Prairie Nursery, P.O. Box 306, Westfield, WI 53964, (800) 476-9453

Prairie Seed Source, P.O. Box 83, North Lake, WI 53064, (262) 673-7166

Seeds of Change, P.O. Box 15700, Santa Fe, NM 87592, (888) 762-7333

Sunlight Gardens, 174 Golden Lane, Andersonville, TN 37705, (800) 272-7396

Asclepias incarnata

Asclepias tuberosa in pod stage

VARIETIES

VARIETY	COLOR	HEIGHT	HARDINESS
Asclepias incarnata			
(Swamp Milkweed)	Purplish pink	60″	−40°F
'Cinderella'	Pinkish white	60″	−40°F
'Ice Ballet'	Creamy white	60″	−40°F
'Soulmate'	Deep rose pink	40″	−40°F

Vanilla-scented purplish pink clusters sway atop sturdy stems in midsummer on this native plant that forms large pods filled with delicate seeds that float away on mild breezes. Named varieties are similar to the parent except for color. Swamp Milkweeds thrive in moist to wet soils and grow wild in marshes and roadside ditches.

VARIETY	COLOR	HEIGHT	HARDINESS
Asclepias tuberosa****			
(Butterfly Milkweed)	Orange	30″	−40°F
'Gay Butterflies'	Orange/red/yellow	30″	−40°F
'Hello Yellow'	Yellow	24″	−40°F

These plants flower for several weeks in midsummer. They grow well in full sun and require dry conditions. Butterfly Milkweed with its deep root resents transplanting. It appears late in spring, so you may want to mark it.

'Alert'

ASTER

(ASS-stir)

ASTER

Bloom Time	Expected Longevity	Maintenance	Years to Bloom	Preferred Light
Summer to late fall	5 to 15 years	Medium	From seed: 2 years From potted plant: 1 year	Full sun

Asters are valued primarily for fall color, although a few varieties do bloom in summer. They are so varied in height that they are useful in the back, mid-, and front sections of gardens. The plants bear a profusion of star-shaped blooms in myriad colors. Many Asters flower over a period of weeks, making them excellent for endless combinations with other perennials. The taller varieties make excellent long-lasting cut flowers. Unfortunately, many Asters are prone to disease, but you can avoid spraying by choosing the most disease-resistant varieties. Most Asters require regular division for best growth. A handful require regular winter protection in cold climates, but most are very durable once mature.

How Asters Grow

There are more than six hundred species of Asters, so the way they grow varies dramatically. Some plants grow quite tall and lanky while others are compact and bushy. Some varieties create large colonies of plants by sending out underground stems or stolons, but most are less aggressive. All produce starry-shaped flowers with rays fanning out from a center that is usually bright yellow or orange. Leaf shape, size, and color vary by variety as does the presence or lack of hairs on plant stems.

Where to Plant

Site and Light Most Asters prefer lots of sun. There are some that tolerate partial shade, and in certain situations, flower color will be richer in light shade. However, tall varieties may become quite lanky if placed in partial shade. Full sun reduces the chance of fungal diseases and promotes abundant flowering. Avoid planting tall varieties in open, windy spots unless you are willing to stake the plants.

Most Asters form flower buds only as days become shorter. Avoid planting them where they'll be exposed to light at night, as this could delay flowering.

Soil and Moisture Asters thrive in moist, cool, but well-drained soils. Avoid boggy or low-lying areas where plants might die from root rot. Add lots of organic matter to the soil to keep it loose and airy. Good soil amendments are compost, leaf mold, peat moss, and rotted horse manure. Asters prefer neutral to slightly acidic soils that naturally occur in most cold-climate areas.

Spacing Space plants according to their potential size. Give all Asters plenty of space for good air circulation to reduce the risk of disease. Bushy Asters often are much wider than they are tall, so take this into consideration at planting time. Plants may take 2 to 3 years to reach maturity.

Companions

Tall, late-summer and fall-flowering varieties are best in the back of the border combined with other tall perennials such as *Cimicifuga/Actaea* (Bugbane), *Rudbeckia* (Coneflower), and **Grasses**. Consider combining some of them with *Euphorbia polychroma* (Cushion Spurge) and *Geranium macrorrhizum* (Bigroot Cranesbill) which have excellent fall foliage color. *Aster novae-angliae* 'Alma Potschke'/'Andenken an Alma Potschke' (New England Aster) combines beautifully with *Artemisia lactiflora* (White Mugwort). Plant more compact forms with *Artemisia absinthium* 'Lambrook Silver' (Common Wormwood), *Chrysanthemum* × *morifolium* (Garden Mum), and reblooming *Hemerocallis* (Daylily). Some varieties flourish in partial shade and make stunning combinations with native wildflowers and **Ferns**.

Planting

Bare Root Plant bare root stock as early as you can work the ground in spring. Remove plants from their shipping package immediately. Snip off broken or damaged root tips. Soak plants overnight in room-temperature water. Place a small amount of superphosphate in the base of the planting hole. Fill the hole. Place the crown about 1 inch (2.5 cm) below the soil surface. Fill in with soil, press firmly with your fingers, and water immediately. Dissolve ½ cup (about 114 g) 10-10-10 fertilizer in a gallon (about 4 liters) of water. Pour ½ cup (about 120 ml) of this starter solution around the base of each plant. If you prefer organic fertilizer, use fish emulsion instead.

Potted Plants Plant potted Asters after all danger of frost has passed in spring. If the soil in the pot is dry, soak it and let drain overnight. The following day, tap the plant out of the pot, keeping the root ball intact. Plant at the same depth as in the pot, after preparing the hole in a similar manner to that for a bare root plant. Firm soil around the plant with your fingers, and water immediately. Pour ½ cup (about 120 ml) of the starter solution around the base of each plant.

How to Care for Asters

Water Most Asters like cool, moist soils and resent drought. Watering the base of the plant instead of overhead sprinkling may help cut down on fungal diseases. Regular watering encourages rapid, vigorous growth and will increase the number and size of blooms in relation to the amount of foliage produced. If Asters are allowed to wilt from lack of water, their lower leaves may turn yellow and drop off. Soak the soil deeply with each watering.

Mulch Mulch keeps the soil cool and moist while preventing annual weed seeds from germinating. After the soil has warmed up in spring, place a 2-inch (5-cm) layer of organic mulch around the base of each plant. Avoid placing the mulch against stems or directly over the crown, as this may cause rot. Good mulches include dried grass clippings, pine needles, and shredded leaves.

Fertilizing Fertilize Asters just as new growth emerges in spring and once again as buds form. Sprinkle 10-10-10 fertilizer around the base of each plant. Water immediately to dissolve the granules and move nutrients into the root zone. Avoid overfertilizing tall varieties, as this often causes stems to become floppy and require staking.

If you prefer organic fertilizers, use alfalfa meal (rabbit pellets), blood meal, bonemeal, compost, fish emulsion, Milorganite, or rotted manures. Bonemeal must be added to the soil at planting time to be effective.

Weeding Mulch helps control the growth of most weeds. Hand pull all others, since Asters have shallow roots which are easily damaged by deep cultivation. Weed control is critical, since Asters compete poorly with weeds for water and nutrients. Furthermore, weeds act as host plants for insects which carry diseases fatal to Asters.

Staking Many of the taller varieties of *Aster novae-angliae* (New England Aster) and *Aster novi-belgii* (New York Aster) will require staking, especially if planted in open, windy locations or if overfertilized. Place stakes next to stems when they are 2 to 4 inches (5 to 10 cm) tall. Tie stems to the stakes at several

places as the plant grows throughout the season. Use materials such as twine, old nylon stockings, or twist-ties tied in a figure-eight pattern. Tie loosely so that the stem will not be restricted as it grows. You can also support a group of stems by placing a stake in the center of the plant and loosely tying the stems to that stake. Do this at several different levels as the stems grow.

Pinching Back Pinching the tips of the growing stems early in the season is recommended for most varieties of Asters. This will cause the plant to form many side branches and be much bushier, which in turn produces additional flowers. Pinching may reduce bloom size on some of the tall varieties that are noted for their large flowers. If you want fewer but larger blooms for cut flowers, then skip this procedure. In cold climates, never pinch stems after the end of June, or you may alter natural bloom dates.

Thinning Mature Asters sometimes form very tight clumps with numerous stems that are extremely close together. Thinning out some of these early in the season will aid air circulation and may help prevent some outbreaks of disease. Never remove more than one-third of the plant's stems.

Deadheading Unless you are growing species Asters that you want to spread, remove all spent blossoms to prevent seeding. The seedlings of named varieties will not be like their parents and may be far inferior. Removing spent blossoms may encourage additional flowering, especially on summer-blooming varieties. Do it on a regular basis for best results.

Winter Protection Most mature Asters are hardy and do not require winter protection other than natural snowfall. If there is no snow by early December, placing 3 to 4 inches (7.5 to 10 cm) of winter mulch over plants is wise. Desirable winter mulches include whole leaves, pine needles, marsh hay, and clean straw. Remove the mulch as soon as the weather begins to warm up in spring to avoid crown rot. No matter how much snow falls, we recommend winter mulch for

Aster × *frikartii* (Frikart's Aster), a plant highly susceptible to winter-kill.

Problems

Insects Insects are generally not a problem with Asters. However, leafhoppers can be a concern, since they transmit an incurable disease called aster yellows. Control them with insecticidal soaps. Japanese beetles have long been a problem in the East and South and are rapidly working their way north and west. Control them by treating lawns with Milky Spore Disease powder or Merit which kills larvae when applied at just the right time in summer. Handpick adults off plants and toss them into salty water or vinegar. Aphids, leaf miners, and thrips occasionally infest plants as well but are generally of minor consequence. Don't spray for them unless you expect perfection from your plants.

Diseases Unfortunately, certain Asters are prone to a number of diseases. Organic gardeners choose varieties with good disease resistance. The most common diseases of Asters are fungal leaf spots, powdery mildew, rust, wilt, and aster yellows. Growing healthy plants and keeping beds clean of debris and weeds dramatically reduces the chance of disease. Leaf spots show as small, defined spots on foliage that, in some cases, kill the leaves. Powdery mildew shows up as a white film on the leaves. It is easier to prevent than to cure. Rust is rare in cold climates and is generally brought in on plants imported from the West. It shows up as orange to yellow spots on the undersides of leaves. Rust, mildew, and leaf spot can be prevented by regular use of fungicides. If a single plant topples over in a group of otherwise healthy plants, chances are that it is infected with a deadly virus know as wilt. Dig it up and destroy it immediately, as there is no cure for wilt. If an entire group of plants wilt, water the plants immediately and see if they revive. Aster yellows stunts or distorts growth, may turn foliage color purple, and often gives a green cast to malformed flowers. Control leafhoppers to prevent this disease, and immediately destroy any infected plants.

Propagation

Division Most Asters require regular division for peak performance. This may be as often as every second or third year. You can dig up the entire plant in early spring and divide it with a sharp knife or spade into sections. Each division should contain a minimum of three to five shoots with ample roots attached. Plant these as you would a bare root plant, and water immediately. For tall varieties used mainly for cut flowers, cut the clump into divisions that consist of one very vigorous, healthy shoot attached to a strong root system. Plant these divisions in a cutting garden. By fall, these plants will produce spectacular bloom. Some plants send out underground stems, or stolons, creating plants off to the side of the mother plant. In early spring, cut into the soil with a sharp spade between the mother plant and the emerging new plant. Try to keep as much soil as possible with the small plant. Plant immediately as you would a bare root plant, and water well.

Cuttings From the tips of young stems, take cuttings with several sets of leaves. Cut a quarter inch (6 mm) below the lowest leaf node. Remove all lower leaves, and dip the cut end of the stem into rooting hormone. Tap off any excess powder, and plant immediately in a sterile, moist rooting medium. Keep the medium evenly moist at all times. When the cuttings have formed strong root systems and start new leaf growth, they can be potted up or planted in a protected spot in the garden. Keep them consistently moist to get them growing well. Taking cuttings will not harm the plant and, on many varieties, will create a bushier, more compact plant with abundant bloom, similar to the effects of pinching and thinning.

Seed Starting species Asters from seed is quite easy. Place moist germination medium in a tray, and sow the seed over it. Barely cover the seed, and place the tray in a plastic bag. Put the seed tray in the crisper of your refrigerator for 3 weeks. Remove the tray after that time, and place it in an area with a temperature between 65°F and 70°F (18°C to 21°C). If the medium is kept evenly moist, germination generally occurs within 14 to 21 days. As soon as the seeds sprout, grow them at 55°F to 60°F (13°C to 16°C). When seedlings have formed their first true leaves, plant them individually in small pots.

Special Uses

Cut Flowers Most Asters make wonderful, long-lasting cut flowers. Cut them as they open, and place the stems into water immediately. Take them indoors, place the stems in 110°F (43°C) water, and keep them submerged overnight. Some growers suggest crushing the bottoms of stems or placing the lower 1 inch (2.5 cm) of stems in boiling water for 2 minutes prior to placing them in tepid water containing ½ cup (about 114 g) sugar per quart (liter).

Dried Flowers Asters also make good dried flowers. Drying individual blooms in a commercial desiccant or cat litter is the preferred method. Insert a 4-inch (10-cm) wire into the base of each flower. Lay the flowers flat in a box, curve the wire upward, and cover them with the desiccant. Leave them alone for at least 6 days, and then begin to check them. You'll know that flowers are completely dry when the outer flower segments are stiff and the petals feel papery. At this point, you can safely remove them from the desiccant, attach them to longer florist wire, and place them in an arrangement. You can also try to dry the entire stem of flowers, but this is not always successful. Some growers place the box with the flowers covered in desiccant in the oven after baking something. Temperatures of 150°F to 200°F (65°C to 93°C) are ideal. The more quickly the flowers dry, the better the color. You can heat them up a number of times over a period of days with this method.

Sources

Ambergate Gardens, 8730 County Rd. 43, Chaska, MN 55318, (877) 211-9769

Bluestone Perennials, 7211 Middle Ridge Rd., Madison, OH 44057, (800) 852-5243

Busse Gardens, 17160 245th Ave., Big Lake, MN 55309, (800) 544-3192

Digging Dog Nursery, P.O. Box 471, Albion, CA 95410, (707) 937-1130

Doyle Farm Nursery, 158 Norris Rd., Delta, PA 17314, (717) 862-3134

Earthly Pursuits, 2901 Kuntz Rd., Windsor Mill, MD 21244, (410) 496-2523

Fairweather Gardens, P.O. Box 330, Greenwich, NJ 08323, (856) 451-6261

Fieldstone Gardens, Inc., 55 Quaker Lane, Vassalboro, ME 04989, (207) 923-3836

ForestFarm, 990 Tetherow Rd., Williams, OR 97544, (541) 846-7269

Joy Creek Nursery, 20300 NW Watson Rd., Scappoose, OR 97056, (503) 543-7474

Outback Nursery, 15280 110th St., Hastings, MN 55033, (651) 438-2771

Roots and Rhizomes, P.O. Box A, Randolph, WI 53956, (800) 374-5035

Spring Hill Nursery, P.O. Box 330, Harrison, OH 45030, (513) 354-1510

'Alma Potschke'/'Andenken an Alma Potschke'

'Purple Dome'

VARIETIES

Recent taxonomic work has resulted in the reclassification of all native American Asters to new groups (genera). The genus *Aster* will undoubtedly continue to be used for some time, but we have included the new scientific names as part of the descriptions for each plant, since in time the name changes will take hold.

VARIETY	COLOR	HEIGHT	HARDINESS
Aster alpinus			
(Alpine Aster)	Purple	12″	−40°F
'Dark Beauty' ('Dunkle Schone')	Dark purple	8″	−40°F
'Goliath'	Light blue	16″	−40°F
'Happy End'	Rose-pink	8″	−40°F

Alpine Aster blooms in early summer with one- to two-inch solitary flowers per stem. It is an excellent rock garden plant, but is short lived unless divided every few years.

Aster azureus/Symphyotrichum oolentangiense			
(Sky Blue Aster)	Sky blue	36″	−40°F

A fine prairie native, this species puts forth a stunning floral display in late summer.

VARIETY	COLOR	HEIGHT	HARDINESS
Aster cordifolius/Symphyotrichum cordifolium			
(Heart-Leaved Aster)	Lavender blue	36″	–40°F
'Avondale'*****	Lavender blue	36″	–40°F

Blooming over a long period in late summer and fall, this native woodland Aster enjoys an evenly moist, highly organic soil in light shade. Plants bloom less and become weak in excessive shade. 'Avondale' blooms prolifically.

Aster divaricatus/Eurybia divaricata			
(White Wood Aster)	White	18″	–30°F

This plant forms clouds of one-inch flowers in late summer and early fall. The stems are purplish to black and grow in a zigzag pattern. The plant grows best in partial shade.

Aster/Symphyotrichum–Dumosus Group			
(Cushion Aster)			
'Alert'*****	Ruby red	10″	–40°F
'Alice Haslam'	Pink	10″	–40°F
'Professor Anton Kippenberg'*****	Lavender	16″	–40°F
'Rosenwichtel'	Deep rose pink	12″	–40°F
'Snow Cushion' ('Schneekissen')*****	White	12″	–40°F
'Starlight'	Purple red	12″	–40°F

These hybrid Asters form dense, compact mounds; bloom in August and September; and need far less space than New England and New York Asters. However, they are prone to the same diseases.

*Aster ericoides/Symphyotrichum ericoides*** **			
(Heath Aster)	White or pale blue	36″	–40°F

This native plant deserves much greater attention. It is multi-branched and covered with a profusion of small flowers in late summer and early fall. This Aster is especially attractive to butterflies and quite disease resistant.

Aster × frikartii			
(Frikart's Aster)			
'Flora's Delight'	Lilac blue	24″	–20°F
'Monch'	Deep lavender	30″	–20°F
'Wonder of Stafa' ('Wunder von Stäfa')	Light lavender	24″	–20°F

This is one of the more popular Asters because it blooms from midsummer into fall. Its two- to three-inch blooms are fragrant and make excellent cut flowers. This plant requires winter protection, but even with that, it often proves short-lived. You may reduce the chance of winter-kill by not cutting stems down in fall. Frikart's Aster is very resistant to powdery mildew.

*Aster laevis/Symphyotrichum laeve*** **			
(Smooth Aster)	Pale blue	48″	–40°F
'Bluebird'	Violet blue	48″	–40°F

This fine native Aster is covered with one-inch flowers in late summer and fall. Smooth Aster is an important food source for late season migrating butterflies, including monarchs. It may require staking if grown in a rich soil.

VARIETY	COLOR	HEIGHT	HARDINESS
Aster lateriflorus/Symphyotrichum lateriflorum			
(Calico Aster)			
'Lady in Black'	Pinkish white	36"	–30°F
'Prince'	Pinkish white	36"	–30°F

Calico Aster is smothered with an abundance of small daisy-like flowers in fall. The glossy foliage of these selections has an attractive mahogany tinge throughout the growing season, especially strong in spring. 'Lady in Black' offers the richest purplish black foliage color. These varieties are usually wider than they are tall and offer good drought and disease resistance.

Aster macrophyllus/Eurybia macrophylla			
(Bigleaf Aster)	Pale blue to white	30"	–40°F

This native woodland Aster forms a dense mound of heart-shaped foliage which hugs the ground. Bigleaf Aster spreads by creeping rhizomes, making it a good ground cover plant in partial shade. Its one-inch flowers bloom in fall.

Aster novae-angliae/Symphyotrichum novae-angliae			
(New England Aster)	Violet to lavender	60"	–40°F
'Alma Potschke'			
('Andenken an Alma Potschke')*****	Salmon rose	36"	–40°F
'Harrington's Pink'	Salmon pink	40"	–40°F
'Hella Lacy'	Purple	42"	–40°F
'Honeysong Pink'*****	Pink	42"	–40°F
'Purple Dome'*****	Deep purple	24"	–40°F
'Red Star' ('Roter Stern')	Maroon	16"	–40°F
'September Ruby' ('Septemberrubin')	Ruby red	36"	–40°F
'Vibrant Dome'*****	Bright pink	24"	–40°F
'Wedding Lace'	White	48"	–40°F

These Asters thrive in rich, moist soils. The multi-stemmed plants form lovely clusters of one- to two-inch blossoms in early fall. They are useful for cutting, but the flowers do close up at night. The taller varieties may need staking unless pinched back early in the growing season. Leaf spot diseases and mildew may be a problem in very wet seasons.

Aster novi-belgii/Symphyotrichum novi-belgii			
(New York Aster)	Light blue	48"	–40°F
'Bonningdale White'*****	White	48"	–40°F
'Crimson Brocade'	Red	36"	–40°F
'Eventide'	Purple	36"	–40°F
'Lady in Blue'	Lavender blue	18"	–40°F
'Marie Ballard'	Blue	30"	–40°F
'Patricia Ballard'*****	Pink	30"	–40°F

Careful selection from this group offers plants of varying heights and an assortment of flower forms, sizes, and colors that add a great deal of interest to the fall landscape. These are not as good for cutting as the named forms of New England Aster. For best results, plant New York Asters in a well-drained soil that remains evenly moist throughout the growing season. Pinching the plants early in the season will encourage bushier growth. Taller forms will probably require staking and frequent division is necessary to keep plants healthy. Powdery mildew and wilt can be problems with this group.

VARIETY	COLOR	HEIGHT	HARDINESS
Aster oblongifolius/Symphyotrichum oblongifolium			
(Aromatic Aster)	Violet blue	30″	−30°F
'Dream of Beauty'*****	Medium pink	18″	−30°F
'October Skies'*****	Light violet blue	24″	−30°F
'Raydon's Favorite'	Violet blue	30″	−30°F

The blooms of this Aster look similar to those of New England Aster, but the plant blooms a bit later and is more tolerant of dry situations. Its short, narrow leaves have a mint-like fragrance and are resistant to pest and diseases.

Aster sedifolius			
(Rhone Aster)			
'Nanus'*****	Lavender blue	24″	−40°F

An uncommon but highly desirable Aster for cold climates, this plant has nice form, abundant bloom in early fall, and good disease resistance.

Aster sericeus/Symphyotrichum sericeum			
(Silky Aster)	Purple	24″	−40°F

Native throughout the central United States, this Aster has very attractive silvery foliage. Silky Aster blooms in very late summer and fall. It requires a well-drained soil in full sun or light shade.

Aster tataricus			
(Tartarian Aster)	Lavender blue	84″	−40°F
'Jindai'	Light lavender blue	60″	−40°F

This plant forms rounded clusters of three-inch flowers in late fall. It is a very tough plant, capable of withstanding drought. Plant it in the back of the border so that foreground plants cover its often barren lower stems. Despite its height, this species rarely needs staking. Unfortunately, it tends to flower a bit too late for gardens in the far north.

Aster umbellatus/Doellingeria umbellata*****			
(Flat-Topped Aster)	White	60″	−40°F

This eastern United States native enjoys a moist soil in full sun or light shade. Flat-Topped Aster has handsome foliage that is pest and disease resistant. Its showy flowers are borne in flattened clusters and bloom in late summer.

Aster/Symphyotrichum–Wood's Series*****			
'Wood's Blue'	Lavender blue	16″	−40°F
'Wood's Light Blue'	Light violet blue	16″	−40°F
'Wood's Pink'	Pink	16″	−40°F
'Wood's Purple'	Purple	16″	−40°F

These varieties are widely valued for their tidy compact habit, a prolific display of blooms for weeks in late summer and fall as well as their attractive, disease-resistant foliage.

'Amethyst'

ASTILBE

(uh-STILL-bee)

FALSE SPIREA

Bloom Time	Expected Longevity	Maintenance	Years to Bloom	Preferred Light
Early to late summer	15+ years	Medium	From seed: 2 to 3 years From potted plant: 1 year	Light to medium shade

False Spireas are among the most delicate and graceful perennials for moist, lightly shaded areas. Varied selections bloom from early to late summer, with flower colors ranging from white to various shades of pink, purple, lavender, and red. The flowers are feathery plumes or panicles of various sizes and shapes, wonderful in fresh or dried arrangements. When not in flower, the plants add distinctive color and texture to the garden with their attractive green to bronze green foliage. False Spireas will live for years and will resist most diseases and insects if grown properly.

How False Spireas Grow

False Spireas grow from a "woody," shallow-rooted crown to form dense mounds of toothed foliage. In the summer months, flower stems that range in height from less than 1 to more than 4 feet (30 to 120 cm) rise out of the foliage mass. If spent flowers are not removed, they develop into dry fruits. Each one of these contains numerous small seeds that are dispersed when the fruits split on one side. The species can be propagated by seed, but most common garden varieties are of hybrid origin and will not come true from seed.

Where to Plant

Site and Light Grow these perennials in light to medium shade for finest bloom and foliage coloration. They look lovely along ponds and streams in wooded areas. In cold climates they thrive in full sun if the soil has been properly prepared and kept evenly moist throughout the growing season.

Soil and Moisture False Spireas require well-prepared soil that is high in organic matter and evenly moist throughout the growing season. It must drain freely, or plants will die in the winter. If you have clay or very rocky soil, replace it with loam or build a raised bed. Add lots of organic matter to the soil. Good amendments include compost, leaf mold, peat moss, and rotted horse manure.

Spacing Spacing depends on the variety. Space very dwarf, slow-growing types as close as 6 inches (15 cm) apart and tall, vigorous-growing varieties 18 inches (45 cm) or more apart. False Spireas look best in groups of at least three to five.

Companions

With their fine-textured foliage, False Spireas contrast nicely with bold-foliaged perennials such as *Hosta* (Hosta) and *Pulmonaria* (Lungwort). Near water they combine well with *Alchemilla* (Lady's Mantle), *Chelone* (Turtlehead), and *Iris* (Siberian Iris). Here are a handful of successful combinations for the more traditional flower garden: *Astilbe* 'Peach Blossom' or 'Cattleya' with *Artemisia schmidtiana* 'Silver Mound'/'Nana'; *Astilbe* 'Fire'/'Feuer' with *Cimicifuga racemosa* (Black Snakeroot); and *Astilbe* 'Professor van der Wielen' combined with *Hosta* 'Royal Standard' (Hosta) and **Ferns**. Many of the later-blooming, dwarf types make fine edging plants or are great additions to the shady rock garden, which is often sorely lacking in flower color in late summer.

Planting

Bare Root Plant bare root stock as soon as you can work the ground in spring. Remove the plants from their shipping package immediately. Snip off broken or damaged root tips. Soak plants in room-temperature water overnight. Place a small amount of superphosphate in the base of the planting hole. Fill the hole with soil. Plant the crown with the buds or eyes 1 inch (2.5 cm) below the soil surface. Fill in with soil, firm with your fingers, and water immediately. Dissolve ½ cup (about 114 g) of 10-10-10 fertilizer in 1 gallon (about 4 liters) of water. Pour ½ cup (about 120 ml) of this starter solution around the base of each plant. If you prefer organic fertilizer, use fish emulsion instead.

Potted Plants False Spireas are widely available as potted plants. Since they are shallow-rooted, plant them early in the season so that they can establish well-developed root systems before the onset of winter. This early-season planting prevents heaving during winter, when plants begin to rise out of the soil. If the soil in the container is dry, soak it overnight before planting. Tap the plant from the pot without shattering the root ball. Plant at the same depth as in the pot, after preparing the hole in a similar manner to that for a bare root plant. Fill in with properly prepared soil, firm with your fingers, and water. Treat with ½ cup (about 120 ml) starter solution.

How to Care for False Spireas

Water False Spireas depend on consistent moisture throughout the growing season. Water frequently if the weather turns hot and dry. If not given enough water, the leaves will turn brown around their edges. If severely stressed, the leaves dry out completely and shrivel up. When you do water, saturate the soil to a depth of 8 to 10 inches (20 to 25 cm).

Mulch Place a 2-inch (5-cm) thick layer of mulch around the base of each plant as soon as the ground warms up in spring. This keeps the soil moist and cool. Good mulches are shredded leaves, dried grass clippings, shredded bark, or pine needles. They also help control the growth of annual weeds, which compete with the plants for nutrients and water.

Fertilizing False Spireas respond well to regular feeding. As plants begin new growth in spring, sprinkle a tablespoon (14 g) of 10-10-10 granular fertilizer around the base of each clump. Water immediately to dissolve the granules and move nutrients into the root zone. Following up with biweekly foliar feedings until late summer helps the plant produce handsome foliage and abundant bloom.

If you prefer organic fertilizers, use alfalfa meal (rabbit pellets), blood meal, bonemeal, compost, fish emulsion, Milorganite, or rotted horse manure. Bonemeal must be mixed into the soil at planting time to be effective.

Weeding Weeds compete with the plants for valuable nutrients and water. Use organic mulches to inhibit their growth. Hand pull any weeds that do germinate to prevent damage to the shallow root systems from close cultivation with a hoe.

Staking Staking is not necessary.

Deadheading Removal of spent flower heads will not extend or promote additional bloom. Whether or not you choose to perform this task is more a matter of aesthetics than anything else. Although most False Spireas are not strong self-seeders, deadheading will prevent any naturally occurring seedlings from popping up in the garden. Since most False Spireas are of hybrid origin, such seedlings will not be true to type.

Winter Protection Cover first-year plantings with a 6-inch (15-cm) layer of clean straw, marsh hay, whole leaves, or pine needles. Apply this once the ground has frozen to a depth of 2 inches (5 cm). Mulch stops young plants from heaving out of the soil, a serious problem with the very shallow-rooted, dwarf False Spireas. If there is fewer than 3 inches (7.5 cm) of snow by early December, cover mature plants as well.

Problems

Insects Spider mites can be a problem in hot, dry periods. Keeping the plants well watered and misting the foliage usually discourages colonies from forming. If they do form, you may have to resort to a miticide to save your plants. There have also been reports of attack by black vine weevil, Japanese beetle, and whitefly, but these are of very minor consequence in cold climates. However, the spread of Japanese beetles is occurring and may require attention such as the use of Milky Spore Disease powder or Merit on lawns to kill insects in the grub stage.

Disease Powdery mildew rarely afflicts certain varieties and is usually a problem only under very humid, wet growing conditions. Rhizoctonia, a rare fungal disease, may also occur in wet seasons. It invades the root system and causes a plant to collapse.

Propagation

Division False Spireas respond well to division every 4 to 5 years. Divided plants seem to grow more vigorously and flower more profusely. This does, however, vary considerably depending on the variety involved, growing conditions, and landscape use. Divide plants in early spring just as they are sending up new growth. Since the crowns become quite woody with age, a sharp spade or knife will be necessary to cut the plant into divisions. Each division should have three to five growth buds and a good supply of roots. This way you will get flowers the same year in which the plants are divided. Do not allow divisions to dry out prior to planting. Handle them as you would a bare root plant.

Seed Named varieties will not come true from seed, so this method of propagation is of value only for gardeners wanting to grow species types or create new forms. The procedure is quite simple except that it may take as long as 80 days for germination to occur. For that reason, False Spireas are best seeded indoors during the winter months. Sow the seed on the surface of the germination medium, and lightly press them in. No additional cover is necessary, since the seeds need light to germinate. Keep the medium evenly moist, and maintain its temperature between 60°F and 70°F (16°C to 21°C). Some gardeners report good results holding the seed tray at that temperature range for 2 weeks, then reducing the temperature to 40°F (4°C) for 4 weeks before returning it to 65°F (18°C). Once seedlings have emerged, maintaining air temperature around 60°F (16°C) will produce the stockiest plants. Don't be in a rush to discard seed trays, as germination may occur over a long period of time. Once seedlings have their first set of true leaves, plant them in individual pots. Harden them off for 14 days, and plant outside after all danger of frost in spring.

Special Uses

Cut Flowers False Spireas make attractive but very short-lived cut flowers. The taller varieties are best for cutting. Harvest stems when the plumes are about half to three-quarters open. There is no single method that works well for conditioning all varieties. Some respond best placed in 110°F (43°C) water, while others do better in cold water. A number will last longer if you char the base of the stem in a flame prior to placing them in water.

Dried Flowers Cut stems when blooms are just opening, and bundle them together after removing all leaves. Hang the bunches upside down in a dark, dry, well-ventilated location for several weeks until dry. Some growers also promote drying the flowers in desiccant. This is done by placing the stems lengthwise on a 2-inch (5-cm) bed of the chosen material in a cardboard box. Gently sift more of the material around the plumes, and continue until they're covered completely to a depth of 2 inches (5 cm). Leave the box uncovered, and carefully check progress once a week. When the individual flowers feel crisp and rigid, carefully remove the stems from the box for arranging. This process may take several weeks.

Many people like using the dried seed heads in fall arrangements. When flowers lose color or turn brown, cut the plumes off. They can be dried either upside down or standing upright. Seed heads often dry well right in the garden. Just cut them off in fall to use in an arrangement.

Sources

Ambergate Gardens, 8730 County Rd. 43, Chaska, MN 55318, (877) 211-9769

Bluestone Perennials, 7211 Middle Ridge Rd., Madison, OH 44057, (800) 852-5243

Busse Gardens, 17160 245th Ave., Big Lake, MN 55309, (800) 544-3192

Fieldstone Gardens, Inc., 55 Quaker Lane, Vassalboro, ME 04989, (207) 923-3836

Mason Hollow Nursery, 47 Scripps Lane, Mason, NH 03048, (603) 878-4347

Sandy Mush Herb Nursery, 316 Surrett Cove Rd., Leicester, NC 28748, (828) 683-2014

Venero Gardens, 5985 Seamans Dr., Shorewood, MN 55331, (952) 474-8550

White Flower Farm, P.O. Box 50, Litchfield, CT 06759, (800) 503-9624

VARIETIES

Choosing the best False Spireas can be extremely difficult as there are so many good choices. Personal tastes and how the plant will be used play a major role. False Spireas are often listed by their breeding background but, for our purposes here, no detailed explanation of this classification system will be given, as this information is primarily of value for historical or hybridizing purposes. We have noted a few characteristics of each group which will aid you in choosing types for your garden. Bloom season extends from early to late summer so varieties marked **E** will bloom in approximately the first third of that period, those marked **M** in the second third, and those marked **L** in the last third. Sometimes there is an overlap in bloom periods and that is indicated by a hyphen, as in **M-L** for mid to late season.

VARIETY	COLOR	BLOOM	HEIGHT	HARDINESS
Astilbe–Arendsii Group				
'America' ('Amerika')	Rich pink	E-M	28″	–40°F
'Amethyst'	Lavender	M	24″	–40°F
'August Light' ('Augustleuchten')	Bright red	M-L	28″	–40°F
'Bergkristall'	Pure white	M	30″	–40°F
'Boogie Woogie'	Rich pink	M	20″	–40°F
'Bressingham Beauty'	Rose pink	E-M	36″	–40°F
'Bridal Veil' ('Brautschleier')*****	Pure white	E-M	20″	–40°F
'Catherine Deneuve'	Rose pink	M	28″	–40°F
'Cattleya'	Rose pink	M	40″	–40°F
'Cotton Candy'	Deep pink	M	16″	–40°F
'Country & Western'*****	Soft pink	E-M	18″	–40°F
'Drum and Bass'	Reddish purple	M	20″	–40°F
'Elizabeth Bloom'	Pure pink	E-M	28″	–40°F
'Erica' ('Erika')	Light pink	E-M	30″	–40°F
'Etna'	Dark red	E-M	24″	–40°F
'Fanal'*****	Carmine red	E-M	24″	–40°F
'Federsee'	Carmine rose	E-M	24″	–40°F
'Fire' ('Feuer')	Coral red	M	30″	–40°F
'Flamingo'	Deep pink	M	18″	–40°F
'Gloria Purpurea'	Rose pink	E-M	24″	–40°F
'Granat'	Dark red	M	28″	–40°F
'Grete Pungel'	Flesh pink	M	28″	–40°F
'Hyacinth' ('Hyazinth')	Lilac rose	E-M	36″	–40°F
'Irrlicht'	Lilac white	M	24″	–40°F
'Jump & Jive'	Pinkish red	M-L	20″	–40°F
'Kvele'	Dark lilac rose	E-M	30″	–40°F
'Lollypop'	Pink blushed white	M	18″	–40°F
'Mars'	Dark lilac rose	E-M	30″	–40°F
'Red Light' ('Rotlicht')	Red	M	20″	–40°F
'Rhythm & Beat'	Purple pink	M	20″	–40°F
'Rhythm & Blues'	Raspberry pink	E-M	24″	–40°F

'Fanal'

'Hennie Graafland'

'Ostrich Plume'/'Straussenfeder'

'Sprite'

VARIETY	COLOR	BLOOM	HEIGHT	HARDINESS
'Rock & Roll'*****	White	M	20"	−40°F
'Sister Theresa'('Zuster Theresa')*****	Salmon pink	E-M	24"	−40°F
'Snowdrift'	Bright white	E-M	24"	−40°F
'Spartan'	Deep red	M	30"	−40°F
'Spinell'	Carmine red	M-L	28"	−40°F
'White Gloria' ('Weisse Gloria')*****	Creamy white	M	20"	−40°F

This is the largest and most well known group of False Spireas. The group was named after the German, George Arends, who bred many hybrids still available today.

Astilbe biternata

(False Goat's Beard)	Creamy white	E-M	48"	−30°F

This tall-growing species is the only native North American False Spirea. It requires soil heavily enriched with organic matter and lots of moisture throughout the entire growing season.

Astilbe chinensis

(Chinese Astilbe)

'Finale'	Light rose	L	20"	−40°F
'Milk and Honey'*****	Soft pink aging white	M-L	28"	−40°F
'Pumila'	Lavender purple	L	12"	−40°F
'Purple Candles' ('Purpurkerze')*****	Reddish purple	M-L	36"	−40°F
'Serenade'	Rose red	M-L	18"	−40°F
'Superba'	Rosy purple	M-L	36"	−40°F
'Veronica Klose'	Red purple	M-L	20"	−40°F
'Visions'*****	Raspberry red	M-L	16"	−40°F
'Vision in Pink'	Pink	M-L	20"	−40°F
'Vision in Red'	Purplish red	M-L	20"	−40°F
'Vision in White'	Creamy white	M-L	24"	−40°F

These varieties are the most drought tolerant of the Astilbes. 'Purple Candles' and 'Visions' have especially intense colors.

Astilbe–Japonica Group

'Avalanche'	Pure white	E-M	20"	−40°F
'Bremen'	Rose pink	M	20"	−40°F
'Deutschland'	White	E-M	24"	−40°F
'Elizabeth Van Veen'	Raspberry purple	M	24"	−40°F
'Ellie'*****	White	E-M	30"	−40°F
'Europa'	Bright rose	E	24"	−40°F
'Gladstone'	White	E-M	20"	−40°F
'Montgomery'*****	Dark red	E-M	24"	−40°F
'Peach Blossom'	Salmon pink	E	24"	−40°F
'Red Sentinel'	Deep red	E-M	24"	−40°F
'Rheinland'*****	Pink rose	E-M	24"	−40°F
'Washington'	White	E	20"	−40°F

'Ellie' has elegant dark foliage and 'Washington' has a wonderful bronzy tone to its leaves.

VARIETY	COLOR	BLOOM	HEIGHT	HARDINESS
Astilbe–Simplicifolia Group				
'Aphrodite'	Rose	M	18″	−40°F
'Bronze Elegance' ('Bronce Elegans')	Light pink	L	14″	−40°F
'Hennie Graafland'	Pink	M-L	16″	−40°F
'Inshriach Pink'	Light pink	M-L	12″	−40°F
'Jacqueline'	Light pink	M	20″	−40°F
'Key Biscayne'	Rose pink	M-L	18″	−40°F
'Key Largo'	Shell pink	M-L	20″	−40°F
'Key West'*****	Carmine red	M-L	20″	−40°F
'Praecox'	Shell pink	M	16″	−40°F
'Sprite'	Pale pink	M	18″	−40°F
'Touch of Pink'	Apricot pink	M	16″	−40°F
'White Sensation'*****	Bright white	L	16″	−40°F
'White Wings'	White blushed pink	M	16″	−40°F

These hybrids have lustrous green foliage and decorative seed pods. A number of them have interesting bronzy tones to their foliage.

VARIETY	COLOR	BLOOM	HEIGHT	HARDINESS
Astilbe–Thunbergii Group				
'Betsy Cuperus'	Blush pink	M-L	36″	−40°F
'Moerheimii'	Creamy white	M	36″	−40°F
'Ostrich Plume' ('Straussenfeder')	Salmon pink	M	30″	−40°F
'Professor van der Wielen'*****	White	M-L	36″	−40°F

These cultivars are of value for their height and later bloom. Their nodding flower clusters are quite large, useful in arrangements, and even ornamental late in the season after they have gone to seed.

VARIETY	COLOR	BLOOM	HEIGHT	HARDINESS
Astilbe (Named varieties and hybrids)				
'Delft Lace'*****	Apricot pink	E-M	36″	−40°F
'Lilliput'	Light salmon pink	E	6″	−40°F
'Maggie Daley'	Purple rose	M	28″	−40°F
'Perkeo'	Rose	E	8″	−40°F
'Radius'	Bright red	M	24″	−40°F
'Rise and Shine'*****	Vibrant pink	E-M	30″	−40°F

'Delft Lace' is known for its unusual blue-green leaves that show red highlights. 'Lilliput' and 'Perkeo' have dark green highly textured foliage. 'Radius' has coppery green foliage in spring. 'Rise and Shine' offers exceptionally sturdy stems and great vigor.

Baptisia australis

BAPTISIA

(bap-TEEJZ-ee-uh)

FALSE INDIGO

Bloom Time	Expected Longevity	Maintenance	Years to Bloom	Preferred Light
Spring to early summer	25+ years	Low	From seed: 3 years From potted plant: 1 to 2 years	Full sun

False Indigos are dramatic plants that bloom for several weeks. Their compound leaves form a mass of blue green foliage that is attractive throughout the season. They are excellent mid- or background plants in the border. They also can act as shrubs and even make good hedges. Their black seedpods are prized in dried arrangements. False Indigos are easy to grow, durable, and problem free. They do take several years to mature before flowering well. Once mature, they thrive for decades.

How False Indigos Grow

False Indigos grow into bushy clumps ranging in height from 24 to 60 inches (60 to 150 cm), depending on the variety. The plant forms from large, fleshy roots, making it difficult to transplant or divide. Its pealike flowers develop on spires 12 inches (30 cm) or more in length. If left on the plant, they form seedpods that slowly blacken and turn brittle by the end of the season. Inside are small seeds that look like dark, immature peas. These fall to the ground and often germinate the following year.

Where to Plant

Site and Light False Indigos prefer full sun but will tolerate light shade. Too much shade results in leggy plants with little bloom. Choose planting sites for these perennials carefully, as they form long roots and don't like to be moved. False Indigos grow nicely in borders, meadows, or on the edges of woodlands. Plants need a fair amount of space, since they get quite large when mature.

Soil and Moisture False Indigos are members of the legume, or pea, family and have the capability of fixing nitrogen in the soil. Still, they prefer deep, rich soils that drain freely. Add lots of organic material to the soil. Good amendments include compost, leaf mold, peat moss, and rotted horse manure. If you have rocky or clay soil, replace it with good soil or build a raised bed.

Spacing False Indigos grow slowly, maturing over years into bushy plants up to 4 or more feet (120 cm) in width. Since they do not like to be disturbed, choose the planting site carefully. Plant large varieties at least 3 feet (90 cm) away from other plants. Smaller varieties can, of course, be somewhat closer.

Companions

Baptisia (False Indigo) combines nicely with *Iris* (Bearded and Siberian Iris), *Paeonia* (Peony), and fine-textured **Grasses**. White or pink Iris and Peonies are especially attractive against the rich blue of *Baptisia australis* (Blue False Indigo). Other suggested companions include *Achillea ptarmica* 'Snowball'/'Boule de Neige' (Sneezewort), *Aquilegia* (Columbine), *Geranium* (Cranesbill), and *Lysimachia punctata* (Yellow Loosestrife).

Planting

Bare Root Plant bare root stock as soon as you can work the ground in spring. Remove the plants from their shipping package immediately. Snip off broken or damaged root tips. Soak plants overnight in room-temperature water. Place a small amount of superphosphate in the base of the planting hole. Fill the hole with soil. Place the crown 1 inch (2.5 cm) below the soil surface. Fill in with soil, firm with your fingers, and water immediately. Dissolve ½ cup (about 114 g) 10-10-10 fertilizer in 1 gallon (about 4 liters) of water. Pour ½ cup (about 120 ml) of this starter solution around the base of the plant. If you prefer organic fertilizer, use fish emulsion instead.

Potted Plants Plant potted False Indigo after all danger of frost in spring. If the soil in the pot is dry, saturate it, and let it drain overnight. Tap the plant out of the pot without disturbing the root ball. Plant it at the same depth as in the pot, after preparing the hole in a similar manner to that for a bare root plant. Fill in with soil, firm with your fingers, and water immediately. Pour ½ cup (about 120 ml) of starter solution around the base of the plant.

How to Care for False Indigos

Water Keep young plants evenly moist throughout the first growing season. Saturate the soil thoroughly every time you water. In subsequent seasons, False Indigos need less frequent watering but should be soaked regularly during extended dry periods.

Mulch Place 2 inches (5 cm) of organic mulch around the base of each plant as soon as the ground warms up in spring. Good mulches are dried grass clippings, shredded leaves, or pine needles. This keeps the soil moist and cool. It also inhibits the growth of annual weeds. Replace the mulch throughout the growing season.

Fertilizing Sprinkle a small handful of 10-10-10 fertilizer around the base of the plant as soon as new growth emerges in spring. Water immediately to dissolve granules and move nutrients into the root zone. Fertilize again after bloom to encourage lush foliage growth.

If you prefer organic fertilizers, use alfalfa meal (rabbit pellets), blood meal, bonemeal, compost, fish emulsion, Milorganite, or rotted manure. Bonemeal must be mixed with the soil at planting time to be effective.

Staking Even the tallest varieties rarely require staking unless you want to limit their horizontal spread. Peony hoops provide good support if you wish to keep these perennials fully upright. However, part of the beauty of the plant is its rounded, free-flowing form. Staking, then, is strictly an aesthetic decision.

Deadheading Cut off faded flowers to prevent plants from self-seeding. You may choose to let some of the flowers form seedpods for use in dried arrangements or for seed to grow new plants.

Winter Protection No winter protection is necessary for mature plants. However, if in the first year of planting there is less than 3 inches (7.5 cm) of snow on the ground by early December, cover the young plants with 4 inches (10 cm) of whole leaves, clean straw, marsh hay, or pine needles. Remove this winter mulch as soon as the weather begins to warm up in spring to avoid crown rot.

Problems

Insects False Indigos are rarely bothered by insects.

Disease These perennials are resistant to most common diseases.

Propagation

Division Division is not necessary for the health of these perennials, and, in fact, is not recommended. However, with plants older than 3 years, division is certainly possible. In spring, just as new growth emerges, dig deeply around the entire plant to expose the extended root system. Keep digging down as far as necessary to remove the entire root system without breaking it. Once the plant is out of the ground and washed clean, cut the woody crown into sections with a sharp knife or saw. Each section should have several shoots and an ample supply of healthy roots. Plant immediately as you would a bare root plant.

Seed If you are going to collect seed, wait until the pods turn crispy black. The seeds rattle inside the pods when they are mature. Ripe seed will be dark brown to black. It is easy to get fresh seed to germinate. Plant it in moist germination medium, and keep the medium evenly moist until seedlings emerge. This usually takes 7 to 14 days. Plant in individual pots when seedlings have a second pair of leaves. Keep them growing under lights until the following spring. Then harden them off for 14 days, and plant them outside after all danger of frost.

You can also sow the fresh seed in late fall in a moist germination medium in a cold frame or bed. Keep the soil evenly moist until it freezes for the winter. The moist chilling of winter will break the seed's dormancy. Seedlings will emerge late the next spring. Transplant to pots or a protected location in the garden when seedlings are 3 inches (7.5 cm) tall.

Purchased or collected seed can be stored until late winter for indoor sowing. Seed should be sown 14 weeks before the last expected frost in spring. With a file or piece of sandpaper, nick the thick seed coat or poke a minuscule hole in the coat with a pin on the opposite side of the seed's eye. This process, known as scarification, allows moisture and oxygen to penetrate the seed coat. Soaking the seed in water for 24 hours is an alternative method, but it is not as effective. Immediately after nicking the seed or soaking it in water, place it in moist germination medium, and barely cover it. Place the seed tray in a plastic bag, and put it in the crisper of your refrigerator for several weeks. After that time, remove it, and keep the medium evenly moist and at 70°F to 75°F (21°C to 24°C) until the seed germinates. After germination, reduce the growing temperature by 10°F (6°C) to produce the stockiest plants. When seedlings have a second pair of leaves, plant them in individual pots.

Special Uses

The sap of *Baptisia australis* (Blue False Indigo) turns purple when exposed to air and is used as a natural dye.

Cut Flowers Although the buds on cut stems do not open well, the open flowers are long-lasting and make excellent additions to arrangements. Cut stems in full bloom for best effect. The fresh foliage is also attractive in arrangements.

Dried Pods, Flowers, and Foliage The dried seedpods are excellent additions to arrangements. Remove them when they reach the stage of maturity you prefer and dry them either hanging upside down or upright in a jar. Fully mature seed heads look like giant, black pea pods. They rattle prior to the seed falling out and were once used as toys for children.

Drying the flowers is difficult, although some people have successfully done it. Cut stems at the stage that appeals to you most and hang them upside down in a well-ventilated, dark, dry location.

Some people also use treated foliage in arrangements. It's best to soak the stems in glycerin as described on commercial containers. The leaves absorb the glycerin and stay pliable for long periods.

Sources

Ambergate Gardens, 8730 County Rd. 43, Chaska, MN 55318, (877) 211-9769

Ion Exchange (seed), 1878 Old Mission Dr., Harpers Ferry, IA 52146, (800) 291-2143

White Flower Farm, P.O. Box 50, Litchfield, CT 06759, (800) 503-9624

Baptisia australis

Seedpods forming on *Baptisia australis*

VARIETIES

VARIETY	COLOR	HEIGHT	HARDINESS
Baptisia australis*****			
(Blue False Indigo)	Indigo blue	48″	−40°F

This tough plant forms a mound of bluish green foliage that has a shrub-like appearance at maturity. It blooms in mid to late spring with spikes of one-inch flowers. It is a foolproof perennial tolerant of a wide range of growing conditions.

Baptisia australis var. *minor******			
(Dwarf False Indigo)	Indigo blue	24″	−40°F

If you don't have the space to afford to large bushy False Indigos, here is a great alternative. This plant has the same flower color and bloom time as Blue False Indigo but it is shorter with appropriately proportioned foliage.

Baptisia bracteata			
(Plains Wild Indigo)	Creamy yellow	24″	−40°F

This compact native species is the earliest member of the group to flower, blooming in early spring. It grows well in full sun or light shade.

Baptisia leucantha			
(Prairie Wild Indigo)	White	48″	−40°F

A mature clump of this perennial boasts a fine display of white flowers from late spring to early summer and attractive seed pods later in the season.

Baptisia leucophaea (see *Baptisia bracteata*)

Baptisia (Named varieties and hybrids)			
'Carolina Moonlight'	Butter yellow	48″	−40°F
Midnite Prairieblues™	Dark blue	48″	−40°F
'Purple Smoke'*****	Purple blue	48″	−40°F
Solar Flare Prairieblues™	Yellow aging to orange	48″	−40°F
Starlite Prairieblues™	Blue/white flush	48″	−40°F
Twilite Prairieblues™	Violet/yellow	60″	−40°F

Originating as a chance seedling, 'Carolina Moonlight' has a strong upright appearance, attractive blue green foliage, and spires of soft yellow pea-like blooms. Midnite Prairieblues™ stands out for the deep blue color of its flowers. A mature specimen of 'Purple Smoke' looks like a rounded shrub with gray-green stems. With its smoky purple this plant is spectacular at peak bloom. The blooms on Solar Flare Prairieblues™ turn color from yellow to orange as they mature. Starlite Prairieblues™ is one of the earliest hybrid False Indigos to come into bloom. Its show of bicolored flowers literally cover the plant. Twilite Prairieblues™ forms a very substantial plant with attractive blue-green foliage. Its violet-purple flowers have a yellow flush at their bases, and the flower spikes can reach two to three feet in length.

'Birch Hybrid'

CAMPANULA

(kam-PAN-you-la)

BELLFLOWER

BLOOM TIME	EXPECTED LONGEVITY	MAINTENANCE	YEARS TO BLOOM	PREFERRED LIGHT
Late spring to late summer	2 to 20 years	Medium	From seed: 2 years From potted plant: 1 year	Full sun to light shade

Bellflowers are a very large and diverse group of perennials offering a wide choice in flower color and form. Many have long bloom periods that can be made even longer by regular deadheading. Certain types make excellent cut flowers. Most Bellflowers are relatively free of insects and disease and, if grown properly, will live for years. Choose varieties carefully, since some need pampering to survive, while others can become weedy. A number are almost irresistible to rabbits.

How Bellflowers Grow

With nearly three hundred species in this group, the way individual plants grow varies dramatically. Some form upright plants, while others mature into spreading clumps. The single leaves all have a jagged or toothed edge. Flowers are star-like or bell-shaped and float above the plant singly or in showy clusters. With some varieties, they face upward, while in others they hang down. If allowed to drop their seed, some varieties will self-sow freely.

Where to Plant

Site and Light Bellflowers thrive in full sun or light shade. They perform best in cold climates, as they do not like extremely high temperatures.

Soil and Moisture Bellflowers prefer loose, organic soils that drain freely. Add lots of organic matter to the soil. Recommended are compost, leaf mold, peat moss, or rotted horse manure. These keep the soil moist and cool.

Spacing Space small, clump-forming types 12 inches (30 cm) apart and those with a tendency to spread no less than 18 inches (45 cm) apart. Place the tallest forms 24 inches (60 cm) away from the nearest plant.

Companions

Campanula (Bellflower) is such a large and diverse group of perennials that potential plant combinations seem almost endless. The tall, summer-blooming types go well in the border with *Achillea* (Yarrow), *Heuchera* (Coral Bells), *Leucanthemum*–Superbum Group (Shasta Daisy), and *Phlox*–Maculata Group (Meadow Phlox). Try *Campanula glomerata* (Clustered Bellflower) along with *Geranium sanguineum* var. *striatum* (Bloody Cranesbill), *Iris* (Siberian Iris), and *Oenothera fruticosa* (Common Sundrops). Low-growing varieties make good edging or front-of-the-border plants as well as being excellent for rock or wall gardens. *Campanula carpatica* (Carpathian Bellflower) is charming planted with *Delphinium grandiflorum* (Chinese Delphinium), *Lilium* (Lily), and *Veronica* 'Pink Damask' (Speedwell Hybrid). The lovely blues of Bellflowers are a wonderful contrast to the white bark of birch trees in more northerly gardens.

Planting

Bare Root Plant bare root stock as soon as you can work the ground in spring. Remove plants from their shipping package immediately. Snip off broken or damaged root tips. Soak plants overnight in room-temperature water. Place a small amount of superphosphate in the base of the planting hole. Fill the hole with soil. Place the crown 1 inch (2.5 cm) below the soil surface. Fill in with soil, firm with your fingers, and water immediately. Dissolve ½ cup (about 114 g) 10-10-10 fertilizer in 1 gallon (about 4 liters) water. Pour ½ cup (about 120 ml) of this starter solution around the base of each plant. If you prefer organic fertilizer, use fish emulsion.

Potted Plants Plant Bellflowers after all danger of frost in spring. If the soil in the pot is dry, water it and let it drain overnight. Tap the plant out of the pot without disturbing the root ball. Plant at the same depth as in the pot, after preparing the hole in a similar manner to that for a bare root plant. Fill in with soil, firm with your fingers, and water immediately. Pour ½ cup (about 120 ml) starter solution around the base of each plant.

How to Care for Bellflowers

Water Keep the soil evenly moist at all times throughout the growing season. Moisture keeps soil temperatures cool, which affects both the beauty and lasting quality of the blossoms. Saturate the soil to a depth of 8 to 10 inches (20 to 25 cm) each time you water.

Mulch Mulch keeps the soil moist and cool in addition to inhibiting weed growth. Place 2 inches (5 cm) of organic mulch around the base of each plant as soon as the ground warms up in spring. Good organic mulches include dried grass clippings, compost, shredded leaves, and pine needles.

Fertilizing Sprinkle 10-10-10 fertilizer around the base of each plant just as new growth emerges in spring. Water immediately to dissolve the granules and carry nutrients to the root zone. A follow-up feeding several weeks later often results in a greater show of flowers. However, some of the taller varieties will get floppy if overfed and need to be staked.

If you prefer organic fertilizer, use alfalfa meal (rabbit pellets), blood meal, bonemeal, compost, cow manure, fish emulsion, Milorganite, or rotted horse manure. Bonemeal must be mixed into the soil at planting time to be effective.

Weeding Weeds compete with Bellflowers for moisture and nutrients. Control them with a layer of mulch and regular hand weeding. Most varieties in this group compete poorly with weeds.

Staking Some of the taller varieties may fall over without staking. Insert stakes into the ground next to stems in early spring. As they grow, attach individual stems to the supports with loose figure-eight knots. Feed less the following year to minimize the need for staking.

Deadheading Remove all dead flowers unless you want seed to form. Regular deadheading will encourage additional bloom in certain varieties.

Winter Protection Most of the varieties described in this section are winter hardy with adequate snowfall. Protect the more tender varieties with 4 inches (10 cm) of marsh hay, whole leaves, or clean straw in late fall. Wait until the ground is frozen to a depth of 2 inches (5 cm) before applying the winter mulch. Remove the cover as soon as the weather warms up in spring to prevent rot.

Problems

Insects In very moist weather, slugs may be a problem. Place boards by the plants being damaged. Turn these over in the morning and pull off the slugs. Toss them into a can of salty water or vinegar. If you use poisoned slug bait, keep it away from pets and wildlife. If slugs become a major nuisance, avoid the use of summer mulch altogether.

Disease There are no serious disease problems with Bellflowers.

Propagation

Division Most Bellflowers will need division every fourth or fifth year to keep them growing well. Dig up the clump just as new growth emerges in spring, and wash off the soil. Cut the clump into sections with a sharp knife, making sure that each section of the crown has a healthy root system. Plant them immediately as you would a bare root plant. *Campanula persicifolia* (Peach-Leaved Bellflower) produces little plantlets (offsets) to the side of the crown. Cut these away with a sharp spade, and plant them immediately in a new location.

Cuttings Take basal cuttings in spring before flower buds form. These cuttings are taken from the base of the plant and include just a tiny bit of tissue from the crown. Cuttings should have several sets of leaves. Remove all but the top set of leaves. Dip the cut end in rooting hormone, and tap off any excess powder. Place it immediately in moist rooting medium. Keep the medium evenly moist and the humidity high until cuttings take root. Once they have formed a clump of roots, transplant them to individual pots or a protected spot in the garden. Keep them consistently moist.

Seed Start seed indoors 10 to 12 weeks before the last expected spring frost. Press seed into moist germination medium, and barely cover it. Germination normally occurs within 21 days at temperatures of 65°F to 70°F (18°C to 21°C). Once seedlings have a second pair of leaves, plant them in pots.

Special Uses

Cut Flowers The tall-growing varieties make excellent cut flowers. Especially good are varieties of *Campanula glomerata* (Clustered Bellflower), *Campanula lactiflora* (Milky Bellflower), *Campanula lat-*

ifolia (Giant Bellflower), and *Campanula persicifolia* (Peach-Leaved Bellflower). Cut these in varied stages of bloom. When conditioning Bellflowers, place the stems in water overnight. The ideal water temperature is different for each Bellflower. Vary the temperature from cold to hot on individual stems to see what produces the best results.

Dried Flowers Bellflowers are not used in dried arrangements, since colors may fade badly. Nevertheless, you may wish to try drying individual blossoms in desiccant. Place the blooms individually in the drying material, and face them up in the exact form desired. Sprinkle the material around the petals and cover them completely. Keep them in the desiccant until they're completely dry.

Sources

Ambergate Gardens, 8730 County Rd. 43, Chaska, MN 55318, (877) 211-9769

Bluestone Perennials, 7211 Middle Ridge Rd., Madison, OH 44057, (800) 852-5243

Busse Gardens, 17160 245th Ave., Big Lake, MN 55309, (800) 544-3192

Digging Dog Nursery, P.O. Box 471, Albion, CA 95410, (707) 937-1130

Joy Creek Nursery, 20300 NW Watson Rd., Scappoose, OR 97056, (503) 543-7474

'Stella'

'White Clips'/'Weisse Clips'

VARIETIES

VARIETY	COLOR	HEIGHT	HARDINESS
Campanula alliariifolia			
(Spurred Bellflower)	Ivory white	30″	−40°F

This species is an adaptable plant with heart-shaped foliage and nodding flowers that bloom for weeks in early summer. The plant spreads to make a good ground cover.

VARIETY	COLOR	HEIGHT	HARDINESS
Campanula carpatica			
(Carpathian Bellflower)			
'Blue Clips' ('Blaue Clips')*****	Violet blue	8″	−40°F
'Karl Foerster'	Cobalt blue	8″	−40°F
'Pearl Deep Blue'*****	Deep violet blue	8″	−40°F
'Pearl White'*****	White	8″	−40°F
'White Clips' ('Weisse Clips')*****	White	8″	−40°F

These are fine border and rock garden plants with bright green, serrated foliage and upward-facing flowers. Plants bloom from spring into late summer if spent blossoms are removed regularly.

VARIETY	COLOR	HEIGHT	HARDINESS
Campanula cochlearifolia			
(Spiral Bellflower)	Violet blue	6″	−30°F
'Bavarian Blue'	Sky blue	6″	−30°F
'Elizabeth Oliver'	Powder blue (D)	4″	−30°F

These Bellflowers bloom with small nodding flowers in mid to late summer. They need good drainage and light shade. 'Elizabeth Oliver' has double (D) flowers.

VARIETY	COLOR	HEIGHT	HARDINESS
Campanula garganica			
(Gargano Bellflower)	Blue/white eyes	6″	−30°F

These plants are best used as ground covers or draped over a retaining wall. They flower in early summer and will die out without a well-drained soil.

VARIETY	COLOR	HEIGHT	HARDINESS
Campanula glomerata			
(Clustered Bellflower)	Violet/purple	36″	−40°F
'Alba'	White	24″	−40°F
'Crown of Snow' ('Schneekrone')*****	White	18″	−40°F
'Joan Elliott'*****	Deep violet blue	18″	−40°F
'Speciosa' (var. *dahurica*)	Dark purple	24″	−40°F
'Superba'	Deep violet	30″	−40°F

This summer-flowering species carries its blooms in clusters at the stem tips and at the leaf nodes, from which it gets its common name. All varieties spread rapidly in moist soil, but 'Superba' is particularly vigorous. Though the plant is somewhat coarse in appearance, it's still lovely in the border and an excellent cut flower.

VARIETY	COLOR	HEIGHT	HARDINESS
Campanula lactiflora			
(Milky Bellflower)	Lavender blue	48″	−30°F
'Alba'	Snow white	30″	−30°F

VARIETY	COLOR	HEIGHT	HARDINESS
'Loddon Anna'	Pale pink	48″	−30°F
'Prichard's Variety'	Violet blue	30″	−30°F

These Bellflowers tend to be short-lived in cold climates, especially if grown in poorly drained soils. They do well in sun or light shade and bloom from June to August. Regular winter protection is advised.

Campanula latifolia

(Giant Bellflower)	Purple/dark blue	48″	−30°F
'Brantwood'	Violet purple	36″	−30°F

Another short-lived Bellflower, this one grows upright with clustered flowers blooming in early to midsummer. Plants thrive in either full sun or light shade. Soil must drain freely and contain lots of organic matter. Winter protection is advised.

Campanula persicifolia

(Peach-Leaved Bellflower)	Light blue	36″	−40°F
'Alba'	White	30″	−40°F
'Blue Eyed Blond'	Deep blue	18″	−40°F
'Chettle Charm'*****	White/blue edge	30″	−40°F
'Coerulea'	Pure blue	30″	−40°F
'Moerheimii'	White (D)	30″	−40°F
'Telham Beauty'	Pale lavender blue	36″	−40°F

This Bellflower produces handsome tufts of lance-shaped, leathery leaves which often remain evergreen, even in cold climates. The saucer-shaped, out-facing flowers bloom at the height of summer and are excellent for cutting. Most of them, except the double forms, are easily grown from seed. These plants may require staking. 'Blue Eyed Blond' has striking yellow foliage.

*Campanula portenschlagiana*****

(Dalmatian Bellflower)	Violet blue	6″	−30°F
'Resholt Variety'	Light violet blue	6″	−30°F

Forming a spreading mat of small green leaves topped with an abundance of upfacing flowers, this Bellflower makes an effective front edge or small-scale ground cover plant. It blooms from late spring into early summer and performs well in full sun or light shade.

Campanula poscharskyana

(Serbian Bellflower)	Lavender blue	12″	−30°F
'Blue Gown' ('Blauranke')	Lavender blue/white	6″	−30°F
Blue Waterfall ('Camgood')*****	Blue violet	10″	−30°F
'E. H. Frost'	Bluish white	6″	−30°F
'Stella'	Lavender blue	8″	−30°F

These sprawling plants make good small-scale ground covers that bloom over a long period in summer.

Campanula punctata

(Spotted Bellflower)			
'Bowl of Cherries'	Purple pink	18″	−30°F
'Cherry Bells'	Cherry pink edged white	24″	−30°F

VARIETY	COLOR	HEIGHT	HARDINESS
'Pantaloons'	Pink purple (D)	24″	–30°F

Spotted Bellflowers are aggressive spreaders and must be placed carefully in the landscape. The plants produce interesting tubular flowers that hang down.

Campanula rotundifolia

(Harebell)	Blue	14″	–40°F
'Alba'	White	14″	–40°F
'Olympica'	Bright blue	12″	–40°F

This Bellflower forms a mound of green foliage out of which rise numerous, wiry stems which carry nodding flowers from midsummer into fall. Plants self-sow freely and naturalize beautifully.

Campanula sarmatica

(Sarmatican Bellflower)	Pale lavender blue	24″	–40°F

Forming a low mound of downy, gray-green leaves, this Bellflower blooms heavily at the height of summer. Its velvety flowers nod to one side of the stem, giving the plant a very distinctive appearance.

Campanula trachelium

(Nettle-leaved Bellflower)

'Bernice'*****	Purple blue (D)	20″	–30°F

This variety has bright green, bristly foliage, and very attractive flowers in mid to late summer. Excellent drainage is crucial to long term survival.

Campanula (Named varieties and hybrids)

'Birch Hybrid'*****	Deep blue	6″	–40°F
'Dickson's Gold'	Lavender blue	6″	–30°F
'Elizabeth'	Pale pink	18″	–30°F
'Hot Lips'	White/pink speckles	12″	–40°F
'Kent Belle'	Violet purple	24″	–40°F
'Pink Octopus'	Pinkish white	14″	–30°F
'Samantha'	Violet blue	8″	–30°F
'Sarastro'*****	Purple blue	18″	–40°F
'Summertime Blues'	Silvery blue	18″	–40°F

'Birch Hybrid' with upward-facing cupped flowers has a long bloom season from spring into summer. 'Dickson's Gold' has striking yellow gold foliage. 'Elizabeth' has long tubular flowers that hang down. 'Hot Lips' spreads nicely and has large tubular flowers. 'Kent Belle' has large nodding flowers. 'Pink Octopus' has slender petals that mimic tentacles. 'Samantha' is a charming plant with upward-facing fragrant blooms. 'Sarastro' produces a terrific display of nodding flowers throughout the summer. 'Summertime Blues' also has nodding flowers that bloom for weeks.

Chelone lyonii

CHELONE

(chuh-LOW-nee)

TURTLEHEAD

Bloom Time	Expected Longevity	Maintenance	Years to Bloom	Preferred Light
Late summer to early fall	25+ years	Low	From seed: 2 to 3 years From potted plant: 1 year	Light shade to full sun

Turtleheads are long-blooming, late-season perennials ideally suited to moist or wet sites. Their dense, dark green foliage is extremely attractive, as are the white or pink blossoms that appear in summer and fall. Their shape simulates the head of a turtle with its mouth wide open, from which we get the common name. One plant will quickly create a colony if kept evenly moist throughout the growing season. Turtleheads are virtually untouched by insects or disease, which contributes to their durability and

longevity. They also make excellent and eye-catching cut flowers.

How Turtleheads Grow

Turtleheads are striking upright plants with thick foliage growing from spreading, fibrous roots. The plants produce flowers at the tips of the stems and where the upper leaves join the stem. They open over a period of days from the bottom up. Plants increase by sending out underground stems, or stolons, to create additional stems each spring. The reddish sprouts may pop up a foot (30 cm) or more away from the parent plant. After flowering, the plant forms seed capsules, which are oval, papery, and tightly arranged around the stem. As the seeds inside mature, the capsules turn brown. Some people cut these for use in dried arrangements.

Where to Plant

Site and Light Turtleheads prefer light shade but can be grown in full sun if the soil remains moist throughout the growing season. If planted in deep shade, the plants often produce lanky stems, which flop over, and produce very few flowers.

Soil and Moisture Turtleheads grow best in consistently moist soil enriched with lots of organic matter. Good soil amendments include compost, leaf mold, peat moss, and rotted horse manure. These perennials grow particularly well along streams or in wetlands where soil moisture is high.

Spacing Space plants 18 inches (45 cm) apart initially. They will quickly fill in the space and create a mass of stems, forming a canopy of leaves.

Companions

This is an especially valuable perennial for damp locations, where it can be planted with *Artemisia lactiflora* (White Mugwort), *Lysimachia clethroides* (Gooseneck Loosestrife), *Tradescantia* (Spiderwort), and numerous varieties of **Ferns**. Use it in the border if you can provide it with consistent moisture. Companions to consider in this case are *Aconitum napellus* (Garden Monkshood), *Deschampsia cespitosa* (Tufted Hair Grass), *Hosta* (Hosta), *Phlox* (Garden Phlox), and *Rudbeckia* (Coneflower).

Planting

Bare Root Plant bare root stock as soon as you can work the ground in spring. Remove the plants from their shipping package immediately. Snip off broken or damaged root tips. Soak plants overnight in room-temperature water. Place a small amount of superphosphate in the base of the planting hole. Fill the hole with soil. Place the crown of the plant about 1 inch (2.5 cm) below the soil surface. Fill in with soil, firm with your fingers, and water immediately. Dissolve ½ cup (about 114 g) 10-10-10 fertilizer in 1 gallon (about 4 liters) of water. Pour ½ cup (about 120 ml) of this starter solution around the base of the plant. If you prefer organic fertilizer, use fish emulsion instead.

Potted Plants Plant after all danger of frost has passed in spring. If soil in the pot is dry, soak it and allow the pot to drain overnight before planting. Remove the plant from the pot without disturbing the root ball. Plant at the same depth as in the pot, after preparing the hole in a similar manner to that for a bare root plant. Fill in with soil, firm with your fingers, and water immediately. Pour ½ cup (about 120 ml) of the starter solution around the base of the plant.

How to Care for Turtleheads

Water Turtleheads thrive in moist to wet soils. Never let the plant dry out completely during drought, as this puts a great amount of stress on it.

Mulch As soon as the ground warms up in spring, surround the base of each stem with a 2-inch (5-cm) layer of mulch to keep the soil moist and cool. The use of rotted oak leaves or pine needles keeps soil slightly acidic, which is just the way Turtleheads like it. Mulch also inhibits the growth of annual weeds.

Fertilizing Sprinkle 10-10-10 fertilizer around the base of the plant just as growth emerges in spring. Water immediately to dissolve the granules and move nutrients into the root zone. Feed plants again just as flower buds begin to form. Using water-soluble fertilizers for foliar feeding throughout the growing season results in exceptionally deep green foliage and lush growth.

If you prefer organic fertilizers, use alfalfa meal (rabbit pellets), blood meal, bonemeal, compost, cow manure, fish emulsion, Milorganite, or rotted horse manure. Bonemeal should be added to the soil at planting time for best results.

Staking Staking is not necessary unless Turtleheads are planted in deep shade.

Pinching Back For a bushier plant, pinch the tips of stems when they are 4 inches (10 cm) tall in spring. This shortens plant height and induces side branching, which makes the plant denser and fuller. If the plant is in the back of the garden where height is important, skip this step.

Deadheading Removing spent blossoms will not induce a second flowering period.

Winter Protection With normal snowfall, mature plants do not need winter protection. If there is no snow cover by early December, it may be good insurance to cover plants with 4 inches (10 cm) of whole leaves, marsh hay, clean straw, or pine needles.

Problems

Insects There are no regular insect pests associated with Turtleheads.

Disease If grown properly, these perennials are rarely bothered by disease.

Propagation

Division Parent plants increase by sending out underground stems, or stolons. Numerous sprouts appear in all directions around the mother plant in early spring. When this new growth is about 1 inch (2.5 cm) high, sever the young plant from the mother by digging down with a spade between the two plants. Plant the young plant immediately as you would a bare root plant.

Cuttings Turtleheads can be propagated by soft-tip cuttings taken in early spring. Take cuttings with three sets of leaves, making the cuts a quarter inch (6 mm) below a leaf node. Remove all but the top leaves, and dip the cut ends in rooting hormone. Tap off any excess powder, and plant immediately in moist rooting medium. Keep the medium consistently moist and humid until roots form. Transplant to pots or a protected location in the garden once the plant is growing vigorously. Keep young plants well watered.

Seed These perennials can be grown from seed, but germination is slow and erratic. Sowing should take place in midwinter. Fill a seed tray with moist germination medium. Press seeds into the surface, and barely cover them. Then slide the tray into a plastic bag, and place it in the crisper of your refrigerator for 6 weeks or longer. After that, place the seed tray in an area with a temperature of 65°F (18°C). After germination, which normally takes 21 to 28 days or longer, grow the young seedlings at 55°F to 60°F (13°C to 16°C). Plant seedlings in individual pots when they have a second set of leaves. Harden them off for 14 days, and plant outside after all danger of spring frost.

Alternatively, sow seeds outdoors in a cold frame or prepared bed immediately after collection in fall. The growing medium should be kept moist until it freezes. Seedlings will emerge in spring when temperatures warm up. When they have formed several sets of leaves and are growing well, plant them in pots or directly in the garden.

Special Uses

Cut Flowers With their unique blooms, wonderful foliage, and long-lasting quality, Turtleheads make superb cut flowers. Cut the stems just as the first flowers open. Remove all leaves that will be submerged in water in the final arrangement. Flowers generally last from 8 to 10 days.

Dried Flowers Although the flowers are not used for this, the mature seedpods are sometimes used in dried arrangements. They can, however, cause skin irritation to certain individuals, so you might want to wear gloves when working with them.

Sources

Fieldstone Gardens, Inc., 55 Quaker Lane, Vassalboro, ME 04989, (207) 923-3836

ForestFarm, 990 Tetherow Rd., Williams, OR 97544, (541) 846-7269

Niche Gardens, 1111 Dawson Rd., Chapel Hill, NC 27516, (919) 967-0078

Chelone lyonii

VARIETIES

VARIETY	COLOR	HEIGHT	HARDINESS
Chelone glabra*****			
(White Turtlehead)	Creamy white	48″	−40°F
'Black Ace'	Creamy white	48″	−40°F

This North American native produces white flowers occasionally tinged rose-pink. The elongated leaves and sturdy stems of 'Black Ace' have a dark black cast when they first emerge, changing to dark green as the season progresses.

Chelone lyonii			
(Pink Turtlehead)	Rose pink	36″	−40°F
'Hot Lips'*****	Deep rose pink	36″	−40°F

Native to the mountains of the southeastern United States, this species is hardy and very attractive in bloom. 'Hot Lips' has deeper green foliage, reddish stems, and bright deep pink flowers.

Chelone obliqua			
(Rose Turtlehead)	Deep rose	36″	−30°F
'Alba'	Pearl white	30″	−30°F

This Turtlehead, native to marshy areas in the southeastern United States, is slightly less winter hardy and a bit later flowering than *Chelone lyonii* (Pink Turtlehead). Its blooms are more deeply colored and abundant.

Foliar feeding with a water-soluble fertilizer also results in lush foliage and abundant bloom.

If you prefer organic fertilizers, use alfalfa meal (rabbit pellets), blood meal, bonemeal, compost, cow manure, fish emulsion, Milorganite, or rotted horse manure. Bonemeal needs to be added to the soil at planting time to be effective.

Weeding Mulch retards most annual weed growth, and any weeds that do sprout are easy to pull by hand. Weeds compete with the plant for valuable water and nutrients, so their control is important in getting peak growth from Bugbanes.

Staking Staking is not normally required for Bugbanes unless they are placed in a windy spot. If necessary, support each flower stem with its own individual stake. Tie the stem loosely to the stake at intervals using a soft material in a figure-eight knot.

Deadheading If you want to collect seed or the dried seedpods, leave the old flower spikes on the plant. Even when finished blooming, these add vertical interest in the garden.

Winter Protection After the plant turns brown, cut it to the ground. Cover first-year plants with 4 inches (10 cm) of clean straw, marsh hay, whole leaves, or pine needles after the ground is permanently frozen. Mature Bugbanes don't normally need winter protection. If there is no snow cover by early December, it may be good insurance to cover crowns with mulch. Remove all mulch as soon as it warms up in spring to prevent crown rot.

Problems

Insects There are no regular insect pests associated with Bugbanes. The flower odor of this perennial is believed to repel them, as noted in the introduction to this section.

Disease Bugbanes experience no common disease problems, but leaf spots and rust have been known to occur. Preventive spraying is not advised.

Propagation

Division Bugbanes are slow to mature and do not require regular division for healthy growth. However, it is possible to increase the number of plants by this means. Dig up the entire clump in early spring, and shake or wash off the soil. With a sharp knife or spade, cut the plant into sections, with each portion containing several shoots and an ample root system. Discard the old central woody core of the plant. Handle the new divisions as you would a bare root plant, planting them immediately and keeping the ground evenly moist until they are growing vigorously.

Seed Bugbanes can be grown from seed, but it must be fresh for best results. Even then, seed germinates erratically, taking from 1 to 12 months to sprout. For best results, sow seeds as soon as they ripen in fall. Start them in sterile, moist germination medium. Cover them to a depth of about $\frac{1}{16}$ inch (2 mm), and place the seed tray in a plastic bag with holes punched in it for ventilation. Keep the medium evenly moist at 60°F to 70°F (16°C to 21°C) for 6 to 10 weeks. After this warm period, put the seed tray in the crisper of your refrigerator for 6 to 8 weeks. Remove it after this period, and place it in an area with a temperature between 55°F and 60°F (13°C to 16°C). Keep the medium consistently moist until germination begins. When each seedling has its second pair of leaves, plant it in a small pot. Harden it off for 14 days before planting it outside in spring after all danger of frost.

If this is too much hassle, you can plant seed in a prepared bed outdoors in the fall. Keep the soil evenly moist until it freezes for the winter. Germination may be stretched out throughout the next spring and summer. As the seedlings emerge, transplant them to pots or to a protected spot in the garden.

Special Uses

Cut Flowers The flowers of Bugbanes can be stunning in arrangements, but they can emit an unpleasant odor. If you choose to try them, cut the stems in full flower, and place them in a pail of water. Transfer them indoors immediately, remove the lower leaves, and place the stems in 110°F (43°C) water. Allow them to remain in the water overnight, and then arrange them the following day. Some gardeners believe it helps to place the bottom 1 inch (2.5 cm) of the stem in boiling water for 30 seconds just prior to arranging.

Dried Flowers Though the flowers do not dry, the mature seed heads of most varieties are useful in dried arrangements.

Sources

Busse Gardens, 17160 245th Ave., Big Lake, MN 55309, (800) 544-3192

Digging Dog Nursery, P.O. Box 471, Albion, CA 95410, (707) 937-1130

Fieldstone Gardens, Inc., 55 Quaker Lane, Vassalboro, ME 04989, (207) 923-3836

Fraser's Thimble Farms, 175 Arbutus Rd., Salt Spring Island, BC V8K 1A3 Canada, (250) 537-5788

Venero Gardens, 5985 Seamans Dr., Shorewood, MN 55331, (952) 474-8550

'Atropurpurea'

Cimicifuga/Actaea racemosa

VARIETIES

Actaea is now the correct name for *Cimicifuga*. It may take some time for the new name to be accepted and/or used in literature and catalogs. Some plants included here were always in the *Actaea* group (genus) and have been added to this edition of the growing guide. Purple foliage color is affected by light and soil conditions!

VARIETY	COLOR	HEIGHT	HARDINESS
Cimicifuga acerina/Actaea acerina			
(Japanese Bugbane)	White	36″	−40°F

This multi-stemmed plant offers lovely dark green foliage and purplish stems. Its fluffy flowers bloom in late summer and early fall in spikes up to two feet long.

Cimicifuga cordifolia (see *Cimicifuga racemosa* var. *cordifolia*/*Actaea racemosa* var. *cordifolia*)

Cimicifuga japonica var. *acerina*/*Actaea japonica* var. *acerina* (see *Cimicifuga acerina*/*Actaea acerina*)

VARIETY	COLOR	HEIGHT	HARDINESS
Actaea pachypoda****			
(White Baneberry)	White	24″	−40°F

This North American plant has green serrated foliage and spring flowers maturing into white berries on bright red stalks (pedicles) in late summer and fall. The poisonous berries have a prominent dark purplish dot at their bases.

VARIETY	COLOR	HEIGHT	HARDINESS
Cimicifuga racemosa/Actaea racemosa			
(Black Snakeroot)*****	White	84″	−40°F
var. *cordifolia*	Greenish white	60″	−40°F

Also a North American native, Black Snakeroot is a standout as a vertical accent plant in a shady place. Its flower spikes, which bloom for several weeks in summer, can be up to two feet long and mature into attractive seed pods.

Cimicifuga ramosa (see *Cimicifuga simplex*/*Actaea simplex*)

VARIETY	COLOR	HEIGHT	HARDINESS
Actaea rubra****			
(Red Baneberry)	White	24″	−40°F

This plant is similar to White Baneberry but its fruits are lustrous red and stalks (pedicels) green.

VARIETY	COLOR	HEIGHT	HARDINESS
Cimicifuga simplex/Actaea simplex			
(Kamchatka Bugbane)	White	48″	−40°F
'Atropurpurea'	Ivory	60″	−40°F
'Black Negligee'*****	White	60″	−40°F
'Brunette'	White	48″	−40°F
'Hillside Black Beauty'*****	White	60″	−40°F
'James Compton'*****	Creamy white	36″	−40°F
'Pink Spike'	White tinged pink	60″	−40°F
'White Pearl' ('Armleuchter')	White	48″	−40°F

These plants bloom so late that they are primarily grown in cold climates for their vertical form and lovely foliage. 'Black Negligee,' 'Hillside Black Beauty,' and 'James Compton' are standouts in that category with their purplish black foliage. All of these plants tolerate more alkaline soil than other members of this overall group (genus).

'Madame Edouard André'

CLEMATIS

(KLEM-uh-tiss)

CLEMATIS

Bloom Time	Expected Longevity	Maintenance	Years to Bloom	Preferred Light
Early summer to fall	25+ years	High	From seed: 3 years From potted plant: 2 years	Full sun to light shade

Clematis are among the most bold and beautiful climbing plants, although a few varieties have a shrubby habit and are suited to flower gardens. Their flower colors are varied and brilliant, and the plants are often covered with a cloud of bloom during peak periods. Flowers vary in size and shape, with some looking like stars and others like hanging bells. In addition to their beautiful flowers, some varieties are delightfully fragrant. Under good conditions, these perennials grow vigorously and produce a magnifi-

cent display of flowers year after year. By choosing a range of varieties, you can extend the bloom season from early summer through fall. Clematis are rarely bothered by disease or insects. They do require maintenance, as they must be pruned and trained each season.

How Clematis Grow

Most Clematis are climbers. They are able to climb only by wrapping their leaf petioles around a means of support such as lattice, wire, or another plant. Maximum height varies by variety. The showy display of flowers is followed by feathery seed heads that remain attractive into fall.

The climbing varieties of Clematis are divided into three groups. The first group flowers on wood grown in the previous season (old wood), and good bloom depends on your ability to protect that wood during the winter. The main flowering period is spring. Because of the difficulty in overwintering the stems, this is the least preferred group for cold climates. The second group flowers on current-year's growth (new wood). The flowering period is usually later, with one main flush of bloom, although some varieties will produce additional flowers as the season progresses. These can be cut to the ground each fall, and you will still get an excellent display of flowers the following season. This is the most reliable group for cold-climate areas. The third group flowers on both old and new wood. In the case of certain varieties, flowers produced on old wood may be different sizes, forms, or colors from those produced on new wood. If the old wood is successfully protected during the winter, these plants will produce flowers in spring and another flush on the new wood during the summer months.

Some varieties of Clematis look more like bushes or low, sprawling plants. These are stunning in the perennial garden. However, many of them need support if you do not want them to take up a large amount of space.

All Clematis are somewhat slow to get going, so don't expect lots of bloom until the second or third year. Once mature, they give you many years of enjoyment.

Where to Plant

Site and Light There's an old saying that Clematis like their heads in the sun and their feet in shade. This remains true today, and the best growth occurs when plants face east to bask in the morning sun. Vining types must have both adequate light and support. They like to trail along fences or climb up trellises.

Shade the base of the plant with a canopy of foliage provided by other plants.

Soil and Moisture Proper soil preparation is critical. Dig a large hole 2 to 3 feet (60 to 90 cm) deep and equally wide. Add lots of compost, well-rotted manure, leaf mold, or other organic materials to the soil. These enable the soil to drain freely yet retain moisture and nutrients. The size of the hole may seem out of proportion to the small size of the initial plant, but as it matures, the plant's root system will spread throughout the entire prepared area and even beyond. Taking time to prepare the soil in the planting hole properly is an important step to long-term success with all varieties of Clematis.

Spacing Space bushy Clematis according to potential height and width, taking into account whether you support the plant or not. Space climbing Clematis 1 foot (30 cm) away from their support, especially from the side of buildings. Lime may leach from concrete walls into the soil and cause a condition called chlorosis.

Companions

The climbing types of **Clematis** (Clematis) lend themselves to numerous uses besides growing up a trellis on the side of the house. Plant them at the base of a shrub or small, flowering tree where they will ramble as a ground cover and clamber up the stems. They look especially nice with **Malus** (Apple), **Rosa** (Rose), and **Taxus** (Yew). These vines are also handsome grown over old stumps and along the rails of fences, decks, and steps. In the garden, grow them up on shrubs or a tall fence that serves as a backdrop for the perennial garden. Choose colors carefully, and plant them close to tall perennials with matching bloom periods. These include **Cimicifuga/Actaea** (Bugbane), **Delphinium** (Larkspur), **Filipendula rubra** (Queen-of-the-Prairie), **Phlox** (Garden Phlox), and **Thermopsis caroliniana** (Carolina Lupine). For late-season interest, combine **Clematis tibetana** ssp. **tangutica** (Golden Chinese Clematis) and **Clematis** *virginiana* (Virgin's Bower) with *Aster/Symphyotrichum ericoides* (Heath Aster), *Rudbeckia laciniata* 'Autumn Sun'/'Herbstsonne' (Cutleaf Coneflower), and **Grasses**. The shrubby forms of *Clematis* (Clematis) are attractive additions to the border, especially if staked upright. *Clematis recta* (Ground Clematis) goes well with *Tanacetum*–Coccineum Group (Painted Daisy) and *Veronica* 'Giles van Hees' (Speedwell). Try *Clematis heracleifolia* 'Davidiana' (Fragrant Tube Clematis) next to *Calamagrostis* ✕ *acutiflora* 'Karl Foerster' (Feather Reed Grass) and *Rudbeckia fulgida* 'Goldsturm' (Orange Coneflower).

Planting

Bare Root Plant bare root stock as soon as you can work the ground in spring. Remove the plants from their shipping package immediately. Snip off broken or damaged root tips. Soak plants overnight in room-temperature water. Place a small amount of superphosphate in the base of the planting hole. Fill the hole with soil. Place the crown about 2 to 3 inches (5 to 7.5 cm) below the soil surface. Fill in the hole, firm with your fingers, and water immediately. Place a short support next to the plant that will lead vining types to their permanent support. Dissolve ½ cup (about 114 g) 10-10-10 fertilizer in 1 gallon (about 4 liters) of water. Pour ½ cup (about 120 ml) of this starter solution around the base of the plant. If you prefer organic fertilizer, use fish emulsion instead.

Clematis have a reputation for being tough to grow from bare root stock. This is usually related to stressed or unhealthy plants. Strong stock will grow well if properly planted in well-drained soil. If plants appear weak upon arrival, you might consider potting them and placing them in a protected spot until they are growing well.

Potted Plants Plant Clematis after all danger of frost in spring. If the soil in the pot is dry, soak it and let it drain overnight. Plant after preparing the hole in a similar manner as that for a bare root plant. The next day, strip off any leaves on the lower 2 inches (5 cm) of stem. Tap the plant out of the pot, keeping the entire root ball intact. Most potted plants come with a little wooden stick supporting the vine. Keep this in place. Place the plant in the prepared hole so that it is 2 to 3 inches (5 to 7.5 cm) below the soil surface. Roots will form from the areas where you stripped off leaves. Firm the soil around the plant with your fingers, and water immediately. Pour ½ cup (about 120 ml) starter solution around the base of the plant.

How to Care for Clematis

Water Clematis flourish in soil kept evenly moist throughout the growing season. If soil has been properly prepared, it is next to impossible to overwater these plants. If you plant Clematis under the eaves of your house, the plants probably will not get enough water from rains. So, you will need to water these frequently even during "wet" summers. When you water these plants, soak the soil deeply. Root systems on mature plants can go down as deep as 2 feet (60 cm) or more.

Mulch Get lush growth from Clematis by keeping the root system moist and cool. As soon as the soil warms up in spring, place 3 inches (7.5 cm) of organic mulch around the base of the plant. Do not place mulch directly over the crown or against the stems, as this can cause disease. Use dried grass clippings, shredded bark, pine needles, or shredded leaves. Mulch also inhibits the growth of most annual weeds.

Fertilizing Sprinkle ½ cup (about 114 g) 10-10-10 fertilizer around the base of the plant just as new growth emerges in spring. Avoid getting the fertilizer on emerging stems, and water immediately to dissolve the granules and move nutrients into the root zone. The regular use of water-soluble fertilizers for foliar feeding through spring and summer will also produce lush foliage and more blooms.

If you prefer organic fertilizer, use alfalfa meal (rabbit pellets), blood meal, bonemeal, compost, fish emulsion, or Milorganite. Bonemeal should be incorporated into the soil at planting time.

Weeding The use of an organic mulch will prevent most annual weeds from growing. A few are likely to break through the mulch, but these can be pulled easily by hand. Avoid deep hoeing, as this may damage the plant's root system.

Support Vining varieties need artificial support.

For vines that flower on new wood, the simplest method is to weave the tip of the vine through the holes in a trellis or wrap it around a stake in early spring. Plants grow at a rapid rate and will quickly climb a support if properly started. If you are planting close to a building, keep the support an inch (2.5 cm) or more away from the wall so that there is free air circulation behind the upper vining portion of the plant. The lower rooted portion should be a foot (30 cm) or so from the building.

For vines that flower on old and new wood, train the vine out in a fan shape on a piece of chicken wire that is attached to the overall support with L-hooks. This method allows you to roll the wire down in the fall for winter protection with minimal damage to the brittle stems. You must preserve the old wood in order to get early flowers. In this case, do not weave the vine through the wire. Just let it attach itself naturally to one side of the support.

For vines that flower on old wood, use a similar system of support. You'll want to lay it down in fall and cover it well with a winter mulch. If you do not protect the stems from winter damage, you will get few, if any, flowers.

Many of the shrubby varieties also need support if you don't want them to ramble. One method is to place a cylinder of chicken wire around the plant in early spring. The plant grows up and around the wire, covering it completely by bloom time. A Peony ring placed around the plant early in the season is another, simple option. Pea stakes placed within the newly emerging shoots accomplish the same function but are best used on varieties such as *Clematis integrifolia* (Solitary Clematis). The growing plants will hide all of these supports in time and look natural once in bloom.

Pinching Back If the plant produces flower buds in its first year, remove them as soon as they appear. This channels all of the plant's energy into establishing a strong root system.

Pinching back selected stems on mature plants is a technique that can be used to get flowers appearing at different heights on a plant, rather than all at the top. You can pinch back some of the stems early in the season while letting others grow naturally. The shorter stems will produce additional growth that will not get as tall and will give you flowers lower on the plant often later in the season. Do this only on varieties that bloom on new wood.

Deadheading Deadheading is such a tedious task that most gardeners skip it, but it can lead to additional bloom. On the other hand, the seedpods are interesting to look at as well, especially on specific varieties, as outlined at the end of the section.

Pruning For vining types: If you're growing a variety that forms flowers on new wood, either cut off the old vines to the ground in the fall as they turn brittle, or, if you prefer, leave the vines on their support. Wait until new growth begins the following spring, and cut back to the highest point where buds emerge from the stem. Types that flower on old and new wood, as well as those that flower on old wood only, should not be pruned until the buds break dormancy in spring. At that point, it is easy to see how far back stems have died. Prune back to live wood, and remove any broken or damaged stems.

For shrubby types: Cut back to ground level in late fall or early spring.

Winter Protection There are three methods of protecting Clematis. Each method is suited to the growing style of the plant.

Plants that flower on new wood may be cut back in late fall or left standing until spring. Protect the root system with a loose mulch after the ground has frozen to a depth of 2 inches (5 cm). Remove the mulch as soon as it begins to warm up in spring.

Plants that flower on new and old wood are harder to protect. One way is to grow them on chicken wire that is held up on a support by L-hooks. At the end of the season, slip the wire off the hooks and roll it loosely to the ground. This method is not perfect but, if done carefully, preserves a good amount of stem tissue through the winter. It may result in some stems being crimped or broken. In late fall, cover the rolled-down plants with 12 inches (30 cm) of mulch. Take the mulch off and hang the wire back up as soon as the weather warms up in spring.

Plants that flower on old wood are the most difficult to protect in cold climates. They can be grown on chicken wire as with the foregoing type but are probably best not rolled down in late fall. Rather, remove the wire from the support, and lay the entire plant flat on the ground. This may require two people working in unison. Cover the whole plant with a 12-inch (30-cm) layer of mulch after the ground is permanently frozen in fall. Good mulches include whole leaves, marsh hay, and clean straw. Remove the mulch as soon as the weather warms up in spring, and hang the wire back on the L-hooks.

Problems

Iron Chlorosis Much garden literature encourages liming your soil. Clematis thrive in slightly acidic soil with a pH ranging from 6 to 6.5. Many soils in colder areas naturally fall into this range. Adding lime to soils with a pH greater than 6.0 often leads to iron chlorosis. The most obvious symptom is yellowing between leaf veins. This condition can also be caused by planting Clematis too close to masonry or stucco walls that leach lime into the soil. Keep Clematis plants at least a foot (30 cm) away from these types of walls. In all but the most severe cases, this problem can be corrected by the use of acid-based fertilizers and iron chelate. Amending soil with acidic peat moss is also recommended.

Insects Insects are rarely a problem with Clematis.

Disease Clematis may be attacked by wilts caused by either bacteria or fungi. The upper portion of stem begins to die, and, eventually, the entire stem turns black. If this occurs, cut the stem all the way back to the crown and destroy the infected upper portion of vine. New growth generally emerges disease-free, and these wilts rarely result in death except for young plants. Although it is rare, powdery mildew occasionally infects plants as well. A whitish film on leaves indicates the problem. Prevent future outbreaks by providing as much air circulation around the plant as possible. Clematis also may, on occasion, be bothered by various leaf spot diseases, but these are generally of minor importance.

Rodents Rodents will nibble on stems during severe winters. If you're laying down plants for winter protection, do so after the ground freezes, and place poisoned baits under the winter mulch to kill rodents. Rabbits often eat freestanding cane in winter, but this is not a problem for plants that produce flowers on new wood. They are simply doing more severe pruning than you might like, not really harming the plant.

Propagation

Division Plants can remain undisturbed for years, but they also can be propagated easily by division. Do this in early spring just as new growth emerges from the soil. Dig up the entire clump, and cut the crown into pieces with a sharp spade or knife. Each portion should have one to three stems attached to a generous amount of roots. Replant as you would a bare root plant, and water immediately.

Cuttings (Leaf Node) In late spring or early summer, cut off an entire stem. Snip off the lower portion if it is very woody, and remove any portion of the recent growth that breaks easily when bent. Cuttings can be taken from the remaining portion of the stem. Make cuts just above and about 2 inches (5 cm) below leaf nodes. Dip the lower cut end of the stem in rooting hormone, and tap off any excess powder.

Place the cutting in a sterile rooting medium up to the point where the leaf meets the stem. Keep the rooting medium moist at all times, and keep humidity high by covering the cuttings with plastic or mist them regularly. Be aware that excess humidity can lead to disease. Cuttings may take from 4 to 12 weeks to root, depending on the variety and growing conditions. Once plants have formed a strong root system, place them in pots, and grow them on until they are big enough to plant in the garden. Clematis are not easy plants to root so expect some failures among your cuttings.

Air Layering In early summer, use a razor or sharp knife to cut a 1-inch (2.5-cm) slit upward toward a leaf node in an upper portion of the stem where the wood is semihard. Angle the slit so that you never cut more than halfway through the stem. Place a toothpick horizontally in the cut, and dust the cut with rooting hormone. Wrap the wound with moist sphagnum moss, and secure it in place with plastic. Use twist-ties or twine to secure the ends of the plastic around the stem. Then wrap aluminum foil around the plastic. Open the top of the plastic each week and check to make sure the moss remains damp. Moisten it if necessary. After 6 to 8 weeks, check to see whether roots have formed. If they have, sever the stem below the cut, and pot the new plant up. Keep the plant consistently moist as it is getting established. This method works best on Clematis that blooms on new and old wood or on old wood only.

Ground Layering Select a stem that, when removed from its support, will allow semihard wood or hard wood to lie on the ground. Make a shallow, slanting cut with a knife just below a leaf node, and place a piece of toothpick horizontally in the cut to keep it open. Dust the wound with rooting hormone, and cover the cut with a couple inches (5 cm) of soil. Pin the plant down or place a rock over the soil. You can do this in several places along the stem if you desire. If kept evenly moist, the cut areas should sprout roots by the end of the summer or the following spring. At that time, cut the entire stem into

sections, making sure that each portion has a strong root system. These are best potted up and grown on before planting in the garden. Though it does require some time, this method, known as *serpentine layering*, is highly effective for all types of Clematis. However, the section lying on the ground should be protected with a thick winter mulch if new plants do not form the first summer.

Seed Grow only the species types from seed. The proper method of growing seed varies highly by species, so we cannot give you one method effective with all. However, you can expect reasonably high success with the following method, especially if the seed is fresh.

Fill a seed tray with moist germination medium. Sow the seed over the medium, covering it no more than ¼ inch (6 mm) deep. Slide the tray into a plastic bag punctured in several places for air circulation. Keep the tray evenly moist and at a temperature of 60°F to 65°F (16°C to 18°C) for 2 to 3 months. Next, place the tray in the crisper of your refrigerator for another 2 to 3 months. Then remove the tray, and place it in an area where the temperature is 70°F to 75°F (21°C to 24°C). Keep the tray enclosed with perforated plastic to keep humidity high and soil moist. Once seeds begin to germinate, remove the plastic. Germination may take up to a year or longer. You may have to moist-chill the tray several times to get seeds to germinate. Check seed trays regularly while they're in the refrigerator. Remove them immediately if seeds begin to germinate. When a seedling has a second pair of leaves, plant it in a small pot. Harden off seedlings for 14 days before planting outside after all danger of frost has passed in spring.

Seed may also be planted outdoors in a prepared bed or cold frame as soon as it is collected. Cover the seed with ¼ inch (6 mm) of germination medium, and keep the medium evenly moist until the soil freezes in fall. The seeds may sprout the following spring and summer or may wait until the following season. Make sure the seedbed remains evenly moist throughout that entire time. After seedlings have grown their second set of leaves, place them in pots, and grow them on until they are large enough to put out into the garden.

Special Uses

Cut Flowers Individual flowers from large-flowered vining types are charming floating in rose bowls or similar shallow containers. You can also cut nearly open blooms with a short section of stem. Remove all the leaves on the stem, and immerse it in water right up to the flower. Let it soak like this overnight before placing it in an arrangement. Some growers boil the lower 1 inch (2.5 cm) of stem for 30 seconds to 3 minutes before standing it in water. In Japan, they place the stems in pure alcohol for a few minutes before placing them in water. You may need to vary your methods to find which works best for you on a given variety.

Some of the bushy types form attractive clusters of flowers that can be used in floral arrangements. Several are quite fragrant as well. Cut stems when flowers are just beginning to open, and condition them overnight in room-temperature water. Remove any leaves that would end up underwater in the final arrangement. *Clematis heracleifolia* (Fragrant Tube Clematis) and *Clematis integrifolia* (Solitary Clematis) are perhaps the best of the bushy types for fresh-cut flowers.

Dried Flowers Though the flowers themselves do not dry well, many varieties form attractive white or silvery seed heads that can be used in fall or winter arrangements. Let the seed heads dry naturally on the vine, then cut them off at the desired stage of development. Spraying them with hair spray or a commercial sealant prevents them from shattering in an arrangement. Another technique worth trying is treating the seed heads with glycerin. Mix 1 part glycerin with 3 parts warm water, and soak the seed head in this solution. It will become quite pliable and should not require any other treatment to keep it intact.

Sources

Bluestone Perennials, 7211 Middle Ridge Rd., Madison, OH 44057, (800) 852-5243

Brushwood Nursery, P.O. Box 483, Unionville, PA 19375, (610) 444-8083

Completely Clematis Specialty Nursery, 217 Argilla Rd., Ipswich, MA 01938, (978) 356-3197

Donahue's, 420 SW 10th St, P.O. Box 366, Faribault, MN 55021, (507) 334-8404

Garden Crossings, LLC, 4902 96th Ave., Zeeland, MI 49464, (616) 875-6355

Klehm's Song Sparrow Perennial Farm, 13101 E Rye Rd., Avalon, WI 53505, (800) 553-3715

Nature Hills Nursery, 3334 N 88th Plaza, Omaha, NE 68134, (888) 864-7663

Rhora's Nut Farm, RR #1, Winfleet, ON L0S 1V0 Canada, (905) 899-3508

Silver Star Vinery, 31805 NE Clearwater Dr., Yacolt, WA 98675 (no telephone by request)

VARIETIES

The Clematis described below are all vining types unless otherwise noted. Select varieties based not only on how they grow but also on flower color and size in addition to overall plant height. In cold climates, it is best to rely on varieties that bloom on new wood. A few flowers are semi-double (SD) or double (D).

VARIETY	COLOR	SIZE	HEIGHT	WOOD	HARDINESS
Clematis alpina					
(Alpine Clematis)	Blue	1″	4′	Old	−20°F
'Frances Rivis'	Light to mid blue	2″	8′	Old	−20°F
'Pamela Jackman'	Mid blue	1½″	8′	Old	−20°F
'Willy'	Pale lavender/pink	3″	10′	Old	−20°F

These plants produce an abundance of lantern-like flowers in spring and are worth the gamble with winter protection.

VARIETY	COLOR	SIZE	HEIGHT	WOOD	HARDINESS
***Clematis*–Atragene Group**					
'Blue Bird'	Mauve blue (SD)	3″	10′	Old	−30°F
'Jan Lindmark'	Plum purple (D)	4″	8′	Old	−30°F
'Maidwell Hall'	Lavender blue (SD)	4″	8′	Old	−30°F
'Markham's Pink'	Pink (SD, D)	3″	10′	Old	−30°F
'White Swan'	White (D)	3″	8′	Old	−30°F

These varieties bloom mainly in spring but may produce some occasional blooms in summer. They have nodding, lantern- or bell-shaped semi-double (SD) to double (D) flowers. Winter protection is necessary.

VARIETY	COLOR	SIZE	HEIGHT	WOOD	HARDINESS
Clematis crispa					
(Curly Clematis)	Purple	1″	10′	New	−30°F

This southeastern United States native is a shrubby climber that offers a nice show of nodding bell-shaped flowers in mid to late summer. The fruits which follow are showy well into the fall months.

VARIETY	COLOR	SIZE	HEIGHT	WOOD	HARDINESS
Clematis heracleifolia					
(Fragrant Tube Clematis)	Blue	½″	4′	New	−40°F
'China Purple'*****	Deep purple blue	1″	3′	New	−40°F
'Davidiana'	Violet blue	½″	4′	New	−40°F
'Wyevale'	Dark blue	1″	4′	New	−40°F

This Chinese native forms a subshrub with clusters of fragrant, hyacinth-like flowers which bloom in August and September. Allow it to ramble across the ground at the base of other shrubs or stake it upright depending upon the look you're after.

VARIETY	COLOR	SIZE	HEIGHT	WOOD	HARDINESS
Clematis integrifolia**✱					
(Solitary Clematis)	Indigo blue	1½″	3′	New	−40°F
'Alba'	White	2″	3′	New	−40°F
'Rosea'	Mauve pink	2″	2′	New	−40°F

These are non-climbing forms. Allow them to ramble over the ground or stake them upright. They are vigorous and easy to grow. Solitary Clematis bloom in early to midsummer with nodding bell-shaped flowers that turn into silvery seedheads.

'Dr. Ruppel'

'Madame Julia Correvon'

Clematis recta

Clematis tibetana ssp. *tangutica*

VARIETY	COLOR	SIZE	HEIGHT	WOOD	HARDINESS
Clematis–Jackmanii Group					
(Jackman's Clematis)					
'Jackmanii'*****	Dark purple	6"	12'	New	−40°F
'Jackmanii Alba'*****	White	5"	12'	New	−40°F
'Jackmanii Rubra'*****	Deep red purple	5"	12'	New	−40°F
'Jackmanii Superba'*****	Violet purple	6"	12'	New	−40°F

These are among the most popular and easy to grow Clematis. They grow vigorously and are ideally suited to cold climates. They bloom profusely on new wood, sometimes for weeks at a time. They are parents to many fine hybrids listed later.

Clematis × *jouiniana*					
(Jouin Clematis)	Purplish white	1½"	10'	New	−30°F
'Mrs. Robert Brydon'	Pale blue	1½"	10'	New	−30°F
'Praecox'*****	Lavender blue	2"	10'	New	−30°F

These vigorous Clematis are especially attractive rambling over a stump or covering a low fence, as they are not strong climbers. They bloom from late summer into fall with 'Praecox' being the first to start flowering.

Clematis maximowicziana (see *Clematis terniflora*)

Clematis orientalis					
(Oriental Clematis)	Yellow	2"	20'	New	−30°F

This Clematis with its small, fragrant flowers blooms profusely during the summer. This plant grows vigorously and is stunning on a fence.

Clematis paniculata (see *Clematis terniflora*)

Clematis recta					
(Ground Clematis)	White	1"	4'	New	−40°F
'Purpurea'*****	White	1"	4'	New	−40°F

This shrub form will sprawl over the ground as a ground cover or form an attractive clump if staked upright. It blooms in early summer with clusters of fragrant flowers which literally cover the plant under ideal growing conditions. 'Purpurea' has lovely, bronzy purple foliage coloration. The fluffy, silver seed heads are also delightful.

Clematis–Tangutica Group					
'Bill MacKenzie'	Bright yellow	3"	20'	New	−40°F
'Golden Harvest'	Deep golden yellow	2"	12'	New	−40°F
Golden Tiara® ('Kugotia')	Bright yellow	3"	12'	New	−40°F
'Grace'	Creamy white	1½"	12'	New	−40°F
'Helios'*****	Bright yellow	2½"	8'	New	−40°F
'Lambton Park'	Buttercup yellow	2"	12'	New	−40°F
My Angel® ('Engelina')	Yellow/purple	1½"	10'	New	−40°F

Members of this group are easy to grow. Their profuse show of nodding blooms lasts well into late summer. The attractive silky seed heads that follow add a great deal of interest to the late-season landscape.

VARIETY	COLOR	SIZE	HEIGHT	WOOD	HARDINESS
Clematis terniflora*****					
(Sweet Autumn Clematis)	Creamy white	¾″	25′	New	−30°F

This vigorous vine blooms heavily with delightfully fragrant flowers in fall. It makes an effective screen, and its fluffy silvery fruits remain showy into late fall and early winter.

Clematis–Texensis Group					
'Duchess of Albany'*****	Two-tone pink	3″	10′	New	−40°F
'Gravetye Beauty'	Ruby red	3″	10′	New	−40°F
'Princess Diana'	Whitish pink/deep pink	3″	8′	New	−40°F
'Sir Trevor Lawrence'	Reddish pink	3″	10′	New	−40°F

These hybrids have the Texas native ***Clematis texensis*** (Scarlet Clematis) in their breeding backgrounds. They have small, tulip-shaped flowers that bloom over a long period in the summer months.

Clematis tibetana ssp. ***tangutica***					
(Golden Chinese Clematis)	Yellow	3″	20′	New	−40°F

This vigorous vine is covered with yellow, lantern-like flowers in late summer. The feathery seed heads are showy from midsummer well into autumn and are sometimes used in dried floral arrangements.

Clematis virginiana					
(Virgin's Bower)	White	½″	20′	New	−40°F

Native to eastern North America, Virgin's Bower is most useful in natural settings. It blooms in August but is perhaps more interesting in fruit than in flower. Some people get skin rashes from handling this plant.

Clematis viticella					
(Italian Clematis)	Purple	2″	12′	New	−40°F
'Abundance'*****	Wine red	3″	12′	New	−40°F
'Alba Luxurians'*****	Ivory white	3″	12′	New	−40°F
'Minuet'*****	White/purple	3″	10′	New	−40°F
'Purpurea Plena Elegans'	Rose purple (D)	3″	12′	New	−40°F
'Royal Velours'*****	Deep reddish purple	3″	10′	New	−40°F
'Venosa Violacea'	Purple/white	4″	10′	New	−40°F

This Eurasian species and its small-flowered descendants are prolific summer bloomers that grow very well in cold-climate areas. They offer excellent vigor and winter hardiness.

Clematis–Viticella Group					
'Betty Corning'*****	Light lavender blue	2″	12′	New	−40°F
'Blue Belle'	Dark purple	4″	12′	New	−40°F
'Carmencita'	Carmine red	4″	12′	New	−40°F
'Etoile Rose'	Rose pink	2″	12′	New	−40°F
'Etoile Violette'*****	Deep purple	4″	12′	New	−40°F
'Huldine'*****	White	4″	15′	New	−40°F
'Madame Julia Correvon'*****	Rosy red	3″	12′	New	−40°F
'Margot Koster'	Pink	4″	12′	New	−40°F
'Pagoda'	Pale purplish pink	2″	10′	New	−40°F
'Perrin's Pride'	Deep purple red	6″	10′	New	−40°F

ied. Some Tickseeds have large, mostly low-growing leaves, while others produce mounds of narrow, fine-textured leaves. Generally, Tickseeds produce seed freely and self-sow in the garden. The mature seeds look somewhat like ticks, from which we get the common name.

Where to Plant

Site and Light Place these plants in full sun. If they are shaded, they often produce little bloom. Being quite short, Tickseeds grow well in windy locations.

Soil and Moisture Loose, airy soils that drain freely are recommended. Sandy loam soils are ideal, but these perennials will grow well in a wide range of soils. Replace clay or rock with good soil or build a raised bed; otherwise, Tickseeds will rot out. Mix lots of organic matter into your soil. Good amendments are compost, leaf mold, or well rotted manure. Tickseeds thrive in moderately fertile soils, and a number of them tolerate dry growing conditions once mature.

Spacing Space according to the potential height and width of the individual variety. Placing plants between 12 and 18 inches (30 to 45 cm) apart works well for most Tickseeds. Plant in groups of three to five for best effect.

Companions

The common bright gold and yellows of these flowers combine beautifully with a wide range of other perennials, including *Campanula* (Bellflower), *Hemerocallis* (Daylily), *Leucanthemum*–Superbum Group (Shasta Daisy), *Lilium* (Lily), *Lysimachia clethroides* (Gooseneck Loosestrife), *Phlox* (Garden Phlox), and *Platycodon* (Balloon Flower). Try *Coreopsis* 'Full Moon' (Tickseed) along with *Artemisia ludoviciana* 'Valerie Finnis' (White Sage), *Echinacea purpurea* (Purple Coneflower), *Helictotrichon sempervirens* (Blue Oat Grass), and *Veronica spicata* 'Icicle' (Spike Speedwell). *Coreopsis grandiflora* (Large-Flowered

Tickseed) and its named varieties are stunning next to *Delphinium* (Larkspur). *Coreopsis rosea* (Pink Tickseed) and *Veronica* 'Purpleicious' (Hybrid Speedwell) offer an interesting contrast in form, texture, and color. *Coreopsis auriculata* 'Zamphir' (Mouse Ear Tickseed) looks lovely with late spring wildflowers planted along walks in natural settings.

Planting

Bare Root Plant bare root stock as soon as you can work the ground in spring. Remove plants from their shipping package immediately. Snip off broken or damaged root tips. Soak plants overnight in room-temperature water. Place a small amount of superphosphate in the base of the planting hole. Fill the hole with soil. Place the crown 1 inch (2.5 cm) below the soil surface. Fill in the hole with soil, press firmly with your fingers, and water immediately. Dissolve ½ cup (about 114 g) 10-10-10 fertilizer in 1 gallon (about 4 liters) water. Pour ½ cup (about 120 ml) of this starter solution around the base of each plant. If you prefer organic fertilizer, use fish emulsion instead.

Potted Plants Plant potted Tickseeds after all danger of frost in spring. If the soil in the pot is dry, water the plant and let it drain overnight. The following day, tap the plant out of the pot, keeping the entire root ball intact. Plant at the same depth as in the pot after preparing the hole in a similar manner to that for a bare root plant. Fill in with soil, firm with your fingers, and water immediately. Pour ½ cup (about 120 ml) starter solution around the base of the plant.

How to Care for Tickseeds

Water Tickseeds thrive if watered on a regular basis, although certain varieties tolerate short dry periods. When watering, saturate the ground thoroughly to a depth of 8 to 10 inches (20 to 25 cm).

Mulch Place 2 inches (5 cm) of mulch around the base of these perennials once the soil has warmed up in spring. Good organic mulches include dried grass clippings, shredded leaves, and pine needles. Dwarf varieties included in rock gardens can be mulched with pea rock or similar materials. Mulch reduces the need for hand watering and inhibits the growth of annual weeds.

Fertilizing Tickseeds prefer soils of medium to low fertility. A small dose of 10-10-10 fertilizer sprinkled around the base of each plant in spring is all that should be necessary for the entire season. Water immediately to dissolve the granules and move nutrients into the root zone. Too much fertilizer can cause plants to become lanky, spindly, and even floppy.

If you prefer organic fertilizers, use alfalfa meal (rabbit pellets), blood meal, bonemeal, compost, cow manure, fish emulsion, Milorganite, or rotted horse manure. Bonemeal should be mixed into the soil at planting time for best results.

Weeding Mulch prevents the growth of many annual weeds. Hand pull any weeds that sprout through or in the mulch. Avoid using hoes close to the base of the plant, since they can hurt the root system.

Staking The tallest varieties may require staking if grown in partial shade, very moist soils, or overly fertile soil.

Deadheading If you want plants to self-sow, let the flowers go to seed. Otherwise, remove spent blossoms, especially on *Coreopsis grandiflora* (Large-Flowered Tickseed) and *Coreopsis lanceolata* (Lance-Leafed Tickseed). Deadheading also prolongs bloom on these varieties.

Winter Protection When the foliage has been killed by frost, cut it back to the ground. If there is no snow by early December, apply a 6-inch (15-cm) layer of mulch over the plants. This is especially important for varieties of *Coreopsis grandiflora* (Large-Flowered Tickseed), *Coreopsis lanceolata* (Lance-Leafed Tickseed), and *Coreopsis* 'Moonbeam,' all of which can suffer damage in very open winters. Use marsh hay, whole leaves, or clean straw. Remove this mulch as soon as it warms up in spring to prevent crown rot.

Problems

Insects *Coreopsis grandiflora* (Large-Flowered Tickseed) and *Coreopsis lanceolata* (Lance-Leafed Tickseed) are occasionally bothered by aphids. You can spray them off the plant with water, or use an insecticidal soap if infestations are severe. A more potent insecticide may be necessary if you let colonies get out of hand. Striped cucumber beetles can also be a problem, especially if you're growing vegetables nearby. Pick these off, and toss them into a can of insecticidal soap. Use an insecticide only if an infestation is extremely severe and threatens plant survival. Flea beetles, a more common nuisance on vegetables, sometimes attack Tickseeds as well. A dusting of diatomaceous earth on foliage is often enough to keep them under control. Some growers prefer using mild insecticides instead, since the dusting is unattractive.

Disease Tickseeds may be affected by root and crown rots as well as viral infections. Rots are common with *Coreopsis grandiflora* (Large-Flowered Tickseed) and *Coreopsis lanceolata* (Lance-Leafed Tickseed) grown in poorly drained soils and may also show up if winter mulches are left over the crowns too long in spring. Viral infections are difficult to prevent unless insects are controlled. Infected plants wilt and turn black. They should be dug up and destroyed immediately. The best way to prevent problems with diseases is to grow the plants properly.

Propagation

Division *Coreopsis grandiflora* (Large-Flowered Tickseed) and *Coreopsis lanceolata* (Lance-Leafed Tickseed) live longer if divided every 2 to 3 years. Dig up the entire clump in early spring just as new growth emerges. Shake excess soil away, or wash the plant clean. With a sharp knife, divide the clump into sections, each containing several growth buds and an ample supply of roots. Plant each section immediately as you would a bare root plant. Other varieties of Tickseeds do not need such regular division for good health but can easily be increased by spring division. Many of these, such as 'Moonbeam,' can be teased apart with your fingers if the plants are first washed clean of soil.

Cuttings The sterile 'Moonbeam' and a number of Tickseeds can be propagated from cuttings. Take these once plants are growing vigorously but before they form flower buds. Cut off the tip of the stem with several sets of leaves. Make your final cut a quarter inch (6 mm) below a leaf node. Remove all but the top set of leaves. Dust the cut end in rooting hormone, and tap off any excess powder. Then place the cuttings in rooting medium that remains evenly moist, and keep the humidity high until roots form. These cuttings often root within a couple of weeks. Once the cuttings are rooted, transplant them to pots before planting them in a permanent location.

Seed Some varieties of Tickseed come reasonably true from seed, with offspring quite similar to the parents. This type of propagation is easily done and an inexpensive way to have a continuous supply of the shorter-lived types. Press the seeds into moist germination medium about 2 months before the last expected frost in your area. Leave the seeds on the soil surface or cover them very lightly. Keep the starting medium moist at all times at a temperature of 65°F to 75°F (18°C to 24°C). Germination normally occurs within 21 days. Once plants have formed a second pair of leaves, plant them in individual pots, and grow them on in a well-lit area. Harden them off for 14 days before planting them in the garden. Do this after all danger of frost has passed in spring.

Special Uses

Cut Flowers Tickseeds make fine cut flowers. Cut stems, and place them in a bucket of water immediately. Once indoors, place the stems in 110°F (43°C) water and let them stand overnight. Some growers place them in cold water containing 1 tablespoon (14 g) salt per quart (liter) of water. The next day, place them in floral arrangements after removing any leaves that would end up underwater.

Dried Flowers No one we know has been particularly successful drying these flowers. You might try using a desiccant with larger individual blooms, especially those of semidoubles or doubles.

Sources

Bluestone Perennials, 7211 Middle Ridge Rd., Madison, OH 44057, (800) 852-5243
Busse Gardens, 17160 245th Ave., Big Lake, MN 55309, (800) 544-3192
Fieldstone Gardens, Inc., 55 Quaker Lane, Vassalboro, ME 04989, (207) 923-3836
ForestFarm, 990 Tetherow Rd., Williams, OR 97544, (541) 846-7269
Goodwin Creek Gardens, P.O. Box 83, Williams, OR 97544, (800) 846-7359
Triple Brook Nursery, 459 State Rte. 34, Colts Neck, NJ 07722, (732) 946-2027
Wayside Gardens, 1 Garden Lane, Hodges, SC 29695, (800) 213-0379

'Moonbeam'

'Sunburst'

VARIETIES

VARIETY	COLOR	FORM	HEIGHT	HARDINESS
Coreopsis auriculata				
(Mouse Ear Tickseed)				
'Zamphir' ('Zamfir')	Yellow orange/orange gold	Single	15″	−30°F

This plant spreads slowly by creeping stems at or just below the soil surface. Bloom peaks in late spring, but expect flowers off and on throughout the summer. The plant grows best in soil kept evenly moist throughout the season.

VARIETY	COLOR	FORM	HEIGHT	HARDINESS
Coreopsis grandiflora				
(Large-flowered Tickseed)				
'Early Sunrise'*****	Gold yellow/yellow	Double	18″	−20°F
'Sunburst'	Gold/gold	Semi-double	24″	−20°F
'Sunfire'*****	Gold yellow/burgundy ring	Single	20″	−20°F

These varieties are short-lived but often self-sow if allowed to go to seed. Death after severe open winters is common, especially in the case of mature clumps. Division of the clumps every two to three years increases the chance of winter survival. These are among the best Tickseeds for cut flowers and often rebloom if regularly deadheaded. 'Early Sunrise' and 'Sunfire,' both award winners, can produce their first flowers in 12 weeks or less after sowing.

VARIETY	COLOR	FORM	HEIGHT	HARDINESS
Coreopsis lanceolata				
(Lance-leafed Tickseed)	Yellow/gold	Single	24″	−30°F
'Ruby Throat' ('Rotkehlchen')	Gold yellow/reddish ring	Double	12″	−30°F
'Sterntaler'	Yellow/brown ring	Double	18″	−30°F

This species is similar to *Coreopsis grandiflora* (Large-flowered Tickseed) but tends to live much longer. Excellent soil drainage and division every two to three years increases longevity. Regular deadheading often results in additional bloom.

Coreopsis palmata				
(Stiff Tickseed)	Bright yellow/gold	Single	36″	−40°F

Blooming for a long period in summer, this native Tickseed is a fairly aggressive spreader that is of greatest value for stabilizing sunny dry slopes. It is good for attracting butterflies to your garden.

Coreopsis rosea				
(Pink Tickseed)	Rose pink/yellow	Single	24″	−30°F

This native has proven surprisingly hardy. It spreads fairly rapidly and tolerates moisture and shade.

Coreopsis tripteris				
(Tall Tickseed)	Bright yellow/brown	Single	96″	−40°F

This tall vertical Tickseed blooms in late summer. Plant it in natural areas where it can self-seed freely.

Coreopsis verticillata*****				
(Thread-leaf Tickseed)	Yellow/gold	Single	24″	−40°F
'Golden Shower' ('Golden Showers')	Gold yellow/gold	Single	24″	−40°F
'Zagreb'	Gold yellow/gold	Single	18″	−40°F

The foliage on these varieties is as fine-textured as that of the well-known named variety 'Moonbeam.' They do not have as long a bloom period but are much hardier. They bloom from mid to late summer. These varieties are very long-lived and tolerate drought quite well.

Coreopsis (Named varieties and hybrids)				
'Creme Brulee'*****	Clear yellow/yellow	Single	20″	−30°F
'Full Moon'	Soft yellow/gold	Single	30″	−20°F
'Galaxy'	Bright yellow/gold	Semi-double	16″	−30°F
'Jethro Tull'	Gold yellow/gold	Single	18″	−30°F
'Moonbeam'	Soft yellow/gold	Single	18″	−30°F
'Moonray'	Cream yellow/gold brown	Single	18″	−30°F
'Sunbeam'	Golden yellow/gold	Single	24″	−30°F

'Creme Brulee,' a long-blooming variety, offers better vigor and longevity than 'Moonbeam.' Its flowers float above bright green lacy foliage as well as down the stems. 'Full Moon' has large blooms that are up to three inches in diameter. 'Galaxy' has a rich yellow flower. 'Jethro Tull' has a neat, tidy appearance; distinctive fluted ray flower petals; and an extended bloom season throughout the summer. Although valued for its extended bloom period, 'Moonbeam' has a tendency to die out during the winter. It's a lovely compact plant with narrow, delicate foliage and ideal for the front of the border. The plant appears sterile to us, so it is curious that seed for this variety is available in some catalogs. 'Sunbeam,' a sport of 'Moonbeam,' has the same narrow delicate foliage but much darker flowers. It blooms all summer and is an excellent choice for hot, dry spots.

Blackmore and Langdon Hybrids

DELPHINIUM

(dell-FIN-ee-um)

LARKSPUR

Bloom Time	Expected Longevity	Maintenance	Years to Bloom	Preferred Light
Late spring to summer	3 to 5 years	High	From seed: 1 to 2 years From potted plant: 1 year	Full sun

Larkspurs are the most beautiful vertical accent plants for late-spring and early-summer bloom. Although available in a number of flower colors, they are most prized for their rich blues. The floral stems are excellent in cut-flower arrangements. Though this is a favorite perennial of many gardeners, it is a difficult one to grow well and tends to be short-lived. While it is somewhat susceptible to pest problems, it is at risk more from hot, dry summers which often lead to its death. Keep the seeds and young plants away from children, since they can cause severe stomach problems and depression if eaten.

How Larkspurs Grow

Larkspurs are clump-forming plants with upright stems that produce dense flower heads at their tops in late spring and early summer. Individual flowers are quite small but bloom in great profusion. The centers, or "bees," of many flowers are contrasting in color. The foliage is mostly at the base of the plant, and individual leaves are shaped like a human hand. These perennials are generally grown from seed, but certain varieties need to be reproduced by division or cuttings to produce offspring identical to the parents. Larkspurs grow from thick, fleshy roots, and, under ideal growing conditions, the crown will get quite large with time. Most types need to be staked to keep their stems upright.

Where to Plant

Site and Light Larkspurs need 6 to 8 hours of sunlight each day for best growth. High light also helps reduce the chance of disease. Avoid placing Larkspurs near trees and shrubs that will compete with the plants for moisture and nutrients. Although the plants need lots of sun, they flourish in cool weather. Avoid windy areas, as even staked stems can get badly damaged in gusts.

Soil and Moisture Larkspurs prefer rich, moist soil that drains freely. Mix lots of organic matter, such as compost, leaf mold, or peat moss, into the soil. Replace clay and rocky soils or build a raised bed. Plants in poorly drained soils often die out during the winter.

Spacing Place the plants 12 to 24 inches (30 to 60 cm) apart, depending on potential height. Giving plants enough space for good air circulation is an important step in preventing diseases. Larkspurs make fine specimen or accent plants but are also stunning in large groups in the border or island beds.

Companions

Place tall varieties of *Delphinium* (Larkspur) at the back of the garden where their vertical spikes can be showcased against some type of background. Some pleasing companion perennials are *Achillea* Anthea and 'Moonshine' (Yarrow), *Filipendula rubra* (Queen-of-the-Prairie), *Geranium × oxonianum* 'Claridge Druce' (Hybrid Cranesbill), *Heuchera* (Coral Bells), *Phlox*–Maculata Group 'Miss Lingard' (Meadow Phlox), *Paeonia* (Peony), *Tanacetum*

(Painted Daisy), and early-blooming varieties of *Lilium* (Lily). *Delphinium grandiflorum* (Chinese Delphinium) is delightful placed near the front of the garden, in a rock garden, or even interplanted among dwarf shrubs such as *Potentilla fruticosa* (Bush Cinquefoil).

Planting

Bare Root Plant bare root stock as soon as you can work the ground in spring. Remove plants from the shipping package immediately. Snip off broken or damaged root tips. Soak plants overnight in room-temperature water. Place a small amount of super-phosphate in the base of the planting hole. Fill the hole with soil. Place the crown 1 inch (2.5 cm) below the soil surface. Fill in with soil, firm with your fingers, and water immediately. Dissolve ½ cup (about 114 g) of 10-10-10 fertilizer in 1 gallon (about 4 liters) of water. Pour ½ cup (about 120 ml) of this starter solution around the base of each plant. If you prefer organic fertilizer, use fish emulsion instead.

Potted Plants Plant Larkspurs after all danger of frost has passed in spring. If the soil in the pot is dry, water it, and let it drain overnight. Tap the plant from the pot without disturbing the root ball. Plant at the same depth as in the pot, after preparing the hole in a similar manner to that for a bare root plant. Fill in with soil, firm with your fingers, and water immediately. Pour ½ cup (about 120 ml) starter solution around the base of each plant.

How to Care for Larkspurs

Water Keep these plants evenly moist throughout the growing season. Even though they require well-drained soil, they need a regular supply of moisture for lush growth. Soak the root system to a depth of 12 inches (30 cm) every time you water. Try to keep the foliage dry, especially if watering in the evening, as this will lessen the chance of infection by disease.

Mulch Surround the base of each plant with 2 inches (5 cm) of mulch as soon as the ground warms up in spring. Good mulches include dried grass clippings, shredded leaves, or pine needles. Mulch keeps the soil cool and moist. It also inhibits the growth of annual weeds, which compete with the plants for food and moisture.

Fertilizing Larkspurs are heavy feeders. Sprinkle 10-10-10 fertilizer around the base of each plant just as growth emerges in spring. Scratch it into the soil, and water immediately to dissolve the granules and move nutrients into the root zone. Follow up with biweekly feedings right through the bloom period. Larkspurs also respond well to foliar feeding with water-soluble fertilizers.

If you prefer organic fertilizer, use alfalfa meal (rabbit pellets), blood meal, bonemeal, compost, cow manure, fish emulsion, Milorganite, or rotted horse manure. Bonemeal must be mixed into the soil at planting time to be effective.

Weeding Using a mulch controls the growth of most annual weeds. Any that do germinate are easily pulled by hand. Weeds compete with the plants for valuable nutrients and moisture. Larkspurs need a great deal of both to grow well, so keep the area around them absolutely weed free.

Staking Most tall varieties need support even when planted in protected areas. Their height, hollow stems, and large flower heads make many of them susceptible to damage in rainstorms. Begin staking individual stems early in the season by placing bamboo, wood, plastic, or metal stakes into the ground just as new growth begins. As they grow, tie the stems to the stakes in loose figure-eight knots.

You can also stake an entire clump by placing long stakes around the outside of the clump. Tie string around the stakes at varying heights. If the plants are in the back of the border, this support is rarely noticed. This is not as effective a method as staking individual stems, however, because strong winds may break stems where they contact the uppermost string.

Thinning Many gardeners reduce the number of stems in a mature clump to three to five. Do this early, when the stems are only 3 to 4 inches (7.5 to 10 cm) high. This practice leads to larger flower heads and also allows better air circulation among the stems, reducing the risk of disease.

Deadheading Removing the main flower head encourages numerous smaller secondary flower heads to bloom. This often carries the bloom period well into the summer months.

Pruning Cutting the plants back to the ground immediately after they flower may result in a second period of bloom in fall. When this happens, it's especially exciting, since the rich blues are rare fall colors.

Winter Protection Remove all dead stems and foliage after a severe frost in fall. When the ground has frozen to a depth of 2 inches (5 centimeters), cover the plants with 6 inches (15 cm) of marsh hay, clean straw, pine needles, or whole leaves. Remove this mulch as soon as the weather warms up in spring to avoid crown or root rot.

Problems

Insects Red spider mites occasionally attack Larkspurs, turning plants a pale yellow color. Spider mites are most common in hot, dry weather. Regular watering during dry periods discourages infestations. In severe cases, the use of a miticide may be necessary. Slugs can be a problem in damp, cool weather, a situation that actually favors good growth in Larkspurs. If they feed on your plants, lay a small board near the base of the plants. After a day or so, lift up the board in early morning and remove any slugs that are hiding on the bottom. Drown them in a can of salty water or vinegar. Repeat this process as necessary. Commercial slug baits are effective, but they must be used carefully so as not to harm pets and wildlife. Aphids may also attack Larkspurs. You can spray them off with a gentle mist of water, or kill them with a mild insecticidal soap. Other insect pests are also known to attack these perennials, but they are rare in cold climates.

Disease Leaf spots can be a problem in certain growing seasons but are not severe enough to warrant preventive spraying. If the foliage is severely damaged, cut stems back to the ground; a new mound of healthy foliage will rapidly take its place. This may have some effect on bloom, depending on when it is done. Powdery mildew does occur but is relatively rare. If it proves to be a routine problem, preventive use of a fungicide may be your only option. Soil care is also important, as poorly drained soils and winter mulches left over the crowns too long in spring can lead to crown and root rot.

Propagation

Division Dividing Larkspurs every 1 to 3 years often prolongs their lives. Dig up the plant in early spring just as new growth emerges, and wash it free of soil. Cut the crown into sections, making sure that each has three to five stems and a healthy root system. Plant them immediately just as you would a bare root plant.

Cuttings Take basal cuttings in early spring when stems are 3 to 4 inches (7.5 to 10 cm) tall. Using a sharp knife, take these cuttings with a small portion of the crown attached. Dip the cut end in rooting hormone, and tap off any excess powder. Place the cuttings in moist rooting medium, and keep the humidity around them high. The cuttings should be rooted in 2 to 3 weeks when they can be potted up for growing on. Plant them into a permanent garden location once they are growing vigorously.

Seed You get the best results from seed that's less than 6 months old. Germination rates fall off dramatically for older seed. Sow seed in midwinter if you hope to get some flowers the first year.

Fill a seed tray with moist germination medium, and press the seed into the surface. Keep the seed exposed, as most Larkspurs require light for germination. Place the seed tray in an area with a temperature of 60°F to 65°F (16°C to 18°C). Germination should take place within 2 to 3 weeks. Seedlings can usually be transplanted about 1 month after sowing.

Older seed may require a moist chilling treatment to encourage germination. Put the seed tray in a perforated plastic bag, and place it in the crisper of your refrigerator for 4 to 6 weeks. Then remove the tray and allow the seeds to germinate as in the preceding paragraph. Once these seedlings have a second pair of leaves, plant them in individual pots. Harden them off for 14 days before planting them outside after all danger of frost has passed in spring.

Special Uses

Cut Flowers Larkspurs make excellent cut flowers. Cut the stems when approximately one-third of the flower buds are open. Place these in water immediately. Remove any lower leaves that might be underwater in the arrangement. Some gardeners suggest that the flower stems hold up longer if the hollow stems are filled with water and then plugged with cotton. You simply hold the stems upside down, pour water into the openings until they're full, and then seal the stems with cotton.

Although the blues are favorites in the garden, whites and pinks are often more desirable in flower arrangements. They retain their color very well, whereas some of the darker colors may turn almost black. The shorter members of the Belladonna Group are particularly recommended for indoor arrangements, as they bloom over a long period, are easier to work with, and have many side branches.

Dried Flowers Although much literature indicates that Larkspurs are not good as dried flowers, that is not true. The dark blues do tend to discolor, but the light blues, whites, and pinks can be dried quite nicely. Cut the flowers at varying stages, and hang them upside down until dry in a dark, well-ventilated area. Some arrangers suggest that the flowers will have a more natural look if they are tipped right side up for a while during the drying process. You can also dry individual flowers in a desiccant for use in potpourris or to be attached to florist wire for special uses. In general, the faster they are dried, the better the color.

Larkspurs also form distinctive seed heads. These dry well right on the plant. Cut them when they're fully dry for use in winter arrangements along with **Grasses** and other fall foliage.

Sources

Ambergate Gardens, 8730 County Rd. 43, Chaska, MN 55318, (877) 211-9769

Blackmore and Langdon, Ltd., Stanton Nurseries, Pensford, Bristol, Somerset BS39 4JL, UK, 01275 332300

Bluestone Perennials, 7211 Middle Ridge Rd., Madison, OH 44057, (800) 852-5243

J.W. Jung, Seed Company, 335 S High St., Randolph, WI 53957, (800) 247-5864

Laporte Avenue Nursery, 1950 Laporte Ave., Fort Collins, CO 80521, (970) 472-0017

Moles Seeds, Ltd., Turkey Cock Lane, Stanway, Colchester, Essex Co3 8PD, UK, 01206 213213

Stokes Seeds, Inc, P.O. Box 548, Buffalo, NY 14240, (800) 396-9238

Swallowtail Garden Seeds, 122 Calistoga Rd. #178, Santa Rosa, CA 95409, (707) 538-3585

White Flower Farm, P.O. Box 50, Litchfield, CT 06759, (800) 503-9624

Delphinium grandiflorum

'Snow White'

VARIETIES

VARIETY	COLOR/BEE (CENTER)	HEIGHT	HARDINESS
Delphinium–Belladonna Group			
'Bellamosum'	Dark blue/blue bee	36″	−40°F
'Casa Blanca' ('Casablanca')*****	White/pale yellow bee	48″	−40°F
'Cliveden Beauty'	Pale blue/bluish white bee	48″	−40°F
'Connecticut Yankee'*****	Mix (blue, purple, white)	30″	−40°F
'Delft Blue'*****	Blue edged white/dark bee	40″	−40°F

These plants have lots of side branches with flowers that open at about the same time as the main flower stalk in late spring into early summer.

Delphinium Blackmore & Langdon Hybrids	Mix	72″	−40°F

Among the loveliest Delphiniums, these English hybrids must be grown from seed and will need to be staked.

Delphinium elatum			
(Bee Delphinium)	Blue violet/dark bee	72″	−40°F

This Siberian species is a parent of many fine hybrids. It is very tall and upright with deeply cut leaves.

Delphinium–Elatum Group			
'Coral Sunset'	Salmon red (D)	48″	−40°F
'Darwin's Blue Indulgence'	Sky blue (D)	48″	−40°F
'Wishful Thinking' ('Dolce Vita')	Light blue violet (D)	48″	−40°F

These plants have deeply-cut green foliage as well as striking double (D) flowers with rich colors.

Delphinium grandiflorum			
(Chinese Delphinium)	Deep blue	30″	−40°F
'Blue Butterfly' ('Butterfly')	Rich blue	24″	−40°F
'Blue Mirror' ('Blauer Spiegel')	Deep blue	24″	−40°F
'Dwarf Blue' ('Blauer Zwerg')	Gentian blue	18″	−40°F
'Summer Blues'*****	Soft sky blue	12″	−40°F
'Summer Morning'*****	Clear pink	12″	−40°F
'Summer Nights'*****	Deep blue	18″	−40°F
Summer Series	Mix	12″	−40°F

These branchy plants with narrow leaves and loose flower heads are usually short-lived but will often self-sow. They come true from seed and will flower the first season if started early enough indoors.

Delphinium–New Millenium Series*****			
'Black Eyed Angels'*****	White/black bee	60″	−40°F
'Blue Lace'	Sky blue/blue to white bee (D)	72″	−40°F
'Blushing Brides'	Lavender pink/dark bee	72″	−40°F
'Double Innocence'*****	White green/greenish bee (D)	48″	−40°F
'Dusky Maidens'	Mulberry pink/brown bee	60″	−40°F
'Green Twist'	White tinged green/greenish bee	72″	−40°F
'Misty Mauves'	Mauve purple/green cream bee (D)	48″	−40°F

VARIETY	COLOR/BEE (CENTER)	HEIGHT	HARDINESS
'Morning Lights'	Mauve lavender blue/white bee	36"	−40°F
'Pagan Purples'*****	Dark blue purple/dark bee (S, D)	72"	−40°F
'Pink Punch'	Mulberry pink/dark bee	60"	−40°F
'Purple Passion'	Purple/white bee	60"	−40°F
'Royal Aspirations'	Blue purple shades/white bee	72"	−40°F
'Sunny Skies'*****	Sky blue/white bee	72"	−40°F
'Sweetheart' ('Sweethearts')	Pink shades/white bee	60"	−40°F

These long-lived Delphiniums prefer cool weather, but still grow well in areas with warm, humid days and nights. They bloom profusely with rich colors. Stems are sturdy but will require staking in windy locations, especially at peak bloom in late spring to early summer. Cutting the plants back may encourage rebloom later in the season.

Delphinium–Pacific Giant Group or Round Table Series

'Astolat'*****	Lavender pink/dark bee	60"	−40°F
'Black Knight'	Dark blue/black bee	60"	−40°F
'Blue Bird'	Greenish blue/white bee	60"	−40°F
'Blue Jay'	Medium blue/dark bee	60"	−40°F
'Camelliard'('Cameliard')	Mid blue/white bee	60"	−40°F
'Galahad'	Pure white	60"	−40°F
'Guinevere'	Blue bicolor	60"	−40°F
'King Arthur'	Royal violet/white bee	60"	−40°F
Pacific Mix	Mix	60"	−40°F
Pennant Mix*****	Mix	30"	−40°F
'Percival'	White/dark bee	60"	−40°F
'Summer Skies'	Sky blue/white bee	60"	−40°F

The Pacific Giant Group is best suited to areas with cool summer nights. You can start plants from a seed mix or as individual colors. These plants do come true from seed. All will require staking as they bloom in late spring to early summer. If they are cut back after first bloom, they form new mounds of foliage which may produce another round of bloom in fall. The Magic Fountains Series are in the Pacific Giant Group but known as Dwarf Pacific Giants. They are generally grown from seed and mature in three years. They make excellent cut flowers. The Magic Fountain varieties are sold as 'Cherry Blossoms,' 'Dark Blue,' 'Fountain' (sky blue), 'Lavender,' 'Pink,' and 'Double White' or 'Snow White.' They range in height from 24" to 30."

Delphinium virescens

(Prairie Larkspur)	Whitish blue	24"	−40°F

This wildflower has long flower spikes covered with Columbine-like blossoms. It blooms in late spring and goes dormant shortly afterward. In fall, a fresh mound of bluish green leaves forms once again, but the plant does not rebloom. Plant it in a dry, sunny portion of the wildflower garden. It demands excellent drainage to grow well and survive.

'Grandchild'

CHRYSANTHEMUM × MORIFOLIUM

(cruh-SAN-thuh-mum more-ih-FOH-lee-uhm)

GARDEN MUM

Bloom Time	Expected Longevity	Maintenance	Years to Bloom	Preferred Light
Late summer to late fall	5+ years	High	From seed: Not applicable From potted plant: 1 year	Full sun

Although they need lots of attention, Garden Mums are one of the most popular plants for fall flowering. These profuse bloomers are available in a wide range of plant types, flower forms, and flower sizes. The predominant flower colors are white, yellow, bronze, pink, red, and purple. All make excellent cut flowers, but taller varieties are favored for this. Most Garden Mums are not winter hardy in cold regions, and these are sometimes grown as annuals. However, the ones listed in this section are hardy if given the correct care and winter protection. They were once classified as *Dendranthema × grandiflora*.

How Garden Mums Grow

Garden Mums grow from short, fibrous roots to form bushy plants with numerous branches and deep green, aromatic foliage. As the growing season progresses, the plants form sizable crowns with an abundance of stems. With longer nights, the plants are triggered to set flower buds and bloom. Flowering will continue until a hard killing frost. If carefully protected through the winter, the plants send off numerous little plantlets to the side of the original mother plant and create an even bushier plant the following season.

Where to Plant

Site and Light Garden Mums are high-light plants and flourish in full sun. Plants grown in shade will have sparse foliage, weak stems, and poor bloom. Since flowering is initiated by long nights, you should avoid planting them near outside lights, as these retard or may even prevent bloom.

Soil and Moisture Garden Mums grow best in rich loam that stays moist throughout the season but drains freely. Mix lots of organic matter into the soil. Good amendments include peat moss, leaf mold, compost, and rotted manure. If you have clay or rocky soil, either replace it or build a raised bed.

Spacing Space plants 12 to 24 inches (30 to 60 cm) apart, depending on the height of the plant and the effect you want to achieve. Proper spacing is key to good air circulation and prevention of fungal diseases.

Companions

Use *Chrysanthemum* ✕ *morifolium* (Garden Mum) for a bold and beautiful effect in mass plantings. They are especially beautiful planted in a wave of one color. Garden Mums combine well with other fall-blooming perennials such as *Aster* (Aster), *Rudbeckia* (Coneflower), *Sedum* (Stonecrop), and various **Grasses**. Don't overlook the dramatic effect of planting them next to woody shrubs bearing colorful foliage and fruits.

Planting

Bare Root Plant bare root stock as soon as you can work the ground in spring. Remove the plants from their shipping package immediately. Snip off broken or damaged root tips. Soak plants overnight in room-temperature water. Place a small amount of superphosphate in the base of the planting hole. Fill the hole with soil. Plant the Mums so that the root system is evenly spread out just under the soil surface. Firm the soil around each plant, and water it immediately. Dissolve ½ cup (about 114 g) 10-10-10 fertilizer in 1 gallon (about 4 liters) of water. Pour ½ cup (about 120 ml) of this starter solution around the base of each plant. If you prefer organic fertilizer, use fish emulsion instead.

Potted Plants Plant potted Garden Mums after all danger of frost has passed in spring. If you purchase potted Garden Mums in spring that have buds or open flowers, pinch all of these off. You want all of the plant's energy to go into forming a healthy root system and ample foliage. After a full season's growth, the lengthening nights will trigger the formation of additional flower buds. If soil in the pot is dry, soak it, and allow the pot to drain overnight before planting. Tap the plant from the pot without disturbing the root ball. Plant it at the same depth as in the pot, after preparing the hole in a similar manner to that for a bare root plant. Fill the hole, firm the soil with your fingers, and water it immediately. Pour ½ cup (about 120 ml) starter solution around the base of each plant.

How to Care for Garden Mums

Water Moisture from spring through fall is critical to lush growth, abundant flowering, and winter survival. Soak the soil to a depth of 6 to 8 inches (15 to 20 cm) each time you water.

Mulch Place 2 inches (5 cm) of mulch around the base of each plant as soon as the ground warms up in spring. A summer mulch keeps the soil moist and cool and encourages the growth of small plantlets to the side of the mother plant. It also inhibits the growth of annual weeds. Good mulches include dried grass clippings, shredded bark, pulverized leaves, and pine needles.

Fertilizing Garden Mums are heavy feeders. Feed them biweekly with a balanced garden fertilizer such as 10-10-10, or apply a slow-release fertilizer in spring that will become available to the plants as they develop through the summer. Some gardeners simply give one feeding of 10-10-10 in spring and another in late summer as bud formation begins. Garden Mums also respond very well to foliar feeding with a water-soluble fertilizer.

If you prefer organic fertilizers, use alfalfa meal (rabbit pellets), blood meal, bonemeal, compost, fish emulsion, Milorganite, or rotted horse manure. Bonemeal should be added to the soil at planting time for maximum effectiveness.

Weeding If you use a summer mulch, annual weeds should be a minor nuisance at worst. Any that do germinate are easily pulled out of the mulch by hand. Garden Mums are quite shallow-rooted, so avoid deep cultivation around their crowns.

Staking Most Garden Mums do not require staking. Some of the tallest varieties may need support if grown in partial shade and not pinched early in the season. If support is necessary, pea stakes stuck into the ground early in the season are a good choice.

Pinching Back Most Garden Mums benefit from pinching back early in the season. This produces shorter, stockier plants with more abundant flowers. While the low cushion forms are already stocky, pinching back produces a greater number of flowers. When plants are 6 inches (15 cm) tall, pinch out the growing tips of the stems just above a leaf node with your fingers or pruning shears. This will force the plant to produce numerous lateral branches. Once these have grown 4 to 6 inches (10 to 15 cm), they can be pinched as well. In colder regions, avoid pinching after July 1, as this may delay or prevent flower bud formation. (See the discussion under "Cuttings" later in this section for information on rooting the stem tips.)

Disbudding Cut-flower growers often remove all side buds on Garden Mums to produce the largest blooms possible. Home gardeners do not generally practice this technique unless they are growing flowers for exhibition.

Deadheading Since these perennials flower so late in the season, removal of spent flowers will not encourage additional bloom and is mainly done for aesthetic reasons. Garden Mums do not self-sow, so this is not a reason for deadheading.

Winter Protection Garden Mums survive winter only with good winter protection. After a severe killing frost, cut the stems back to the ground. Do not disturb the green growth at the base of the plant, since it will produce flower stems the following year. When the ground freezes to a depth of 2 inches (5 cm), cover Garden Mums with a 6- to 8-inch (15- to 20-cm) layer of mulch. Marsh hay, clean straw, whole leaves, and pine needles work well. In many instances, it is not cold that causes damage, but rather water loss, as the plants are heaved out of the ground by alternate freeze–thaw cycles. The purpose of the mulch is to protect the plants from winter cold and to keep the ground frozen until the warm weather of spring arrives. Remove the mulch as soon as the weather warms up in spring to prevent rot.

Problems

Insects Garden Mums are host to a wide range of insects. These include aphids, leafhoppers, plant bugs, leaf miners, red spider mites, and caterpillars. Most are not serious or common, and control is often for aesthetic reasons. Aphids and leafhoppers serve as carriers of a viruslike disease called aster yellows, and you may need to control them in certain seasons with the use of an insecticidal soap. The best nonchemical way to ward off insects is to grow strong, vigorous plants which can withstand attacks. Wash off light insect infestations with spray from a hose. Though not a true insect, some mention of nematodes is in order. These microscopic worms sometimes feed on plants. Garden Mums are occasionally bothered by a foliage-eating nematode that leaves brown wedges of dead tissue where they enter the plant. This damage occurs first on leaves nearest the ground. Control this pest by early removal and destruction of infested leaves. The use of a summer mulch and watering the plants without getting the foliage wet also help stop the spread of these invaders. Use systemic insecticides or nematicides if these worms become a regular or serious pest.

Diseases Garden Mums are prone to a number of diseases, including leaf spots, bacterial blight, powdery mildew, rust, various wilts, and aster yellows. Most of these are quite uncommon with well-grown plants and normal weather conditions. Aster yellows, though, is not. It results in abnormal or stunted growth, a purplish cast to the foliage, and malformed flowers with a greenish cast. Since there is no cure for this disease, you should immediately dig up and destroy any Garden Mums showing these symptoms. This pathogen is carried by leafhoppers and aphids from surrounding weeds. Killing off weeds and these insects will help prevent outbreaks of this deadly disease in the first place.

Frost Damage Garden Mums take light frosts well, but many have blossoms that will turn brown in heavy frost. To extend their bloom period as late into the fall as possible, protect them from hard frosts. Cover the plants on very cold nights with old sheets, blankets, rugs, or commercial covers. This extra care usually extends the bloom period by several weeks during typical Indian summers.

Propagation

Division Garden Mums will survive for the longest period and be most vigorous if divided and replanted each spring. Garden Mums form a loose mat of roots with new stems coming up off to the side of the mother plant. As soon as new growth begins, dig up the entire clump, and shake or wash off all surplus soil. Cut off the areas of new growth from the old central core. Keep as many roots with each new section of growth as possible. Discard the old portion of plant. These new divisions should be replanted immediately and kept consistently moist.

Cuttings Garden Mums are also easy to propagate by cuttings. If these cuttings are taken in early spring, they will produce a good show of flowers that first fall. Take cuttings with three sets of leaves. Make cuts a quarter inch (6 mm) below leaf nodes, and strip off all but the top set of leaves. Though Garden Mums will root well without a rooting hormone, its use may speed the process along. Dip the bottoms of the cuttings in the rooting hormone, and tap off excess powder. Then stick the cuttings into a rooting medium, and keep them moist and humid throughout the rooting process. This usually takes only a couple of weeks. Once they have rooted, transplant the young plants to individual pots for further growing on or directly into the garden. Cuttings can continue to be taken until early summer, and, in fact, the tips that are removed in the pinching process (see "Pinching Back") are sometimes rooted to produce additional plants. However, these later cuttings often do not produce flowers that first season.

Seed Garden Mums are so quick and easy to propagate by division and cuttings that seed is of little value. Most seed-grown strains also lack the quality that most gardeners are after. Seedling populations often show great variability in development and poor plant growth. In addition, they are less hardy than plants propagated by division or cuttings.

Special Uses

Cut Flowers Garden Mums make excellent, long-lasting cut flowers that blend well with other fall flowers, foliage, and fruits. Harvest them just as the main flower reaches maturity. The numerous side buds will open later to put on a fine display. Condition the stems by placing them in a pail of warm sugar water and allowing them to stand overnight in a cool, dark place. Use ½ cup (about 114 g) sugar per quart (4 liters) of water. Crushing the lower part of stems helps them absorb water. Remove any leaves that will be below the water line in the arrangement.

Dried Flowers Though Garden Mums are not normally recommended for this use, you may try drying individual flowers in a desiccant.

Sources

Busse Gardens, 17160 245th Ave., Big Lake, MN 55309, (800) 544-3192

King's Mums LLC, 14857 S Brunner Rd., Oregon City, OR 97045, (503) 656-2078

Mums by Paschke, 12286 E Main Rd., North East, PA 16428, (814) 725-9860

Mums of Minnesota-Faribault Growers, Inc., 3135 227th St. E, Faribault, MN 55021, (507) 334-6220

VARIETIES

Northern hybridizing programs have resulted in a wonderful assortment of Garden Mums well suited to the shorter seasons of colder climates. Especially important is the breeding work which has been carried on at the University of Minnesota. Available named varieties (cultivars) offer a myriad of choices of flower color, flower type and size, plant height, and time of bloom. The farther north you live, the more important it is to choose varieties which bloom early. The bloom seasons given in the following list are based on data collected in southern Minnesota (USDA Zone 4) and correspond to the following calendar dates: **Early** (before September 1), **Mid** (September 1–15), and **Late** (after September 15). All plants listed are hardy to –30 and some to –40 with good winter protection.

The flowers of Garden Mums are described using a number of terms. Here is a brief explanation of the flower types included in this varietal listing (there are others, but they are not suited to cold climates): **Decorative**—Fairly large double flowers generally blooming on taller plants; **Intermediate incurved**—Flowers with petals curving toward the center in a somewhat uniform manner; **Pompon**—Abundant small flowers whose petals hug the centers very tightly; **Quill**—Flowers with long tubular petals; **Single**—Daisy petaled flowers with flat or slightly rounded central disks; **Spoon**—Flowers with tubular petals whose ends flare into the shape of a spoon.

Mammoth™ Mums are extremely large plants once mature and showered with blossoms. They are not currently available through mail-order sources but distributed in retail outlets. Consider all of them five star (*****) plants. We have included five from this series in the following chart.

VARIETY	COLOR	TYPE	SIZE	HEIGHT	SEASON
'Autumn Fire'	Burnt orange	Decorative	3½"	18"	Mid
'Autumn Sunset'	Red, gold, yellow	Decorative	3"	16"	Mid
'Bristol White'	White	Decorative	4"	16"	Mid
'Burnt Copper'	Orange bronze	Pompon	3"	18"	Mid
'Centennial Sun'	Golden yellow	Decorative	1½"	16"	Early
'Centerpiece'*****	Rose lavender	Quill	4"	24"	Early/mid
'Dolliette'	Yellow bronze tipped red	Spoon	2½"	18"	Late
'Dorothy Dean'('Degn')*****	Bright red	Pompon	2½"	24"	Early/mid

'Centerpiece'

'Minnruby'

'Minnyellow'

'Sea Urchin'

VARIETY	COLOR	TYPE	SIZE	HEIGHT	SEASON
'Gold Country'	Golden yellow	Incurved (D)	4½″	20″	Mid
'Golden Star'*****	Rich yellow	Spoon	3½″	16″	Early
'Goldstrike'	Golden yellow	Pompon	2″	16″	Early
'Grandchild'	Lavender pink	Decorative	2½″	18″	Early
'Grape Glow'*****	Rose purple	Decorative	3½″	16″	Mid
'Inca'	Bronzy orange	Pompon (D)	2″	12″	Early
'Irish Linen'	Ivory	Incurved (D)	5″	24″	Early
'Lemonsota'	Lemon yellow	Pompon	1″	12″	Mid
Mammoth™ Coral Daisy	Coral pink	Single	2½″	36″	Early/mid
Mammoth™ Dark Pink Daisy	Lavender pink	Single	2½″	36″	Early/mid
Mammoth™ Lavender Daisy	Rich lavender	Single	2½″	36″	Early/mid
Mammoth™ Red Daisy	Medium red	Single	2½″	36″	Early/mid
Mammoth™ Yellow Quill	Bright yellow	Quill	2½″	36″	Early/mid
'Matchstick'*****	Yellow tipped red	Quill	2″	16″	Mid
'Maroon Pride'	Dark red	Decorative	3½″	18″	Early
'Mellow Moon'*****	Cream	Int. incurve (D)	4½″	18″	Mid
'Minnautumn'	Reddish bronze	Decorative	2½″	16″	Mid
'Minngopher'	Crimson red	Decorative	2¼″	16″	Mid
'Minnpink'	Rose pink	Decorative	2″	16″	Early
'Minnqueen'*****	Bright rose pink	Decorative	3″	12″	Mid
'Minnruby'*****	Ruby red	Decorative	2″	12″	Mid
'Minnwhite'	White	Decorative	2″	12″	Early
'Minnyellow'	Lemon yellow	Decorative	2″	12″	Early
'Peach Centerpiece'	Peach/gold	Quill	4″	24″	Mid
'Pilgrim'	Dark red	Decorative	2″	16″	Mid
'Quarterback'	Rose pink	Int. incurve	5″	30″	Mid
'Rose Blush'*****	Bright pink mauve	Decorative	3″	16″	Early
'Rose Grenadine'	Rose pink gold	Decorative	2″	24″	Mid
'Rosy Glow'	Rose pink	Int. incurve	4″	16″	Early
'Royal Knight'*****	Burgundy	Decorative	3½″	20″	Mid
'Ruby Mound'	Ruby red	Decorative	2″	18″	Late
'Sea Urchin'	Greenish yellow	Quill	4″	16″	Mid
'Sesquicentennial Sun'	Bright yellow	Pompon	2″	16″	Mid
'Snowscape'*****	White tinged purple	Decorative (SD)	3″	14″	Early
'Snowsota'*****	White	Pompon	1½″	16″	Early
'Sun Spider'	Bright yellow	Quill-like	5″	18″	Mid
'Wayzata'	Bright yellow	Decorative	3″	24″	Early
'White Grandchild'	White	Decorative	2½″	16″	Early
'Yellow Giant'	Bright yellow	Int. incurve	5″	26″	Mid
'Yellow Glow'	Rich yellow	Decorative	2¾″	20″	Mid
'Zonta'	Apricot bronze	Pompon	2½″	18″	Mid

'Clara Curtis'

CHRYSANTHEMUM SPECIES

(Dendranthema)

(den-DRAN-thee-muh)

HARDY MUM

Bloom Time	Expected Longevity	Maintenance	Years to Bloom	Preferred Light
Late summer to late fall	10+ years	Medium	From seed: 2 years From potted plant: 1 year	Full sun

These fine perennials are in the same group as Garden Mums, but they are much hardier and require less care. All are former members of the genus *Dendranthema*, a group eliminated with recent reclassification. Hardy Mums have lovely foliage and richly colored flowers, bloom profusely over a long period of time, are easy to propagate, and make lovely cut flowers. They provide wonderful fall color and are rarely bothered by insects and disease. They will live for years if properly cared for.

How Hardy Mums Grow

Hardy Mums have a fibrous root system. The different varieties of *Chrysanthemum*–Rubellum Group (Hardy Garden Mum) grow in varied ways from bushy to quite upright, but all have deeply indented leaves. They bloom in late summer and fall with numerous, attractive daisylike flowers that have showy eyes. *Chrysanthemum weyrichii* (Miyabe) has shiny green foliage, blooms in late fall, and has a distinctive creeping habit. These plants spread out to become quite wide over the years.

Where to Plant

Site and Light Hardy Mums need full sun to bloom profusely. If planted in partial shade, they respond with poor and reduced bloom. The plants also may be leggy and require staking.

Soil and Moisture Hardy Mums like loose, rich soils that drain freely. If you have clay or rocky soil, replace it or build a raised bed. Mix lots of organic matter into the soil. Good amendments include peat moss, leaf mold, compost, and rotted manure.

Spacing Spacing plants from 12 to 18 inches (30 to 45 cm) apart is a good rough guide. Remember, however, that these perennials form clumps quickly and, to prevent disease, they should not be crowded.

Companions

Chrysanthemum weyrichii (Miyabe) is ideal for late-season color in rock or wall gardens. It serves as a delightful edging plant in beds and borders and looks wonderful in larger groupings. *Chrysanthemum*--Rubellum Group (Hardy Garden Mum) combines beautifully with *Artemisia* (Wormwood), *Rudbeckia* (Coneflower), *Sedum* (Stonecrop), and **Grasses**.

Planting

Bare Root Plant bare root stock as soon as you can work the ground in spring. Remove plants from their shipping package immediately. Snip off broken or damaged root tips. Soak plants overnight in room-temperature water. Place a small amount of superphosphate in the base of the planting hole. Fill the hole with soil. Place the crown 1 inch (2.5 cm) under the soil surface. Fill in with soil, firm with your fingers, and water immediately. Dissolve ½ cup (about 114 g) 10-10-10 fertilizer in 1 gallon (about 4 liters) of water. Pour ½ cup (about 120 ml) of this starter solution around the base of each plant. If you prefer organic fertilizer, use fish emulsion instead.

Potted Plants Plant potted Hardy Mums after all danger of frost in spring. If the soil in the pot is dry, water it, and let it drain overnight. Tap the plant out of the pot, without disturbing the root ball. Plant at the same depth as in the pot, after preparing the hole in a similar manner to that for a bare root plant. Fill in with soil, firm with your fingers, and water immediately. Pour ½ cup (about 120 ml) starter solution around the base of each plant.

How to Care for Hardy Mums

Water Keep the soil around Hardy Mums evenly moist throughout the season for lush foliage and abundant bloom. When you water, soak the soil to a depth of 6 to 8 inches (15 to 20 cm) each time.

Mulch Place 2 inches (5 cm) of mulch around the base of each plant as soon as the ground warms up in spring. This keeps soil moist and cool while inhibiting the growth of annual weeds. Good mulches include dried grass clippings, shredded leaves and bark, compost, and pine needles.

Fertilizing Sprinkle 10-10-10 fertilizer around the base of each plant just as new growth emerges in spring. Water immediately to dissolve the granules and move nutrients into the root zone. Hardy Mums respond well to light feedings every other week until late summer. If you prefer organic fertilizer, use alfalfa meal (rabbit pellets), blood meal, bonemeal, compost, cow manure, fish emulsion, Milorganite, or rotted horse manure. Bonemeal must be mixed into the soil at planting time to be effective.

Weeding Summer mulch stops most annual weed growth. Avoid any hoeing around the base of the plants, since the roots are very shallow and easily damaged.

Staking Hardy Mums should not require staking if they are grown properly.

Pinching Back The *Chrysanthemum*–Rubellum Group (Hardy Garden Mum) may benefit from pinching. Pinching results in plants that are shorter and denser with greater bloom. When the stems are 6 to 8 inches (15 to 20 cm) tall, remove their growing tips with your fingernails. This forces lateral branches to form that can be pinched again as they develop. Stop all pinching by early July to allow flower buds to develop.

Deadheading Since the plants bloom so late in the season, deadheading does not result in additional bloom. Hardy Mums do not self-sow, so deadheading is not important in that regard, either.

Winter Protection Cover first-year plants with a 6-inch (15-cm) layer of winter mulch once the ground has permanently frozen in late fall. Good mulches include marsh hay, clean straw, whole leaves, and pine needles. Remove these as soon as the ground warms up in spring. Mature Hardy Mums are rarely damaged by winter cold, but even these older plants are so shallow-rooted that a winter mulch may stop them from heaving from the ground during alternate freezing and thawing of the soil in late winter and early spring.

Problems

Insects One of the great attractions of these plants is that they are rarely bothered by insects.

Disease Leaf spot diseases can infect foliage. These occur most often in prolonged, wet weather. Avoid most problems by keeping lots of space between the plants for good air circulation.

Propagation

Division Dig up a clump in early spring just as new growth starts. Cut the clump into sections, making sure that each contains several growth eyes and a healthy supply of roots. Plant these immediately as you would a bare root plant and keep them well watered to get them off to a good start.

Cuttings Hardy Mums are very easy to propagate by cuttings. Take these from spring into early summer. The cuttings should have several sets of leaves. Make a final cut about a quarter inch (6 mm) below a leaf node. Remove all but the top pair of leaves, then dip the cut end in rooting hormone. Tap off any excess powder, and place the cuttings in moist rooting medium. Keep the medium evenly moist and the humidity around the cuttings high while they are forming roots. This usually takes only 2 to 4 weeks. Once cuttings have rooted, place the plants in individual pots or plant them in the garden. Keep the soil evenly moist around these young plants until they are growing vigorously. Cuttings taken in early spring will produce some bloom the first fall.

Seed Only the species *Chrysanthemum weyrichii* (Miyabe) can be grown from seed and expected to be similar to the parents. Propagate all other named varieties by division or cuttings if you want identical offspring. Start seed indoors about 12 weeks before the last expected frost in spring. Sow the seed over moist germination medium, and barely cover it. Keep the medium at a temperature of 68°F to 72°F (20°C to 22°C), and germination should take place within 3 weeks. When the seedlings have a second pair of leaves, plant them in individual pots. Harden them off for 14 days before planting them outside after all danger of frost has passed in spring.

Special Uses

Cut Flowers *Chrysanthemum*–Rubellum Group (Hardy Garden Mum) is one of the finest choices for late-season cut flowers. Cut the stems just as the main flower reaches maturity. The side buds open after cutting for a wonderful display. Condition the stems by placing them in a pail of warm sugar water and allowing them to stand overnight in a cool, dark place prior to arranging. Use ½ cup (about 114 g) sugar per quart

'Mary Stoker'

(4 liters) of water. Remove any foliage that would end up below the water line in the arrangement.

Dried Flowers Hardy Mums are not normally used in dried arrangements.

Sources

Bluestone Perennials, 7211 Middle Ridge Rd., Madison, OH 44057, (800) 852-5243

Busse Gardens, 17160 245th Ave., Big Lake, MN 55309, (800) 544-3192

Joy Creek Nursery, 20300 NE Watson Rd., Scappoose, OR 97056, (503) 543-7474

Siskiyou Rare Plant Nursery, 2115 Talent Ave., Talent, OR 97540, (541) 535-7103

Southview Nurseries (seed), Chequers Lane, Eversley Cross, Hook, Hampshire RG27 0NT England, 0118-973-2206

VARIETIES

VARIETY	COLOR	HEIGHT	HARDINESS
Chrysanthemum–Rubellum Group			
(Hardy Garden Mum)			
'Clara Curtis'*****	Light apricot pink	24″	−30°F
'Duchess of Edinburgh'	Pinkish red (D)	24″	−30°F
'Mary Stoker'	Buff yellow	30″	−30°F
'Paul Boissier'	Bright orange	30″	−30°F

These are extremely tough perennials that deserve much greater use as replacements for the common but less dependable Garden Mum. They form neat, bushy plants with deeply indented leaves and flowers from late summer into fall. The blooms are two inches or more wide. Division every three to four years keeps plants healthy and blooming abundantly. 'Duchess of Edinburgh' has unique, double (D) flowers.

VARIETY	COLOR	HEIGHT	HARDINESS
Chrysanthemum weyrichii			
(Miyabe)	White aging pink	18″	−40°F
'Pink Bomb'	Rosy pink	10″	−40°F
'White Bomb'	Creamy white	12″	−40°F

These plants are excellent rock garden plants with shiny green foliage and a profusion of flowers in fall. They may still be blooming when a severe frost hits. Plants creep along the ground and quickly form attractive clumps.

'Bath's Pink'

DIANTHUS

(dye-AN-thus)

PINKS

Bloom Time	Expected Longevity	Maintenance	Years to Bloom	Preferred Light
Spring to summer	2 to 10+ years	Medium	From seed: 1 to 2 years From potted plant: 1 year	Full sun

This large group of perennials is a favorite of many gardeners for their pleasing garden show, delightful fragrance, and value as cut flowers. They bloom over a long period in the spring and summer months. Most have white, pink, or red flowers. Some Pinks have rather demanding cultural needs and may prove to be short-lived if these needs are not met. Depending on the variety, they can be used in the rock garden, in the cutting garden, as edging plants, or even as ground covers. Pinks are rarely bothered by insects or disease.

How Pinks Grow

Pinks grow from fibrous roots, maturing into mat-forming or mounded plants with grasslike foliage that may be green, bluish green, gray, or blue. The mat-forming Pinks are fairly rapid spreaders with good longevity, and many of them make fine ground covers. Mound-forming types generally have a handsome, compact foliage habit, are slower growing, and are prone to be short-lived, especially in heavy soils. The flowers of Pinks may be borne solitary or in loose heads, and many have fringed or frilled petals that look as though they have been trimmed by a pinking shears. Pinks come in single, semidouble, or fully double forms, and a number of them have center eyes that are contrasting in color. Most varieties produce cylindrical capsules containing small seeds, while a few species produce one-seeded nutlets. Certain varieties will self-sow freely in the landscape.

Where to Plant

Site and Light Pinks grow best in full sun, although performance may be acceptable in very light shade. Even though good drainage is essential, these perennials do not do well in extremely hot, dry areas.

Soil and Moisture Pinks relish light, loose soils that drain freely. Sandy loams are ideal but not essential. The plants can be successfully grown in heavier soils that have been amended with generous amounts of organic matter such as compost, rotted manure, or leaf mold. If you are going to grow Pinks in heavy soils, raise the bed and add lots of organic matter to the soil. Excellent drainage during the dormant season is crucial to long-term survival of many varieties. Pinks require regular watering during extended dry periods, especially if grown in lighter soils.

Spacing Space according to the growth habit of the plant. The very small mound-forming types may need to be as close as 6 inches (15 cm) apart, while spreading forms can be placed 12 to 15 inches (30 to 37.5 cm) apart if you do not require an immediate full effect. The spreading forms will grow quite rapidly, filling in whatever space has been given them, so don't worry about the initial gaps between plants.

Companions

Many of the named varieties go well with other perennials such as *Aquilegia* (Columbine), *Artemisia* (Wormwood), *Campanula carpatica* (Carpathian Bellflower), *Coreopsis auriculata* 'Zamphir' (Mouse Ear Tickseed), *Festuca* (Fescue Grass), *Geranium cinereum* (Grayleaf Cranesbill) or *Geranium dalmaticum* (Dalmatian Cranesbill), *Iris* (Bearded Iris), *Sedum* (Stonecrop), and *Veronica austriaca* 'Crater Lake Blue' (Hungarian Speedwell). All of these plants are appropriate as front-of-the-border or edging plants in well-drained soils. Types such as *Dianthus alpinus* (Alpine Pink) and *Dianthus pavonius* (Cushion Pink) are best in rock gardens next to plants such as *Achillea tomentosa* (Woolly Yarrow) and *Phlox divaricata* 'Chattahoochee' (Woodland Phlox). Many Pinks also make excellent container plants.

Planting

Bare Root Plant bare root stock as soon as you can work the ground in spring. Remove plants from their shipping package immediately. Snip off broken or damaged root tips. Soak plants overnight in room-temperature water. Place a small amount of superphosphate in the base of the planting hole. Fill the hole with soil. Place the crown just below the soil surface. Fill in with soil, firm with your fingers, and water immediately. Dissolve ½ cup (about 114 g) 10-10-10 fertilizer in 1 gallon (about 4 liters) of water. Pour ½ cup (about 120 ml) of this starter solution around the base of each plant. If you prefer organic fertilizer, use fish emulsion instead.

Potted Plants Plant potted *Dianthus* after all danger of frost has passed in spring. If the soil in the pot is dry, water it, and let it drain overnight. Tap the plant from the pot without disturbing the root ball. Plant it at the same depth as in the pot, after preparing the hole in a similar manner to that for a bare root plant. Fill in with soil, firm with your fingers, and then water immediately. Pour ½ cup (about 120 ml) starter solution around the base of each plant.

How to Care for Pinks

Water Keeping the soil evenly moist throughout the growing season will encourage lushest growth as well as abundant and extended bloom. Remember, however, that excellent drainage is also necessary. Short dry periods will not affect plant growth as long as soil temperatures are not excessively high. When you do water, soak the soil to a depth of at least 6 to 8 inches (15 to 20 cm).

Mulch Mulch can be used to help keep the soil moist and cool as well as to prevent the germination of many weeds. Since many of the Pinks are very short, mulch is also important in preventing mud from splashing on the flowers during heavy rainstorms. One to 1½ inches (2.5 to 4 cm) of mulch around each plant should do the job. Organic mulches such as dried grass clippings, shredded leaves, or pine needles are very effective, but pea gravel or similar materials may be preferred in rock gardens for aesthetic reasons. Keep mulch away from the crown of the plant to avoid encouraging the development of crown rot during very humid or wet periods.

Fertilizing Sprinkle 10-10-10 fertilizer around the base of each plant in early spring just as new growth begins to emerge. Water immediately to move the fertilizer into the root zone. A follow-up feeding just prior to the bloom period will encourage strong flowering.

If you prefer organic fertilizer, use alfalfa meal (rabbit pellets), blood meal, bonemeal, compost, cow manure, fish emulsion, Milorganite, or rotted horse manure. Bonemeal must be mixed into the soil at planting time to be effective.

Weeding The use of a summer mulch should minimize any weed problems. Any weeds that do sprout are easily pulled by hand. Take a careful look for invading grasses, as they can be difficult to spot in the Pinks whose foliage is very narrow.

Staking Staking is not necessary for Pinks.

Deadheading Remove spent blossoms regularly to keep plants looking their best. In the case of certain varieties, this may also help in extending the bloom season. If you are trying to encourage a species type to self-sow, you will obviously want to allow the old flowers to remain and develop their seedpods.

Winter Protection Many of the Pinks have evergreen foliage that needs some sort of cover to bring it through harsh winters in cold climates. If there is no snow by early December, cover the plants with a 4- to 6-inch (10- to 15-cm) layer of winter mulch. Good mulches include marsh hay, clean straw, oak leaves, and pine needles. Remove the mulch as soon as the weather begins to warm up in spring to prevent crown rot. This is crucial with Pinks, as many are very susceptible to rot.

Problems

Insects Insect pests are rare on these perennials under good culture. Red spider mites are known to attack the foliage during very hot, dry periods, but regular watering of the foliage should ward them off. Thrips are known to feed on the flowers, and slugs may find a suitable home under the generous foliage canopies, but their control is rarely warranted.

Disease Crown rot can be the most troubling disease of these perennials, and it can lead to death of the plants. It can be prevented by siting plants correctly and growing them according to their cultural needs. Wilts, rust, and yellows are other known diseases of Pinks, but they are generally of very minor concern in the home garden.

Propagation

Division Many Pinks are short-lived plants by nature, but their longevity can often be extended by dividing them every few years. Dig up a mature plant in early spring just as new growth starts. Pull or cut it into sections, making sure that each one has a number of strong growth eyes and a healthy root system. Plant them immediately as you would a bare root plant. On some varieties it is possible to dig under the mother plant with a trowel and simply pull off a piece of the plant without disturbing it very much.

Cuttings Taking cuttings is the preferred commercial method for propagating named varieties, as most Pinks are very easy to root from cuttings throughout the growing season. A number of different types of cuttings can be taken with good results. *Heel cuttings* consist of short shoots cut off with some stem tissue, a bit of the lowest portion of the plant. *Pipings* are tip cuttings that are taken by holding the stem in one hand while pulling at its top with the other. This forces the shoot to break at a node, a location where roots will readily form. Traditional stem cuttings about 2 inches (5 cm) in length taken in the summer months also work very well.

Cuttings should be stuck in a moist rooting medium, making sure that any foliage that would be buried has been removed. Keep the humidity around the cuttings high while they are rooting. Once they have formed a strong root system, pot them up for further growing. Plant them in a permanent garden location once they are growing vigorously.

Ground Layering Varieties with long, lax stems can also be propagated by layering. Cut about one-third of the way through the underside of a prostrate stem at a 45-degree angle. Stick a piece of toothpick in the wound to keep it open, and then peg the stem to the ground. Cover it with soil. Check it regularly for root formation. Once the stem is well rooted,

sever it from the mother plant, then pot it up like any other cutting.

Seed Pinks are easy to grow from seed. However, since most named varieties will not come true from seed, this method is of most value for species types. Seed started indoors 10 to 12 weeks before the last expected frost in spring may result in some flowers the first season. Sow them in a seed flat, and cover them with about ¼ inch (6 mm) of moist germination medium. Slide the seed flat into a plastic bag, and keep it at 68°F to 70°F (20°C to 21°C). Germination often takes place within a week or 2, and seedlings are usually ready for transplanting within 2 to 3 weeks of sowing. Once they are well rooted in individual pots, they can be hardened off for 14 days and then planted outdoors after all danger of frost has passed in spring.

Special Uses

Cut Flowers Carnations are well-known Pinks popular as cut flowers. Unfortunately, they are not hardy in cold climates. Other hardy Pinks with longer stems match the beauty of carnations as cut flowers. Condition the stems by placing them in 110°F (43°C) water and allowing them to stand overnight in a cool, shaded area. Alternatively, mix ½ teaspoon (2.5 ml) boric acid to 2 quarts (about 2 liters) water, and boil the base of the stems in this solution for 2 minutes.

Dried Flowers Individual blooms of large-flowered Pinks are good candidates for drying in a desiccant. Stick a 4-inch (10-cm) piece of florist wire into each blossom, and bend it so that the flower can face straight up. Place the flower on a bed of desiccant, and carefully fill around it until the bloom is completely covered with the drying agent. Allow each flower to dry as long as necessary to get rid of all moisture. Once the blossom is completely dry, carefully remove it from the desiccant and attach the wire to a longer and thicker florist wire for use in a dried arrangement.

Sources

Ambergate Gardens, 8730 County Rd. 43, Chaska, MN 55318, (877) 211-9769

Arrowhead Alpines, P.O. Box 857, Fowlerville, MI 48836, (517) 223-3581

Bluestone Perennials, 7211 Middle Ridge Rd., Madison, OH 44057, (800) 852-5243

W. Atlee Burpee & Co., 300 Park Ave., Warminster, PA 18991, (800) 888-1447

Busse Gardens, 17160 245th Ave., Big Lake, MN 55309, (800) 544-3192

Earthly Pursuits, 2901 Kuntz Rd., Windsor Mill, MD 21244, (410) 496-2523

Fieldstone Gardens, Inc., 55 Quaker Lane, Vassalboro, ME 04989, (207) 923-3836

ForestFarm, 990 Tetherow Rd., Williams, OR 97544, (541) 846-7269

Greer Gardens, 1280 Goodpasture Island Rd., Eugene, OR 97401, (800) 548-0111

Goodwin Creek Gardens, P.O. Box 83, Williams, OR 97544, (800) 846-7359

Inter-State Nurseries, 1800 E Hamilton Rd., Bloomington, IL 61704, (309) 663-6797

J. L. Hudson Seedsman, P.O. Box 337, La Honda, CA 94020

Joy Creek Nursery, 20300 NW Watson Rd., Scappoose, OR 97056, (503) 543-7474

Mt. Tahoma Nursery, 28111 112th Ave., Graham, WA 98338, (253) 847-9827

Niche Gardens, 1111 Dawson Rd., Chapel Hill, NC 27516, (919) 967-0078

Roots and Rhizomes, P.O. Box A, Randolph, WI 53956, (800) 374-5035

White Flower Farm, P.O. Box 50, Litchfield, CT 06759, (800) 503-9624

Whitney Gardens & Nursery, P.O. Box 170, Brinnon, WA 98320, (360) 796-3556

VARIETIES

VARIETY	COLOR	FORM	HEIGHT	HARDINESS
Dianthus × *allwoodii*				
(Allwood Pink)				
'Frosty Fire'*****	Deep red pink	Double	6″	−30°F
'Helen'	Salmon pink	Double	8″	−30°F

This group of hybrids has its origins in breeding work started in the 1920s. The lance-shaped leaves are bluish green and form a dense mat of foliage. The flowers usually bloom in pairs and are highly fragrant. Plants bloom for several weeks in the summer. Regular deadheading and an even supply of moisture will prolong the bloom season.

VARIETY	COLOR	FORM	HEIGHT	HARDINESS
Dianthus alpinus				
(Alpine Pink)	Pink	Single	6″	−40°F

Though sometimes short-lived, especially if soil drainage is not excellent, this remains a fine addition to the rock garden, and it also makes a nice edging plant. Its narrow leaves are bright green and form quite a large mat. The scentless flowers appear over a long period in spring and early summer.

VARIETY	COLOR	FORM	HEIGHT	HARDINESS
Dianthus arenarius				
(Sand Pink)	White	Single	8″	−40°F

This species forms a mat of foliage similar to that of the more well known *Dianthus deltoides* (Maiden Pink), but it has larger flowers and blooms later. Its fragrant flowers have distinctly notched petals and green eyes.

Dianthus caesius (see *Dianthus gratianopolitanus*)

Dianthus deltoides

Dianthus superbus

'Tiny Rubies'

'Zing Rose'

VARIETY	COLOR	FORM	HEIGHT	HARDINESS
Dianthus deltoides				
(Maiden Pink)	Red, pink, or white	Single	12″	−40°F
'Arctic Fire'	White/magenta eye	Single	8″	−40°F
'Brilliant'	Bright red	Single	6″	−40°F
'Flashing Light' ('Leuchtfunk')	Bright pink	Single	4″	−40°F
'Nelli'	Bright red	Single	8″	−40°F
'Zing Rose'*****	Deep rose red	Single	8″	−40°F

These perennials form low, dense foliage mats with leaves tinged purplish red in the cooler seasons. They are profuse bloomers in late spring and early summer, often reblooming if deadheaded. If allowed to form seed, they will self-sow freely. They are valuable as a ground cover for small areas or cascading over rock ledges. Keep these plants consistently moist for best results.

VARIETY	COLOR	FORM	HEIGHT	HARDINESS
Dianthus gratianopolitanus				
(Cheddar Pink)	Rose pink	Single	12″	−40°F
'Bath's Pink'	Pink/darker eye	Single	10″	−40°F
'Bewitched'*****	Light pink/magenta ring	Single	8″	−40°F
'Dottie'	White/maroon bicolor	Single	4″	−40°F
'Eydangeri' ('Compactus Eydangeri')	Medium pink	Single	6″	−40°F
'Firewitch' ('Feuerhexe')*****	Raspberry red	Single	10″	−40°F
'Pink Feather' ('Rosa Feder')	Rose pink	Single	10″	−40°F
'Spotty'	Red spotted white	Single	6″	−40°F
'Tiny Rubies'	Rose pink	Double	6″	−40°F

With their fragrant showy flowers and easy culture, these selections deserve to be much more widely grown. Their blue to gray green leaves form neat mounds of evergreen foliage, and they flower from late spring into early summer. If planted in a well-drained soil, these will prove to be long-lived perennials.

VARIETY	COLOR	FORM	HEIGHT	HARDINESS
Dianthus knappii				
(Hairy Garden Pink)	Sulphur yellow	Single	18″	−40°F

This species is very hardy, but it often looks scruffy and dies after flowering. It is of value for its unique coloration among the Pinks. Its scentless flowers bloom in early to midsummer, and it produces a plentiful crop of seeds which self-sow freely.

Dianthus neglectus (see *Dianthus pavonius*)

VARIETY	COLOR	FORM	HEIGHT	HARDINESS
Dianthus pavonius				
(Cushion Pink)	Cherry red/blue eye	Single	8″	−30°F

Though this species is best grown in the rock garden, it is such a treasure that it deserves to be much more widely known. The blue-green leaves are very fine-textured and form an attractive ground-hugging mat. It flowers in early summer and performs best in lean well-drained soils.

VARIETY	COLOR	FORM	HEIGHT	HARDINESS
Dianthus–Plumarius Group				
'Charles Musgrave' ('Musgrave's Pink')	White/green eye	Single	10″	−30°F
'Desmond'*****	Red	Double	12″	−30°F
'Doris'*****	Salmon pink/deeper eye	Double	16″	−30°F

VARIETY	COLOR	FORM	HEIGHT	HARDINESS
'Essex Witch'*****	Rose pink	Semi-double	6″	–30°F
'Fire Star' ('Devon Xera')	Fire red/crimson red	Single	8″	–30°F
'Her Majesty'	White	Double	10″	–30°F
'Horatio'*****	Rose pink/maroon eye	Double	8″	–30°F
'Little Jock'	Rose pink/crimson eye	Semi-double	4″	–30°F
'Margaret Curtis'*****	White/burgundy eye	Single	8″	–30°F
'Mrs. Sinkins' ('Aqua')	White	Double	12″	–30°F
'Neon Star'	Magenta	Single	6″	–30°F
'Oakington'	Rose pink	Double	6″	–30°F
'Pike's Pink'	Soft pink	Double	6″	–30°F
'Rachel'	Deep pink	Double	6″	–30°F
'Raspberry Surprise' ('Yolande')*****	Pink/burgundy red eye	Double	6″	–30°F
'Raspberry Swirl' ('Devon Siskin')	White/magenta edge	Single	8″	–30°F
'Rose de Mai'	Pale pink	Double	12″	–30°F
'Roshish One'	Velvet red edged pink	Single	10″	–30°F
'Sops in Wine'	Pink spotted white	Single	8″	–30°F
'Spangled Star'	Red/pink throat/white spots	Single	8″	–30°F

These perennials demand good drainage, especially in their dormant period, to ensure long life. They tend to be larger and somewhat less vigorous than the Allwood Pinks. Stems often carry more than one flower and are showy in early to midsummer. Most are extremely fragrant. Regular removal of spent flowers and cool weather will prolong the bloom season.

Dianthus simulans

	COLOR	FORM	HEIGHT	HARDINESS
(Cushion Alpine Pinks)	Light rose	Single	4″	–30°F

The species has short, narrow leaves that give it an unusual moss-like appearance. It blooms with small flowers in spring.

Dianthus superbus

	COLOR	FORM	HEIGHT	HARDINESS
(Lilac Pink)	Lilac, pink, or white	Single	18″	–30°F

This is one of the most fragrant of the Pinks and easily recognized for its shaggy flowers which bloom in the summer. It is such a heavy bloomer that it can flower itself to death, but, it is very easy and quick to grow from seed.

Dianthus (Named varieties and hybrids)

VARIETY	COLOR	FORM	HEIGHT	HARDINESS
'Chili'	Dark coral	Double	4″	–20°F
'Coconut Punch'	White edged maroon	Double	10″	–30°F
'Coconut Surprise'	White/burgundy center	Double	8″	–30°F
'Cranberry Ice'	Pink edged rose/deep rose	Single	8″	–30°F
'Crimson Treasure'	Velvety red	Single	10″	–30°F
'Dad's Favorite'	White/maroon edges	Double	8″	–30°F
'Dale Lindgren'	Medium pink	Semi-double	18″	–30°F
'First Love'*****	White aging to rose	Single	14″	–40°F
'Fizzy'	Pale lavender/maroon eye	Double	6″	–20°F
'Frosty'	Pure white	Double	6″	–20°F

VARIETY	COLOR	FORM	HEIGHT	HARDINESS
'Greystone'	White	Single	12″	−30°F
'Inchmery'	Shell pink	Double	12″	−30°F
'Itsaul White'*****	White	Double	8″	−30°F
'Karliks' ('Karlik')	Medium pink/darker ring	Single	6″	−30°F
'Laced Romeo'	Pink edged rose/white spots	Double	14″	−30°F
'Lady Granville'	White/deep rose	Semi-double	18″	−30°F
'Mountain Mist'	Soft silvery pink	Single	12″	−30°F
'Neon Star'	Magenta	Single	6″	−30°F
'Radiance'	Crimson red	Double	6″	−20°F
'Sangria Splash'	Deep pink edged purple	Single	12″	−30°F
'Sherbet'	Deep pink	Double	4″	−20°F
'Strawberry Sorbet'	Red/edged and spotted pink	Single	14″	−30°F

The above selections are hybrids and many of their backgrounds are undocumented, so there is no way to be sure of their origins. A number of them are newer introductions whose hardiness in the far north has yet to be adequately tested. As with most Pinks, good drainage during the winter months is critical to survival. Many of these hybrids offer striking flower coloration, long bloom, and an attractive appearance throughout the growing season.

'Gold Heart'

DICENTRA

(dye-SEN-truh)

BLEEDING HEART

Bloom Time	Expected Longevity	Maintenance	Years to Bloom	Preferred Light
Spring to summer	3 to 10+ years	Medium	From seed: 2 years From potted plant: 1 year	Light to full shade

Bleeding Hearts are among the finest perennials for shady areas of the garden. These easy-to-grow plants offer lovely, delicate, blue green foliage and uniquely shaped flowers dangling from arching stems. The blooms are a delightful addition to floral arrangements. These perennials may self-sow under good growing conditions, with little plants springing up in the most unusual places. Some varieties go into dormancy shortly after flowering, while the foliage of others persists throughout the growing season if plants are properly placed and cared for. All parts of these plants are poisonous and can cause convulsions if eaten. Wildlife and grazing animals avoid native American *Dicentra canadensis* (Squirrel Corn) and *Dicentra cucullaria* (Dutchman's Breeches) for this reason. The sap also can cause dermatitis in sensitive individuals, so wear gloves when working with them.

How Bleeding Hearts Grow

Bleeding Hearts are generally grown from seed or divisions, but *Dicentra spectabilis* (Common Bleeding Heart) can also be reproduced from cuttings. All form handsome mounds of deeply divided, fernlike foliage growing from thick, fleshy roots or creeping, tuberous rhizomes. Clumps get larger each season as root systems expand and new eyes are formed on the outside edges of the plants. The graceful flowers bloom in abundance in the spring months, but the display continues into summer with certain varieties. If not deadheaded, the plants form small pods that drop their seed as they dry and mature. This seed will germinate the following spring if the ground is not disturbed.

Where to Plant

Site and Light Bleeding Hearts thrive in light to full shade and prefer cool weather. If *Dicentra spectabilis* (Common Bleeding Heart) is grown in full sun, the foliage often has a yellowish color, and the plant may even go dormant in summer. Ideal growing conditions are in woodland gardens, in shaded rocky areas, and along the east and north sides of buildings.

Soil and Moisture Bleeding Hearts grow rapidly in a loose, evenly moist, organic soil that drains freely. Add lots of compost, rotted manure, leaf mold, or peat moss to the soil. These retain necessary moisture and help keep the soil cool but allow surplus water to move away from the root zone. Heavy, compacted clays can lead to rot problems and may need to be replaced or at least formed into a raised bed.

Spacing Large plants such as *Dicentra spectabilis* (Common Bleeding Heart) should stand 2 or more feet (60 cm) apart, while smaller ones can be placed as close as 1 foot (30 cm) away from surrounding plants.

Companions

Interplant *Dicentra canadensis* (Squirrel Corn) and *Dicentra cucullaria* (Dutchman's Breeches) with perennials to fill voids when these two natives go dormant. Good companions include small **Ferns**, *Hosta* (Hosta), and *Pulmonaria* (Lungwort). Vari-

eties of *Dicentra eximia* (Fringed Bleeding Heart) and *Dicentra formosa* (Western Bleeding Heart) are delightful planted with spring-flowering bulbs, *Luzula nivea* (Snowy Woodrush Grass), and *Phlox stolonifera* (Creeping Phlox). Try *Dicentra spectabilis* (Common Bleeding Heart) in light shade along with *Aquilegia* (Columbine), *Filipendula vulgaris* 'Multiplex' (Dropwort), *Geranium* (Cranesbill), *Hosta* (Hosta), *Phlox stolonifera* 'Pink Ridge' (Creeping Phlox), and **Ferns**.

Planting

Bare Root Plant bare root stock as soon as you can work the ground in spring. Remove plants from their shipping package immediately. Snip off broken or damaged root tips. Soak plants in room-temperature water overnight. Place a small amount of superphosphate in the base of the planting hole. Fill the hole with soil. Place the crown 1 inch (2.5 cm) below the soil surface. Fill in with soil, firm with your fingers, and water immediately. Dissolve ½ cup (about 114 g) 10-10-10 fertilizer in 1 gallon (about 4 liters) of water. Pour ½ cup (about 120 ml) of this starter solution around the base of each plant. If you prefer organic fertilizer, use fish emulsion.

Potted Plants Plant Bleeding Hearts after all danger of frost has passed in spring. If the soil in the pot is dry, water it, and let it drain overnight. Tap the plant out of the pot without disturbing the root ball. Plant it at the same depth as in the pot, after preparing the hole in a similar manner to that for a bare root plant. Fill in with soil, firm with your fingers, and water immediately. Pour ½ cup (about 120 ml) starter solution around the base of each plant.

How to Care for Bleeding Hearts

Water Keep the soil evenly moist at all times throughout the growing season. Moisture aids in keeping soil temperatures cool and is critical to *Dicentra eximia* (Fringed Bleeding Heart), *Dicentra* *formosa* (Western Bleeding Heart), and the Hearts series if you want spring bloom to continue into the summer. Saturate the soil to a depth of 8 to 12 inches (20 to 30 cm) each time you water.

Mulch Spread 2 inches (5 cm) of mulch around the base of each plant as soon as the ground warms up in spring. Good organic mulches include dried grass clippings, shredded leaves, and pine needles. Mulch keeps soil moist and cool.

Fertilizing Sprinkle 10-10-10 fertilizer around the base of each plant just as new growth emerges in spring. Water immediately to dissolve the granules and move nutrients into the root zone.

If you prefer organic fertilizer, use alfalfa meal (rabbit pellets), blood meal, bonemeal, compost, cow manure, fish emulsion, Milorganite, or rotted horse manure. Bonemeal must be mixed into the soil at planting time to be effective.

Weeding Summer mulch inhibits weed growth. Any weeds that do sprout are best pulled by hand, as deep hoeing can damage the plant's root system.

Staking *Dicentra spectabilis* (Common Bleeding Heart) may spread out in heavy winds or rains, but is difficult to stake. Placing a peony hoop around it in early spring is one way to control its floppiness.

Deadheading Remove spent flowers on all varieties of *Dicentra eximia* (Fringed Bleeding Heart), *Dicentra formosa* (Western Bleeding Heart), and the Hearts Series to encourage additional bloom. Other Bleeding Hearts do not require deadheading, as aged flowers and seedpods are rather inconspicuous. Nor does deadheading of the latter result in additional bloom.

Winter Protection If there is no snow by early December, covering the plants with a 6-inch (15-cm) layer of winter mulch may be good insurance against winter damage. Recommended mulches include marsh hay, clean straw, whole leaves, and pine needles. Remove the mulch as soon as the weather warms up in spring to prevent crown rot.

Problems

Insects There are no serious insect problems with Bleeding Hearts, although *Dicentra eximia* (Fringed Bleeding Heart) is occasionally bothered by aphids. A few aphids can be washed off with a hose. Use insecticidal soap to control more severe infestations.

Disease New gardeners sometimes think that a plant going naturally dormant is diseased. Understanding the growth pattern of each variety will clear up this confusion. When conditions are right, dormant plants will spring back to life.

Propagation

Division Most varieties of Bleeding Heart can be divided every few years to increase stock. However, you can leave plants undisturbed for years without affecting their health. If you wish to divide a plant, dig up the clump just as new growth emerges in spring. Shake off or wash away all excess soil, and cut the plant into sections (eyes) with a sharp knife, making sure that each division has several growth buds and a healthy root system. Plant these immediately as you would a bare root plant. Remember that the roots are quite brittle, so handle them carefully. Many books recommend fall division, but in cold climates spring division is much better, since it gives the plant a chance to establish a strong root system prior to the onset of winter.

Stem Cuttings *Dicentra spectabilis* (Common Bleeding Heart) can be grown from stem cuttings taken in spring or after flowering. Cuttings root best if taken early in the season. Take cuttings 2 to 3 inches (5 to 7.5 cm) long, making the cut a quarter inch (6 mm) below a leaf node. Remove the lower leaves, and dip each cut end in rooting hormone. Tap off any excess powder, place the cuttings in moist rooting medium, and keep the humidity around them high. Once they have developed a strong root system, plant them in pots or a protected location in the garden. Keep the soil around the young plants consistently moist.

Root Cuttings *Dicentra spectabilis* (Common Bleeding Heart) can be reproduced from root cuttings. Dig up the plant in very early spring before active growth. Remove several roots the size of your small finger, and replant the mother plant immediately. Cut these roots into 2- to 3-inch (5- to 7.5-cm) sections, and plant each one vertically in a moist, well-drained medium in a flat or cold frame. Treating cut ends with rooting hormone may speed up the rooting process. Place the end of the cutting that was nearer the crown up when planting. Firm the medium around the cuttings, and keep it cool and evenly moist until new growth emerges. After about 4 to 8 weeks, the young plants can generally be transplanted to pots or a protected garden location.

Seed Fresh seed germinates faster than old seed, normally taking less than 50 days at temperatures between 55°F and 65°F (13°C to 18°C). Be patient, as germination can be erratic, even with fresh seed.

Fill a seed tray with moist germination medium, and sow the seed over this. Press the seed into the medium, barely covering it. Then slide the tray into a perforated plastic bag. Keep the medium moist and at a temperature of 60°F to 65°F (16°C to 18°C) for a few weeks. If no germination occurs, place the seed tray in the crisper of your refrigerator for 6 weeks. Then remove it, and place it in an area with a temperature around 60°F (16°C). If no germination has occurred after several weeks, put the seed tray back in the refrigerator crisper. Check the tray regularly, and remove it immediately if seedlings start to sprout or after 2 to 4 weeks. Sometimes, seeds need several cycles of the warm–cold treatment to break their dormancy.

Once germination occurs, grow the seedlings on at a temperature of 65°F to 70°F (18°C to 21°C). As the seedlings develop their second pair of true leaves, plant them in individual pots. Harden them off for 14 days before planting them outdoors after all danger of frost has passed in spring.

Seed can also be sown in an outdoor seedbed or cold frame. Collect seed in late summer or early fall upon its maturity, and sow it immediately. Keep the germination medium evenly moist until it freezes for the winter. The seedlings will emerge the following spring. Transplant them to pots, or place them in their permanent garden locations.

Note that many varieties self-seed freely without help. Simply let seed mature and fall to the ground. In spring, do not cultivate around the plant; just pull weeds by hand. Avoid chemical fertilizer, which can kill germinating seeds and seedlings. Once the little plants begin to form, feed the mother plant and offspring with dilute solutions of fertilizer.

Special Uses

Medicinal The crushed leaves of Bleeding Hearts are said to relieve the pain caused by touching or brushing your skin against Stinging Nettles.

Cut Flowers All varieties produce excellent cut flowers, but taller forms are of greatest value. Cut the stems just above a leaf, and place them in a container filled with 110°F (43°C) water. Let the cut stems remain in this water overnight in a cool, shaded spot. Arrange them the following day after removing all leaves that would end up underwater.

Dried Flowers These perennials are not of value for dried flowers.

Sources

Ambergate Gardens, 8730 County Rd. 43, Chaska, MN 55318, (877) 211-9769

Busse Gardens, 17160 245th Ave., Big Lake, MN 55309, (800) 544-3192

Fraser's Thimble Farms, 175 Arbutus Rd., Salt Spring Island, BC V8K 1A3 Canada, (250) 537-5788

Fritz Creek Gardens, P.O. Box 15226, Homer, AK 99603, (907) 235-4969

Roots and Rhizomes, P.O. Box A, Randolph, WI 53956, (800) 374-5035

Dicentra spectabilis

Dicentra spectabilis 'Alba'

VARIETIES

VARIETY	COLOR	HEIGHT	HARDINESS
Dicentra canadensis			
(Squirrel Corn)	White tipped pink	12″	–30°F

Named for its underground tubers resembling corn kernels, this North American native blooms with fragrant flowers in spring. The finely cut, blue-green leaves disappear shortly after the plant produces seed.

Dicentra cucullaria***			
(Dutchman's Breeches)	White tipped yellow	12″	–40°F

This perennial has lacy foliage and small flowers whose spurs look like pantaloons, from which comes its common name. Since it goes dormant shortly after flowering in spring, you should plant it among other perennials in a shady, natural location. The plant prefers slightly acidic soil, so add lots of peat moss at planting time.

Dicentra eximia			
(Fringed Bleeding Heart)	Rosy pink	15″	–40°F
'Alba'	White suffused pink	12″	–40°F

VARIETY	COLOR	HEIGHT	HARDINESS
'Snowdrift'	Pure white	12"	−40°F

Native to the eastern part of the United States, this species and its named varieties offer a long flowering period, which extends from May to August in cool climates. The "ferny" foliage is bluish green and forms a handsome mound. Removing spent flowers encourages extended bloom. Plant in rich, moist loam with lots of organic matter mixed in. To survive plants need consistent moisture throughout the summer and soil that drains freely in winter. Plants may self-sow freely under good growing conditions.

Dicentra formosa

	COLOR	HEIGHT	HARDINESS
(Western Bleeding Heart)	Rosy pink	15"	−40°F
'Adrian Bloom'	Ruby red	15"	−40°F
'Bacchanal'	Dark red	15"	−40°F
'Bountiful'	Bright pink	15"	−40°F
'Langtrees' ('Pearl Drops')*****	Ivory white	12"	−40°F
'Luxuriant'*****	Cherry red	15"	−40°F

As does its East Coast counterpart *Dicentra eximia* (Fringed Bleeding Heart), this plant thrives in soil that drains freely and is rich in organic matter. However, these varieties are more drought tolerant. They bloom most freely in spring but often produce additional flowers throughout summer, especially if spent blossoms are removed regularly. All have attractive, blue-gray leaves of varying intensity, while 'Bacchanal' has an interesting bronze tinge to its foliage. Grown properly, these plants spread by creeping rhizomes and, therefore, are often recommended for use as a ground cover. 'Luxuriant' is among the most free-flowering and vigorous of the group.

Dicentra–Hearts Series

	COLOR	HEIGHT	HARDINESS
'Burning Hearts'*****	Deep rose red	10"	−40°F
'Candy Hearts'	Bright rose pink	12"	−40°F
'Ivory Hearts'	Ivory white	12"	−40°F
'King of Hearts'	Rosy pink	15"	−40°F

Akira Shiozaki bred these plants in Japan. These are hybrids of native American species and the Japanese *Dicentra peregrina* (Japanese Bleeding Heart). The heart-shaped flowers are delightful. All form compact tidy mounds of finely cut leaves, but the blue-gray foliage color of 'Burning Hearts' and 'Ivory Hearts' is particularly striking. Like other Fringe-leaved Bleeding Hearts, these selections bloom profusely during late spring and early summer in northern locations. They will also produce some flowers throughout the balance of the growing season under ideal care and growing conditions.

Dicentra spectabilis*****

	COLOR	HEIGHT	HARDINESS
(Common Bleeding Heart)	Rose pink	36"	−40°F
'Alba'	Pure white	30"	−40°F
'Gold Heart'	Rose pink	30"	−40°F

This perennial looks almost like a shrub. In cool climates, it blooms from late spring into early summer. However, it may go dormant by midsummer if placed in full sun or if under watered. The white flowered form has lighter green foliage and is less vigorous. 'Gold Heart' is a gold-foliaged selection whose coloration is most prominent early in the season. If grown properly, these Bleeding Hearts will live for many years.

'Coconut Lime'

ECHINACEA

(ek-uh-NAY-see-uh)

PURPLE CONEFLOWER

Bloom Time	Expected Longevity	Maintenance	Years to Bloom	Preferred Light
Early summer to fall	15+ years	Low	From seed: 1 to 2 years From potted plant: 1 year	Full sun

Purple Coneflowers are wonderfully drought-resistant prairie wildflowers that adapt beautifully to the border. They have a long bloom period that extends from early summer to first frost. Regular removal of spent flowers encourages additional bloom. Purple Coneflowers are resilient and will even grow well in hot, windy sites. They will live for many years and form attractive colonies if properly cared for. The foliage, though somewhat coarse, offers deep green coloration. The large, colorful flowers attract butterflies and are excellent in cut-flower arrangements. Many of the modern hybrids have a lovely honeylike fragrance. Use these perennials in many areas, from beds and borders to meadows and prairies.

How Purple Coneflowers Grow

Purple Coneflowers grow into plants with oval to lance-shaped, coarse-textured, dark green leaves. Their crowns are fleshy, and the thick, dark roots form a very fibrous network. Stiff flower stems that stand up to 4 feet (120 cm) tall rise above the main mound of foliage. The primary flowers bloom at the ends of these stems, but numerous secondary blossoms emerge where leaves join the stem. The daisylike flowers have prickly central domes with ray petals that usually recurve downward and range in color from purplish pink to white. As the flower matures, the central cones blacken, and, if left to dry on the plant, the cones feel and look much like sea urchins or elongated cones on the doubles by the end of the growing season. These mature fruits contain numerous thin black seeds that scatter around the parent plant and germinate freely. The crowns of Purple Coneflowers also increase in size annually to form large colonies over a period of years under ideal growing conditions.

Where to Plant

Site and Light Purple Coneflowers like it sunny and hot. These perennials tolerate light shade, but the number of blossoms decreases there, and the stems may be somewhat lanky and floppy.

Soil and Moisture Purple Coneflowers thrive in well-drained, loamy soils. They prefer lighter soils but will grow well in other types if lots of organic matter is added to them. Highly recommended soil amendments are compost, peat moss, leaf mold, or rotted manure. Avoid planting these perennials in soggy soils that do not drain well, as this will cause them to rot out. Mature Purple Coneflowers can tolerate long dry periods.

Spacing Space Purple Coneflowers from 18 to 24 inches (45 to 60 cm) apart, depending on the variety. Plants look best in groupings of at least 3 and are very effective in mass. Crowding the plants together too tightly can lead to outbreaks of fungal leaf spots in moist, humid seasons.

Companions

Echinacea (Purple Coneflower) combines well with numerous summer- and fall-blooming perennials but is especially impressive planted with some of the following: *Asclepias tuberosa* (Butterfly Milkweed),

Chrysanthemum–Rubellum Group (Hardy Garden Mum), *Heliopsis* (Oxeye), *Liatris* (Gayfeather), *Monarda* (Bee Balm), *Phlox* (Garden Phlox), and *Platycodon* (Balloon Flower). If you find *Echinacea* (Purple Coneflower) to be somewhat coarse and rigid, try planting soft-textured perennials such as *Achillea* (Yarrow), *Artemisia schmidtiana* 'Silver Mound'/'Nana,' *Euphorbia corollata* (Flowering Spurge), or **Grasses** next to it.

Planting

Bare Root Plant bare root stock as soon as you can work the ground in spring. Remove plants from their shipping package immediately. Snip off broken or damaged root tips. Soak plants overnight in room-temperature water. Place a small amount of super-phosphate in the base of the planting hole. Fill the hole with soil. Place with the crown 1 inch (2.5 cm) below the soil surface. Fill in with soil, firm with your fingers, and water immediately. Dissolve ½ cup (about 114 g) 10-10-10 fertilizer in 1 gallon (about 4 liters) of water. Pour ½ cup (about 120 ml) of this starter solution around the base of each plant. If you prefer organic fertilizer, use fish emulsion instead.

Potted Plants Plant potted Purple Coneflowers after all danger of frost has passed in spring. If the soil in the pot is dry, saturate it, and let drain overnight before planting. Tap the plant out of the pot, keeping the root ball intact. Plant it at the same depth as in the pot, after preparing the hole in a similar manner to that for a bare root plant. Fill in with soil, firm with your fingers, and water immediately. Pour ½ cup (about 120 ml) starter solution around the base of the plant.

How to Care for Purple Coneflowers

Water Water newly planted Purple Coneflowers regularly until they have established strong root systems. Mature plants do tolerate drought, but for the lushest growth and most abundant bloom, water them regularly during dry periods. When you water, saturate the soil to a depth of at least 8 to 10 inches (20 to 25 cm).

Mulch Purple Coneflowers, which grow so well on drier soils, do not require an organic mulch to keep soil moist and cool. However, a light mulch inhibits the growth of competing weeds. Surround the plants with 1 inch (2.5 cm) of dried grass clippings, shredded leaves, or pine needles for this reason alone.

Fertilizing Sprinkle 10-10-10 fertilizer around the base of each plant just as new growth emerges in spring. Water immediately to dissolve the granules and move nutrients into the root zone. Since Purple Coneflowers are not heavy feeders, this should satisfy their needs for the entire growing season. Overfertilizing can cause stems on taller varieties to become floppy and require staking.

If you prefer organic fertilizers, use alfalfa meal (rabbit pellets), blood meal, bonemeal, compost, cow manure, fish emulsion, Milorganite, or rotted horse manure. Bonemeal must be added to the soil at planting time to be effective.

Weeding Controlling weeds reduces competition for nutrients and moisture and also helps prevent outbreaks of a disease called aster yellows. Many common weeds serve as hosts for the organism responsible for this disease. So, keep the area around Purple Coneflowers weed free.

Staking Avoid partially shaded sites, overfeeding, and overwatering, and it's unlikely you'll have to stake even the tallest Purple Coneflowers.

Pinching Back Pinching back Purple Coneflowers in spring creates bushier plants with smaller but more numerous blooms. Pinch the growing tip off each stem in late spring to induce formation of many side branches. Leave the plant alone if you want it to be taller and more natural looking.

Deadheading Unless you want flowers to form seed heads for propagation or for dried floral arrangements, remove all spent flowers. This will encourage additional bloom. You get the best of both worlds by removing early bloom and allowing only later blooms to form attractive seed heads.

Winter Protection After a killing frost in fall, cut the leaves and stems to the ground. Bear in mind, however, that the rich black seed heads are decorative and add interest to the winter garden. If there is no snow cover by early December, it may be wise to cover the plants with a 6-inch (15-cm) layer of marsh hay, clean straw, whole leaves, or pine needles. This is especially important with some of the modern varieties. Remove winter mulch as soon as it starts to warm up in early spring.

Problems

Insects Purple Coneflowers occasionally attract Japanese beetles. These insects have been spreading in recent years and are becoming a common pest in cold climates. Pick off adult beetles, and toss them into a can of salty water or vinegar. Using Milky Spore Disease powder on lawns over a period of years will often kill this insect in its grub stage. Merit, an inorganic control, is extremely effective used in a similar fashion. Leafhoppers serve as carriers for a disease called aster yellows and should be controlled with timely use of insecticidal soap.

Disease Leaf spots are an occasional problem related to poor care and unusually high humidity. During a severe outbreak, cut the plant back to ground level; destroy the diseased foliage. The plant will resprout a healthy mound of foliage, but you may lose out on bloom that year, depending on when the plant is cut back. Aster yellows, a viruslike pathogen, often infects this perennial. Symptoms are abnormal or stunted growth, a purplish cast to the foliage, or malformed flowers that often have a greenish cast. Since there is no cure for this disease, you should immediately dig up and destroy any plants showing these symptoms. Keeping the garden weed free and destroying leafhoppers, which live on weeds, are keys to avoiding aster yellows.

Propagation

Division Although Purple Coneflowers can remain undisturbed for years, division every fourth or fifth year is highly advised for the plant's health. As the plant starts growing in spring, dig it up, and shake off all loose soil. With a sharp spade or knife, slice the crown into sections. Make sure that each contains several healthy growth eyes and ample root tissue. Plant these immediately as you would a bare root plant.

Stem Cuttings Propagate these perennials from basal-stem or tip cuttings taken in spring or summer. You will have best luck with basal cuttings taken in spring as new growth emerges from the plant's crown. Basal cuttings should include a small portion of the crown. Stuck in a moist rooting medium, these will usually root within 2 to 3 weeks. Tip cuttings can be taken later in spring or in early summer. Make the cuttings a quarter inch (6 mm) below a leaf node and long enough so that each cutting has several sets of leaves. Remove all but the top set of leaves, and dip the cut end in rooting hormone. Tap off any excess powder, and plant the cuttings in moist rooting medium. During the rooting process, keep the medium evenly moist and the humidity high. Once the cuttings have formed a strong root system, place them in pots or transplant them to a protected spot.

Root Cuttings Though not commonly done, you also can propagate Purple Coneflowers by root cuttings. Lift a mature plant as soon as you can dig in the garden in early spring. Cut off several of the largest roots, and replant the clump immediately. Cut these roots into 2-inch (5-cm) sections, and plant each one vertically in a moist, well-drained medium in a pot or cold frame. Place the end of the cutting that was nearer the crown up when planting. Keep the rooting medium evenly moist during the rooting process. Transplant the cuttings to pots or a garden location once they have established a strong root system and begun to grow foliage.

Seed It's easy to grow these perennials from seed. However, not all named Purple Coneflowers will come true from seed. Exceptions are the well-known varieties 'Magnus,' 'Ruby Star,' and 'White Swan.' In late winter, fill a seed tray with moist germination medium. Scatter the seeds over the surface, and barely cover them. Then slide the tray into a plastic bag perforated for good air circulation. Keep the medium moist and at a temperature of 65°F to 70°F (18°C to 21°C). Germination normally takes place in 10 to 15 days. When seedlings have a second pair of leaves, plant them in individual pots. This is usually about 20 to 30 days after sowing. Harden them off for 14 days before planting outside after all danger of frost in spring.

If seeds do not germinate within a month of sowing, place the seed tray in the crisper of your refrigerator for 4 to 6 weeks. A moist chilling should overcome the seeds' dormancy. After the cool period, again place the seed tray where the temperature will remain at 65°F to 70°F (18°C to 21°C).

Purple Coneflowers will self-sow freely if seed heads are allowed to mature on the plant. Seed may also be collected and started in a prepared bed or cold frame. In late fall, sow the seed over moist germination medium. Keep the medium moist until it freezes. The seedlings will emerge the following spring as the weather warms up. Transplant them to pots or a protected location for growing on once they have formed a second set of leaves.

Special Uses

Native American Plains Indians used Purple Coneflower to cure a variety of ailments. Studies on the plant's medicinal properties are now taking place. The plant appears to contain chemical compounds that stimulate the human immune system.

Cut Flowers Purple Coneflowers make excellent, long-lasting cut flowers. 'Magnus' and 'Ruby Giant' are particularly prized for this use, since they have large blooms whose ray petals do not droop as much as the other varieties. Condition the stems by placing them in cool water overnight before arranging. Remove any foliage that will be below water level in the arrangement. **Note:** Some arrangers deliberately remove all petals, leaving only the central cone, for a unique look in arrangements. The cone has a lovely shape, prickly texture, and rich coloration.

Dried Flowers Individual flowers can be dried in a desiccant. Insert a 4-inch (10-cm) piece of florist wire into the flower. Then place the flower face up on a bed of desiccant. Cover it carefully with more material, making sure the petals are appropriately arranged. Allow it to remain in place until the petals are brittle. The short wire can then be attached to a longer one for use in arrangements. The mature seed heads are also useful in dried arrangements; harvest these when they turn black or deep brown. Cut them

at different stages if you would like to get slightly different colorations from the seed heads.

Sources

Ambergate Gardens, 8730 County Rd. 43, Chaska, MN 55318, (877) 211-9769

Bluestone Perennials, 7211 Middle Ridge Rd., Madison, OH 44057, (800) 852-5243

Busse Gardens, 17160 245th Ave., Big Lake, MN 55309, (800) 544-3192

Fieldstone Gardens, Inc., 55 Quaker Lane, Vassalboro, ME 04989, (207) 923-3836

Prairie Nursery, W5875 Dyke Ave., Westfield, WI 53964, (608) 296-3679

'Sunrise'

'White Swan'

VARIETIES

From the recent explosion of Coneflower introductions we have selected some of the best. The flower colors of Coneflowers vary by the stage of maturity, often becoming more pale with age. Fragrance is being bred into Coneflowers. It can be subtle and tends to be more noticeable on mature plants. The lovely doubles (D) may take two years to form double flowers. Newer introductions are hardy to −20°F in open winters, to −30°F if there is adequate snow cover during cold spells. Plants will survive *if* your soil drains freely, *if* you buy vernalized plants (ones that growers have artificially chilled at 40°F for up to ten weeks), and *if* you get plants into the ground early in the season. Chilling is particularly important for plants grown by tissue culture rather than from seed.

VARIETY	FLOWER/CONE	HEIGHT	HARDINESS
Echinacea angustifolia			
(Narrow-leafed Coneflower)	Pale rosy pink/gold brown	24″	−40°F
This is a good prairie plant with peak bloom in midsummer.			
Echinacea pallida			
(Pale Purple Coneflower)	Pale pink/brown black	48″	−40°F
This variety, suited to natural settings, has large flowers with narrow, drooping petals and blooms June through July.			
Echinacea (Named varieties and hybrids)			
(Purple Coneflower)	Lavender pink/gold brown	36″	−40°F
'Coconut Lime'	Greenish white	24″	−30°F
'Elton Knight'*****	Vibrant pink/gold orange	24″	−30°F
'Fatal Attraction'*****	Bright purple pink/reddish gold	26″	−30°F
'Fragrant Angel'	White/yellow orange	24″	−30°F
Harvest Moon™ ('Matthew Saul')	Gold/gold orange	30″	−30°F
'Hot Papaya'	Orange red/red gold (D)	30″	−30°F
'Hot Summer'	Yellow to orange red/brown	36″	−30°F
'Magnus'	Rose pink/copper orange	36″	−40°F
'Meringue'	White/creamy yellow (D)	18″	−30°F
'Milkshake'	White/white to orange (D)	34″	−30°F
'Pica Bella'*****	Bright pink/red orange	30″	−30°F
'Pink Double Delight'	Light pink/dark pink (D)	30″	−30°F
Pixie Meadowbrite™*****	Deep pink/rose (D)	24″	−30°F
'Prairie Splendor'	Rich rose pink/rose gold	24″	−30°F
'Ruby Giant'	Deep rose pink/reddish gold (large)	30″	−30°F
'Ruby Star' ('Rubinstern')	Carmine red/copper orange	36″	−30°F
Summer Sky™ ('Katie Saul')*****	Peach rose/gold brown	34″	−30°F
'Sunrise'	Butter yellow/green to gold	30″	−30°F
'Vintage Wine'*****	Intense reddish pink/copper orange gold	30″	−30°F
'White Swan'	White/greenish gold	30″	−40°F

Euphorbia polychroma

EUPHORBIA

(ewe-FOR-bee-uh)

SPURGE

Bloom Time	Expected Longevity	Maintenance	Years to Bloom	Preferred Light
Spring to summer	10+ years	Low	From seed: 2 years From potted plant: 1 year	Full sun

There are well over fifteen hundred native species of Spurges throughout the world, but only a few are hardy enough for cold-climate gardens. These long-lived, durable plants are valued for both their attractive foliage and bracts (brightly colored leaves that look like flowers). The true flowers are inconspicuous and are barely noticed by most people. The stems can be used in arrangements if conditioned properly, but wear gloves, since the milky sap causes skin irritation in some people. These tough plants are rarely bothered by diseases and insects.

How Spurges Grow

Each of the varieties described in this section has its own distinctive foliage and way of growing. *Euphorbia corollata* (Flowering Spurge), a native prairie plant, looks like a vase with small, white bracts. *Euphorbia cyparissias* (Cyprus Spurge) has delicate foliage and dainty flowers. It makes a good ground cover. *Euphorbia myrsinites* (Myrtle Spurge) has grayish blue foliage and trailing growth. *Euphorbia polychroma* (Cushion Spurge) looks like a dwarf shrub with dense foliage that takes on an attractive reddish orange fall color. If planted in well-drained soils, these perennials live for years, forming individual or spreading clumps that get larger each season. Spurges form seed capsules that explode when mature, scattering numerous seeds in the garden.

Where to Plant

Site and Light Spurges grow best in full sun but tolerate light shade. Plant *Euphorbia myrsinites* (Myrtle Spurge) in a protected spot, as it is the least hardy of the varieties included here. All of the Spurges tolerate hot, dry sites.

Soil and Moisture Spurges prefer light, loose soils. Ideally, place plants in sandy loam that drains rapidly. Replace clay and rocky soil, or build a raised bed. Mix lots of organic matter into the soil. Good amendments include compost, rotted horse manure, leaf mold, and peat moss. Once mature, these perennials tolerate dry spells well.

Spacing In general, Spurges should stand 12 to 18 inches (30 to 45 cm) away from the nearest plant. Some will spread to fill up more than their allotted space and must be either checked or used as a ground cover.

Companions

Spring-blooming members of this group combine well with many shrubs, bulbs, and other perennials such as *Artemisia absinthium* 'Lambrook Silver' (Common Wormwood), *Festuca glauca* 'Elijah Blue' (Blue Fescue grass), and *Iris* (Bearded Iris). *Euphorbia myrsinites* (Myrtle Spurge) is delightful with *Dianthus* (Pinks), *Geranium cinereum* 'Ballerina' (Grayleaf Cranesbill), *Phlox borealis* (Arctic Phlox), and *Sedum* (Stonecrop) at the front of the border or in the rock garden. *Euphorbia corollata* (Flowering Spurge) works nicely with *Lilium* (Lily), *Lysimachia punctata* (Yellow Loosestrife), *Monarda* (Bee Balm), and *Veronica longifolia* 'Blue John' or 'White Jolanda' (Longleaf Speedwell).

Planting

Bare Root Plant bare root stock as soon as you can work the ground in spring. Remove plants from their shipping package immediately. Snip off broken or damaged root tips. Soak plants overnight in room-temperature water. Place a small amount of superphosphate in the base of the planting hole. Fill the hole with soil. Place the crown 1 inch (2.5 cm) below the soil surface. Fill in with soil, firm with your fingers, and water immediately. Dissolve ½ cup (about 114 g) 10-10-10 fertilizer in 1 gallon (about 4 liters) of water. Pour ½ cup (about 120 ml) of this starter solution around the base of each plant. If you prefer organic fertilizer, use fish emulsion instead.

Potted Plants Plant Spurges in the garden after all danger of frost in spring. If the soil in the pot is dry, water it, and let it drain overnight. Tap the plant from the pot without disturbing the root ball. Plant it at the same depth as in the pot, after preparing the hole in a similar manner to that for a bare root plant. Fill in with soil, firm with your fingers, and water immediately. Pour ½ cup (about 120 ml) starter solution around the base of each plant.

How to Care for Spurges

Water Once mature, these perennials can tolerate dry conditions. However, they grow best if kept evenly watered during hot, dry spells. Whenever you water, saturate the soil thoroughly.

Mulch Place 2 inches (5 cm) of mulch around the base of each plant as soon as the weather warms up in spring. Use dried grass clippings, shredded leaves, or pine needles. The mulch keeps soil moist and cool while inhibiting the growth of most annual weeds.

Fertilizing Sprinkle 10-10-10 fertilizer around the base of each plant in early spring just as new growth emerges. Water immediately to dissolve the granules and move nutrients into the root zone. Avoid further feeding, since these plants grow well with low amounts of nutrients and can become floppy if overfed.

If you prefer organic fertilizer, use alfalfa meal (rabbit pellets), blood meal, bonemeal, compost, cow manure, fish emulsion, Milorganite, or rotted horse manure. Bonemeal must be mixed into the soil at planting time to be effective.

Weeding Control the growth of annual weeds with a summer mulch. Pull up any weeds that do appear by hand. Remove even the smallest weeds from the spreading types to keep the ground cover most attractive.

Staking Too much fertilizer and water can cause stems of some varieties to become floppy. However, this is rarely a problem.

Deadheading The old bracts are not an eyesore. They seem to shrivel and melt away on their own. However, if you do not want these perennials to self-sow, clip off the bracts once they lose their color.

Winter Protection Most mature Spurges with the exception of *Euphorbia myrsinites* (Myrtle Spurge) are quite hardy and do not require winter protection other than normal snowfall. If there is no snow by early December, cover plants with 6 inches (15 cm) of winter mulch. Always winter protect Myrtle Spurge no matter what the amount of expected snowfall. Good mulches include marsh hay, clean straw, whole leaves, or pine needles. Remove the mulch as soon as the weather begins to warm up in spring to prevent crown and root rot.

Problems

Insects Spurges are rarely bothered by insects.

Disease Diseases are also very uncommon.

Propagation

Division Spurges can be propagated by division, but with the less aggressive types this is not easy. Dig up the plant in early spring just as new growth starts, and wash the roots clean of soil. The thick, fleshy roots of certain Spurges are quite brittle and must be handled very carefully. Cut the plant into sections with a sharp knife, making sure that each division has several growth eyes and a healthy root system. Discard the old central woody core of the plant. Plant these new divisions immediately as you would a bare root plant.

If the Spurge is a spreader, simply remove little plantlets off to the side of the mother. Plant these immediately as you would a bare root plant.

Cuttings Stem cuttings are the preferred propagation method for most Spurges. Tip cuttings taken in spring before flower buds set have the greatest chance of rooting. These should have three sets of leaves. Cut about a quarter inch (6 mm) below a leaf node. Remove the lower leaves, and dip the cut end in rooting hormone. Tap off any excess powder, and place the cutting in moist rooting medium. Once the young plants have formed a strong root system, plant them in pots or in a protected site outdoors.

Stem cuttings taken from semimature stems in early to midsummer on varieties such as *Euphorbia corollata* (Flowering Spurge) and *Euphorbia polychroma* (Cushion Spurge) will also take root. Another method worth trying is to take basal cuttings when the stems are 3 to 4 inches (7.5 to 10 cm) high. Make sure that a small portion of the crown is attached to each cutting. Handle both types of cuttings as you would tip cuttings.

Seed Start seed indoors about 12 weeks before the last expected frost in spring. Stored seed will require a moist chilling period to increase the chance of germination. Fill a seed tray with sterile, moist, germination medium, and sow the seed over this surface. Just press the seed onto the surface of the medium. Slip the seed tray into a perforated plastic bag, and put it in the crisper of your refrigerator for 3 to 4 weeks. After that time, take it out, and place it in an area with a temperature of 68°F to 70°F (20°C to 21°C). Seedlings should sprout in about 10 to 15 days and be ready for transplanting to pots in another 10 to

15 days. Grow the young seedlings on at a fairly cool temperature, and allow them to dry out slightly between waterings. Harden them off for 14 days before planting outdoors after all danger of frost has passed in spring. Most Spurges will self-sow readily in the garden if not deadheaded. If you want seedlings from the mother plant, allow seedpods to form, avoid the use of mulch, and never sprinkle inorganic fertilizer around the base of the plant, since it will kill germinating seed and seedlings.

Special Uses

Cut Flowers The bracts of the larger Spurges look lovely in cut arrangements. Wear gloves when handling the stems to avoid skin irritation. Sear the cut end of each stem with a flame until it glows to prevent the sap from coming out. Place the stems in 110°F (43°C) water, and allow them to stand overnight. Arrange them the next day, removing any leaves that would be underwater in the arrangement.

Dried Flowers Spurges make poor dried flowers.

Sources

Bluestone Perennials, 7211 Middle Ridge Rd., Madison, OH 44057, (800) 852-5243

Greer Gardens, 1280 Goodpasture Island Rd., Eugene, OR 97401, (800) 548-0111

Prairie Moon Nursery, 32115 Prairie Lane, Winona, MN 55987, (866) 417-8156

Variegated Foliage Nursery, 245 Westford Rd., Eastford, CT 06242, (860) 974-3951

Euphorbia cyparissias

Euphorbia polychroma bract

VARIETIES

VARIETY	COLOR	HEIGHT	HARDINESS
Euphorbia corollata*****			
(Flowering Spurge)	White	36″	−40°F

This is a very lovely, delicate native perennial that blooms for two to three weeks in summer. It resembles Baby's breath in flower and is a good substitute for it.

Euphorbia cyparissias			
(Cyprus Spurge)	Yellow	6″	−40°F

Its delicate foliage and dainty, mustard-colored flowers make this an attractive ground cover. The plant spreads rapidly through underground stolons and needs room to roam.

Euphorbia dulcis			
(Purple Spurge)			
'Chameleon'	Chartreuse	12″	−40°F

A fine foliage perennial, this plant has whorls of leaves that emerge gray-purple and mature to deep purple. It spreads slowly by creeping underground stems and makes a delightful mass planting. Deadheading the plant after its late spring to early summer bloom period will prevent its tendency to self-sow.

Euphorbia epithymoides (see *Euphorbia polychroma*)

Euphorbia griffithii			
(Griffith's Spurge)			
'Fireglow'	Orange	36″	−30°F

Common in English gardening literature, this plant is now making its way into the American marketplace. It forms a shrub-like mound of foliage with red-veined leaves and produces fiery orange bracts in early summer. Place it carefully since its spreading habit can be a nuisance under good growing conditions.

Euphorbia myrsinites			
(Myrtle Euphorbia)	Yellow	10″	−20°F

This trailing species has interesting bluish green leaves that spiral around the stems. The yellow bracts (look like flowers) are showy over a period of two to three weeks in spring. Plant it in rock gardens and walls for a spectacular effect.

Euphorbia polychroma*****			
(Cushion Spurge)	Yellow	18″	−40°F
'Bonfire'	Yellow	12″	−40°F
'First Blush'	Yellow	12″	−40°F

The most well-known and popular Spurge for cold climates, this perennial has something to offer throughout the entire growing season. It bears colorful bracts for four to six weeks in spring and then forms a neat mound of foliage. As fall arrives, the whole plant turns a wonderful reddish orange color. When planted in a well-drained soil, this perennial is long-lived and actually resents being disturbed. The foliage of 'Bonfire' takes on purple, red, and orange tones as it matures. It is an exceptional foliage plant from early spring until a hard freeze in fall. 'First Blush' has light green leaves (pinkish in spring) with creamy white edges during summer and fall.

Matteuccia struthiopteris

FERNS

Bloom Time	Expected Longevity	Maintenance	Years to Maturity	Preferred Light
Not applicable	25+ years	Low	From spores: 2 to 7 years From potted plant: 2 years	Light to full shade

Ferns are often taken for granted, and their landscape potential is not fully understood. Many of the taller types make excellent background or companion plants, while low-growing, vigorous spreaders serve as effective ground covers. Approximately one hundred different Ferns are suitable for cold-climate areas. They are available in a wide range of sizes, forms, and textures. Although their basic color is green, it is one of many different shades. Ferns are minimal-maintenance plants that offer excellent disease and insect resistance. Some are slow to mature, but most are very long-lived if their specific needs are met. Fern fronds (leaves) are often sought after for use in fresh arrangements, but only a handful of varieties hold up well. The mature spore stalks of some varieties are suitable for dried arrangements.

How Ferns Grow

Based on the way they grow, Ferns are divided into two groups: clump-formers and spreading types. The clump-formers grow from a crown, which increases in size each year but does not cover a very large area.

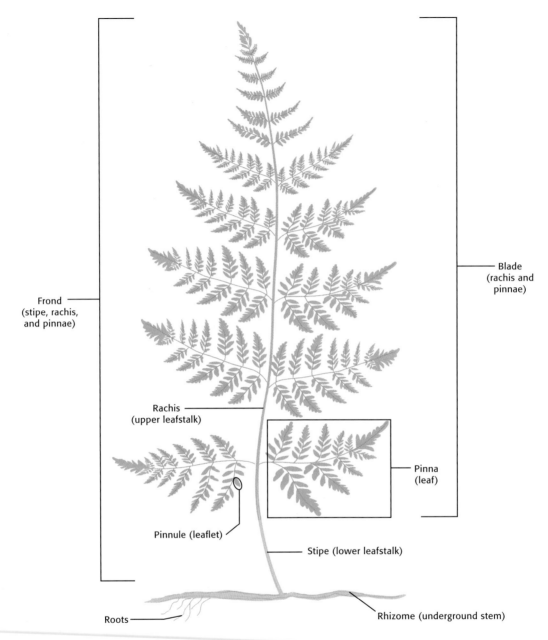

Frond
(stipe, rachis,
and pinnae)

Blade
(rachis and
pinnae)

Rachis
(upper leafstalk)

Pinna
(leaf)

Pinnule (leaflet)

Stipe (lower leafstalk)

Roots

Rhizome (underground stem)

Most gardeners are unfamiliar with the different parts of a **Fern**. This illustration will help you to understand them.

Spreading types, on the other hand, may form large colonies through the growth of underground stems, or rhizomes. Mature Ferns do not produce seed, but rather spores. These are small, nonsexual fruits or cells that function as seeds. These dustlike particles are produced on the undersides of the leaves or on separate specialized fronds. Once mature, spores fall to the ground. If conditions are right, they will begin to grow. Initial growth is into tiny, heart-shaped plantlets about a quarter inch (6 mm) wide that are individually known as prothallium. This is the sexual life stage of Ferns, and these tiny plants produce eggs and sperm. Once fertilization takes place, tiny Ferns begin to develop. These mature over the years into the adult Ferns familiar to all. Some varieties of Ferns also produce little bulblets in the axils of their leaves or pinnae. These fall to the ground and grow into new plants under the right conditions.

Where to Plant

Site and Light Most Ferns are low- to medium-light plants, and they thrive in shade or filtered light. However, Ferns that grow naturally in the wild in the crevices of rocks often do well in full sun. Others can also be grown in full sun if the planting site is evenly moist throughout the growing season. However, their color is often yellowish green, and they will brown readily during exceptionally hot summers. Ferns can be planted in a variety of locations in the garden, but they grow best in shady spots high in humidity and protected from strong winds.

Soil and Moisture Ferns thrive in consistently moist soil. The ideal soil for most types is a loam made up of at least 50 percent organic matter. Mix generous amounts of compost, peat moss, or leaf mold into your soil. This organic matter keeps the soil light and fluffy, allows for excellent moisture and air penetration, and keeps humidity high. Avoid heavy, compacted clays, or replace them with loam. Most Ferns grow well on the neutral to slightly acidic soils that are common in colder climates. However, some varieties require alkaline or highly acidic soils. Consider this when choosing varieties. Types that grow in rocks are tolerant of drier soils and, in fact, often grow well with very little soil. The exact needs of each Fern are outlined in the Varieties table at the end of the section.

Spacing Space according to the potential size and spread of the plants at maturity. Give the largest types up to 36 inches (90 cm) of space to develop fully. Space the very dwarf, rock-garden types from 6 to 12 inches (15 to 30 cm) apart.

Companions

With their various foliage colors and textures, Ferns add a refreshing contrast to flowering perennials and also to the bold foliage of other nearby plants. Use them to fill spaces left by *Narcissus* (Daffodil) and *Tulipa* (Tulip) bulbs, which go dormant in early summer. Ferns are particularly effective combined with *Aconitum* (Monkshood), *Chelone* (Turtlehead), *Hosta* (Hosta), *Lamium* (Dead Nettle), *Pulmonaria* (Lungwort), *Tradescantia* (Spiderwort), and many shade-loving native American wildflowers. Ferns suited to rocky areas look nice with dwarf varieties of *Astilbe* (False Spirea), *Campanula* (Bellflower), *Phlox* (Creeping Phlox), and *Hosta* (Hosta).

Planting

Bare Root Plant bare root stock as soon as you can work the ground in spring. Remove plants from their shipping package immediately. Snip off broken or damaged root tips. Soak plants overnight in room-temperature water. Place a small amount of superphosphate in the base of the planting hole. Fill the hole with soil. Place the crown just under the soil surface. Fill in with soil, firm with your fingers, and water immediately. Dissolve ½ cup (about 114 g) 10-10-10 fertilizer in 1 gallon (about 4 liters) of water. Pour ½ cup (about 120 ml) of this starter solution around the base of each plant. If you prefer organic fertilizer, use fish emulsion instead.

Potted Plants Plant potted Ferns after all danger of frost has passed in spring. Mature fronds of many varieties break easily, so try to purchase plants before they are fully developed. If soil in the pot is dry, soak it, and let it drain overnight. Tap the plant from the pot, keeping the root ball intact. Plant it at the same depth as in the pot, after preparing the hole in a similar manner to that for a bare root plant. Fill in with soil, firm with your fingers, and water immediately. Pour ½ cup (about 120 ml) starter solution around the base of each plant.

How to Care for Ferns

Water Keep the soil evenly moist throughout the growing season for most Ferns. Most will turn brown and go dormant as a way of surviving if they don't get enough water. When you water, soak the soil deeply and thoroughly each time.

Mulch The regular use of a summer mulch will conserve soil moisture, keep humidity high, and help control weeds. Spread a 2-inch (5-cm) layer of mulch around the base of each plant after the ground warms up in spring. Good mulches are compost, dried grass clippings, leaf mold, shredded leaves, decomposed wood chips, or pine needles.

Fertilizing Ferns grow well without lots of fertilizer as long as the soil was properly prepared prior to planting. A small amount of 10-10-10 fertilizer sprinkled around the base of mature plants in early spring is all that's needed. Too much chemical fertilizer may burn the foliage. Water immediately to dissolve the granules and move nutrients into the root zone. Ferns react well to foliar feeding with dilute solutions of water-soluble fertilizers.

If you prefer organic fertilizer, use alfalfa meal (rabbit pellets), blood meal, bonemeal, compost, fish emulsion, Milorganite, or rotted horse manure. Bonemeal must be mixed into the soil at planting time to be effective.

Weeding Weeds are generally a minor concern, as they rarely can tolerate the shady conditions where Ferns grow. However, avoid cultivating around Ferns so as not to damage their shallow roots. The use of mulch inhibits the growth of annual weeds. Hand pull any that do pop up through the mulch.

Staking If plants are properly placed, there should be no need for staking. Avoid very open windy locations, especially for the taller varieties.

Deadheading Since these perennials do not produce flowers, deadheading is not necessary.

Winter Protection Properly selected Ferns are very hardy and do not need winter protection other than normal snowfall. Ferns planted late in the season will benefit from being covered with 6 inches (15 cm) of mulch once the ground has permanently frozen in late fall. Good winter mulches include marsh hay, clean straw, whole leaves, and pine needles. Remove the mulch as soon as the weather warms up in spring.

Problems

Insects Ferns are free of insect pests but are bothered by slugs. Slugs love the cool, moist conditions in which Ferns grow so well. Place boards by the plants being damaged. Turn these over in the morning and pull off the slugs. Toss them into a can of salty water or vinegar. If you use poisoned slug bait, keep it away from pets and wildlife.

Diseases These perennials are not bothered by disease. If planted in too much light or underwatered, the foliage may turn yellowish to brown. Inexperienced gardeners sometimes interpret this as a symptom of disease, rather than a problem caused by lack of water or too much sun.

Propagation

Division Ferns do not require frequent division for their health, but they are generally easily propagated by this means. Dig up a plant in early spring just as growth starts. Pull or cut the plant into sections, making sure that each has several emerging fronds and plenty of fibrous roots. Plant these sections immediately as you would a bare root plant. For Ferns that spread by long underground rhizomes, you can dig a portion without disturbing the mother plant. Simply sever one of these rhizomes to the side of the mother plant with a spade, and dig it up with as much soil as possible. Replant it immediately in its new location, and water it well.

Bulblets Several Ferns produce little bulblets in the axils of their pinnae that serve as means of propagation. Upon maturity, these will fall to the ground and grow into young plants that can be dug up and moved to new locations. You could also collect the mature bulblets and scatter them in another location.

Spores Starting Ferns from spores is for the patient gardener, as it can take several years to get mature plants. However, it is an important technique, as it serves as a means of propagating large numbers of plants. Spores must be collected immediately upon their maturity, or they will be scattered and lost in the garden. The timing of this varies greatly by variety, so you have to check plants regularly as spores mature. Collect fronds when most of the spore cases are turning light to medium brown. Place them in a white envelope or between sheets of white paper in a dry, warm area. After drying for 3 to 4 days, the spores drop (dehisce) from the frond and will be visible as fine, dustlike particles on the white paper. Remove all nonspore material to reduce contamination by algae, fungi, and mosses.

The variety of containers and media that will work for growing Ferns from spores is limited only by your imagination. *The single most important factor for success is that both container and medium be sterile.* You may want to start with a mixture of peat moss, perlite, and fine vermiculite. Place this medium in a cake pan, moisten it thoroughly, and sterilize it in an oven. The starting medium must reach 180°F (82°C) and remain at that temperature for 30 minutes. You may have to experiment with a meat thermometer to find the right settings on your unit. After cooking, place the medium in a container, and pour boiling water through it several times to ensure sterility. Cover the container to avoid airborne impurities. Once the medium has cooled, sow the spores sparsely and evenly over its surface.

Cover the container with plastic or glass, place it under fluorescent lights set for 16-hour days, and keep it at 65°F to 70°F (18°C to 21°C). Within 1 to 4 months, you should see a pale green film on the surface of the medium. These are the young sexual plants that will produce new Ferns, or sporophytes, upon fertilization. Freestanding moisture is essential to successful fertilization, and it may be necessary for you to mist these tiny plantlets with distilled or boiled cooled water during this period.

When the new Ferns are a couple of inches (5 cm) tall, they can be separated and transplanted to individual pots. For a couple of weeks prior to doing this, you should gradually acclimate the plants to lower humidity. You may want to transplant the young Ferns as small groups instead of taking them out as single plants. They seem to resent being detached from their siblings at a very young age. Once well established, the young Ferns can be transplanted outdoors, but they will need to be acclimated to cooler temperatures and should not be put out until all danger of frost has passed in spring. Keep the soil around them consistently moist throughout the growing season. It usually takes 2 to 3 years before these new Ferns are mature enough to produce their first crop of spores.

Special Uses

The emerging fronds, or fiddleheads, of certain Ferns are edible and considered a delicacy. *Matteuccia struthiopteris* (Ostrich Fern) is particularly prized for this use. They are typically steamed until tender and served with butter and grated Parmesan cheese, but they can also be included in soups, salads, and quiche as well as numerous other recipes.

Cut Foliage The foliage of most garden Ferns does not hold up well in fresh arrangements. Among the best Ferns to experiment with are *Adiantum pedatum* (Maidenhair Fern), *Athyrium filix-femina* (Lady Fern), *Athyrium niponicum* var. *pictum* (Japanese Painted Fern), *Athyrium pycnocarpon* (Narrow-Leafed Spleenwort), *Dryopteris marginalis* (Marginal Wood Fern), and *Polystichum acrostichoides* (Christmas Fern). Cut fronds and place them in 110°F (43°C) water in a cool spot for several hours or longer prior to arranging. You could also try soaking the entire frond in cold water for 4 hours or longer before placing it in a plastic bag overnight. Alternative methods that can be successful with certain varieties include treating fronds with 110°F (43°C) water for several hours prior to placing them in a plastic bag in a cool location, or submerging fronds in a solution of 7 teaspoons (35 g) of powdered fabric starch per gallon (4 liters) of water.

Dried Fronds The mature spore-bearing fronds of *Matteuccia struthiopteris* (Ostrich Fern), *Onoclea sensibilis* (Sensitive Fern), and *Osmunda cinnamomea* (Cinnamon Fern) are prized for use in dried arrangements. Simply harvest these in fall and use them to add form and rich, chocolate brown color to floral designs. Pressed dry fronds of *Athyrium filix-femina* (Lady Fern), *Dryopteris marginalis* (Marginal Wood Fern), *Osmunda cinnamomea* (Cinnamon Fern), and *Osmunda regalis* (Royal Fern) are also sought after for dried arrangements. Harvest the fronds, and lay them between sections of newspaper. Make sure each leaflet is lying completely flat, and place a weight over them. Some people just slide the newspaper under a heavy rug once the fronds are properly placed. Allow

them to remain between the paper until completely dry. Harvesting fronds at different stages of development can result in a variety of color shades.

Sources

The Crownsville Nursery, P.O. Box 309, Strasbourg, VA 22657, (540) 631-9411

Fraser's Thimble Farms, 175 Arbutus Rd., Salt Spring Island, BC V8K 1A3, Canada, (250) 537-5788

Greer Gardens, 1280 Goodpasture Island Rd., Eugene, OR 97401, (541) 686-8266

Mason Hollow Nursery, 47 Scripps Lane, Mason, NH 03048, (603) 878-4347

Siskiyou Rare Plant Nursery, 2115 Talent Ave., Talent, OR 97540, (541) 535-7103

Sunlight Gardens, 174 Golden Lane, Andersonville, TN 37705, (800) 272-7396

Triple Brook Farm, 37 Middle Rd., Southampton, MA 01073 (413) 527-4626

VARIETIES

VARIETY	FOLIAGE COLOR	HEIGHT	HARDINESS
Adiantum pedatum*****			
(Northern Maidenhair Fern)	Light green	24″	–40°F
Among the most beautiful of our native Ferns with its lacy fronds on shiny black stems. It grows very well in a moist soil rich in organic matter.			
Asplenium platyneuron			
(Ebony Spleenwort)	Deep green	18″	–40°F
This Fern grows upward with long, narrow spore-bearing fronds. The sterile fronds are much shorter and evergreen. Grow it in a rock garden with alkaline soil. Ebony Spleenwort will tolerate short dry spells quite well.			
Asplenium trichomanes			
(Maidenhair Spleenwort)	Dark green	6″	–40°F
Maidenhair Spleenwort is found in the wild on limestone rocks, but it grows well in other soil types. It has attractive evergreen fronds and dark stems. Provide it with consistent moisture and shade.			

VARIETY	FOLIAGE COLOR	HEIGHT	HARDINESS
Athyrium filix-femina*****			
(Lady Fern)	Medium green	36″	−40°F
'Dre's Dagger'*****	Medium green	36″	−40°F
'Frizelliae'	Medium green	18″	−40°F
'Lady in Red'*****	Bright green	24″	−40°F
'Victoriae'	Medium green	24″	−40°F

The fronds of this Fern are finely cut, very lacy in appearance and, contrary to most Ferns, produced throughout the summer months. Lady Fern grows easily in a wide range of conditions, even in full sun if the soil remains moist throughout the entire growing season. The leaflets (pinnae) of 'Dre's Dagger' and 'Victoriae' have a crisscross pattern while the fronds themselves have crested tips. The pinnae of 'Frizelliae' are tightly rolled up giving the fronds a unique look. Mature plants of 'Lady in Red' have deep burgundy red stems.

Athyrium goeringianum (see *Athyrium niponicum*)

Athyrium niponicum			
(Japanese Painted Fern)			
'Applecourt' ('Apple Court')	Gray green	18″	−30°F
'Burgundy Lace'	Gray green	18″	−30°F
'Pewter Lace'	Pewter silver	18″	−30°F
var. *pictum******	Silver green purple	24″	−30°F

These are among the most popular perennials due to the unique coloration of their fronds. The frond tips of 'Applecourt' are crested. They are loveliest once fully mature.

Athyrium pycnocarpon*****			
(Narrow-leafed Spleenwort)	Dark green	24″	−40°F

This attractive Fern is not well known or readily available but well worth seeking out. It requires lots of organic matter in the soil and must be kept evenly moist throughout the growing season. It grows from a creeping rootstock which forms an impressive clump over time.

Athyrium thelypteroides			
(Silvery Glade Fern)	Light green	36″	−30°F

Spreading from a slender rootstock, this species is easily grown in rich, damp soils and looks at home along the banks of a pond or stream in partial shade.

Athyrium (Hybrids)			
'Branford Beauty'	Silvery gray	24″	−40°F
'Branford Rambler'	Dark green	24″	−40°F
'Ghost'*****	Silvery white	24″	−40°F
'Ocean's Fury'	Silver green	36″	−40°F

'Branford Beauty' with its stunning foliage and reddish stems is an ideal accent plant in a shade garden. 'Branford Rambler' is suited to mass plantings. It too has distinctive red to maroon stems. 'Ghost' is aptly named with silvery white fronds and pinkish purple stems. 'Ocean's Fury' has crested silver green fronds.

Adiantum pedatum

Athyrium niponicum var. *pictum*

Onoclea sensibilis

Osmunda claytoniana

Phegopteris connectilis

Polystichum braunii

VARIETY	FOLIAGE COLOR	HEIGHT	HARDINESS
Camptosorus rhizophyllus (Walking Fern)	Dark green	12″	−40°F

This Fern has narrow, triangular, evergreen fronds which, under favorable conditions, will root at their tips to form new plants, thus "walking" to new locations. Plant Walking Fern in moist, neutral soil among limestone rocks in partial shade.

VARIETY	FOLIAGE COLOR	HEIGHT	HARDINESS
Cystopteris bulbifera (Bulblet Fern)	Pale green	36″	−40°F

Bulblet Fern grows very well in a variety of soils as long as it is planted in a damp, shady location. It propagates readily from pea-size bulblets formed in the axils on the underside of the fronds. These drop to the ground when mature, take root, and serve to increase the size of the colony.

VARIETY	FOLIAGE COLOR	HEIGHT	HARDINESS
Cystopteris fragilis (Fragile Fern)	Bright green	10″	−40°F

This wild Fern with finely cut foliage is found most commonly on moist, shady, rocky slopes, but it also grows well in a shady woodland garden. Keep the soil consistently moist throughout the growing season.

VARIETY	FOLIAGE COLOR	HEIGHT	HARDINESS

Dennstaedtia punctilobula

| (Hay-scented Fern) | Light green | 36″ | −40°F |

This Fern has long-creeping rhizomes which roam freely making it a good ground cover. The dainty fronds smell like newly-mown hay from which we get the common name. Hay-scented Fern will grow in partial shade or full sun, but it needs plenty of moisture.

Dryopteris cristata

| (Crested Wood Fern) | Dark green | 30″ | −40°F |

This Fern has two different frond types, with the spore-bearing ones being taller and more erect than the shorter, sterile, evergreen ones. It grows in a wide variety of areas but prefers rich, moist soils with lots of organic matter.

Dryopteris filix-mas

| (Male Fern) | Shiny green | 36″ | −40°F |

Male Fern is one of the easier Ferns to grow in partial shade. The crown increases in size slowly, and this Fern does best in moist soil rich in organic matter.

*Dryopteris goldiana*****

| (Goldie's Wood Fern) | Deep green | 48″ | −40°F |

A large Fern with leathery fronds that can be more than a foot wide, this species forms a most impressive plant. It needs a cool, moist, shaded location to grow well.

Dryopteris intermedia

| (Evergreen Wood Fern) | Dark green | 24″ | −40°F |

The fronds of this Fern are leathery, nearly evergreen, and form a vase-shaped plant. It grows slowly and requires lots of moisture to do well.

*Dryopteris marginalis*****

| (Marginal Wood Fern) | Dark bluish green | 18″ | −40°F |

The fronds of this clump-forming plant are evergreen and leathery making them ideal for cutting. Marginal Wood Fern requires a shady location with consistently moist soil throughout the growing season.

Dryopteris spinulosa

| (Spinulose Wood Fern) | Deep green | 30″ | −40°F |

The nearly evergreen fronds of this Fern have a much lacier appearance than the other species of *Dryopteris*. It likes a damp shady area where it spreads slowly to form a handsome specimen plant.

Gymnocarpium dryopteris

| (Oak Fern) | Yellow green | 10″ | −40°F |
| 'Plumosum' | Apple green | 8″ | −40°F |

This diminutive Fern with wiry stems and triangular fronds grows from long, creeping rhizomes. In time, it forms an attractive ground cover if planted in a rich, woodsy soil. It also grows well in rocks and will tolerate partial sun if the soil is kept consistently moist.

VARIETY	FOLIAGE COLOR	HEIGHT	HARDINESS
Matteuccia struthiopteris			
(Ostrich Fern)	Bright green	60″	−40°F
'The King'	Bright green	72″	−40°F

This may be the most well-known Fern and one of the easiest to grow. Ostrich Fern forms a large, vase-shaped plant with erect, brown fertile fronds good for drying. The fiddleheads of the sterile fronds are excellent to eat. This plant spreads rapidly from a creeping rootstock to form a dense ground cover. It thrives in evenly moist to wet soils.

Onoclea sensibilis			
(Sensitive Fern)	Medium green	24″	−40°F

The sterile fronds of this species are quite coarse. Its spores appear in clusters at the top of separate fronds. These fertile fronds turn brown, last throughout the winter, and are sometimes used in dried arrangements. The plant is called Sensitive Fern because when the sterile fronds are picked, the edges roll up slightly and because it is one of the first Ferns struck down by fall frosts. It does best in marshy soils in full sun or light shade.

Osmunda cinnamomea*****			
(Cinnamon Fern)	Yellow green	60″	−40°F

This attractive vase-shaped Fern is named for the color of its "cinnamon-stick" fertile fronds. It grows wild in swampy places in open woods. It prefers slightly acidic, consistently moist soil. The plant will be much shorter in drier soils.

Osmunda claytoniana			
(Interrupted Fern)	Yellow green	48″	−40°F

The general appearance of the sterile fronds is very similar to that of Cinnamon Fern. However, the frond is "interrupted" in the middle by a spore-bearing segment that resembles brown clusters of miniscule grapes once mature. This Fern tolerates many types of soils but needs lots of moisture.

Osmunda regalis*****			
(Royal Fern)	Light green	60″	−40°F

This may be the most attractive member of this fine group. The leaves or pinnae are carried on wiry, upright stems with the spore bearing segments clustered at the tips of the fronds. This gives rise to its nickname, the "flowering" Fern. It requires lots of moisture and thrives along the banks of streams or edges of ponds if kept in partial shade.

Pellaea atropurpurea			
(Purple Cliff-brake)	Bluish green	10″	−40°F

A fine rock garden Fern, Purple Cliff-brake is easily recognized by its purple-brown, hairy stems and bluish to olive green, leathery leaves. Plant it in neutral to slightly acidic, woodsy soil among rocks. It is difficult to transplant.

Pellaea glabella			
(Smooth Cliff-brake)	Bluish green	10″	−40°F

This differs from the preceding species in that the stem is dark brown and lacks hairs. It will grow on limestone or sandstone rocks in both damp and quite dry exposed locations.

VARIETY	FOLIAGE COLOR	HEIGHT	HARDINESS

Phegopteris connectilis*****
(Narrow Beech Fern)   Light green   24″   −40°F

This species is similar to New York Fern except that its fronds are triangular in shape. Narrow Beech Fern spreads by underground rhizomes and makes a nice dense ground cover. Planted in a good soil with abundant organic matter, it is one of the easiest Ferns to grow; but, like the New York Fern, requires evenly moist soil.

Polypodium virginianum
(Common Polypody)   Dark green   12″   −40°F

The fronds of this Fern are very leathery and evergreen. It grows best if planted in a rocky location in partial shade. It can be grown in higher light, but the foliage will have a distinct yellow-green color. The root system is shallow, and the plant spreads through creeping rhizomes.

Polystichum acrostichoides
(Christmas Fern)   Dark green   30″   −40°F

The evergreen fronds of this species exhibit sprawling rather than upright growth. These fronds are favored by arrangers and those interested in making wreaths. This Fern does very well in a woodland soil that is not overly fertile. It can tolerate some sun during the summer months if the soil is moist enough.

Polystichum braunii*****
(Braun's Holly Fern)   Deep green   24″   −40°F

This is among the most beautiful of hardy garden Ferns. Though not evergreen, the fronds are quite leathery and very lustrous with stems covered by brown scales. Plant this fern in a cool, moist, partially shaded location with lots of mulch around the base of the plant.

Thelypteris noveboracensis
(New York Fern)   Yellow green   24″   −40°F

This is also known as the Tapering Fern because the leaf is widest in the middle. New York Fern spreads rapidly and has the unfortunate characteristic of turning brown early in the fall. Plant in fertile loam and keep it consistently moist throughout the season.

Thelypteris palustris
(Marsh Fern)   Light green   30″   −40°F

Plant this Fern in a marsh or at the edge of a pond or stream where it will spread rapidly through creeping rhizomes. It does very well in full sun as long as the soil is wet.

Thelypteris phegopteris (see *Phegopteeris connectilis*)

Woodsia ilvensis
(Rusty Cliff Fern)   Gray green   6″   −40°F

The undersides of the fronds and stems are rusty colored on mature plants. Plant in a rock garden in a moist neutral soil in open shade. If not kept well watered, this Fern will go dormant during extended dry periods.

Woodsia obtusa
(Blunt-lobed Cliff Fern)   Pale gray green   12″   −40°F

Larger than the above species, Blunt-lobed Cliff Fern is easily grown in a wide variety of soils in the rock garden. It thrives in partial shade but also tolerates full sun if kept evenly moist.

Filipendula rubra

FILIPENDULA

(fill-ee-PEND-you-luh)

MEADOWSWEET

Bloom Time	Expected Longevity	Maintenance	Years to Bloom	Preferred Light
Early to midsummer	15+ years	Low	From seed: 2 to 3 years From potted plant: 1 year	Full sun to light shade

Meadowsweets are stunning perennials both in and out of bloom. Their attractive leaves are deep green and hold up well throughout the season. The flowers bloom in feathery, terminal clusters and are excellent for cutting. Certain varieties exude a lovely fragrance. Meadowsweets tend to be long-lived and require minimal maintenance. If properly grown, they are rarely bothered by insects or disease.

How Meadowsweets Grow

Meadowsweets grow from fibrous roots into plants of varying forms. *Filipendula vulgaris* (Dropwort) forms a delicate plant with a rosette of fernlike foliage and clusters of dainty blossoms carried on short stems. Most of the other Meadowsweets develop into bushy plants with bold foliage and tall flowering stems. As they mature, these perennials spread by creeping stems and can form sizable clumps. Self-seeding in the garden is not common but does occur.

Sources

Ambergate Gardens, 8730 County Rd. 43, Chaska, MN 55318, (877) 211-9769

Busse Gardens, 17160 245th Ave., Big Lake, MN 55309, (800) 544-3192

ForestFarm, 990 Tetherow Rd., Williams, OR 97544, (541) 846-7269

Spring Hill Nursery, P.O. Box 330, Harrison, OH 45030, (513) 354-1510

VARIETIES

VARIETY	COLOR	HEIGHT	HARDINESS
Filipendula digitata (see *Filipendula palmata*)			
Filipendula hexapetala (see *Filipendula vulgaris*)			
Filipendula palmata			
(Siberian Meadowsweet)	Soft pink	48″	–40°F
'Elegans' (see *Filipendula purpurea* 'Elegans')			
'Nana'	Pale to medium pink	10″	–40°F

Siberian Meadowsweet has leaflets covered with dense white hairs on the undersides and blooms in summer.

Filipendula purpurea			
(Japanese Meadowsweet)	Medium pink	36″	–40°F
'Alba'	White	30″	–40°F
'Elegans'	White/red stamens	36″	–40°F

This species has smooth leaflets and crimson red stems. It blooms in early to midsummer.

Filipendula rubra			
(Queen-of-the-Prairie)	Medium pink	60″	–40°F
'Venusta' ('Venusta Magnifica')*****	Deep pink	60″	–40°F

This plant may be too large for small gardens, but it is excellent as an accent or specimen plant and rarely requires support. The flowers bloom in large, feathery plumes about midsummer and rise well above the mound of mid-green leaves. This perennial will quickly form impressive clumps in an evenly moist soil.

Filipendula ulmaria			
(Queen-of-the-Meadow)	Creamy white	48″	–40°F
'Aurea'	Creamy white	30″	–40°F
'Plena' ('Flore Pleno')	Creamy white (D)	36″	–40°F
'Variegata' ('Aureo-variegata')	Creamy white	30″	–40°F

This Eurasian native forms long, erect flower stems rising out of the foliage mound in early to midsummer. 'Aurea' has golden yellow leaves which hold their color in light shade. 'Plena' has fully double (D) flowers, while 'Variegata' has dark green leaves with creamy yellow variegation in their centers. These named varieties should not be allowed to self-sow, since seedlings will not be identical to their parents.

Filipendula rubra

Filipendula vulgaris 'Multiplex'

VARIETY	COLOR	HEIGHT	HARDINESS
Filipendula vulgaris			
(Dropwort)	Creamy white	30″	−40°F
'Multiplex' ('Flore Pleno') ('Plena')*****	Creamy white (D)	18″	−40°F

The rich green, finely divided leaves of this perennial are among the first to appear in spring and the last to disappear in fall. The slender roots have interesting tuber-like structures hanging from their ends. These plants are much more tolerant of dry conditions than other members of this overall genus (group). The species blooms in early summer, while 'Multiplex' with its fully double (D), sterile flowers offers a more extended bloom period. The lovely foliage of 'Multiplex' combined with its compact growth and tendency to spread mildly make it a fine ground cover.

VARIETY	COLOR	HEIGHT	HARDINESS
Filipendula (Hybrid)			
'Kahome' ('Kakome')*****	Rosy pink	12″	−40°F

This delightful dwarf has pale green foliage and produces fragrant flowers in early to midsummer.

Geranium ibericum

GERANIUM

(jer-AYE-knee-um)

CRANESBILL

Bloom Time	Expected Longevity	Maintenance	Years to Bloom	Preferred Light
Spring to late summer	15 to 20+ years	Low	From seed: 2 to 3 years From potted plant: 1 year	Full sun to light shade

The plants that most people commonly refer to as Geraniums are not true Geraniums, but rather varieties of *Pelargonium*, a large group of plants killed by winter cold. True Geraniums are commonly known as Cranesbills, and many of them are hardy in cold climates. They are generally vigorous plants, often spreading steadily to cover quite an area. Certain varieties have aromatic foliage, while others stand out for fall color. Many of them, particularly the taller forms, can be used in floral arrangements. Cranesbills are free-flowering plants that bloom from spring through summer, and many rebloom if they are deadheaded. These easily grown perennials do not require a lot of maintenance and offer good pest resistance. Do not let children play with the foliage, since, if eaten, the leaves can cause diarrhea, nausea, and vomiting.

How Cranesbills Grow

Many Cranesbills grow from rather thick rhizomes with small, wiry roots. Some types are running in nature, and others have prominent taproots. Plant forms range from trailing to mounded to upright. The leaves mimic the shape of your hand, are grayish green, and generally remain attractive throughout the season. The flowers have five distinct petals and are normally saucer-shaped and about 1 to 2 inches (2.5 to 5 cm) across. Flower colors range from white to blue, purple, pink, mauve, or magenta, and many have interesting veining. If spent flowers are not removed, they will form beaklike fruits which burst at maturity to spread their seed around the garden. It is the shape of these fruits that has given rise to the common name of these fine perennials. Some varieties will self-sow freely in the garden.

Where to Plant

Site and Light Cranesbills grow best in full sun or light shade. Dense shade produces leggy plants with sparse foliage and few flowers. Avoid sunny areas that are extremely hot and dry, as these perennials are natives of temperate zones and prefer cooler growing conditions.

Soil and Moisture Cranesbills grow well in many different types of soil, but they demand good drainage. Add lots of organic matter to the soil. Good amendments are compost, leaf mold, rotted horse manure, and peat moss. Avoid boggy soils where these plants grow poorly and often die.

Spacing Space upright and mound-forming plants 12 to 18 inches (30 to 45 cm) apart. Plant the vigorous trailing or spreading varieties no less than 2 feet (60 cm) away from the nearest plants. A number of Geraniums make good ground covers.

Companions

With such great diversity within this group, it is possible to find a *Geranium* (Cranesbill) to fill virtually any need. Some such as *Geranium* × *cantabrigiense* (Hybrid Cranesbill) and *Geranium macrorrhizum* (Bigroot Cranesbill) are delightful among *Rosa* (Roses) along with *Artemisia* (Wormwood) and *Nepeta* (Catmint). Try *Geranium ibericum* (Iberian

Cranesbill) next to varying colors of *Iris* (Bearded Iris), or *Geranium sanguineum* var. *striatum* (Bloody Cranesbill) planted with *Dianthus gratianopolitanus* 'Bewitched' (Cheddar Pink) and *Helictotrichon sempervirens* (Blue Oat Grass). Other perennials to use as companions include *Alchemilla* (Lady's Mantle), *Campanula* (Bellflower), *Delphinium* (Larkspur), *Iris* (Siberian Iris), *Phlox* (Garden Phlox), and various **Grasses**. Partially shaded areas are excellent locations for a number of varieties. *Geranium maculatum* (Wild Cranesbill) is especially beautiful next to *Phlox stolonifera* (Creeping Phlox), available in a number of colors. *Geranium phaeum* (Mourning Widow) is dramatic next to yellow-foliaged *Hosta* (Hosta). Combine varieties noted for fall foliage color with fall-blooming perennials, colorful grasses, and woody shrubs. Use the trailing types as ground covers on slopes and as living waterfalls over walls.

Planting

Bare Root Plant bare root stock as soon as you can work the ground in spring. Remove plants from their shipping package immediately. Snip off broken or damaged root tips. Soak plants overnight in room-temperature water. Place a small amount of superphosphate in the base of the planting hole. Fill the hole with soil. Place the crown 1 inch (2.5 cm) below the soil surface. Fill in with soil, firm with your fingers, and water immediately. Dissolve ½ cup (about 114 g) 10-10-10 fertilizer in 1 gallon (about 4 liters) of water. Pour ½ cup (about 120 ml) of this starter solution around the base of each plant. If you prefer organic fertilizer, use fish emulsion instead.

Potted Plants

Plant Geraniums after all danger of frost has passed in spring. If the soil in the pot is dry, water it, and let it drain overnight. Tap the plant from the pot without disturbing the root ball. Plant it at the same depth as in the pot, after preparing the hole in a similar manner to that for a bare root plant. Fill in with soil, firm with your fingers, and water immediately. Pour ½ cup (about 120 ml) starter solution around the base of each plant.

How to Care for Cranesbills

Water Most Cranesbills thrive in evenly moist soil throughout the growing season. Some, however, will tolerate short dry periods. When you water, soak the soil to a depth of 8 to 10 inches (20 to 25 cm).

Mulch Place 2 inches (5 cm) of mulch around the base of each plant after the ground warms up in spring. This keeps the soil moist and cool, a condition Cranesbills enjoy. It also stops many annual weeds from growing. Dried grass clippings, shredded leaves, compost, or pine needles are all effective mulches.

Fertilizing Sprinkle 10-10-10 fertilizer around the base of each plant in early spring just as new growth emerges. Water immediately to dissolve the granules and move nutrients into the root zone. Fertilizing most varieties once each season is usually enough. Too much fertilizer may lead to lush growth, but, especially for plants that grow upright (rather than spreading outward), it also produces weak stems that flop over.

If you prefer organic fertilizers, use alfalfa meal (rabbit pellets), blood meal, bonemeal, compost, cow manure, fish emulsion, Milorganite, or rotted horse manure. Bonemeal must be mixed into the soil at planting time to be effective.

Weeding The regular use of an organic mulch should keep annual weed populations in check. Any that do sprout are easily pulled by hand.

Staking Unless upright forms of Cranesbills are fertilized too heavily, these plants rarely require staking. The one exception is *Geranium psilostemon* (Armenium Cranesbill). Consider placing a peony hoop around the plant in early spring, or tie individual stems to stakes at varying heights as they grow.

Deadheading Removing spent flowers may encourage additional bloom on some varieties. If you want the plant to develop seed, let the spent flowers form seedpods.

Cutting Back Cut back some geraniums after flowering to encourage the growth of a fresh mound of foliage. Do this with 'Johnson's Blue' and *Geranium × oxonianum* varieties.

Winter Protection Mature plants are hardy, but, if there is no snow cover by early December, it may be good insurance to cover plants with 6 inches (15 cm) of marsh hay, clean straw, whole leaves, or pine needles. Remove the mulch as soon as the weather begins to warm up in spring.

Problems

Insects Cranesbills are rarely bothered by insects, with the exception of Japanese beetles. These beetles are spreading into colder climates. They get concentrated in specific areas within each state. They are most lethargic in the morning, which is the ideal time to pick them off plants by hand. Toss them into a can filled with soapy water or vinegar. Prevent their spread by treating lawns with Milky Spore Disease powder or the inorganic insecticide Merit.

Disease Leaf spots and botrytis are known to occur on Cranesbills, but they are rare. Rust is even rarer and usually found only on stock grown on the West Coast. Unless outbreaks are severe, keeping the bed clean and removing diseased foliage is all that's advised.

Propagation

Division These perennials can remain undisturbed for 6 to 10 years before division may be necessary. Most, except taprooted types, are easily propagated by division if you want to increase the number of your plants.

Dig up a mature plant in early spring just as new growth starts, and wash it free of soil. Some varieties can be pulled apart by hand, while others will need to be cut apart with a sharp knife or pruning shears. Make sure each division has a number of strong growth eyes and a healthy root system. Plant the new divisions immediately as you would bare root plants. Any broken pieces of root may be worth replanting, as they often have buds that will sprout to form new plants. These are known as *adventitious buds*, since they occur where buds normally are not found.

Some of the strongly rhizomatous varieties produce new shoots away from the crown of the plant. Dig these up, keeping as many roots as possible without disturbing the mother plant, and place them immediately in a rooting medium kept consistently moist. Keep the humidity high around the plantlets as they establish a new root system. Once these young plants are actively growing, place them in a permanent location.

Stem Cuttings Depending on the variety, Cranesbills can be increased by basal or tip cuttings taken in spring or summer. Basal cuttings taken between April and June are preferred. Using a sharp knife, take these cuttings from the numerous shoots emerging from the crown. Take them just above the soil line when the shoots are 4 inches (10 cm) tall. Dip the cut end in rooting hormone, and tap off any excess powder. Place each in moist rooting medium, and keep the humidity around the cuttings high. Once they have formed a strong root system, plant them in individual pots. Harden them off for 14 days before planting outside.

Root Cuttings Varieties with thick, fleshy roots can also be propagated by root cuttings. In very early spring before the plant begins growth, dig it up, and cut off several roots about the size of your little finger. Replant the rest of the plant immediately, and water it well. In the case of taprooted types, you may not be able to save any of the parent plant. Cut the severed roots into pieces 2 to 3 inches (5 to 7.5 cm) long, and plant each one vertically in a moist, well-drained medium in a pot or cold frame. Place the end of the cutting that was nearer the crown up when planting. Keep the medium consistently moist until the cuttings form a solid root ball. Transplant the cuttings to pots or a garden location once they have established a strong root system and begun to grow foliage.

Seed Cranesbills can be easily grown from seed. If you are going to collect seed on your plants, you must check the pods regularly as they mature. It is easy to lose a seed crop: when the pods are ripe, they burst and scatter seeds in all directions. Store seed in a cool, dark location. You can sow it in a bed or cold frame in fall for germination the following spring. The key is to keep the growing medium moist until it freezes. Normally, however, seed is sown indoors in mid- to late winter.

Sow the seed over moist germination medium, barely covering it. Place the seed tray in a plastic bag with a few small holes punched through it. Keep the growing medium evenly moist at a temperature of 55°F to 60°F (13°C to 16°C). If no germination has taken place after 6 to 8 weeks, slide the tray into the crisper of your refrigerator for 6 to 8 weeks. This should overcome the seeds' dormancy. Remove the tray after this time, and place it back in an area with a temperature of 55°F to 60°F (13°C to 16°C). Once seedlings sprout, give them plenty of light and keep the medium moist at all times. After they have developed a second pair of leaves, pot them in individual pots.

Special Uses

Cut Flowers Although a number of varieties make good cut flowers, *Geranium himalayense* (Lilac Cranesbill), *Geranium pratense* (Meadow Cranesbill), and *Geranium sanguineum* (Bloody Cranesbill) are among the most popular. Cut the flower stems when flowers are just reaching peak bloom, and place them into water immediately. Once indoors, put the bottom 1 inch (2.5 cm) of each stem in boiling water for a few seconds. Then allow the stems to stand in warm water overnight before arranging. Another conditioning method is to split the base of each stem with a sharp knife, and place it in cold water for several hours.

The foliage is also of value in arrangements, but it is, unfortunately, not long-lasting. The handsome fall color of certain varieties is particularly interesting in late-season arrangements.

Dried Flowers The flowers are not suitable for drying. However, the seedpods on some types are large enough to blend nicely into dried arrangements.

Sources

Bluestone Perennials, 7211 Middle Ridge Rd., Madison, OH 44057, (800) 852-5243

Busse Gardens, 17160 245th Ave., Big Lake, MN 55309, (800) 544-3192

Digging Dog Nursery, P.O. Box 471, Albion, CA 95410, (707) 937-1130

Fritz Creek Gardens, P.O. Box 15226, Homer, AK 99603, (907) 235-4969

Geraniaceae Nursery, 122 Hillcrest Ave., Kentfield, CA 04904, (415) 461-4168

Roots & Rhizomes, P.O. Box A, Randolph, WI 53956, (800) 374-5035

White Flower Farm, P.O. Box 50, Litchfield, CT 06759, (800) 503-9624

'Alpenglow'

'Johnson's Blue'

VARIETIES

VARIETY	COLOR	HEIGHT	HARDINESS
Geranium × *cantabrigiense*			
(Hybrid Cranesbill)	Bright pink	12″	−40°F
'Biokovo'*****	White flushed pink	12″	−40°F
'Cambridge'	Soft pink	10″	−40°F
'Karmina'*****	Lavender pink	12″	−40°F
'Rosalina'	Light blue pink/pink	8″	−40°F

These are among the most easily grown and desirable of the Cranesbills. They spread in neat clumps and bloom in late spring and early summer. Their glossy, nearly evergreen foliage turns an attractive red in fall.

VARIETY	COLOR	HEIGHT	HARDINESS
Geranium cinereum			
(Grayleaf Cranesbill)			
'Ballerina'	Lilac pink/darker veins	6″	−20°F
'Lawrence Flatman'	Lilac pink/crimson veins	6″	−20°F
'Purple Pillow'	Purple/black center	8″	−20°F

These are compact, neat plants with attractive deeply cut, gray-green foliage. They are garden favorites because of their showy flowers which bloom from June to September. Well-drained, gritty soils are essential to long life, as is good winter protection. 'Ballerina' is a nearly sterile hybrid with a very long bloom season.

VARIETY	COLOR	HEIGHT	HARDINESS
Geranium clarkei			
(Clarke's Cranesbill)			
'Kashmir Pink'	Pink/darker veins	18″	−30°F
'Kashmir Purple'	Deep purple blue	18″	−30°F
'Kashmir White'	White/lilac veins	18″	−30°F

Blooming in late spring and early summer, these named varieties are among the most free-flowering of the Cranesbills. Plants have a loose look with large, deeply cut leaves.

VARIETY	COLOR	HEIGHT	HARDINESS
*Geranium dalmaticum*****			
(Dalmatian Cranesbill)	Mauve pink	6″	−30°F
'Album'	White tinged pink	6″	−30°F

This low grower is best in the front of borders or in rock gardens. It blooms in late spring and early summer with flowers up to one inch across. The fragrant, rounded leaves take on a reddish orange fall color. This perennial spreads by creeping rhizomes, but 'Album' is less vigorous than the species.

VARIETY	COLOR	HEIGHT	HARDINESS
Geranium endressii			
(Pyrenean Cranesbill)			
'Wargrave Pink'	Salmon pink/darker veins	18″	−30°F

This is a very popular perennial, but often short-lived in compacted soils. In cold climates, it flowers over a long period in the summer months.

Geranium grandiflorum (see *Geranium himalayense*)

Geranium grandiflorum var. *alpinum* (see *Geranium himalayense* 'Gravetye')

VARIETY	COLOR	HEIGHT	HARDINESS
Geranium himalayense			
(Lilac Cranesbill)	Violet blue	16″	−30°F
'Birch Double' ('Plenum')*****	Purplish pink (D)	16″	−30°F
'Gravetye'	Blue/purple-red center	12″	−30°F

Forming sprawling plants, these perennials bloom for several weeks in late spring and early summer. This is another group with reddish orange fall foliage. 'Birch Double' is a sterile, double (D) flowered selection with a longer bloom period.

Geranium ibericum			
(Iberian Cranesbill)	Violet blue	18″	−30°F
'Genyel'	Deep purple/darker veins	18″	−30°F

Not the showiest of Cranesbills, this is still an important plant for cold-climate gardeners because it is vigorous and tolerates drought. Its leaves are dark green, quite hairy, and take on a pleasing fall color. Iberian Cranesbill flowers in early summer.

*Geranium macrorrhizum*****			
(Bigroot Cranesbill)	Magenta	18″	−40°F
'Album'	Bluish white/pink	18″	−40°F
'Bevan's Variety'	Crimson purple	12″	−40°F
'Ingwersen's Variety' ('Walter Ingwersen')	Soft pink	18″	−40°F
'Variegatum'	Light magenta	12″	−40°F
'White Ness'	Pure white	10″	−40°F

With its spreading underground stems, this is the best of the Cranesbills for use as a ground cover. This species and its named varieties can be recognized by the unique but pleasant odor of their crushed foliage. The plant blooms from late spring to early summer and has yellow or reddish orange foliage in fall. It grows well in dry, lightly shaded areas.

Geranium maculatum			
(Wild Cranesbill)	Clear pink	24″	−30°F
'Album'	White	24″	−30°F
'Espresso'	Pale lavender pink	16″	−30°F

This Cranesbill is common in meadows and along the edges of woods where it blooms from late spring into early summer. It is an excellent plant for the wild garden or in natural settings. It prefers moist soils in full sun or light shade.

Geranium × *magnificum*****			
(Showy Cranesbill)	Violet blue/darker veins	24″	−40°F

This sterile hybrid offers excellent hardiness, handsome hairy foliage, good vigor, and clusters of showy flowers in early summer. Cut it back after flowering if a tidy look is important to you.

Geranium × *oxonianum*			
(Hybrid Cranesbill)			
'A.T. Johnson'	Silver pink	18″	−30°F
'Claridge Druce'	Deep pink/purplish veins	24″	−30°F
'Katherine Adele'	Pale pink/purple veins	16″	−30°F

Similar in appearance to *Geranium endressii* (Pyrenean Cranesbill), one of the parents. 'Claridge Druce' forms a vigorous clump of large, gray-green leaves and tolerates some shade. Though these plants flower heavily in early summer, they do bloom on and off for the rest of the season. Cut back after flowering.

VARIETY	COLOR	HEIGHT	HARDINESS
Geranium phaeum			
(Mourning Widow)	Dark maroon	24″	−30°F
'Album'	White/brown veins	24″	−30°F
'Lily Lovell'	Deep mauve	30″	−30°F
'Samobor'	Purple brown	24″	−30°F

The appearance of the very dark, nodding flowers which first open in late spring give this plant its common name. These are very tough plants which tolerate some shade and fairly dry soils. They have a look totally unlike any of the other Cranesbills. They do have a tendency to self-seed.

Geranium platypetalum			
(Broad-petaled Cranesbill)	Deep purple	24″	−40°F

This is a fine plant flowering from late spring into early summer.

Geranium pratense			
(Meadow Cranesbill)			
'Black Beauty'*****	Lavender blue	16″	−30°F
'Hocus Pocus'	Lavender blue	16″	−30°F
'Midnight Reiter'	Lavender blue	8″	−30°F
'Mrs. Kendall Clark'	Sky blue with white veins	24″	−30°F
'Okey Dokey'	Purple blue	20″	−30°F

These are vigorous, upright plants which flower in late spring. They will sometimes rebloom if old flower stalks are removed. All have distinctive, purplish foliage with the exception of 'Mrs. Kendall Clark.'

Geranium psilostemon			
(Armenium Cranesbill)	Magenta/black center	48″	−30°F

This tall Cranesbill has striking two-inch flowers that appear in midsummer on stems which may require support.

Geranium rectum var. *album* (see *Geranium clarkei* 'Kashmir White')

*Geranium renardii******	White/violet veins	12″	−30°F

Although this species is valued mostly for its foliage, it does produce attractive flowers in late spring. Its gray-green, lobed leaves have a delightful velvety appearance throughout the season. This plant grows slowly and demands a well-drained soil.

*Geranium sanguineum******			
(Bloody Cranesbill)	Reddish purple	12″	−40°F
'Album'	White	16″	−40°F
'Alpenglow'	Rose red	18″	−40°F
'Ankum's Pride'	Bright pink/rose veins	8″	−40°F
'Cedric Morris'	Reddish purple	12″	−40°F
'Drake's Pink'	Soft pink/pink veins	12″	−40°F
'Elke'	Rich pink edged white	10″	−40°F
'Elsbeth'	Dark magenta	18″	−40°F
'John Elsley'	Carmine	10″	−40°F
'Max Frei'	Reddish purple	10″	−40°F
'New Hampshire Purple'	Deep reddish purple	18″	−40°F

VARIETY	COLOR	HEIGHT	HARDINESS
'Purple Flame'	Reddish purple/red veins	12″	−40°F
'Shepherd's Warning'	Deep rose pink	6″	−40°F
var. *striatum* (var. *lancastriense*)	Pale pink/crimson veins	8″	−40°F
'Vision'	Magenta/purple veins	14″	−40°F

These Cranesbills form low mounds of deeply lobed, dark green foliage which turns deep red in autumn. They make good ground covers and flower profusely in early summer. Many of the named varieties like 'Alpenglow,' 'Cedric Morris,' and 'New Hampshire Purple' will continue to flower intermittently throughout the rest of the summer. 'Shepherd's Warning' is best as a rock garden plant. Bloody Cranesbills are remarkably tolerant of dry sites.

Geranium sylvaticum

(Wood Cranesbill)	Violet blue/white center	30″	−40°F
'Album'	White	24″	−40°F
'Amy Doncaster'	Violet blue/white center	24″	−40°F
'Mayflower'	Light blue/white center	24″	−40°F

This upright Cranesbill blooms for a number of weeks in spring. It requires evenly moist soil and light shade.

Geranium wallichianum

(Wallich Cranesbill)			
'Buxton's Variety' ('Buxton's Blue')*****	Clear blue/white center	8″	−30°F

This is a low trailing plant with leaves marked by silky white hairs. It flowers in late summer and takes on an attractive fall foliage color. Wallich Cranesbill prefers a cool moist soil in full sun or light shade.

Geranium (Named varieties and hybrids)

'Brookside'	Sapphire blue/white center	18″	−30°F
'Carol'	Fuchsia purple/wine veins	8″	−20°F
'Dily's'	Reddish purple	12″	−30°F
'Johnson's Blue'	Clear blue/white center	18″	−30°F
'Jolly Bee'*****	Lavender blue/white center	24″	−30°F
'Nimbus'	Blue rose/reddish veins	24″	−30°F
'Orion'*****	Mid blue/reddish veins	24″	−30°F
'Patricia'	Magenta/maroon center	24″	−30°F
'Phillippe Vapelle'	Bluish purple/dark veins	16″	−40°F
'Rozanne'	Violet blue/lighter center	20″	−25°F
'Spinners'	Purple blue	30″	−30°F
'Tiny Monster'	Purple red/dark veins	18″	−30°F

'Brookside' has a nice rounded form. 'Johnson's Blue' sprawls a bit so cut it back after flowering. 'Brookside,' 'Nimbus,' and 'Orion' are proving to be superior to 'Johnson's Blue.' 'Orion' also appears to tolerate heat and humidity well. 'Rozanne,' with its rich color and long bloom season, is one of the most popular geraniums.

'Silver Feather'/'Silberfeder'

GRASSES

Bloom Time	Expected Longevity	Maintenance	Years to Bloom	Preferred Light
Spring to fall	25+ years	Low	From seed: 3 to 5 years From potted plant: 2 years	Variable

Grasses are grown for their varied foliage and unique flowers. Their leaves provide pleasing form and texture throughout the growing season and well into winter. Foliage colors range from shades of green to yellow, tan, bronze, blue, and reddish purple. Some blend colors in distinctive patterns. The flowers range from bold to subtle, and the seed heads that follow can vary as well. The mature seed plumes of certain varieties are highly valued for use in dried arrangements. Many Grasses wave gracefully and rustle in even the slightest breeze, bringing landscapes to life. They are easy to grow, increase rapidly, require minimal maintenance, last for years, and are generally disease and insect free. In recent years, Grasses have undergone widespread field testing in cold climates, and many are proving hardier than once believed.

How Grasses Grow

Each Grass has its own distinct pattern of growth. Most form clumps, but a handful spread rapidly by creeping rhizomes to form large colonies. Place these

'Elijah Blue'

'Karl Foerster'

'Malepartus'

Miscanthus sinensis 'Variegatus'

VARIETY	FOLIAGE COLOR	HEIGHT	HARDINESS

Andropogon scoparius (see *Schizachyrium scoparium*)

Andropogon sibiricus (see *Spodiopogon sibiricus*)

Arrhenatherum elatius

(Bulbous Oat Grass)	Deep green	12″	–30°F
'Variegatum'*****	Green/white striping	12″	–30°F

This cool-season Grass with stunning foliage but insignificant flowers thrives in most soils except heavy clay and does well in full sun or light shade. Keep the soil evenly moist at all times. If foliage is damaged by drought, cut it back to the ground.

Asperella patula (see *Hystrix patula*)

Bouteloua curtipendula

(Side Oats Gramma)	Gray green	24″	–40°F

This clump-forming, warm-season Grass gets its name from the way its midsummer flowers are arranged on one side of the stem. These mature into seed heads that remain attractive into fall. This Grass grows best in full sun and tolerates dry sites.

Bouteloua gracilis

(Blue Gramma)	Light green gray	24″	–40°F

This fine-textured, warm-season Grass has curious blooms attached to stems at a right angle. The silvery white flowers appear in summer and mature into purplish seed heads when mature. Plant in well-drained soils and full sun.

Briza media

(Quacking Grass)	Green	24″	–30°F

A clump-forming, cool-season plant, Quacking Grass produces interesting heart-shaped seeds in summer which make a "quacking" noise in wind. This plant will grow in poor soils, but prefers full sun.

Calamagrostis × *acutiflora*****

(Feather Reed Grass)			
'Avalanche'	Green/white centers	60″	–40°F
'Eldorado'	Green/gold centers	60″	–40°F
'Karl Foerster' ('Stricta')	Medium green	72″	–40°F
'Overdam'	Green/white margins	60″	–40°F

Feather Reed Grass is a superb cool-season Grass that makes an excellent vertical accent plant. Bronzy purple flower heads appear in early summer and fade to an attractive light buff. This Grass will grow in many soil types and is best planted in full sun for finest flowering. Keep the soil evenly moist for best results.

Calamagrostis brachytricha

(Fall-blooming Reed Grass)	Deep green	48″	–30°F

This Korean native warm-season Grass has proven to be much hardier than first expected. Flowers open in fall with a greenish cast quickly turning into a wonderful rose purple at peak bloom. The fluffy seed heads which follow are buff with a light lavender cast, but they are only showy for a brief period. Place this plant where it can self-sow freely. This Grass grows best in full sun but tolerates light shade.

VARIETY	FOLIAGE COLOR	HEIGHT	HARDINESS
Carex caryophyllea			
(Mop-headed Sedge)			
'Beatlemania'*****	Green/yellow margins	6″	−30°F
'The Beatles'	Green	6″	−30°F

This cool-season European Sedge is grown for its long, narrow, cascading leaves that create a mop head effect. It spreads slowly into an attractive small-scale ground cover. Place it in light shade and keep the soil consistently moist.

Carex flacca			
(Blue Sedge)	Blue gray	6″	−30°F
'Blue Zinger'	Blue gray	10″	−30°F

This is another cool-season European sedge with nicely textured foliage. It makes a good ground cover in full sun or light shade. 'Blue Zinger' forms an upright, tight clump of foliage. Keep the soil evenly moist throughout the season.

Carex glauca (see *Carex flacca*)

*Carex muskingumensis*****			
(Palm Sedge)	Green	36″	−40°F
'Ice Fountains'	Green/vareigated white in spring	24″	−40°F
'Little Midge'	Green	12″	−40°F
'Oehme'	Green/yellow margins	20″	−40°F
'Wachtposten'	Green	36″	−40°F

This cool-season Sedge has foliage reminiscent of palm fronds and turns yellowish green in bright light. 'Wachtposten' has the most upright form. Palm Sedge grows well in full sun or light shade but requires consistently moist soil.

Carex nigra			
(Black-flowering Sedge)	Blue gray	9″	−30°F
'Variegata'	Blue gray/gold edges	9″	−30°F

Black-flowering Sedge is valued for its wonderful foliage color and its ability to grow in light shade. The flowers are insignificant. This cool-season Sedge requires constant moisture and will even grow in shallow water.

*Carex pensylvanica*****			
(Pennsylvania Sedge)	Dark green	12″	−40°F

This cool-season species native to woodlands in the Eastern United States has fine textured foliage but insignificant flowers. It spreads slowly and tolerates dry sites.

Carex siderosticha			
(Variegated Broad-leaved Sedge)			
'Variegata'	Green/edged cream/white centers	12″	−30°F

Grown for attractive foliage, this cool-season Sedge is a durable ground cover in evenly moist, partially shaded locations.

Chasmanthium latifolium

(Northern Sea Oats)	Green	48″	–30°F

This lovely warm-season Grass with its unusual oat-shaped seeds is prized for fresh and dried arrangements. It may die out, but is likely to self-seed. It needs moist to wet soils and will grow in a wide variety of light conditions.

Chondrosum gracile (see *Bouteloua gracilis*)

Chrysopogon nutans (see *Sorghastrum nutans*)

---

*Deschampsia cespitosa******

(Tufted Hair Grass)	Deep green	36″	–40°F
'Bronze Veil' ('Bronzeschleier')	Deep green	36″	–40°F
'Gold Pendant' ('Goldgehänge')	Deep green	36″	–40°F
'Schottland'	Deep green	48″	–40°F

This is a fine-textured, cool-season Grass with nearly evergreen foliage. Flowers appear in early summer with seed heads lasting well into fall. Most of the varieties were selected for their flower colors: 'Bronze Veil' (bronze yellow), 'Gold Pendant' (golden yellow), and 'Schottland' (chartreuse yellow). The flowers and seed heads are delightful in arrangements. These plants will grow in full sun or light shade but require evenly moist soil throughout the growing season. These plants are most commonly sold under their German names.

Elymus arenarius (see *Leymus arenarius*)

Elymus glaucus (see *Leymus arenarius*)

Festuca amethystina

(Sheep's Fescue)			
'Bronzeglanz'	Green blue	12″	–30°F
'Klose'	Olive green shaded blue	10″	–30°F

This is a striking cool-season Grass grown more for its fine texture and foliage color than for its early summer flowers. It survives only in well-drained soil in full sun. To prolong its life, divide every third year.

Festuca glauca

(Blue Fescue)			
'Boulder Blue'*****	Intense silvery blue	10″	–30°F
'Elijah Blue'	Silvery blue	10″	–30°F
'Harz'	Olive green	10″	–30°F
'Sea Blue' ('Meerblau')	Blue green	10″	–30°F
'Sea Urchin' ('Seeigel')	Steel blue	10″	–30°F
'Solling'	Blue gray	8″	–30°F
'Superba'	Blue green	12″	–30°F

These cool-season Grasses form compact clumps that are most intensely colored in spring. They are grown for their foliage, not for their flowers. 'Solling' is a very fine-textured selection that does not even produce flowers. The plants do best in full sun. They need well drained soil or they may die out.

Festuca ovina var. *glauca* (see *Festuca glauca*)

VARIETY	FOLIAGE COLOR	HEIGHT	HARDINESS

Glyceria aquatica 'Variegata' (see *Glyceria maxima* 'Variegata')

Glyceria maxima
(Variegated Manna Grass)

'Variegata'	Green/creamy striping	36″	–30°F

This cool-season Grass relishes very moist soils like those found on the edges of ponds and streams. It is a vigorous spreader and should be planted in full sun to enhance variegation.

Hakonechloa macra
(Hakone Grass)

	Olive green	24″	–30°F
'Aureola'	Yellow/green striping	24″	–30°F

Grown for its handsome arching leaves (not flowers), this slow-growing, warm-season Japanese native adds texture to the landscape. Plant this Grass in soil with lots of organic matter. Place it in light shade and keep the soil evenly moist.

*Helictotrichon sempervirens*****
(Blue Oat Grass)

	Glaucous blue	36″	–30°F
'Sapphire' ('Sparkling Sapphire')			
('Saphirsprudel')	Deep blue	36″	–30°F

This cool-season Grass rarely blooms in cold climates. The mound of blue foliage has a medium to fine texture. When planted in a well-drained soil in full sun, this Grass will grow well for years without division. It can tolerate dry conditions.

Hystrix patula
(Bottlebrush Grass)

	Olive green	36″	–40°F

This cool-season Grass can be short-lived, but usually self-seeds. Its greenish, bottlebrush-like flowers are lovely in summer. It prefers light shade and a moist yet well-drained soil. It can be grown in full sun if the soil is kept consistently moist.

Leymus arenarius
(Blue Lyme Grass)

	Glaucous blue	36″	–40°F
'Blue Dune'	Bright blue gray	36″	–40°F

The foliage color on this cool-season Grass is striking, but flowers minimal. Blue Lyme Grass can be valuable in controlling soil erosion since it spreads aggressively. Plant it where this will not be a problem.

Luzula nivea
(Snowy Woodrush)

	Gray green	24″	–30°F

Most Grasses grow best in full sun, but this cool-season Grass actually prefers partial shade. The leaves are edged with soft white hairs, and small plumes of showy white flowers appear in spring. Keep soil evenly moist throughout the season.

Miscanthus
(Red Flame Miscanthus)

'Purpurascens'*****	Medium green	60″	–40°F

The foliage of this very fine warm-season Grass takes on a reddish cast by midsummer if grown in an evenly moist soil. Its silvery white plumes are particularly showy in late summer and early fall. This Grass grows best in full sun.

VARIETY	FOLIAGE COLOR	HEIGHT	HARDINESS
Miscanthus sinensis			
(Japanese Silver Grass)			
'Far East' ('Ferner Osten')	Green/white midrib	60″	−20°F
'Graziella'	Green/white midrib	66″	−20°F
'Helga Reich'	Green/white midrib	60″	−20°F
'Herkules'	Green/white midrib	66″	−20°F
'Kirk Alexander'	Green/horizontal yellow bands	66″	−20°F
'Little Dot' ('Puenktchen')	Green/horizontal yellow bands	66″	−20°F
'Malepartus'*****	Green/white midrib	96″	−30°F
'Positano'	Green/white midrib	72″	−20°F
'Purpurascens' (see *Miscanthus* 'Purpurascens')			
'Red Silver' ('Rotsilber')	Green/white midrib	66″	−30°F
'Silver Arrow' ('Silberpfeil')*****	Dark green/white striping	66″	−30°F
'Silver Feather' ('Silberfeder')	Green/white midrib	120″	−30°F
'Silver Spider' ('Silberspinne')	Green/white midrib	66″	−20°F
'Undine'	Green/white midrib	66″	−20°F
'Variegatus'	Dark green/white striping	84″	−20°F

These warm-season Grasses are grown for their lovely flowers but are marginally hardy with 'Malepartus' and 'Silver Feather' proving to be the hardiest. These plants need warm soil temperatures to get them off to a good start in spring. They prefer moist, rich soil in full sun. Place them where possible self-seeding will not be a problem.

Molinia altissima (see *Molinia arundinacea*)			
*Molinia arundinacea*****			
(Tall Moor Grass)			
'Bergfreund'	Light gray green	84″	−30°F
'Karl Foerster'	Light gray green	84″	−30°F
'Skyracer'	Light gray green	96″	−30°F
'Transparent'	Light gray green	72″	−30°F
'Windspiel'	Light gray green	84″	−30°F

These cool-season Grasses are particularly lovely when back- or side-lit against a dark background. They have been referred to as "see-through" Grasses because of their very tall, fine-textured blooms held on long stems well above the low foliage mounds. They have wonderful architectural qualities and sway seductively in the breeze. The flowers open with a purplish cast turning golden yellow by fall. Plant them in full sun or light shade in consistently moist soil.

*Molinia caerulea*****			
(Purple Moor Grass)			
'Moorflamme'	Light green	48″	−30°F
'Moorhexe'	Light green	36″	−30°F
'Strahlenquelle'	Light green	48″	−30°F
'Variegata'	Light green/white striping	30″	−30°F

These cool-season Grasses are easy to grow, mature slowly, but are worth the wait. The foliage and the summer-blooming flower heads are fine-textured. 'Variegata' requires light shade. Grow them in moist, fertile soil.

VARIETY	FOLIAGE COLOR	HEIGHT	HARDINESS

Molinia litoralis (see *Molinia arundinacea*)

Panicum virgatum

(Switch Grass)	Green	84″	−40°F
'Cheyenne Sky'	Green/reddish purple tones	36″	−40°F
'Dallas Blues'	Blue	72″	−30°F
'Haense Herms' ('Rotstrahlbusch')	Green	48″	−40°F
'Heavy Metal'	Metallic blue	60″	−30°F
'Northwind'*****	Blue green	60″	−40°F
'Shenandoah'	Green/reddish purple tones	36″	−40°F
'Strictum'	Light blue green	72″	−30°F

This warm-season prairie native forms handsome upright clumps with pleasing fall color. The airy flower heads, appearing in late summer, are green with a pinkish cast most prominent in varieties whose foliage takes on reddish tones. 'Heavy Metal' is stiffly upright with metallic blue leaves that turn bright yellow in fall. 'Northwind' is the best upright Switch Grass for cold climate regions. The foliage of 'Cheyenne Sky' and 'Shenandoah' shows reddish purple tones by midsummer. Switch Grasses grow well in a variety of soil conditions but need sun for best color.

Phalaris arundinacea

(Ribbon Grass)			
'Feesey' ('Strawberries and Cream')	White striped blushed pink	30″	−40°F
'Picta'	Green/white striping	48″	−40°F

This cool-season Grass grown for its variegated foliage (not flowers) can spread aggressively. 'Feesey' is slightly less invasive and offers a better and longer lasting variegation, often pink early in the season. If foliage turns pure green, cut the plant down. Variegated leaves will reappear. Plant Ribbon Grass in a moist soil in full sun or light shade.

Schizachyrium scoparium

(Little Bluestem)	Light green to blue	48″	−40°F
Blue Heaven™*****	Blue gray	48″	−40°F
'Carousel'	Blue green	30″	−40°F

This warm-season, prairie Grass forms a dense clump of medium-textured leaves. The silvery white seed heads and its foliage color make this a knockout in the fall landscape. 'Carousel' has a vertical look and fall color that includes shades of copper, pink, beige, and mahogany. Blue Heaven™ also has a strong upright appearance, but its fall foliage color is a stunning burgundy red with purplish violet highlights. These plants need good soil drainage to flourish.

*Sesleria autumnalis*****

(Autumn Moor Grass)	Yellow green	18″	−30°F

This cool-season Grass forms a neat mound of foliage with yellow-green leaves of medium to fine texture and insignificant flowers. Plant this Grass in full sun or very light shade and provide it with consistent moisture.

Sesleria caerulea

(Blue Moor Grass)	Bluish green	15″	−30°F

The foliage of this cool-season Grass is lovely. Place the plant in full sun or light shade and keep soil evenly moist.

Sorghastrum avenaceum (see *Sorghastrum nutans*)

VARIETY	FOLIAGE COLOR	HEIGHT	HARDINESS
Sorghastrum nutans*****			
(Indian Grass)	Green to blue gray	84″	−40°F
'Sioux Blue'	Metallic blue	84″	−40°F

This fine, upright warm-season Grass produces bronzy yellow flowers in late summer and early fall. The flowers with bright yellow protruding anthers are simply stunning at peak bloom. Fall foliage color varies from golden yellow to almost burnt orange, and the golden brown seed heads remain showy into early winter. This plant is easy to grow and will tolerate considerable drought once mature. It is valuable in both fresh and dried arrangements.

Spartina michauxiana (see *Spartina pectinata*)

Spartina pectinata			
(Prairie Cord Grass)	Glossy green	96″	−40°F
'Aureomarginata' ('Variegata')	Green/narrow gold margins	84″	−40°F

This is a spreading warm-season Grass native to the wet prairies and sloughs of North America. It has wonderful, arching leaves which seem to be moving even when there is no breeze. It blooms in late summer with purplish green flowers, and the leaves turn bright yellow in fall. It is best planted along the edges of ponds and streams in full sun.

Spodiopogon sibiricus*****			
(Silver Spike Grass)	Dark green	60″	−40°F

This warm-season Grass makes an excellent specimen plant with bold horizontal foliage contrasting beautifully with vertical, fine-textured blooms. The flowers appear in summer and the seed heads generally shatter by late fall. If Silver Spike Grass is planted in full sun, the foliage often turns reddish purple in fall. This Grass prefers cool, moist sites.

Sporobolus heterolepis*****			
(Prairie Dropseed)	Emerald green	36″	−40°F
'Tara'	Emerald green	24″	−40°F

This delightful, warm-season prairie native is fine-textured in all respects. Its narrow leaves form a low mound of foliage that appears to have been swirled in place by the wind. The plant blooms from late summer to early fall and is noted for the popcorn-like fragrance of its seed heads. The foliage turns golden orange in fall and is dramatic in the early morning or late afternoon light. 'Tara' has a more upright appearance. Consider these plants as replacements for the popular but tender *Pennisetum alopecuroides* (Fountain Grass). Prairie Dropseed prefers full sun and is quite drought tolerant.

'Karat'

HELIOPSIS HELIANTHOIDES

(hee-lee-OP-suhs heel-lee-ann-THOY-dees)

OXEYE

Bloom Time	Expected Longevity	Maintenance	Years to Bloom	Preferred Light
Summer to early fall	10+ years	Low	From seed: 2 years From potted plant: 1 year	Full sun to light shade

Oxeye is among the earliest blooming of the summer-flowering yellow daisies. It offers bright color, a long bloom season, good pest resistance, and excellent cut flowers. Oxeye produces flowers up to 4 inches (10 cm) across. The blooms come in single, semidouble, and double forms. The named varieties are preferable to the species, since they are more compact and less likely to require staking.

How Oxeyes Grow

Oxeye develops from strong, fibrous roots into a bushy plant with deep green, toothed leaves. The flowers look like small Sunflowers, with centers often deeper in color than the ray petals. The plant increases quickly and produces more stems and flowers each year. Any naturally occurring seedlings from the named selections probably will not be identical to their parents.

Where to Plant

Site and Light Oxeye can be grown in full sun or light shade but flowers much more freely in bright light. Avoid very windy areas, or you may have to stake the plants.

Soil and Moisture Oxeye is a tough plant capable of surviving in a wide range of soils. It prefers average to highly fertile soil with lots of organic matter. Mix leaf mold, compost, rotted manure, or peat moss into the soil. Replace clay or rocky soil with good soil or build a raised bed. Oxeyes die out in compacted soils. Although Oxeye tolerates short dry periods, it does poorly in droughts.

Spacing Place Oxeye approximately 18 to 24 inches (45 to 60 cm) from the nearest plant. These perennials form large clumps as they mature and need adequate space to develop fully.

Companions

Heliopsis (Oxeye) is stunning placed next to pastel colors, especially pinks of perennials such as *Achillea* (Yarrow), *Hemerocallis* (Daylily), and *Phlox* (Garden Phlox). Other good companions are *Aster* × *frikartii* (Frikart's Aster), *Leucanthemum*–Superbum Group (Shasta Daisy), *Liatris* (Gayfeather), *Monarda* (Bee Balm), and *Veronica* (Speedwell). Oxeyes also look great with showy summer **Grasses** such as *Calamagrostis* × *acutiflora* 'Overdam' (Feather Reed Grass) and *Miscanthus* 'Purpurascens' (Red Flame Miscanthus).

Planting

Bare Root Plant bare root stock as soon as you can work the ground in spring. Remove plants from their shipping package immediately. Snip off broken or damaged root tips. Soak plants overnight in room-temperature water. Place a small amount of superphosphate in the base of the planting hole. Fill the hole with soil. Place the crown 1 inch (2.5 cm) below the soil surface. Fill in with soil, firm with your fingers, and water immediately. Dissolve ½ cup (about 114 g) 10-10-10 fertilizer in 1 gallon (about 4 liters) of water. Pour ½ cup (about 120 ml) of this starter solution around the base of each plant. If you prefer organic fertilizer, use fish emulsion instead.

Potted Plants Plant potted Oxeyes after all danger of frost has passed in spring. If the soil in the pot is dry, soak it, and let it drain overnight. Tap the plant from the pot without disturbing the root ball. Plant it at the same depth as in the pot, after preparing the hole in a similar manner to that for a bare root plant. Fill in with soil, firm with your fingers, and water immediately. Pour ½ cup (about 120 ml) starter solution around the base of each plant.

How to Care for Oxeyes

Water Keep the soil evenly moist throughout the growing season for best results. Saturate the soil to a depth of 8 inches (20 cm) each time you water.

Mulch Place 2 inches (5 cm) of mulch around the base of each plant as soon as the ground warms up in spring. Good mulches include dried grass clippings, shredded leaves, pine needles, and shredded bark.

Fertilizing Oxeyes are heavy feeders. Sprinkle 10-10-10 fertilizer around the base of each plant just as new growth emerges in spring. Water immediately to dissolve the granules and move nutrients into the root zone. Follow up with light biweekly applications of 10-10-10 right into the flowering season, or alternate with liquid foliar feeding.

If you prefer organic fertilizer, use alfalfa meal (rabbit pellets), blood meal, bonemeal, compost, cow manure, fish emulsion, Milorganite, or rotted horse manure. Bonemeal must be mixed into the soil at planting time to be effective.

Weeding The use of a summer mulch keeps most annual weeds in check. Any that do sprout are easily pulled by hand. Avoid deep cultivation around these perennials, as they are fairly shallow-rooted.

Staking The named selections are the most compact and sturdy. However, in very windy locations, even these may require staking. Tie the stems loosely to stakes in loose, figure-eight knots.

Deadheading Regular removal of all spent flowers encourages additional bloom and extends the flowering season. It also makes plants much more attractive and prevents the named selections from self-sowing.

Winter Protection Mature plants are very hardy and should not require any winter protection other than normal snowfall. If there is no snow by early December, it may be good insurance to cover the crowns with 6 inches (15 cm) of mulch. Recommended are marsh hay, clean straw, pine needles, or whole leaves. Remove the mulch as soon as the weather begins to warm up in spring.

Problems

Insects Oxeye is occasionally bothered by aphids, especially during hot, dry spells. In most cases, you can wash these away with spray from a hose or kill them with an insecticidal soap. Fourlined plant bug is another nuisance. It causes spotting on the upper leaf surface that may mimic fungal leaf spot diseases. This is usually more of an aesthetic rather than a health issue. We don't recommend spraying for this.

Disease These tough, durable plants are rarely bothered by disease.

Propagation

Division Although Oxeye does not require frequent division for good health, it is very easily propagated by this means. Also, if you notice a clump beginning to die out in the center, it is time to divide it. Dig up the plant in early spring just as new growth begins.

Knock off excess soil, and wash the clump clean to make division easier. With a sharp spade or knife, cut the clump into sections, making sure that each one has three or four shoots and a healthy root system. Discard the old central portion of the crown. Plant these new divisions in the same way as you would a bare root plant.

Cuttings Oxeye is very easy to root from cuttings. Take cuttings from early to midspring before the plants start to form flower buds. Each cutting should have several sets of leaves. Make the final cut a quarter inch (6 mm) below a leaf node. Remove all but the upper set of leaves. Dip the cut ends in rooting hormone, and tap off any excess powder. Plant the cuttings in rooting medium, and keep the medium evenly moist with high humidity around the cuttings as they root. After the cuttings have formed strong root systems, pot them up.

Seed This perennial germinates very readily from seed, but only the species, 'Midwest Dreams,' and 'Summer Sun' are normally true to type. Seed started about 12 weeks before the last expected frost in spring may result in some flowers late the first year. Sow over moist germination medium, leaving the seed uncovered. Slip the tray into a plastic bag, and keep the temperature at 68°F to 70°F (20°C to 21°C). Seed generally sprouts between 3 and 14 days after sowing, and the seedlings should be ready for transplanting 2 to 3 weeks after this. Grow them on in individual pots in a bright, warm area. Harden them off for 14 days before planting outside after all danger of frost has passed in spring.

Special Uses

Cut Flowers Oxeye produces attractive daisylike flowers which are excellent for cutting. Cut the stems just as the first flowers are opening, and place them in a bucket of water immediately. Take the cut stems indoors, and put them into 110°F (43°C) water. Let the stems sit in this water overnight, and arrange them the following day. Remove foliage that would end up below the water in the final arrangement.

Dried Flowers This perennial is not generally recommended for drying. However, you could certainly try to dry individual flowers in a desiccant if you choose.

Sources

Ambergate Gardens, 8730 County Rd. 43, Chaska, MN 55318, (877) 211-9769

Bluestone Perennials, 7211 Middle Ridge Rd., Madison, OH 44057, (800) 852-5243

Busse Gardens, 17160 245th Ave., Big Lake, MN 55309, (800) 544-3192

Garden Place, 6780 Heisley Rd., PO Box 388, Mentor, OH 44061

White Flower Farm, P.O. Box 50, Litchfield, CT 06759, (800) 503-9624

'Karat'

VARIETIES

VARIETY	FLOWER/FOLIAGE	FORM	HEIGHT	HARDINESS
Heliopsis helianthoides				
(False Sunflower)	Golden yellow/green	Single	60″	−40°F
'Asahi'	Golden yellow/green	Double pompon (large)	30″	−40°F
'Ballerina' ('Spitzentanzerin')*****	Orange yellow/green	Semi-double	48″	−40°F
'Bressingham Doubloon'	Golden yellow/green	Semi-double	60″	−40°F
'Golden Plume' ('Goldgefieder')	Golden yellow/green	Double (large)	30″	−40°F
'Gold Greenheart' ('Goldgrunherz')	Yellow with green center/green	Double	40″	−40°F
'Loraine Sunshine'	Gold yellow/white green veins	Single	36″	−40°F
'Karat'	Bright golden yellow/green	Single (very large)	48″	−40°F
'Midwest Dreams'	Orange yellow/green	Single	36″	−40°F
'Prairie Sunset'	Gold yellow/green/purple stems	Single	60″	−40°F
'Summer Nights'*****	Gold yellow/green/purple stems	Single	48″	−40°F
'Summer Sun' ('Sommersonne')	Yellow gold/green	Semi-double	40″	−40°F
'Tuscan Sun'	Golden yellow/green	Single	20″	−30°F
'Venus'*****	Clear yellow/green	Semi-double (very large)	36″	−40°F

'Raspberry Frolic'

HEMEROCALLIS

(hem-er-oh-KAL-us)

DAYLILY

BLOOM TIME	EXPECTED LONGEVITY	MAINTENANCE	YEARS TO BLOOM	PREFERRED LIGHT
Spring to late summer	25+ years	Low	From seed: 3 years From potted plant: 1 year	Full sun to light shade

Daylilies have taken the country by storm, becoming one of the most popular hardy perennials. The plants are not true Lilies but produce a lilylike bloom, occasionally with a fragrant scent. Daylilies are a tough plant, withstand considerable abuse, and spread prolifically, virtually lasting forever. Their blooms come in a stunning array of colors and, although short-lived, are replaced almost immediately by new blooms. The individual blooms are among the most beautiful in the garden, and collectively form one of the most magnificent displays imaginable.

How Daylilies Grow

Most Daylilies form a thick, fibrous root system with tuberous-like structures. These roots are connected to stem tissue (a crown) from which springs a thick clump of pointed leaves. Flower stems (scapes) shoot up from the clumps and are usually leafless. Each stem can produce up to 30 flowers, although a few will top 100. Most of the blooms last only a day (a few last 36 hours), which is why these plants are commonly called Daylilies. Although most Daylilies bloom during the day, several varieties bloom at night. The plants form increasingly larger clumps as they mature.

Where to Plant

Site and Light In cooler areas, Daylilies prefer full sun all day long. If your summers tend to be hot and dry, Daylilies prefer full sun during the morning and some shade in the afternoon.

Light does affect flower color. On a cloudy day or in partial shade, colors may be different from the way they appear in full sun. Some growers recommend placing certain-colored Daylilies in shade to get a richer color. Generally, this is not applicable in colder climates. Plants grow more vigorously in full sun, and this is a more important consideration.

Soil and Moisture Daylilies do well in a wide variety of soils, but they need good drainage. Do not plant them in soggy lowlands. If soil is too compacted, the roots will rot during the winter. Compaction is common in clay soils. Replace these with loam or build a raised bed. To any soil, add copious amounts of organic material, such as compost, peat moss, rotted manures, and leaf mold. Ideal soil amendments are peat moss and rotted oak leaves, since they are slightly acidic—the soil condition favored by Daylilies.

Spacing Space according to the potential size of the plant. Plants spread widely, so give them plenty of room for good air circulation. Plant in groups of three to five for best effect.

Companions

Hemerocallis (Daylily) are stunning in mass plantings or drifts along walls, streams, or ponds, or in the shrub border. On slopes, they are effective as a living mulch which not only stabilizes the soil but also provides a beautiful display of flowers. Use them to hide the dying foliage of spring bulbs such as *Narcissus* (Daffodil) and *Tulipa* (Tulip). Those with repeat bloom make good container plants. In the border, they look best in groups or as bold specimen plants combined with *Asclepias tuberosa* (Butterfly Milkweed), *Echinacea* (Purple Coneflower), *Geranium* (Cranesbill), *Heliopsis* (False Sunflower), *Leucanthemum*–Superbum Group (Shasta Daisy), *Liatris* (Gayfeather), *Nepeta* (Catmint), *Phlox* (Garden Phlox), *Platycodon* (Balloon Flower), and *Tradescantia* (Spiderwort).

Planting

Bare Root Plant bare root stock as soon as you can work the ground in spring. Remove the plants from their shipping package immediately. Snip off broken or damaged root tips. Soak plants overnight in room-temperature water. Place a small amount of superphosphate in the base of the planting hole. Fill the hole with soil. Place the crown just barely below the soil surface. Fill in with soil, firm with your fingers, and water immediately. Dissolve ½ cup (about 114 g) 10-10-10 fertilizer in 1 gallon (about 4 liters) of water. Pour ½ cup (about 120 ml) of this starter solution around the base of the plant. If you prefer organic fertilizer, use fish emulsion instead.

Potted Plants Plant potted Daylilies after all danger of frost has passed in spring. If the soil in the pot is dry, soak it, and let the plant drain overnight. Tap the plant out of the pot the following day, keeping the entire root ball intact. Plant it at the same depth as in the pot, after preparing the hole in a similar manner to that for a bare root plant. Fill in with soil, firm with your fingers, and water immediately. Pour ½ cup (about 120 ml) starter solution around the base of each plant.

How to Care for Daylilies

Water Water young plants consistently. Mature Daylilies are drought tolerant but will drop buds if conditions are too dry.

Mulch Daylilies respond well to mulch, which keeps the soil moist and cool around the base of the plant. Mulch also stops many weeds from sprouting and competing with the Daylilies for nutrients and water. Use organic mulches such as dried grass clippings, shredded leaves (especially oak), pine needles, or compost. Avoid placing the mulch against the crown of the plant.

Andre Viette Farm & Nursery, P.O. Box 1109, Fishersville, VA 22939, (540) 943-2315

Archway Daylily Gardens, 700 Gillespie Dr., Manhattan, KS 66502, (785) 539-7772

Bloomingfields Farm, P.O. Box 5, Gaylordsville, CT 06755, (860) 354-6951

Bloom River Gardens, 39744 Deerhorn Rd., Spriongfield, OR 97478, (541) 726-8997

Crochet Daylily Garden, P.O. Box 425, Prairieville, LA 70769, (225) 673-8491

Day Bloomers Garden, 883 Oconee Springs Rd., Eatonton, GA 31024, 706) 485-2175

Edith's Daylilies, 2145 Hwy 255, Clarkesville, GA 30523, (706) 947-3683

Fieldstone Gardens, Inc., 55 Quaker Lane, Vassalboro, ME 04989, (207) 923-3836

Garden Perennials, 85261 Hwy 15, Wayne, NE 68787, (402) 375-3615

Gilbert H. Wild & Son, 2994 State Hwy 37, Reeds, MO 64859, (888) 449-4537

Gold City Flower Gardens, 6298 Gold City Rd., Franklin, KY 42134, (270) 776-6584

Gratrix Garden Lilies, P.O. Box 186, Coldwater, ON LoK 1E0 Canada, (705) 835-6794

Hornbaker Gardens, 22937 1140 N Ave., Princeton, IL 61356, (815) 659-3282

Klehm's Song Sparrow Perennial Farm, 13101 E Rye Rd., Avalon, WI 53505, (800) 553-3715

LaCygne Daylily Farm, 21117 E 2100 Rd., LaCygne, KS 66040, (913) 757-2030

Midnight Gardens, 16869 SW 65th Ave., Lake Oswego, OR 97035, (503) 889-6819

North Pine Gardens, P.O. Box 595, Norfolk, NE 68701, (402) 371-3895

Oakes Daylilies, P.O. Box 268, Corryton, TN 37721, (800) 532-9545

Olalie Daylily Gardens, 129 Augur Hole Rd., South Newfane, VT 05351, (802) 348-6614

Renaissance Garden, 1047 Baron Rd., Weddington, NC 28173, (704) 843-5370

Ric-A-Tee Daylily Gardens, 4007 State Hwy 134E, Headland, AL 36345, (334) 693-3055

Rock Island Wildflowers, P.O. Box 57, Rock Island, TN 38581, (931) 686-2360

Roycroft Daylily Nursery, 942 Whitehall Ave., Georgetown, SC 29440, (843) 527-1533

Seawright Gardens, 201 Bedford Rd., Carlisle, MA 01741, (978) 369-1900

Soules Garden, 5809 Rahke Rd., Indianapolis, IN 46217, (317) 786-7839

Spring Fever Daylilies, 12 Loys Lane, Plains, MT 59859, (406) 826-3214

Sterrett Gardens, P.O. Box 85, Craddockville, VA 23341, (757) 442-4606

Tranquil Lake Nursery, 45 River St., Rehoboth, MA 02769, (508) 252-4002

Walnut Hill Gardens, 999 - 310th St., Atalissa, IA 52720, (563) 946-3471

White Oak Nursery, 1 Oak Park Lane, Metamora, IL 61548, (309) 822-8477

Wildwood Gardens, P.O. Box 250, Molalla, OR 97038, (503) 829-3102

Willow Bend Farm, 2331 J Rd., Grand Junction, CO 81505, (970) 263-4138

VARIETIES

More than fifty thousand Daylilies are registered with the American Hemerocallis Society, and well in excess of one thousand new ones are introduced annually.

Breeders have successfully developed virtually every flower color in Daylilies except for true blue, and that will probably come in time. When selecting Daylilies, consider not only bloom color but also other characteristics including flower form and shape, the number of flower stems (scapes), bud count, the size of the bloom, flower substance (thickness), petal surface texture, fragrance, the height of the plant, and ploidy—whether the plant is diploid or tetraploid. Plants carrying the normal number of chromosomes are *diploid*. *Tetraploids* have had their chromosome count artificially doubled: many of these have more vigorous growth, larger flowers, more intense color, and a greater number of bloom stems with better branching and higher bud counts. However, tetraploid does not always indicate a superior plant, and there are numerous excellent diploid Daylilies. Tetraploids are indicated by an asterisk (*) after the flower color in the following varieties table.

The peak bloom period for Daylilies in colder climates is July and early August. Within that period you can select plants which bloom in early-, mid-, or late-season periods. If possible, try to see Daylilies in bloom before making a selection. Many public gardens and local growers have an excellent assortment of Daylilies to view in season.

If you were to ask 20 different people to list their 25 favorite Daylilies, you might end up with a list of 500 varieties. The following selections have been made for cold-climate gardeners based on these qualities: hardiness, plant vigor, number of buds, quality of bloom color, fragrance, repeat bloom, strength of scapes, beauty of foliage, and proportion of flower size to the plant. The Daylilies listed here are all stunning in cold climates.

The following Daylilies are all hardy to −40°F and are among the loveliest for home gardeners. Whether a variety will bloom off and on in the season or is fragrant is noted under the "Fragrance" and "Rebloom" columns. Doubles (D) have double the average number of petals on a typical Daylily. Spiders have elongated petals that hang down. These characteristics are noted in the "Color" column.

VARIETY	COLOR/PLOIDY	HEIGHT	FRAGRANCE	REBLOOM
Hemerocallis citrina				
(Citron Daylily)	Light yellow	48″	Yes	No
Of Chinese origin, this species blooms in mid to late summer. It is very fragrant, blooms at night, and has semi-evergreen foliage.				
Hemerocallis dumortieri				
(Early Daylily)	Yellowish orange	24″	Yes	No
This plant flowers in spring with small, funnel-shaped, pale orange flowers. It is extremely winter hardy, but, unfortunately, carries its flowers down in or just barely above its foliage.				
Hemerocallis flava (see *Hemerocallis lilio-asphodelus*)				
Hemerocallis lilio-asphodelus				
(Lemon Daylily)	Chrome yellow	36″	Yes	No
Another spring-blooming plant, the flowers of this species stay open more than one day. With the wide range of hybrid cultivars available, this fine perennial has gone out of favor. Considering its form and lovely, fragrant flowers, it deserves your attention.				

'Charles Johnston'

Hemerocallis middendorfii

'Satin Silk'

'Sigudilla'

VARIETY	COLOR/PLOIDY	HEIGHT	FRAGRANCE	REBLOOM

Hemerocallis middendorfii

(Middendorff Daylily)	Yellow or pale orange	30″	Yes	Yes

This species flowers between *Hemerocallis dumortieri* (Early Daylily) and *Hemerocallis lilio-asphodelus* (Lemon Daylily). The closely clustered flowers bloom well above the foliage on unbranched stems. This native of Siberia and Japan will occasionally rebloom in cold climates.

Hemerocallis minor

(Grass-leaf Daylily)	Yellow	18″	Yes	No

Blooming in spring, this dwarf Daylily from eastern Siberia and Japan has fine grassy foliage and numerous flowers that open in the afternoon and last longer than a day.

Hemerocallis thunbergii

(Thunberg Daylily)	Lemon yellow	36″	Yes	No

This plant, a native of China and Korea, has dark green foliage with yellow flowers that open at night and close during the early part of the day.

Hemerocallis (Named varieties and hybrids)

VARIETY	COLOR/PLOIDY	HEIGHT	FRAGRANCE	REBLOOM
'All American Chief'*****	Rich red/deep yellow*	32″	No	Yes
'Artist Etching'	Cream pink/green*	28″	Yes	No
'Asiatic Pheasant'	Russet yellow/green yellow (spider)	22″	Yes	No (long bloom)
'Autumn Minaret'	Gold/rust/yellow	70″	No	No
'Bama Music'	Pink bitone/lemon yellow/green	36″	No	No
'Barbara Mitchell'*****	Lavender pink/yellow green	24″	No	Yes
'Bela Lugosi'*****	Dark purple/yellow green*	32″	No	No
'Bertie Ferris'	Persimmon orange/orange	20″	No	No (long bloom)
'Bitsy'*****	Lemon yellow/lemon yellow	30″	No	Yes
'Buttered Popcorn'*****	Butter yellow/green*	30″	Yes	No (long bloom)
'Charles Johnston'	Cherry red*	24″	Yes	Yes
'Corryton Pink'	Pearl pink/green*	32″	No	No
'Designer Gown'	Lavender pink/dark eye/lemon green	30″	No	No
'Dorethe Louise'	Light yellow/yellow green*	18″	Yes	No
'Dream Souffle'*****	Rose pink/cream yellow (D)	20″	No	Yes
'Dublin Elaine'	Whitish light pink/yellow green (D)	32″	No	Yes
'Fairy Tale Pink'	Peach pink/yellow/green	24″	No	Yes
'Frances Joiner'	Rose apricot/light yellow green (D)	24″	Yes	Yes
'Going Bananas'*****	Canary yellow/light yellow	20″	Yes	Yes
'Happy Returns'	Light yellow/light yellow	18″	Yes	Yes
'Holly Dancer'	Brilliant red/green (spider)	32″	No	No
'Hush Little Baby'	Rose pink/yellow green	24″	No	No (long bloom)
'Hyperion'	Lemon yellow/greenish	42″	Yes	No
'Joan Senior'*****	Near white/yellow green	24″	No	No (long bloom)
'Judith'*****	Lavender pink/green	24″	No	Yes
'Kindly Light'	Medium yellow/green (spider)	30″	No	No

VARIETY	COLOR/PLOIDY	HEIGHT	FRAGRANCE	REBLOOM
'Lady Lucille'*****	Deep orange/gold*	26"	No	Yes
'Lavender Stardust'	Lavender blend/yellow/green	24"	No	Yes
'Leebea Orange Crush'	Cream orange/red/yellow green*	24"	Yes	Yes
'Little Grapette'	Grape purple/green	12"	No	No
'Lullaby Baby'	Cream pink/green	20"	Yes	No
'Mary Todd'*****	Buff yellow/buff yellow*	26"	No	No
'Moonlit Masquerade'*****	Cream white/dark purple/green*	28"	No	Yes
'Pardon Me'	Medium red/yellow green	18"	No	Yes
'Parade Queen'*****	Cream yellow/pale green	20"	Yes	Yes
'Plum Perfect'	Plum/black purple/gold	22"	No	Yes
'Prairie Moonlight'	Pale yellow/green	34"	Yes	No
'Primal Scream'	Tangerine orange/green*	34"	No	No
'Raspberry Candy'	Cream/red maroon/green	26"	Yes	No
'Raspberry Frolic'	Rose lavender blend/gold*	24"	Yes	Yes
'Red Volunteer'*****	Crimson red/gold/reddish orange*	30"	No	No
'Rocket City'	Brilliant orange/orange yellow*	36"	No	No (long bloom)
'Rosy Returns'	Rose pink/rose purple/yellow	18"	No	Yes
'Ruby Spider'	Ruby red/yellow (spider)*	34"	No	No
'Ruby Stella'	Dark red/yellow	14"	Yes	Yes
'Satin Silk'	Pink blend*	32"	No	No
'Sigudilla'	Bronze red*	22"	No	No
'Siloam Double Classic'*****	Peach pink/yellow/green (D)	26"	Yes	No
'Siloam June Bug'	Gold yellow/maroon	24"	No	Yes
'Siloam Virginia Henson'	Pink/ruby red/green	18"	No	No
'Skinwalker'	Lavender yellow/green (spider)	32"	No	No
'Stella de Oro'	Golden yellow	18"	No	Yes
'Stella Supreme'	Lemon yellow/pale green	18"	Yes	Yes
'Strawberry Candy'*****	Coral pink/rose red/yellow green*	26"	No	No (long bloom)
'Strutter's Ball'*****	Black purple/lemon green*	30"	No	No (long bloom)
'Summer Valentine'	Pink/magenta eye and edges/green*	24"	No	No
'Swirling Water'	Blue purple/white splashes	24"	No	No
'White Temptation'*****	Near white/pale yellow green	32"	No	No
'Wineberry Candy'*****	Orchid pink/wine red/green*	22"	No	No
'Woman's Work'	Medium pink/yellow	20"	Yes	No

'Chocolate Ruffles'

HEUCHERA

(HUE-ker-uh)

CORAL BELLS

Bloom Time	Expected Longevity	Maintenance	Years to Bloom	Preferred Light
Summer	5 to 10 years	Low	From seed: 2 years From potted plant: 1 year	Full sun to light shade

Coral Bells are easy to grow in cold climates. Their foliage and dainty flowers are delightful. Both are useful in floral arrangements. In fact, some varieties are grown for their unique foliage only. The flowers, which come in a wide range of colors, often attract hummingbirds. Plants are rarely bothered by insects or disease, but they tend to be short-lived unless divided on a regular basis and properly winter protected to prevent heaving.

How Coral Bells Grow

Coral Bells grow from slender, fibrous roots into low-growing plants with lovely, maple- to heart-shaped leaves. This foliage varies in coloration and is even mottled in some varieties. Each plant forms a circular mound of airy foliage. Dozens of small, delicate flowers appear on leafless wandlike stems (scapes), which rise up from the base. If the spent blossoms are not removed, they form oval seed capsules, which are dark brown when mature. Inside are minuscule black seeds. The roots spread slowly but deliberately under good growing conditions.

Where to Plant

Site and Light Coral Bells grow best in light shade. They also thrive in full sun if the ground is kept consistently moist throughout the growing season. If grown in full sun without adequate moisture, leaves may turn brown and wither.

Soil and Moisture Coral Bells thrive in rich, well-drained soil high in organic matter. Ideal soil amendments are compost, leaf mold, rotted manures, and peat moss. These retain moisture but drain freely. If you have clay or rocky soil, remove it and replace it with loam or build a raised bed.

Spacing Space plants 12 to 18 inches apart (30 to 45 cm) on the average. Small, rock-garden plants can be much closer. Plant in groups of three to five for best effect.

Companions

Heuchera (Coral Bells) is valuable as both a border and an edging plant. Specific combinations include *Heuchera micrantha* 'Molly Bush' (Small-Flowered Alumroot) with *Athyrium niponicum* var. *pictum* (Japanese Painted Fern), *Geranium* 'Orion' (Cranesbill), and *Lamium maculatum* 'White Nancy' (Spotted Dead Nettle); *Heuchera* 'Frosted Violet' (Hybrid Coral Bells) planted next to *Hemerocallis* 'Happy Returns' (Daylily); *Heuchera* 'Pretty Polly' (Hybrid Coral Bells) combined with *Geranium sanguineum* 'New Hampshire Purple' (Bloody Cranesbill) and *Oenothera fruticosa* (Common Sundrops); and *Heuchera americana* 'Dale' (American Alumroot) interplanted with *Pulmonaria* (Lungwort) and *Gymnocarpium dryopteris* (Oak Fern). *Heuchera* can also combine well with woodland plants and spring-blooming bulbs.

Planting

Bare Root Plant bare root stock as soon as you can work the ground in spring. Remove the plants from their shipping package immediately. Snip off broken or damaged root tips. Soak plants overnight in room-temperature water. Place a small amount of superphosphate in the base of the planting hole. Fill the hole with soil. Place the crown 1½ inches (4 cm) below the soil surface. Fill in with soil, firm with your fingers, and water immediately. Dissolve ½ cup (about 114 g) 10-10-10 fertilizer in 1 gallon (about 4 liters) of water. Pour ½ cup (about 120 ml) of this starter solution around the base of each plant. If you prefer organic fertilizer, use fish emulsion instead.

Potted Plants Plant Coral Bells after all danger of frost in spring. If the soil in the pot is dry, water it, and let it drain overnight. Plant at the same depth as in the pot after preparing the hole in a similar manner to that for a bare root plant. Fill in with soil, firm with your fingers, and water immediately. Pour ½ cup (about 120 ml) starter solution around the base of each plant.

How to Care for Coral Bells

Water Coral Bells need moist soil to do well. Water them frequently. Keep the soil evenly moist throughout the growing season, especially if you are growing plants in full sun. Lots of organic matter in the soil and a good mulch help cut down on the amount of watering. Whenever you water, saturate the soil to a depth of 18 inches (45 cm). Never let these plants dry out.

Mulch Place a 3-inch (7.5-cm) layer of mulch around the base of each plant as soon as the ground warms up in spring. Avoid touching the crown of the plant with the mulch. Good organic mulches include compost, dried grass clippings, shredded leaves, sawdust, pine needles, and chipped bark. If you use either sawdust or bark, add more fertilizer than normal, since these deplete nitrogen from the soil.

Fertilizing Sprinkle 10-10-10 fertilizer around the base of each plant just as new growth emerges in spring. Water immediately to dissolve granules and carry nutrients into the root zone. Do this again just as buds form.

If you prefer organic fertilizers, use alfalfa meal (rabbit pellets), blood meal, bonemeal, compost, cow manure, fish emulsion, Milorganite, or rotted horse manure. Bonemeal must be mixed into the soil at planting time to be effective.

Weeding Mulch inhibits most weed growth, but a few weeds will still sprout. Pull these by hand to avoid harming the shallow root system of the plant. Weeds compete with the plant for moisture and nutrients.

Staking The flower scapes of Coral Bells do flop over regularly, but staking these plants makes no sense at all. The way the stems drift back and forth in a breeze like colorful wands is part of their magic.

Deadheading Remove spent flowers unless you want seed to form. Cut the flower stalks off at their base. This rarely induces a second round of bloom.

Replanting The crown of this plant has a tendency to rise out of the ground as it matures. When this happens, you can either fill in with additional soil around the crown, replant it, or divide the plant. Otherwise, during the winter it will be highly exposed to fluctuating temperatures, which can cause it to heave out of the ground and die as it dehydrates in winter cold and drying winds.

Winter Protection During the first year, cover the plants with a 4-inch (10-cm) winter mulch of clean straw, whole leaves, or pine needles when the ground has frozen to a depth of 3 inches (7.5 cm). This prevents the young plants from heaving during winter freezes and thaws. If in subsequent years there is no snow by mid-December, apply a 4-inch (10-cm) mulch at that time. Remove mulch as soon as the weather warms up in early spring to prevent crown rot.

Problems

Insects Insects rarely bother Coral Bells.

Disease Although rarely bothered by disease, plants must have good drainage to prevent crown rot during the winter.

Propagation

Division Divide Coral Bells every 2 to 3 years for the plant's health. The central portion of the plant often turns woody and can be discarded after division. Younger plants seem to be hardier than older ones. Just as new growth emerges in spring, dig up the entire clump, and divide it with a sharp knife into sections. Each division should contain several stems connected to an ample supply of roots. Plant the sections immediately as you would a bare root plant. Keep them consistently moist once planted.

Cuttings Coral Bells can be propagated by leaf heal cuttings. In midsummer, cut a leaf from the base of the plant, taking a small portion of the crown with the stem of the leaf. Dust the cut end with rooting hormone. Tap off any excess powder. Plant it in moist growing medium, keeping humidity high and the medium consistently moist. Once the plant is growing well and has formed a solid root ball, plant it as you would a bare root plant.

This can also be done in fall if you would like to grow plants indoors during the winter. This gives them a long time to mature, and it is sometimes easier to start older leaves in this manner. Of course, you need space and time to care for plants during the entire winter season, and that's not easy for most home gardeners.

Seed Grow species (wild) and a few named varieties from seed. To do so, place moist peat moss in a tray. Press the seed into the surface of the growing medium without covering it, since it needs light to germinate. Then slide the tray into a plastic bag perforated for good air circulation. Keep temperatures above 65°F (18°C). Germination usually occurs within 21 to 60 days. If after 9 weeks the seed has not germinated, place the tray in the crisper of your refrigerator for 6 weeks. Remove the tray after this moist chilling, and keep it above 65°F (18°C) again until seeds germinate. Once seedlings have a second pair of leaves, plant them in individual pots. Do not discard the smallest seedlings if you're growing plants for foliage color; these often have the deepest coloration. Lower the temperature to 55°F (13°C) if possible. Keep the pots consistently moist. Harden the seedlings off for 14 days before planting them outdoors after all danger of frost has passed in spring.

Another method is to plant seed in moist growing medium in a cold frame or prepared bed outdoors in late fall when it is already extremely cold. Press the seed into the surface of the medium. Temperatures will fluctuate throughout the winter and spring. Once temperatures rise in spring, keep the medium consistently moist until germination begins. Once seedlings germinate, care for them as outlined in the preceding paragraph.

Special Uses

Cut Flowers Coral Bells are grown for both cut flowers and foliage. Cut either of these at the base of the plant. Place them in water immediately. Transfer them indoors, and put the flower or foliage stems in 110°F (43°C) water for conditioning overnight before arranging the following day.

When using leaves alone, place the base of the stem in boiling water for a few seconds before conditioning as outlined in the previous paragraph. Some varieties do well without any conditioning at all and just need to be kept in cool water.

Dried Flowers The flowers of Coral Bells are very dainty and best dried by dehydration in a desiccant. Hold the flower stem in place as you gently pour desiccant over it. Cover the entire stem. Let the stem dry until all parts of the flowers are crisp and brittle.

Sources

Ambergate Gardens, 8730 County Rd. 43, Chaska, MN 55318, (877) 211-9769

Bluestone Perennials, 7211 Middle Ridge Rd., Madison, OH 44057, (800) 852-5243

Busse Gardens, 17160 245th Ave., Big Lake, MN 55309, (800) 544-3192

Fieldstone Gardens, Inc., 55 Quaker Lane, Vassalboro, ME 04989, (207) 923-3836

ForestFarm, 990 Tetherow Rd., Williams, OR 97544, (541) 846-7269

RareFind Nursery, 957 Patterson Rd., Jackson, NJ 08527, (732) 833-0613

Venero Gardens, 5985 Seamans Dr., Shorewood, MN 55331, (952) 474-8550

Heuchera sanguinea

'Palace Purple'

VARIETIES

The following species (wild plants) have been used to create a wide range of Coral Bells either grown for their flowers, foliage, or a combination of both. Breeding has resulted in a fascinating range of foliage coloration as you will tell from the table. The tops and bottoms of leaves are indicated by a separation (/) in the list when significant. Leaves often change color as the season progresses. In the varietal list "green to purple" would indicate leaves changing color from green to purple over time. An asterisk (*) after the flower color indicates a plant with especially lovely flowers or one that makes a unique impression when in bloom. Most gardeners cut off insignificant or unsightly flowers on plants grown primarily for foliage coloration. Plant heights include the length of the flower stems (scapes). Heights vary so much that these should be considered no more than approximate guides.

VARIETY	FOLIAGE	FLOWER	HEIGHT	HARDINESS
Heuchera americana				
(American Alumroot)	Bright green	Greenish white	24″	−30°F
'Dale' ('Dale's Strain')	Green blue/marbled green	Greenish white	18″	−30°F
'Ring of Fire'	Silver/green	Pinkish white	26″	−30°F

American Alumroot is grown primarily for its scalloped foliage mottled silver with purplish red fall color. Its lantern-like flowers sway on greenish red stems.

VARIETY	FOLIAGE	FLOWER	HEIGHT	HARDINESS
Heuchera × brizoides				
(Queen of Hearts Coral Flower)				
'Mt. St. Helens'*****	Deep green	Bright red*	16″	–30°F
This variety forms a compact mound of foliage and is among the showiest of the Coral Bells in bloom.				
Heuchera cylindrica				
(Poker Alumroot)	Dark green	Greenish white	10″	–30°F
This species with its puffy flowers is native to northwestern North America, but it grows well in most cold-climates areas.				
Heuchera micrantha				
(Small-flowered Alumroot)	Green with reddish tones	Yellow white pink	12″	–30°F
'Molly Bush'	Dark purple	Greenish white	18″	–30°F
'Palace Purple'	Mahogany red	Yellowish white	18″	–30°F
These are attractive plants with clean foliage, reddish stems, and insignificant flowers.				
Heuchera richardsonii				
(Prairie Alumroot)	Medium green	Greenish white	24″	–40°F
This prairie native is noted for its deeply veined foliage, greenish red stems, and spikes of dainty flowers that bloom in spring.				
Heuchera sanguinea				
(Coral Bells)	Medium green	Crimson red	18″	–40°F
Bressingham Hybrids	Green	Red/pink/white*	24″	–40°F
'Ruby Bells'*****	Green	Blood red*	16″	–40°F
'Snow Angel'	Green spotted white	Medium pink	12″	–30°F
The common name for ***Heuchera*** comes from this southwestern native. The flowers hang from stiff reddish stems like little coral bells. Its scalloped foliage is sometimes marbled red.				
Heuchera villosa				
(Hairy Alumroot)	Light to medium green	White to pink	36″	–40°F
This is a threatened species native to the southeast. It has fuzzy leaves and bristly stems. It has been used extensively in breeding to increase the vigor of hybrid introductions.				
Heuchera (Named varieties and hybrids)				
'Amethyst Mist'*****	Purplish silver	Insignificant	26″	–30°F
'Berry Smoothie'	Rose pink purple	White	18″	–30°F
'Beaujolais'	Burgundy silver	Creamy	24″	–30°F
'Black Beauty'*****	Blackish red	White	24″	–30°F
'Blackout'	Purplish black	Cream	18″	–30°F
'Brownies'	Chocolate green	Cream	30″	–30°F
'Canyon Melody'	Dark green	Medium pink*	18″	–30°F
'Caramel'*****	Apricot caramel	Cream	16″	–30°F
'Champagne Bubbles'*****	Light green	White to rose*	30″	–30°F

VARIETY	FOLIAGE	FLOWER	HEIGHT	HARDINESS
'Cherries Jubilee'*****	Dusty bronze purple	Cherry red	16″	−30°F
'Chocolate Ruffles'	Chocolate purple	Yellowish brown	30″	−40°F
'Chocolate Veil'	Chocolate black	Greenish white	24″	−30°F
'Christa'*****	Peach orange	Pinkish	16″	−30°F
'Dark Secret'	Bronze purple	Cream	16″	−30°F
Dolce® Creme Brulee	Medium bronze	Pinkish	18″	−30°F
'Electra'*****	Gold with red veins	White	12″	−30°F
'Encore'	Rose purple	Creamy	18″	−30°F
'Fire Chief'	Wine red	Pink white bicolor	18″	−30°F
'Frosted Violet'*****	Burgundy violet	Light pink*	30″	−30°F
'Geisha's Fan'*****	Purple black silver overlay	Pale pink	18″	−30°F
'Georgia Peach'	Reddish peach	Cream	30″	−30°F
'Green Spice'*****	Green purple/silver	Insignificant	28″	−30°F
'Jade Gloss'	Glossy silver green	Pale pink*	18″	−30°F
'Melting Fire'	Red to maroon	White	18″	−30°F
'Midnight Rose'	Black purple spotted rose	Insignificant	24″	−30°F
'Miracle'	Chartreuse red to red purple	Pink	16″	−30°F
'Mocha'*****	Bronze purple	Cream	30″	−30°F
'Montrose Ruby'	Bronze purple	Greenish white	30″	−30°F
'Obsidian'*****	Satiny black purple	Insignificant	24″	−30°F
'Paris'	Silvery white	Rose (rebloom)*	16″	−30°F
'Petite Pearl Fairy'*****	Plum purple	Medium pink*	12″	−30°F
'Pewter Moon'	Silver green purple	Pink	18″	−30°F
'Pewter Veil'	Pewter purple silver	Purplish white*	20″	−30°F
'Pinot Gris'	Silvery rose	Cream	18″	−30°F
'Pinot Noir'	Silvery black purple	White	18″	−30°F
'Pistache'	Lime to chartreuse	Cream	18″	−30°F
'Plum Pudding'*****	Plum purple	Insignificant	26″	−30°F
'Plum Royale'	Purple silver	Pinkish white	18″	−30°F
'Pretty Polly'	Medium green	Pale pink*	12″	−40°F
'Raspberry Ice'	Silver gray green	Pink	24″	−30°F
'Raspberry Regal'	Green mottled silver	Raspberry red*	42″	−40°F
'Rave On'	Silver green	Dark pink*	18″	−30°F
'Regina'	Silver burgundy	Light pink*	36″	−30°F
'Silver Lode'	Silver green	White	30″	−30°F
'Silver Scrolls'*****	Metallic silver/purple	Light pink	24″	−30°F
'Silver Veil'	Silver with dark green veins	Red*	20″	−30°F
'Southern Comfort'	Peach orange copper pink	Creamy white	18″	−30°F
'Sparkling Burgundy'	Coppery purple	White	18″	−30°F
'Starry Night'	Dark purple	White	12″	−30°F
'Velvet Night'	Satiny bluish purple	Greenish white	30″	−30°F

'Wide Brim'

HOSTA

(HOS-tuh)

HOSTA

Bloom Time	Expected Longevity	Maintenance	Years to Bloom	Preferred Light
Early summer to late fall	25+ years	Low	From seed: 4 years From potted plant: 2 years	Light to medium shade

Hostas are one of the most popular perennial plants. Known primarily as foliage plants, they are now being developed with highly decorative or scented flowers. The stunning variation of Hostas is part of their attraction. The range in foliage color, form, size, and texture is remarkable. Flowers also vary in color, form, and fragrance. Most Hostas are sturdy, long-lived, reliable plants that grow rapidly and are relatively maintenance free and easy to grow. They are resistant to disease and almost pest free. They are extremely easy to propagate through division. Hummingbirds are often attracted to their flowers. A number of Hostas are edible, served as delicacies in China and Japan. Hostas can be somewhat finicky about where they are planted. If they're given too much sun, burning or bleaching of leaves is common in many varieties. Hostas can be infected by viral diseases. Once quite rare, this is becoming increasingly common and, in some cases, quite serious.

How Hostas Grow

Hostas grow from fleshy roots and produce clumps with leaves emerging from a central crown. Individual plants are erect, flat, moundlike, or rounded in form. New leaves emerge from the center of newly planted plants as they mature. The leaves are extremely diverse. They have been described as broad, crinkled, cupped, curly, curving, dimpled, edged, frosty, glossy, heart-shaped, lancelike, mottled, pointed, puckered, ribbed, round, ruffled, seersuckered, sharp, shiny, smooth, splashed, splotched, streaked, twisted, variegated, veined, waffling, wavy, and waxy. Flower stalks, known as scapes or racemes, rise from the center of the plant during the blooming period, which varies with each variety. Flowers are usually bell-shaped and hang from arching stems. The flowers are described as funneled, lilylike, trumpet-shaped, or tubular. The height and attractiveness of blooms are related to the variety you choose. A number of varieties have fragrant blossoms. Note that prices of Hostas are often related directly to how fast they grow. Blues are generally more expensive, because they are the slowest to mature. Most Hostas will form seedpods if the spent blooms are left on the plant. However, not all Hostas form viable seed.

Where to Plant

Site and Light Almost all gardening publications refer to Hostas as shade-loving plants. Actually, the amount of light needed varies with each variety. Most Hostas will survive in deep shade, but plants will be smaller, as will individual leaves. The color of the leaves may also be affected by extremely low-light conditions.

The majority of Hostas prefer filtered light or semishade that gives them a little sun during part of the day. These plants grow larger than those in deep shade and have good coloration. Yellow and gold Hostas often need 2 to 3 hours of direct sun daily to develop their richest coloration. Thick-leafed Hostas also can stand more direct sun than thinner-leafed varieties.

The blue Hostas are tricky. The bluish coloration comes from a coating on the leaf that you can actually rub off with your fingers. This coating will wear off from strong sun, high heat, and heavy rains. For this reason, blue Hostas are best planted in protected areas, such as under tree canopies. Blues are always at their peak early in the season. The blue coloration tends to weaken as the season progresses because the coating on the leaves may disappear. You're not doing anything wrong when this happens; it's in the nature of the plant.

Fragrant plants are best located along shaded walkways where the scent can be enjoyed by all. Hostas like it cool, and that's part of the reason they do not tolerate full sun well during heat waves.

Soil and Moisture Hostas thrive in rich, well-drained soil. If your soil is rocky or clay, replace it with loam or build a raised bed. Add lots of organic matter to the soil to retain moisture. Peat and well-rotted oak leaves are both excellent soil amendments because they are slightly acidic. Hostas are often planted under trees which provide shade or semi-shade. This is fine for their light requirements but presents a problem in regard to moisture. Be sure to keep the soil evenly moist throughout the entire growing season. Drench it to a depth of 18 inches (45 cm) or more when watering. Deep watering results in lush leaf growth and bushy plants.

Spacing There is no set rule on spacing other than to give each plant enough room to expand to its natural size. Some Hostas are enormous, others tiny. Space them according to their potential size. When you're planting potentially large Hostas, the initial space between plants may appear unnatural. However, if you space plants correctly to begin with, you avoid having to transplant them at a later date.

Companions

Hostas fulfill a variety of needs. They are good edgers, accent plants, ground covers, or background subjects. They are delightful massed in light to medium shade as a minimal-maintenance ground cover or bold design statement. Plant a range of spring flowering bulbs among the clumps to give an early show of bloom. Hostas are very effective in masking the aging foliage of common bulbs such as *Narcissus* (Daffodil) or *Tulipa* (Tulip). Plant fragrant varieties where you can appreciate their delightful aroma. Hostas combine gracefully with numerous other shade-tolerant perennials including *Aconitum* (Monkshood), *Alchemilla* (Lady's Mantle), *Astilbe* (False Spirea), *Chelone* (Turtlehead), *Cimicifuga/Actaea* (Bugbane), *Geranium* (Cranesbill), *Lamium* (Dead Nettle), *Lysimachia nummularia* 'Aurea' (Moneywort), *Phlox divaricata* (Woodland Phlox), *Pulmonaria* (Lungwort), *Tradescantia* (Spiderwort), a wide variety of **Ferns**, and select **Grasses** such as *Carex nigra* (BlackFlowering Sedge), *Hystrix patula* (Bottlebrush Grass), and *Luzula nivea* (Snowy Woodrush Grass).

Planting

Bare Root Plant bare root stock as soon as you can work the ground in spring. Remove the plants from their shipping package immediately. Snip off broken or damaged root tips. Soak plants overnight in room-temperature water. Place a small amount of superphosphate in the base of the planting hole. Fill the hole with soil. Place the crown even with the surrounding soil. The growing tips should be right at the soil surface. Fill in with soil, firm with your fingers, and water well. Dissolve ½ cup (about 114 g) of 10-10-10 fertilizer in 1 gallon (about 4 liters) of water. Pour ½ cup (about 120 ml) of this starter solution around the base of the plant. If you prefer organic fertilizer, use fish emulsion instead.

Potted Plants Plant Hostas after any danger of frost has passed in spring. If the soil in the container is dry, soak the plant overnight, and let it drain thoroughly. Carefully tap the plant out of the pot to prevent damage to the root ball. Plant it at the same depth as in the pot, after preparing the hole in a manner similar to that for a bare root plant. Fill in with soil, firm with your fingers, and water immediately. Fertilize with a starting solution as outlined for bare root plants.

How to Care for Hostas

Water Keep the soil moist throughout the growing season. Once mature, Hostas can stand some dry weather, but it's best to soak the plants at least once a week to a depth of 18 inches (45 cm) or more. These plants need lots of water. So, water frequently. Be especially attentive to Hostas planted under eaves or trees; even after a heavy rain, these areas are often quite dry.

Mulch Hostas like evenly moist soils. Surround the base of the plant with an organic mulch after the soil warms up in late spring or early summer. Avoid getting mulch over the shoots that emerge from the side of the mother plant. Good mulches include shredded leaves, dried grass clippings, pine needles, and shredded bark. The latter lasts the longest and looks very good in contrast to the foliage. Bulk hardwood bark is available in most nurseries at a reasonable price. If you have a problem with slugs, pine needles are a good deterrent. Pine needles are also slightly acidic, which benefits the soil.

Fertilizing Fertilize Hostas at least twice a year, more often if possible (every 3 weeks is ideal). Just as new growth emerges in spring, sprinkle 10-10-10 fertilizer around the edge of the crown. Avoid getting granules into the crown of the plant itself. Water immediately to dissolve the granules and carry nutrients into the root zone. Fertilize again just before the plant flowers by sprinkling fertilizer around the base of the plant. If you prefer organic fertilizers, use alfalfa meal (rabbit pellets), blood meal, bonemeal, compost, cow manure, fish emulsion, Milorganite, or rotted horse manure. Bonemeal must be added to the soil at planting time to be effective.

Weeding Use mulch around Hostas to inhibit growth of annual weeds. Hand pull any weeds that sprout through the mulch.

Staking Hostas do not require staking.

Deadheading Each variety of Hosta flowers differently. On some of the varieties the flower is not particularly attractive, while on others it is not only beautiful but scented as well. If the flowers seem ugly to you, then remove them immediately just as they form. If the flowers are lovely, wait until they die to remove the stem which shoots up from the center of the plant. Just snip each stem off at the base with pruning shears or scissors. If you want a plant to self-sow, leave the flowers on to form seedpods. However, some varieties are sterile.

Pruning Some of the lower leaves may turn yellow or brown as the season progresses, even on perfectly healthy plants. Pull these off.

Winter Protection A number of Hostas will not survive in colder climates. The ones listed in this section usually do. *Hosta plantaginea, Hosta sieboldiana*, and *Hosta* 'Tokudama' should have winter protection. As soon as the ground has frozen to a depth of 3 inches (7.5 cm), remove all dead leaves and stems before covering the plants with a thick layer of whole leaves, marsh hay, straw, or pine needles. Remove the covering as soon as the weather begins to warm up in spring to prevent crown rot.

Problems

Insects Slugs and snails chew holes in leaves at night and hide during the day. Poisonous slug baits are effective, but dangerous. Organic controls include sprinkling diatomaceous earth around the base of each plant; placing beer in shallow dishes at ground level to attract and drown slugs; laying boards down to give slugs a hiding place, then turning them over to kill the slugs. Begin slug control early in the season. They multiply quickly.

Disease Once thought of as a disease-free plant, Hostas are now threatened by several different viruses, the most serious of which is known as Hosta Virus (HVX). Sap from one plant carries the virus to another. Telltale signs of infection include blue, green, or dark blotches on leaves (called "inkbleed"); irregular spotting on leaves; unusual changes in leaf texture atypical for that plant; death of leaves for no

apparent reason; and, finally, death of the plant. Since the signs of infection may not show up for a year or longer, many infected plants are still being sold. Once infected, plants should be destroyed immediately by burning or disposal in the trash. The work of Dr. Ben Lockhart at the University of Minnesota indicates that Hostas vary in their susceptibility to this incurable and sometimes fatal disease. Some Hostas listed in the table have shown potential resistance: 'Blue Angel,' 'Frances Williams,' 'Frosted Jade,' 'Love Pat,' 'Sagae,' and *Hosta sieboldiana* 'Elegans.' Tests for the disease are available, but they are expensive and may not be conclusive.

Nematodes Foliar nematodes (*Aphelencoides*) are miniature worms that cause mature leaves to have yellowish stripes by midsummer. Nematodes are relatively rare, but the problem has been showing up more often in recent years. Although nematodes rarely kill plants, we suggest you dig up an infected plant, clean up the area around it completely, and destroy all tissue to protect the rest of your bed.

Spotted, mottled, and distorted leaves can be signs of frost damage, iron chlorosis, or viral infections. Take a leaf to a nursery for help in identifying the problem.

Sun Scorch If specific Hostas are placed in too strong light and stressed by lack of water, their leaves may turn yellow and then brown. This looks like a disease but is not. Either move the plants to a more shaded site or keep the soil consistently moist.

What may look like a disease is often sun scorch, caused by lack of water or too much sun.

Animals Deer, rabbits, and woodchucks love eating Hostas. A single deer can destroy an entire bed overnight. Trap rabbits and woodchucks early in the season. Sprinkle Milorganite around the base of each Hosta regularly. This not only fertilizes the plant but also scares deer off with the scent. However, deer will eventually get used to the scent. Vary Milorganite with blood meal, human hair, and even thin soap scrapings to keep them away from plants. Alternatively, use a commercial deer repellent. Varying repellents, rather than using just one, is most effective.

Propagation

Division Hostas generally mature in 3 to 5 years, but some types take much longer. Most Hostas do not need to be divided for good health. However, if the centers of the plants begin to get bare, you should dig the plants up, cut out the center, and replant the outer, healthier portions. Hostas are extremely easy to divide. Dig up the clump in early spring just as new growth emerges. Slice the mature plant into divisions, each containing no fewer than three shoots. Plant each division immediately as you would a bare root plant. Cutting larger plants is easiest with a sharp spade. For smaller plants, use a sharp knife.

Seed It is possible to grow Hostas from seed, but unless the seed is from species (wild) varieties, it rarely comes true.

Sow the seed indoors in February, covering it with $\frac{1}{16}$ inch (2 mm) of growing medium. Keep the medium moist at all times and covered with glass or plastic to ensure high humidity. Maintain temperatures of 50°F to 70°F (10°C to 21°C). If seedlings do not appear within 90 days, place the container in your refrigerator for a month or more. Keep the medium moist during this chilling process. Then place back into higher heat and try again. Keep the medium moist at all times. Germination is often erratic and irregular.

Rossizing Rossizing, named after Henry Ross, is the unusual term for the following process. In early spring, dig the soil away from the base of a plant with a single crown. Poke a sharp knife into the crown under one of the little growing tips. Now cut straight down through the roots. On a larger crown you can do this in three or four places. Dust the cuts with fungicide. Replace the soil, and grow the plant on as you would a normal Hosta. The following year, the plant will produce several plantlets from the cut crown. Cut these apart, and plant each as a bare root plant.

Tissue Culture Commercially, it is now possible to get hundreds of thousands of plants from one plant using the sophisticated technique known as tissue culture. For the home gardener, this is an interesting fact but much too difficult to attempt on your own.

Special Uses

Cut Flowers and Leaves Some Hostas provide nice cut flowers, which are lovely, scented, but not long-lasting. It may help to place stems in 100°F to 110°F (38°C to 43°C) water overnight before using them in arrangements. The leaves are also highly valued in floral arrangements and much longer-lasting. Just soak them in cold water for several hours before arranging. Or, if you have tried this and failed, place the leaves in a plastic bag, and keep them cool for 2 days in a refrigerator. Then arrange. If this fails, place the base of the stems in 1 inch (2.5 cm) of boiling water for 30 seconds before placing them in cold water. You'll get firm, not floppy, leaves through one of these methods.

Dried Flowers, Foliage, and Seed Heads Some of the flowers dry quite nicely in a desiccant. Try varied flowers to see which ones do the best for you. Arrange individual blooms in place, and fill in around them, shaping the petals as you do this. Cover them completely, and allow them to dry out for as long as necessary. The more delicate varieties are easiest to dry.

To dry leaves, pick them just as they begin to fade. Leaves chosen for drying should be spotless and undamaged in any way. Place the leaves between sheets of newspaper and set them under a rug until completely dry. You also can use a commercial press if you prefer.

Pick seed heads just as they begin to dry. Place them so that the lower stems are in 1 inch (2.5 cm) of water. Let them dry standing up in as hot a spot as you have in the house. Let them cure for as long as necessary. Some varieties are sterile and do not produce seed heads.

Food *Hosta montana* and *Hosta sieboldiana* are two varieties grown as food crops in China and Japan. Young shoots, leaves, or flower buds are often covered in light batter and fried in hot oil as tempura. Shoots are also good in salads. Boil them briefly, remove the skin, and cut them into small pieces before mixing with other vegetables.

Sources

A & D Nursery, P.O. Box 2338, Snohomish, WA 98291, (360) 668-9690

Ambergate Gardens, 8730 County Rd. 43, Chaska, MN 55318, (877) 211-9769

André Viette Farm & Nursery, 608 Longmeadow Rd., Fishersville, VA 22939, (540) 943-2315

Contrary Mary's Plants, 2735 Rte. 52, Minooka, IL 60447, (815) 521-9535

Daylily & Hosta Gardens, 2396 Roper Mountain Rd., Simpsonville, SC 29681, (864) 297-9043

Direct Source Hostas, 2773 Granite Ct., Prairie Grove, IL 60012, (815) 356-8280

Frida's Hostas, 3324 Diehn Ave., Davenport, IA 52802, (563) 326-4590

Glenbrook Farm, 142 Brooks Rd., Fultonville, NY 12072, (518) 922-5091

Green Hill Farm, Inc, 66 Codys Way, Franklinton, NC 27525, (919) 494-7178

Green Mountain Hosta Nursery, P.O. Box 97, East Dover, VT 05341, (802) 348-6368

Homestead Division, 9448 Mayfield Rd., Chesterland, OH 44026, (440) 729-9838

Homestead Farms Nursery, 3701 Hwy EE, Owensville, MO 65066, (573) 437-4277

Hornbaker Gardens, 22937 1140 N Ave., Princeton, IL 61356, (815) 659-3282

HostasDirect, Inc, 19 Mid Oaks Rd., Roseville, Roseville, MN 55113 (no phone)

Hosta Hideaway, 511 E Salem, Indianola, IA 50125, (515) 961-8213

Jim's Hostas, 11616 Robin Hood Dr., Dubuque, IA 52001, (563) 588-9671

Klehm's Song Sparrow Perennial Farm, 13101 E Rye Rd., Avalon, WI 53505, (800) 553-3715

Kuk's Forest Nursery, 10174 Barr Rd., Brecksville, OH 44141, (440) 546-2675

Land of the Giants Hosta, 9106 N Raven Ct., Milton, WI 53563, (608) 580-0190

Made in the Shade, 16370 W 138th Terrace, Olathe, KS 66062, (913) 829-0760

Naylor Creek Nursery, P.O. Box 309, Chimacum, WA 98325, (360) 732-4983

New Hampshire Hostas, 73 Exeter Rd., South Hampton, NH 03826, (603) 879-0085

North Pine Gardens, P.O. Box 595, Norfolk, NE 68701, (402) 371-3895

Pine Forest Gardens, 556 Ellison Rd., Tyrone, GA 30290, (866) 605-5418

Plant Delights, 9241 Sauls Rd., Raleigh, NC 27603, (919) 772-4794

Savory's Gardens, Inc., 5300 Whiting Ave., Edina, MN 55439, (952) 941-8755

Seawright Gardens, 201 Bedford Rd., Carlisle, MA 01741, (978) 369-1900

Soules Garden, 5809 Rahke Rd., Indianapolis, IN 46217, (317) 786-7839

The Hosta Patch, 23720 Hearthside Dr., Deer Park, IL 60010, (847) 540-8051

Walnut Hill Gardens, 999 - 310th St., Atalissa, IA 52720, (563) 946-3471

White Oak Nursery, 1 Oak Park Lane, Metamora, IL 61548, (309) 822-8477

VARIETIES

Following are some of the best and most readily available Hostas. This list includes top-notch varieties. Breeders are paying much greater attention to Hosta flowers, and recent introductions offer larger, much showier blooms. There are a number of both old and new varieties which have wonderful fragrance. Those are indicated by an asterisk (*) after their flower color.

Choose varieties by foliage color, the beauty of the flowers, the size of the plant, and hardiness. The plant size given here relates to the mature height of the foliage mound: D (dwarf) = 3″–6″, S (small) = 7″–12″, M (medium) = 13″–24″, and L (large) = 25″–36+″ tall. The naming of Hostas can be a bit confusing. For example, 'Aureomarginata' could be *Hosta montana* 'Aureomarginata' or *Hosta ventricosa* 'Aureomarginata.' Within the chart that follows you'll find appropriate cross references, some of which are to the list of named varieties at the end of the chart itself.

VARIETY	FOLIAGE	FLOWER	SIZE	HARDINESS
Hosta caerulea (see *Hosta ventricosa*)				
Hosta clausa*****	Green	Reddish purple	M	–40°F

This Hosta has a creeping growth pattern, making it an excellent medium-sized ground cover. It has narrow green leaves and reddish purple flower buds that never open.

VARIETY	FOLIAGE	FLOWER	SIZE	HARDINESS
Hosta fluctuans 'Variegated' (see 'Sagae' in the list of named varieties)				
Hosta montana	Green	Pale lavender	L	–40°F
'Aureomarginata'*****	Green/cream yellow edge	Pale lavender	L	–40°F

Both of these Hostas mature into dramatic specimens with glossy foliage. The leaves of 'Aureomarginata' are edged bright yellow in spring and, as the summer heat arrives, they fade to a pleasing creamy white.

VARIETY	FOLIAGE	FLOWER	SIZE	HARDINESS
Hosta nakaiana*****	Green	Deep lavender	S	–40°F

This dwarf species has green, heart-shaped leaves and deep lavender flowers. If deadheaded, this Hosta may reward you with a second crop of flowers.

VARIETY	FOLIAGE	FLOWER	SIZE	HARDINESS
Hosta plantaginea*****	Light green	White*	L	–30°F
'Aphrodite'	Light green	White (D)*	ML	–30°F

This popular Hosta is valued for its impressive display of highly fragrant, trumpet-like flowers in late summer and also its shiny, light green leaves. It grows best in an eastern exposure where it gets lots of morning sun. 'Aphrodite' is much the same as its parent and also grown for its intense fragrance. However, its flowers are double.

VARIETY	FOLIAGE	FLOWER	SIZE	HARDINESS
Hosta sieboldiana	Bluish green	Near white	L	–30°F
'Elegans'*****	Blue gray	Near white	L	–30°F

These are popular Hostas offering large rounded leaves and early summer bloom. They grow slowly, but mature into handsome specimen plants.

VARIETY	FOLIAGE	FLOWER	SIZE	HARDINESS
Hosta tardiflora (see 'Tardiflora' in the list of named varieties)				
Hosta tokudama 'Aureo-nebulosa' (see 'Tokudama Aureonebulosa' in the list of named varieties)				
Hosta tokudama 'Flavo-circinalis' (see 'Tokudama Flavocircinalis' in the list of named varieties)				
Hosta undulata 'Albo-marginata' (see 'Undulata Albomarginata' in the list of named varieties)				

'Frances Williams'

'Green Gold'

Hosta plantaginea

Hosta ventricosa 'Aureomaculata'

'Beverly Sills'

IRIS

(EYE-ris)

BEARDED IRIS

Bloom Time	Expected Longevity	Maintenance	Years to Bloom	Preferred Light
Spring to early summer	10+ years	High	From seed: 4 years From potted plant: 1 year	Full sun

The blooms of Bearded Iris are among the most beautiful in the perennial garden. The range of colors and possible combinations on individual blossoms is amazing. The plants reproduce vigorously, making them one of the top choices or mainstays in your garden. The blooms come in at varied times, depending on the plants selected, so that bloom time can be extended over a period of weeks. Unfortunately, Bearded Irises are susceptible to disease and insect infestations. However, if you follow good cultural procedures, you'll often avoid many problems.

How Bearded Irises Grow

Bearded Irises grow from thick, fleshy stems called rhizomes. Roots go down while leaves grow up from these stems, which often lie just under or on the surface of the ground. The stems look like tubes and are food-storage units for the leaves. The leaves are quite wide, pointy, and firm. Flower stems (scapes) shoot up from these leaves to produce striking blossoms. The flowers are "bearded" in the sense that they have raised hairs near the flower's throat. After the flowers wither, they may produce seedpods. As individual plants mature, they form large clumps as the fleshy stems spread out in all directions from the parent plant.

Where to Plant

Site and Light This is a plant that thrives in full sun, so give it lots of light. Don't let it get shaded by other plants.

Soil and Moisture Bearded Irises thrive in rich, well-drained soil. If your soil is clay or rock, replace it or make a raised bed. If soil does not drain properly, the Iris will die out from root rot. Add lots of organic matter. Good choices are compost, peat moss, rotted manure, and shredded leaves.

Spacing Bearded Irises need lots of sun to do well. They also require good air circulation around the leaves and stems to avoid foliar diseases. Give them lots of space.

Companions

Plant Bearded Irises with perennials of similar cultural needs. Match bloom times, as the flowering period for Bearded Iris runs from spring to early summer. The early season bloomers combine beautifully with small bulbs, including many of the miniature varieties of *Narcissus* (Daffodil) and wild (species) forms of *Tulipa* (Tulip). Plant intermediate types with *Dianthus deltoides* (Maiden Pink), *Euphorbia polychroma* (Cushion Spurge), *Phlox divaricata* 'Chattahoochee' (Chattahoochee Phlox), and standard named varieties (cultivars) of *Tulipa* (Tulip). The possibilities for plant combinations with the late-spring bloomers is quite large, as there are so many more perennials blooming at that time. Suggestions include *Aquilegia* (Columbine), *Artemisia* (Wormwood), *Baptisia* (False Indigo), *Campanula glomerata* (Clustered Bellflower), *Dianthus gratianopolitanus* (Cheddar Pink), *Geranium sanguineum* (Bloody Cranesbill), *Hemerocallis* (Daylily), *Heuchera* (Coral Bells), *Leucanthemum*–Superbum Group (Shasta Daisy), *Nepeta* (Catmint), *Paeonia* (Peony—especially singles, Japanese, and hybrids),

Salvia (Sage), *Tanacetum*–Coccineum Group (Painted Daisy), and *Veronica prostrata* (Harebell Speedwell).

Planting

Bare Root Plant bare root stock when it becomes available, usually in July or early August. Remove the rhizomes from their shipping package immediately. Snip off broken or damaged root tips. Do *not* soak these plants overnight as you would most other perennials. Let rhizomes dry in the sun for 7 to 14 days before planting. If they get rained on, just let them dry out. Place a small amount of superphosphate in the base of the planting hole. Fill the hole with soil. Place the rhizome so that it is barely under the soil surface. Fill in with soil, firm with your fingers, and water immediately. Dissolve ½ cup (about 114 g) 10-10-10 fertilizer in 1 gallon (about 4 liters) of water. Pour ½ cup (about 120 ml) of this starter solution around each plant. If you're an organic gardener, use fish emulsion instead.

Potted Plants Plant Bearded Iris after all danger of frost has passed in spring. If the soil in the pot is dry, water it, and let it soak overnight. Tap the plant out of the pot, being careful not to disturb the root ball. Plant it at the same depth as in the pot, after preparing the hole in a manner similar to that for a bare root plant. The rhizome should be at or just under the soil surface. Fill in with soil, firm with your fingers, and water immediately. Pour ½ cup (about 120 ml) of starter solution around each plant.

How to Care for Bearded Irises

Water Keep the soil evenly moist around Bearded Iris from the beginning of the season until the end of flowering. Once plants have finished blooming, slowly reduce watering. During midsummer, these plants go into semidormancy. If you water too much during this time, you could cause rot. When the plants resume growth later in the season, begin regular watering once again.

Mulch A thin layer of mulch around these plants is fine, but they need a somewhat dry period in mid-summer. For this reason, avoid thick mulches at that time. Good organic mulches include dried grass clippings, compost, shredded leaves, and pine needles. Never place any mulch over the crown of the plant. This may cause rot.

Fertilizing Sprinkle 5-10-10 fertilizer around the base of each plant in early spring just as growth begins. Water immediately to dissolve the granules and carry nutrients to the root zone. Fertilize again just as the flower scapes emerge from the leaves.

If you prefer organic fertilizers, use alfalfa meal (rabbit pellets), blood meal, bonemeal, compost, cow manure, fish emulsion, Milorganite, or rotted horse manure. Bonemeal must be added to the soil at planting time to be effective. Some garden writers insist that horse manure may cause bacterial soft rot. We have not experienced this as long as the manure has been properly composted.

Weeding Kill off all perennial weeds before planting Bearded Iris. The rhizomes are often above soil level, so be careful when weeding. Hand pull all weeds that are close to the plant to avoid harm. Getting rid of all weeds around these plants is important not only to stop competition for water and nutrients but also to prevent disease and infestations of iris borers. A weed-free Iris bed is absolutely critical to good growth, since Irises cannot stand competition with other plants. Many growers use herbicides in their Iris beds for this reason. Preemergent herbicides are generally applied just as new growth of the perennial begins in spring, but read labels carefully for proper procedure.

Staking Many varieties need no staking, but the tall Bearded Irises may need support even when planted in full sun. In early spring, push bamboo stakes into the ground next to the plants. Attach the stems to the stakes with a soft material tied in a figure-eight knot.

Deadheading Cut or pinch off all blooms as they fade. This is both aesthetically pleasing and stops the plant from forming seed. You may have to do this each day as with Daylilies for a really good-looking garden. Carry a bucket with you, since you don't want to leave the blooms on the soil, which could cause disease. Once all blooms have faded on the stem (scape), cut the entire stem off at its base.

Pruning If plants are diseased or attacked by insects, causing discoloration or spotting of the foliage, cut the foliage back only as far as necessary to reach healthy tissue, the green and firm portion without spots. Remove dead or yellowing leaves by pulling them off the plant. They'll slide up from the base with a firm tug. Leave only healthy, unblemished leaves or portions of leaves on the plant.

If a plant is healthy, leave it alone. The leaves form food for the rhizomes, and this is what gives your plant lots of bloom in the following season. Do not cut these plants back automatically, even though this is suggested in many publications. The more leaves on a plant, the better. Also, the longer the leaves last each season, the better. Always remove dead foliage either at the end of the season or in early spring. It may harbor diseases and insect eggs.

Winter Protection Bearded Irises are very hardy plants. However, because they grow just on the surface of the soil, fluctuating winter soil temperatures may cause the plants to heave out of the soil, where they dry out and die. The following steps are recommended to protect your plants: After a hard frost, cut off all leaves as they wither. Then cover the plants with a 6-inch (15-cm) blanket of marsh hay, clean straw, pine needles, or whole leaves. Remove these as soon as the weather starts to warm in late winter or early spring to prevent rot. Generally, this winter protection is essential only in the first year, but advised in subsequent seasons with little snow.

Problems

Insects Iris borer is a serious problem with Bearded Iris. A moth (*Macronoctua onusta*) lays minuscule cylindrical eggs in the fall, which hatch the following spring. At this stage, they are iris borers (larvae).

They generally attack the central leaf, which is the most tender. As they tunnel down toward the rhizome, they're a half-inch (12 mm) long and no wider than a pin, whitish to pink with a brownish head. The borers may enter the rhizome and tunnel it out. This creates an ideal environment for bacterial soft rot. After the Iris blooms, the borers pupate and now have a hard brown shell. They emerge in fall as grayish moths to start the cycle anew.

Organic gardeners can kill borers by looking for them early in the season. Infected leaves may have jagged edges or be soft in the center, which feels wettish and is slightly different in color. Simply squeeze the leaf, running your fingers up and down the edges and center to squish the bug. Mature borers do their damage in the rhizomes, creating mushy holes which often leads to problems with disease. Cut out the creamy pink larvae and kill them.

Inorganic gardeners often use a systemic insecticide, one absorbed into the plant tissue, to kill borers. Apply it when the plants are 3 inches (7.5 centimeters) tall and once again just before bloom. Follow the directions on the label exactly.

Both organic and inorganic gardeners are wise to do the following: Clean up all debris around the Bearded Iris in fall or early spring; reduce watering after bloom; and divide the plants every 3 to 5 years to keep the bed healthy and clean. If you clean up the area around the plants in spring and fall, you often get rid of material harboring iris borer eggs. This cleanup includes the removal of dead foliage.

Aphids are also a problem because they carry disease. They are often discouraged by misting plants regularly during dry periods. However, it is sometimes necessary to use mild insecticidal soaps to kill these voracious feeders.

Disease Good cultural practices will prevent many diseases. Give plants lots of space, plant them in full sun, get rid of all weeds, clean up around the plant at all times, disinfect tools with bleach, and use fungicides if absolutely necessary.

By planting Bearded Iris in soil with excellent drainage, you'll avoid root rot. Don't water during the semidormant period after the plant blooms. Also,

avoid placing too much mulch around the base of the plant, and never put any mulch over the rhizomes (tuberous stems).

If Iris leaves get spotted during the season, cut them back just below the lowest yellow or brown spots. Otherwise, leave healthy leaves alone.

If you notice rot (bacterial or fungal) on your rhizomes, don't dig them up unless the plants are clearly dying or dead. Instead, scrape out the soft material with a spoon. Keep scraping out all soft tissue until you get to a firm portion. Then swab the wound with bleach or dust it with chlorinated cleanser. Leave the area exposed. Remove all flower stems to the base of the rhizome so that the plant's energy will go into healing itself for the next season.

Bearded Irises are notorious for getting leaf spot diseases. The most common are caused by a fungus carried by aphids, another by a bacteria, and a third by a virus (mosaic). If you're an inorganic gardener, you can control fungal and bacterial problems with regular spraying. If you're an organic gardener, the simplest solution is to cut off any diseased portion of a leaf. Grass clippers work well for this, but dip them in a chlorine solution (1 part bleach, 9 parts water) as you do this. If leaves are completely shriveled, dry, or dead, just pull them off the plant. On healthier leaves, remove only the spotted areas. The more foliage you can leave on a plant, the better. Never, ever cut off healthy foliage!

Some diseases have no cure. Plants die back or die out. If this happens, dig out the dead plant. Do not plant Bearded Iris in this same spot. Instead, use the area for a different perennial.

Propagation

Division Divide a mature plant whenever it starts to have fewer blossoms. Poor bloom indicates a need for rejuvenation. Division every 3 to 5 years is a good average. Proper division gives each plant more light and better air circulation around the leaves to prevent disease. It also gets rid of debris where moths can lay eggs, and it helps plants bloom more profusely.

Divide the rhizomes 4 to 6 weeks after the flowers have finished blooming. This is usually in July or early August, in their semidormant period. If division is done later than this, you may reduce your chances for bloom in the following season.

First, cut existing foliage back to a fan shape 3 to 6 inches (7.5 to 15 cm) tall. This minimizes water loss from the new divisions (fans). Remove any yellowing or dead leaves. Then dig up the rhizomes. Cut them apart, saving only the more vigorous, outer growth. Use a sharp knife for a smooth cut. Each rhizome should be 3 to 4 inches (7.5 to 10 cm) long, have a fan of leaves or a growing point, and have ample roots. Divisions of dwarf varieties will be smaller. Feel free to trim the roots to 2 inches (5 cm). Discard the older part of the plant. Plant each new division as a bare root plant. If you've been having disease problems, dip each fan into a solution containing bleach or Lysol (1 part bleach or Lysol to 9 parts water), and let it dry for several hours. Alternatively, spray divisions with a commercial fungicide before planting.

Seed If you buy seed, follow the directions on the package. Soaking seed is often helpful in getting it off to a good start. Bearded Iris seed is finicky, and germination can take anywhere from 1 month to 2 years. Planting in flats and following the directions outlined here is a good alternative to starting seeds indoors.

You can create your own new hybrid by crossing two flowers. Choose two different varieties of Bearded Iris. Select a flower just opening on one. Remove the falls, the petals hanging down. Then snip off the anthers, the parts with pollen. From the other variety, remove an anther with a pair of tweezers. Rub it on the stigma of the denuded first flower. Do this when the stigma are sticky. Random pollination is so rare that you do not have to cover the flower with aluminum foil as often recommended for other flowers or shrubs. In about a week, the part below the flower should begin to swell. This is the ovary. If it swells, your attempt at pollination has been suc-

cessful. Normally, the ovary will take about 6 weeks to form seed.

Seedpods turn brown and begin to split open when fully mature. Pick them at this stage. Remove the seeds, and place them in an opaque container for at least a month. Keep them cool and completely dry.

After the ground has frozen outdoors, fill a flat with sterilized soil or peat moss. Moisten it so that it's damp, not soggy. Place the seeds about ¾ inch (18 mm) deep and 1 inch (2.5 cm) apart. Cover the flat with solid plastic. The growing medium will freeze. The following spring, keep the growing medium moist at all times until seedlings start to sprout. When seedlings are 6 inches (15 cm) tall, plant them in a location where you can give them special attention. Sometimes seeds do not germinate the first year but do sprout in the following year. Seedlings take about a year to form an adult rhizome.

Special Uses

Cut Flowers These plants make lovely cut flowers. Cut stems just as the first bud starts to unfurl. Place the stem in water immediately. As flowers die off in the final arrangement, snip them off. Other buds may flower. Although this is not a long-lasting cut flower, it is still one of the most impressive for brief displays. Some people suggest that the flowers will last a little longer if you cut the bottom of the stem at a slant. Conditioning in warm water overnight often works as well.

Dried Pods Bearded Iris are not normally used for dried flowers. However, if you don't remove spent blossoms, some varieties will form seedpods, and these can be used in dried arrangements. Simply hang them upside down in a well-ventilated area, or let them dry right on the plant.

Sources

Aitken's Salmon Creek Garden, 608 NW 119th St., Vancouver, WA 98685, (360) 573-4472

Anderson Iris Gardens, 22179 Keather Ave. N, Forest Lake, MN 55025, (651) 433-5268

André Viette Farm & Nursery, P.O. Box 1109, Fishersville, VA 22939, (800) 575-5538

Argyle Acres, 910 Pioneer Circle E, Argyle, TX 76226, (940) 464-3680

Bay View Gardens, 1201 Bay St., Santa Cruz, CA 95060, (831) 423-3656

Bluebird Haven Iris Garden, 6940 Fairplay Rd., Somerset, CA 95684, (530) 620-5017

Blue J Iris, 955 Cody Ave., Alliance, NE 69301, (308) 762-4420

Cape Iris Gardens, 822 Rodney Vista Blvd., Cape Girardeau, MO 63701, (573) 334-3383

Chapman Iris, RR#1, 8790 WR 124, Guelph, ON N1H 6H7 Canada, (519) 856-4424

Comanche Acres Iris Gardens, 12421 SE State Rte 116, Gower, MO 64454, (816) 424-6436

Cooley's Iris Gardens, 11553 Silverton Rd. NE, P.O. Box 126, Silverton, OR 97381, (503) 873-5463

Dowis Ranch, P.O. Box 124, Marseilles, IL 61341, (815) 795-5681

Draycott Gardens, 16815 Falls Rd., Upperco, MD 21155, (410) 374-4788

Ferncliff Gardens, 8502 McTaggart St., Mission, BC V2V 6S6 Canada, (604) 826-2447 (604) 826-2447

Friendship Gardens, 341 Schwartz Rd., Gettysburg, PA 17325, (717) 338-1657

Hank's Iris Garden, 6119 Walnut Ave., Chino, CA 91710, (909) 945-2148

Hearthstone Legacy Iris Gardens, 12383 Hearthstone, Higginsville, MO 64037, (660) 584-6309

Holly Lane Iris Garden, 10930 Holly Lane, Osseo, MN 55369, (763) 420-4876

Hornbaker Gardens, 22937 1140 N Ave., Princeton, IL 61356, (815) 659-3282

Iris City Gardens, 502 Brighton Pl., Nashville, TN 37205, (800) 934-4747

Iris Sisters Farm, 16124 Shirley St., Omaha, NE 68130, (402) 330-1287

Iris Test Gardens, Rte 1, Box 4. Saint John, WA 99171, (509) 648-3873

Keith Keppel, P.O. Box 18154, Salem, OR 97305, (503) 391-9241

Long's Gardens, P.O. Box 19, Boulder, CO 80306, (866) 442-2353

Maple Tree Garden, P.O. Box 547, Ponca, NE 68770, (402) 755-2615

Mid-America Garden, LLC, P.O. Box 9008, Salem, OR 97305, (503) 390-6072

Misty Hill Farms, P.O. Box 1521, Healdsburg, CA 95448, (707) 433-8408

My Wild Iris Rows, 4919 Rincon Ave., Santa Rosa, CA 95409, (707) 537-7346

Napa Country Iris Gardens, 9087 Steele Canyon Rd., Napa, CA 94558, (707) 255-7880

Nicodemus Iris Garden, 124 State Rd. EE, Buffalo, MO 65622, (417) 345-8697

Nicholls Gardens, 4724 Angus Dr., Gainesville, VA 20155, (703) 754-9623

North Pine Iris Gardens, P.O. Box 595, Norfolk, NE 68701, (402) 371-3895

Painted Acres Faerm, 1711 SE State Rte EE, Weatherby, MO 64497, (816) 449-2975

Pleasure Iris Gardens, 425 E Luna Azul Dr., Chaparral, NM 88021, (505) 824-4299

Riverdale Iris Gardens, 4652 Culver Ave. NW, Buffalo, MN 55313, (320) 960-6810

Roris Gardens, 8195 Bradshaw Rd., Sacramento, CA 95829, (916) 689-7460

Sandhollow Iris Gardens, 14000 Oasis Rd., Caldwell, ID 83607, (208) 459-7185

Schreiner's Iris Gardens, 3625 Quinaby Rd. NE, Salem, OR 97303, (800) 525-2367

Spruce Gardens, 2317 3rd Rd., Wisner, NE 68791, (402) 529-6860

Superstition Iris Gardens, 2536 Old Hwy, Cathey's Valley, CA 95306, (209) 966-6277

Sutton's Iris Garden, 16592 Rd. 208, Porterville, CA 93257, (888) 558-5107

Wildwood, 33326 S Dickey Prairie Rd., Molala, OR 97038, (503) 829-3102

Willow Bend Farm, 1154 Hwy 65, Eckhert, CO 81418, (970) 263-4138

Zebra Gardens, 9130 N 5200 W, Elwood, UT 84337, (435) 257-0736

VARIETIES

Tens of thousands of named varieties of Bearded Irises have been bred and introduced over the years. In order to deal with this vast array of plants, the American Iris Society has devised a classification system, which groups Bearded Irises based primarily on the season of bloom and the height of bloom scapes (stems or flower stalks). Following is a brief explanation of the classification system as used in the table. Fragrance is noted by the initial (F) after the bloom color in the varietal chart.

Arilbred (AB): Although more difficult to grow, this is an interesting group of Irises with uniquely colored and patterned blooms. They get their name from the white collar or aril around each seed. Excellent soil drainage throughout the growing season is essential to success with these types. They grow best in areas with hot, dry summers. Their bloom season is classified as mid.

Border Bearded (BB): In the 15 to 27 inch height range, these Irises are like smaller versions of Tall Bearded Irises with flower size reduced proportionately to the height of their scapes. They bloom at the same time as Tall Bearded Irises and are quite attractive planted in front of them. However, they do not require staking to keep them upright as so many of the Tall Bearded Irises do. Their bloom season is classified as late.

Intermediate Bearded (IB): This is an important group of Irises for filling the bloom gap between Dwarf and Tall Bearded Irises. They range in height from 15 to 27 inches with flowers four to five inches across. As a group these are vigorous, heavy blooming, well-branched plants with flowers nicely proportioned to the plant size. They rarely require staking and their bloom season is classified as mid.

Miniature Dwarf Bearded (MDB): These are the smallest and earliest blooming of the Bearded Irises. They range in height from four to eight inches with flowers two to three inches across. Their flower scapes are unbranched but produced in great quantities on mature plants. They form nice clumps very quickly and are ideal in rock gardens. Their bloom season is classified as early.

Miniature Tall Bearded (MTB): These are commonly referred to as Table Irises because their size and proportion make them excellent for use in fresh floral arrangements. They range in height from 15 to 27 inches with flowers not more than six inches in combined height and width. They have six to twelve buds per stem and bloom along with Tall Bearded Irises. The wiry flower scapes are quite slender and extend nicely above the foliage. The overall effect of these irises is very dainty and airy. Their bloom season is classified as late.

Standard Dwarf Bearded (SDB): These bloom after Miniature Dwarf Bearded Irises and range in height from 8 to 15 inches. They flower along with many of our common spring-flowering bulbs and make good companions for them. Their flowers are larger than those of the Miniature Dwarf Bearded Iris and generally have two blooms at the tip of the stem and one on the side. They are vigorous growers and have good disease resistance. Their bloom season is classified as early.

Tall Bearded (TB): This is the group of Bearded Irises most well-known to gardeners. They are over 27 inches in height and are the last of the Bearded Irises to flower, blooming in late spring. They produce numerous flowers up to seven inches across and their bloom stems often require support. Their bloom season is classified as late.

VARIETY	CLASS	SEASON	COLOR (FALLS/STANDARD)	HEIGHT	HARDINESS
'Aachen Elf'	MTB	Late	Lavender/yellow	20″	−40°F
'Absolute Joy'	SDB	Early	Lavender edged pink/pink	12″	−40°F
'Again and Again'	TB	Late	Medium yellow/white	36″	−40°F
'Alpenview'	TB	Late	Light blue/white	40″	−40°F

VARIETY	CLASS	SEASON	COLOR (FALLS/STANDARD)	HEIGHT	HARDINESS
'Altruist'	TB	Late	Flax blue/white	36"	−40°F
'Apricot Drops'*****	MTB	Late	Orange pink	18"	−40°F
'Autumn Bugler'	TB	Late	Violet purple	28"	−40°F
'Az Ap'	IB	Mid	Cobalt blue	22"	−40°F
'Be My Baby'	BB	Late	Pale pink white	24"	−40°F
'Belvi Queen'	TB	Late	Cinnamon yellow (F)	42"	−40°F
'Best Bet'	TB	Late	Light blue/deep blue	36"	−40°F
'Bethany Clair'	TB	Late	Wisteria blue/white	40"	−40°F
'Beverly Sills'*****	TB	Late	Flamingo pink	36"	−40°F
'Blackbeard'	BB	Late	Light blue/black	26"	−40°F
'Blushing Kiss'	TB	Late	Light pink/dark pink	36"	−40°F
'Breakers'	TB	Late	Deep blue	36"	−40°F
'Bride's Halo'	TB	Late	White edged yellow	36"	−40°F
'Brother Carl'	TB	Late	White/pale yellow	36"	−40°F
'Bubbling Over'	TB	Late	Sky blue lilac	36"	−40°F
'Buckwheat'	TB	Late	Cream yellow/yellow	36"	−40°F
'California Style'	IB	Mid	Orange white	22"	−40°F
'Camelot Rose'	TB	Late	Pink lilac/burgundy	30"	−40°F
'Champagne Elegance'	TB	Late	White/light apricot	32"	−40°F
'Cheers'	IB	Mid	White/orange beard	24"	−40°F
'Cherry Smoke'	TB	Late	Purple red	34"	−40°F
'Chocolate Moose'	TB	Late	Brown silver streaks	30"	−40°F
'Copper Classic'	TB	Late	Burnt orange	30"	−40°F
'Crinkled Joy'	TB	Late	Lilac	34"	−40°F
'Crowned Heads'	TB	Late	Blue/bluish white	38"	−40°F
'Dazzling Gold'	TB	Late	Yellow/red brown markings	30"	−40°F
'Deep Currents'	TB	Late	Reddish purple/cream	30"	−40°F
'Deep Dark Secret'	TB	Late	Dark blue purple (F)	34"	−40°F
'Domaine'	IB	Mid	Raspberry red	26"	−40°F
'Dusky Challenger'	TB	Late	Silky rich purple	40"	−40°F
'Eagle's Flight'	TB	Late	Purple white/sky blue	36"	−40°F
'Eastertime'	TB	Late	Cream/white edged gold	38"	−40°F
'Edith Wolford'	TB	Late	Blue violet/yellow	40"	−40°F
'Everything Plus'	TB	Late	Deep blue white/sky blue	34"	−40°F
'Extravagant'	TB	Late	Pale pink/red purple	36"	−40°F
'Fashion Queen'	TB	Late	Apricot/purple	40"	−40°F
'Fire Coral'	SDB	Early	Burgundy/vibrant orange	12"	−40°F
'Fogbound'	TB	Late	Wisteria blue/white	40"	−40°F
'Gay Parasol'	TB	Late	Lavender/rose violet	35"	−40°F
'Going My Way'	TB	Late	White/purple rim	36"	−40°F
'Golden Knight'	TB	Late	Rich yellow	30"	−40°F

'Cheers'

'Honey Glazed'

'Jesse's Song'

'Joyce Terry'

'Lemon Mist'

'New Idea'

'Raspberry Ripples'

'Tides In'

VARIETY	CLASS	SEASON	COLOR (FALLS/STANDARD)	HEIGHT	HARDINESS
'Golden Panther'*****	TB	Late	Golden bronze	34″	−40°F
'Grand Waltz'	TB	Late	Lavender orchid	34″	−40°F
'Hagar's Helmet'*****	IB	Mid	Medium yellow	20″	−40°F
'Happenstance'*****	TB	Late	Rich pink	36″	−40°F
'Harvest of Memories'*****	TB	Late	Medium yellow (VF)	36″	−40°F
'Heartstring Strummer'	TB	Late	White lavender	40″	−40°F
'Hollywood Nights'	TB	Late	Purple black	32″	−40°F
'Honey Glazed'	IB	Mid	Butterscotch/cream	26″	−40°F
'I Bless'	IB	Mid	Cream/light yellow	18″	−40°F
'I Do'	TB	Late	White/greenish yellow	30″	−40°F
'Immortality'	TB	Late	White tinged blue (F)	30″	−40°F
'Imposter'	TB	Late	Apricot/purplish red	36″	−40°F
'Jean Guymer'	TB	Late	Apricot pink/tangerine	36″	−40°F
'Jesse's Song'	TB	Late	White/violet	36″	−40°F
'Joyce Terry'*****	TB	Late	Yellow edged white	38″	−40°F
'Laced Cotton'	TB	Late	White	34″	−40°F
'Lacy Snowflake'	TB	Late	White	38″	−40°F
'Lady Friend'	TB	Late	Garnet red	38″	−40°F
'Late Lilac'	TB	Late	Lilac/lavender (F)	30″	−40°F
'Lemon Mist'	TB	Late	Soft Yellow	30″	−40°F
'Limonada'	IB	Mid	Lemon yellow	24″	−40°F
'Lorna's Jennifer'	TB	Late	Light pink/lavender (F)	36″	−40°F
'Lorilee'	TB	Late	Rose orchid	36″	−40°F
'Lovely Senorita'	TB	Late	Burgundy/orange	40″	−40°F
'Lyrique'	BB	Late	Silver lilac/burgundy	20″	−40°F
'Maid of Orange'	BB	Late	Orange/tangerine	24″	−40°F
'Matinata'*****	TB	Late	Deep violet purple	40″	−40°F
'Mary Frances'*****	TB	Late	Light blue orchid	38″	−40°F
'Morning Frost'	TB	Late	Lavender/pale white	38″	−40°F
'Mulberry Echo'	TB	Late	Maroon orange (F)	36″	−40°F
'Mulled Wine'	TB	Late	Raspberry burgundy	30″	−40°F
'Mystique'	TB	Late	Blue/deep blue purple	36″	−40°F
'New Idea'	MTB	Mid	Rose mulberry	26″	−40°F
'Novella'	BB	Late	Cranberry (F)	24″	−40°F
'Olympiad'	TB	Late	Pale blue/darker center	38″	−40°F
'Orinoco Flow'*****	BB	Late	White edged blue	24″	−40°F
'Paul Black'	TB	Late	Deep purple (F)	42″	−40°F
'Pretty Pixie'	MDB	Early	Brass bronze edged white/white	8″	−40°F
'Pure As Gold'	TB	Late	Deep gold	34″	−40°F
'Quantum Leap'	TB	Late	Plum white	36″	−40°F
'Queen Anne's Lace'*****	TB	Late	White	38″	−40°F

VARIETY	CLASS	SEASON	COLOR (FALLS/STANDARD)	HEIGHT	HARDINESS
'Queen Dorothy'	TB	Late	White violet/yellow (F)	28″	−40°F
'Queen In Calico'	TB	Late	Apricot/red violet	34″	−40°F
'Queen's Circle'	TB	Late	White edged blue (F)	32″	−40°F
'Raptor Red'	TB	Late	Velvet red	34″	−40°F
'Rare Edition'	IB	Mid	White/mulberry	24″	−40°F
'Raspberry Ripples'	TB	Late	Rose purple	36″	−40°F
'Red Zinger'	IB	Mid	Burgundy red	26″	−40°F
'Ringo'	TB	Late	White/grape edged white	36″	−40°F
'Rosette Wine'	TB	Late	Petunia purple/white	36″	−40°F
'Ruffled Ballet'*****	TB	Late	Blue white/medium blue	30″	−40°F
'Sea Power'*****	TB	Late	Cornflower blue edged white	38″	−40°F
'Season Ticket'	IB	Mid	Apricot	36″	−40°F
'September Replay'	TB	Late	Golden tan/white	30″	−40°F
'Silverado'	TB	Late	Light blue	38″	−40°F
'Skating Party'	TB	Late	White	36″	−40°F
'Song Of Norway'*****	TB	Late	Light powder blue	38″	−40°F
'Sonja's Selah'*****	BB	Late	Tan rose/cream	24″	−40°F
'Stairway to Heaven'*****	TB	Late	White/blue	38″	−40°F
'Starring'	TB	Late	White/near black	34″	−40°F
'Stepping Out'*****	TB	Late	White/blue violet	38″	−40°F
'Study In Black'	TB	Late	Deep red black	36″	−40°F
'Superstition'	TB	Late	Ebony	36″	−40°F
'Supreme Sultan'	TB	Late	Yellow/crimson	40″	−40°F
'Summer Olympics'*****	TB	Late	Yellow/white	30″	−40°F
'Synergy'	IB	Mid	Golden rose lilac	24″	−40°F
'Tides In'	TB	Late	Blue	36″	−40°F
'Tiny Titan'	MDB	Early	Peach orange	8″	−40°F
'Titan's Glory'	TB	Late	Dark violet	36″	−40°F
'Trans Orange'	TB	Late	Orange/white	36″	−40°F
'Tuxedo'	TB	Late	Sky blue	22″	−40°F
'Uncle Charlie'	TB	Late	Silvery blue white	34″	−40°F
'Victoria Falls'*****	TB	Late	Blue/white spot	40″	−40°F
'Violet Returns'	TB	Late	Violet/yellow	30″	−40°F
'Virginia Lyle'	MTB	Late	Medium blue	24″	−40°F
'Whoop 'Em Up'	BB	Late	Golden yellow/maroon	26″	−40°F
'Yaquina Blue'	TB	Late	Marine blue	36″	−40°F
'Zipper'*****	MDB	Early	Pale yellow (F)	8″	−40°F

'Steve Varner'

IRIS

(EYE-ris)

SIBERIAN IRIS

Bloom Time	Expected Longevity	Maintenance	Years to Bloom	Preferred Light
Late spring to early summer	25+ years	Low	From seed: 3 years From potted plant: 2 years	Full sun

Siberian Irises are extremely hardy, easy to grow, and trouble free. Mature plants are lush with long, thin leaves and covered with spectacular bloom during a short period of time. Blooms lack the fuzzy beards of Bearded Iris and so are often referred to as Beardless Iris. The foliage remains attractive throughout the season. Siberian Irises make good, if short-lived, cut flowers. Dried stems with seedpods are cherished in floral arrangements. Plants are extremely long-lived, are rarely bothered by disease or insects, and don't need regular division to do well. However, they do require consistent moisture throughout the growing season.

How Siberian Irises Grow

Siberian Irises, unlike Bearded Irises, have fibrous roots. As each plant matures, it grows into a large clump with tall, thin leaves. From this clump spring willowy stems with long, delicate buds unfurling into beautiful beardless flowers. These stay open for days and then begin to wither. If left on the plant, they form pods with three distinct chambers. When the plant is mature, each section is filled with a row of dark brown seeds. Clumps increase in size yearly, looking like large upright vases.

Where to Plant

Site and Light This high-light plant thrives in full sun. Without direct sun, plants will be less vigorous and produce far fewer blossoms. A well-grown plant will produce numerous stalks and prolific bloom.

Soil and Moisture Siberian Irises flourish in rich, well-drained, slightly acidic soil (pH of 5.5 to 6.5). Add lots of organic matter to the soil. Compost, rotted manure, shredded leaves, and peat moss are all good. Shredded oak leaves or peat moss are the best because they are slightly acidic. This organic matter is essential, since it retains moisture. Siberian Irises need lots of water, especially prior to bloom.

Spacing Although bare root plants are small, they will form extensive clumps over a period of a few years. Give the plants plenty of space in which to mature.

Companions

Siberian Irises have stunning flowers and fine foliage. Striking companions are *Alchemilla* (Lady's Mantle), *Aquilegia* (Columbine), *Baptisia* (False Indigo), *Campanula* (Bellflower), *Dianthus* (Pinks), *Filipendula vulgaris* (Dropwort), *Geranium* (Cranesbill), *Heuchera* (Coral Bells), *Nepeta* (Catmint), *Paeonia* (Peony), *Salvia* (Sage), *Tanacetum*–Coccineum Group (Painted Daisy), *Tradescantia* (Spiderwort), and *Veronica* (Speedwell). Following are specific combinations to consider: *Iris* 'Dancing Nanou' (Siberian Iris) with *Alchemilla mollis* (Lady's Mantle) and *Paeonia* 'Norma Volz' (Peony); *Iris* 'Butter and Sugar' (Siberian Iris) planted with *Artemisia schmidtiana* 'Silver Mound'/'Nana' (Wormwood) and *Geranium* × *magnificum* (Showy Cranesbill); and *Iris* 'Pink Haze' (Siberian Iris) next to *Campanula glomerata* (Clustered Bellflower) and *Dianthus*–Plumarius Group 'Margaret Curtis' (Hardy Garden Pink). With their excellent golden yellow fall color, Siberian Irises should also be considered for combination with other plants with interesting fall foliage color. Among the perennials to consider are *Euphorbia polychroma* (Cushion Spurge), *Geranium* (Cranesbill), *Lysimachia clethroides* (Gooseneck Loosestrife), *Paeonia* (Peony), *Platycodon grandiflorus* (Balloon Flower), and **Grasses**. Siberian Irises are also lovely planted in sunny locations along streams or ponds. The mass effect can be breathtaking.

Planting

Bare Root Plant bare root stock as soon as it arrives, generally in late summer or early fall (a few mail-order sources offer plants in spring). Remove the plants from their shipping package immediately. Snip off broken or damaged root tips. Soak plants overnight in room-temperature water. Place a small amount of superphosphate in the base of the planting hole. Fill the hole with soil. Place the crown just under the soil surface. Fill in with soil, firm with your fingers, and water immediately. Dissolve ½ cup (about 114 g) 10-10-10 fertilizer in a gallon (about 4 liters) of water. Pour ½ cup (about 120 ml) of this starter solution around each plant. If you're an organic gardener, use fish emulsion instead.

Potted Plants Plant Siberian Iris after all danger of frost has passed in spring. If the soil in the pot is dry, water it, and let it drain overnight. Tap the plant out of the pot, being careful not to disturb the root ball. Plant it at the same depth as in the pot, after preparing the hole in a manner similar to that for a bare root plant. Fill in with soil, firm with your fingers, and water immediately. Pour ½ cup (about 120 ml) of starter solution around each plant.

How to Care for Siberian Irises

Water Siberian Irises are moisture-loving plants. Keep the soil moist around the plants, especially prior to their bloom period. Whenever you water, saturate the soil to a depth of 18 inches (45 cm). If you prepare the soil properly, it will retain moisture but drain freely.

Mulch Mulch is highly recommended to keep moisture in the soil. Good organic mulches include dried grass clippings, compost, shredded leaves, and pine needles. Mulch has the added benefit of controlling annual weeds and making weeding easier.

Fertilizing Sprinkle 10-10-10 fertilizer around the base of each plant in early spring just as growth begins. Water immediately to dissolve the granules and carry nutrients to the root zone. Do this again just before the plant blooms. Frequent small feedings (every 2 weeks) are a fine alternative.

If you prefer organic fertilizers, use alfalfa meal (rabbit pellets), blood meal, bonemeal, compost, cow manure, fish emulsion, Milorganite, or rotted horse manure. Bonemeal must be added to the soil at planting time to be effective.

Weeding Kill all perennial weeds before planting, with Roundup® or a similar systemic herbicide. Hand weed around the base of the plant to disturb its root system as little as possible. If weeds sprout up inside the clump, simply pull them out.

Staking Staking is rarely needed unless plants are placed in too much shade.

Deadheading Cut off all blooms as they fade. This is both aesthetically pleasing and stops the plant from forming seed. If you want seed, let a few blossoms remain on the plant. Or, if you want dried pods for floral arrangements, leave the number of stems needed for such use.

Winter Protection Siberian Irises are extremely hardy and rarely require any winter protection.

Problems

Insects Iris borers are not a common problem for Siberian Iris. Clean up all debris around the plants when you cut them back in fall. This material can harbor eggs that develop into borers. Aphids can also be an occasional nuisance. Gentle misting deters most aphid infestations. If plants do get covered with aphids, use mild insecticidal soaps to kill them.

Disease Siberian Iris are very disease resistant, which make them a good choice for purely organic gardeners, who will most likely need to use pesticides to grow Bearded Iris well.

Rodents Rodents often use mature beds of Siberian Iris for their winter home. They also munch on crowns for their food supply. Rarely do they kill the entire plant, but they'll often do so much damage that you get little or no bloom. To prevent this, cut the foliage back to ground level late in the fall after a hard frost when the foliage withers and turns yellow to brown. It's easiest to do this with hedge pruners. Then compost the dead leaves.

Propagation

Division Siberian Irises form a mat of fibrous rhizomes. In early spring, dig up the entire plant when leaves are just beginning to show. Sever the thick mat of roots (rhizomes) with a knife or spade. Each section should have at least six stems attached to a healthy bunch of roots. Plant these divisions (fans) immediately as you would a bare root plant. Be sure to keep them moist at all times. Note that if you wait until the plant has leaves taller than 3 to 4 inches (7.5 to 10 cm), you've waited too long. Division can stop bloom for an entire season if done too late.

However, you have a second chance to divide this plant. In very late summer to early fall, cut the foliage back to 6 to 12 inches (15 to 30 cm). This minimizes water loss from the leaves. Dig up the plant, divide it, and plant the sections as you would in spring. Most commercial growers divide late in the season with excellent survival rates even in cold climates, as long as clumps contain three or more fans.

Seed The species (wild) Siberian Iris come true from seed. To propagate these plants, fill a tray with moist peat moss. Cover the seed slightly. Then slide the tray into a plastic bag perforated for good air circulation. Place the tray in the crisper of your refrigerator for 6 to 8 weeks. After this time, remove the tray, and keep it at temperatures above 55°F (13°C) until seedlings emerge. Remove the bag, but keep the medium moist at all times. Give the young plants plenty of light until they are growing vigorously. After any chance of frost, plant the seedlings outdoors once they are 3 to 4 inches (7.5 to 10 cm) tall. Harden them off for 14 days.

The species Siberian Iris and a number of the named varieties will self-sow if seedpods are allowed to remain on the plant. This is the easiest way to get new seedlings. Seeds fall to the ground and begin to grow the following season. Use organic fertilizer around the plants in the spring if you want these young seedlings to survive. Inorganic fertilizer often kills seedlings. Do not expect seedlings to have flowers identical to the parents if you're growing named varieties (cultivars).

Special Uses

Cut Flowers These make excellent but relatively short-lived cut flowers. Cut stems just as buds start to unfurl to get longest life in the arrangement. Place them directly in an arrangement, or condition them in warm water overnight. The buds are as beautiful as the flowers in arrangements and will open up in about a day.

Dried Pods Siberian Iris are not normally used for dried flowers. However, stems with dried seedpods are attractive in floral arrangements. Let the stems and pods dry and turn brown before cutting them off the plant. If you wait too long, the pods often split open. Both closed and open pods are quite lovely.

Sources

Aitken's Salmon Creek Garden, 608 NW 119th St., Vancouver, WA 98685, (360) 573-4472

Ambergate Gardens, 8730 County Rd. 43, Chaska, MN 55318, (877) 211-9769

Bountiful Bulbs, 427 E 500 N, Rupert, ID 83350, (208) 532-4500

Busse Gardens, 17160 245th Ave., Big Lake, MN 55309, (800) 544-3192

Chehalem Gardens, P.O. Box 693, Newberg, OR 97132, (503) 538-8920

Deer-resistant Landscape Nursery, 3200 Sunstone Ct., Clare, MI 48617, (800) 595-3650

Draycott Gardens, 16815 Falls Rd., Upperco, MD 21155, (410) 374-4788

Eartheart Gardens, 1709 Harpswell Neck Rd., Harpswell, ME 04079, (207) 833-6905

Ensata Gardens, 9823 E Michigan Ave., Galesburg, MI 49053, (269) 665-7500

EZ Iriz, 31726 Sunrise Ave., Dowagiac, MI 49047, (866) 797-7909

Fieldstone Gardens, 55 Quaker Lane, Vassalboro, ME 04989, (207) 923-3836

Greenhorn Valley Iris, P.O. Box 19609, Colorado City, CO 81019, (719) 671-3675

Holly Lane Gardens, 10930 Holly Lane, Osseo, MN 55369, (763) 420-4876

Homestead Farms Nursery, 3701 Hwy EE, Owensville, MO 65066, (573) 437-4277

Iris City Gardens, 7675 Younger Creek Rd., Primm Springs, TN 38476, (800) 934-4747

Joe Pye Weed's Garden, 337 Acton St., Carlisle, MA 01741, (978) 371-0173

Klehm's Song Sparrow Perennial Farm, 13101 E Rye Rd., Avalon, WI 53505, (800) 553-3715

Mid-America Garden, LLC, P.O. Box 9008, Salem, OR 97305, (503) 390-6072

Nicholls Gardens, 4724 Angus Dr., Gainesville, VA 20155, (703) 754-9623

Reath's Nursery, N-195 Cty Rd. 577, Vulcan, MI 49892 (906) 563-9777

Schreiner's Iris Gardens, 3625 Quinaby Rd. NE, Salem, OR 97303, (800) 525-2367

Siberian Iris Gardens, P.O. Box 101, Hannibal, NY 13074, (888) 761-8782

Tranquil Lake Nursery, 45 River St., Rehoboth, MA 02769, (508) 252-4002

Walnut Hill Gardens, 999 310th St., Atalissa, IA 52720, (563) 946-3471

'Dreaming Yellow'

'Little White'

VARIETIES

When selecting varieties, consider the following characteristics: flower color, flower shape and substance (thickness), plant height, length of bloom season, foliage quality, and chromosome count. Plants carrying a single complement of chromosomes are diploid. Tetraploids have had their chromosome numbers artificially doubled. The latter are stouter with more upright foliage. Their larger flowers have richer colors, more flaring falls, and heavier texture. The tetraploids do require a more even supply of moisture throughout the season. Tetraploids are marked with an asterisk (*) next to plant color in the list below. If you like ruffled flowers, try 'Blueberry Fair,' 'Coronation Anthem,' 'Jeweled Crown,' 'Magnum Bordeaux,' 'Over in Gloryland,' and 'Strawberry Fair.' Some Siberian Iris varieties rebloom in certain parts of the country, but this is not a reliable characteristic in cold-climate areas. Genetics and overall plant health as well as climatic and soil conditions play a significant role in this phenomenon. A few varieties like 'Dancing Nanou,' 'Heliotrope Bouquet,' 'Indy,' and 'White Swirl' stand out for extended periods of bloom.

VARIETY	COLOR/PLOIDY	HEIGHT	HARDINESS
Iris sanguinea			
(Oriental Iris)	Intense blue	30″	−30°F

This species has reed-like leaves and fairly large flowers blooming just above the foliage. The flower stems (scapes) are generally unbranched but plentiful. It is an important parent in breeding named varieties of Siberian Iris.

Iris sibirica			
(Siberian Iris)	Violet blue	36″	−30°F

The primary species used in breeding modern Siberian Iris, *Iris sibirica* has erect, grassy foliage, and numerous small flowers blooming well above the foliage.

Iris typhifolia			
(Cattail Iris)	Rich violet blue	24″	−30°F

This early-blooming species has also become an integral part of Siberian Iris breeding programs. It has twisted, very narrow foliage and many, medium-sized flower scapes.

Iris (Named varieties and hybrids)			
'Aqua Whispers'	Lavender pink/rose blush	36″	−40°F
'Band of Angels'	Deep blue violet/light blue edges*	30″	−40°F
'Blueberry Fair'*****	Blue violet/white*	32″	−40°F
'Butter and Sugar'	Yellow/creamy white	28″	−40°F
'Caesar's Brother'	Deep purple	36″	−40°F
'Careless Sally'	Light rose lavender/pink lavender	26″	−40°F
'Cheery Lyn'*****	Pinkish lavender white/yellow	36″	−40°F
'Coronation Anthem'*****	Medium blue/white center*	32″	−40°F
'Dancing Nanou'*****	Blue violet/purple	34″	−40°F
'Dewful'	Medium blue/light blue	40″	−40°F
'Dreaming Spires'	Lavender/royal blue	36″	−40°F
'Dreaming Yellow'	White/creamy yellow	30″	−40°F
'Ego'	Rich blue	32″	−40°F
'Ewen'	Wine red/whitish yellow*	32″	−40°F
'Flight of Butterflies'	Violet blue/white veins	36″	−40°F

VARIETY	COLOR/PLOIDY	HEIGHT	HARDINESS
'Fond Kiss'	White/lavender pink blush	32″	−40°F
'Forrest McCord'	Dark blue/white edge	36″	−40°F
'Frosted Cranberry'	Medium rose pink	32″	−40°F
'Gull's Wing'*****	Pure white/pale yellow base	36″	−40°F
'Harpswell Happiness'	Creamy white/yellow*	30″	−40°F
'Heliotrope Bouquet'*****	Light mauve	32″	−40°F
'Indy'	Medium deep red violet	32″	−40°F
'Isabelle'*****	Creamy white/light yellow	26″	−40°F
'Jamaican Velvet'*****	Red violet	30″	−40°F
'Jeweled Crown'*****	Deep wine red/white yellow*	24″	−40°F
'Lady Vanessa'	Wine red/white base	36″	−40°F
'Lavender Bounty'	Lavender pink/whitish yellow	36″	−40°F
'Little White'	Bright white/gold	12″	−40°F
'Mabel Coday'	Rich medium blue/white base	30″	−40°F
'Magnum Bordeaux'	Reddish purple	36″	−40°F
'Moon Silk'	Pale yellow/creamy white	28″	−40°F
'Orville Fay'	Violet blue/dark veins*	36″	−40°F
'Over in Gloryland'	Dark royal purple/cream yellow base*	34″	−40°F
'Pas de Deux'	Lemon yellow/white	26″	−40°F
'Percheron'*****	Dappled blue violet/pale blue	35″	−40°F
'Pink Haze'	Clear lavender pink	38″	−40°F
'Regency Belle'	Blue violet bitone*	28″	−40°F
'Roaring Jelly'	Red purple maroon/lighter center	36″	−40°F
'Ruffled Velvet'	Velvety purple/white yellow base	24″	−40°F
'Sally Kerlin'	Clear pale blue	28″	−40°F
'Shaker's Prayer'	White veined lilac/violet	36″	−40°F
'Ships Are Sailing'	Blue violet/light blue	35″	−40°F
'Shirley Pope'*****	Rich wine purple/white	28″	−40°F
'Silver Edge'	Medium blue/silver edge*	28″	−40°F
'Springs Brook'	Silvery blue violet	40″	−40°F
'Steve Varner'	Bright lavender/pale blue	30″	−40°F
'Strawberry Fair'*****	Ruffled rose violet/white yellow*	30″	−40°F
'Sultan's Ruby'	Deep reddish violet/gold	30″	−40°F
'Summer Revels'	Medium yellow/white tinged yellow	28″	−40°F
'Super Ego'	Light blue bitone	30″	−40°F
'Tealwood'	Dark velvet blue purple/white	27″	−40°F
'Temper Tantrum'	Deep purplish red/purple veins	36″	−40°F
'Trim the Velvet'	Blue purple/white edge	40″	−40°F
'Where Eagles Dare'	Dark blue violet	40″	−40°F
'White Swirl'	Ivory white/white yellow	40″	−40°F
'Windwood Spring'	Light blue/white center*	28″	−40°F

Lamium maculatum

LAMIUM MACULATUM

(LAY-mee-um maah-cue-LAY-tuhm)

SPOTTED DEAD NETTLE

Bloom Time	Expected Longevity	Maintenance	Years to Bloom	Preferred Light
Late spring to early summer	5 to 10+ years	Low	From seed: 2 years From potted plant: 1 year	Light shade

Spotted Dead Nettle is a durable perennial that grows well in partial shade. Though related to **Urtica dioica** (Stinging Nettle), it lacks any stinging hairs. It is a superb ground cover. The various selections offer a wide variety of foliage colors and patterns as well as several flower colors. Spotted Dead Nettle is rarely bothered by insects or diseases, and the cut stems, though somewhat short, are lovely in floral arrangements.

How Spotted Dead Nettles Grow

Spotted Dead Nettle grows readily from a young plant with short, fibrous roots into a low wide-spreading colony of plants. Each plant has square stems and oval-shaped leaves that, in most cases, are mottled or striped with silver. In mild climates, this perennial remains evergreen, but our difficult winters usually result in dieback to ground level. Its small, hooded flowers are reminiscent of Snapdragons, and they bloom in late spring and early summer. They are typically mauve pink or some similar shade, but there are a number of attractive white-flowered forms as well. In cool, moist seasons, sporadic blooms appear throughout the entire summer. Spotted Dead Nettle will self-sow quite freely, but the named selections will not come true to type.

Where to Plant

Site and Light Although best grown in light shade, this perennial grows well in full sun in cold climates if the soil is kept evenly moist throughout the season. Deep shade results in lanky growth and poor flowering. This is a terrific plant to use as a ground cover under flowering trees and shrubs.

Soil and Moisture Spotted Dead Nettle thrives in evenly moist soil that drains freely. Replace clay or rocky soil with good soil or build a raised bed. Mix in lots of organic matter. Recommended amendments are compost, leaf mold, rotted manure, and peat moss. Keep the soil evenly moist all season long for best bloom. A number of varieties, especially the more vigorous forms, tolerate short, dry periods as mature plants.

Spacing Space plants 8 to 12 inches (20 to 30 cm) apart, depending on the variety. The plants will quickly fill in any available space, covering the ground with a dense mat of striking foliage.

Companions

Lamium maculatum (Spotted Dead Nettle), despite its unpleasant common name, makes an attractive ground cover under small ornamental trees such as *Malus* (Crabapple) or spring-flowering shrubs such as *Viburnum* (Viburnum). It also intermingles beautifully with other perennials such as *Dicentra* (Bleeding Heart), *Hosta* (Hosta), *Pulmonaria* (Lungwort), *Tradescantia* (Spiderwort), spring flowering bulbs, and **Ferns**. Specific combinations worth trying are *Lamium maculatum* 'White Nancy' (Spotted Dead Nettle) planted with *Geranium* 'Orion' (Cranesbill) and *Heuchera micrantha* 'Molly Bush' (Small Flowered Alumroot) or *Lamium maculatum* 'Beedham's White' (Spotted Dead Nettle) used as a ground cover between *Dicentra eximia* 'Snowdrift' (Fringed Bleeding Heart) and *Hosta* 'Gold Standard' (Hosta).

Planting

Bare Root Plant bare root stock as soon as you can work the ground in spring. Remove plants from their shipping package immediately. Snip off broken or damaged root tips. Soak plants overnight in room-temperature water. Place a small amount of superphosphate in the base of the planting hole. Fill the hole with soil. Place the crown just under the soil surface. Fill in with soil, firm with your fingers, and water immediately. Dissolve ½ cup (about 114 g) 10-10-10 fertilizer in 1 gallon (about 4 liters) of water. Pour ½ cup (about 120 ml) of this starter solution around the base of each plant. If you prefer organic fertilizer, use fish emulsion instead.

Potted Plants Plant potted plants after all danger of frost has passed in spring. If the soil in the pot is dry, water it, and let it drain overnight. Tap the plant out of the pot without disturbing the root ball. Plant it at the same depth as in the pot, after preparing the hole in a manner similar to that for a bare root plant. Fill in with soil, firm with your fingers, and water immediately. Pour ½ cup (about 120 ml) starter solution around the base of each plant.

How to Care for Spotted Dead Nettle

Water Although Spotted Dead Nettle will tolerate short dry spells, the lushest growth and most abundant flowering takes place in soils kept evenly moist throughout the growing season. Saturate the soil to a depth of 8 to 10 inches (20 to 25 cm) each time you water.

Mulch Place 2 inches (5 cm) of mulch around the base of each plant as soon as the soil warms up in spring. Good materials include leaf mold, shredded bark, and pine needles. Mature plants cover the ground so well that their foliage acts as a summer mulch. Mulch keeps the soil moist and cool while inhibiting the growth of annual weeds.

Fertilizing Sprinkle 10-10-10 fertilizer over the mass of plants just as new growth begins to emerge in spring. Water immediately to dissolve the granules and to move nutrients into the root zone. Immediate watering also prevents fertilizer burn of new shoots. Following up with a second feeding several weeks later results in lush foliage and better bloom.

If you prefer organic fertilizers, use alfalfa meal (rabbit pellets), blood meal, bonemeal, compost, cow manure, fish emulsion, Milorganite, or decomposed horse manure. Bonemeal must be mixed into the soil at planting time to be effective.

Weeding When using Spotted Dead Nettle as a ground cover, eliminate perennial weeds from the site prior to planting. If this is not done, portions or all of the planting may be overwhelmed by undesirable plants. Use a mulch around young plants to prevent germination of annual weeds. As Spotted Dead Nettle fills in an area, its dense foliage will prevent most weeds from germinating. Any that do grow can be removed easily by hand.

Staking Staking is not required.

Deadheading Remove the small dead blossoms to keep plants tidy, encourage additional bloom, and prevent self-sowing. Deadheading is certainly not critical for the long-term health of these plants.

Pruning If you want to keep plants more dense and compact, cut them back partially with hedge shears immediately after the main flush of bloom. Plants sheared back in this fashion may reward you with some flowers again later in the season.

Winter Protection Mature Spotted Dead Nettle does sometimes suffer damage in very open, difficult winters. Protect plants in open sites. Cover them with a 4-inch (10-cm) layer of marsh hay, whole leaves, or clean straw after the ground has permanently frozen in late fall. Remove this as soon as the weather starts to warm up in spring.

Problems

Insects Spotted Dead Nettle is rarely bothered by insects. Slugs may make their home under the dense foliage, but they do not find the bristly textured leaves appetizing.

Disease Plants grown under good culture are virtually disease free.

Propagation

Division Though not requiring frequent division for its health, Spotted Dead Nettle is very easy to propagate by this method. The best time to divide is in early spring, but these tough perennials can be divided in midsummer if they are cut back and watered well while they are taking root. The low-growing stems often root where leaf nodes touch the ground. These rooted plants can be severed and dug up without disturbing the mother clump. Plant them immediately as you would a bare root plant.

Cuttings Spotted Dead Nettle roots easily from cuttings. Take tip cuttings from new shoots in early spring, or stem cuttings after summer flowering. Both types root well without rooting hormone, but its use often speeds up the process. Remove the lower leaves from the cuttings prior to sticking them in a moist rooting medium. Within several weeks, they will be rooted well enough that they can be transplanted into pots or into the garden where they must be kept evenly moist to get off to a good start.

Seed Seed-grown plants vary considerably in foliage color from their parents and often are not as compact and tidy as ones grown from divisions or cuttings. Spotted Dead Nettle is, however, easy to grow from seed and does not require special treatments.

Special Uses

Cut Flowers Most gardeners rarely think of using Spotted Dead Nettle in fresh arrangements, mainly because it's so short. However, the plant makes a good cut flower as long as it is conditioned properly. Cut stems as long as possible, get them into a bucket of water immediately, get them out of direct sun as soon as possible, and then set the bottom inch (2.5 cm) or so of each stem in boiling water for a few seconds. Finally, submerge the stems in warm water for about 12 hours. After that, place them in an arrange-ment, stripping off any leaves that will end up below the water line.

Dried Flowers Spotted Dead Nettle is not used for dried arrangements.

Sources

Bluestone Perennials, 7211 Middle Ridge Rd., Madison, OH 44057, (800) 852-5243

Busse Gardens, 17160 245th Ave., Big Lake, MN 55309, (800) 544-3192

Fieldstone Gardens, Inc., 55 Quaker Lane, Vassalboro, ME 04989, (207) 923-3836

Joy Creek Nursery, 20300 NW Watson Rd., Scappoose, OR 97056, (503) 543-7474

Variegated Foliage Nursery, 245 Westford Rd., Eastford, CT 06242, (860) 974-3951

'Beacon Silver'

'White Nancy'

VARIETIES

VARIETY	FOLIAGE	COLOR	HEIGHT	HARDINESS
Lamium maculatum				
(Spotted Dead Nettle)	Green dabbed silver	Mauve pink	12″	−40°F
'Album'	Green dabbed silver	White	8″	−40°F
'Anne Greenaway'	Greens edged yellow/silver white stripe	Mauve pink	8″	−40°F
'Aureum'	Golden yellow/white stripe	Lavender pink	6″	−40°F
'Beacon Silver'	Silver edged green	Purple pink	10″	−40°F
'Beedham's White'	Golden yellow/white stripe	Pure white	8″	−40°F
'Brocade'	Silver edged green	Rose pink	8″	−40°F
'Chequers'	Green/silver slashes	Amethyst violet	12″	−40°F
'Cosmopolitan'	Highly silvered	Light pink	6″	−40°F
'Ghost'	Silver barely edged green	Orchid purple	12″	−40°F
'Lemon Frost'	Yellowish green/white stripe	Lavender rose	8″	−40°F
'Orchid Frost'*****	Silver edged green	Orchid pink	8″	−40°F
'Pink Pewter'	Silver edged green	Soft pink	8″	−40°F
'Purple Dragon'	Silver edged green	Deep purple	8″	−40°F
'Red Nancy'*****	Silver edged green	Rose pink	8″	−40°F
'Shell Pink'	Green/white slashes	Medium pink	12″	−40°F
'White Nancy'	Silver edged green	Pure white	8″	−40°F

The species is a very vigorous plant that makes a fine ground cover for large areas. Only about half of seed-grown 'Album' will bloom white. 'Anne Greenaway' has light and dark green leaves edged chartreuse yellow with a silver white central stripe. 'Aureum' requires protection from hot afternoon sun to look its best and is not as vigorous as 'Beedham's White.' 'Beacon Silver' is similar to the species but with almost entirely silver leaves. The foliage of 'Brocade' is gorgeous, but it blooms sparsely. 'Chequers' is a vigorous grower and makes a good large-scale ground cover. 'Cosmopolitan' is ideal for containers. 'Ghost' has noticeably large leaves. 'Lemon Frost' has new growth which is lime green to chartreuse with a central white stripe. 'Orchid Frost' is a profuse bloomer. 'Purple Dragon' stands out for its distinctly larger individual blooms and more substantial flower spikes. 'Shell Pink' is similar to the species but is more compact with truer pink flowers. 'White Nancy' has lovely pure white flowers.

iccant. Then cover it carefully with more material, making sure the petals are appropriately arranged. Allow it to remain in place until totally dry. The short wire can then be attached to a longer one if necessary for any given use.

Sources

Ambergate Gardens, 8730 County Rd. 43, Chaska, MN 55318, (877) 211-9769

W. Atlee Burpee & Co., 300 Park Ave., Warminster, PA 18991, (800) 888-1447

Bluestone Perennials, 7211 Middle Ridge Rd., Madison, OH 44057, (800) 852-5243

Busse Gardens, 17160 245th Ave., Big Lake, MN 55309, (800) 544-3192

Dayton Nurseries, 3459 Cleveland-Massilon Rd., Norton, OH 44203, (330) 825-3320

ForestFarm, 990 Tetherow Rd., Williams, OR 97544, (541) 846-7269

Fraser's Thimble Farms, 175 Arbutus Rd., Salt Spring Island, BC V8K 1A3, Canada, (250) 537-5788

Fritz Creek Gardens, P.O. Box 15226, Homer, AK 99603, (907) 235-4969

Roots and Rhizomes, P.O. Box A, Randolph, WI 53956, (800) 374-5035

Stokes Seeds, Inc., P.O. Box 548, Buffalo, NY 14240, (800) 396-9238

White Flower Farm, P.O. Box 50, Litchfield, CT 06759, (800) 503-9624

Whitney Gardens & Nursery, P.O. Box 170, Brinnon, WA 98320, (360) 796-4411

'Aglaya'/'Aglaia'

'Alaska'

VARIETIES

VARIETY	COLOR	FORM	HEIGHT	HARDINESS
Leucanthemum–Superbum Group				
(Shasta Daisy)				
'Aglaya' ('Aglaia')	White/light yellow	Double (frilly)	30″	−20°F
'Alaska'	White/deep yellow	Single (large)	24″	−30°F
'Amelia'*****	White/gold yellow (large)	Single	40″	−20°F
'Banana Cream'	Lemon yellow/yellow	Single	18″	−20°F
'Becky'*****	White/bright yellow	Single	40″	−20°F
Broadway Lights™	White/cream/yellow	Single	24″	−20°F
'Crazy Daisy'	White/yellow	Double (twisting)	30″	−20°F
Gold Rush (Goldrausch)	White yellow/yellow	Double (fringed)	16″	−20°F
'Northern Light' ('Nordlicht')	White/gold	Single	30″	−20°F
'Rijnsburg Glory'	White	Single	30″	−20°F
'Silver Princess' ('Silberprinzesschen')	White/yellow	Single	18″	−20°F
'Snowcap'	White/deep yellow	Single (large)	18″	−20°F
'Snowdrift'	White/gold	Double (frilly)	34″	−20°F
'Snow Lady'	White/yellow	Single	24″	−20°F
'Summer Snowball'	White/white	Double (pompon)	30″	−20°F
'Sunny Side Up'	White/bright yellow	Semi-double (crested)	36″	−20°F
'Sunshine' ('Sonnenschein')	Lemon yellow/gold yellow	Single	36″	−20°F
'Switzerland'	White/gold yellow	Single (large)	30″	−20°F
'Thomas Killen'*****	White/medium yellow	Single (crested)	24″	−20°F
'Tinkerbelle'	White/deep yellow	Single	16″	−20°F
'White Knight'*****	White/yellow	Single (large)	24″	−20°F
'Wirral Pride'	White/medium yellow	Double (crested)	36″	−20°F

'Amelia' gets high ratings for its vigor and classic look. 'Becky' and 'White Knight' are both known for their prolific bloom while 'Thomas Killen' stands out for its unique, showy flowers.

'Kobold'

LIATRIS

(lye-ATE-riss)

GAYFEATHER

Bloom Time	Expected Longevity	Maintenance	Years to Bloom	Preferred Light
Midsummer to early fall	15 years	Low	From seed: 2 years From potted plant: 1 year	Full sun

Gayfeathers are durable, care-free, native American perennials that thrive for many years if grown properly. They make wonderful vertical accent plants for the mid- to back sections of the flower garden. These perennials mature slowly into striking plants whose dense heads of flowers are quite attractive to bees and butterflies. They bloom from midsummer to early fall and are widely recognized as excellent fresh-cut and dried flowers.

How Gayfeathers Grow

Gayfeathers grow from root structures known as corms or rhizomes, which lie just under the soil surface. These fleshy structures produce rosettes of narrow foliage out of which rise vertical stems with alternate, dark green, narrow leaves. Individual flowers (florets) are quite small but bloom generously in dense spikes at the top of the stems. Mature plants range in height from 1 to 5 feet (30 to 150 cm). Most Gayfeathers bloom from the top of the spikes down, in direct contrast to most other plants with this bloom arrangement. If spent flower spikes are not removed, Gayfeathers will produce a heavy crop of seed. However, many of the named selections will not come true from seed.

Where to Plant

Site and Light Gayfeathers flourish in full sun. Although plants will flower fairly well in light shade, taller varieties will usually require staking under low-light conditions.

Soil and Moisture Gayfeathers prefer soils that drain freely. Sandy loams are ideal, but many other soil types are fine if amended with organic matter. Replace clay or rocky soils with good soil or build a raised bed. Gayfeathers often die out in compacted soils during the winter. Mix generous amounts of materials such as compost, leaf mold, peat moss, or rotted manure into the soil. Most Gayfeathers thrive in soil kept consistently moist throughout the growing season.

Spacing Space plants 8 to 12 inches (30 to 45 cm) apart, depending on the potential height of individual varieties. Clumps increase slowly but still need enough room to expand comfortably in time.

Companions

If you want to attract butterflies, include this perennial in either a meadow garden or a more formal border. It combines well with some of the following plants: *Artemisia* (Wormwood), *Coreopsis* 'Full Moon' (Tickseed), *Echinacea* (Purple Coneflower), *Hemerocallis* (Daylily), *Leucanthemum*–Superbum Group (Shasta Daisy), *Phlox*–Paniculata Group (Summer Phlox), and *Rudbeckia* (Coneflower). Try *Liatris pycnostachya* (Kansas Gayfeather) with *Heliopsis* (False Sunflower) and *Monarda fistulosa* (Wild Bergamot). The tall purple-flowered types contrast nicely with the rounded form and medium texture of *Helictotrichon sempervirens* (Blue Oat Grass).

Planting

Bare Root Plant bare root stock as soon as the ground can be worked in spring. Remove the corms or rhizomes from their shipping package as soon as they arrive, and soak them overnight in room-temperature water. Place a small amount of superphosphate in the base of the planting hole. Place the corm or rhizome in the planting hole so that the top is about 1 to 2 inches (2.5 to 5 cm) below the soil surface. Fill in with soil, firm with your fingers, and water immediately. Dissolve ½ cup (about 114 g) 10-10-10 fertilizer in 1 gallon (about 4 liters) of water. Pour ½ cup (about 120 ml) of this starter solution around the base of each plant. If you prefer organic fertilizer, use fish emulsion instead.

Potted Plants Plant potted Gayfeathers after all danger of frost has passed in spring. If the soil in the pot is dry, soak it, and let it drain overnight. Tap the plant out of the pot without disturbing the root ball. Plant it at the same depth as in the pot, after preparing the hole in a manner similar to that for a bare root plant. Fill in with soil, firm with your fingers, and water immediately. Pour ½ cup (about 120 ml) starter solution around the base of each plant.

How to Care for Gayfeathers

Water Water needs vary somewhat by variety, but most enjoy regular moisture right up until their bloom period. Excess moisture may cause tall varieties to become floppy and require staking. Most Gayfeathers tolerate limited periods of drought once mature, but *Liatris scariosa* (Tall Gayfeather) stands out in this regard.

Mulch Place 2 inches (5 cm) of mulch around the base of each plant as soon as the ground warms up in spring. Use materials such as dried grass clippings, shredded leaves, compost, or pine needles. The main purpose of this mulch is to reduce the need for hand watering and weeding. Since some Gayfeathers prefer rather hot, dry conditions, you should avoid using too deep a mulch around these.

Fertilizing Sprinkle 10-10-10 fertilizer around the base of each plant as soon as growth emerges in spring. Water it immediately to dissolve the granules and move nutrients into the root zone. Foliar feeding with water-soluble fertilizers is also fine. The plants need regular feeding, but do not overfeed, since this can lead to weak stems, requiring support. If your plants tend to flop over, fertilize less the following year.

If you prefer organic fertilizers, use alfalfa meal (rabbit pellets), blood meal, bonemeal, compost, cow manure, fish emulsion, Milorganite, or rotted horse manure. Bonemeal must be mixed into the soil at planting time to be effective.

Staking Staking is not necessary on shorter varieties. The taller species (wild) Gayfeathers as well as 'September Glory' and 'White Spire' often need support. If staking is required, place green stakes next to individual stems early in the season. Avoid spearing the corm or rhizome when doing this. Tie the stems to the stakes at different heights as they grow, using loose, figure-eight knots.

Deadheading Unless you want a seed crop, remove flower heads as the last blooms fade. Although this does not encourage additional bloom, it improves the appearance of the plants. Cut the bloom spikes off just below the bottom flowers with pruning shears or a sharp knife.

Winter Protection Mature plants do not require any winter protection beyond normal snowfall. If there is no snow by early December, it may be good insurance to cover the plants with 6 inches (15 cm) of marsh hay, clean straw, whole leaves, or pine needles.

Remove these as soon as the weather warms up in spring.

Problems

Insects Gayfeathers are rarely bothered by insects.

Disease Root and crown rots can be a problem in poorly drained soils. If the soil does not drain freely in winter, plants will die out. Avoid problems by preparing soil correctly in the first place.

Animals Rabbits and deer relish the tender young shoots. Keep them away with physical barriers or commercial repellents.

Propagation

Division Gayfeathers should be divided every 4 to 5 years for best health. Although they can remain undisturbed for longer periods, bloom quantity and quality diminish. Divide plants just as new growth emerges in spring. Dig up the plant, and wash it free of soil. Cut the corms or rhizomes into sections with a sharp knife. Make sure that each division has several strong shoots. We suggest dusting cut ends with a general-purpose fungicide. Plant these new divisions immediately as you would a bare root corm or rhizome.

Seed Species types are easily grown from seed and usually flower in their second year. Fall-collected seed can be sown in a cold frame or outdoor seedbed. Keep the germination medium evenly moist until it freezes for the winter. The seed will germinate the following spring as the weather warms up. When seedlings are 2 to 3 inches (5 to 7.5 cm) tall, transplant them into pots or a protected spot in the garden. Keep the soil evenly moist to get them off to a good start.

Seed can also be planted indoors during the winter months. If you start it about 12 weeks before the last expected frost in spring, you may get a few flowers late in the first season. Seed should be left exposed to light during germination, so do not cover it with any medium. Germination is often erratic, taking 21 to 28 days or longer at 65°F to 70°F (18°C to 21°C). Dropping night temperature by 10°F (6°C) may speed up germination, but a moist-chilling period may prove even more helpful. After sowing, slide the seed tray into a perforated plastic bag, and place this in the crisper of your refrigerator for 4 to 6 weeks. Then return it to the warm temperature described earlier. Once the young seedlings are 2 to 3 inches (5 to 7.5 cm) tall, transplant them to pots for growing on. Harden them off for 14 days before planting them outside after all danger of frost has passed in spring.

Special Uses

Cut Flowers Gayfeathers make striking, long-lived cut flowers. Cut them when the topmost flowers begin to open, and place the cut stems in water immediately. Never cut more than two-thirds of the plant stem to ensure that there is ample foliage left to manufacture food for the following year. Keep the stems in cool water for as long as possible before arranging.

Dried Flowers Once again, cut the stems just as the top buds start to open. Strip off all the foliage, and hang the stems upside down in a dark, dry, well-ventilated area. Some arrangers also have good luck standing the flower spikes straight up to dry. In general, the white varieties do not dry as well as the purplish pink or lavender purple ones.

Sources

Ambergate Gardens, 8730 County Rd. 43, Chaska, MN 55318, (877) 211-9769

Busse Gardens, 17160 245th Ave., Big Lake, MN 55309, (800) 544-3192

Goodness Grows, 332 Eberton Rd., Lexington, GA 30648, (706) 743-5055

Outback Nursery, 15280 110th St. S, Hastings, MN 55033, (651) 438-2771

Prairie Moon Nursery, 32115 Prairie Lane, Winona, MN 55987, (866) 417-8156

Thompson & Morgan (seed), P.O. Box 4086, Lawrenceburg, IN 47025, (800) 274-7333

Liatris spicata 'Alba'

VARIETIES

VARIETY	COLOR	HEIGHT	HARDINESS

Liatris aspera
(Rough Gayfeather)	Lavender purple	48″	−40°F

This Gayfeather is native over a large area in eastern North America. Its spikes have an open, airy appearance, and the clusters of blooms look like large frilly buttons. Nearly all the flowers open at the same time in mid- to late summer. This variety does very well on dry soils and is best suited to meadows where its spindly stems are supported by grasses.

Liatris cylindracea
(Cylindric Gayfeather)	Light purple	24″	−40°F

Noted for its compact growth and large clusters of flowers in late summer, Cylindric Gayfeather is best grown on dry gravelly soils. Unless soil conditions are ideal, it commonly dies out.

Liatris ligulistylis*****
(Meadow Gayfeather)	Purplish pink	60″	−40°F

Similar in appearance to Cylindric Gayfeather, this species has fuller bloom spikes and much darker flowers. It is found native on higher moisture soils, making it more adaptable to a wider range of situations in the landscape. It is the favorite Gayfeather of monarch butterflies.

Liatris punctata
(Dotted Gayfeather)	Rosy purple	18″	−40°F

This Gayfeather forms a dwarf clump with its flower heads tightly packed onto short spikes. It blooms in late summer and tolerates dry sites.

Liatris pycnostachya
(Kansas Gayfeather)	Purplish pink	48″	−40°F
'Alba'	Creamy white	36″	−40°F
'Eureka'	Reddish purple	60″	−40°F

Native to the central states, this plant bears dense flower spikes that are showy in August and September. It is a good cut flower and also retains its color well when dried. The species has such heavy flower heads that it may require staking. If the soil does not drain freely, this perennial will die out in winter.

Liatris scariosa
(Tall Gayfeather)	Purple red	36″	−30°F
'Alba'	White	36″	−30°F
'Gracious'	White	36″	−30°F
'September Glory'	Deep purple	48″	−30°F
'White Spire' ('White Spires')	White	48″	−30°F

This species is similar to *Liatris pycnostachya* (Kansas Gay Feather) but it is more compact and later blooming. It may be the most drought tolerant of the Gayfeathers. 'September Glory' and its sport 'White Spires' are both taller growing and may require staking.

VARIETY	COLOR	HEIGHT	HARDINESS
Liatris spicata			
(Spike Gayfeather)	Lavender purple	36″	−40°F
'Alba'	White	36″	−40°F
'Floristan Violet' ('Floristan Violett')*****	Violet	24″	−40°F
'Floristan White' ('Floristan Weiss')	White	36″	−40°F
'Kobold'	Mauve purple	30″	−40°F
'Kobold Original'*****	Mauve purple	15″	−40°F

With their ability to tolerate higher soil moisture, this species and its selections may be the most versatile Gayfeathers. Their stiff stems rarely require staking. 'Floristan Violet' and 'Floristan White' are valued mainly as cut flowers. 'Kobold' is commonly grown from seed and shows a wide variability in height while 'Kobold Original' is a true dwarf selection that is propagated by division.

'Black Beauty'

LILIUM

(LIL-ee-um)

LILY

Bloom Time	Expected Longevity	Maintenance	Years to Bloom	Preferred Light
Early summer to early fall	10 to 15+ years	Medium	From seed: 3 to 4 years From potted plant: 1 year	Variable

With more than two hundred species of Lilies and an astonishing number of hybrids, you have an incredible variety of plants from which to choose. Some are strikingly beautiful, while others are noted for fragrance. Lilies offer a remarkable variety of forms, as well as a range of colors second only to Iris, with no true blue available. Blooms last a long time and make excellent cut flowers. Lilies are easy to grow and long-lived but a delicacy to deer, which invade gardens to nibble off buds just before they bloom. Each type of Lily may require slightly different care. Special information in this regard is included in the Varieties table at the end of the section. Lilies are an extremely good value for your money.

How Lilies Grow

Lilies grow from scaly bulbs best planted in September or October. The following spring, bulbs produce shoots bearing bright, glossy green leaves that are somewhat whimsical in appearance. These shoots, or stems, grow upward and finally produce flowers which vary in shape according to the species or variety. Typical shapes are bowl, dahlia, slipper, spider, turban, and trumpetlike. Underneath the soil, the bulbs are maturing and producing additional lily bulbs along the underground stem. These tiny bulbs are called *bulblets*. Some lilies produce tiny bulbs, or *bulbils*, above ground where leaves join the stem. These can be taken from the plant when they're mature and planted to produce offspring. The root system of a few species grows horizontally, creating underground stems, or rhizomes, to the side of the mother plant. All mature into attractive clumps with age.

Where to Plant

Site and Light Most Lilies grow well in high-light conditions. They will do best when planted in full sun, although a few will grow in either full sun or partial shade. Some varieties prefer partial shade. The specific light needs of different types are included in the Varieties table at the end of the section. Lilies do well on slopes. A north-facing slope is ideal, since the Lilies will emerge only after any danger of frost in spring. The smaller varieties look best when planted with rocks as a backdrop.

Avoid planting taller varieties in windy spots. By planting them in a protected area, you'll avoid some of the need for staking.

Soil and Moisture Lilies thrive in well-drained soil. If you have clay or rocky soils, replace these with loam. If this is impractical, build a raised bed. You should have at least 12 inches (30 cm) of loose soil for best growth. Bulbs will rot out in compacted soils. Work lots of organic matter into your soil before planting. Most Lilies do well in slightly acidic soil, although many do well in neutral soil as well. Add peat moss or rotted oak leaves to the soil regularly to keep it loose and acidic. Some Lilies need especially acidic soil to do well. You can sprinkle an acidifying agent into the soil at regular intervals to ensure the right conditions for growth. Products recommended for soils around Azaleas or Rhododendrons work well. You can buy these in any nursery. Whether a plant needs this special treatment or not is included

in the Varieties table. **Note:** Never add lime or wood ash to the soil. These are alkaline, not acidic.

Spacing All Lilies need lots of space. Don't crowd them too close to other plants. Most get quite large and don't want to compete for nutrients and water. Furthermore, good air circulation around the plants prevents disease. Most packages come with explicit directions on how far apart to plant bulbs.

Lilies look best if planted in groups of three or more. Some growers like to plant them in separate beds. Others plant Lilies in waves, naturalizing them like Daffodils. But there is no reason why they cannot be combined with other perennials in the garden as long as they are given plenty of space to mature properly.

Companions

The landscape uses of *Lilium* (Lily) are quite broad, as these plants are fine in both formal and informal settings. Combine shade-tolerant types in the woodland garden along with perennials such as *Aquilegia* (Columbine), *Astilbe* (False Spirea), *Hosta* (Hosta), *Lamium* (Dead Nettle), and **Ferns**. Oriental Lilies, with their wonderful fragrance and specific cultural needs, make good container plants for the entryway or patio. Groupings of Asiatic, Orienpets, or Trumpet hybrids combine beautifully with numerous summer-flowering perennials in the border. The following are among the best companions: *Achillea* (Yarrow), *Alchemilla* (Lady's Mantle), *Coreopsis* (Tickseed), *Delphinium* (Larkspur), *Geranium* (Cranesbill), *Heliopsis* (Oxeye), *Heuchera* (Coral Bells), *Leucanthemum*–Superbum Group (Shasta Daisy), *Monarda* (Bee Balm), *Nepeta* (Catmint), *Phlox* (Garden Phlox), *Salvia* (Sage), *Veronica* (Speedwell), and **Grasses**.

Planting

Bulbs Ideally, bulbs should be planted in late summer or early fall. Note, however, that some bulbs are for sale in spring as well. If you buy bulbs in spring, make sure they are not already sprouting in the plastic package. Buy them as soon as they come into the store. We advise calling ahead for specific arrival dates.

You want fresh bulbs from a reputable source, whether local or mail-order. Bulbs look like globe artichokes with their fleshy, overlapping scales and should be firm—no bruises, no rot, and no shriveling. If they feel mushy or are moldy, don't buy them, or send them back if ordered through the mail. The bigger the bulbs, the better. Really large bulbs are rare. You'll usually be able to get these only from other Lily growers in your area. These people are often members of the local Lily society. Ideally, bulbs should have lots of roots.

Bulbs are alive. Treat them with care. Do not expose them to sunlight for long periods of time. Don't let them dry out. Do not overheat or freeze them. If you must store them for a while, put them in damp peat moss in a plastic bag in the crisper of your refrigerator. The temperature should not drop below 32°F (0°C). Do not store them next to fruit, which gives off damaging ethylene gas.

Prepare beds in advance so that as soon as the bulbs arrive you can get them into the soil. Immediate planting is best.

Plant bulbs to a depth roughly equivalent to three times their diameter. When planting, dig a hole to a depth six times the diameter of the bulb. Sprinkle 2 tablespoons (30 ml) of bonemeal, or an appropriate amount of superphosphate, and a little 10-10-10 fertilizer at the base of the hole. Then fill the hole halfway with soil. Compact the soil to form a firm base. Set the bulb with the fat end down. Push the bulb into the soil so that only the pointed end sticks up. Fill the hole with water, letting it soak down into the soil. Then fill the hole to the top with soil, firm it with your fingers, and water it again. Let the soil settle and dry out. If necessary, fill in with soil and water again later. Firming the soil and watering in stages gets rid of any air pockets. You want the bulb to be firmly in place, completely surrounded by soil, not air.

If your variety needs support, push in a bamboo stake or similar support behind the planting hole before planting the bulb. This avoids root disturbance or damage to the bulb once it has been covered with soil. **Note:** If you plant bulbs extremely late in the season, it's best to apply a thick winter mulch over the planting bed. This will keep the soil warmer into fall and early winter. It will also delay warming of the bed in spring. These conditions favor proper growth of late-planted bulbs. This is important information for cold-climate gardeners because some of the best and biggest bulbs are available only late in the season, which is far too late for ideal planting.

Potted Plants A number of varieties are sold already potted in spring, especially Oriental (Division VII) and Trumpet Lilies (Division VI). Choose plants with lush, green foliage. If foliage is yellow or brownish, the plants are stressed from either improper watering, lack of fertilizer, or disease. Since it's hard to tell which, you're better off avoiding these altogether.

Also, check plants carefully for insect infestations. If Lilies are covered with aphids, do not buy them. Aphids carry serious diseases, which could devastate Lilies already growing in your garden or harm the ones you're buying.

If plants are in bloom, snip off all blooms and buds. This goes against the grain but helps the plant grow properly the first year. If the soil in the pot is dry, soak it, and let it drain overnight. Tap the plant out of the pot the following day without disturbing the root ball. Place it in a properly prepared hole as outlined under planting bulbs. Plant it at the same depth as in the pot. Firm the soil around the base of the plant, and water it immediately.

How to Care for Lilies

Water Lilies like it moist and cool, so water regularly during dry spells. If you keep the soil evenly moist throughout the growing season, you'll have luxuriant foliage. Good leaf growth provides more food for the underground bulb for much better bloom the following season.

Mulch Mulching is a good idea, since it keeps soil moist and cool. It also reduces weed growth. A mulch

3 inches (7.5 cm) deep is fine around most Lilies. Good mulches include compost, dried grass clippings, shredded leaves, and pine needles. If any weeds do pop up, they are easy to pull out by hand. Apply mulch around but not against the stems to avoid disease.

Fertilizing Add 10-10-10 fertilizer to the soil during the preparation of the bed. In following years, sprinkle granules around the base of each stem as it emerges from the ground. Avoid getting fertilizer on the young shoots. Water immediately after fertilizing to dissolve the granules and carry nutrients into the root zone. Fertilize again just as buds are forming to encourage prolific bloom. Do not overfertilize.

If you prefer organic fertilizers, use alfalfa meal (rabbit pellets), blood meal, bonemeal, compost, cow manure, fish emulsion, Milorganite, or rotted horse manure. A combination of these is best. Bonemeal must be added to the soil at planting time to be effective.

Weeding Kill off any perennial weeds such as quack grass or thistle with Roundup®. Do this in the spring to prepare for late-summer or fall planting. Once plants are growing, pull weeds close to the stem by hand to avoid injuring the plant. Most gardeners mark the location of Lilies to avoid damaging the underground bulbs during spring cleaning. Lilies often emerge later than other types of perennials, and they are easy to cut into while digging in the garden.

Staking Some of the taller varieties require staking. They have such tall stems and large flower heads that they will topple over without support. Use thin bamboo stakes or similar supports, and tie the stem of the plant to the stake with something soft. Pieces of old nylon are recommended. Tie the plant to the stake in a figure-eight knot. This allows the plant to move slightly. Avoid tight knots. As mentioned earlier, you should always place stakes into the ground at the time of planting. Otherwise, you might skewer the bulb, as some of them get very large as they mature.

Deadheading Unless you're saving seed, remove all blooms after they have withered by cutting the stem just below the lowest bloom. Do not cut any lower than this, as the foliage along the stem produces food necessary for good bulb formation. Good bulbs produce better blooms. You can also handpick individual withered blossoms by snapping them off with a quick twist of your hand.

Winter Protection Cover fall-planted bulbs immediately after planting with a 6-inch (15-cm) layer of whole leaves, clean straw, or pine needles. This will prevent the soil from freezing early. This delay allows the bulbs to take root. Unfortunately, early mulch sometimes attracts rodents, but this is a risk worth taking in the first year. You may want to place poison bait in the mulch to kill off these marauders.

In subsequent seasons, winter protection is necessary only for Division VI (Trumpet) and Division VII (Oriental) Lilies. These are more susceptible to winter damage than the other divisions.

Remove the mulch only after danger of frost has passed in late spring. During an unexpected cold snap, put an inverted basket over the plants in the early afternoon before the temperature drops. This traps heat from the soil. Frost on young shoots can damage plants.

Problems

Insects You'll avoid most insect problems with Lilies if they are planted in soil that drains freely, are given plenty of space for good light and air circulation, and are kept in weed-free beds.

Aphids are a serious problem in the Lily garden because they carry viral diseases. Some growers spray routinely to prevent infestations, while others prefer to use chemicals only if aphids form large colonies. Mild insecticidal soaps are often enough to kill these tiny insects.

Disease Botrytis (gray mold), a fungal disease, produces circular spots with a reddish brown tinge on the leaves. It is best prevented with a routine spraying of an appropriate fungicide.

Mosaic virus is carried by aphids. Plants often have twisted, distorted, streaked, and stunted leaves. Our recommendation is to dig up and destroy the plant. Plant a different perennial in that spot. Avoid mosaic virus by buying healthy plants and killing aphids.

Lilies will rot out in heavily compacted or soggy soils. Prevent this rot by adding lots of organic matter to the soil, by using raised beds, and by not overwatering. It is hard to overwater if soil drains well.

Animals Lilies exude an odor attractive to deer. You may have to fence in your flower garden if deer are a nuisance. A loose dog in the fenced-in area at night will scare off any deer tempted to hop the fence. Some growers insist that Milorganite, scrapings of scented soaps, and human hair are good deterrents. Milorganite has an advantage in that it's a fertilizer; its primary nutrient is nitrogen. Lilies do need lots of nitrogen. But, Milorganite does have an unpleasant odor.

Fences also deter rabbits, a real nuisance to young Lilies. Entire books have been written on natural ways to keep rabbits away from vegetables and flowers, but the only method that works well is a fence. Trap and destroy them if necessary.

Woodchucks also can devastate a Lily crop. Fencing helps keep them out of the garden, but they can tunnel under it if so inclined. Live trapping is the easiest way to get rid of them.

Propagation

Lilies can be propagated in a fascinating variety of ways. The following sections discuss the plant parts used in this process.

Bulbils A few Lilies produce tiny bulbs (bulbils) where leaves join the stems. They may be close to the ground or quite high up on the stem. These bulbils generally turn dark brown or black as they mature. When fully mature, they'll actually drop off onto the ground. Pick these off the stem, and plant them about 1 inch (2.5 cm) deep and 3 inches (7.5 cm) apart in a place set aside for starting plants from scratch. Keep the growing medium moist at all times. These bulbils will then produce roots until late fall. After the chilling period of winter, they will begin to grow in spring. After 2 years of growing the plants in your special bed, dig them up in midsummer or early fall, and plant them in the perennial garden. **Tip:** If you have a plant that creates bulbils, you can increase their number by snipping off all flower buds as they form. The energy normally spent on creating flowers will go into increasing the number of bulbils.

Bulblets All Lilies eventually produce tiny little bulbs on the underground stems of the parent plant. In mid- to late summer, dig up your mature Lily plant and look for bulblets. Remove these, and plant them as you would bulbils. Immediately replant the mature Lily bulb.

Bulblets

Scales Most Lilies look like garlic bulbs with many individual sections. The individual sections of the bulb are known as *scales*. Each scale will produce a new plant if removed from the mother bulb. In mid- to late summer, dig up a fully mature plant, ideally 2 weeks after bloom. Cut off the stem. Remove the outer scales. Discard these, since they have the greatest chance of being infected with disease. Use the inner scales for new plants. Plant them as you would bulblets or bulbils. Some gardeners remove no more than a few scales from each bulb so that they can replant the mother bulb immediately.

Division Dividing Lilies is the simplest way to get

Bulbils

new plants. Dig up a large clump in late summer or early fall, and divide it into individual bulbs. Plant these bulbs as outlined earlier. Such division is good for the health of certain types of Lilies, which can get too crowded over a period of years.

Cuttings Commercial growers have been working with stem and leaf cuttings for years. Research continues into this method of propagation that is not yet practical for home gardeners.

Seed You can grow Lilies from seed. This requires patience and quite a bit of time, but many people enjoy the process. Not all Lilies grow the same way from seed. They are classified as either quick-germinating (epigeal) or slow-germinating (hypogeal). This quality is included in the individual write-ups for species Lilies in the table at the end of the section. Following are proven methods for growing both types.

There are two ways to grow quick-germinating Lilies. You can start them indoors (harder but with quicker results) or outdoors (easier but slower). Let's start with the easier but slower method.

To start quick-germinating Lilies outdoors: Prepare a seedbed in a shaded area. The soil should be extremely loose and drain freely. About a third of the soil should be peat. Place a fungicidal powder and seeds in a plastic bag, then shake the bag. This will cover each seed with a light dusting of the chemical.

Seed

After all danger of frost in spring, scatter the seed over the bed. Cover the seed with ½ inch (12 mm) of potting soil. Firm the soil with your hands. Then gently sprinkle the soil with water. Keep it damp at all times; never let it dry out. As soon as the seeds begin to sprout, feed them with water-soluble fertilizer at a low dosage. Do this every few weeks throughout the growing season. In late fall, cover the plants with an extra inch (2.5 cm) of soil. Then cover the entire bed with a 6-inch (15-cm) layer of whole leaves, clean straw, or pine needles. Remove the mulch as soon as the weather begins to warm up in spring. Dig up the tiny bulbs before new growth emerges. Plant them 2 inches (5 cm) deep and about 6 inches (15 cm) apart throughout the bed. Follow this routine until bulbs are large enough to plant in the perennial garden.

To start quick-germinating Lilies indoors (sow in midwinter): Fill your growing container with growing medium. A combination of peat, vermiculite, perlite, and sterilized potting soil is ideal. Moisten the medium with hot water. Cover the surface with ¼ inch (6 mm) of peat. Then moisten it again with hot water (peat does not absorb cool water easily). Scatter fungicide-dusted seeds (see the previous paragraph) over the surface of the peat. Then cover them with another ¼ to ½ inch (6 to 12 mm) of premoistened peat. Place the container in a plastic bag with a few holes punched in it. This keeps the humidity high. Check the peat often to make sure it never dries out. Ideal temperatures for germination range from 50°F to 60°F (10°C to 16°C). As soon as the seedlings begin to pop up, usually within 30 days, remove the bag, but continue to keep the peat moist. Give the young seedlings lots of light, using grow lights if necessary. Every few weeks, feed the seedlings with a dilute solution of water-soluble fertilizer. At some point the leaves will start to turn color and die back, indicating that the plants are going into a dormant period. Stop watering and feeding at this time. Place the container in a plastic bag. Put it in the crisper of your refrigerator for no less than 6 to 8 weeks. Remove the container after this period, dig up the small bulbs, and plant them in an outdoor seedbed. Follow directions for care outlined in the previous paragraph.

Slow-germinating Lilies require yet a different method: Dust seeds with a fungicide, as explained for quick germinators. Fill a plastic bag with peat moss, vermiculite, and perlite in equal parts. Barely moisten the mixture with water containing a small amount of water-soluble fertilizer. Toss the seeds into the bag, and shake it until they are evenly distributed throughout the growing medium. Tie the bag closed, but check frequently to make sure that the medium stays moist. Usually within 3 months you'll see the seeds form minuscule bulbs that look like tiny grains of rice or wheat. When this happens, place the bag in the crisper of your refrigerator for 6 to 8 weeks. Prepare a container filled with growing medium and covered with peat as outlined in the previous paragraph. Plant the little bulbs under ¼ to ½ inch (6 to 12 mm) of damp peat, and treat them now as you would quick-growing seeds as outlined.

Warning: If seeds begin to grow and then topple over, you've got a problem with *damping off*. This is not one disease, but rather a group of diseases that attack young plants. Spray the seedlings with a fungicide recommended at a nursery for this problem. Until you get the fungicide, let the growing medium dry out slightly. This often stops the spread of the disease from one plant to the next. Better yet, have the fungicide on hand for immediate use.

Special Uses

Cut Flowers Lilies make excellent cut flowers. They are very heat tolerant, perfect for hot summer bridal bouquets.

Cut no more than one-third of the stem when harvesting cut flowers. You will weaken next year's growth if you cut more than this. Remember that Lilies need leaves to produce food for their bulbs which create lots of bloom in subsequent seasons. Cut stems when the first buds start to open, since the remaining buds will continue to open indoors. Remove stamens, the parts covered with pollen, since pollen causes stains. Clip them off with cuticle scissors, pull them off with tweezers, or just flip them off with a fork.

When cutting Lilies, place stems immediately in a bucket of room-temperature water. Once indoors, cut the stems under cold water at a slant, and use them in arrangements immediately. Remove any leaves that would end up submerged in the final arrangement. Conditioning in cool, not cold, water for a few hours is recommended if your Lilies don't seem to last. Another trick is to run warm water over the blossoms and foliage while holding them upside down, then splitting the lower portion of the stem with a knife, and finally placing them in cold water overnight.

Dried Flowers Lilies are difficult to dry. You can try to dry individual blossoms in a desiccant. When doing this, place the flower up. Remove the stamens. Fill in around the flower, and form the petals into the desired shape as you go. Let the flower dry for as long as it takes to get rid of all moisture.

The seed heads of *Lilium martagon* (Martagon Lily) are easy to dry. Simply hang them upside down in a dry, well-ventilated area.

Sources

Ambergate Gardens, 8730 County Rd. 43, Chaska, MN 55318, (877) 211-9769

B & D Lilies, P.O. Box 2007, Port Townsend, WA 98368, (360) 765-4341

Bluestone Perennials, 7211 Middle Ridge Rd., Madison, OH 44057, (800) 852-5243

Brent & Becky's Bulbs, 7900 Daffodil Lane, Gloucester, VA 23061, (804) 693-3966

Crossview Gardens, 1801 Lower Elmore Mountain Rd., Morrisville, VT 05661, (802) 888-2409

Dutch Gardens, P.O. Box 2999, Bloomington, IL 61702, (800) 944-2250

Faraway Flowers, 9 Pleasant Ave., Cape Elizabeth, ME 04107, (207) 767-3889

Fritz Creek Gardens, P.O. Box 15226, Homer, AK 99603, (907) 235-4969

Gilbert H. Wild & Son, 2994 State Hwy 37, Reeds, MO 64859, (888) 449-4537

Goodness Grows, P.O. Box 311, Lexington, GA 30648, (706) 743-5055

Gratrix Garden Lilies, P.O. Box 186, Coldwater, ON Canada l0K 1E0, (705) 835-6794

Hartle-Gilman Garden, 2100 W 106th St., Bloomington, MN 55431, (952) 884-8254

John Scheepers, Inc., 23 Tulip Dr., Bantam, CT 06750, (860) 567-0838

The Lily Garden, 4902 NE 147th Ave., Vancouver, WA 98682, (360) 253-6273

The Lily Nook, P.O. Box 846, Neepawa, MB Canada R0J 1H0, (204) 476-3225

The Lily Pad, 3403 Steamboat Island Rd. NW #374, Olympia, WA 98502, (360) 866-0291

McClure & Zimmerman, P.O. Box 368, Friesland, WI 53935, (800) 883-6998

Old House Gardens, 536 Third St., Ann Arbor, MI 48103, (734) 995-1486

S-W Gardens, 22507 Kenesserie Rd., Thamesville, ON Canada N0P 2K0, (519) 692-5580

VARIETIES

Consider the following characteristics when choosing varieties: height of the plant, bloom time, color of bloom, size of bloom, fragrance, and hardiness. The flowering season for Lilies extends from early summer to early fall. By planting a wide variety of Lilies, you can have an extremely long period of bloom.

Lilium lancifolium (Tiger Lily), an old-fashioned favorite, can harbor viruses without showing symptoms and is best segregated from other Lilies. Aphids can spread the virus from one Lily variety to another as they feed.

Over the years, thousands of varieties of Lilies have been hybridized. Lilies have been classified into nine divisions. *Lilium* species, varieties, and forms fall into **Division IX** and are followed by *Lilium* (named varieties in **Divisions I** through **VIII**) in the following chart. A few of the named varieties are not in single quotes and followed by the word "strain" in parenthesis, such as Citronella (strain). These represent seed-grown strains. Such strains may vary slightly in flower color and height, but despite their minimal lack of uniformity are well worth growing.

"Recurved" describes flowers which curve backward, inward, or outward. "Reflexed" is very similar to recurved, generally meaning curved backward or downward. These curving forms appeal to the eye. Following is a brief explanation of Lily classification:

Division I: Asiatic Hybrids

Asiatics are the most common and easily grown Lilies. The species in their backgrounds are found growing wild throughout Asia. Most of them bloom in early to midsummer, but plant breeders are developing new varieties to extend the season even further. These Lilies come in a wide variety of colors. They should be grown in full sun to partial shade depending upon the variety. They do best in neutral to slightly acidic soils. Divide them every three to five years. They are subdivided as follows:

> Ia - upfacing flowers
>
> Ib - sidefacing flowers
>
> Ic - downfacing flowers

Division II: Martagon Hybrids

These hybrids come from woodland Lilies native to Europe and Asia. They tend to be tall plants and have attractive foliage swirling around the stems. Martagons bloom in early summer with small hanging blooms. They grow well in shade gardens in neutral to slightly alkaline soils. They increase in size slowly, but are very disease free and long-lived.

Division III: Candidum Hybrids

These Lilies originated from European natives like *Lilium candidum* (Madonna Lily). They grow best in full sun in neutral to acidic soil. Most are not suited to cold climates, and none are included in the list which follows.

Lilium auratum

'Black Dragon'

'Claude Shride'

'Dandy Lion'

'Enchantment'

'Indian Brave'

'Star Gazer'

'White Henryi'

Division IV: American Hybrids

This group contains all hybrids originating from North American native Lilies. They are quite difficult to find and equally difficult to grow. They should be planted in an acidic soil in either full sun or light shade. None are included in the list which follows.

Division V: Longiflorum Hybrids

These are familiar to most gardeners as Easter Lilies, an important holiday pot crop. They are not well suited to growing outdoors in cold climates.

Division VI: Trumpet Hybrids

Trumpets are tall plants blooming in midsummer with large, fragrant flowers. They are not quite as winter-hardy as Asiatics, but an annual winter mulch will usually take care of this. They grow best in full sun in neutral to slightly acidic soils. With their huge flower heads, they will require staking and shelter from winds to keep them upright. They are subdivided as follows:

> VIa - trumpet-shaped flowers
> VIb - bowl-shaped flowers
> VIc - flat flowers (or only the tips recurved)
> VId - flowers with petals distinctly recurved

Division VII: Oriental Hybrids

These are hybrids derived from Far Eastern species like ***Lilium auratum*** (Goldband Lily) and ***Lilium speciosum*** (Showy Japanese Lily). They bloom in late summer with exotic looking, large flowers noted for their wonderful fragrance and excellent coloration. Unfortunately, they are neither as easy to grow nor as winter-hardy as the Asiatic hybrids. They require full sun and an acidic soil with lots of organic matter added to grow well. In addition, they are susceptible to viral diseases which do kill them off. This division is subdivided as follows:

> VIIa - trumpet-shaped flowers
> VIIb - bowl-shaped flowers
> VIIc - flat flowers (or only the tips recurved)
> VIId - flowers with petals distinctly recurved

Division VIII: Miscellanous Hybrids

This division contains all hybrids which do not fit into any of the other categories, including crosses between divisions such as Asiapets (crosses between Asiatic and Trumpet Hybrids), Longiflorum-Asiatic Lilies (crosses between Longiflorum and Asiatic Hybrids), and Orienpets (crosses between Asiatic and Trumpet Hybrids). These are very popular. Hybridizers are making other interesting crosses which will, undoubtedly, result in a whole new range of exciting Lily varieties. Most of the Lilies in this division grow best in full sun and prefer soils which range from neutral to slightly acidic.

Division IX: Species Lilies

All naturally occurring species, varieties, and forms are placed in this division.

VARIETY	DIVISION	SEASON	COLOR	HEIGHT	HARDINESS
Lilium amabile*****					
(Korean Lily)	IX	Early	Orange red	36″	−40°F
var. *luteum*	IX	Early	Orange yellow	36″	−40°F

This Lily produces heavy bloom noted for its shiny colorations. It tolerates dry soils in full sun or light shade and is very easy and quick to grow from seed. It is a fast germinator.

Lilium auratum					
(Goldband Lily)	IX	Late	White/yellow band	72″	−30°F
var. *platyphyllum*	IX	Late	White/yellow band	72″	−30°F

Not an easy Lily to grow, but still a favorite of many. The flowers are very fragrant, bowl-shaped, and dotted with crimson-red spots. The var. *platyphyllum* is hardier and has more blossoms. This Lily thrives in coarse, acidic soils in full sun. Unfortunately, Goldband Lily is susceptible to die off from viral infections. A winter mulch is strongly recommended in cold climates. It is a slow germinator.

Lilium canadense					
(Canada Lily)	IX	Early/Mid	Yellow, orange, or red	60″	−40°F

It blooms with up to 20 hanging, bell-shaped flowers per stem and requires an evenly moist yet well-drained, acidic soil. Canada Lily does well in full sun or light shade. It is a slow germinator.

Lilium davidii****					
(David's Lily)	IX	Mid	Vermilion to scarlet	48″	−30°F

This is an easily grown Lily that offers a pyramidal head of 20 or more blooms. The dainty flowers have strongly reflexed petals that are covered with numerous, small, black spots. This lily prefers full sun and a soil which ranges from neutral to slightly acidic. It is a fast germinator.

Lilium henryi****					
(Henry Lily)	IX	Mid/Late	Orange	96″	−30°F

This Chinese lily is among the toughest and longest lived of the species Lilies. A well-grown stem can carry up to two dozen brown-spotted flowers. It will grow in a wide range of soils in either full sun or light shade. It is a fast germinator.

Lilium lancifolium					
(Tiger Lily)	IX	Mid/Late	Orange-red	48″	−40°F

This Lily has long been valued for food in China and Japan. Its spotted orange to red blooms are familiar to many since it grows so freely across the country. This Lily reproduces rapidly from its black-brown stem bulbils. Unfortunately, it carries viruses deadly to many Lilies and may be best avoided unless grown on its own. Tiger Lily does well in full sun or light shade in any well-drained soil. It is a fast germinator.

Lilium martagon					
(Martagon Lily)	IX	Early	Purplish rose	60″	−40°F
var. *album******	IX	Early	White	48″	−40°F

This species is perhaps the most widely distributed Lily in the world as it occurs naturally throughout most of Europe and Asia. Martagon Lilies bloom with numerous, small, heavy-substanced, Turk's cap-type flowers. They prefer light shade and neutral to slightly alkaline soils. Bulbs are somewhat slow to mature but can be left undisturbed for many years. It is a slow germinator.

VARIETY	DIVISION	SEASON	COLOR	HEIGHT	HARDINESS

Lilium michiganense

(Michigan Lily)	IX	Early/Mid	Red orange	60″	−40°F

Michigan Lily is closely related to **Lilium canadense** (Canada Lily). The flower form and bloom season are similar to that species, but the plant produces fewer buds. It prefers neutral to slightly acidic, loamy soils in full sun or very light shade. It is a slow germinator.

Lilium pumilum***

(Coral Lily)	IX	Early	Red	18″	−40°F

Though often short-lived, this Lily is easy to grow and quick to mature from seed. Up to 20 nodding, fragrant flowers sway atop a short stem covered with grass-like leaves. This Lily makes an excellent cut flower. It thrives in neutral to slightly acidic soils and should be grown in full sun. It is a fast germinator.

Lilium regale***

(Regal Lily)	IX	Mid	White	72″	−40°F

Regal Lily produces highly fragrant, trumpet-shaped flowers flushed rose-purple on the outside. It produces up to ten flowers per stem. It prefers full sun and neutral to slightly acidic soils high in organic matter. This Lily is very long-lived if cared for properly. It is a fast germinator.

Lilium speciosum

(Showy Japanese Lily)	IX	Late	Pink/white margins	48″	−30°F
var. **album**	IX	Late	White	48″	−30°F
var. **rubrum**	IX	Late	Carmine/white margins	48″	−30°F

This Lily is highly favored for its rich colors and delightful fragrance. The flowers are twisted and reflexed with numerous raised, crimson-red spots. It is susceptible to viruses and often short-lived. Plant it in full sun in an acidic soil with lots of organic matter. Feed regularly with an acid-based fertilizer recommended for Azaleas and Rhododendrons. It is a slow germinator.

Lilium superbum

(American Turk's Cap Lily)	IX	Mid/Late	Orange	84″	−30°F

This east coast native blooms with as many as 40 flowers on a stem and requires a rich, moist, acidic soil to flourish. Grow it in full sun or light shade, but keep it cool and moist with regular watering and an organic mulch. It is a slow germinator.

Lilium tenuifolium (see **Lilium pumilum**)

Lilium tigrinum (see **Lilium lancifolium**)

Lilium (Named varieties and hybrids in **Divisions I** through **VIII**)

Note: An asterisk (*) after the Division classification indicates an Asiapet, two asterisks (**) a Longiflorum-Asiatic, and three asterisks (***) an Orienpet. Doubles (D) have double the complement of petals. This is indicated after flower color.

'Acapulco'	VIIb	Mid/late	Pink/deeper center	48″	−40°F
'America'	Ia	Mid	Maroon	36″	−40°F
'Anastasia'*****	VIII***	Late	White/pink center	60″	−40°F
'Arabesque'	VIII***	Late	Rose red	60″	−40°F

VARIETY	DIVISION	SEASON	COLOR	HEIGHT	HARDINESS
'Ariadne'*****	Ic	Early	Rose/creamy peach center	60″	−40°F
'Black Beauty'*****	VIId	Very late	Red/white/green	48″	−40°F
'Black Dragon'	VIa	Late	White/maroon	72″	−30°F
'Blackout'	Ia	Early/mid	Dark red	40″	−40°F
'Brunello'	Ia	Mid	Pure orange	36″	−40°F
'Cancun'	Ia	Mid	Magenta/yellow center	36″	−40°F
'Caravan'	VIII***	Mid/late	Yellow/red center	60″	−40°F
'Casa Blanca'*****	VIIb	Late	White	36″	−30°F
'Cathedral Windows'	Ia	Early/mid	Red orange/plum/yellow	48″	−40°F
'Centerfold'	Ia	Early/mid	White/maroon strokes	30″	−40°F
'Ceres'	Ia	Mid	Rose pink (D)	36″	−40°F
Citronella (strain)	Ic	Mid	Gold to lemon yellow	42″	−40°F
'Claude Shride'*****	II	Early	Dark red	60″	−40°F
'Commander in Chief'	Ia	Early/mid	Bright red	40″	−40°F
'Conca d'Or'*****	VIII***	Mid/late	Lemon yellow	48″	−40°F
'Connecticut King'*****	Ia	Mid	Yellow orange	30″	−40°F
Copper King (strain)	VIa	Late	Orange apricot	60″	−30°F
'Dandy Lion'*****	Ib	Mid	Yellow/brown flush	30″	−40°F
'Dazzle'	VIII**	Mid	Cream yellow	34″	−30°F
'Dimension'	Ia	Mid	Black cherry	40″	−40°F
'Dizzy'	VIId	Mid/late	White/red bands	40″	−30°F
'Doeskin'	Ic	Early	Creamy fawn	30″	−40°F
'Dolly Madison'	Ia	Mid	Magenta pink	40″	−40°F
'Double Pleasure'	Ia	Early/mid	Lavender red/white (D)	40″	−40°F
'Dreamcatcher'	VIII**	Early	Salmon pink	24″	−30°F
'Earlibird'	Ib	Very early	Apricot	32″	−40°F
'Elodie'	Ia	Early/mid	Pale pink (D)	40″	−40°F
'Enchantment'*****	Ia	Mid	Orange red	40″	−40°F
'Endless Love'	Ia	Early	White	36″	−40°F
'Eurydice'	Ic	Mid	Raspberry red	48″	−40°F
'Fata Morgana'	Ia	Mid	Yellow (D)	36″	−40°F
'Giraffe'	Ia	Mid	Golden yellow/red tips	48″	−40°F
'Gironde'	Ia	Mid	Golden yellow	36″	−40°F
Golden Splendor (strain)	VIa	Late	Golden yellow	60″	−30°F
'Grand Cru' ('Gran Cru')	Ia	Early/mid	Yellow/red marks	36″	−40°F
'Indian Brave'	Ia	Late	Yellow tan	42″	−40°F
'Indian Maid'	Ia	Mid	Clear yellow	36″	−40°F
'Iowa Rose'*****	Ib	Mid	Dark pink	40″	−40°F
'Jacqueline'	Ia	Mid	Red orange/yellow	30″	−40°F
'Journey's End'*****	VIId	Late	Rose red edged white	42″	−30°F
'Landini'*****	Ia	Early/mid	Black mahogany	40″	−40°F
'Last Dance'	Ic	Late	Lemon yellow	48″	−40°F

VARIETY	DIVISION	SEASON	COLOR	HEIGHT	HARDINESS
'Lennox'	Ia	Mid	Clear white	24″	−40°F
'Leslie Woodriff'*****	VIII***	Mid/late	White/scarlet/green	60″	−40°F
'Lollipop'*****	Ia	Early/mid	White/rose tips	24″	−40°F
'Loreto'	Ia	Mid	Golden orange/plum strokes	36″	−40°F
'Matrix'	Ia	Early/mid	Red/orange marks	20″	−40°F
'Monte Negro'	Ia	Early/mid	Velvety red	40″	−40°F
'Montreux'	Ia	Early/mid	Pink	36″	−40°F
'Mount Duckling'	Ia	Mid	Magenta rose	24″	−40°F
'Mrs. R.O. Backhouse'	II	Early	Yellow/purplish spots	60″	−40°F
'Navona'	Ia	Mid	Pure white	36″	−40°F
'New Wave'	Ia	Early/mid	Pure white	24″	−40°F
'Orange Matrix'	Ia	Early/mid	Bright orange	18″	−40°F
Pink Perfection (strain)	VIa	Late	Orchid purple	72″	−30°F
Pixie Series	Ia	Mid	Varied	24″	−40°F
'Pizzaz'	VIII***	Mid/late	Orange/red center	60″	−40°F
'Pollyana'	Ia	Mid	Bright yellow/gold	36″	−40°F
'Red Velvet'*****	Ib	Mid	Red	48″	−40°F
'Renoir'	Ia	Mid	Soft pink/white center	36″	−40°F
'Rosella's Dream'	Ib	Mid	Pink/yellow strokes	40″	−40°F
'Sally'	Ic	Mid	Orange pink	48″	−40°F
'Scheherazade'*****	VIII***	Late	Deep red/gold edges	72″	−40°F
'Seafarer'	VIII*	Mid/late	Cantaloupe orange	48″	−30°F
'Silk Road'*****	VIII***	Mid/late	White/intense crimson	60″	−40°F
'Starburst Sensation'*****	VIII***	Mid/late	Pink/crimson center	48″	−40°F
'Star Gazer'*****	VIIc	Late	Red/white margins	36″	−30°F
'Sterling Star'	Ia	Mid	White	36″	−40°F
'Strawberry & Cream'	Ia	Mid	Cream pink speckled red	36″	−40°F
'Sunlight'	VIb	Late	Sulphur yellow	48″	−30°F
'Sweet Surrender'	Ic	Mid	Cream/plum spots	48″	−40°F
'Tiger Babies'	Ic	Mid	Salmon peach	36″	−40°F
'Timepiece'	Ia	Mid	Orange spotted maroon	40″	−40°F
'Toronto'	Ia	Mid	Rose pink/cream center	36″	−40°F
'Val di Sole'	Ia	Mid	Bright yellow/green	40″	−40°F
'Vermeer'*****	Ia	Mid	Pink white/raspberry	36″	−40°F
'White Henryi'*****	VIc	Late	White	48″	−30°F
'White Pixels'	Ia	Mid	White burgundy	36″	−40°F
'Willow Wood'	Ia	Mid	Yellow/red marks/pink	30″	−40°F

Lysimachia punctata

LYSIMACHIA

(liss-uh-MAH-kee-uh)

LOOSESTRIFE

Bloom Time	Expected Longevity	Maintenance	Years to Bloom	Preferred Light
Summer to late summer	25+ years	Medium	From seed: 2 years From potted plant: 1 year	Full sun to light shade

Loosestrifes are ideally suited to informal garden settings. They are tough, easy-to-grow perennials with attractive foliage and showy flowers in the summer months. Most Loosestrifes spread rapidly and need lots of space to roam. Control their spread by regular division. Loosestrifes require little care and are rarely bothered by insects or diseases. Since they grow in so many different ways, these plants can serve many purposes in landscape design.

How Loosestrifes Grow

Loosestrifes grow from creeping fibrous roots into a wide variety of forms from low creeping to quite tall vertical plants. All have attractive leaves that spiral around the stems. Their small, rounded flowers are white or yellow and bloom singly or in elongated spikes. All flower freely. They form stunning clumps or widespread colonies quite quickly. Loosestrifes produce seed but do not self sow as commonly as many other perennials.

Where to Plant

Site and Light Loosestrifes grow well in full sun or light shade. Certain varieties selected for their foliage color depend on protection from hot afternoon sun for best results. If you plant rapid-spreading types in the flower garden, restrict their spread with a physical barrier if you are not able to divide them regularly. Many of them are ideally located next to water.

Soil and Moisture Loosestrifes thrive in rich, moist soils. Add generous amounts of organic matter such as compost, leaf mold, rotted manure, or peat moss to the soil. They will survive on drier sites but at the expense of good foliage and abundant flowers.

Spacing Space low, mat-forming types about a foot (30 cm) apart. Place the larger-growing, rapid-spreading varieties farther apart.

Companions

Since most varieties of *Lysimachia* (Loosestrife) prefer moist soils, they do well in mass plantings near ponds and streams, where they combine effectively with *Asclepias incarnata* (Swamp Milkweed), *Chelone* (Turtlehead), *Filipendula* (Meadowsweet), *Iris* (Siberian Iris), *Monarda* (Bee Balm), and **Grasses** such as *Glyceria maxima* 'Variegata' (Variegated Manna Grass) or *Spartina pectinata* (Prairie Cord Grass). Certain species, such as *Lysimachia ciliata* (Fringed Loosestrife) and *Lysimachia punctata* (Yellow Loosestrife), are also appropriate in the border and look handsome next to *Campanula persicifolia* (Peach-Leaved Bellflower), *Geranium* (Cranesbill), and *Heuchera* (Coral Bells). *Lysimachia clethroides* (Gooseneck Loosestrife) takes on a dramatic reddish orange fall color and can be placed around woody ornamentals and **Grasses**, which offer complementary foliage and fruit coloration.

Planting

Bare Root Plant bare root stock as soon as you can work the ground in spring. Remove plants from their shipping package immediately. Snip off broken or damaged root tips. Soak plants overnight in room-temperature water. Place a small amount of superphosphate in the base of the planting hole. Fill the hole with soil. Place the crown just below the soil surface. Fill the hole with soil, firm with your fingers, and water immediately. Dissolve ½ cup (about 114 g) 10-10-10 fertilizer in 1 gallon (about 4 liters) of water. Pour ½ cup (about 120 ml) of this starter solution around the base of the plant. If you prefer organic fertilizer, use fish emulsion instead.

Potted Plants Plant potted Loosestrifes after all danger of frost has passed in spring. If the soil in the pot is dry, water it, and let drain overnight. Tap the plant out of the pot without disturbing the root ball. Plant it at the same depth as in the pot, after preparing the hole in a similar manner to that for a bare root plant. Fill in the hole, firm the soil with your fingers, and water immediately. Pour ½ cup (about 120 ml) of the starter solution around the base of the plant.

How to Care for Loosestrifes

Water Loosestrifes prefer evenly moist soils throughout the growing season. Moisture encourages lush growth and prolific bloom but will also speed up the spreading tendencies of certain varieties. If not watered during hot, dry spells, plants may die out.

Mulch Place 2 inches (5 cm) of mulch around the base of young plants as soon as the ground warms up in spring. Good mulches include dried grass clippings, shredded leaves, and pine needles. Mulch keeps the soil moist and cool while inhibiting the growth of annual weeds. Mature plantings of Loosestrifes cover the ground so effectively that they act as their own living mulch.

Fertilizing Sprinkle 10-10-10 fertilizer over the planting in early spring. Water immediately to dissolve granules and move the fertilizer down into the root zone. Immediate watering also stops the fertilizer from burning tender new growth. Biweekly feedings through the summer months with a dilute solution of water-soluble fertilizer will encourage very lush growth.

If you prefer organic fertilizers, use alfalfa meal (rabbit pellets), blood meal, bonemeal, compost, fish emulsion, Milorganite, or rotted horse manure. Bonemeal must be mixed into the soil at planting time to be effective.

Weeding Spreading types are vigorous enough to choke out most annual weeds. Place mulch around vertical types to inhibit weed growth.

Staking Staking is not necessary.

Deadheading Removal of dead flowers, particularly on taller varieties, will keep plants looking their best. Deadheading rarely induces a new round of flowering.

Winter Protection Mature plants are quite winter hardy and survive well with normal snowfall. If there is no snow cover by early December, it may be good insurance, especially with *Lysimachia nummularia* (Moneywort), to cover the plants with 6 inches (15 cm) of marsh hay, clean straw, pine needles, or whole leaves. Remove this winter protection as soon as the weather warms up in early spring.

Problems

Insects Loosestrifes are rarely bothered by insects.

Disease Leaf spot diseases are primarily an aesthetic concern. You may have to spray *Lysimachia punctata* (Yellow Loosestrife) for use as a cut flower.

Propagation

Division Loosestrifes benefit from division about every 6 to 10 years. Divide these perennials in early spring just as they begin growth. Dig up the entire plant, and wash it free of soil. Tease the plant apart with your fingers, or cut it into sections with a knife or pruning shears. Make sure each section has several shoots and an ample supply of roots. Plant these new divisions immediately as you would a bare root plant.

Cuttings Most Loosestrifes can be easily propagated by stem cuttings taken in spring and early summer before the plants are budded or flowering. However, only *Lysimachia nummularia* (Moneywort) and *Lysimachia punctata* (Yellow Loosestrife) seem to be commonly propagated in this way. Take terminal cuttings, making sure that each one has three sets of leaves. Strip off all but the top set of leaves, and dip the cut end in rooting hormone. Tap off any excess powder, and plant the cutting immediately in moist rooting medium. Adequate rooting usually occurs within 2 to 4 weeks. Once a strong root system has formed, transplant the young plants to pots or a protected location in the garden. Keep the soil evenly moist to get the young plants off to a good start.

Ground Layering If the soil remains evenly moist, spreading varieties will naturally form roots where leaf nodes touch the ground. Sever the young plantlets from the mother plant, and either plant them in a pot or move them to a new garden location. You can propagate the taller varieties in this way if you simply peg a stem down to the ground. Make a shallow cut at a leaf node, and bury that area in the soil. Roots will form where you make the cut. You can use a rooting hormone to speed up the process.

Seed Seed of Loosestrifes other than *Lysimachia clethroides* (Gooseneck Loosestrife) and *Lysimachia punctata* (Yellow Loosestrife) is not commonly available. Start seed indoors about 12 weeks before the last expected frost in spring. Sow the seed over moist germination medium, and keep it evenly moist at 55°F to 65°F (13°C to 18°C). Germination is often irregular, taking from 30 to 120 days. Once seedlings emerge, drop the growing temperature by 10°F (6°C) to produce the stockiest plants. Seedlings can be transplanted to individual pots once they have developed their first set of true leaves.

Special Uses

Cut Flowers With their abundant and showy blooms, Loosestrifes make excellent cut flowers. Each variety offers its own distinctive habit and bloom arrangement. Cut the stems at the peak of bloom, and place them into water immediately. They hold up for a long time in arrangements without any special conditioning as long as any foliage that would be below the water level has been removed.

Dried Flowers Loosestrifes generally are not suitable for drying.

Sources

Bluestone Perennials, 7211 Middle Ridge Rd., Madison, OH 44057, (800) 852-5243

Fieldstone Gardens, Inc., 55 Quaker Lane, Vassalboro, ME 04989, (207) 923-3836

Fraser's Thimble Farms, 175 Arbutus Rd., Salt Spring Island, BC V8K 1A3 Canada, (250) 537-5788

Niche Gardens, 1111 Dawson Rd., Chapel Hill, NC 27516, (919) 967-0078

'Aurea'

Lysimachia clethroides

VARIETIES

VARIETY	COLOR	HEIGHT	SPREADING HABIT	HARDINESS
Lysimachia ciliata				
(Fringed Loosestrife)	Yellow	36″	Slow	−40°F
'Firecracker'	Yellow	36″	Slow	−40°F
'Purpurea'	Yellow	36″	Slow	−40°F

This northeastern United States native is an elegant plant with a willowy appearance and small yellow flowers in midsummer. 'Firecracker' and 'Purpurea' are both named for the chocolate purple color of their foliage.

VARIETY	COLOR	HEIGHT	SPREADING HABIT	HARDINESS
Lysimachia clethroides				
(Gooseneck Loosestrife)	White	36″	Rapid	−40°F
'Geisha'	White	30″	Rapid	−40°F

This species produces uniquely shaped, arching white flower heads in mid to late summer. It is stunning in mass plantings but needs to be placed carefully since it can be invasive. The handsome foliage is attractive all season and turns a beautiful, tannish orange in fall. 'Geisha' has green leaves that are irregularly edged cream.

VARIETY	COLOR	HEIGHT	SPREADING HABIT	HARDINESS
Lysimachia japonica var. *minutissima*				
(Miniature Japanese Loosestrife)	Bright yellow	1″	Slow	−40°F

Although a summer bloomer, this plant is a good substitute for *Lysimachia nummularia* (Moneywort), which can be invasive. Consider this diminutive perennial with its tiny bright green leaves for use in the rock garden or among stepping stones. It prefers shade but takes morning sun.

VARIETY	COLOR	HEIGHT	SPREADING HABIT	HARDINESS
Lysimachia nummularia				
(Moneywort)	Yellow	4″	Rapid	−30°F
'Aurea'	Yellow	2″	Rapid	−30°F

A well-known ground cover, this plant produces its display of small, fragrant flowers in late spring. The golden foliage of 'Aurea' brightens up lightly shaded areas. In very open, severe winters, this plant may suffer some winter damage, but it normally recovers.

VARIETY	COLOR	HEIGHT	SPREADING HABIT	HARDINESS
Lysimachia punctata				
(Yellow Loosestrife)	Bright yellow	30″	Rapid	−30°F
'Alexander'	Golden yellow	24″	Rapid	−30°F
Golden Alexander ('Walgoldalex')	Golden yellow	24″	Rapid	−30°F

Flowering in late spring and early summer, this species will tolerate drier sites than other Loosestrifes, especially when planted in partial shade. It is very popular in cold climates because it is so easy to grow. 'Alexander' has a striking pink blush to its emerging stems and creamy leaf edges that age to white. Golden Alexander has yellow leaf edges that fade to cream. Both of these varieties need to be grown in a bit of shade.

'Cambridge Scarlet'

MONARDA

(moh-NAR-duh)

BEE BALM

Bloom Time	Expected Longevity	Maintenance	Years to Bloom	Preferred Light
Summer	20 years	High	From seed: 2 years From potted plant: 1 year	Full sun

Bee Balms are tough, vigorous, attractive perennials with bright coloration and interestingly shaped blooms. The flowers are favorites of bees, butterflies, and hummingbirds and are also good for cutting. The foliage is known for a pleasing mintlike aroma released when it is crushed, bruised, or even brushed against as you work in the garden. Bee Balms spread rapidly, requiring frequent division to keep them under control. Most of the standard varieties are quite susceptible to powdery mildew, a disease that often discolors or even defoliates the plant, especially if it is underwatered. However, some of the more recent releases in this group are relatively disease resistant.

How Bee Balms Grow

Bee Balms grow from a shallow, spreading root system into plants standing from 1 to 4 feet (30 to 120 cm) tall. Each plant produces numerous square stems that are hollow inside. The stems are clothed in dark green, toothed, hairy leaves. The tubular-shaped flowers bloom in a wide range of colors and in round clusters at the tops of the stems. These clusters of blooms give the plant a shaggy appearance when it flowers during the summer months. Bee Balms spread quickly by underground stems, or stolons, to form large clumps, but they do not self-sow freely.

Where to Plant

Site and Light Bee Balms prefer full sun but tolerate light shade. Too much shade results in weak stems, a poor show of flowers, and greater susceptibility to powdery mildew. Plant them in natural settings or in the border, but give them plenty of space to spread. They flourish on the edge of water in full sun.

Soil and Moisture Bee Balms thrive in rich, evenly moist soils. Soil type is not as important as consistent moisture. Add lots of organic matter such as peat moss, compost, leaf mold, or rotted manure to the soil. Dry soils increase the likelihood of powdery mildew.

Spacing Space plants 15 to 18 inches (37.5 to 45 cm) apart in groups of three to five. They will quickly fill the space and appear as one showy colony. Don't crowd Bee Balms with neighboring plants, as this may prevent proper growth and increase the likelihood of disease.

Companions

The wild species of *Monarda* (Bee Balm) naturalize well in meadows and prairies and on the edges of woodlands. Named selections do well in lightly shaded borders combined with *Chelone* (Turtlehead), *Cimicifuga/Actaea* (Bugbane), *Filipendula* (Meadowsweet), *Lysimachia* (Loosestrife), and *Tradescantia* (Spiderwort). In sunnier spots, you may try combining them with *Asclepias tuberosa* (Butterfly Milkweed), *Echinacea* (Purple Coneflower), *Heliopsis* (Oxeye), *Hemerocallis* (Daylily), *Lilium* (Lily), *Phlox*–Paniculata Group (Summer Phlox), and

Platycodon (Balloon Flower). As one specific combination, try *Monarda* 'Jacob Cline' with *Achillea* 'Sunny Seduction' (Hybrid Yarrow) and *Platycodon grandiflorus* 'Komachi' (Balloon Flower).

Planting

Bare Root Plant bare root stock as soon as you can work the ground in spring. Remove plants from their shipping package immediately. Snip off broken or damaged root tips. Soak plants overnight in room-temperature water. Place a small amount of superphosphate in the base of the planting hole. Fill the hole with soil. Place the crown 1 inch (2.5 cm) below the soil surface. Fill in with soil, firm with your fingers, and water immediately. Dissolve ½ cup (about 114 g) 10-10-10 fertilizer in 1 gallon (about 4 liters) of water. Pour ½ cup (about 120 ml) of this starter solution around the base of the plant. If you prefer organic fertilizer, try using fish emulsion instead.

Potted Plants Plant potted Bee Balms after all danger of frost has passed in spring. If the soil in the pot is dry, water it, and let it drain overnight. Tap the plant out of the pot without disturbing the root ball. Plant it at the same depth as in the pot, after preparing the hole in a similar manner to that for a bare root plant. Fill in the hole, firm the soil with your fingers, and water immediately. Pour ½ cup (about 120 ml) of starter solution around the base of the plant.

How to Care for Bee Balms

Water Bee Balms require an abundant supply of moisture throughout the growing season. If these plants dry out they may lose leaves, have less abundant bloom, and be more susceptible to disease. *Monarda fistulosa* (Wild Bergamot) and *Monarda punctata* (Spotted Bee Balm) tolerate slightly drier growing conditions, but even they resent extended dry periods. When you water, soak the soil to a depth of 6 to 8 inches (15 to 20 cm).

Mulch Place a 2-inch (5-cm) layer of mulch around each plant after the ground warms up in spring. Good mulches are pine needles, shredded leaves, or dried grass clippings. Mulch keeps the soil moist and cool while inhibiting annual weed growth. Young plantings are easy to mulch, but old clumps really don't need it. The dense foliage often acts as a living mulch. If you do mulch mature plants, just spread material around the outer edge of the plant, never over the intricate pattern of spreading stolons.

Fertilizing Bee Balms respond well to regular feeding. Sprinkle 10-10-10 fertilizer around the base of the plants as growth emerges in spring. Water immediately to dissolve the granules and move the fertilizer into the root zone. Give them another light feeding about a month later, or foliar feed them with a water-soluble fertilizer every 2 weeks through their bloom period.

If you prefer organic fertilizers, use alfalfa meal (rabbit pellets), blood meal, bonemeal, compost, fish emulsion, Milorganite, or rotted manure. Bonemeal must be mixed into the soil at planting time to be effective.

Weeding The roots of Bee Balms are very shallow and easily damaged during cultivation. Mulches prevent the growth of most annual weeds. Any weeds that do sprout are easily pulled by hand. Old plantings form such dense foliage canopies that few weeds sprout other than around the outside edges of the clump. Again, control these by hand pulling.

Staking By not planting these lovely perennials in deep shade or in a windy spot, you can avoid staking altogether. The stems of some varieties get very tall in moist soil and bright light, but they stand up well without any support.

Deadheading Removing spent flowers improves the plant's appearance and lengthens the bloom period.

Winter Protection Cut the stems to the ground in late fall, and destroy them. This gets rid of some of the disease-causing agent (inoculum) that results in powdery mildew. Winter protection other than natural snowfall is not required on mature plants.

Problems

Insects Bee Balms are not regularly bothered by insects, although purple scale and stalk borer are known pests.

Disease Many of the standard Bee Balm varieties are susceptible to powdery mildew. Though this fungus rarely kills plants, it leaves an unsightly frosty white growth on leaf surfaces. Providing good air circulation, watering consistently, picking up all fallen leaves, and removing all foliage at the end of the season help limit the spread of this disease. Fungicides are effective against powdery mildew and best used to prevent rather than control the

This plant is infected by powdery mildew, with its characteristic white powdery look. The disease can affect other plants as well, especially *Phlox*.

disease. Recent Bee Balm introductions offer better disease resistance. Among them are 'Coral Reef,' the Grand™ Series, 'Jacob Cline,' 'Marshall's Delight,' 'Purple Mildew Resistant,' 'Raspberry Wine,' and 'Violet Queen.' Resistance does not mean that they can not get powdery mildew, but rather that they get it less often and tolerate it better than other varieties.

Rusts and leaf spots occasionally infect Bee Balms. Both are related to weather conditions and are not common problems. Their damage is more of an aesthetic rather than a health concern. Spraying is rarely warranted.

Propagation

Division Bee Balms are very easy to propagate by division, and a mature clump yields dozens of plants. In borders, these perennials require division every 1 to

3 years to limit their spread and keep them healthy. The centers of older clumps often die out, leaving the plants with a somewhat strange appearance. Divide plants in early spring just as new growth emerges. Dig up the plant, and cut it into sections with a sharp spade. In many cases the growth is on the soil surface, and you can just pull the little plantlets apart. Take divisions from the newest growth at the outside of the clump. Plant these divisions immediately as you would a bare root plant.

Cuttings Stem cuttings taken in spring, well before plants have formed buds, root easily and quickly. Cuttings should have several sets of leaves. Make the final cut a quarter inch (6 mm) below a leaf node. Strip off all but the top set of leaves, and dip the cut end in rooting hormone. Tap off any excess powder, and stick the cuttings in moist rooting medium. Keep the medium evenly moist through the 2 to 4 weeks that it takes for cuttings to root. At that time, place them in pots or a protected garden location. Keep the soil evenly moist during this transition to get the plants off to a good start.

Seed Of the varieties described in the table, only the three species (native plants) come true from seed. Sowing should take place about 10 weeks before the last expected frost in spring. The seed can be either left exposed or lightly covered. Keep the medium evenly moist at 70°F to 75°F (21°C to 24°C), and germination should take place within 5 to 8 days. The young seedlings should be ready for transplanting to individual pots within 3 to 4 weeks of sowing. Harden seedlings off for 14 days before planting them outside after all danger of frost has passed in spring.

Special Uses

Cut Flowers Bee Balms are excellent for cutting as long as the foliage is not infected by powdery mildew. The mintlike aroma of the leaves adds to the loveliness of the showy flowers. Cut the stems just before or right at peak bloom, and put them into cool water immediately. Once indoors, place the bottom inch (2.5 cm) of each stem in boiling water for several seconds or longer. Then place the stems in room-temperature water overnight before arranging the following day. Remove any leaves that would be underwater in the arrangement. Some gardeners claim that the flowers last longer if the hollow stems are turned upside down, filled with water, and sealed with cotton before being placed in an arrangement.

Dried Flowers Bee Balms are not the easiest flowers to dry, but it can be done. Cut stems just as the flowers start to open. Hang them upside down in a dark, dry, well-ventilated area. Be aware that colors often change dramatically during the drying process.

Food Bee Balms have been used for making herbal teas since colonial times. If you want to try it yourself, cut the stems, and hang them upside down for about 10 days. Then remove the leaves and shred them into tiny pieces. Use 1 teaspoon (5 g) of leaves per cup (about 240 ml) of water, and steep for 3 to 5 minutes. The French sometimes use the leaves of Bee Balms in salads or to flavor wine and fruit drinks.

Sources

Ambergate Gardens, 8730 County Rd. 43, Chaska, MN 55318, (877) 211-9769

Bluestone Perennials, 7211 Middle Ridge Rd., Madison, OH 44057, (800) 852-5243

Busse Gardens, 17160 245th Ave., Big Lake, MN 55309, (800) 544-3192

Earthly Pursuits, 2901 Kuntz Rd., Windsor Mill, MD 21244, (410) 496-2523

Fieldstone Gardens, Inc., 55 Quaker Lane, Vassalboro, ME 04989, (207) 923-3836

ForestFarm, 990 Tetherow Rd., Williams, OR 97544, (541) 846-7269

Goodwin Creek, P.O. Box 83, Williams, OR 97544, (800) 846-7359

Well-Sweep Herb Farm, 205 Mount Bethel Rd., Port Murray, NJ 07865, (908) 852-5390

'Blue Stocking'/'Blaustrumpf'

'Violet Queen'

VARIETIES

VARIETIES	COLOR	HEIGHT	HARDINESS

Monarda didyma

(Oswego Tea)	Scarlet red	48″	−30°F

Plant this eastern United States native in a natural area where it will attract hummingbirds and butterflies.

Monarda fistulosa

(Wild Bergamot)	Soft lavender	48″	−40°F

Wild Bergamot fits nicely into natural areas. It resists drought better than *Monarda didyma.*

Monarda punctata

(Spotted Bee Balm)	Greenish yellow/spotted purple	36″	−40°F

This Bee Balm with its unique blooms often lives a brief life. It tolerates drought and is quite disease-resistant.

Monarda (Named varieties and hybrids)

'Aquarius'	Violet	42″	−30°F
'Blue Stocking' ('Blaustrumpf')	Violet purple	36″	−30°F
'Cambridge Scarlet'	Scarlet	36″	−30°F
'Colrain Red'	Deep purplish red	36″	−30°F
'Coral Reef'*****	Coral pink	36″	−30°F
'Dark Ponticum'	Rich purple	36″	−30°F
'Fireball'	Reddish purple	20″	−30°F
'Gardenview Scarlet'	Bright red	48″	−30°F
Grand Marshall™	Fuchsia purple	24″	−30°F
Grand Mum™	Soft pink	20″	−30°F
Grand Parade™*****	Lavender purple	18″	−30°F
'Jacob Cline'*****	Deep red	48″	−30°F
'Kardinal'	Purplish red	48″	−30°F
'Marshall's Delight'	Bright pink	42″	−30°F
'Petite Delight'	Lavender rose	14″	−30°F
'Petite Wonder'	Pink	12″	−30°F
'Pink Lace'	Light pink/purple center	18″	−30°F
'Prairie Night' ('Prarienacht')	Deep purple	48″	−30°F
'Purple Mildew Resistant'	Purple	36″	−30°F
'Raspberry Wine'*****	Bright purplish red	48″	−30°F
'Snow White' ('Schneewittchen')	Creamy white	42″	−30°F
'Squaw'	Clear red	48″	−30°F
'Stone's Throw Pink'	Purplish pink	48″	−30°F
'Sunset'	Purple red	42″	−30°F
'Thundercloud' ('Donnerwolke')	Violet purple	36″	−30°F
'Violet Queen'*****	Deep purple	42″	−30°F

Although all Bee Balms attract hummingbirds, those with red flowers are by far the most popular.

'Mount Hood'

NARCISSUS

(nar-SIS-us)

DAFFODIL

Bloom Time	Expected Longevity	Maintenance	Years to Bloom	Preferred Light
Spring	5 to 25 years	Medium	From seed: 3 to 6 years From bulb: 1 year	Full sun

Fields of Daffodils evoke spring. The flowers' color and sweet scent are best appreciated when they are planted in waves. Daffodils are ideal for naturalizing. In good weather, the plants have an extended bloom period. Properly planted, they are long lived. They are wonderful cut flowers. They also are generally insect and disease free. By choosing varieties from different classifications, you will have a long season of bloom. However, Daffodils can be expensive, and preparation for proper planting is a chore. Do not let bulbs lie around. They can be confused with edible plants. If eaten, bulbs cause nausea, vomiting, and even death. Do not let kids play with them. If you store them for a short time in your refrigerator before planting, mark them with a poison sign. This characteristic is an advantage outdoors in that it discourages rodents and deer from eating the foliage and bulbs as they do with Tulips.

How Daffodils Grow

Daffodils are spring-flowering plants that grow from bulbs. These are planted in the fall. The following spring, the bulbs send up leaves. A stem shoots up between these leaves and forms buds, each of which turns into a flower or several flowers, depending on the variety. The outside petals of the flower are known as the *perianth* and may be a different color from the inside trumpet or cup, known as the *corona*. The many variations of color give this group of flowers great appeal. Underground, the bulb absorbs food manufactured by the leaves after flowering. This goes on for 7 weeks or longer. The leaves then fade and finally flop onto the ground as the plant enters its dormant period. Each year the bulb forms one or more bulblets, or *offsets*. Later in the fall, the bulb begins to grow new roots and prepare itself for flowering the following spring.

Where to Plant

Site and Light Daffodils do best in full sun, although they tolerate light shade. If you plant Daffodils under trees, consider trimming off the lower tree limbs to give them more light.

Soil and Moisture Daffodils require soils that drain freely. If you have clay or rocky soil, replace it with loam or build a raised bed. If soils are soggy, bulbs will rot out. Daffodils may die out in alkaline soils, ones with a pH above 7.3. If concerned and planting many bulbs, have a soil test done.

All bulb plantings require good soil preparation. This can be tough the first time, especially in clay or rocky soil. If you're planting a large grouping, which looks best, this will be a chore.

Dig up the entire bed to a depth of 12 inches (30 cm), deeper if you have the energy. Pile the soil off to one side of the large trench on a plastic tarp. Keep only dark, rich loam. Get rid of clay or rock. Turn the soil at the bottom of the trench over. Mix organic matter into the loosened soil. Once you do this, do not step on it again. The soil must be loose at the bottom. Break this soil up either with a garden rake, with the tip of your spade, or by hand as you turn it.

Sprinkle superphosphate, 10-10-10 fertilizer, and peat moss at the bottom of the trench. Potash is also helpful. Sources include New Jersey green sand, gran-ite sand, or small amounts of wood ash. Work these into the soil with a garden rake. Do not step into the trench. If you prefer organic fertilizers, add blood meal, bonemeal, compost, cow manure, Milorganite, or rotted horse manure.

Fill up the trench with soil until it is 8 inches (20 cm) from the surface. The soil should be mixed with peat moss at the ratio of 1 part peat moss to 2 parts soil. Peat moss is recommended because it is slightly acidic. The ideal soil will also contain lots of other organic matter, such as compost or rotted manure. If your soil is bad, you may have to buy some from a garden center.

The remaining soil needed to fill the trench should be amended with peat moss at the appropriate ratio. Use this in the final planting stage as described later in the section.

Spacing Space bulbs as recommended on the package, generally 3 to 4 inches (7.5 to 10 cm) apart and 5 to 8 inches (12.5 to 20 cm) deep, depending on the variety. Flowers look more natural if planting is not uniform. If you naturalize bulbs, strew them on the ground, then plant them wherever the bulbs land. This gives a disorganized feel to the planting and is much more appealing than rigid, uniform spacing. This technique works just as well in trench planting.

Companions

Use *Narcissus* (Daffodil) in many creative ways. They are wonderful massed at the bases of spring-flowering shrubs or small ornamental trees such as *Malus* (Crab Apple). They are also lovely along walks and at entryways where they capture attention. Place groupings in the border next to other perennials blooming at the same time. These would include *Dicentra* (Bleeding Heart), *Euphorbia polychroma* (Cushion Spurge), *Pulmonaria* (Lungwort), and *Tulipa* (Tulip). The smaller types are perhaps most appropriate in rock gardens or at least in special settings where they are not overwhelmed by larger plants.

When planting these bulbs, keep in mind that they go dormant in early summer and that for many weeks their foliage is unattractive. Mask the dying foliage and bare spots later in the season by careful companion planting. Some good choices to do this are *Alchemilla mollis* (Lady's Mantle), *Hemerocallis* (Day-lily), *Hosta* (Hosta), *Lamium* (Dead Nettle), *Nepeta* (Catmint), *Phlox divaricata* (Woodland Phlox), *Pulmonaria* (Lungwort), **Ferns**, and **Grasses**.

Planting

Bulbs Always check all bulbs before planting. If you purchase them locally, check them in the store. Buy the largest available bulbs of any given variety. Feel the base of the bulb; if it's soft, don't buy it. Look for a dark brown to almost black color at the lower, largest end of the bulb; if the area is discolored, don't buy it. Watch out for any mold. Call stores to find out exact arrival dates of bulbs, and buy them as soon as they arrive. They deteriorate in heat and humidity. Check mail-order bulbs on receipt. If they are bad, send them back. They aren't going to get better.

As soon as you get bulbs, plant them. Prepare the bed in advance so that there is no waiting time after they are purchased or shipped. Bulbs are alive. They do not like to be warm or exposed to humidity. Reputable dealers know this and keep them in cool, well-ventilated conditions until shipped. If you have to, you can keep bulbs in the crisper of your refrigerator for a few days. Try not to do this, though, since they can be harmed by ethylene gas given off by fruits. Also, as mentioned in the introduction, they are highly toxic, so be sure to mark the stored package with a symbol indicating this.

The very latest that bulbs should be planted is the early part of October. This is very late, since bulbs need 10 to 12 weeks to form roots properly.

Plant bulbs with the fat end down at the bottom of the trench, generally 5 to 8 inches (12.5 to 20 cm) deep, depending on the variety. Press the bulbs into the soil to get rid of any air pockets. Fill the trench with water and let it recede. Then fill the trench to the top with soil mixed with peat moss at the proper ratio. Water the soil again until it's thoroughly soaked.

You can extend bloom time with one variety by varying the planting depth of individual bulbs. The deeper you plant bulbs, the later they bloom. However, don't plant deeper than recommended, since this could stop the bulb from blooming at all; just vary the depth of planting by an inch or 2 (2.5 to 5 cm). You can also extend bloom by varying the depth of the winter mulch: the deeper the winter mulch, the later it can stay on in spring, which results in later bloom.

How to Care for Daffodils

Water Water the buried bulbs frequently during the fall after planting. The bulbs need water to send out roots at this time. Fall watering is critical to good root growth but is often ignored because gardeners forget that the bulbs are growing underground. Proper watering and root growth at that time help protect bulbs from winter cold.

Water generously again in spring. Then cut back on watering as foliage dies down during the dormant period later in the season. Flower buds begin forming in the underground bulbs in late summer, so begin regular watering again at that time. Continue watering through fall.

Mulch As soon as the leaves are 3 to 4 inches (7.5 to 10 cm) high, place a 1-inch (2.5-cm) layer of organic mulch around the base of each plant without touching the leaves. This keeps the soil moist and cool. It also prevents annual weeds from sprouting. In large beds or naturalized areas, this is not practical but is certainly helpful if you have the time and energy.

Fertilizing In early spring before growth appears, sprinkle 5-10-10 fertilizer over the bed at a rate of 2 pounds (about 1 kg) per 100 square feet (9 square meters). When using chemical fertilizers, water immediately to dissolve the granules and carry nutrients to the root zone. If any new growth is showing, avoid touching it with chemicals. If you do fertilize when new growth is already showing, water right away.

Chemicals coming into contact with foliage can cause burn. Holland Bulb Booster (9-9-6) is coated with a polymer and is highly recommended as a slow-release fertilizer.

If you prefer organic fertilizers, use alfalfa meal (rabbit pellets), blood meal, bonemeal, compost, cow manure, fish meal, Milorganite, or rotted horse manure. Bonemeal must be mixed into the soil at planting time to be effective. Spread these over the soil surface before Daffodils begin to sprout. Soak the soil immediately to get nutrients into the root zone.

Follow the same fertilizing procedure in early fall after the plants have had a period of rest during the summer. Apply 3 pounds (about 1.5 kg) of 5-10-10 fertilizer per 100 square feet (9 square meters). Begin deep watering at this time to carry the nutrients down into the soil to feed the bulbs. Again, this step is commonly overlooked by the home gardener because foliage has long ago disappeared. Bulbs, however, are begging for water and nutrients at this time!

Weeding Daffodils look great in large clumps or undulating drifts, but these can become infested with perennial weeds. Wait until the leaves die down to use a systemic herbicide to kill the weeds off. We recommend Roundup®. If you allow weeds to spread in the patch, the plants can be suffocated from the competition, or they may not bloom well in spring.

Always cultivate the surface of the soil lightly after the foliage dies down. This covers openings left by the decaying stem. Covering these holes stops bulb flies from laying eggs in them.

Staking Daffodils sometimes flop over, but no one stakes them. Their somewhat lax growth is part of their beauty.

Deadheading Snip off spent blossoms for aesthetic reasons. Do not remove foliage until it begins to turn yellow and ugly.

Pruning Many people plant Daffodils in natural settings, often on the edge of lawns by woods. This is fine as long as you do not mow the leaves down after the plants flower. Let them die back naturally as they would in the wild. This generally takes about 7 weeks or longer from the time of last flowering. Once foliage yellows, you can cut it off without doing damage to bulbs.

Do not twist the foliage into a knot as illustrated in a number of gardening books. The idea is to leave foliage alone so that it can produce food for the underground bulbs. By damaging or removing it, you reduce the food source to the bulbs, which need it for vigorous growth and good bloom.

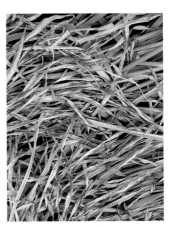

Remove the leaves of Daffodils only after they have turned brown and dropped to the ground.

Winter Protection If you plant bulbs late in the season, protect them with a deep winter mulch, certainly no less than 6 inches (15 cm). This allows the underground bulbs to form roots over a longer period of time. Good protective mulches include whole leaves, clean straw, pine needles, and pine boughs. Bark and wood chips also work well. Remove this winter cover as soon as the weather gets warm in spring. Do this before the bulbs start to sprout, which can be quite early in spring. If you wait too long, you'll damage the tender new growth.

Winter protection is not practical for naturalized bulbs. When naturalizing, get bulbs in as early as possible in the fall to give them enough time to form an extensive root system. Late plantings may not survive.

Late spring frosts may damage leaves. By using a winter mulch each year, you stop premature emergence in spring. The mulch holds frost in the ground for a longer period of time than if the area were left exposed to the sun. However, mulch must be removed when it thaws out to prevent rot of emerging leaves and damage to sprouting plants.

Problems

Insects Bulb fly maggots come from flies that lay eggs on the base of leaves and in the holes left as stems die back in summer. Cultivate lightly after foliage dies back to cover these openings. The maggots eat bulb tissue, often hollowing out and destroying the bulb in the process. Apply insecticide to the soil if this ever occurs.

Disease Plants are sometimes affected by underwatering, a severe frost just as new growth emerges, or a premature heat wave. Any of these can cause foliage to yellow. However, if none of these conditions exist, yellowing foliage early in the season is a sign of trouble. It is nothing to worry about weeks after the plant flowers when it goes into a dormant state. Leaves turn yellow, then brown, and die at this time.

If yellowing occurs early in the season, dig one of the bulbs up. If the soil is soggy, bulbs may be infected by botrytis blight or fusarium bulb rot. If the bulb is rotted, dig up the entire bed. Discard all rotted bulbs.

Rodents Rodents like Tulip bulbs but are not attracted to Daffodils, which are very toxic. So, these are good plants for wild areas where deer, rabbits, and woodchucks destroy many other types of perennials.

In early fall, you can dig up the mother plant and divide the numerous small bulbs to create a larger patch of bulbs.

Propagation

Division Each mother bulb produces smaller bulbs off to its side each year known as offsets. Each offset will produce a new plant if taken from the mother bulb and planted as a new bulb. These offsets produce plants identical to the parent plant. It is said that shallow planting of bulbs increases the number of offsets. So, if you're interested in getting lots of plants quickly, this might be a good tip. However, bulbs must be deep enough to survive cold winters.

Leave Daffodils alone until clumps get thick and blooms start to dwindle in size. These are signs that it's time to divide the Daffodils for their good health.

Dig up plants in early fall. Try not to cut or bruise any bulbs while digging. Start digging at the edge of the bed, and work in with your spade. Separate the small bulbs from the larger parent bulb; simply pull the roots of each bulb apart gently. Plant the offsets and parent bulbs immediately in a newly prepared bed, or rejuvenate the old bed. Never leave the bulbs and offsets exposed to light and heat for any extended period of time. Keep them covered in a cool, shady spot. Get them into the ground as quickly as possible, and water the bed immediately.

Seed Only species (wild) Daffodils will come true to seed. Seed may take up to 6 years to form blooming plants. Plant seed in the fall so that it can be moist-chilled (stratified) in the ground during the winter. Plant seed in a bed especially prepared for this. Note that wild Daffodils are not recommended in this guide, since most are too tender for colder climates.

Special Uses

Cut Flowers Daffodils make wonderful cut flowers. Some of them are sweetly scented and fill the room with aroma. Harvest them just as the buds begin to open. Simply reach down to the base of the stem and pull up. The stem will snap. Place the stems into water immediately. The stems produce a slime, which affects other cut flowers, such as Tulips. Add 5 drops of household bleach per quart (liter) of water to take care of this. Cut-flower preservatives also work fine. Do not mix Daffodils with other flowers unless you follow the previous steps. Many arrangers suggest that Daffodils last best in shallow, rather than deep water. For this reason the smaller varieties are often preferred to larger ones if long-lasting bloom is your goal.

Dried Flowers You can freeze-dry Daffodils, but few gardeners have the equipment for this. Traditional drying methods used by the home gardener for other perennials rarely result in decent dried Daffodils.

Sources

ADR Bulbs, Inc., 49 Black Meadow Rd., Chester, NY 10918, (800) 990-9934

Bluestone Perennials, 7211 Middle Ridge Rd., Madison, OH 44057, (800) 852-5243

Breck's Bulbs, P.O. Box 65, Guilford, IN 47022, (513) 354-1511

Brent & Becky's Bulbs, 7900 Daffodil Lane, Gloucester, VA 23061, (877) 661-2852

Cherry Creek Daffodils, 21700 SW Chapman, Sherwood, OR 97140, (503) 625-3379

Colorblends, 747 Barnum Ave., Bridgeport, CT 06608, (888) 847-8637

Daffodils and More, P.O. Box 495, Dalton, MA 01227, (413) 443-1581

Dutch Gardens, 4 Currency Dr., Bloomington, IL 61704, (800) 944-2250

Holland Bulb Farms, 8480 N 87th St., Milwaukee, WI 53224, (414) 355-3774

Jacques Amand, LLC, P.O. Box 4000, Ancramdale, NY 12503, (480) 656-6151

John Scheepers, Inc. (Van Engelen), 23 Tulip Dr., Bantam, CT 06750, (860) 567-0838

McClure & Zimmerman, 335 S High St., Randolph, WI 53956, (800) 883-6998

Messelaar Bulb Co., P.O. Box 269, Ipswich, MA 01938, (978) 356-3737

Mitsch Daffodils, P.O. Box 218, Hubbard, OR 97032, (503) 651-2742

Nancy Wilson Species & Miniature Narcissus, 6525 Briceland-Thorn Rd., Garberville, CA 95542, (707) 923-2407

Oakwood Daffodils, 2330 W Bertrand Rd., Niles, MI 49120, (269) 684-3327

Old House Gardens, 536 Third St., Ann Arbor, MI 48103, (734) 995-1486

Ringhaddy Daffodils, 60 Ringhaddy Rd., Killinchy, Co Down, BT23 6TU Northern Ireland, +44(0) 289754 1007

Terra Ceia Farms, 3810 Terra Ceia Rd., Pantego, NC 27860, (800) 858-2852

Tulips.comRoozengarde, P.O. Box 1248, Mount Vernon, WA 98273, (866) 488-5477

Tulip World Holland Bulbs, 8480 N 87th, Milwaukee, WI 53224, (866) 688-9547

Van Bourgondien Bros., P.O. Box 2000, Virginia Beach, VA 23450, (800) 622-9997

Veldheer Tulip Gardens, 12755 Quincy St., Holland, MI 49424, (616) 399-1900

White Flower Farm, P.O. Box 50, Litchfield, CT 06759, (800) 503-9624

Wooden Shoe Tulip Farm, 33814 S Meridian Rd., Woodburn, OR 97071, (800) 711-2006

VARIETIES

Most people purchase Daffodils according to flower color, but there are many other considerations. These are outlined for you in the way Daffodils have been classified into divisions by the Royal Horticultural Society in Great Britain. With thousands of varieties available, we have suggested some of the very best for cold-climate gardeners. The classification system is as follows:

Division I: Trumpet Daffodils

These varieties have one flower per stem with the trumpet (corona) as long as or longer than the outer petals (perianth). The large blooms are excellent for cutting and the bulbs multiply freely. The entire group is hardy to –40°F.

Division II: Long-cupped Daffodils

These varieties have one flower per stem with the cup (corona) more than one third (but less than equal to) the length of the outer petals (perianth). This group contains a large number of varieties hardy to –40°F.

Division III: Short-cupped Daffodils

These varieties have one flower per stem with the cup (corona) not more than one third the length of the outer petals (perianth). The flowers in this group are very refined and delicate looking. Plants are all hardy to –40°F.

Division IV: Double Daffodils

These varieties have double flowers. They may have one or more flowers per stem. Doubles grow better in cooler climates but are easily damaged by heavy rains and storms. They are hardy to –40°F.

Division V: Triandrus Daffodils

These Daffodils, like the species ***Narcissus triandrus*** (Angel's tears), have two to three small, nodding flowers per stem. They are available mainly in white and shades of yellow and are rather scarce because of the strong demand for them. They are hardy to –40°F.

Division VI: Cyclamineus Daffodils

These varieties have slightly nodding flowers with medium to long trumpets (coronas) and reflexed outer petals (perianth). Their appearance is similar to ***Narcissus cyclamineus*** (Cyclamen-flowered Daffodil) from which the group name is derived. They are among the earliest Daffodils to bloom in spring. These Daffodils are not as hardy as many others but are certainly worth growing in protected areas. They are hardy to –30°F.

Division VII: Jonquilla Daffodils

These Daffodils have small, clustered, fragrant flowers and rush-like leaves similar to that of ***Narcissus jonquilla*** (Jonquil). They are available in a wide color range and are prized for indoor use because of their sweet scent. They are hardy to –40°F.

Division VIII: Tazetta Daffodils

These hybrids have fragrant, clustered flowers similar to those of ***Narcissus tazetta*** (Polyanthus Daffodil). The true Tazetta Daffodils are not reliably hardy in cold climates and are usually used for indoor forcing only. Some of the Tazetta Daffodils were crossed with ***Narcissus poeticus*** (Poet's Daffodil) to create a new group called Poetaz. Many of these are hardy in cold climates, but very few are sold today. We have included one of them, 'Geranium,' in the varietal listing.

Division IX: Poeticus Daffodils

These Daffodils, like the species *Narcissus poeticus* (Poet's Daffodil), have fragrant flat flowers with small cups (coronas) that are rimmed red. They are among the latest of the Daffodils to flower and increase slowly. The group is hardy to −40°F.

Division X: Species, Wild Forms, and Wild Hybrid Daffodils

This group includes over 50 naturally occurring species and their forms. Many of them are difficult to grow because of very specific growing requirements. They also don't live very long in average cold-climate gardens. We have not included any for that reason.

Division XI: Split-corona Daffodils

These varieties have cups (coronas) that are split for a least one third of their length and reflexed to resemble additional petals. These Daffodils are available in many color combinations and are favorites of arrangers. They are hardy to −40°F.

Division XII: Miscellaneous Daffodils

This group includes all Daffodils which do not fit into any of the above divisions. Very few are presently recommended for cold climates, but some are being developed which may soon be.

The bloom season descriptions given below are relative to the overall bloom season of Daffodils and will help you choose varieties to get the longest bloom season possible. *Under color, we have separated the outer petals (perianth) and trumpet or cup (corona) colors by a hyphen (-).* The first color describes the outer petals, and the color(s) following the hyphen describe the trumpet or cup (corona) from the inside out. You will note that certain Daffodils go through a progression of color from the heart of the cup to the outside.

A few of the listed daffodils are miniatures, including 'Chit Chat,' 'Hawera,' 'Sun Disc,' and 'Tête à Tête.' These are delightful in rock gardens.

Many Daffodils naturalize very well. Among the best are 'Accent,' 'Actaea,' 'Arctic Gold,' 'Barrett Browning,' 'Cantabile,' 'Carbineer,' 'Carlton,' 'Cheerfulness,' 'Daydream,' 'Dutch Master,' 'Flower Record,' 'Fortune,' 'Geranium,' 'Golden Harvest,' 'Ice Follies,' 'Kissproof,' 'Mount Hood,' 'Orangery,' 'Peeping Tom,' 'Saint Patrick's Day,' 'Salome,' 'Spellbinder,' 'Suzy,' 'Sweetness,' 'Tête à Tête,' 'Tresamble,' 'Unsurpassable,' and 'Yellow Cheerfulness.'

VARIETY	CLASS	SEASON	COLOR	HEIGHT	HARDINESS
'Accent'	II	Mid	White-Pink	18″	−40°F
'Acropolis'	IV	Mid/late	White-Red	18″	−40°F
'Actaea'*****	IX	Mid	White-Green/Yellow/Red	14″	−40°F
'Aircastle'	III	Mid/late	White-Yellow	22″	−40°F
'Altun Ha'	II	Mid/late	Yellow-White	18″	−40°F
'Ambergate'	II	Mid/late	Orange-Red	14″	−40°F
'Apricot Whirl'	IV	Mid/late	Pale pink-Deep pink apricot	12″	−40°F
'Arctic Gold'*****	I	Early/mid	Yellow-Yellow	16″	−40°F
'Barrett Browning'	III	Mid	White-Deep orange	16″	−40°F
'Camelot'	II	Mid/late	Yellow-Gold	18″	−40°F
'Cantabile'	IX	Late	White-Green/Green/Red	16″	−40°F
'Carbineer'	II	Mid	Yellow-Orange	18″	−40°F

'Accent'

'Acropolis'

'Carlton'

'Geranium'

'Jenny'

'Merlin'

'Sugarbush'

'Thalia'

Fertilizing Sprinkle just a little bit of 10-10-10 fertilizer around the base of each plant just as new growth emerges in spring. Water immediately to dissolve the granules and move nutrients into the root zone. If you overfeed these plants, they get weak, floppy stems.

If you prefer organic fertilizer, use alfalfa meal (rabbit pellets), blood meal, bonemeal, compost, cow manure, fish emulsion, Milorganite, or rotted horse manure. Bonemeal must be mixed into the soil at planting time to be effective.

Weeding The regular use of a summer mulch will inhibit most annual weed growth. Any weeds that do sprout are easily pulled by hand.

Staking Taller forms may require support, especially if overfertilized. For these taller plants, place pea stakes around the small stems in early spring. As the foliage develops, it hides the stakes which act as hidden support throughout the growing season.

Deadheading Once the primary bloom period has ended, cut off old flower heads in mass with grass clippers or hedge pruners. This will usually encourage additional bloom later in the season.

Pruning If plants sprawl or become floppy, cut them back by half after flowering. This "shearing back" results in compact plants that may rebloom.

Winter Protection Mature plants rarely need winter protection other than natural snow cover. If there is no snow by early December, cover the crowns with 6 inches (15 cm) of loose winter mulch. Good materials include marsh hay, clean straw, whole leaves, and pine needles. Remove winter mulch as soon as the weather warms up in early spring.

Problems

Insects Catmints are rarely bothered by insects.

Disease Diseases are a minor concern.

Propagation

Division Catmints are easy to propagate by division. Dig up a clump in early spring just as growth emerges, and cut it into sections with a sharp spade or knife. Make sure that each division has a number of young shoots and a strong root system. Plant these immediately as you would a bare root plant. Catmints can even be divided after their primary bloom period if they are cut back hard and carefully watered as they reestablish themselves. Prostrate stems often root where they touch the ground. Sever plantlets from the mother plant.

Cuttings Cuttings root readily if taken from vigorous shoots prior to flowering. Tip cuttings should have several sets of leaves. Make the final cut ¼ inch (6 mm) below a node. Remove all but the top set of leaves, and dip the cut end in rooting hormone. Tap off any excess powder, and plant the cutting immediately in moist rooting medium. If kept moist and humid, cuttings should be well-rooted within several weeks.

Seed Only species Catmints, not named varieties, can be grown from seed. *Nepeta cataria* (Catnip), an invasive species, is not included in this guide. However, it is very easy to uproot, so cat lovers may want to grow it. The other species are more suitable for a perennial garden. Start Catmints indoors about 12 weeks before the last expected frost in spring. Barely cover the seed in moist germination medium. Slip the seed tray into a clear plastic bag, and place it in an area with a temperature of 68°F to 72°F (20°C to 22°C).

Seeds usually germinate within 7 to 21 days. When the seedlings have developed their first set of true leaves, transplant them to individual pots. Harden young plants off for 14 days before planting them outside after all danger of frost has passed in spring.

Special Uses

Cut Flowers The flower spikes of Catmints can be used in arrangements without any special conditioning. Remove any leaves that will be underwater. Try them with pink or white *Dianthus* (Pinks) for an especially pleasing combination.

Dried Flowers To dry the flower spikes, cut them just as they reach peak bloom. Hang them upside down in a dark, well-ventilated place until they are totally dry. The leaves usually turn papery and crumble, but the dried flowers hold their color well.

Sources

Bluestone Perennials, 7211 Middle Ridge Rd., Madison, OH 44057, (800) 852-5243

Deer-resistant Landscape Nursery, 3200 Sunstone Ct., Clare, MI 48617, (800) 595-3650

Digging Dog Nursery, P.O. Box 471, Albion, CA 95410, (707) 937-1130

Fieldstone Gardens, Inc., 55 Quaker Lane, Vassalboro, ME 04989, (207) 923-3836

High Country Gardens, 2902 Rufina St., NM 87507, (800) 925-9387

'Blue Wonder'

VARIETIES

VARIETY	COLOR	HEIGHT	HARDINESS
Nepeta–Faassenii Group			
'Dropmore'	Lavender blue	18″	−40°F
'Kit Cat'	Purplish lavender blue	16″	−40°F
'Select Blue'*****	Deep lavender blue (close to true blue)	16″	−40°F
'Six Hills Giant'*****	Lavender blue (long flower spikes)	30″	−40°F
'Walker's Low'*****	Deep lavender blue	24″	−40°F

Lovely aromatic gray-green foliage as well as prolific and extended bloom make these choice garden plants. 'Six Hills Giant' has strong stems that do not require staking while the arching stems of 'Walker's Low' may.

VARIETY	COLOR	HEIGHT	HARDINESS
Nepeta grandiflora			
(Caucasus Catmint)			
'Dawn to Dusk'	Pale pink/violet calyces	30″	−40°F
'Pool Bank'	Lavender blue/mulberry calyces	40″	−40°F
'Wild Cat'	Dark lavender blue/purplish red calyces	40″	−40°F

Though not particularly free flowering, these plants offer interesting flower colors and forms (calyces look like little petals (sepals) at the base of the flower). If plants flatten out after flowering, shear them back for better form.

VARIETY	COLOR	HEIGHT	HARDINESS
Nepeta racemosa			
(Raceme Catmint)			
'Blue Wonder'	Lavender blue	18″	−40°F
'Little Titch'	Rich purple blue	10″	−40°F
'Snowflake'	Creamy white	12″	−40°F

These plants form attractive mounds of serrated gray-green leaves and bloom profusely from late spring into summer. They often rebloom later in the season even if not sheared back after initial bloom. Mature plants are drought tolerant.

VARIETY	COLOR	HEIGHT	HARDINESS
Nepeta sibirica			
(Siberian Catmint)	Purplish blue	42″	−40°F
'Souvenir d'André Chaudron'*****	Medium blue	30″	−40°F

This upright Catmint has light green lance-shaped leaves and large flower spikes that stay in bloom for weeks. 'Souvenir d'André Chaudron' has larger tubular flowers and deeper green foliage. Mature plants are drought-tolerant.

VARIETY	COLOR	HEIGHT	HARDINESS
Nepeta subsessilis			
(Japanese Catmint)	Lavender blue	30″	−40°F
'Candy Cat'	Pale violet	24″	−40°F
'Cool Cat'	Lavender blue speckled white	30″	−40°F
'Sweet Dreams'	Clear pink	30″	−40°F

These plants are noted for large dark green leaves with serrated edges, large flowers, and tolerance of moist soils.

VARIETY	COLOR	HEIGHT	HARDINESS
Nepeta (Named hybrid)			
'Joanna Reed'*****	Lavender blue/pink in throats	24″	−40°F

Attractive gray-green foliage, bright flowers in bloom for weeks, and strong stems make this plant a winner.

Oenothera fruticosa

OENOTHERA

(ee-no-THAIR-ruh)

EVENING PRIMROSE, SUNDROPS

Bloom Time	Expected Longevity	Maintenance	Years to Bloom	Preferred Light
Spring to summer	25 years	Medium	From seed: 2 years From potted plant: 1 year	Full sun

Many varieties of *Oenothera* are native prairie plants. Flower coloration and shape are unique to each variety. Some make excellent cut flowers. Only a few of them are truly hardy in cold climates, and these are listed in the table at the end of the section. Foliage is often reddish in cool weather. Most varieties are extremely durable and maintenance free. Most are also long lived and spread freely. Rarely are these plants bothered by disease or insects.

How *Oenothera* Grow

The growing habits of *Oenothera* vary by the species. All grow from fibrous to fleshy roots into upright or ground-hugging plants with stems varying from winding and firm to stiff and wiry. The upright plants are more vigorous growers. Blossoms also vary, although many are funnel- or cup-shaped. All have four petals. Seedpods vary in shape, but some look like wings. Some varieties will self-sow, but this is not particularly common.

Where to Plant

Site and Light A high-light plant, *Oenothera* thrives in full sun but tolerates light shade. A south-facing slope is ideal. Protected areas along fences or walls are excellent for more tender varieties. Plants do well in rock gardens where soil temperatures tend to soar.

Soil and Moisture Plant these perennials in soil that drains freely. Sandy loam is ideal. Replace clay or rock with loam. If that's not practical, build a raised bed. Add lots of organic matter to any soil. Good amendments include compost, peat moss, and rotted manure. These retain moisture during drought but drain freely, keeping soil light and airy. These plants will die in compacted or boggy soils.

Spacing Plant most varieties 12 to 15 inches (30 to 37.5 cm) apart. Some spread quickly, filling up the space around them in one season. Others roam, with elongated, ground-hugging stems. Allow for these tendencies when planting perennials nearby.

Companions

Plant *Oenothera fruticosa* (Common Sundrops) with perennials such as *Campanula* (Bellflower), *Geranium* (Cranesbill), *Heuchera* (Coral Bells), *Iris* (Bearded Iris), *Nepeta* (Catmint), *Phlox*–Maculata Group (Meadow Phlox), *Salvia* (Sage), or *Veronica* (Speedwell). Summer-blooming types such as *Oenothera macrocarpa* (Ozark Sundrops) pair up nicely with fine-textured **Grasses** and such specific perennials as *Artemisia ludoviciana* 'Valerie Finnis' (White Sage), *Lilium* 'Elodie' (Lily), *Platycodon grandiflorus* (Balloon Flower), and *Veronica spicata* 'Icicle' (Spike Speedwell). *Oenothera fruticosa* (Common Sundrops) placed around a clump of birches is very pleasing and an often overlooked combination in the far north.

Planting

Bare Root Plant bare root stock as soon as the soil can be worked in spring. Remove plants from packages as soon as they arrive. Snip off any broken or diseased root tips. Soak the entire plant in room-temperature water overnight. Place a small amount of superphosphate in the base of the planting hole. Fill the hole with soil. Place the crown 1 inch (2.5 cm) below the soil surface. Fill in with soil, firm with your fingers, and water immediately. Dissolve ½ cup (about 114 g) 10-10-10 fertilizer in 1 gallon (about 4 liters) of water. Pour ½ cup (about 120 ml) of this starter solution around the base of each plant. If you prefer organic fertilizer, use fish emulsion instead.

Potted Plants Plant *Oenothera* after all danger of frost has passed in spring. If the soil in the pot is dry, water it, and let it drain overnight. Tap the plant out of the pot without disturbing the root ball. Plant it at the same depth as in the pot, after preparing the hole in a manner similar to that for a bare root plant. Fill in with soil, firm with your fingers, and water immediately. Pour ½ cup (about 120 ml) of starter solution around the base of each plant.

How to Care for *Oenothera*

Water Water frequently when plants are young. Mature plants are drought tolerant but do best with consistent moisture in well-drained soil. Plants will rot out in soggy, boggy soils.

Mulch Surround the base of each plant with a 1-inch (2.5-cm) layer of organic mulch. Good mulches are dried grass clippings, shredded leaves, or pine needles. These help keep soil moist and cool during hot spells. They also inhibit annual weed growth.

Fertilizing Sprinkle 10-10-10 fertilizer around the base of each plant in early spring just as new growth emerges. Water immediately to dissolve granules and carry nutrients into the root zone. Use water-soluble fertilizers for foliar feeding to create lush growth.

If you prefer organic fertilizers, use alfalfa meal (rabbit pellets), blood meal, bonemeal, compost, cow manure, fish emulsion, Milorganite, or rotted horse manure. Bonemeal must be mixed into the soil at planting time to be effective.

Staking These perennials do not need support.

Deadheading Deadheading may encourage repeat bloom on some varieties. If you want seedpods, do not deadhead.

Winter Protection When top growth dies in late fall, cut it off. Leave any green or reddish foliage at the base of the plant over winter. When the ground freezes to a depth of 3 inches (7.5 cm), cover the plants with a 6-inch (15-cm) layer of clean straw, whole leaves, or pine needles. Covering should be fluffed up and airy, not wet and matted. Remove winter mulch in early spring as soon as the weather starts to warm up to prevent rot. Winter protection is strictly optional for the hardier varieties but highly recommended for the more tender ones. If there is no snow by early winter, it is especially important to provide winter protection for the latter.

Problems

Insects *Oenothera* are generally not bothered by insects at all.

Disease You may occasionally see a few spots on leaves caused by foliar diseases, but this is so rare as not to be of concern.

Propagation

Division Varieties vary in growth habits. Quick spreaders form mats of new plants at the base of the parent plant. Dig up these small plants and pull them apart just as growth starts in early spring. Plant each as a bare root plant. Other varieties take 3 years to mature into a large crown. Divide the central crown in early spring just as growth starts. Plant each division as you would a bare root plant. *Oenothera macrocarpa* does not divide well, so avoid disturbing this plant at all once it matures.

Seed Start seed indoors 12 weeks before the last expected frost in spring. Press seeds into a moist growing medium, but do not cover them at all. Place them in light to speed germination. Keep the growing medium consistently moist at 65°F to 75°F (18°C to 24°C) with a drop of 10°F (6°C) at night. Germination normally takes from 15 to 30 days. Once seeds are sprouting, reduce the temperature to 55°F (13°C). When seedlings form a second pair of leaves, plant them in individual pots. Harden them off for 14 days before planting them outdoors after all danger of frost has passed in spring.

Stem Cuttings For varieties with upright growth, remove the tip of the growing stem when the plant is 12 inches (30 cm) high. The tip cutting should have three sets of leaves. Cut ¼ inch (6 mm) below a leaf node. Remove the lower leaves, and dust the cut end in rooting hormone. Tap off any excess powder. Then plant the cutting in a moist growing medium. Keep the medium evenly moist at all times until a root ball forms. Plant the rooted cutting in a pot or directly in the garden at that time. Keep the soil moist.

Special Uses

Food Indians ate the roots of some varieties as a vegetable.

Cut Flowers The upright-growing varieties produce excellent stems for cut-flower arrangements. The wide range of bud coloration adds a special dimension to floral arrangements and a wonderful contrast to the fully open blossoms. Many of the flaring, funnel-, or cup-shaped flowers exude a sweet scent, making them lovely floating in a bowl of water. When cutting stems, keep the cut ends in water at all times. Once indoors, place the bottom 1 inch (2.5 cm) of each stem in boiling water for a few seconds or longer, then plunge them into cool water up to the base of the flowers for a few hours. Remove any leaves that would be underwater in the final arrangement. *Oenothera fruticosa* (Common Sundrops) is excellent both in full bloom and in the green seed-head stage. If you pick it just as the first buds begin to open, the others will open indoors over a period of days.

Dried Flowers Some growers pick these flowers in the green, seed-head stage for drying. Cut the stems, remove all leaves, and hang the stems upside down in a dry, well-ventilated area. The seedpods of *Oenothera macrocarpa* (Ozark Sundrops) look like small, indented wings. These are popular in arrangements. Pick these at the end of the season when they're completely dry.

Sources

Ambergate Gardens, 8730 County Rd. 43, Chaska, MN 55318, (877) 211-9769

Earthly Pursuits, 2901 Kuntz Rd., Windsor Mill, MD 21244, (410) 496-2523

Fieldstone Gardens, Inc., 55 Quaker Lane, Vassalboro, ME 04989, (207) 923-3836

Siskiyou Rare Plant Nursery, 2115 Talent Ave., Talent, OR 97540, (541) 535-7103

Sunlight Gardens, 174 Golden Lane, Anderesonville, TN 37705, (800) 272-7396

Oenothera macrocarpa/Oenothera missouriensis

'Rosea'

VARIETIES

VARIETY	COLOR	HEIGHT	HARDINESS
Oenothera fruticosa			
(Common Sundrops)	Yellow	24″	−40°F
'Fireworks' ('Feuerverkeri')*****	Deep yellow	18″	−40°F
'Highlight' ('Hohes Licht')	Bright yellow	18″	−40°F
'Spring Gold' ('Fruhlingsgold')	Yellow	14″	−40°F
'Summer Solstice' ('Sonnenwende')*****	Bright yellow	20″	−40°F

These perennials produce countless reddish buds which open into bright yellow blossoms. The flowers are open during daylight hours, and the plants are showy over a period of weeks in late spring and early summer. The deep dark green foliage takes on an attractive reddish purple color in fall. This old-fashioned perennial spreads rapidly and requires frequent division. 'Fireworks' has reddish bronze-tipped leaves while those of 'Highlight' are pure green. The foliage of 'Spring Gold' shows pink and white highlights in spring, changing to green with creamy white margins as it matures. 'Summer Solstice' has leaves that are deep ruby red as they emerge in spring.

VARIETY	COLOR	HEIGHT	HARDINESS
*Oenothera macrocarpa*******			
(Ozark Sundrops)	Lemon yellow	12″	−30°F
'Comanche Campfire'	Bright yellow	14″	−30°F
'Lemon Silver'	Pale yellow	8″	−30°F
'Silver Blade'	Lemon yellow	6″	−30°F

The sprawling Ozark Sundrops are ideal for the front of a border. In summer, reddish buds open into large, day-flowering, lemon yellow blooms. These mature into interesting winged seed pods. This perennial is a superb choice for hot dry locations. It resents transplanting and emerges late in spring. 'Comanche Campfire' has bright ruby red stems. 'Lemon Silver' has a compact appearance and silvery green leaves. 'Silver Blade' offers silvery blue foliage and is even shorter.

Oenothera missouriensis (see *Oenothera macrocarpa*)

VARIETY	COLOR	HEIGHT	HARDINESS
Oenothera perennis			
(Nodding Sundrops)	Yellow	14″	−40°F

This species often lives only two years. It quickly forms a clump of wiry stems with narrow leaves. The nodding buds appear in summer, and the cup-shaped flowers are open only during the day.

Oenothera pumila (see *Oenothera perennis*)

VARIETY	COLOR	HEIGHT	HARDINESS
Oenothera speciosa			
(Showy Evening Primrose)	White to rose pink	18″	−20°F
'Rosea'	Pink	18″	−20°F
'Siskiyou'	Pale pink	18″	−20°F
'Woodside White'	White	18″	−20°F

Though not reliably winter hardy, these perennials may survive in protected areas with winter cover. They spread quickly by running roots and needs lots of space to roam.

'Wilford Johnson'

PAEONIA

(pay-OWN-ee-uh)

PEONY

Bloom Time	Expected Longevity	Maintenance	Years to Bloom	Preferred Light
Late spring to early summer	25+ years	Low	From seed: 5 to 7 years From potted plant: 2 to 3 years	Full sun

Peonies are favorites of many gardeners because they grow so well and for so long with minimal care. Their sweet-scented flowers are magnificent and bloom in great abundance each spring but, individually, may be short lived especially after heavy rains or thunderstorms. Their flowers, available in pink, red, white, and pale yellow, are among the best for fresh-cut use, and some can even be dried. The foliage of many Peony varieties has red or pink tones as it emerges in spring and generally remains an asset in the garden throughout the season. Some varieties have desirable fall foliage color. Peonies are excellent as accent or specimen plants, mixed in perennial borders, or even as informal hedges. Most Peonies, but especially the double-flowered types, need support to keep their flowers from flopping over. Grown properly, Peonies are rarely bothered by insects or disease and often outlive their owners. While they are low maintenance plants once mature, they do demand excellent soil preparation and patience for them to reach peak performance.

How Peonies Grow

Peonies require a certain number of chilling hours under 40°F (4°C) each winter in order to break dormancy and grow well the following season. For this reason they are one of the finest perennials for cold climates. Peonies develop slowly from swollen, tuberous roots. These structures perform all the tasks of typical root systems but also serve as food-storage organs. The tuberous roots have prominent buds, or eyes, at their tops. These sprout into stems which are reminiscent of Asparagus shoots as they emerge in spring. The plant matures into a dwarf shrublike form with shiny, dark green leaves. Large, prominent flower buds form at and near the tips of the stems and burst into bloom in late spring and early summer. The plant slowly increases in size each year, forming an extensive root system, and can remain undisturbed for decades. The seedpods, which ripen later in the season, are often used in dried arrangements. Mature seeds are quite large with thick seed coats and are usually brown or black.

Where to Plant

Site and Light Peonies require at least 6 to 8 hours of sunlight each day for best growth. Avoid planting Peonies under large woody plants which, besides blocking necessary sunlight, compete for water and nutrients. The highest-quality Peonies are grown in cultivated beds, not surrounded by grass where they have to compete for water and nutrients. Choose a spot protected from strong winds, but avoid areas with poor air circulation. Select planting sites very carefully, as these perennials are quite permanent and do not like to be moved once mature.

Soil and Moisture Peonies prefer medium- to fine-textured soils as long as they drain freely. They will, however, grow in a wide range of soils, especially if the soils contain organic matter. Mix in lots of peat moss, leaf mold, or compost. In the case of Peonies some growers will not use rotted manures, insisting that they may contain fungal spores that can lead to disease. The addition of organic matter, and lots of it, is critical to good growth.

Spacing Space Peonies 3 to 4 feet (90 to 120 cm) from other plants. The amount of space appears unnatural, but Peonies will fill in this area completely as they mature. Also, the plants need good air circulation around foliage. Without it, they may develop fungal diseases, especially during wet seasons.

Companions

Paeonia (Peony) combines readily with a wide range of perennials and woody plants. Early-flowering types are attractive near flowering trees such as *Crataegus* (Hawthorn) or shrubs such as late-blooming *Syringa* (Lilac). Use them to create stunning garden pictures with common perennials such as *Aquilegia* (Columbine), *Heuchera* (Coral Bells), *Iris* (Bearded and Siberian Iris), and *Nepeta* (Catmint). They also go well with sun-tolerant **Ferns** and bulbs, especially *Narcissus* (Daffodil). Their rich mound of foliage does an excellent job of masking dying bulb leaves. Here are a handful of specific combinations to consider: *Paeonia* 'Red Charm' with *Artemisia absinthium* 'Lambrook Silver' (Common Wormwood) and *Nepeta racemosa* 'Blue Wonder' (Raceme Catmint); *Paeonia* 'Sea Shell' with *Dicentra formosa* 'Luxuriant' (Western Bleeding Heart); and *Paeonia* 'Prairie Moon' combined with *Iris* 'Queen Anne's Lace' and 'Titan's Glory' (Tall Bearded Iris), and *Heuchera sanguinea* 'Ruby Bells' (Coral Bells).

Planting

Bare Root Although Peonies are at times available as bare root plants in spring, we recommend fall planting. The ideal planting time is late August through September, as this allows adequate rooting time before winter arrives.

Each Peony division should have three to five eyes or buds along with a firm sound root structure. Eyes look like small little points, often white, pink, or red. Divisions with fewer than three eyes will take several extra years to produce an abundant show of flowers. Those with more than five eyes have a tendency to live off their stored food reserves in their first growing season and not produce a strong root system. A properly sized division should produce only a few stems its first year. Such plants spend their first growing season forming an extensive root system, which is the key to the long life and good performance of this perennial.

Prepare the planting hole several weeks in advance to allow soil to settle completely. Dig holes 18 to 24 inches (45 to 60 cm) deep and 24 inches (60 cm) wide. Fill in all but the top 8 inches (20 cm) with loose soil mixed together with compost, leaf mold, or peat moss and ½ cup (about 114 g) of superphosphate or 1 cup (about 228 g) of bonemeal. Fill the balance of the hole with well-prepared but unfertilized soil, and water soil well to eliminate any air pockets.

When the plant arrives, remove it immediately from its shipping package. Handle it carefully so as not to break off any eyes. Trim off any soft or rotted sections of root tissue. If the plant appears dry, soak it for several hours in water until it's firm. Redig the hole, and spread the roots out over a cone of loose soil, with the eyes 1½ to 2 inches (4 to 5 cm) below the final grade. If you plant Peonies too deep, they often produce flower buds that turn brown and never open, or simply do not form buds at all. Fill around the plant with just enough soil to hold it in place, and then fill the hole with water. Wait until the water soaks in, and then check to see whether eyes are at the proper depth. Fill the hole, firm the soil around the plant, and soak it immediately.

All of this is a lot of work, but strong divisions, good soil conditions, and proper planting will lead to vigorous plants with an abundance of bloom. However, do not expect prolific bloom until the third season after initial planting. A few Peonies even take longer than that to bloom well.

Potted Plants Potted Peonies are often available from local retail outlets throughout the growing season, but they are best planted early in the year. Prepare the bed as you would for a bare root plant.

If the soil in the pot is dry, water it, and let it drain overnight. Check the plants carefully to see that the eyes are not deeper than 2 inches (5 cm) in the soil. Tap the plant from the pot, trying not to disturb the root ball. Keep the eyes at the correct planting depth. Fill the hole around the plant with well-prepared soil, firm with your fingers, and water immediately.

How to Care for Peonies

Water Water carefully after planting to encourage development of a strong root system. Watering mature plants regularly will encourage heavier and longer bloom. When you water, soak the soil to a depth of at least 12 inches (30 cm). Plants stressed by drought, even though mature, will have fewer and smaller flowers the following season.

Mulch Place 2 inches (5 cm) of mulch around the base of each plant as soon as the ground warms up in spring. Good mulches are dried grass clippings, pine needles, compost, or shredded bark. Mulch keeps the soil cool and moist and reduces competition from weeds. Replace the mulch as necessary throughout the season.

Fertilizing Add phosphorus fertilizer to the soil at planting time as indicated earlier. Each spring, sprinkle half a handful of 10-10-10 fertilizer around the outside of each plant just as the shoots start to emerge from the ground. Water immediately to dissolve the granules and move nutrients into the root zone. Immediate watering is especially important if you sprinkle fertilizer over the tender growing tips. You can do this, but it may burn plant tissue unless the fertilizer is dissolved quickly. For top-quality flowers, feed again just as flower buds begin to form. Foliar feeding with water-soluble fertilizers also deepens foliage color and encourages greater bloom.

If you prefer organic fertilizers, use alfalfa meal (rabbit pellets), blood meal, bonemeal, compost, fish emulsion, or Milorganite. Bonemeal must be mixed into the soil at planting time for maximum effectiveness.

Weeding Mulch inhibits the growth of most annual weeds. Any weeds that do pop up through the mulch are best pulled by hand. Be particularly careful when working around young shoots, which are easily damaged or broken off. They snap like the tips of Asparagus, and you can lose a stem in the process.

Staking Staking is necessary, especially for double-flowered types and tall weak-stemmed varieties. The most commonly used support is a metal peony hoop placed over the plant in early spring. The stems grow up inside the rings or can be trained inside. They are then held in place during the entire season. The foliage virtually hides the metal support system but not entirely. Unfortunately, even the hoops are not without problems, as stems are often bent over during strong winds at the point where they contact the upper metal ring. As clumps get larger, it may be hard to contain all the stems inside the rings of the commonly available peony hoops. There is definitely a need for several sizes of these rings. There are other systems of support as well, but most are not as successful as the metal hoops. No matter which system is used, the key is to have it in place before the stems have reached their ultimate height and are loaded with blooms. Trying to stake Peonies at that point always leads to an unnatural look and damage to the plant.

Growing single and Japanese flowering Peonies minimizes the need for staking, as their smaller flowers are less prone to flopping over. However, even these may require support to get them through the worst storms.

Disbudding Removal of all flower buds for the first few years after planting helps plants mature and ensures better bloom in the future. If you want large, specimen-size flowers on mature plants, remove all side buds below the terminal bud as soon as they are visible. Simply pinch them out with your thumb and forefinger. This technique is commonly used by people growing flowers for cut use or for exhibition in flower shows. If you are more interested in a shower of smaller blooms, then leave the plant alone. Some of the hybrid Peonies naturally form only one terminal bud and do not require disbudding.

Deadheading Unless you want seed to form, remove all spent blossoms as they fade. This prevents formation of seedpods and allows the plant to channel energy into the root system for next year's growth. Never cut stems back before they freeze in fall. The plant needs its foliage for the entire growing season to manufacture food reserves for the next year's growth and flowering.

Winter Protection In the fall, cut off all stems to the ground as soon as they turn brown and begin to flop over. At this time, you may see newly forming eyes just below the surface of the soil. Use scissors or pruning shears to cut the stems, but do not disturb the reddish buds off to the sides, since they will produce stems the following spring. Mature plants generally do not need winter protection other than natural snowfall. However, alternate freezing and thawing of the soil in late winter often pushes young plants out of the ground, causing them to dehydrate. A 6-inch (15-cm) layer of marsh hay, clean straw, whole leaves, or pine needles applied after the ground has frozen to a depth of 2 to 3 inches (5 to 7.5 cm) will prevent this from happening. Remove the mulch early in spring as soon as the weather begins to warm up. Be careful not to disturb the small young shoots emerging from the ground at this time. Remember how easy they are to break off.

Problems

Insects Insects are rarely a problem, although rose chafers, scale, thrips, and fourlined plant bug are some of the insects known to cause damage to Peonies. Ants are probably the most common insect seen on these perennials. They are attracted to sweet secretions produced by the flower buds, which become sticky at this time. Control is not normally necessary, although some evidence suggests that ants may spread the fungal disease botrytis blight. To get ants off flower buds or out of flowers, just shake the stems before bringing them indoors. Or dip them in warm sudsy water, and rinse.

Disease Peonies are susceptible to a number of diseases but rarely to severe outbreaks. Avoid most problems by purchasing disease-free or disease-resistant stock, planting Peonies in the proper location, caring for them as outlined, and keeping the bed clean of debris.

One of the most common diseases is botrytis blight. Symptoms to watch for include sudden wilting and collapsing of young stems, leaves and stems covered with a brown mass of spores, and young buds turning black and drying up. Outbreaks of this disease occur during wet weather, especially in spring. Since the fungal spores overwinter in plant tissue, late fall cleanup is the best control. Proper plant spacing is also helpful, since it allows air to circulate freely around the plants. In certain seasons, it may be necessary to spray with a fungicide as suggested by your local garden center or nursery.

Other known diseases include phytophthora blight, which causes infected tissue to blacken and become leathery; verticillium wilt, which causes wilting of stems and foliage during bloom season; various leaf spot diseases; stem and crown rots; and several viral diseases. Most are problems only under poor growing conditions. Viral diseases such as mosaic and leaf curl have no cure and are uncommon. Plants infected by virus should be destroyed, and Peonies should not be planted in that same location.

Propagation

Division Peonies do not like to be disturbed. Division is suggested only as a means to increase your stock. Dividing an old clump is a major job and is best done in early fall. Cut stems level with the ground, and dig up the entire plant. You will need to dig deeply, as Peonies have extensive root systems. Once the clump is out of the ground, wash it clean with a hose. Then, with a sharp knife, cut the plant into sections. Each division should have three to five eyes (small white,

pink, or red points) at the top of the tuberous root. Remove any diseased or broken portion of root tissue, always leaving neat, clean cuts. Do not touch the eyes or bump them, as they will break off easily. Dipping the roots into a broad-spectrum fungicide prior to replanting is good insurance against infection of wounds. Replant immediately as you would a bare root plant.

Seed Growing Peonies from seed is suggested for only the most patient gardeners, since it may take from 5 to 7 years to get a flowering-size plant from seed. Of course, for those interested in growing unusual species or hybridizing, it is a necessity. Fresh seed will give the quickest and best results. It often takes 2 years to get germination, as seeds may need to be exposed to several moist-chilling periods with warmth in between.

Fill a seed tray with moist germination medium. Sow the seed, covering it with about ½ inch (12 mm) of medium. Slide the tray into a plastic bag perforated for good air circulation. Keep the medium moist at all times and at a temperature between 55°F and 60°F (13°C to 16°C) for 3 months. Then slide the tray into the crisper of your refrigerator for 3 to 4 months. After that time, take the seed tray out of the refrigerator, and keep it at 55°F to 60°F (13°C to 16°C) again for another 3 months. If germination does not occur, place the seed tray back in the refrigerator for another chilling period. Check it regularly, and remove it from the refrigerator immediately if seedlings start to emerge. Nicking the seed coat with a file prior to moist-chilling may speed up germination, especially for older seed.

Perhaps the simplest method for germinating Peony seeds is to plant them immediately after collection in fall. Sow them in a well-prepared outdoor seedbed, and allow nature to take its course. Keep the soil evenly moist at all times. It may take up to 2 years or longer for the seedlings to emerge under such conditions. Keeping the soil moist during that period is quite difficult but is the key to success with these finicky seeds.

Special Uses

Cut Flowers Peonies are among the finest flowers for fresh-cut use, as they have a long vase life if handled properly. If you cut them in the soft bud stage (when the bud is the size of a golf ball) and lay them dry on the shelf of a cooler, they can last for weeks before use in arrangements. For immediate use, cut the blooms early in the day when they are about three-quarters open. Strip the lower leaves off of the stems, and immediately put the stems into 110°F (43°C) water. After bringing cut Peonies indoors, some arrangers place the bottom 1 inch (2.5 cm) of the stems in boiling water for 30 seconds or char the bases in a flame to prolong the life of the blooms. Conditioning the stems by placing them in a cool room for several hours before arranging will also help them to last much longer. When cutting flowers, leave three or four sets of leaves on each stem of the plant, and do not cut more than one-third of the blooms on any given plant if you want good flowering the next season.

Dried Flowers Peonies are not often thought of as appropriate for drying, but local growers have been doing it for years. Harvest flowers on a dry day, just as the buds start to loosen up. Hang them upside down in a clean, warm, dry, well-ventilated area. Use a dehumidifier if necessary to keep humidity as low as possible. Do not hang the flowers in a sunny location, as that damages petals and fades color. The single and Japanese types will dry the best, but full doubles can be dried as well. In terms of flower color, the reds seem to hold the best, while whites often turn brown unless they are dried very quickly. Some gardeners have also had success drying mature blooms in desiccants. The ripe seedpods of Peonies are of value as well in dried floral work and are especially attractive mixed into wreaths.

Sources

A & D Nursery, P.O. Box 2338, Snohomish, WA 98291, (360) 668-9690

Adelman Peony Gardens, 5690 Brooklake Rd. NE, Salem, OR 97305, (503) 393-6185

Anderson Iris Gardens, 22179 Keather Ave. N, Forest Lake, MN 55025, (651) 433-5268

Andre Viette Nursery, 608 Longmeadow Rd., Fishersville, VA 22939, (540) 943-2315

Bannister Garden Center, 10001 E Bannister, Kansas City, MO 64134, (816) 763-4664

Brother's Peonies, Inc, P.O. Box 1370, Sherwood, OR 97140, (503) 625-7548

Buck Canyon Gardens, P.O. Box 1242, Cave Junction, OR 97523, (541) 592-6115

Countryside Gardens, 10602 Fenner Ave. SE, Delano, MN 55328, (952) 955-2283

Full Bloom Farm, 2330 Tuttle Lane, Lummi Island, WA 98262, (360) 758-7173

Gilbert H. Wild & Son, 2994 State Hwy 37, Reeds, MO 64859, (888) 449-4537

Gold City Flower Gardens, 6298 Gold City Rd., Franklin, KY 42134, (270) 776-6584

Hidden Springs Flower Farm, 813 Elm St., Spring Grove, MN 55303, (763) 218-4540

Hollingsworth Nursery, 28747 290 St., Maryville, MO 64468, (660) 562-3010

Klehm's Song Sparrow Perennial Farm, 13101 E Rye Rd., Avalon, WI 53505, (800) 553-3715

La Pivoinerie D'Aoust, P.O. Box 220, Hudson Heights, QB Canada J0P 1J0, (450) 458-2759

Nicholls Gardens, 4724 Angus Dr., Gainesville, VA 20155, (703) 754-9623

The Peony Farm, 80A Old Main Rd., Little Compton, RI 02837, (401) 592-0002

Peony Meadows, 4344 Stony Point Rd., Keswick, VA 22947, (434) 973-3431

Reath's Nursery, N195 County Rd. 577, Vulcan, MI 49892, (906) 563-9777

Sevald Nursery, 4937 3rd Ave. S, Minneapolis, MN 55419, (612) 822-3279

Swenson Gardens, P.O. Box 209, Howard Lake, MN 55349, (763) 350-2051

VARIETIES

Choose Peonies by flower form, flower color, height, and bloom season. Following are descriptions of Peony flower forms:

Single: One row of broad (guard) petals surrounds a center made up of yellow gold stamens. These are the male portion of the flower consisting of a filament tipped with pollen-bearing anthers (little gold sacks).

Semi-double: Several rows of petals surround the center with clearly visible pollen-bearing stamens mixed in with some filaments that have been transformed into petal-like structures (petaloides).

Japanese: Five or more broad petals surround a mound of modified stamens (stamenoides) that stand out by their "lacy" form and mix of colors. A stamenoide is simply a stamen without pollen-producing anthers.

Anemone: Outer petals surround a center in which all stamens have been transformed into narrow petal-like structures (petaloides). The outer petals and petaloides may be different colors.

Double: Five or more guard petals surround stamens that have all been transformed into petal-like structures (petaloides) similar in coloration to the outer petals and making up the bulk of the flower.

Bomb: Outer petals surround a central "snowball" of petals (petaloides). These blooms may also be called "double bomb."

The following list includes superior plants for cold climates. It does not include many of the old workhorse varieties like 'Felix Crousse,' 'Festiva Maxima,' 'Karl Rosenfield,' 'Monsieur Jules Elie,' and 'Sarah Bernhardt.' These are all lovely plants with great color and fragrance but with a tendency to topple, especially in rain. Still, they make wonderful cut flowers. If a plant is a hybrid, it is noted in parentheses after the flower's name. The colors of hybrids are especially brilliant.

VARIETY	FORM	COLOR/CENTER	HEIGHT	BLOOM	HARDINESS
Paeonia lobata (see *Paeonia peregrina*)					
Paeonia peregrina					
(Balkan Peony)	Single	Vibrant red/gold	24″	Mid	−40°F

This is one of the most beautiful Peony species with its glossy green foliage and cupped flowers.

Paeonia tenuifolia					
(Fern Leaf Peony)	Single	Bright red/gold	18″	Early	−40°F
'Plena'	Double	Bright red	24″	Early	−40°F

These are long-time favorites for their finely divided foliage and very early bloom. Unfortunately, the bloom period is quite brief. These plants may go dormant if conditions are especially hot and dry.

Paeonia (Named varieties and hybrids)					
'Amalia Olson'*****	Double	White	30″	Mid	−40°F
'Angel Cheeks'*****	Bomb	Pink cream	26″	Mid/late	−40°F
'Big Ben'*****	Bomb	Blackish red	48″	Mid	−40°F
'Bouquet Perfect'	Japanese	Deep pink/yellow	24″	Mid	−40°F
'Bowl of Cream'*****	Double	Cream white	30″	Mid	−40°F
'Burma Ruby' (hybrid)	Single	Bright red/gold	24″	Early	−40°F
'Charm'*****	Japanese	Black red/black red gold	30″	Late	−40°F

VARIETY	FORM	COLOR/CENTER	HEIGHT	BLOOM	HARDINESS
'Coral Sunset' (hybrid)*****	Semi-double	Deep coral/yellow	32"	Early	−40°F
'Cytherea' (hybrid)*****	Semi-double	Rich rose/gold	24"	Early/mid	−40°F
'Diana Parks' (hybrid)	Bomb	Dark red	36"	Mid	−40°F
'Do Tell'*****	Japanese	Light pink/pink red white	36"	Mid	−40°F
'Duluth'	Double	White	36"	Late	−40°F
'Gardenia'	Double	Blush white	34"	Early/mid	−40°F
'Kansas'	Double	Maroon red	30"	Mid	−40°F
'Kay Tischler'	Japanese	Bright pink/pink yellow	36"	Mid	−40°F
'Le Charme'*****	Japanese	Pink/pink gold	36"	Mid/late	−40°F
'Little Red Gem' (hybrid)	Single	Crimson red/yellow	16"	Early	−40°F
'Lorelei' (hybrid)	Bomb	Red orange	26"	Early/mid	−40°F
'Mackinac Grand' (hybrid)*****	Semi-double	Dark red/yellow	36"	Early/mid	−40°F
'Many Happy Returns'(hybrid)*****	Bomb	Scarlet red	30"	Mid	−40°F
'Miss America'	Semi-double	White/gold	30"	Early/mid	−40°F
'Moonrise' (hybrid)	Single	Soft yellow/yellow gold	24"	Early	−40°F
'Nick Shaylor'*****	Double	Light pink	34"	Mid/late	−40°F
'Norma Volz' *****	Double	White pink	36"	Mid	−40°F
'Paula Fay' (hybrid)*****	Semi-double	Vibrant pink/gold	36"	Early	−40°F
'Pink Hawaiian Coral' (hybrid)*****	Semi-double	Medium coral/yellow	36"	Early	−40°F
'Prairie Moon' (hybrid)*****	Semi-double	Pale yellow/gold	30"	Early/mid	−40°F
'Red Charm' (hybrid)*****	Bomb	Dark red	36"	Early	−40°F
'Red Grace' (hybrid)	Bomb	Burgundy red	36"	Early	−40°F
'Red Red Rose' (hybrid)*****	Semi-double	Deep red/gold	30"	Early/mid	−40°F
'Requiem' (hybrid)	Single	White/gold	30"	Early	−40°F
'Rozella' (hybrid)*****	Double	Dark pink	30"	Late/mid	−40°F
'Salmon Dream' (hybrid)*****	Semi-double	Salmon pink/yellow	36"	Early/mid	−40°F
'Sea Shell'	Single	Medium pink/yellow	36"	Mid	−40°F
'Terry Grudem'	Japanese	Medium red/reddish gold	36"	Mid	−40°F
'Topeka Garnet'*****	Single	Dark red/yellow	30"	Mid	−40°F
'White Cap'*****	Anemone	Raspberry/white pink	32"	Mid	−40°F
'White Frost'	Double	White	30"	Late/mid	−40°F
'Wilford Johnson'	Double	Rose	30"	Mid	−40°F

'Burma Ruby'

'Do Tell'

'Kay Tischler'

'Paula Fay'

'Red Charm'

'Requiem'

'Sea Shell'

'Terry Grudem'

'Home Fires'

PHLOX

(flocks)

CREEPING PHLOX, GARDEN PHLOX, WOODLAND PHLOX

Bloom Time	Expected Longevity	Maintenance	Years to Bloom	Preferred Light
Spring to fall	10+ years	Low to medium	From seed: 2 years From potted plant: 1 year	Variable

Some of the taller varieties are referred to as Garden Phlox. These produce masses of blooms during the summer with brilliant coloration and often fragrant scent. The flowers are attractive to butterflies and hummingbirds and bloom over a long period of time. The central eye of flowers on many varieties is a different color, making these striking additions to the border. Unfortunately, some varieties of *Phlox*–Paniculata Group (Summer Phlox) are extremely susceptible to powdery mildew and attacks by red spider mites. However, breeding has resulted in some selections with greater powdery mildew resistance.

The low-growing Phlox that do best in sun are commonly referred to as Creeping Phlox. These perennials form large mats of foliage covered with masses of tiny flowers in varied colors. They are among the best perennials for spring color. They also make ideal ground covers and can prevent erosion on banks. They are durable and relatively maintenance free if you get them off to a good start. Problems with either disease or insects are rare.

The low-growing Phlox that do best in shade are often called Woodland Phlox. These plants produce lovely, fragrant blooms from spring to early summer. These shade-loving perennials are much less susceptible to powdery mildew than Garden Phlox and quite resistant to insects. They make excellent ground covers and are good in rock gardens.

How Phlox Grow

The taller varieties are clump-forming plants. Stems are quite rigid and produce large clusters of small flowers during an extended bloom period. Clumps get larger each year as more stems form around the crown or base of the plant.

Some of the ground-hugging varieties of Phlox send out underground stems, or stolons, from the mother plant to create new plants. From just a few plants in spring, you may have dozens of plants by fall. Small stems emerge from the mat of foliage and produce brilliant carpets of colored, small blooms. Some varieties do produce seed and self-sow.

Where to Plant

Site and Light The needs of Phlox vary dramatically by group. Whether a plant needs shade or sun is covered in the plant descriptions in the table. Avoid placing all varieties of *Phlox*–Paniculata Group (Summer Phlox) next to stone or brick walls. These stop air circulation and retain moisture, the combination of which promotes the spread of powdery mildew.

Soil and Moisture All Phlox do well in medium-rich soil, which drains freely but retains moisture. Add lots of organic matter, such as compost, leaf mold, peat, or rotted manure to the soil. Best are peat and rotted oak leaves, which are slightly acidic. Replace clay and rocky soils with loam or build a raised bed.

Spacing Some varieties of Phlox creep along the ground. Plant them 8 to 12 inches (20 to 30 cm) apart to begin with, and they will soon fill in the gaps. These plants look best in large masses or drifts of color. Plant taller, clump-forming varieties 18 inches (45 cm) or farther apart in all directions. Give these plants enough space for good air circulation to prevent disease.

Companions

Early-summer-blooming types such as *Phlox*–Arendsii Group (Arend's Phlox) and *Phlox*–Maculata Group (Meadow Phlox) combine nicely with *Aquilegia* (Columbine), *Campanula persicifolia* (Peach-Leaved Bellflower), *Clematis integrifolia* (Solitary Clematis), *Delphinium* (Larkspur), *Geranium* (Cranesbill), *Lysimachia punctata* (Yellow Loosestrife), *Nepeta* (Catmint), *Oenothera fruticosa* (Common Sundrops), *Salvia* (Sage), *Tanacetum corymbosum* (Caucasian Daisy), and *Thermopsis caroliniana* (Carolina Lupine).

Phlox–Paniculata Group (Summer Phlox) goes well with mid- to late-summer-blooming plants such as *Achillea* (Yarrow), *Asclepias tuberosa* (Butterfly Milkweed), *Coreopsis* 'Sunbeam' (Tickseed), *Echinacea* (Purple Coneflower), *Heliopsis* (Oxeye), *Hemerocallis* (Daylily), *Leucanthemum*–Superbum Group (Shasta Daisy), *Liatris* (Gayfeather), *Lilium* (Lily), *Monarda* (Bee Balm), and numerous **Grasses**. One particularly striking combination that merits mentioning: *Phlox*–Paniculata Group 'Dodo Hanbury Forbes' (Summer Phlox) planted next to *Artemisia absinthium* 'Lambrook Silver' (Common Wormwood), *Echinacea purpurea* 'White Swan' (Purple Coneflower), and *Monarda* 'Violet Queen' (Bee Balm).

The creeping, sun-loving varieties of Phlox are versatile. Use the spring-blooming members of this group along the edges of walkways or as a carpet underneath pockets of bulbs at the front of the border. They are also good selections for rock and wall gardens. Potential companion plants include *Aquilegia* (Columbine), *Campanula* (Bellflower), *Dianthus* (Pinks), *Euphorbia* (Spurge), and *Iris* (Dwarf Bearded Iris). Consider planting *Phlox pilosa* (Prairie Phlox) among shrub-type roses along with *Artemisia stelleriana* (Beach Wormwood). *Phlox divaricata*

'Chattahoochee' (Woodland Phlox) is stunning next to *Aquilegia canadensis* (Canadian Columbine), *Dicentra formosa* 'Luxuriant' (Western Bleeding Heart), and *Veronica repens* 'Sunshine' (Creeping Speedwell).

The shade-loving varieties stand out in the woodland garden or as ground covers under spring-blooming shrubs. *Phlox divaricata* (Woodland Phlox) goes well with spring bulbs, native wildflowers, and **Ferns** as well as specific perennials such as *Aquilegia canadensis* (Canadian Columbine) and *Dicentra eximia* (Fringed Bleeding Heart). Try *Phlox stolonifera* (Creeping Phlox) with *Hosta* (Hosta), especially types that offer intense gold or variegated foliage early in the season, and *Pulmonaria* (Lungwort). *Phlox stolonifera* 'Home Fires' (Creeping Phlox) looks delightful with early-blooming *Astilbe* (False Spirea) and *Geranium macrorrhizum* (Bigroot Cranesbill) as a ground cover under small flowering trees.

Planting

Bare Root Plant bare root stock as soon as you can work the ground in spring. Remove plants from their shipping packaging immediately. Snip off broken or damaged root tips. Soak plants overnight in room-temperature water. Place a small amount of superphosphate in the base of the planting hole. Fill the hole with soil. Place the crown 1½ inches (4 cm) below the soil surface for taller varieties, and just under the soil surface for creeping varieties. Fill in with soil, firm with your fingers, and water immediately. Dissolve ½ cup (about 114 g) 10-10-10 fertilizer in 1 gallon (about 4 liters) of water. Pour ½ cup (about 120 ml) of this starter solution around the base of each plant. If you prefer organic fertilizer, use fish emulsion instead.

Potted Plants Plant Phlox after all danger of frost has passed in spring. If the soil in the pot is dry, water it, and let it drain overnight. Tap the plant from the pot without disturbing the root ball. Plant it at the same depth as in the pot, after preparing the hole in a manner similar to that for a bare root plant. Fill in

with soil, firm with your fingers, and water immediately. Pour ½ cup (about 120 ml) starter solution around the base of each plant.

How to Care for Phlox

Water Keep these plants consistently moist at all times.

Water taller varieties by hand soaking the base of the plant without getting the foliage wet. The theory is to "keep the feet wet, the clothing dry" to avoid powdery mildew. **Note:** Some growers believe that the disease is caused more by hot, dry conditions around the roots rather than moist, humid conditions around the foliage. No one has yet proved which theory is correct.

During hot, dry periods, mist the foliage of taller varieties early in the morning to discourage red spider mites, which appear during these times. The foliage will dry out quickly in the morning sun.

Mulch Place a 2-inch (5-cm) layer of organic mulch around the base of each young plant as soon as the ground warms up in spring. Good mulches include compost, shredded leaves, dried grass clippings, and pine needles. The mulch keeps the soil moist and cool. Add mulch throughout the season as needed for the taller varieties.

Mulch encourages rapid root growth and spread of creeping varieties that soon fill in gaps between original plantings. Mulch also inhibits weed growth, which can be a problem in ground covers. Once creeping varieties have spread, their foliage acts as a living mulch, shutting off light to annual weed seeds.

Fertilizing Sprinkle 10-10-10 fertilizer around the base of each plant just as growth emerges in spring. Water immediately to dissolve the granules and carry nutrients into the root zone. Do this again just before the plant flowers or after deadheading to initiate a second round of flowering in certain varieties.

If you prefer organic fertilizers, use alfalfa meal (rabbit pellets), blood meal, bonemeal, compost, cow manure, fish emulsion, Milorganite, or rotted horse manure. Bonemeal must be mixed into the soil at planting time to be effective.

Weeding Use a mulch to control the growth of most annual weeds. If a few pop through, pull these by hand.

Staking Some taller varieties may need support, especially if planted in windy locations. Begin staking individual stems early in the season by placing bamboo stakes or similar supports in the ground just as new growth begins. Tie the stems to the stakes at varying heights for support. Use soft material or twine tied in a loose figure-eight knot. Staking is a chore and can be avoided by planting taller varieties in more protected sites or by buying shorter varieties if your garden is like a wind tunnel.

Deadheading Cutting off faded flowers keeps plants tidy and may stimulate a second round of bloom in some varieties. Deadheading also stops plants from self-sowing. Most seedlings of hybrids will not match the beauty of parent plants. If you want to maintain a certain coloration, deadheading is critical. Note that some varieties are sterile, so that this is of no concern. Deadheading ground covers is a chore. Using grass clippers helps speed things up.

Pruning When plants of *Phlox*–Paniculata Group (Summer Phlox) are 6 inches (15 cm) tall, cut out all but five stems per plant. This creates better, bigger, and longer-lasting bloom. It also reduces the chance of mildew by increasing air circulation around individual stems.

Pinch off the growing tips of the remaining stems. This will create bushier, sturdier plants with fuller bloom. Do this early in the season, certainly no later than 6 weeks before normal bloom time.

Phlox–Arendsii Group (Arend's Phlox) can be sheared back after they flower to create new growth. How far to shear back varies garden by garden. Experiment with different levels to see which produces the best round of bloom for you. Generally, the farther south you are, the more you shear the plants back. In the far North, you're better off just removing spent blossoms.

Experiment with shearing back other groups as well. You may get good results.

Winter Protection Remove all dead foliage after a severe frost in fall. Cover plants with 6 inches (15 cm) of winter mulch, such as clean straw, pine needles, or whole leaves. Remove mulch as soon as the weather warms up in spring to avoid crown rot.

Problems

Insects Red spider mites often attack *Phlox*–Paniculata Group (Summer Phlox), turning plants a pale yellow color. These are most common in hot, dry weather. Mist foliage lightly each morning during these periods to discourage infestations. If the problem becomes too severe, use a miticide. Red spider mites occasionally attack other groups as well.

Disease Powdery mildew, a white film on foliage and stems, is a serious problem on certain varieties of *Phlox*–Paniculata Group (Summer Phlox). Preventive measures include planting in a deeply prepared, highly organic soil; allowing for good air circulation around the plants; thinning the number of stems in a clump each spring to no more than five; and dividing mature plants every third year.

Leaf spotting is not quite as common but still occurs. The only sure way of stopping these problems is with the regular use of fungicides. Begin using these early in the year, since prevention is always easier than cure. Also vary the type of fungicide used for best results. One week use one kind, the next week another. All-purpose sprays containing fungicides, insecticides, and miticides are a good alternative. Read all pesticide labels carefully, as some chemicals badly damage Phlox.

Leaf Drop When leaves start to drop off of plants for no apparent reason, you may have a physiological problem called "leaf drop." Prevent it by using mulch and dividing older plants.

Rabbits Rabbits do like to nibble on new growth, especially of ***Phlox divaricata*** (Woodland Phlox). Either fence them out or trap them.

Propagation

Division Divide taller plants every 2 to 4 years for best health. Dig up the plant in early spring just as new growth starts. Cut the crown into sections, each with three to five stems attached to ample roots. Plant as you would bare root plants. Discard the central core if it is woody or dead.

The creeping varieties tend to spread rapidly, rooting where leaf nodes come in contact with the ground. Cut off rooted sections to the side of the mother plant. Do this just after the plant flowers. Plant them as you would a bare root plant.

Stem Cuttings When the plant is tall enough so that the tip of the stem snaps off but is somewhat firm (like a green bean), cut off a section with three sets of leaves. Cut ¼ inch (6 mm) below a leaf. Remove all but the top leaves. Dip the cut end in rooting hormone. Tap off any excess powder. Then place the cutting in moist growing medium. Keep it in partial shade at high humidity. Keep the medium consistently moist until roots form. Plant outside when the cutting has a solid root ball.

If early cuttings fail, wait until the plant blooms. After it is done blooming, remove the entire flower head. Take a cutting from the remaining portion of stem as outlined in the previous paragraph. The stem will be more mature and may root more easily.

Cuttings rooted late in the season must be winter protected, preferably in a cold frame. Expect rapid growth the following spring.

Root Cuttings Root cuttings can be taken with some of the taller varieties. In very early spring, dig up one side of a mature plant. Dig deeply, trying to get as many roots up as possible. Tilt the plant upward and sideways. You'll see many fibrous roots. Cut off several of the thickest and longest. Let the plant drop back into place. Fill in around it with fresh soil. It will barely notice the operation. Cut the roots into 2-inch (5-cm) sections. Lay these horizontally 1 inch (2.5 cm) deep in moist growing medium. Keep the medium consistently moist. Each root cutting will produce a new plant. Dig up and plant these young plants when they form several sets of leaves.

Another technique is to dig around the plant with a spade in fall. Completely encircle the plant while digging at an angle under it. You'll cut through some of the roots, which will produce young shoots off to the side of the parent plant the following spring. Dig these up and plant as you would bare root plants.

Seed Fill a tray with moist germination medium. Press the seed into it. Slide the tray into a bag perforated for good air circulation. Then put the tray in the crisper of your refrigerator for 6 weeks. Remove the tray 12 weeks before the last expected frost in spring. Keep it completely dark until seedlings emerge. Germination normally takes from 25 to 30 days at 68°F (20°C), but may take longer. Once the seedlings are germinating, move them into light. When the seedlings have a second pair of leaves, plant them in individual pots. Harden them off for 14 days before planting them outside after all danger of frost has passed in spring.

Special Uses

Cut Flowers Although these flowers are lovely and often have a nice fragrance, they tend to drop florets quickly, even if handled well. Cut flowers just as they reach peak bloom. Hammer the base of each stem gently, just breaking up the woody texture. This helps the stem take in water. Place the stems in warm water for several hours before placing them in an arrangement. Remove any flowers that begin to drop florets immediately. If the warm-water treatment doesn't work, try cold water instead. Do not expect long-lasting bloom.

Dried Flowers No Phlox is really suited for drying. If you have discovered a successful method, please let us know.

Sources

Ambergate Gardens, 8730 County Rd. 43, Chaska, MN 55318, (877) 211-9769

Bluestone Perennials, 7211 Middle Ridge Rd., Madison, OH 44057, (800) 852-5243

Busse Gardens, 17160 245th Ave., Big Lake, MN 55309, (800) 544-3192

Earthly Pursuits, 2901 Kuntz Rd., Windsor Mill, MD 21244, (410) 496-2523

Fieldstone Gardens, Inc., 55 Quaker Lane, Vassalboro, ME 04989, (207) 923-3836

ForestFarm, 990 Tetherow Rd., Williams, OR 97544, (541) 846-7269

Fritz Creek Gardens, P.O. Box 15226, Homer, AK 99603, (907) 235-4969

Perennial Pleasures Nursery, P.O. Box 147, East Hardwick, VT 05836, (802) 472-5104

Siskiyou Rare Plant Nursery, 2115 Talent Ave., Talent, OR 97540, (541) 535-7103

Spring Hill Nursery, P.O. Box 330, Harrison, OH 45030, (513) 354-1510

Sunlight Gardens, 174 Golden Lane, Andersonville, TN 37705, (800) 272-7396

Triple Brook Nursery, 459 State Rte 34, Colts Neck, NJ 07722, (732) 946-2027

Variegated Foliage Nursery, 245 Westford Rd., Eastford, CT 06242, (860) 974-3951

Woodlanders Inc., 1128 Colleton Ave. SE, Aiken, SC 29801, (803) 648-7522

VARIETIES

VARIETY	COLOR	HEIGHT	HARDINESS
Phlox–Arendsii Group			
(Arend's Phlox)			
'Baby Face'*****	Pink/rosy red eye	30″	–40°F
'Eye Catcher'	White/red eye	20″	–40°F
'Ping Pong'	Light pink/rose red eye	20″	–40°F
'Pink Attraction'	Pink	24″	–40°F
'Sabine'	Bluish pink	20″	–40°F

Arend's Phlox is a cross between *Phlox divaricata* (Woodland Phlox) and *Phlox*–Paniculata Group (Summer Phlox). These varieties are intermediate in height and flowering characteristics between the two species. If deadheaded after bloom, they will often produce additional flowers later in the season. They like full sun for best bloom.

VARIETY	COLOR	HEIGHT	HARDINESS
Phlox bifida			
(Sand Phlox)	Lavender to white	8″	–30°F
'Betty Blake'	Sky blue	8″	–30°F
'Starbrite'	Lavender/purple center	4″	–30°F

This Midwest native prefers sandy soil and relatively low fertility. The flowers have notched petals, bloom in spring, and occasionally rebloom later in summer. It grows best in full sun.

VARIETY	COLOR	HEIGHT	HARDINESS
Phlox borealis*****			
(Arctic Phlox)	Lavender pink	6″	−40°F

Arctic Phlox forms a compact mound similar to that of *Phlox*–Subulata Group, but it is superior because its deep green leaves hold their color throughout the season. If only it were available in more colors! It grows best in rich, well-drained soil in full sun.

Phlox carolina			
(Carolina Phlox)			
'Magnificence'	Dark carmine	42″	−40°F
'Miss Lingard'*****	White/gold stamens	36″	−40°F

These varieties resemble *Phlox*–Paniculata Group (Summer Phlox), but their leaves are thicker and their showy clusters of flowers start blooming earlier in summer. Both are quite resistant to powdery mildew.

Phlox divaricata			
(Woodland Phlox)	Bluish purple	18″	−40°F
'Blue Moon'	Dark bluish purple	12″	−40°F
'Blue Perfume'*****	Lilac blue	15″	−40°F
'Chattahoochee'	Lavender blue/deep purple eye	12″	−40°F
'Clouds of Perfume'	Lavender	15″	−40°F
'London Grove Blue'	Dark blue	12″	−40°F
'Lousiana Blue'	Dark blue	12″	−40°F
'Manita'*****	White/purple eye	12″	−40°F
'May Breeze'	Pale blue	10″	−40°F
'Parksville Beach'	Purple pink	8″	−40°F
'Plum Perfect'	Plum purple/darker eye	10″	−40°F
ssp. *laphamii*	Dark blue	15″	−40°F
'White Perfume'*****	White	15″	−40°F

This woodland plant is native to a large portion of the eastern United States. It spreads slowly by creeping rhizomes and is highly desirable as a ground cover. The flowers are fragrant with 'Blue Perfume' being, perhaps, the most fragrant variety. 'Manita' is an exciting choice with noticeably larger and unusually colored flowers. Woodland Phlox needs an evenly moist soil, otherwise it may be plagued by mildew.

Phlox–Douglasii Group			
'Crackerjack'*****	Crimson red	4″	−40°F
'May Snow'	White/purple eye	5″	−40°F
'Rose Cushion'	Rose pink	4″	−40°F

These compact plants produce numerous clusters of flowers in spring. They require well-drained soil and full sun.

Phlox–Maculata Group			
(Meadow Phlox)			
'Alpha'	Rose pink/darker eye	40″	−40°F
'Flower Power'	White tinged pink	40″	−40°F
'Natascha'	Pink and white bicolor	36″	−40°F

'Bright Eyes'

'Chattahoochee'

'Miss Lingard'

'The King'

VARIETY	COLOR	HEIGHT	HARDINESS
'Omega'	White flushed violet	32"	−40°F
'Rosalinde'	Purplish pink	36"	−40°F

Varieties of Meadow Phlox offer glossier and darker green foliage along with an earlier bloom season than the more well-known varieties of *Phlox*–Paniculata Group (Summer Phlox). The fragrant flowers appear in early summer, and the plants will often rebloom if cut back after flowering. These plants flourish in full sun and, like Summer Phlox, powdery mildew can be a problem in some growing seasons.

Phlox–Paniculata Group
(Summer Phlox)

VARIETY	COLOR	HEIGHT	HARDINESS
'Becky Towe'	Salmon pink/darker eye	30"	−40°F
'Blue Boy'	Mauve blue	36"	−40°F
'Blue Paradise'*****	Bluish purple/white eye	42"	−40°F
'Bright Eyes'*****	Pink/red eye	36"	−40°F
Candy Store™ Coral Creme Drop	Coral/rose eye	36"	−40°F
Candy Store™ Grape Lollipop	Grape purple/white/darker eye	36"	−40°F
'David'*****	White	42"	−40°F
'David's Lavender'	Deep lavender pink	42"	−40°F
'Delta Snow'	White/purple eye	30"	−40°F
'Dodo Hanbury Forbes'	Bright pink/darker eye	40"	−40°F
'Eva Cullum'	Pink/red eye	30"	−40°F
Flame® Lilac	Lilac purple/white eye	18"	−40°F
Flame® Pink	Rose pink/darker eye	18"	−40°F
Flame® Purple	Violet purple/darker eye	18"	−40°F
Flame® White	White/small green eye	18"	−40°F
'Flamingo'	Shrimp pink/red eye	30"	−40°F
'Franz Schubert'*****	Lilac	30"	−40°F
'Fujiyama' ('Mount Fuji')	White	42"	−40°F
'Juliet'	Pale pink	24"	−40°F
'Junior Dance'	Salmon pink	20"	−40°F
'Junior Dream'	Purple	20"	−40°F
'Katherine'*****	Lavender blue/white eye	30"	−40°F
'Laura'	Fuchsia purple/white eye	30"	−40°F
'Little Princess'	Pink/white eye	24"	−40°F
'Lizzy'	Pink/white eye	36"	−40°F
'Natural Feelings'	Green/white/ pink bracts	30"	−40°F
'Nicky'*****	Magenta purple	42"	−40°F
'Norah Leigh'*****	Pinkish white/pink eye	36"	−40°F
'Orange Perfection'	Salmon orange	30"	−40°F
'Peppermint Twist'	Pink and white bicolor	18"	−40°F
'Pinafore Pink'	Pink/red eye	18"	−40°F
'Pixie Miracle Grace'	Lavender purple/white eye	20"	−40°F
'Pixie Twinkle'	Pink/darker eye	20"	−40°F

VARIETY	COLOR	HEIGHT	HARDINESS
'Red Riding Hood'*****	Cherry red	24″	−40°F
'Rijnstroom'	Deep rose pink	36″	−40°F
'Shortwood'	Medium pink/dark pink eye	42″	−40°F
'Shorty White'	White	15″	−40°F
'Speed Limit'	Pink flushed white	48″	−40°F
'Tenor'	Rose suffused scarlet	24″	−40°F
'The King'	Deep violet	30″	−40°F

By choosing a range of these varieties, you can have bloom from midsummer to early fall. Unfortunately, as a group, Summer Phlox are susceptible to diseases like powdery mildew. The degree of infection varies by region so a variety which shows resistance in one geographic area may not in another. Climatic conditions in any given season along with culture also play a role in infection rates. Many of the varieties listed here have shown relatively good disease resistance in the upper Midwest. Summer Phlox require full sun and good air circulation to thrive. The leaf edges of 'Becky Towe' are gold while those of 'Norah Leigh' are creamy white.

Phlox pilosa

VARIETY	COLOR	HEIGHT	HARDINESS
(Prairie Phlox)	Pink, purple, white	18″	−40°F
'Eco Happy Traveler'	Deep rose	18″	−40°F

Prairie Phlox has downy stems and leaves. It is best grown in a well-drained soil in more informal settings. It needs full sun and blooms in early summer. 'Eco Happy Traveler' makes a lovely semi-evergreen ground cover.

Phlox × *procumbens*

VARIETY	COLOR	HEIGHT	HARDINESS
(Trailing Phlox)			
'Variegata'*****	Rose pink	6″	−40°F

This is a hybrid between *Phlox stolonifera* and the *Phlox*–Subulata Group (Creeping Phlox) that combines the flowering habit of the former with the vigor of the latter. 'Variegata' has deep green leaves edged creamy white. Light shade during the hottest part of the day helps it retain this coloration.

Phlox stolonifera

VARIETY	COLOR	HEIGHT	HARDINESS
(Creeping Phlox)	Lavender blue	6″	−40°F
'Blue Ridge'	Pale blue	8″	−40°F
'Home Fires'*****	Deep pink	8″	−40°F
'Irridescens'	Lavender	10″	−40°F
'Pink Ridge'	Deep pink	8″	−40°F
'Sherwood Purple'*****	Purple blue	10″	−40°F

Perhaps the most shade-tolerant of the Phloxes, this perennial should be used much more frequently as a ground cover. It spreads by creeping stems, which root at their nodes, and forms a dense cover of foliage very close to the ground. The flowers are carried atop small stems, which rise out of the foliage in mid spring.

Phlox–Subulata Group

VARIETY	COLOR	HEIGHT	HARDINESS
(Creeping Phlox)			
'Atropurpurea'	Rose	6″	−40°F
'Betty'	Blue	3″	−40°F
'Blue Hill' ('Blue Hills')	Steel blue	6″	−40°F

VARIETY	COLOR	HEIGHT	HARDINESS
'Candy Stripes'	White/pink stripes	6"	−40°F
'Coral Eye'*****	Pinkish white/coral eye	6"	−40°F
'Crimson Beauty'	Purple red	6"	−40°F
'Emerald Cushion Blue' ('Blue Emerald')	Lavender blue	6"	−40°F
'Emerald Pink' ('Pink Emerald')	Pink	6"	−40°F
'Fort Hill'	Deep pink	6"	−40°F
'Laurel Beth'	Rose pink/purplish eye	6"	−40°F
'Millstream Daphne'	Hot pink/dark eye	6"	−40°F
'Millstream Jupiter'	Blue/yellow center	6"	−40°F
'Moerheim Beauty'	Pinkish white	6"	−40°F
'Nettleton Variation'	Bright pink	6"	−40°F
'Red Wings'	Crimson/dark center	6"	−40°F
'Scarlet Flame'*****	Vibrant pink red	6"	−40°F
'Schneewittchen'*****	Pure white	3"	−40°F
'White Delight'	White	6"	−40°F

The best-known and most popular of the Creeping Phloxes, this perennial offers sheets of color in spring and good winter hardiness, although very cold, open winters can cause some injury. The stiff needle-like leaves are mid-green, but have a tendency to turn an unattractive yellow green later in the season if not watered regularly. 'Laurel Beth' and 'Nettleton Variation' have green and white variegated foliage. Although these plants are often recommended as a ground cover, the foliage is not dense enough to crowd out weeds. Shearing after bloom may help correct this. *Phlox*–Subulata Group is quite tolerant of alkaline soils, but sharp drainage is critical to good growth. Plants thrive in full sun.

Phlox (Named hybrid)

VARIETY	COLOR	HEIGHT	HARDINESS
'Minnie Pearl'*****	White	18"	−30°F

'Minnie Pearl' has fragrant flowers and glossy green foliage that is very disease-resistant. It blooms for several weeks in summer, generally before varieties of *Phlox*–Paniculata Group (Summer Phlox) come into flower.

'Mariesii'

PLATYCODON GRANDIFLORUS

(plah-tee-KOH-dun gran-duh-FLOR-us)

BALLOON FLOWER

Bloom Time	Expected Longevity	Maintenance	Years to Bloom	Preferred Light
Midsummer to late summer	25+ years	Low	From seed: 2 years From potted plant: 1 year	Full sun

Balloon Flowers provide some of the best mid- to late-summer-blooming perennials for cold climates. Their flowers are available in single, semidouble, or double forms and range in color from violet blue to pink and white. Under good growing conditions, the bloom period is quite long. These tough, long-lived plants are slow to mature and prefer to remain undisturbed. Balloon Flowers are rarely bothered by either insects or disease. They make fine cut flowers if conditioned properly. Young children are intrigued by these plants because when they squeeze the flower buds, they pop.

How Balloon Flowers Grow

Balloon Flowers grow from fleshy, carrotlike roots into shrublike plants of varying heights. Their stems are quite slender and covered with gray green leaves that have whitish undersides. Large swollen flower buds looking like small balloons float near the tops of the stems. These open into bell-like blooms that are 2 to 3 inches (5 to 7.5 cm) across. If allowed to form, the swollen seedpods will drop their seed around the base of each plant, and these will germinate the following season. Balloon Flowers are very late to begin growth each spring, so you must be careful not to damage the growth eyes when working in the garden at that time.

Where to Plant

Site and Light Balloon Flowers thrive in full sun, but adequate flowering occurs in light shade. In fact, pale-colored forms such as 'Fuji Pink' and 'Shell Pink' produce better and longer-lasting color in a bit of shade.

Soil and Moisture Balloon Flowers grow best in slightly acidic soils that drain freely. Replace clay or rocky soil with good soil or build a raised bed. Mix lots of organic matter into the soil. Good soil amendments include compost, cow manure, leaf mold, peat moss, and rotted horse manure. Peat moss is preferred, since it's acidic. Balloon Flowers will die out during the winter in compacted soils.

Spacing Plant Balloon Flowers carefully, since they do not like being moved. Space dwarf types a foot (30 cm) away from the nearest plant, the tallest forms 18 inches (45 cm) or more apart. Although standard Balloon Flowers are most often used as specimen or accent plants, dwarf types are ideal for mass plantings.

Companions

Platycodon grandiflorus (Balloon Flower) has the look somewhat of a dwarf, woody shrub and can be used in place of one. In the border, it combines well with numerous late-summer-blooming perennials such as *Achillea* (Yarrow), *Artemisia* (Wormwood),

Chrysanthemum–Rubellum Group (Hardy Garden Mum), *Hemerocallis* (Daylily), *Liatris* (Gayfeather), *Lysimachia clethroides* (Gooseneck Loosestrife), *Monarda* (Bee Balm), and *Phlox*–Paniculata Group (Summer Phlox). Many of the dwarf types grow well in containers and can be used to add color to decks and patios. The fall foliage color of this perennial can be quite eye-catching in combination with **Grasses**, *Aster* (Aster), and *Sedum* (Stonecrop).

Planting

Bare Root Plant bare root stock as soon as you can work the ground in spring. Remove the plants from their shipping package immediately. Snip off broken or damaged root tips. Soak plants overnight in room-temperature water. Place a small amount of superphosphate in the base of the planting hole. Fill the hole with soil. Place the crown no deeper than 1 inch (2.5 cm) below the soil surface. Fill in with soil, firm with your fingers, and water immediately. Dissolve ½ cup (about 114 g) 10-10-10 fertilizer in 1 gallon (about 4 liters) of water. Pour ½ cup (about 120 ml) of this starter solution around the base of each plant. If you prefer organic fertilizer, use fish emulsion instead.

Potted Plants Plant potted Balloon Flowers after all danger of frost has passed in spring. If the soil in the pot is dry, water it, and let drain overnight. Tap the plant out of the pot without disturbing the root ball. Plant it at the same depth as in the pot, after preparing the hole in a similar manner to that for a bare root plant. Fill in around the plant with soil, firm with your fingers, and water immediately. Pour ½ cup (about 120 ml) starter solution around the base of the plant.

How to Care for Balloon Flowers

Water Keep the soil around Balloon Flowers consistently moist throughout the growing season. Saturate the soil to a depth of 8 to 10 inches (20 to 25 cm) each time you water.

Mulch Place 2 inches (5 cm) of mulch around the base of each plant as soon as the ground warms up in spring. Good mulches are shredded leaves, dried grass clippings, or pine needles. The mulch keeps the soil moist and cool and inhibits the growth of annual weeds. If you want the plants to self-sow, remove mulch as soon as seedpods form. Otherwise the mulch may interfere with seeds making proper contact with the soil.

Fertilizing Sprinkle 10-10-10 fertilizer around the base of each plant just as growth emerges in spring. Water immediately to dissolve granules and move nutrients into the root zone. Feed again just as buds begin to form. Foliar feeding with water-soluble fertilizer is also highly recommended.

If you prefer organic fertilizers, use alfalfa meal (rabbit pellets), blood meal, bonemeal, compost, fish emulsion, Milorganite, or rotted manures. Bonemeal must be mixed into the soil at planting time to be effective.

Weeding Balloon Flowers emerge late in the spring, so be very careful when working around the crowns early in the season. In fact, marking the location of this perennial is highly recommended to avoid damaging it in early cultivation. The regular use of a mulch controls most annual weeds. Any that do germinate are easily pulled by hand.

Staking The tallest forms may require support. A peony ring placed around a clump generally provides all the support necessary and becomes relatively inconspicuous by bloom time. Alternative methods include pea stakes and bamboo stakes with twine tied between them. No matter which method you use, get it in place when the plant is small so that it will be covered by the time the plant matures.

Deadheading Spent flowers do not really detract from the beauty of these perennials, but their removal may prolong the bloom season. If you want to collect seed or encourage the plants to self-sow, leave some of the spent flowers on the plant.

Winter Protection Mature Balloon Flowers are very hardy and do not require any winter protection other than natural snowfall. It may be a good idea to mulch young plantings with 6 inches (15 cm) of marsh hay, clean straw, pine needles, or whole leaves during the first season. Apply this cover once the ground has frozen in late fall. Remove it in early spring as soon as the weather warms up to avoid crown rot.

Problems

Insects Balloon Flowers are very rarely bothered by insects.

Diseases These perennials are very much disease free if grown properly. Soils that do not drain freely lead to crown and root rot.

Propagation

Division Balloon Flowers prefer to remain undisturbed, and division is not necessary for the plant's health. However, division is possible. Do not expect bloom from divisions for a year or two. Lift clumps in early spring just as new growth emerges. Dig deeply so that you get as much of the fleshy root system as possible. Wash the plant free of soil, and cut it into sections with a sharp knife. Make sure that each one has several strong shoots and an ample amount of fleshy root tissue. Any cuts or breaks on the root system should be trimmed flush so that they heal in the shortest possible time. Plant these new divisions immediately as you would a bare root plant.

Cuttings Though not commonly done, Balloon Flowers can be propagated by cuttings. When the young stems are 6 to 8 inches (15 to 20 cm) tall, take tip cuttings long enough so that they have about three sets of leaves. Make the final cut ¼ inch (6 mm) below a leaf node. Remove the lower leaves, and dust the cut end in rooting hormone. Tap off any excess powder, and stick the cuttings in moist rooting medium. Maintain high humidity around the cuttings, and keep the medium evenly moist throughout the rooting process. Once the cuttings have formed a strong root mass, place them in individual pots for growing on.

Seed Balloon Flowers are easy to start from seed without any special pretreatments. However, not all varieties will come 100 percent true from seed. If you want to be sure that offspring are identical to the parent plant, propagate by division or cuttings.

Start seed indoors 8 weeks before the last expected frost in spring. Press the seed into the surface of moist germination medium. Do not cover it. Put a piece of plastic over the seed tray, and keep it at 65°F to 70°F (18°C to 21°C). Germination normally takes place within 1 to 2 weeks, but older seed may take longer. Once seed has germinated, lower the growing temperature by 10°F (6°C) to produce the stockiest plants. Seedlings are generally ready for transplanting about 3 to 4 weeks after sowing. Harden them off for 14 days before planting them outside after all danger of frost has passed in spring.

As mentioned, Balloon Flowers will self-sow quite freely in the garden. If you want to encourage this, do not remove spent flowers, do not mulch heavily, and avoid the use of preemergent herbicides and chemical fertilizers around the base of the plant.

Special Uses

Cut Flowers Balloon Flowers make excellent cut flowers if handled properly. These perennials exude a milky substance that can clog stems if their bases are not seared with a flame prior to being placed in water. Allow the stems to stand overnight in a bucket of warm water before arranging. Remove any leaves that would be below the water line in the final design. Handled in this fashion, Balloon Flowers last about 1 week.

Dried Flowers Individual flowers can be dried in a desiccant. Pick flowers at peak bloom, and attach a 4-inch (10-cm) piece of florist wire to each of them. Place them face up on a bed of desiccant, and fill around the petals with the drying agent, making sure they are properly arranged as you cover them. They should be completely covered when you are done. Let the blooms remain in this agent until they are completely dry. Once they are removed from the desiccant, you can attach a longer wire to the short piece if necessary for a specific use.

Sources

Bluestone Perennials, 7211 Middle Ridge Rd., Madison, OH 44057, (800) 852-5243

Busse Gardens, 17160 245th Ave., Big Lake, MN 55309, (800) 544-3192

Fieldstone Gardens, Inc., 55 Quaker Lane, Vassalboro, ME 04989, (207) 923-3836

ForestFarm, 990 Tetherow Rd., Williams, OR 97544, (541) 846-7269

Goodness Grows, P.O. Box 311, Lexington, GA 30648, (706) 743-5055

Well-Sweep Herb Farm, 205 Mount Bethel Rd., Port Murray, NY 07865, (908) 852-5390

'Double Blue'

'Shell Pink'

VARIETIES

VARIETY	COLOR	HEIGHT	HARDINESS
Platycodon grandiflorus			
(Balloon Flower)	Violet blue	40"	−40°F
'Albus'	White	36"	−40°F
'Astra Blue'/'Astra Pink'/'Astra White'*****	Rich blue/light pink/white	18"	−40°F
'Astra Blue Double'/'Astra Lavender Double'/ 'Astra Double White'*****	Rich blue (D)/lavender (D)/ white (D)	12"	−40°F
'Blue Bell' ('Blaue Glocke')	Purple blue	36"	−40°F
'Double Blue'/'Double White'	Violet blue (D)/white (D)	24"	−40°F
'Fairy Snow'	White with blue veins	18"	−40°F
'Fuji Blue'/'Fuji Pink'/'Fuji White'	Violet blue/shell pink/white	30"	−40°F
'Hakone Blue'/'Hakone White'*****	Violet blue (D)/white (D)	36"/20"	−40°F
'Komachi'	Lavender blue	36"	−40°F
'Mariesii'	Rich violet blue	18"	−40°F
'Misato Purple'	Violet purple	24"	−40°F
'Mother of Pearl' ('Perlmutterschale')	Lilac pink	36"	−40°F
Sentimental Hybrids*****	Blue, white, pink	18"	−40°F
'Shell Pink'	Soft pink	24"	−40°F

Doubles (D) look like a flower within a flower. All of the Astra single and double Balloon Flowers are five-star plants.

'Mrs. Moon'

PULMONARIA

(puhl-muhn-AIR-ee-uh)

LUNGWORT

Bloom Time	Expected Longevity	Maintenance	Years to Bloom	Preferred Light
Early spring	25 years	Low	From seed: 2 years From potted plant: 1 year	Light to medium shade

Lungworts are among the finest early-blooming spring plants. Their flowers are an attractive blue, pink, white, or reddish hue. The foliage is especially appealing as long as the plants are grown properly. Lungworts are easy to grow and propagate. Most are virtually maintenance free and rarely affected by disease or insects. They spread evenly and are not invasive. They make an excellent ground cover in shady areas, especially along the edges of woods. Although their flowers are small, they attract hummingbirds, another magical touch to the spring garden.

How Lungworts Grow

Lungworts grow from thick, fibrous roots into low-growing plants with lovely foliage. Leaves are small to begin with, but quite long and large by the end of the season for most varieties. Some varieties have mottled coloration and silky hairs. The plant forms a dense, circular mound of foliage. Small, delicate flowers appear on short stems above the foliage in early spring. The plant has crowns that spread slowly but deliberately under good growing conditions.

Where to Plant

Site and Light Lungworts grow best in light shade. Plants will grow in full sun if the ground is kept consistently moist throughout the growing season. When grown in such a site with proper watering, they will often be larger than plants grown in the shade. However, if Lungworts are grown in full sun without adequate moisture, their leaves turn brown and wither. They may also get mildew. The ideal location is on the edge of woods where plants can spread freely over the years. Here they have a rich supply of humus from decaying leaves.

Soil and Moisture Lungworts thrive in rich, well-drained soil high in organic matter. Ideal soil amendments are compost, leaf mold, rotted manures, and peat moss. These retain moisture but drain freely. The plant needs moist soil for good foliage growth. If you have clay or rocky soil, remove it and replace it with loam or build a raised bed.

Spacing Space plants 12 to 18 inches (30 to 45 cm) apart. Plant in groups of three to five at the minimum, since the plant looks best this way. *Pulmonaria* makes a nice, specimen plant in the shade garden as long as it is kept moist at all times.

Companions

These perennials are good companions to spring bulbs such as *Narcissus* (Daffodil) and *Tulipa* (Tulip), as well as other early-season perennials such as *Phlox stolonifera* (Creeping Phlox). The colorful foliage is a bonus throughout the season and combines in a unique manner with other foliage perennials such as *Athyrium niponicum* var. *pictum* (Japanese Painted Fern), *Filipendula ulmaria* 'Variegata' (Queen-of-the-Meadow), *Heuchera* 'Plum Pudding' (Hybrid Coral Bells), *Hosta* (Hosta), *Lamium maculatum* 'Pink Pewter' (Spotted Dead Nettle), *Luzula nivea* (Snowy Woodrush Grass), *Lysimachia ciliata* 'Purpurea' (Fringed Loosestrife), and *Phlox × procumbens* 'Variegata' (Trailing Phlox). Lungworts are great ground covers for use under small trees and shrubs. They are particularly effective with gray-barked plants such as *Amelanchier* (Juneberry) and *Carpinus caroliniana* (Blue Beech).

Planting

Bare Root Plant bare root stock as soon as you can work the ground in spring. Remove plants from their shipping package immediately. Snip off broken or damaged root tips. Soak plants overnight in room-temperature water. Place a small amount of superphosphate in the base of the planting hole. Fill the hole with soil. Place the crown 1 inch (2.5 cm) below the soil surface. Fill in with soil, firm with your fingers, and water immediately. Dissolve ½ cup (about 114 g) 10-10-10 fertilizer in 1 gallon (about 4 liters) of water. Pour ½ cup (about 120 ml) of this starter solution around the base of each plant. If you prefer organic fertilizer, use fish emulsion instead.

Potted Plants Plant Lungworts after all danger of frost in spring. If the soil in the pot is dry, water it, and let drain overnight. Plant it at the same depth as in the pot, after preparing the hole in a manner similar to that for a bare root plant. Fill in with soil, firm with your fingers, and water immediately. Pour ½ cup (about 120 ml) starter solution around the base of each plant.

How to Care for Lungworts

Water Lungworts need moist soil throughout the season to do well. Water them frequently, keeping the soil evenly moist, especially if you are growing plants in full sun. Lots of organic matter in the soil and a good mulch help cut down on the amount of watering needed. Whenever you water, saturate the soil to a depth of 18 inches (45 cm).

Mulch Place a 2-inch (5-cm) layer of mulch around the base of the plants as soon as the ground warms up in spring. Avoid touching the crown of the plant with the mulch. Good organic mulches include compost, dried grass clippings, shredded leaves, sawdust, pine needles, and chipped bark. If you use either sawdust or bark, add more fertilizer than normal, because these materials draw nitrogen from the soil.

Fertilizing Sprinkle 10-10-10 fertilizer around the base of each plant just as new growth emerges in spring. Water immediately to dissolve granules and carry nutrients into the root zone.

If you prefer organic fertilizers, use alfalfa meal (rabbit pellets), blood meal, bonemeal, compost, cow manure, Milorganite, or rotted horse manure. Bonemeal must be mixed into the soil at planting time to be effective. Fish emulsion is excellent for foliar feeding.

Weeding Kill all perennial weeds before planting. Mulch inhibits most weed growth, but a few annual weeds will still sprout. Pull these by hand to avoid harming the plant's root system. Weeds compete with the plant for moisture and nutrients.

Staking This is a low-growing or mound-forming plant. It never requires staking.

Deadheading When the clusters of flowers have finished blooming, remove them unless you want seed to form. Cut the stalks off at their base.

Winter Protection During the first year, cover the plants with a 4-inch (10-cm) winter mulch of clean straw, whole leaves, or pine needles. If in subsequent years there is no snow by mid-December, apply a 4-inch (10-cm) mulch at that time. Remove mulch as soon as the weather warms up in early spring to prevent crown rot. Plants will bloom extremely early and can be damaged by winter mulch if it is left on too long.

Problems

Insects Lungworts are rarely bothered by insects, although some gardeners occasionally have problems with slugs. Place boards out at night. Lift them in early morning, and destroy the pests that take cover under them. Since slugs are slimy, some people wear gloves to toss the pests into salt water or vinegar.

Disease Lungworts are a disease-resistant group. If foliage dies out, it's usually because the plant is in direct sun and not getting enough water. Plants not given enough water may also develop mildew.

Propagation

Division After the plants have flowered in spring, dig up the entire clump, and divide it with a sharp knife into sections. Each section should contain several stems connected to an ample supply of roots. Plant the divisions immediately as you would a bare root plant. Keep the soil consistently moist.

Root Cuttings Some Lungworts are quite easy to start from root cuttings. Remove roots from the mother plant as soon as the frost gets out of the ground in spring. Cut roots into small sections and plant immediately. This technique works best for *Pulmonaria longifolia* (Long-Leaved Lungwort) and quite well for *Pulmonaria angustifolia* (Blue Lungwort).

Seed To start seed, barely cover it in moist peat moss in a tray. Cover the tray with perforated plastic. Keep the seed moist and at room temperature for 2 to 4 weeks. Then slide it into the crisper of your refrigerator for 4 to 6 weeks. After this period, remove the tray, and set it in an area where the temperature stays between 60°F and 65°F (16°C to 18°C). Germination should occur within a month, but some seed may sprout later. Once plants have a second set of leaves, plant them in individual pots. Harden plants off for 14 days before planting them outdoors after all danger of frost has passed in spring. Plants of some varieties self-sow readily in the garden, but may not be identical to the parent plants.

Special Uses

Cut Flowers Neither the leaves nor the flowers of Lungworts are easy to use in arrangements. You might try a few cuttings of flowers early in the season, but don't expect them to last long.

Dried Flowers Lungworts are not grown for this purpose.

Sources

Bluestone Perennials, 7211 Middle Ridge Rd., Madison, OH 44057, (800) 852-5243

Fieldstone Gardens, Inc., 55 Quaker Lane, Vassalboro, ME 04989, (207) 923-3836

Joy Creek Nursery, 20300 NW Watson Rd., Scappoose, OR 97056, (503) 543-7474

Klehm's Song Sparrow Perennial Farm, 13101 E Rye Rd., Avalon, WI 53505, (800) 553-3715

Plant Delights, 9241 Sauls Rd., Raleigh, NC 27603, (919) 772-4794

Roots & Rhizomes, P.O. Box A, Randolph, WI 53956, (800) 374-5035

Sandy Mush Herb Nursery, 316 Surrett Cove Rd., Leicester, NC 28748, (828) 683-2014

Variegated Foliage Nursery, 245 Westford Rd., Eastford, CT 06242, (860) 974-3951

'Spilled Milk'

'Mrs. Moon' flower cluster

VARIETIES

VARIETY	COLOR	HEIGHT	HARDINESS
Pulmonaria angustifolia			
(Blue Lungwort)	Deep blue	12″	−40°F
'Blaues Meer'*****	Gentian blue	10″	−40°F
'Johnson's Blue'	Blue	10″	−40°F

This species and its selections are vigorous growing plants that form sprawling mats of foliage. Their dark green, bristly leaves are rarely spotted and make a good ground cover among shrubs. The nodding flowers are pink in bud and mature to the colors described above.

VARIETY	COLOR	HEIGHT	HARDINESS
Pulmonaria azurea (see *Pulmonaria angustifolia*)			

VARIETY	COLOR	HEIGHT	HARDINESS
Pulmonaria longifolia			
(Long-leaved Lungwort)	Purple blue	12″	−40°F
'E.B. Anderson' ('Bertram Anderson')*****	Violet blue	12″	−40°F
'Diana Clare'	Violet blue	10″	−40°F
subsp. *cevennensis*****	Cobalt blue	16″	−40°F

These Lungworts are distinguished by their long narrow leaves that are marked with silver. 'E.B. Anderson' has narrower leaves and flower stems that are not as floppy as the species. The narrow leaves of 'Diana Clare' are mostly silver with green margins. *Pulmonaria longifolia* subsp. *cevennensis* offers perhaps the longest bloom season of all the Lungworts as well as interesting silvery gray markings on its elongated spear-shaped green leaves.

VARIETY	COLOR	HEIGHT	HARDINESS
Pulmonaria officinalis			
(Jerusalem Cowslip)	Violet blue	24″	−40°F
'Sissinghurst White'	White	10″	−40°F

These Lungworts have rough leaves heavily spotted in spring, but subdued by summer. They thrive in soils high in organic matter and evenly moist throughout the growing season. Though 'Sissinghurst White' is a fine long-blooming variety, it is sometimes bothered by mildew.

VARIETY	COLOR	HEIGHT	HARDINESS
Pulmonaria rubra			
(Red Lungwort)	Coral red	24″	−30°F
'David Ward'	Coral red	12″	−30°F
'Redstart'	Salmon red	16″	−30°F

The species has hairy, dull green leaves and spreads rapidly, making it a fine ground cover among shrubs. Named varieties are less aggressive and produce more and larger flowers on stronger flower stems (scapes). Red Lungworts are among the earliest members of this group to bloom in spring. 'David Ward' has pale green leaves that are edged silvery white.

VARIETY	COLOR	HEIGHT	HARDINESS
Pulmonaria saccharata			
(Bethlehem Sage)	Blue	18″	−40°F
'Argentea' ('Argentifolia')	Blue	12″	−40°F
'Dora Bielefeld'*****	Pink	16″	−40°F
'Janet Fisk'	Blue	12″	−40°F

VARIETY	COLOR	HEIGHT	HARDINESS
'Mrs. Moon'	Pink fading to blue	12″	−40°F
'Pierre's Pure Pink'*****	Pale salmon pink	12″	−40°F
'Silverado'*****	Blue	12″	−40°F

These Lungworts have oval-shaped leaves highlighted by silvery white coloration. All are purplish pink in bud, but their flowers mature to the given colors. 'Argentea,' 'Janet Fisk,' and 'Silverado' have silvery foliage that is ideal for brightening up dark sites.

Pulmonaria vallarsae

'Margery Fish'*****	Pink aging violet blue	12″	−40°F

The species is a native to Italy, but seldom grown. 'Margery Fish,' one of its offspring, is quite vigorous, with large silvery spots on its broad, hairy leaves.

Pulmonaria (Named varieties and hybrids)

'Benediction'*****	Cobalt blue	12″	−40°F
'Berries and Cream'	Rosy pink	12″	−40°F
'Blue Ensign'	Rich blue	12″	−40°F
'Dark Vader'	Pink aging dark blue	12″	−40°F
'Excalibur'	Pink aging dark blue	10″	−40°F
'Little Star'*****	Cobalt blue	10″	−40°F
'Majeste'*****	Pink aging blue pink	12″	−40°F
'Moonshine'	Pale blue	8″	−40°F
'Polar Splash'	Blue aging to pink	10″	−40°F
'Raspberry Splash'*****	Raspberry pink	12″	−40°F
'Roy Davidson'*****	Sky blue	12″	−40°F
'Silver Bouquet'	Pink aging blue	10″	−40°F
'Smokey Blue'*****	Pink aging soft blue	10″	−40°F
'Spilled Milk'	Blue pink	10″	−40°F
'Trevi Fountain'	Cobalt blue	12″	−40°F

The foliage of 'Benediction' is dark green with silver speckles, but it really stands out for its generous display of richly colored blooms. 'Berries and Cream' offers mostly silver foliage that is marked with green splotches along with wavy leaf edges. The broad green leaves of 'Blue Ensign' are unspotted and the flower color is among the most intense of the Lungworts. 'Dark Vadar' has deep green foliage generously speckled with silver. 'Excalibur' has silver leaves edged in green. It makes a good ground cover in a shady dark corner of the garden. 'Little Star' has lance-shaped leaves with small silver spots. The flowers are quite large and remain in bloom for a long time. 'Majeste' has lance-shaped leaves that are silvery gray with a slight sheen and very narrow green edges. 'Polar Splash' has, perhaps, the most distinctive spotting pattern on its foliage of any of the Lungworts. The foliage of 'Raspberry Splash' is noticeably more upright than many other forms of Lungwort. The leaves of this variety are long, narrow, sharply pointed and marked with a distinct pattern of silver spots. 'Roy Davidson,' as evidenced by the shape of its leaves, has *Pulmonaria longifolia* (Long-leaved Lungwort) as one of its parents. The spotting pattern on the leaves is very regular and uniform. 'Silver Bouquet,' with its dynamic floral display and long, narrow, silvery foliage, is a very fine shade perennial. 'Smokey Blue' has silver-spotted, dark green foliage and is a fairly prolific bloomer. 'Trevi Fountain,' with its abundant bloom and lance-shaped, green leaves that are spotted silver, is another choice perennial for the shade garden.

'Gold Drop'/'Goldquelle'

RUDBECKIA

(rude-BECK-ee-uh)

CONEFLOWER

Bloom Time	Expected Longevity	Maintenance	Years to Bloom	Preferred Light
Late summer to early fall	25+ years	Low	From seed: 2 years From potted plant: 1 year	Full sun

Coneflowers are noted for their brilliant golden yellow colors. Blossoms are often big, bright, and splashy. Bold drifts of these perennials create a wave of gold late in the season and last for a long time. Individual blossoms often have a different-colored center, which makes them interesting in floral arrangements. Most Coneflowers are easy to grow. Many attract butterflies. Some are quite short lived, others more permanent, depending on the variety. They are relatively carefree with the exception of the tallest varieties, which may need staking in windy sites or if overfed or overwatered. Some, unfortunately, are prone to powdery mildew.

How Coneflowers Grow

The perennial Coneflowers grow from strong, fibrous roots into plants with wiry stems and bold blossoms. Leaves can be somewhat sparse and often hairy. The crowns spread but are not invasive. Blossoms may be up to 5 inches (12.5 cm) wide. Mature plants form multistemmed clumps which give a bold effect in perennial borders.

Where to Plant

Site and Light Coneflowers are high-light plants and thrive in full sun. They like it very hot as well. The more sun, the better the bloom. Avoid planting taller varieties in windy locations, since they will topple over unless staked.

Soil and Moisture Most varieties thrive in rich, well-drained soils high in organic matter. Add lots of compost, rotted manure, or peat moss to the soil at planting time to keep it loose but moisture retentive. Coneflowers like consistent moisture throughout the growing season, although a few tolerate dry conditions.

Spacing Space the plants approximately 18 inches (45 cm) apart. Allow enough space from walls or other structures for good air circulation, since, as noted, some varieties are prone to powdery mildew.

Companions

These bright-flowered perennials are often used in mass to make a statement in the landscape during late summer and fall. *Rudbeckia laciniata* 'Autumn Sun'/'Herbstsonne' (Cutleaf Coneflower) looks especially impressive with *Artemisia lactiflora* (White Mugwort) and *Miscanthus sinensis* 'Silver Feather'/'Silberfeder' (Japanese Silver Grass). Try *Rudbeckia fulgida* 'Goldsturm' (Orange Coneflower) in combination with *Hemerocallis* 'Joan Senior' (Daylily), *Phlox*–Paniculata Group 'Red Riding Hood' (Summer Phlox), and *Platycodon grandiflorus* (Balloon Flower). Other good perennials to consider as companions include *Asclepias tuberosa* (Butterfly Milkweed), *Aster* (Aster) *Chrysanthemum*–Rubellum Group (Hardy Garden Mum), *Echinacea* (Purple Coneflower), *Liatris* (Gayfeather), *Lysimachia clethroides* (Gooseneck Loosestrife), *Monarda* (Bee Balm), and *Sedum* (Stonecrop).

Planting

Bare Root Plant bare root stock as soon as you can work the ground in spring. Remove plants from their shipping package immediately. Snip off broken or damaged root tips. Soak plants overnight in room-temperature water. Place a small amount of super-phosphate in the base of the planting hole. Fill the hole with soil. Place the crown 1 inch (2.5 cm) below the soil surface. Fill in with soil, firm with your fingers, and water immediately. Dissolve ½ cup (about 114 g) 10-10-10 fertilizer in 1 gallon (about 4 liters) of water. Pour ½ cup (about 120 ml) of this starter solution around the base of each plant. If you prefer organic fertilizer, use fish emulsion instead.

Potted Plants Plant Coneflowers after all danger of frost in spring. If the soil in the pot is dry, soak it, and let it drain overnight. Plant potted Coneflowers at the same depth as in the pot, after preparing the hole in a manner similar to that for a bare root plant. Fill in with soil, firm with your fingers, and water immediately. Pour ½ cup (about 120 ml) starter solution around the base of each plant.

How to Care for Coneflowers

Water In their early stage of growth, water plants frequently. Once mature, they require less water. They are often listed as drought tolerant, but they actually grow much better if watered regularly throughout the season.

Mulch Place a 2-inch (5-cm) layer of organic mulch around the base of each plant as soon as the ground warms up in spring. Use dried grass clippings, pine needles, compost, or shredded leaves. Avoid touching the crown of the plant with the mulch. Mulch keeps the soil moist and cool while preventing annual weed growth.

Fertilizing Sprinkle 10-10-10 fertilizer around the base of each plant just as new growth emerges in spring. Water immediately to dissolve granules and carry nutrients to the root zone. If plants were lanky in the previous season, fertilize less or not at all. This is especially important on taller varieties.

If you prefer organic fertilizers, use alfalfa meal (rabbit pellets), blood meal, bone meal, compost, cow manure, Milorganite, or rotted horse manure. Bonemeal must be mixed into the soil at planting time to be effective.

Weeding Kill all perennial weeds before planting. Mulch inhibits the growth of most annual weeds. If a few pop up, pull them out of the moist ground by hand. Weeds compete with the plants for valuable nutrients and moisture. Never use a hoe around the base of these plants; the roots are quite shallow and can easily be damaged by the blade.

Staking Staking is often necessary for the tallest varieties. Place the support next to the stem in early spring. Tie the stem to the support at different heights as the plant matures. Use soft fabric or twine in a loose figure-eight knot for ties. Note that too much moisture or too much fertilizer can cause spindly growth in taller varieties. If this is a problem, cut back on feeding the following year.

Deadheading Pinch off all spent blossoms to keep the area clean.

Winter Protection During the first year, cover all plants with 4 inches (10 cm) of clean straw, whole leaves, or pine needles. If there is no snow by mid-December in subsequent years, do the same. Remove all winter mulch by early spring as the weather begins to warm up to prevent crown rot.

Problems

Insects Leaf miners or aphids can be a problem. Spray aphids off with a hose. If the infestation is severe, cut the plants back to a healthy area. Dispose of diseased tissue. The plant will regrow vigorously. Mild insecticidal soaps are highly recommended if the foliage has not already been damaged. Use more potent insecticides only as a last resort.

Disease Powdery mildew can damage some varieties. Prevent it by giving plants plenty of space. If the disease returns each year, prevent it with the use of an appropriate fungicide.

Propagation

Division Divide plants every 4 years for good health and to increase the number of plants. As soon as new growth emerges in early spring, dig up the entire clump getting as much of the root system as possible. Wash the soil off with a hose. Then cut the clump into sections, each one with several stems attached to a healthy clump of roots. Plant the sections immediately as you would a bare root plant.

Stem Cuttings When plants are 12 inches (30 cm) tall, remove the tip of each stem. Cut ¼ inch (6 mm) below a leaf node. Each cutting should have three sets of leaves. Remove the lower leaves. Dust the cut end in rooting hormone. Tap off any excess powder. Plant cuttings in moist growing medium. Keep the medium consistently moist until a root ball forms. Then plant the cuttings in pots or in a permanent spot in the garden, keeping the soil moist at all times until the plant is growing vigorously.

Seed Start seed of species types indoors approximately 8 weeks before the last expected frost in spring. Press the seed into moist germination medium, and keep it at 68°F (20°C). Germination normally takes from 14 to 21 days. As soon as seedlings have a second pair of leaves, plant them in individual pots.

Many varieties self-seed if spent blossoms are not removed. Do not use chemical fertilizers in spring if you would like seedlings to germinate around the parent plants. The young flowers often vary considerably from their parents, but many people enjoy the surprise. If you want flowers more uniform in appearance, remove all spent blooms to prevent self-seeding.

Special Uses

Cut Flowers These are among the best perennials for cut flowers. Cut stems just as they reach peak bloom. Some of the stems are quite stiff; sharp pruning shears help in harvesting them. Place stems in water immediately. Strip off any leaves that will be underwater in the final arrangement. Place the bottom 1 inch (2.5 cm) of each stem in boiling water for a few seconds or longer. Then submerge the entire stem up to the flowers in cool water for several hours. Arrange them only after this conditioning.

Dried Flowers In floral arrangements, stems with either entire flowers or only the dark central disks are equally interesting. If keeping the stem attached to an entire flower, doubles are your best choice. Petals on these often twist and form a strange look. Cut flowers in peak bloom, save or remove petals as desired, strip off all leaves from the stem, and hang them upside down in a dry, dark, well-ventilated area.

You can also dry individual flowers with stems removed. If you attach a 4-inch (10-cm) piece of florist wire to each flower before drying, you make the job of creating artificial stems much easier. Place the flower in the desiccant face up. Bend the wire up to the side. Fill in around the flower and between the petals. Cover the entire flower completely and allow it to dry until it becomes brittle. Remove it from the desiccant, clean it carefully with a soft brush, and then attach a thicker wire to the short piece of wire with floral tape.

Sources

Ambergate Gardens, 8730 County Rd. 43, Chaska, MN 55318, (877) 211-9769

Busse Gardens, 17160 245th Ave., Big Lake, MN 55309, (800) 544-3192

Prairie Moon Nursery, 32115 Prairie Lane, Winona, MN 55987, (866) 417-8156

'Goldsturm'

'Autumn Sun'/'Herbstsonne'

VARIETIES

VARIETY	COLOR	FORM	HEIGHT	HARDINESS
Rudbeckia fulgida				
(Orange Coneflower)	Golden yellow	Single	36″	−40°F
'Goldsturm'	Golden yellow	Single	36″	−40°F
var. *fulgida*	Golden yellow	Single	30″	−40°F
var. *speciosa******	Golden yellow	Single	30″	−40°F
var. *sullivantii*	Golden yellow	Single	36″	−40°F
'Viette's Little Suzy'*****	Golden yellow	Single	18″	−40°F

These perennials have flowers with brown or black central cones and bloom profusely from mid to late summer. Overuse of 'Goldsturm' has made it prone to leaf spot diseases. Replace it with the more refined and longer blooming var. *fulgida*. Var. *speciosa* spreads more slowly than the others. Var. *sullivantii* is more upright with larger flowers than the species. 'Viette's Little Suzy' is ideal for the front of borders.

	COLOR	FORM	HEIGHT	HARDINESS
Rudbeckia laciniata				
(Cutleaf Coneflower)	Clear yellow	Single	72″	−40°F
'Autumn Sun' ('Herbstonne')*****	Bright yellow	Single	60″	−40°F
'Gold Drop' ('Goldquelle')*****	Bright yellow	Double	36″	−40°F
'Golden Glow' ('Hortensia')	Lemon yellow	Double	60″	−40°F

The species gets its name from its irregular indented (cut) leaves. The ray flowers droop down from a cylindrical green cone. The flowers of 'Autumn Sun' resemble those of the species. The doubles 'Gold Drop' and 'Golden Glow' provide superb cut flowers. The cones on these named varieties are green, turning dark with age. These perennials spread quickly but can remain undisturbed for years. They prefer an evenly moist soil.

	COLOR	FORM	HEIGHT	HARDINESS
Rudbeckia maxima*****				
(Great Coneflower)	Golden yellow	Single	72″	−30°F

This late summer blooming plant has gold flowers with dark brown central cones. They make a nice contrast to a low mound of grayish green, oval-shaped leaves that are up to 18 inches long. This species thrives in evenly moist soils. Finches love it.

Rudbeckia newmanii (see *Rudbeckia fulgida* var. *speciosa*)

	COLOR	FORM	HEIGHT	HARDINESS
Rudbeckia nitida				
(Shining Coneflower)	Bright yellow	Single	48″	−30°F

This species has large flowers with petals drooping down from a central greenish cone. The foliage is an attractive deep green color. The flowers shine from mid- to late summer. 'Autumn Sun' is often incorrectly placed with this species.

	COLOR	FORM	HEIGHT	HARDINESS
Rudbeckia subtomentosa				
(Sweet Black-eyed Susan)	Golden yellow	Single	60″	−30°F
'Henry Eilers'	Golden yellow	Single	60″	−30°F

The brilliant display of flowers with reddish brown cones makes this native species a standout for weeks in late summer. 'Henry Eilers' has quilled ray petals that give blooms a unique look.

Rudbeckia sullivantii (see *Rudbeckia fulgida* var. *sullivantii*)

'East Friesland'/'Ostfriesland'

SALVIA

(SAL-vee-uh)

SAGE

Bloom Time	Expected Longevity	Maintenance	Years to Bloom	Preferred Light
Early summer to late summer	10 to 15 years	Low	From seed: 2 years From potted plant: 1 year	Full sun

Sages are a good choice for vertical accent plants. Their colors are deep and rich. Only a few varieties are truly hardy in cold climates, but they are long-flowering and very showy. Foliage is often grayish green and aromatic. The combination of spectacular color and scented foliage makes Sage an ideal choice for cut flowers. It is also highly attractive to butterflies. Sage has a reputation for being short lived. By following the correct growing information outlined in this section, you'll overcome this objection to a large degree.

How Sages Grow

Sage grows from fibrous roots into plants producing floral spikes on squarish stems. These are almost frilly looking, with spires covered with tiny, tubular-shaped blossoms, often deep blue or purple. Leaves are grayish green and have an attractive aroma, noticed easily if you rub a leaf between your fingers. Mature plants form an attractive clump of foliage and flowers. Although many Sages are short lived, those listed in the table at the end of the section have a greater chance of living longer than many others not listed.

Where to Plant

Site and Light Give Sages lots of sun: the more, the better. Depending on the height of the plant, vary the location in the border. Plants thrive in high heat, so if they are next to a protected wall or fence, they react well, as long as there is good air circulation to prevent mildew. Keep the taller varieties out of windy sites.

Soil and Moisture Soil must drain freely if Sage is to survive. This is critical to success with this plant. Avoid planting it in boggy areas. If you have clay or rocky soil, replace it with loam or build a raised bed. Add in lots of organic matter. Good soil amendments include compost, peat moss, leaf mold, and rotted manure. All of these help soil retain moisture during dry periods but drain freely.

Spacing Space Sages according to the potential height and width of the plant. Each variety varies. Do not crowd the plants. Give each as much space as possible, since good air circulation helps prevent mildew, which can be a problem with this plant.

Companions

Combine *Salvia* (Sage) with perennials such as *Achillea* (Yarrow), *Asclepias tuberosa* (Butterfly Milkweed), *Coreopsis* (Tickseed), *Euphorbia* (Spurge), *Iris* (Bearded Iris), *Oenothera macrocarpa* (Ozark Sundrops), *Tanacetum corymbosum* (Caucasian Daisy), and *Sedum* (Stonecrop). Here are several particularly effective combinations: *Salvia nemorosa* 'May Night'/'Mainacht' (Violet Sage) planted behind *Coreopsis auriculata* 'Zamphir' (Mouse Ear Tickseed); *Salvia nemerosa* 'Lubeca' (Violet Sage) with *Geramium clarkei* 'Kashmir White' (Clark's Cranesbill) and *Oenothera fruticosa* 'Fireworks'/'Feuerverkeri' (Common Sundrops); and *Salvia koyamae* (Yellow Sage) combined with *Aster divaricatus/Eurybia divaricata* (White Wood Aster) and *Hosta clausa* (Hosta). Many of the early-summer-flowering types fit nicely into the rose garden combined with silver-leaved perennials such as *Artemisia* (Wormwood).

Planting

Bare Root Plant bare root stock as soon as you can work the ground in spring. Remove the plants from their shipping packaging immediately. Snip off broken or damaged root tips. Soak plants overnight in room-temperature water. Place a small amount of superphosphate in the base of the planting hole. Fill the hole with soil. Place the crown 1 inch (2.5 cm) below the soil surface. Fill in with soil, firm with your fingers, and water immediately. Dissolve ½ cup (about 114 g) 10-10-10 fertilizer in 1 gallon (about 4 liters) of water. Pour ½ cup (about 120 ml) of this starter solution around the base of each plant. If you prefer organic fertilizer, use fish emulsion instead.

Potted Plants Plant Sages after all danger of frost in spring. If the soil in the pot is dry, soak it, and let it stand overnight. Plant potted Sages at the same depth as in the pot, after preparing the hole in a manner similar to that for a bare root plant. Fill in with soil, firm with your fingers, and water immediately. Pour ½ cup (about 120 ml) starter solution around the base of each plant.

How to Care for Sages

Water Sage is drought tolerant when mature, but it really prefers evenly moist soil throughout the growing season. As long as the soil drains freely, it is hard to overwater this plant. So, saturate the soil to a depth of 12 to 18 inches (30 to 45 cm) each time you water.

Mulch Place 2 inches (5 cm) of organic mulch around the base of each plant as soon as the ground warms up in spring. Use compost, dried grass clippings, shredded leaves, or pine needles. Mulch keeps the soil moist and cool while inhibiting annual weed growth.

Fertilizing Sprinkle 10-10-10 fertilizer around the base of each plant as soon as new growth emerges in spring. Water immediately to dissolve the granules and carry nutrients to the root zone.

If you prefer organic fertilizers, use alfalfa meal (rabbit pellets), blood meal, bonemeal, compost, cow manure, fish emulsion, Milorganite, or rotted horse manure. Bonemeal must be mixed into the soil at planting time to be effective.

Weeding Weeds compete with the plants for valuable nutrients and moisture. Kill all perennial weeds before planting. Mulch will stop the growth of most annual weeds. If a few sprout, pull them out by hand to prevent damaging the plant's root system.

Staking Sages rarely require staking, although some of the taller varieties may need support if planted in windy sites. If they do, stake them early in the season. Tie the stems in several places to the support using soft material and figure-eight knots.

Pinching Back When plants of taller varieties are 6 inches (15 cm) tall, pinch off the growing tips to make bushier plants. If you take stem cuttings (see "Propagation"), this will result in the same thing.

Deadheading Cut off spent blossoms as soon as all flowers fade. With conscientious deadheading, some varieties bloom almost the entire season.

Winter Protection After the soil freezes to a depth of 3 inches (7.5 cm), place a 4-inch (10-cm) layer of winter mulch over the plants. Use clean straw, marsh hay, whole leaves, or pine needles. Remove this mulch as soon as the weather warms up in spring to avoid crown rot. Winter protection will be of little value if soil drains poorly. Protection is critical for more tender varieties.

Problems

Insects Sages are rarely bothered by insects.

Disease Powdery mildew is a problem with a number of Sages. It shows up as a whitish film on the leaves. Prevent it by giving the plant lots of light and plenty of room for good air circulation. If the outbreak is severe, cut the plant back, and destroy the diseased foliage. If the plant regrows and is still infected, use an appropriate fungicide to kill the dis-

ease. If the problem is recurring, use a preventive spraying program or grow different varieties.

Propagation

Division Mature plants sometimes begin to die out in the center. This is an indication that it is time to divide the plant for its own health. Dig up the entire clump just as new growth emerges in spring. Cut the clump into sections, each containing several stems attached to ample roots. Plant the sections immediately as you would a bare root plant.

Stem Cuttings Before the plants begin to set flower buds, cut off the tips of stems. Each cutting should have three pairs of leaves. Make the final cut ¼ inch (6 mm) below a leaf node. Remove the lower leaves. Dust the cut end in rooting hormone, and tap off any excess powder. Then plant the cuttings in pots containing moist growing medium. Keep the medium consistently moist until a root ball forms.

Seed Many of the named varieties will not come true from seed or are sterile. However, the species and certain named varieties do come true and are easy to grow from seed. Recommended are *Salvia nemerosa*, 'Blue Queen'/'Blaukönigen' and 'Rose Queen'/'Rosekönigen' (Perennial Sage).

Start seed indoors 12 weeks before the last expected frost in spring. Press seeds into moist growing medium. Do not cover them, since they need light to germinate. Keep them consistently moist, but not soggy, at a temperature above 68°F (20°C). Seed may take up to 3 months to germinate. Once seedlings emerge, reduce the temperature by 10°F (6°C). When seedlings have a second pair of leaves, plant them in individual pots.

Special Uses

Cut Flowers Cut the flower spires at whatever stage is most appealing to you. They make a nice vertical accent in arrangements. The blue or purple varieties are particularly sought-after. The soft leaves are also aromatic.

Dried Flowers The dried flowers are lovely in dried bouquets and wreaths. Cut the stems of deeper colors in full bloom. Dry these in an upright position. Cut the stems of paler varieties in an earlier stage of bloom. Hang these upside down in a dry, dark, well-ventilated area. Removing the leaves from the stems is important to prevent mildew.

Sources

Ambergate Gardens, 8730 County Rd. 43, Chaska, MN 55318, (877) 211-9769

Bluestone Perennials, 7211 Middle Ridge Rd., Madison, OH 44057, (800) 852-5243

Busse Gardens, 17160 245th Ave., Big Lake, MN 55309, (800) 544-3192

Deer-resistant Landscape Nursery, 3200 Sunstone Ct., Clare, MI 48617, (800) 595-3650

Earthly Pursuits, 2901 Kuntz Rd., Windsor Mill, MD 21244, (410) 496-2523

Fieldstone Gardens, Inc., 55 Quaker Lane, Vassalboro, ME 04989, (207) 923-3836

Niche Gardens, 1111 Dawson Rd., Chapel Hill, NC 27516, (919) 967-0078

Well-Sweep Herb Farm, 205 Mount Bethel Rd., Port Murray, NJ 07865, (908) 852-5390

'Blue Hill'/'Blauhugel'

'Lubeca'

VARIETIES

VARIETY	COLOR	HEIGHT	HARDINESS
Salvia koyamae			
(Yellow Sage)	Pale yellow	24″	−30°F

Not well-known in cold climates, this Japanese woodland plant is worth a gamble. It has bold-textured green foliage and blooms from late summer into fall. With its trailing stems, Yellow Sage has potential as a ground cover in light shade. It requires a well-drained soil with lots of organic matter added to it.

VARIETY	COLOR	HEIGHT	HARDINESS
Salvia nemorosa			
(Perennial Sage)			
'Amethyst'	Light purple	36″	−40°F
'Blue Hill' ('Blauhugel')	Deep sky blue	24″	−40°F
'Blue Queen' ('Blaukönigin')	Rich violet	30″	−40°F
'Caradonna'*****	Violet purple/dark stems	24″	−40°F
'East Friesland' ('Ostfriesland')	Violet purple	24″	−40°F
'Lubeca'	Violet purple	28″	−40°F
Marcus™ ('Heumanarc')	Rich violet purple	12″	−40°F
'May Night' ('Mainacht')*****	Deep violet	24″	−40°F
'Pink Friesland'*****	Rose pink	18″	−40°F
'Plumosa'	Deep rose purple	18″	−40°F
'Rose Queen' ('Rosakönigen')	Rose pink	30″	−40°F
'Sensation Rose'	Rose pink	12″	−40°F
'Snow Hill' ('Snow Mound') ('Schneehugel')	White	24″	−40°F
'Vesuvius' ('Wesuwe')	Deep violet	24″	−40°F
'Viola Klose'*****	Violet purple	18″	−40°F

These selections are among the best Sages for gardeners in cold climates. They are quite hardy, bloom freely, and mature into nice clumps. If sheared back after flowering, they will often rebloom. The deep purple stems of 'Caradonna' enhance the flower color while 'May Night'/'Mainacht' has flowers which are noticeably larger than the others. 'Viola Klose' is perhaps the earliest of these varieties to flower.

VARIETY	COLOR	HEIGHT	HARDINESS
Salvia pratensis			
(Meadow Sage)	Violet blue	36″	−30°F

Although hardier than most people believe, this tall bushy plant still tends to be short-lived. Fortunately, it often self-sows. It flowers in early summer and will often rebloom if deadheaded.

VARIETY	COLOR	HEIGHT	HARDINESS
Salvia verticillata			
(Lilac Sage)			
'Endless Love'	Violet blue	22″	−30°F
'Purple Rain'*****	Smoky purple	24″	−30°F

These selections have a nice vertical look, showy flowers, and a long bloom period during the summer.

VARIETY	COLOR	HEIGHT	HARDINESS
Salvia (Named hybrid)			
'Eveline'	Lavender pink	24″	−40°F

Numerous spikes of small blooms rise above a mound of dark green foliage in early to midsummer.

'Dragon's Blood'/'Schorbuser Blut'

SEDUM

(SEE-dum)

STONECROP

Bloom Time	Expected Longevity	Maintenance	Years to Bloom	Preferred Light
Spring to fall	25+ years	Low	From seed: 2 to 3 years From potted plant: 1 year	Full sun

Stonecrops are among the easiest of all perennials to grow. They are nearly indestructible. Most varieties have fleshy leaves and clusters of tiny star-like flowers. Both foliage and flowers come in a wide variety of colors and the latter are attractive to butterflies. The scent of some is exquisite. Stonecrops with their varied growth patterns are among the most versatile of perennials, with virtually every possible use. Some make excellent cut flowers. A few are ideal accent plants with a long bloom period. Most varieties spread but are not invasive in the border. These make wonderful ground covers. All are rarely harmed by insects or disease.

How Stonecrops Grow

Stonecrops divide into two overall groups: The first includes varieties that form neat clumps of upright stems with fleshy leaves. Each stem flowers with a cluster of tiny blossoms. This group is most suited for perennial borders. The second group includes low growers, making them good ground covers. These spread rapidly, sending out roots wherever nodes touch the soil. This group is good for rock gardens and rock crevices and on slopes to prevent erosion.

Where to Plant

Site and Light Stonecrops thrive in full sun, but they tolerate filtered light. They will grow in a wide range of temperatures. They truly comprise one of the most versatile groups of plants.

Soil and Moisture Stonecrops are extremely adaptable to varying soil conditions. The upright types will grow much larger in rich soil. The ground-hugging varieties thrive in rich soil and spread rapidly. The ideal soil is loose, rich, and well drained. Drainage is extremely important or plants may die out in wet winter soils. Add lots of organic matter to the soil. Good amendments include compost, peat moss, and rotted manure. These keep the soil moist throughout the season but drain freely. If you have clay or rocky soil, replace it with loam or build a raised bed.

Spacing The clump-forming varieties should be spaced approximately 18 to 24 inches (45 to 60 cm) from the nearest plant. Place the ground-hugging varieties 12 inches (30 cm) apart. They will spread and fill in any open space in a short time. Plant them only where they are free to roam. Some can be mildly invasive if planted in a perennial border.

Companions

With a bloom season extending from spring through fall, these plants combine well with a wide range of other perennials. Many of the tiny forms are best in rock or wall gardens combined with *Achillea tomentosa* (Wooly Yarrow), *Alchemilla alpina* (Mountain Mantle), *Aquilegia alpina* (Alpine Columbine), *Delphinium grandiflorum* (Chinese Delphinium), *Dianthus arenarius* (Sand Pink), *Geranium cinereum* (Grayleaf Cranesbill), *Phlox bifida* (Sand Phlox),

Veronica pectinata (Wooly Creeping Speedwell), and small **Grasses**. The spreading forms are good ground covers and, if not too aggressive, are good choices along edges of walks and flower borders. Most of the upright types bloom late in the season and look lovely with a host of other perennials, including *Aster* (Aster), *Chrysanthemum × morifolium* (Garden Mum), *Chrysanthemum*–Rubellum Group (Hardy Garden Mum), *Echinacea* (Purple Coneflower), *Heliopsis* (Oxeye), *Rudbeckia* (Coneflower), *Phlox* (Phlox), *Platycodon grandiflorus* (Balloon Flower), and numerous varieties of **Grasses**. Don't neglect compositions based on foliage color, for example, *Sedum* 'Xenox' planted next to *Coreopsis* 'Creme Brulee' (Tickseed). *Helictotrichon sempervirens* (Blue Oat Grass) and *Salvia nemerosa* 'Blue Hill'/'Blauhugel' (Violet Sage) make a delightful combination of color and texture throughout the growing season.

Planting

Bare Root Plant bare root stock as soon as you can work the ground in spring. Remove plants from their shipping package immediately. Snip off broken or damaged root tips. Soak plants overnight in room-temperature water. Place a small amount of superphosphate in the base of the planting hole. Fill the hole with soil. Place the crown 1 inch (2.5 cm) below the soil surface. Fill in with soil, firm with your fingers, and water immediately. Dissolve ½ cup (about 114 g) of 10-10-10 fertilizer in 1 gallon (about 4 liters) of water. Pour ½ cup (about 120 ml) of this starter solution around the base of each plant. If you prefer organic fertilizer, use fish emulsion instead.

Potted Plants Plant Stonecrops after all danger of frost in spring. If the soil in the pot is dry, water it, and let it drain overnight. Plant potted Stonecrops at the same depth as in the pot, after preparing the hole in a manner similar to that for a bare root plant. Fill in with soil, firm with your fingers, and water immediately. Pour ½ cup (about 120 ml) starter solution around the base of each plant.

How to Care for Stonecrops

Water Stonecrops thrive in moist conditions, although they are remarkably drought tolerant. High amounts of moisture will encourage border plants to be taller and ground-hugging varieties to spread more rapidly. Foliage is also more lush in moist conditions. Saturate the soil thoroughly whenever it gets dry.

Mulch Stonecrops do not demand mulch; however, mulch inhibits weed growth and is still a good idea. Place 1 inch (2.5 cm) of organic mulch around the base of each plant as soon as the ground warms up in spring. Good mulches include compost, shredded leaves, pine needles, and dried grass clippings. Replace mulch around upright varieties as it disappears throughout the growing season. The ground-hugging varieties will spread to become a living mulch as the season progresses.

Fertilizing Stonecrops grow well without large amounts of fertilizer. The ground-hugging varieties will spread more rapidly if given regular feedings. The upright types may occasionally get lanky and flop over if given too much nitrogen. If this happens, cut down on fertilizer in the following season.

In general, sprinkle 10-10-10 fertilizer around the base of each plant just as new growth emerges in spring. Water immediately to dissolve the granules and carry nutrients to the root zone.

If you prefer organic fertilizers, use alfalfa meal (rabbit pellets), blood meal, bonemeal, compost, cow manure, fish emulsion, Milorganite, or rotted horse manure. Bonemeal must be mixed into the soil at planting time to be effective.

Weeding Kill all perennial weeds before planting Stonecrops. This is critical if you are covering a large area with ground-hugging varieties. Use organic mulch to inhibit annual weed growth. If weeds pop through the mulch, pull them up by hand from the moist earth. Weeds are extremely unattractive in ground covers. Remove them immediately so that the ground cover can expand and smother other annual weeds about to sprout.

Staking The upright plants rarely require staking, but occasionally this is helpful if plants have become floppy. When this happens, divide them the following spring, and fertilize less.

Deadheading Removing spent blossoms is unnecessary on the ground-hugging varieties. Whether you remove blossoms on the larger clump-forming plants is an aesthetic choice. Many of the seed heads are quite attractive if left on the plant. They make for interesting patterns in the fall and winter garden. However, removing them is fine.

Winter Protection Stonecrops vary slightly in their hardiness. Most do not require winter protection. In severe open winters, it is good insurance to cover the more tender varieties with a thick layer of mulch, such as marsh hay, clean straw, or whole leaves. Remove these as soon as the weather warms up in spring to prevent rot.

Problems

Insects Some Stonecrops are occasionally infested with aphids. Spray them off with water. If they persist, use an insecticidal soap. In extreme situations, use more potent insecticides. Aphids do carry viral diseases and should be controlled.

Disease These plants resist most disease, but they will rot out if soil does not drain freely in winter.

Propagation

Division Divide the clump-forming varieties every few years to keep them at a desirable size. Some of them become quite large with age and their stems fall over. If this happens, divide them in early spring just as new growth emerges. Dig up the plant, and cut it into sections, each one having several stems attached to a healthy clump of roots. Plant each division as you would a bare root plant.

For the ground-hugging varieties, simply dig or pull off the plantlets to the side of the mother plant.

Plant these as you would a bare root plant. Water immediately.

Stem Cuttings Take cuttings from clump-forming varieties when the stems are 12 inches (30 cm) tall. Each cutting should have three sets of leaves. Make the final cut ¼ inch (6 mm) under a node. Remove the lower leaves. Let the cuttings rest in a cool, dry place for several days to form a callus, like a scab, over the cut end. Then place them in moist growing medium. Let this medium dry out slowly, then moisten it lightly again. Keep it just between slightly moist and dry for best results. If the soil is soggy, the cuttings are likely to rot out. When the plant forms a root ball, plant it in a permanent location.

Seed Seed is available for the species (wild) varieties. Propagate named varieties through cuttings or division only.

Plant seed indoors 16 weeks before the last expected spring frost. Sow them in moist growing medium just under the surface. Keep them evenly moist and at temperatures between 70°F (21°C) and 80°F (27°C). Use bottom heat if necessary to maintain this temperature. When seedlings emerge, keep the soil barely damp, never soggy. Harden seedlings off for 14 days before planting them outside after all danger of frost has passed in spring.

Special Uses

Cut Flowers The clump-forming varieties produce nice stems for floral arrangements, and they are extremely long lasting. *Sedum* 'Autumn Joy'/'Herbst-freude' is one of the all-time favorite cut flowers. Leaves and flowers are quite unusual on many varieties and make a good contrast to other perennials. Cut stems when the flower color is most appealing to you. Keep them in water at all times. Just before arranging them, cut the lower stem at a slant underwater. Also remove all leaves that would be underwater in the final arrangement. Keep flowers in cool water for best color and longest life.

Dried Flowers Many varieties produce clusters of flowers at the tips of the stems. If left outdoors on the plant, these often dry into interesting seed heads. Cut these off at the end of the season for use in arrangements.

You can also cut stems earlier in the season if you prefer. After cutting stems, strip off the leaves. Then hang the stems upside down in a warm, well-ventilated area until they're completely dry. Flowers often fade considerably.

Sources

Bluestone Perennials, 7211 Middle Ridge Rd., Madison, OH 44057, (800) 852-5243

ForestFarm, 990 Tetherow Rd., Williams, OR 97544, (541) 846-7269

Joy Creek Nursery, 20300 NW Watson Rd., Scappoose, OR 97056, (503) 543-7474

Siskiyou Rare Plant Nursery, 2115 Talent Ave., Talent, OR 97540, (541) 535-7103

Squaw Mountain Gardens, P.O. Box 496, Estacada, OR 97023, (503) 630-5458

Venero Gardens, 5985 Seamans Dr., Shorewood, MN 55331, (952) 474-8550

VARIETIES

VARIETY	COLOR	HEIGHT	HARDINESS
Sedum acre			
(Goldmoss Stonecrop)	Bright yellow	4″	−40°F
'Aureum'	Light yellow	4″	−40°F

Goldmoss Stonecrop is a very vigorous spreader. Its overlapping leaves are very small but so dense as to make this an effective ground cover. It flowers heavily in early summer. The young shoots and leaves of 'Aureum' are edged in gold in cool spring weather.

VARIETY	COLOR	HEIGHT	HARDINESS
Sedum aizoon			
(Aizoon Stonecrop)	Yellow	14″	−30°F
'Aurantiacum'	Orangish yellow	14″	−30°F

This Stonecrop falls somewhere between a ground-hugging and upright type. 'Aurantiacum' has reddish stems and deeper colored flowers.

VARIETY	COLOR	HEIGHT	HARDINESS
Sedum alboroseum/Hylotelephium erythrostictum			
'Mediovariegatum'	Pink	14″	−40°F

This selection has bluish green leaves with creamy yellow centers and blooms in fall. It does have a tendency to revert to green, and, though short, may need to be staked.

VARIETY	COLOR	HEIGHT	HARDINESS
Sedum album			
(White Stonecrop)	White	6″	−40°F
'Coral Carpet'*****	White	6″	−40°F
'Murale'	White	4″	−40°F

White Stonecrop is a good ground cover blooming in early summer. The foliage of 'Coral Carpet' is tinted salmon orange in spring while 'Murale' has a lovely maroon hue in its stems and leaves throughout the season.

VARIETY	COLOR	HEIGHT	HARDINESS
Sedum cauticola/Hylotelephium cauticola			
'Lidakense'*****	Rose red	4″	−40°F

A wonderful plant for rock or wall gardens, this Stonecrop is a vigorous spreader. It has small, rounded leaves that are tinged purple in cooler seasons and flowers in late summer. It tolerates higher soil moisture than most other Stonecrops.

VARIETY	COLOR	HEIGHT	HARDINESS
Sedum floriferum			
(Bailey's Gold Stonecrop)			
'Weihenstephaner Gold'*****	Yellow	4″	−40°F

Making an excellent fine-textured ground cover, this Stonecrop is a prolific bloomer with attractive dark green leaves. The foliage shows red tones in cool weather, and the flower buds and seed heads are also red.

VARIETY	COLOR	HEIGHT	HARDINESS
*Sedum kamtschasticum******			
(Kamschatka Stonecrop)	Yellow	6″	−40°F
'Variegatum'	Orange yellow	4″	−40°F

The species has dark green, sharply toothed leaves while 'Variegatum' is noted for its creamy white variegated leaves that are often tinged pink. These plants bloom in early summer.

VARIETY	COLOR	HEIGHT	HARDINESS
Sedum nevii			
(Nevius Stionecrop)	White	4″	−30°F

VARIETY	COLOR	HEIGHT	HARDINESS
Silver Frost™	Starry white	4″	−30°F

This Virginia native forms a mound of green leaves that are tinged purple. It blooms in early summer and tolerates light shade. Silver Frost™ with its thick leaves also hugs the ground and is great in the rock garden.

Sedum reflexum

(Recurved Yellow Stonecrop)	Golden yellow	12″	−40°F
'Angelina'	Golden yellow	6″	−30°F

Native to Europe, this plant has narrow, waxy, grayish colored leaves and colorful flowers in midsummer. The leaves are served in soups and salads abroad. The golden foliage of 'Angelina' takes on amber tones in cool fall weather.

Sedum sexangulare

(Hexagon Stonecrop)	Yellow	4″	−40°F

This is a tidy little plant with greenish leaves that curl up around the stem. It blooms in early to mid summer.

Sedum sieboldii/Hylotelephium sieboldii

(October Daphne)	Pink	8″	−40°F
'Mediovariegatum'*****	Pink	6″	−40°F
'Nana'	Pink	4″	−40°F

Blooming in September and October, this is one of the last of the low Stonecrops to flower. 'Mediovariegatum' has rounded, gray leaves that are variegated white. 'Nana' is delightful in the garden and can also be used in containers.

Sedum spectabile/Hylotelephium spectabile

(Showy Stonecrop)

'Brilliant'	Deep pink	20″	−40°F
'Hot Stuff'	Purplish pink	12″	−40°F
'Meteor'	Carmine red	20″	−40°F
'Neon'*****	Bright purplish pink	20″	−40°F
'Pink Chablis'	Vibrant pink	16″	−40°F
'Stardust'	Pale pink to white	20″	−40°F

'Variegatum' (see *Sedum alboroseum* 'Mediovariegatum')

'Hot Stuff' is a sturdy, compact plant selection ideal for containers. 'Neon' is the showiest of these varieties in bloom. 'Pink Chablis' has bluish green leaves with variable white margins. They all bloom in late summer and fall.

Sedum spurium

(Two Row Stonecrop)	Pink	6″	−40°F
'Bronze Carpet'	Red	4″	−40°F
'Dragon's Blood' ('Schorbuser Blut')	Rose red	4″	−40°F
'Elizabeth'	Deep red	4″	−40°F
'Fire Glow' ('Fulda Glow') ('Fuldaglut')	Rose red	4″	−40°F
'Green Mantle'	Light pink	4″	−40°F
'John Creech'	Rose pink	4″	−40°F
'Red Carpet'	Rosy red	4″	−40°F
'Ruby Mantle'*****	Cerise	6″	−40°F
'Tricolor'	Pale pink	4″	−40°F

Two Row Stonecrop is popular for its summer flowers and interesting leaf colorations. It forms a vigorous, tangled mat of foliage valued as a ground cover. 'Bronze Carpet' has thick green leaves that turn bronzy as the season pro-

'Autumn Joy'/'Herbstfreude'

Sedum kamtschaticum

Sedum reflexum

'Ruby Glow'/'Robustum'

gresses. 'Dragon's Blood' ('Schorbuser Blut') describes both the flowers and the tone of the green foliage. 'Elizabeth' has green leaves with red margins while the green foliage of 'Fire Glow' shows reddish orange tones. 'Green Mantle' and 'John Creech' have attractive deep green foliage. Both form dense mats, making them excellent for use as ground covers. The leaves of 'Red Carpet' are a deep red burgundy. 'Ruby Mantle' has consistently red foliage. 'Tricolor' rarely flowers, and its leaves are a mixture of green, pink, and white.

VARIETY	COLOR	HEIGHT	HARDINESS
Sedum telephium/Hylotelephium telephium			
(Upright Stonecrop)			
'Atropurpureum'	Pale pink	24″	−40°F

'Atropurpureum' is grown more for foliage color than for its flowers. The heavy textured leaves are mahogany red. Note that 'Atropurpureum' will get floppy if overwatered and overfertilized!

Sedum ternatum			
(Whorled Stonecrop)	White	6″	−30°F
'Larinem Park'	White	6″	−30°F

These plants are covered with starry flowers in spring and are perhaps the most shade tolerant of the Stonecrops. The fleshy leaves are green but may have darker tones in cool weather. This is an excellent rock garden plant.

Sedum/Hylotelephium (Named varieties and hybrids)			
Autumn Charm™ ('Lajos')	Bronze pink	18″	−40°F
Autumn Delight™ ('Beka')	Light pink	24″	−40°F
'Autumn Fire'*****	Bronze pink	24″	−40°F
'Autumn Joy' ('Herbstfreude')	Bronze pink	24″	−40°F
'Bertram Anderson'*****	Dusky pink	6″	−40°F
'Carl'*****	Bright pink	20″	−40°F
'Cloud Walker'	Mauve	16″	−40°F
'Elsie's Gold'	Dark pink	18″	−40°F
'Lynda Windsor'	Ruby red	14″	−40°F
'Maestro'*****	Light pink	24″	−40°F
'Matrona'	Pale pink	30″	−40°F
'Mr. Goodbud'	Purplish pink	18″	−40°F
'Postman's Pride'	Pinkish red	20″	−40°F
'Purple Emperor'	Light pink	16″	−40°F
'Red Cauli'	Pinkish red	16″	−40°F
'Rosy Glow'	Ruby red	8″	−40°F
'Ruby Glow' ('Robustum')	Ruby red	12″	−40°F
'Vera Jameson'	Dusky pink	12″	−40°F
'Xenox'*****	Medium to dark pink	18″	−40°F

Autumn Charm™ has green leaves with creamy yellow edges while those of Autumn Delight™ have chartreuse yellow centers and blue green edges. 'Autumn Fire' is similar to 'Autumn Joy' but is sturdier. 'Bertram Anderson' has small, rounded smoky purple leaves, bright flowers, and excellent vigor and is a much better garden plant than the well-known 'Vera Jameson.' 'Carl' has pinkish stems and rich gray green leaves with pinkish edges. It is a sturdy, vigorous plant. 'Elsie's Gold' has green leaves edged yellow fading to cream as the season progresses. The foliage of 'Maestro' is a distinctive bluish green. while its stems are bright purple. 'Lynda Windsor,' 'Matrona,' 'Postman's Pride,' 'Purple Emperor,' 'Red Cauli,' and 'Xenox' all have purplish foliage. These plants do best in full sun in soils that drain freely. Do not overwater or overfertilize them as this will cause stems to be floppy.

'Eileen May Robinson'

TANACETUM

(tan-uh-SEE-tum)

CAUCASIAN DAISY, PAINTED DAISY, SNOW DAISY

Bloom Time	Expected Longevity	Maintenance	Years to Bloom	Preferred Light
Early summer	10+ years	Medium	From seed: 2 years From potted plant: 1 year	Full sun

These perennials are hardy, have stunning flowers, bloom profusely, are easy to propagate, and make lovely cut flowers. They are easy to grow and rarely bothered by insects or disease. The foliage of these plants will be unattractive if stressed by high heat or drought. Overcome this tendency with proper care and lots of water. Also, these Daisies can be somewhat difficult to find, but are well worth seeking out.

How These Daisies Grow

These plants have fibrous roots, which form a dense mat as they mature. Foliage varies from feathery and carrot-like to rounded and deeply indented. Stems may be long and wiry or multi-branched and dense. Flowers range in size from button-like to as wide as 3 to 5 inches (7.5 to 12.5 cm). Many of these have yellow to gold centers for a lovely contrast to the outer petals. Some of these Daisies self-seed freely if spent blossoms are not removed.

Where to Plant

Site and Light These Daisies are high-light plants. They produce abundant foliage and bloom in full sun. If placed in shade, plants get leggy, bloom less, and often require staking.

Soil and Moisture All of these Daisies like a loose, rich soil that drains freely. If you have clay or rocky soil, replace it with loam or build a raised bed. Add lots of organic matter to any soil. Good amendments include peat moss, compost, and rotted manure. These keep the soil moist and cool but allow it to drain freely. The loose soil encourages rapid root growth, which results in lush foliage and plentiful bloom. If soil is not properly prepared, the plants will die out in winter.

Spacing Space Daisies in relation to the overall height of the plant, giving taller varieties more room than smaller ones. Each plant will spread out with time, taking up more space than you might think from the original size of the plant.

Companions

These Daisies combine beautifully with a wide range of perennials, including *Aquilegia* (Columbine), *Baptisia* (False Indigo), *Clematis recta* (Ground Clematis), *Delphinium* (Larkspur), *Dianthus* (Pinks), *Geranium* (Cranesbill), *Heuchera* (Coral Bells), *Iris* (Siberian Iris), *Nepeta* (Catmint), *Paeonia* (Peony), *Salvia* (Sage), *Thermopsis caroliniana* (Carolina Lupine), and *Veronica* (Speedwell). Although the possibilities are numerous, consider the following suggestions as a starting point from which you can develop additional combinations: *Tanacetum*–Coccineum Group 'Robinson's Rose' (Painted Daisy) planted with *Baptisia australis* (Blue False Indigo) and *Iris* 'Gull's Wing' (Siberian Iris); or *Tanacetum*

niveum (Snow Daisy) combined with *Paeonia* 'Nick Shaylor' (Peony) and *Thermopsis caroliniana* (Carolina Lupine).

Planting

Bare Root Plant bare root stock as soon as you can work the ground in spring. Remove plants from their shipping package immediately. Snip off broken or damaged root tips. Soak plants overnight in room-temperature water. Place a small amount of superphosphate in the base of the planting hole. If you're an organic gardener, use bone meal instead. Fill the hole with soil. Place the crown 1 inch (2.5 cm) under the soil surface. Fill in with soil, firm with your fingers, and water immediately. Dissolve ½ cup (about 114 g) 10-10-10 fertilizer in 1 gallon (about 4 liters) of water. Pour ½ cup (about 120 ml) of this starter solution around the base of each plant. If you prefer organic fertilizer, use fish emulsion instead.

Potted Plants Plant Daisies after all danger of frost has passed in spring. If the soil in the pot is dry, water it, and let it drain overnight. Tap the plant out of the pot without disturbing the root ball. Plant it at the same depth as in the pot, after preparing the hole in a manner similar to that for a bare root plant. Fill in with soil, firm with your fingers, and water immediately. Pour ½ cup (about 120 ml) of the starter solution around the base of each plant.

How to Care for Daisies

Water Water is critical to rapid and lush growth. Daisies form foliage that is thick and deep green, and form a mass of flower buds when properly watered. Water whenever the soil starts to dry out. If you prepare the soil properly, it will never be soggy. These plants are often listed as drought tolerant; this is true, but they will look much better if watered regularly.

Mulch Place a 2-inch (5-cm) layer of organic mulch around the base of plants when the ground warms up in spring. Good mulches include dried grass clippings, pulverized leaves, and pine needles. Mulch keeps the soil moist and cool and inhibits annual weed growth.

Fertilizing Painted Daisies are heavy feeders. They respond well to frequent small feedings. Sprinkle tiny amounts of 10-10-10 fertilizer around the base of each plant every other week. Water immediately to dissolve the granules and carry nutrients into the root zone.

If you prefer organic fertilizers, use alfalfa meal (rabbit pellets), blood meal, bonemeal, compost, cow manure, fish emulsion, Milorganite, or rotted horse manure. Bonemeal must be mixed into the soil at planting time to be effective.

Weeding Kill perennial weeds before planting Daisies. Use mulch to control annual weeds. Occasionally, a weed or two will spring up close to the main stem of the flower. Pull these by hand. The earth under mulch stays moist, which makes weeding easy.

Staking Some of the taller varieties may require staking, but this is usually the case only if they are planted in too much shade. Tie their stems to the stakes with soft material in loose figure-eight knots. Pea stakes work well as hidden supports for bushier varieties.

Deadheading Some of these Daisies self-seed aggressively and can become quite invasive. As soon as blossoms fade, pinch them off immediately unless you want a colony of seedlings around the mother plant.

Cutting Back Cut Painted Daisies back to the ground after the first flowers fade if the foliage begins to look ratty. New growth will emerge and be more attractive. Paying more attention to watering may eliminate the need for cutting plants back.

Winter Protection In the first year, cover plants with a 6-inch (15-cm) layer of winter mulch after the ground freezes to a depth of 3 inches (7.5 cm). Good mulches include marsh hay, clean straw, whole leaves, and pine needles. Remove these as soon as the ground warms up in spring to prevent crown rot. In subsequent years, you need not provide winter protection if there is snow by mid-December.

Problems

Insects Parts of these Daisies are used in organic insecticides. Insects do not damage them.

Disease Disease is rarely a problem. If foliage turns yellow or begins to look bedraggled, it's generally due to extreme heat or lack of water. Cut the plant back to the ground as outlined under "Cutting Back."

Propagation

Division Divide mature plants every 2 to 4 years for the overall health of the plant and also to increase stock. Dig up clumps in early spring just as new growth starts. Cut the clump into sections, each containing several stems attached to a healthy supply of roots. Plant these divisions immediately as you would a bare root plant. Keep the soil consistently moist.

Stem Cuttings Take cuttings early in the season when the plant is growing vigorously. Remove cuttings from stem tips. Each cutting should have three sets of leaves. Make the final cut ¼ inch (6 mm) below a node. Remove the lower leaves. Dip the cut end in rooting hormone, and tap off any excess powder. Then place cuttings in moist growing medium until the plants form solid root balls. Place them in a permanent location at this time.

Seed The species (wild plants) and some of the named varieties, which may only be available as seed, come true. Plant seed indoors 12 weeks before the last expected frost in spring. Press the seed into moist growing medium, barely covering it. Keep plants at temperatures above 68°F (20°C). Germination normally occurs within 20 days. When the seedlings have a second pair of leaves, plant them in individual pots. Harden them off for 14 days before planting them outdoors after all danger of frost has passed in spring.

Special Uses

Cut Flowers Daisies are among the finest perennials for cut flowers. Cut stems when flowers are at their peak. Keep the stems in water until moving them indoors. Then place the stems in 110°F (43°C) water. Then put that container in a cool spot for several hours or longer, allowing the water to cool down gradually before arranging.

Dried Flowers Unfortunately, these Daisies resist drying. Try drying individual flowers in a desiccant, but expect flowers to fade badly.

Sources

Ambergate Gardens, 8730 County Rd. 43, Chaska, MN 55318, (877) 211-9769

B & T World Seeds, Paguignan, 34210 Aigues-Vives, France (00 33 04 68 91 29 63)

Crimson Sage, P.O. Box 83, Orleans, CA 95556, (530) 627-3457

Fieldstone Gardens, Inc., 55 Quaker Lane, Vassalboro, ME 04989, (207) 923-3836

Green Mountain Transplants, Inc., 670 Alfred Rd., Arundel, ME 04046, (207) 282-6444

Park Seed Co., 1 Parkton Ave., Greenwood, SC 29649, (800) 213-0076

The Sandy Mush Herb Nursery, 316 Surrett Cove Rd., Leicester, NC 28748, (828) 683-2014

Well-Sweep Herb Farm, 205 Mt. Bethel Rd., Port Murray, NJ 07865, (908) 852-5390

'Robinson's Crimson'

VARIETIES

Most of these plants were once classified as **Chrysanthemums** and may appear in publications and source lists that way.

VARIETY	COLOR	HEIGHT	HARDINESS
Tanacetum–Coccineum Group			
(Painted Daisy)			
'Brenda'	Cerise pink/gold	24″	–40°F
'Duro'*****	Purple red/gold	30″	–40°F
'Eileen May Robinson'	Salmon pink/gold	24″	–40°F
'James Kelway'	Dark red/gold	36″	–40°F
'Mont Blanc'	White/creamy yellow (D)	24″	–40°F
'Robinson's Crimson'	Crimson/gold	24″	–40°F
'Robinson's Pink'	Light pink/gold	24″	–40°F
'Robinson's Red'*****	Scarlet red/gold	24″	–40°F
'Robinson's Rose'	Rose pink/gold	24″	–40°F
Robinson's Mix	Varied/gold	24″	–40°F

These perennials bloom early in the summer and are excellent for cutting. The deep-green leaves are finely divided and remain attractive as long as you water plants well. Robinson's Mix is a seed-grown strain that produces plants with light pink, deep pink, red, white, and near-white flowers.

Tanacetum corymbosum			
(Caucasian Daisy)	White/gold	36″	–40°F

This plant hugs the ground with a mound of deep-green, finely divided foliage. It blooms in midsummer with numerous small, daisy-like flowers. It can self-seed and be invasive if not deadheaded.

*Tanacetum niveum******			
(Snow Daisy)	White/gold	24″	–30°F
'Jackpot'	White/gold	24″	–30°F

Despite its somewhat short life span, this fine perennial deserves to be much more widely grown. It has finely divided, silvery green aromatic foliage and blooms with numerous small flowers in early to midsummer. 'Jackpot' is an exceptionally heavy blooming variety that may only be available as seed. Snow Daisy thrives in a variety of soil types as long as drainage is good. Both may self-seed.

Tanacetum parthenium			
(Midsummer Daisy)			
'Snowball'	Ivory white/light yellow (D)	24″	–30°F

The species produces frilly white flowers with bright gold centers but is very invasive. 'Snowball' has multi-branched stems; deep-green leaves that are toothed, hairy, and pungent; and small double (D) pompom flowers that bloom in mid- to late summer. It will self-seed and can be invasive if spent blossoms are not removed.

Tanacetum vulgare			
(Common Tansy)			
'Isla Gold'	Yellow gold (button)	24″	–40°F

The species is very invasive, although prized by organic gardeners as a refuge for beneficial insects. 'Isla Gold' is less aggressive; has bright yellow, ferny foliage; and clusters of button-like flowers. Its foliage is most striking early in the season. It blooms from mid- to late summer.

Thermopsis caroliniana

THERMOPSIS

(thur-MOP-suhs)

FALSE LUPINE

Bloom Time	Expected Longevity	Maintenance	Years to Bloom	Preferred Light
Early summer	25 years	Low	From seed: 2 years From potted plant: 1 year	Full sun

False Lupine is an easily grown, vertical accent plant with many potential uses. It grows well where true Lupines (*Lupinus*) don't. False Lupine has green to gray green, cloverlike leaves and showy spires of yellow, pealike flowers. The flowers are good for cutting, and the mature seedpods are an interesting addition to dried arrangements. False Lupine is a long-lived perennial that endures considerable neglect and offers excellent pest resistance.

How False Lupines Grow

False Lupine grows from thick, fleshy roots into a vertical plant with numerous stems. With age, root systems become semiwoody and quite wide-spreading. Each stem develops an elongated flower head similar in shape to those of Lupines. After the blossoms fade, narrow, flat seedpods form, which turn brittle and brown by the end of the season. These contain numerous round, dark brown seeds which, if allowed to fall to the ground, will germinate freely.

period. As with the outdoor method, sow the seed over moist germination medium in a seed tray; cover them about ⅛ inch (3 mm) deep. Then slide the tray into a perforated plastic bag, and place it in the crisper of your refrigerator for about 6 weeks. Some gardeners have reported success putting the seed tray in the freezer for 7 to 14 days. After this moist-chilling, remove the seed flat, and place it in an area with a temperature of about 70°F (21°C). Seedlings should emerge within 15 to 20 days and can be planted in individual pots as they develop their first set of true leaves. Harden them off for 14 days prior to planting them outside after all danger of frost has passed in spring.

For uniform germination, old seed may require *scarification* in addition to a moist-chilling period. Commercially this is often done by treatment with sulfuric acid, but that is not a practical process for home gardeners. Nicking the hard seed coat prior to sowing is a much safer method. Opposite the eye on the seed, barely file, prick, or scratch through the seed coat. Sometimes, just soaking the seed of False Lupines in warm water for 24 hours will do the job. Either method allows moisture to enter the seed and begin the germination process.

The other easy way to increase the number of plants by seed is to let plants self-sow in the garden. Seed will fall to the ground in fall, and winter will provide the necessary moist-chilling period. Seedlings will emerge the next spring and can be transplanted in a fashion similar to other methods. Avoid the use of summer mulches late in the season and preemergent herbicides at any time if you wish to encourage self-sowing in this way.

Special Uses

Cut Flowers Both the flower spikes and gray green leaves of False Lupine are desirable in floral arrangements. Cut the stems just as the bottom florets open, and place them in water immediately. The flowers do well in arrangements without special conditioning.

Dried Pods If old flower spikes are allowed to remain on the plant, they will develop into attractive seed heads made up of flattened, narrow, upright pods clustered together. These add an interesting vertical accent to fall and winter gardens. They can also be cut for use in fresh and dried arrangements. By late in the season, these seedpods will turn brown and crack open to spread their seed onto the ground.

Sources

Fieldstone Gardens, Inc., 55 Quaker Lane, Vassalboro, ME 04989, (207) 923-3836

ForestFarm, 990 Tetherow Rd., Williams, OR 97544, (541) 846-7269

Niche Gardens, 1111 Dawson Rd., Chapel Hill, NC 27516, (919) 967-0078

Prairie Moon Nursery, 32115 Prairie Lane, Winona, MN 55987, (866) 417-8156

RareFind Nursery, 957 Patterson Rd., Jackson, NJ 08527, (732) 833-0613

VARIETIES

VARIETY	COLOR	HEIGHT	HARDINESS
*Thermopsis caroliniana***** (Carolina False Lupine)	Rich yellow	48″	−40°F

*Thermopsis caroliniana*****
(Carolina False Lupine)
This, one of the best vertical accent plants, also happens to be nearly maintenance free. The plant's early summer lupine-like flowers mature into narrow, flattened seed pods later in the season. The pods change color as they mature and are wonderful in both fresh and dried floral arrangements.

Thermopsis caroliniana

Immature seedpods of *Thermopsis caroliniana*

VARIETY	COLOR	HEIGHT	HARDINESS
Thermopsis chinensis			
(Chinese False Lupine)	Bright yellow	24″	−40°F
'Sophia'	Bright canary yellow	18″	−40°F

With its bushy compact appearance, Chinese False Lupine is an excellent fit in urban gardens. It offers compound, fine-textured foliage and numerous spikes of brilliant colored blooms in late spring and early summer. It thrives in full sun and tolerates dry conditions once mature. Soil should drain freely.

Thermopsis lanceolata			
(Lanceleaf False Lupine)	Sulfur yellow	18″	−40°F

Despite interesting flowers and unique seed pods, this plant often loses its leaves after bloom in midsummer. Unfortunately, it is sometimes sold as Carolina Lupine. The latter is bolder, more vigorous, and a much better plant.

Thermopsis lupinoides (see ***Thermopsis lanceolata***)

Thermopsis montana			
(Mountain False Lupine)	Deep yellow	24″	−30°F

This western species is closely related to *Thermopsis caroliniana* (Carolina Lupine). It has a compact, upright appearance with deep green foliage contrasting beautifully to the spires of deep yellow flowers that bloom earlier than its cousin.

Thermopsis villosa (see ***Thermopsis caroliniana***)

'Red Cloud'

TRADESCANTIA

(treh-des-KANTJ-ee-uh)

SPIDERWORT

Bloom Time	Expected Longevity	Maintenance	Years to Bloom	Preferred Light
Early summer to early fall	5 years	Medium	From seed: 2 years From potted plant: 1 year	Light shade to full sun

Spiderworts are unusual-looking perennials that bloom freely over a long period in summer. Blooms are especially brilliant during cool, moist weather. The flowers open in the morning, only to melt away later in the day. This characteristic is either magical or maddening, depending on your point of view. The shape of the plant's foliage resembles that of the indoor Spider Plant, making it somewhat whimsical in nature. The plant grows vigorously with proper care. It is also very disease and insect resistant. However, if neglected, the plant may die back and look bedraggled by midsummer. Spiderworts also can suffer damage in cold climates during severe winters with little snow.

How Spiderworts Grow

Spiderworts grow rapidly from generally white, fleshy roots into dense clumps of narrow, arching leaves. At the tips of stems a tight cluster of buds forms. These do not bloom all at once, but instead intermittently throughout the season from early summer to early fall. Although each individual flower lasts only one day, these perennials produce such an abundance of buds that plants are showered in dainty blooms during the peak season. If allowed to form seed, Spiderworts self-sow very freely, but seedlings from the named selections will not be identical to their parents.

Where to Plant

Site and Light In cold climates, Spiderworts will grow in a wide range of light conditions. Best flowering occurs in full sun, but only if plants are kept consistently moist. Lightly shaded areas provide cool, moist growing conditions with less fuss and still result in good bloom. Placing Spiderworts in natural areas and near woods works well if they have enough water.

Soil and Moisture These perennials relish evenly moist soils with good drainage. Highly fertile, moist soils will lead to very rapid spread of Spiderworts. Amend soils with compost, leaf mold, peat moss, or rotted manure to help soils drain freely but retain moisture.

Spacing Plants spread quickly and mature by the end of their first season. Space them 18 to 24 inches (45 to 60 cm) apart in groups of three to five plants, or mass them in wild areas for a stunning effect.

Companions

Tradescantia (Spiderwort) combines well with *Alchemilla mollis* (Lady's Mantle), *Astilbe* (False Spirea), *Filipendula vulgaris* (Dropwort), *Geranium* (Cranesbill), *Heuchera micrantha* 'Palace Purple' (Small-Flowered Alumroot), *Hosta* (Hosta), *Lamium maculatum* (Spotted Dead Nettle), *Phlox stolonifera* (Creeping Phlox), and *Pulmonaria* (Lungwort).

Planting

Bare Root Plant bare root stock as soon as you can work the ground in spring. Remove the plants from their shipping package immediately. Snip off broken or damaged root tips. Soak plants overnight in room-temperature water. Place a small amount of superphosphate in the base of the planting hole. Fill the hole with soil. Place the crown about 1 inch (2.5 cm) below the soil surface. Fill in with soil, firm with your fingers, and water immediately. Dissolve ½ cup (about 114 g) 10-10-10 fertilizer in 1 gallon (about 4 liters) of water, and pour ½ cup (about 120 ml) of this solution around the base of each plant. If you prefer organic fertilizer, use fish emulsion instead.

Potted Plants Plant potted Spiderworts after all danger of frost has passed in spring. If the soil in the pot is dry, soak it, and let it stand overnight. Plant Spiderworts at the same depth as in the pot, after preparing the hole in a manner similar to that for a bare root plant. Fill in with soil, firm with your fingers, and water immediately. Pour ½ cup (about 120 ml) of starter solution around the base of each plant.

How to Care for Spiderworts

Water Spiderworts require evenly moist soil throughout the growing season. Regular watering during dry periods prevents foliage from going dormant during the heat of summer. If plants do not receive enough water, they will turn brown and look awful. They are not diseased, just stressed. When you water, soak the soil to a depth of 8 to 10 inches (20 to 25 cm) each time. It is impossible to overwater this plant if the soil drains freely.

Mulch A summer mulch keeps the soil moist and cool while inhibiting weed growth. Apply a 2-inch (5-cm) layer of dried grass clippings, shredded leaves, compost, shredded bark, or pine needles around the base of each plant after the soil has warmed up in late spring or early summer. Replace the mulch as necessary throughout the growing season. Mulching Spiderworts is one of the best ways to keep them looking their best.

Fertilizing Sprinkle 10-10-10 fertilizer around the base of each plant just as growth starts in early spring. Water immediately to dissolve the granules and move the nutrients into the root zone. Give Spiderworts a second feeding of granular fertilizer as the buds begin to form, or foliar feed every 2 weeks with a water-soluble fertilizer right through the bloom period.

If you prefer organic fertilizers, use alfalfa meal (rabbit pellets), blood meal, bonemeal, compost, fish emulsion, Milorganite, or rotted manures. Bonemeal must be mixed into the soil at planting time to be effective.

Staking The natural growth of Spiderworts is somewhat lax and floppy, but staking is not necessary. If you don't like the plant's look, place it in natural settings rather than in the border. Plants placed in such areas are frequently neglected. Make sure to water them consistently, especially if placed under trees.

Deadheading Removal of blossoms is generally not necessary for aesthetic reasons, as the old blossoms seem to melt away as they fade each afternoon. However, to prevent self-seeding, you should remove the seedpods before they turn brown.

Pruning Foliage will turn brown and look messy if the plants don't get enough water. If this happens, cut them back to within 4 inches (10 cm) of the ground. This drastic pruning results in a fresh new mound of foliage if the plant is properly watered. You may even be rewarded with some additional flowers late in the season. This shearing often prevents Spiderworts from self-seeding.

Winter Protection Since open, excessively cold winters can damage Spiderworts, be sure to cover these perennials with 6 inches (15 cm) of mulch if there is little snow by early winter. Use marsh hay, clean straw, whole leaves, or pine needles. Do not apply the cover until the ground has permanently frozen, and remove it as soon as the weather warms up in early spring to prevent crown rot.

Problems

Insects Spiderworts are rarely bothered by insects, although certain mealybugs and caterpillars are known to feed on them on occasion.

Disease Botrytis blight can infect Spiderworts, but this is rare. Remove and destroy any infected plant parts. These perennials should recover without any other treatment. Usually, if the plant turns brown, it's from lack of water rather than from a disease.

Propagation

Division Division is the preferred method for propagating named selections of Spiderworts, since they do not come true from seed. Divide the plants every 2 to 3 years to control their spread and to keep plants healthy. They are best divided just as new growth begins in spring. Dig up the entire plant, and use a sharp knife or spade to cut it into sections. Make sure each division has several strong shoots and a healthy root system. Plant these new divisions immediately as you would a bare root plant.

Cuttings Although not commonly done, Spiderworts can be increased by stem cuttings. These root most easily and quickly if taken prior to the formation of flower buds. Cuttings should have no fewer than two leaf nodes. Cut just under the lower node. Dust the cut end in rooting hormone, and tap off any excess powder. Then stick the cutting in rooting medium. Keep the medium evenly moist during the rooting process, which usually takes 1 to 2 weeks. Transplant rooted cuttings to pots or a protected garden location once a healthy mass of roots has formed.

Seed Seed propagation is not recommended for named varieties, as it will not produce plants similar to the parents. If you don't care about that or if you want to grow wild species, then propagate Spiderworts from seed. Sow the seed 12 weeks before the last expected frost in spring. Press the seed into moist germinating medium. Then place the seed tray in an area with a temperature between 70°F and 72°F (21°C to

22°C) during the day with about a 10°F (6°C) drop at night. Germination typically occurs within 1 to 2 weeks, and the seedlings are ready for planting in pots in about 3 to 4 weeks. Harden young plants off for 14 days before planting them outside after all danger of frost has passed in spring.

Special Uses

Cut Flowers Since individual blooms are so short-lived, the usefulness of Spiderworts as cut flowers is limited. Nevertheless, some arrangers use these perennials in fresh arrangements if only for the unusual foliage and unique clusters of buds.

Dried Flowers The blooms of Spiderworts are not good for drying.

Sources

Bluestone Perennials, 7211 Middle Ridge Rd., Madison, OH 44057, (800) 852-5243

ForestFarm, 990 Tetherow Rd., Williams, OR 97544, (541) 846-7269

Fraser's Thimble Farms, 175 Arbutus Rd., Salt Spring Island, BC V8K 1A3, Canada, (250) 537-5788

Goodness Grows, P.O. Box 311, Lexington, GA 30648, (706) 743-5055

Niche Gardens, 1111 Dawson Rd., Chapel Hill, NC 27516, (919) 967-0078

Well-Sweep Herb Farm, 205 Mt Bethel Rd., Port Murray, NJ 07865, (908) 852-5390

'Zwanenburg Blue'

Typical bud cluster

VARIETIES

VARIETY	COLOR	HEIGHT	HARDINESS
Tradescantia–Andersoniana Group			
'Bilberry Ice'	White/lavender splash	18″	−30°F
'Blushing Bride'	White	18″	−30°F
'Concord Grape'*****	Rich purple	18″	−30°F
'Danielle'	White	18″	−30°F
'Hawaiian Punch'	Pinkish red	24″	−30°F
'Innocence'	Creamy white	24″	−30°F
'Iris Prichard'	White suffused violet	18″	−30°F
'Leonora'	Violet blue	18″	−30°F
'Little Doll'	Light pink blue	14″	−30°F
'Osprey'	White blue	24″	−30°F
'Pauline'	Mauve pink	18″	−30°F
'Purple Dome'	Rosy purple	24″	−30°F
'Purple Profusion'	Deep blue purple	24″	−30°F
'Red Cloud'	Rose red	18″	−30°F
'Red Grape'*****	Red violet	24″	−30°F
'Satin Doll'	Pink	16″	−30°F
'Snowcap'*****	Pure white	18″	−30°F
'Zwanenburg Blue'*****	Blue violet	24″	−30°F

These named varieties are among the best for use in cold climates. However, in severe winters they may die out if not protected with a winter mulch. 'Concord Grape' and 'Red Grape' both have lovely bluish green foliage. The small size of 'Little Doll' and 'Satin Doll' make them excellent choices as container plants. The leaves of 'Blushing Bride' emerge with pink blotches at their bases. As the foliage matures, the pink coloration changes to white.

Tradescantia ohiensis			
(Ohio Spiderwort)	Blue, pink, purple, white	30″	−40°F

This eastern U.S. native blooms from late spring into summer. Ohio Spiderwort is far more sun and drought tolerant than the commonly available forms of this perennial. It is ideally suited to use in meadows and similar natural sites.

Tradescantia (Named variety)			
'Blue and Gold' ('Sweet Kate')	Deep blue	18″	−30°F

The golden foliage of this variety is most pronounced early in the season. Provide protection from afternoon sun to maintain that color.

'Greenland'/'Groenland'

TULIPA

(TEW-lih-puh)

TULIP

Bloom Time	Expected Longevity	Maintenance	Years to Bloom	Preferred Light
Early to late spring	5 to 15 years	High	From seed: 5 to 7 years From bulb: 1 year	Full sun

Since Tulip bulbs need a period of winter chill, these plants thrive in cold climates. For spring color, Tulips are hard to beat. They come in a wide variety of colors, heights, and shapes. By mixing varieties, you'll have extended bloom over a period of weeks. Tulips also make excellent cut flowers. Some varieties are especially fragrant. Although some gardeners plant hybrid Tulips as annuals, others get years of beautiful bloom through extra care. The species or wild Tulips are ideal for rock gardens and often spread quickly. They are extremely long-lived. Most Tulips are insect and disease resistant as well.

How Tulips Grow

Tulips grow from fall-planted bulbs, which, like onions, are composed of fleshy scales surrounding a preformed flower bud. The scales provide food storage for the bulbs. At their base is a flat spot known as the basal plate. Once planted, bulbs grow roots from this flat area until winter cold stops their underground growth. At the right soil temperature, in spring the bulbs produce stems which pop through the ground. Each stem produces one or more flowers. The leaves produce food to be stored in the bulbs, then turn yellow and die back. Flowers of species Tulips produce capsules containing flat, winged seeds. All Tulip bulbs produce smaller bulbs, known as offsets, which in turn grow into new plants. Hybrid Tulips will often diminish in vigor if not grown properly. Species Tulips can live for many years. They also reproduce quickly by sending out underground stems, or stolons, that produce numerous bulblets. These little bulbs in turn mature, giving a mass effect in the garden. Since species Tulips are generally small, they look best in large groups. They require little maintenance and are gaining in popularity.

Where to Plant

Site and Light Tulips thrive in full sun but tolerate some shade during the hottest part of the day.

Where you plant Tulips affects the time of year they come into bloom. Plants on south-facing slopes or near concrete foundations come into bloom early because of additional warmth. This can be a problem for very early- to early-blooming varieties, since they may be damaged by a late unexpected frost.

Soil and Moisture Dig a trench as wide as the area you intend to plant with bulbs. Dig it 12 inches (30 cm) deep. This is a lot of work, but Tulips can last for years if properly planted in the first place. Keep all dark topsoil. Place it on a tarp to the side of the trench to make cleaning up easier. Get rid of poor subsoil, especially clay and rocks. Replace these with loam, either purchased locally or brought in from another area of the garden. Add as much compost, rotted manure, leaf mold, or peat as necessary to make the soil light and fluffy. You should be able to dig into it with your bare hand. The addition of organic matter is extremely important. It helps drainage and retains moisture during dry periods while releasing nutrients to the bulbs slowly over a period of several years. A bed that is 50 percent loam and 50 percent organic matter is ideal.

Build a raised bed if the soil is compacted or rocky. Good drainage is critical to Tulips. This, of course, requires buying and hauling in lots of topsoil, but this is often the easiest and most effective way to get a large bed quickly.

Mix 6 cups (about 1.5 kilos) of 10-10-10 fertilizer into every 100 square feet (9 square meters) of bed. Holland Bulb Booster is a good alternative. If you are an organic gardener, mix blood meal, manure, and bonemeal into the soil. If you're planting individual bulbs, give 1 teaspoon (5 g) of fertilizer per bulb. Place fertilizer in the soil 3 inches (7.5 cm) below the bulb, where the roots will get to it within a few weeks of planting. Never place fertilizer in direct contact with the bulb, since it can burn the emerging roots.

Spacing You can space bulbs according to recommendations on the package, or ignore these recommendations if you're after a more natural look. Tulips look best in large groups. For example, curving beds planted with numerous tulips are stunning. Typically, instructions are to plant tulips 5 to 6 inches (12.5 to 15 cm) apart. For a more showy display plant them closer than this. The outside of the bulbs will be 2 to 4 inches (5 to 10 cm) apart with the distance related to the size of the bulbs.

Companions

The larger varieties are often planted in masses for a bold effect. Mass plantings of one color or a few highly complementary colors is most highly recommended. Mix many colors only in the cutting garden. Tulips combine well with other spring-flowering bulbs, woody plants, and perennials such as *Aquilegia* (Columbine), *Dianthus* (Pinks), *Dicentra* (Bleeding Heart), *Euphorbia* (Spurge), *Iris* (Bearded Iris), *Phlox borealis* (Arctic Phlox), *Phlox*–Subulata Group (Creeping Phlox), and *Pulmonaria* (Lungwort). The smaller and wild types are ideal in rock gardens or tucked at the base of spring-flowering shrubs.

When planting Tulips, keep in mind that they go dormant in late spring or early summer. During this period, the foliage is unattractive. Mask the dying foliage and bare spots later in the season by careful companion planting. Some good choices for this are *Alchemilla mollis* (Lady's Mantle), *Geranium* (Cranesbill), *Hemerocallis* (Daylily), *Hosta, Lamium* (Dead Nettle), *Nepeta* (Catmint), *Rudbeckia* (Coneflower), *Salvia* (Sage), *Tradescantia* (Spiderwort), and **Grasses**. Often overlooked is how well many Tulips grow in containers. These add color to decks and patios during the early part of the year, only to be removed when foliage dies back.

Planting

Bulbs Buy quality bulbs from a reputable source, either mail-order or local. Bulbs deteriorate if exposed to humidity and to temperatures above 70°F (21°C). Sources should keep bulbs cool and ventilated. Buy bulbs as soon as available in the fall. Call ahead for exact arrival dates in order to get the freshest bulbs.

Check for blemishes, bruises, decay, or mold. Bulbs should be firm. Size will vary by variety.

Get bulbs into the ground as soon as they are available. Late plantings are risky. If you know that bulbs will be arriving late, prepare the bed, and cover it with a thick mulch to prevent the soil from freezing.

Plant the bulbs according to the depth recommended on the package for that variety. If there is no recommendation, plant bulbs about five times as deep as their width at the widest point. Depth of planting does make a difference: the deeper you plant bulbs, the later they'll bloom. For varied bloom time, plant bulbs at different depths. Shallow planting can result in rodent damage and winterkill, but it does encourage the production of more offsets, or new bulbs. And it will result in earlier bloom.

Plant bulbs with the pointed top up. Sometimes it's hard to tell which side is the top unless a little bit of green is showing there. Tiny bumps, or hairy growth (dried roots) are at the base of the bulb. Plant these down. Push the bulb into soil at the bottom of the trench and compress a little soil around the bulb to keep it firmly in place.

Most packages indicate spacing at 5 to 6 inches (12.5 to 15 cm). Tighter spacing results in spectacular masses of color.

Water the bulbs before covering them with soil.

Fill up the entire trench with water, and let it soak in. If the drainage is good, this will take only a few minutes.

Then cover the bulbs with topsoil mixed with peat, compost, and rotted manure. Allow the top 2 inches (5 cm) of soil to freeze before covering the area with 6 inches (15 cm) or more of mulch. Good winter covers include marsh hay, whole leaves, clean straw, and pine needles. This mulch prolongs the period in which bulbs can form roots—especially important if you plant bulbs late in the season.

How to Care for Tulips

Water Water the newly planted bulbs immediately after planting, and keep watering them throughout the fall to stimulate underground root growth. Water frequently the following spring. Stop watering after the leaves have died down. Begin watering again in early fall. Watering should be deep.

Mulch Mulch helps retain moisture in the soil. Tulips need moisture in spring and fall to survive and produce abundant bloom year after year. Use dried grass clippings, bark, shredded leaves, or pine needles only for a short period in spring. This early mulch stops the growth of annual weeds, which compete with the actively growing plants for moisture and nutrients.

Fertilizing After the first season fertilize the bed each fall by sprinkling several cups (about a kilo) of 10-10-10 fertilizer over each 100 square feet (9 square meters) of bed. Scratch the fertilizer lightly into the soil, and water immediately to dissolve granules and carry nutrients to the bulbs. This early fall feeding helps underground bulbs take root in the coming months.

Fertilize in spring just as the tiny tips shoot through the soil. Sprinkle 3 cups (700 g) 10-10-10 fertilizer per 100 square feet (9 square meters) around the emerging plants. Holland Bulb Booster is a good alternative. Water immediately so that the granules dissolve into the soil.

Substitute organic fertilizers for chemicals if you

prefer. Good organic fertilizers include alfalfa meal (rabbit pellets), blood meal, cow manure, fish emulsion, Milorganite, and rotted horse manure.

Never fertilize with chemicals during or right after bloom. This can cause fusarium bulb rot and botrytis blight.

Staking Staking is not necessary for most varieties of Tulips but helpful on the taller varieties in bad weather. Many gardeners cut the stems of the taller varieties for indoor use just to avoid the chore of staking.

Deadheading Remove all spent flowers except on species (wild) Tulips. Cutting stems for bouquets actually helps plants. Energy goes into bulb rather than seed formation. Leave seedpods on species Tulips to form seed and self-sow.

Pruning Many gardeners are tempted to cut down the foliage after bloom. Although it is unattractive, do not remove or disturb it. Leaves make food for the underground bulbs. If you cut the leaves off, then there is no way for the bulb to produce food. No food results in poor bloom the following year.

Many gardening books suggest braiding or tying leaves together. Do not do this. If you play games with the foliage, you end up damaging it, which reduces the food produced for the bulbs. The solution is to plant perennials in front of the bulbs to mask the foliage later in the season.

Once the foliage has died completely, remove and compost it. Dead foliage invites disease and insects.

Bed Renewal Tulips often bloom poorly after 3 or 4 years. Dig up the entire bed in early fall. Remake the bed as outlined earlier, and replant the bulbs. You can make Tulips last for years if you go to the trouble of digging and replanting them regularly.

Winter Protection Cover the planting bed with a 6-inch (15-cm) or more layer of mulch as soon as the top 2 inches (5 cm) of soil freeze. Once the ground is frozen, mice, which love winter mulch, will not dig into the ground and harm the bulbs. Remove this winter mulch as soon as the weather starts to warm up in early spring.

Mulch also affects bloom time. Winter mulch keeps the soil cool later into spring. This retards blooming. Vary the depth of winter cover to extend the season of Tulip bloom. Varieties that bloom very early in spring may be damaged by a late unexpected frost. Covering them with an extra-thick layer of mulch in the winter may prevent this.

Problems

Insects Tulips rarely are attacked by insects.

Disease Fertilizing during or immediately after bloom may cause fusarium bulb rot and botrytis blight. Prepare the bed as outlined to prevent rots caused by poor drainage.

All Tulips die back in the summer after bloom. Leaves turn yellow and then brown. This is completely normal. The plant is simply going into a dormant period.

Rodents Mice, moles, and voles can easily work their way through soil to nibble on Tulip bulbs. Castor oil and commercial products such as Mole-Med may help prevent damage. Fine, sharp, crushed gravel placed around bulbs can be effective. *Scilla* (Squill) bulbs planted with Tulips may also act as an organic deterrent. Some gardeners use poisoned baits or traps for control.

Chipmunks and squirrels often dig up newly planted bulbs. Some gardeners discourage them by placing bulbs in a chicken-wire cage. This is effective but a hassle. Others cover the soil with hardware cloth and keep it in place with rocks. Unless you remove the top of the cage or the hardware cloth before bulbs sprout in spring, stems often get entangled in the wire. Live traps, of course, are available and work well.

Deer, rabbits, and woodchucks eat new growth in spring. You can trap rabbits and woodchucks, but keeping deer away can be frustrating. Some gardeners insist that Milorganite, human hair, and scented soap scrapings placed around the beds will stop deer. A number of commercial products, such as Hinder, may be more effective if applied regularly.

Varying the repellent each year tends to be the most effective treatment.

Propagation

Division Tulip bulbs produce small bulbs (bulblets or offsets) to the side of the mother bulb. Each will produce a young plant.

Dig bulbs in early fall. Start from the outside of the bed and work in to avoid cutting any bulbs. The roots of the mother bulb and its offsets may be entwined. Gently pull them apart. Replant all bulbs immediately.

Seed Tulips take 5 to 7 years to mature from seed, which is a good way to propagate species Tulips. Check seedpods to see if seeds are forming. Just before they turn black, plant them in a moist growing medium outdoors in a cold frame or specially prepared bed. Do not dry them out. Plant them just as you remove them from the pod. Keep the medium moist at all times. It will freeze during the winter. With luck, Tulips will emerge the following spring.

If you buy seed, plant it ⅛ inch (3 mm) deep in a moist growing medium. Keep it at 50°F (10°C) unless the package indicates a higher temperature. Germination is irregular, taking from 1 to 4 months. Once plants sprout, feed them lightly with highly diluted fertilizer. Keep them in high light to help leaf formation. Separate the little plants when they're growing vigorously, and plant them in individual pots.

Special Uses

Cut Flowers Cut stems just above the ground as the flower begins to open. Never pull stems up from the plant, as you may pull off leaves in the process. Using a knife, make a slanting cut to sever the stem. Place the cut flowers in a bucket of cold water. Work quickly to get the cut flowers indoors as soon as possible.

Once indoors, wrap the flowers firmly in paper, leaving the lower 3 to 4 inches (7.5 to 10 cm) of stems exposed and soaking in tepid water. Some arrangers add 1 tablespoon (15 ml) alcohol per pint (⅛ liter) of water. Place the cut flowers in a cool spot for several hours. Wait until the flowers take in water and have stiff stems, then arrange them.

Use a clean vase and cut-flower preservative in fresh, cool water. If you have no preservative, use 1 teaspoon (5 g) sugar and a drop of bleach or 1 aspirin per quart (liter) of water. Fill the vase no more than one-third full. Change the water daily, refilling to the exact same level.

If flowers wilt, cut ½ inch (12 mm) off the bottom of each stem, and recondition them. Tulips properly conditioned will last 7 days or longer.

Many varieties of Tulips are fragrant, so if that is important to you, buy ones noted for scent. The Japanese often push petals backward for floral arrangements. This makes the Tulip look like an entirely different flower.

Tulips look lovely arranged by themselves or with other flowers. Taking a few leaves from the plants is okay to make the arrangement more attractive, but don't take many, since the leaves are so important in manufacturing food critical to next year's bloom.

Dried Flowers Some people dry Tulips in desiccant with painstaking effort. If petals break off, glue them back on.

Sources

ADR Bulbs, Inc., 49 Black Meadow Rd., Chester, NY 10918, (800) 990-9934

Bluestone Perennials, 7211 Middle Ridge Rd., Madison, OH 44057, (800) 852-5243

Breck's Bulbs, P.O. Box 65, Guilford, IN 47022, (513) 354-1511

Brent & Becky's Bulbs, 7900 Daffodil Lane, Gloucester, VA 23061, (804) 693-3966

Colorblends, 747 Barnum Ave., Bridgeport, CT 06608, (888) 847-8637

Dutch Gardens, 4 Currency Dr., Bloomington, IL 61704, (800) 944-2250

Holland Bulb Farms, 8480 N 87th St., Milwaukee, WI 53224, (414) 355-3774

Hudson, J. L., Seedsman, P.O. Box 337, La Honda, CA 94020 (a seed bank)

Jacques Amand, LLC, P.O. Box 4000, Ancramdale, NY 12503, (480) 656-6151

John Scheepers, Inc. (Van Engelen), 23 Tulip Dr., Bantam, CT 06750, (860) 567-0838

Landreth, D, Seed Co, 60 E High St., Bldg #4, New Freedom, PA 17349, (800) 654-2407

McClure & Zimmerman, 335 S High St., Randolph, WI 53956, (800) 883-6998

Messelaar Bulb Co., P.O. Box 269, Ipswich, MA 01938, (978) 356-3737

Odyssey Bulbs, P.O. Box 382, South Lancaster, MA 01561, (508) 335-8106

Old House Gardens, 536 Third St., Ann Arbor, MI 48103, (734) 995-1486

Terra Ceia Farms, 3810 Terra Ceia Rd., Pantego, NC 27860, (800) 858-2852

Tulips.comRoozengarde, P.O. Box 1248, Mount Vernon, WA 98273, (866) 488-5477

Tulip World Holland Bulbs, 8480 N 87th, Milwaukee, WI 53224, (866) 688-9547

Van Bourgondien Bros. (Van Dykes), P.O. Box 2000, Virginia Beach, VA 23450, (800) 622-9997

Veldheer Tulip Gardens, 12755 Quincy St., Holland, MI 49424, (616) 399-1900

White Flower Farm, P.O. Box 50, Litchfield, CT 06759, (800) 503-9624

Wooden Shoe Tulip Farm, 33814 S Meridian Rd., Woodburn, OR 97071, (800) 711-2006

VARIETIES

As with many large and complex groups of perennials, a classification system exists. This system helps you sort through the many Tulips introduced over centuries of breeding and selection. There are tens of thousands of varieties and perhaps several thousand of those are being sold today. The flowering season for Tulips extends from early through late spring in colder climates. To extend the overall bloom season, buy Tulips which bloom at varying times. Noting the class of Tulip also helps you understand what the Tulip will look like once mature. Few people think of Tulips as being fragrant, but two with intense fragrance are 'Monte Carlo' and 'Peach Blossom.' Following is a brief explanation of this classification system.

Division 1: Single Early Tulips

Noted for their fragrant flowers and early bloom, these short Tulips are good for both bedding and forcing indoors. This group includes some types once known as Mendels.

Division 2: Double Early Tulips

These short-stemmed, early-blooming Tulips have double flowers that are usually fragrant. They are particularly valuable for use in beds and borders.

Division 3: Triumph Tulips

Noted for their large flowers, midseason bloom, and strong stems that stand 18 to 24 inches tall, these Tulips are excellent as garden plants, for cut flowers, and for indoor forcing. This group includes some types once known as Mendels.

'Angelique'

'Fantasy'

'General de Wet'

'Juan'

Tulipa saxatilis 'Lilac Wonder'

'Lustige Wittwe'

'Peach Blossom'

'Queen of Bartigons'

'Red Riding Hood'

'Shakespeare'

'Union Jack'

'West Point'

Division 4: Darwin Hybrid Tulips

These Tulips are noted for their large showy flowers, excellent vigor, and stems that stand 20 to 30 inches tall. They bloom in midseason and often require staking in bad weather.

Division 5: Single Late Tulips

This group includes Tulips derived from the now obsolete Breeder, Cottage, and Darwin classifications. They all flower late in the Tulip season and make good bedding plants and cut flower subjects. They offer a wide color range, tall stems, and vigorous growth.

Division 6: Lily-flowered Tulips

The petals of these late-flowering tulips are long, pointed, reflexed, and brilliantly colored. They grow 20 to 24 inches tall and are excellent in the garden or as cut flowers. These come from a classification once known as Cottage Tulips.

Division 7: Fringed Tulips

This group includes all hybrids whose petals are edged with crystal-shaped fringes. They flower late in the season with long-lasting blooms. Their stems grow 20 to 24 inches high.

Division 8: Viridiflora Tulips

This late-flowering group is easily recognized by the green stripes or flares in the petals. The flowers are large, brightly colored, and oval-shaped with curving petals. Viridiflora Tulips grow 16 to 20 inches tall and are sometimes listed as Single Late Tulips in catalogs.

Division 9: Rembrandt Tulips

Rembrandts have multicolored streaks on their petals and are often referred to as "broken tulips." They were derived from the now obsolete Breeder, Cottage, and Darwin classifications. Since a virus was responsible for this breaking pattern, these Tulips are no longer sold. Gardeners desiring this "broken" look should select modern varieties that have been bred to resemble Rembrandts but are not infected with the virus. Two good examples included in our list are the Single Late Tulips 'Shirley' and 'Union Jack.'

Division 10: Parrot Tulips

Parrot Tulips have large flowers with a frilly, feathery appearance with exotic markings. They flower late, grow 20 to 24 inches tall, and are excellent for cutting. They may require staking in bad weather.

Division 11: Double Late Tulips

These stunning Tulips produce extremely large, heavy blooms easily damaged by wind and rain. Often referred to as peony-flowered Tulips, they bloom late and stand 14 to 20 inches tall.

Division 12: Kaufmanniana Tulips

These hybrids, sometimes referred to as Waterlily Tulips, bloom early, have broad pointed buds, and flat flowers. Their foliage is often mottled or striped brown. They stand about 4 to 8 inches tall and are excellent in rock gardens where they spread rapidly.

Division 13: Fosteriana Tulips

The tallest of the early Tulips, these hybrids are noted for large, elongated flowers and clear colored blooms. They grow 14 to 24 inches tall and some have mottled or striped foliage while others have grayish green leaves. As a group, these tend to spread well and live long. This division includes what once were known as Emperor Tulips.

Division 14: Greigii Tulips

These Tulips bloom early in the season. They grow about 8 to 16 inches tall, have mottled foliage occasionally striped purple, and long lasting flowers.

Division 15: Wild Species Tulips

All species, varieties, forms, and cultivar selections of the species are placed in this division. All bloom early and are long lived. Most also spread rapidly.

VARIETY	DIVISION	SEASON	COLOR	HEIGHT	HARDINESS
Tulipa acuminata					
(Horned Tulip)	15	Early	Yellow/red lines	18″	−40°F
This Turkish species has very slender leaves and long pointed flowers with twisted petals.					
Tulipa bakeri (see *Tulipa saxatilis*)					
Tulipa batalinii****					
(Batalin Tulip)	15	Early	Pale yellow	6″	−40°F
'Bright Gem'	15	Early	Bright yellow	6″	−40°F
This is a superb plant for the rock garden where it can live undisturbed for years.					
Tulipa clusiana****					
(Clusius Tulip)	15	Early	White/red stripes	12″	−40°F
This delightful Tulip is a favorite for rock gardens. A well grown clump also makes a dramatic statement in the garden. The blooms are shaped like urns and quite fragrant.					
Tulipa dasystemon (see *Tulipa tarda*)					
Tulipa eichleri****					
(Eichler Tulip)	15	Early	Deep red	12″	−30°F
This is a showy Tulip with broad leaves and large flowers, both blue-black at their bases.					
Tulipa greigii					
(Greig Tulip)	15	Very early	Orange scarlet	12″	−30°F
Greig Tulip is native to Turkestan and has dark green, fairly broad leaves and flowers with dark blotches at their bases.					
Tulipa humilis var. *pulchella*					
(Ground Tulip)	15	Early	Violet	6″	−30°F
Native to Persia, this Tulip has narrow, strap-like leaves and flowers often yellow at the bases.					
Tulipa kaufmanniana					
(Waterlily Tulip)	15	Very early	Creamy yellow/red	10″	−30°F
Parent to many fine hybrids, Waterlily Tulip is worth growing in its own right as it produces abundant flowers in early spring.					
Tulipa kolpakowskiana					
(Kolpak Tulip)	15	Early	Buttercup yellow	6″	−40°F
This Tulip has narrow, pointed leaves and cup-shaped flowers often marked red or purple on the outside.					

VARIETY	DIVISION	SEASON	COLOR	HEIGHT	HARDINESS
Tulipa linifolia*****					
(Slimleaf Tulip)	15	Early	Bright red	4″	−30°F

This gem has grass-like foliage and glossy flowers with a black base. Despite its beauty, it remains undiscovered by many.

Tulipa praestans					
(Leather-bulb Tulip)					
'Fusilier'	15	Early	Reddish orange	12″	−40°F
'Unicum'	15	Early	Reddish orange	10″	−40°F

These Tulips produce one to four elongated flowers per stem. 'Unicum' has variegated foliage which contrasts nicely with its red flowers. All are delightful in rock gardens.

Tulipa pulchella (see *Tulipa humilis*)

Tulipa saxatilis	15	Early	Mauve/yellow base	18″	−30°F
'Lilac Wonder'*****	15	Early	Lilac/yellow base	8″	−30°F

This plant usually produces two flowers to a stem. Each of these is fragrant, shallow, and cup-like opening almost flat. This Tulip will live for years and produces an impressive clump, but it needs to be kept on the dry side during the summer months.

Tulipa tarda*****					
(Daystemon Tulip)	15	Early	White/yellow center	4″	−40°F

A native of Turkestan, the readily available Daystemon Tulip usually bears several starry flowers per stem. It will live for years and tends to spread freely.

Tulipa (Named varieties in Divisions 1 through 14)					
'African Queen'	3	Mid	Red purple	16″	−40°F
'Alladin'	6	Late	Scarlet/gold edge	18″	−40°F
'Angelique'*****	11	Late	Soft pink/rose	14″	−40°F
'Apeldoorn'*****	4	Mid	Red	18″	−40°F
'Apricot Beauty'	1	Early	Apricot pink	14″	−40°F
'Apricot Delight'	4	Mid	Light pink apricot	22″	−40°F
'Apricot Emperor'	13	Early mid	Salmon pink	14″	−40°F
'Apricot Parrot'	10	Late	Apricot yellow	24″	−40°F
'Asta Nielsen'	5	Late	Yellow	22″	−40°F
'Ballade'	6	Late	Red/violet/white	28″	−40°F
'Ballerina'*****	6	Mid late	Apricot orange	22″	−40°F
'Beauty Queen'	1	Early	Pink apricot	18″	−40°F
'Big Chief'	4	Mid	Rose	24″	−40°F
'Black Parrot'	10	Late	Dark purple	24″	−40°F
'Blue Aimable'*****	5	Late	Smoky lilac	24″	−40°F
'Blueberry Ripple'	3	Mid	White/purple flames	20″	−40°F
'Blue Heron'	7	Late	Lilac purple	22″	−40°F
'Blue Parrot'	10	Late	Lavender violet	24″	−40°F
'Burgundy Lace'*****	7	Late	Deep red	28″	−40°F

VARIETY	DIVISION	SEASON	COLOR	HEIGHT	HARDINESS
'Candy Apple Delight'	4	Mid	Red/white	14″	−40°F
'Calgary'	3	Mid	White	10″	−40°F
'China Pink'	6	Mid late	Light pink	18″	−40°F
'China Town' ('Chinatown')	8	Late	Pink cream blend	16″	−40°F
'Cream Lizard'	10	Mid late	Yellow tinged pink	14″	−40°F
'Daydream'	4	Mid	Medium yellow orange	18″	−40°F
'Diana'	1	Early	White	14″	−40°F
'Dordogne'	5	Late	Rose blend	26″	−40°F
'Dreaming Maid'	3	Mid	Lavender/white	18″	−40°F
'Early Harvest'*****	12	Very early	Orange red	10″	−40°F
'Elizabeth Arden'*****	4	Mid	Salmon pink	22″	−40°F
'Esperanto'	8	Late	Green/red	14″	−40°F
'Estella Rijnveld'	10	Late	Red/white	24″	−40°F
'Esther'	5	Late	Silvery pink	24″	−40°F
'Fancy Frills'*****	7	Late	White pink	18″	−40°F
'Fantasy'	10	Late	Rosy pink/green	22″	−40°F
'Flair'	1	Early	Yellow red	12″	−40°F
'Flaming Parrot'	10	Late	Yellow/red	24″	−40°F
'Foxtrot'	2	Early	Rose cream	12″	−40°F
'General de Wet'*****	1	Early	Orange	12″	−40°F
'Georgette'	5	Late	Yellow edged red	18″	−40°F
'Golden Melody'*****	3	Mid	Lemon yellow	18″	−40°F
'Golden Oxford'	4	Mid	Golden yellow	24″	−40°F
'Golden Parade'*****	4	Mid	Yellow	18″	−40°F
'Greenland' ('Groenland')	8	Late	Green/pink	22″	−40°F
'Halcro'	5	Late	Red	26″	−40°F
'Heart's Delight'*****	12	Very early	Red yellow	8″	−40°F
'Ile de France'	5	Late	Red	20″	−40°F
'Indian Summer'	3	Mid	Yellow pink	12″	−40°F
'Jewel of Spring'*****	4	Mid	Cream	28″	−40°F
'Juan'*****	13	Early	Red/yellow	16″	−40°F
'Lilac Perfection'	11	Late	Purplish lilac	20″	−40°F
'Lucky Strike'	3	Mid	Red edged white	24″	−40°F
'Lustige Wittwe'*****	3	Mid	Red edged white	16″	−40°F
'Madame Lefeber'	13	Mid	Deep red orange tones	14″	−40°F
'Madonna'	9	Mid late	White green	18″	−40°F
'Marjolein Bastin'	3	Mid	White edged pink green	18″	−40°F
'Mariette'	6	Late	Rose	24″	−40°F
'Marilyn'	6	Late	White flamed red	22″	−40°F
'Maureen'	5	Late	White	28″	−40°F
'Merry Widow'*****	3	Mid	Red edged white	16″	−40°F
'Monte Carlo'	2	Early	Golden yellow	20″	−40°F
'Montreux'	2	Early	White yellow pink	18″	−40°F

VARIETY	DIVISION	SEASON	COLOR	HEIGHT	HARDINESS
'Mount Tacoma'*****	11	Late	White	18"	−40°F
'Mrs. J. T. Scheepers'	5	Late	Yellow	26"	−40°F
'Negrita'*****	3	Mid	Deep purple	18"	−40°F
'New Design'	3	Mid	Pink	14"	−40°F
'Orange Emperor'*****	13	Early	Orange/yellow	18"	−40°F
'Orange Monarch'	3	Mid	Orange	18"	−40°F
'Orange Princess'	11	Late	Orange purple	14"	−40°F
'Oratario'	14	Mid	Rose pink	14"	−40°F
'Oxford'	4	Mid	Scarlet red	24"	−40°F
'Parade'*****	4	Mid	Red	18"	−40°F
'Peach Blossom'	2	Early	Soft pink	12"	−40°F
'Peerless Pink'	3	Mid	Satiny pink	18"	−40°F
'Pieter de Leur'	6	Early mid	Red	12"	−40°F
'Pink Supreme'	5	Late	Rose	28"	−40°F
'Pinocchio'	14	Early	Red/yellow	11"	−40°F
'Princess Irene'	3	Mid	Orange/purple flames	12"	−40°F
'Queen of Bartigons'	5	Late	Salmon	24"	−40°F
'Queen of Night'*****	5	Late	Black maroon	26"	−40°F
'Queen of Sheba'	6	Late	Red	26"	−40°F
'Queensland'	7	Mid late	Reddish pink	14"	−40°F
'Red Emperor'*****	13	Early	Red	18"	−40°F
'Red Parrot'	10	Late	Raspberry red	24"	−40°F
'Red Riding Hood'*****	14	Early	Red/black	8"	−40°F
'Red Shine'*****	6	Late	Red	20"	−40°F
'Renown'	5	Late	Red	26"	−40°F
'Salmon Pearl'	3	Mid	Coral rose	16"	−40°F
'Shakespeare'*****	12	Early	Rose red	7"	−40°F
'Shirley'	9	Late	White edged purple	24"	−40°F
'Showwinner'	12	Early	Red/yellow	6"	−40°F
'Silverado'	5	Late	Soft pink	18"	−40°F
'Smiling Queen'	5	Late	Pink	28"	−40°F
'Spring Green'*****	8	Late	Green/cream	20"	−40°F
'Stresa'	12	Early	Yellow blotched red	8"	−40°F
'Sweetheart'	12	Early	Yellow cream white	14"	−40°F
'Temple of Beauty'	5	Late	Salmon	30"	−40°F
'Tom Pouce'	3	Mid	Deep yellow pink	18"	−40°F
'Toronto'*****	14	Early	Rose/vermilion	12"	−40°F
'Union Jack'	9	Late	Red flamed white	24"	−40°F
'West Point'*****	6	Late	Yellow	26"	−40°F
'White Emperor'*****	13	Early	White	18"	−40°F
'White Parrot'	10	Late	White	22"	−40°F
'White Triumphator'*****	6	Late	White	26"	−40°F

'Icicle'

VERONICA

(ver-ON-ih-kuh)

SPEEDWELL

Bloom Time	Expected Longevity	Maintenance	Years to Bloom	Preferred Light
Late spring to fall	20 years	Low	From seed: 2 years From potted plant: 1 year	Full sun

Speedwell is an excellent, easy-to-grow vertical accent plant. It grows quickly, forming lovely clumps or ground covers. The plant often blooms for an extended period of time. Flowers are varied in color, but the richness of the blues stands out. Cut flowers are excellent. Foliage is usually attractive and deep green. Speedwell is rarely bothered by disease or insects. The varying forms make this one of the more versatile perennials for garden design and use. The varieties listed at the end of the section are long-lived in colder areas, as long as soil drains freely during the winter months.

How Speedwell Grow

Speedwell grows from fibrous roots into either upright, clump-forming or ground-hugging plants. Clumps spread slowly, creating more erect stems each year. The lower-growing plants spread rapidly and are excellent for ground covers. Foliage is usually narrow and toothed but occasionally rounded. The stems are topped with spikes covered with small flowers. Some varieties will self-seed if not deadheaded.

Where to Plant

Site and Light Speedwell thrives in full sun. It tolerates partial shade but the number of blooms will be reduced.

Soil and Moisture Speedwell prefers medium-rich soils that drain freely. Replace clay or rocky soils with loam or build a raised bed. Add lots of organic matter, such as compost, peat, rotted manure, or leaf mold. All help drainage but retain moisture during hot, dry periods. Speedwell likes consistent moisture throughout the growing season.

Spacing Plant larger Speedwells approximately 12 to 15 inches (30 to 37.5 cm) apart. Smaller varieties can be closer.

Companions

The spiky form of *Veronica* (Speedwell) combines well with the mounded form of many of our common perennials. Among those are *Alchemilla* (Lady's Mantle), *Baptisia* (False Indigo), *Campanula* (Bellflower), *Coreopsis* (Tickseed), *Echinacea purpurea* 'White Swan' (Coneflower), *Geranium* (Cranesbill), and *Oenothera* (Evening Primrose). Here are several suggested combinations using these fine perennials: *Veronica spicata* 'Glory' (Spike Speedwell) planted along with *Achillea* 'Paprika' (Yarrow), *Hemerocallis* 'Dorethe Louise' (Daylily), and *Phlox*–Paniculata Group 'David' (Summer Phlox); *Veronica austriaca* 'Crater Lake Blue' (Hungarian Speedwell) combined with *Iris* 'Queen Anne's Lace' (Tall Bearded Iris) and *Dianthus*–Plumarius Group 'Essex Witch' (Hardy Garden Pink); and *Veronica longifolia* 'White Jolanda' (Longleaf Speedwell) surrounded by *Coreopsis verticillata* 'Golden Shower' (Thread-Leaf Coreopsis), *Heliopsis helianthoides* 'Venus' (Oxeye), and *Monarda* 'Jacob Cline' (Bee Balm). The dwarf types with rich green foliage throughout the growing season suit border edges.

Planting

Bare Root Plant bare root stock as soon as you can work the ground in spring. Remove plants from their shipping packaging immediately. Snip off broken or damaged root tips. Soak plants in room-temperature water overnight. Place a small amount of superphosphate in the base of the planting hole. Fill the hole with soil. Place the crown 1 inch (2.5 cm) below the soil surface. Fill in with soil, firm with your fingers, and water immediately. Dissolve ½ cup (about 114 g) of 10-10-10 fertilizer in 1 gallon (about 4 liters) of water. Pour ½ cup (about 120 ml) of this starter solution around the base of each plant. If you prefer organic fertilizer, use fish emulsion instead.

Potted Plants Plant Speedwell after all danger of frost in spring. If the soil in the pot is dry, water it, and let it drain overnight. Tap the plant from the pot without disturbing the root ball. Plant it at the same depth as in the pot, after preparing the hole in a manner similar to that for a bare root plant. Fill in with soil, firm with your fingers, and water immediately. Pour ½ cup (about 120 ml) starter solution around the base of each plant.

How to Care for Speedwells

Water Water regularly when plants are young. Mature plants are quite drought tolerant, although they prefer consistent moisture. Soak the soil to a depth of 8 to 10 inches (20 to 25 cm) each time you water.

Mulch Surround the base of each plant with a 2-inch (5-cm) layer of organic mulch as soon as the ground warms up in spring. Good mulches are shredded leaves, grass clippings, pine needles, and compost. Mulch inhibits annual weed growth and keeps soil moist and cool.

Fertilizing Sprinkle 10-10-10 fertilizer around the base of each plant just as new growth emerges in spring. Water immediately to dissolve the granules and move nutrients into the root zone. If taller varieties of Speedwell grown in full sun appear lanky or spindly, reduce fertilizer the following year.

If you prefer organic fertilizers, use alfalfa meal (rabbit pellets), blood meal, bonemeal, compost, cow manure, fish emulsion, Milorganite, or rotted horse manure. Bonemeal must be mixed into the soil at planting time to be effective.

Staking Staking is not required for most varieties. If taller ones become floppy, stake them. The following year reduce the amount of fertilizer. Stake early in the season with pea stakes. These support stems but are not visible once the plant matures.

Deadheading Cut off entire flower spikes as they fade to induce rebloom on some varieties.

Pruning Cutting back taller varieties of Speedwell after they bloom may result in multibranched stems and create a fuller look. Pinching off growing tips when the plants are only 8 inches (20 cm) tall may also induce side branching for more prolific first bloom.

Winter Protection If there is no snow by mid-December, cover the plants with a 6-inch (15-cm) layer of marsh hay, clean straw, pine needles, or whole leaves. Remove this winter mulch by early spring as soon as the weather warms up to prevent crown rot.

Problems

Insects Speedwells are rarely bothered by insects.

Disease If foliage browns, cut it back, and remove any discolored portions of the plant. The plant will regenerate if kept consistently moist.

Propagation

Division Divide clumps every 3 to 4 years for the health of the plant. Dig up the mature plant in early spring just as new growth starts. Cut the crown into several sections, each with several shoots connected to an ample supply of roots. Plant the divisions as

you would a bare root plant. Keep them consistently moist for quick rooting.

Stem Cuttings Cut off the growing tip of 8-inch (20-cm) stems. Take cuttings with three sets of leaves. Make your final cut ¼ inch (6 mm) below a leaf node. Strip off the lower leaves. Dip the cut end in rooting hormone. Tap off any excess powder. Then place the cutting in moist growing medium. Keep the humidity high and the soil consistently moist until roots form.

Layering The creeping varieties send out growth to the side of the parent plant. Pin stems down at leaf nodes, the place where leaves join the stem, or watch where they root naturally. Cut off rooted portions. Plant these portions as you would a bare root plant.

Seed Seed is best used only for species (wild) Speedwells. Most of the named varieties do not come true from seed and are best reproduced by stem cuttings or division. Some gardeners enjoy surprises and let named varieties self-seed. Let seed drop to the ground. Avoid fertilizing the area until seedlings emerge in spring. Or, collect seed as it matures late in the season to be grown as outlined in the following paragraph.

Start seed indoors 12 weeks before the last expected frost in spring. Press the fine seed into moist growing medium. Varieties vary in their need for light to germinate properly. If unsure, cover some lightly and leave others exposed. Keep them moist and in high humidity at 68°F (20°C) during the day, with a drop of 10°F (6°C) at night. Germination normally takes 15 to 30 days but in some species is highly irregular, taking much longer. Once seedlings are sprouting, keep them at 55°F to 60°F (13°C to 16°C). When seedlings have a second pair of leaves, plant them in individual pots. Harden them off for 14 days before planting outside after all danger of frost has passed in spring.

Special Uses

Cut Flowers All taller varieties are good for flower arrangements. *Veronica longfolia* 'Eveline' and

'Purpleicious' (Longleaf Speedwell) are outstanding for cut flower use. Many other varieties listed under *Veronica spicata* are also good. Cut stems when flowers reach peak bloom and richest color. Place them in water immediately, and arrange them once indoors.

Dried Flowers Cut floral spikes when flowers are partially open. Pick them when coloration is at its richest. You may want to cut stems at varying times, since color may vary once the flowers dry. Bunch stems into clumps, and hang them upside down in a dry, dark, well-ventilated area. Stems also dry well when placed in desiccant. The latter is actually preferred over hang-drying. The faster the stems dry, the better the color. Cover the flower spikes completely with desiccant until they become dry and brittle. Many arrangers insist that pinks are preferable to other colors.

Sources

Ambergate Gardens, 8730 County Rd. 43, Chaska, MN 55318, (877) 211-9769

Bluestone Perennials, 7211 Middle Ridge Rd., Madison, OH 44057, (800) 852-5243

Fieldstone Gardens, Inc., 55 Quaker Lane, Vassalboro, ME 04989, (207) 923-3836

ForestFarm, 990 Tetherow Rd., Williams, OR 97544, (541) 846-7269

Roots & Rhizomes, P.O. Box A, Randolph, WI 53956, (800) 374-5035

'Heavenly Blue'

'Minuet'

VARIETIES

VARIETY	COLOR	HEIGHT	HARDINESS
Veronica alpina			
(Alpine Speedwell)			
'Alba'	White	8″	−40°F

This is a choice rock garden or front of the border plant. It has wonderful deep green foliage and slowly spreads into a handsome clump. Alpine Speedwell has a long flowering period in summer if spent flowers are removed.

Veronica austriaca			
(Hungarian Speedwell)			
'Crater Lake Blue'*****	Intense blue	24″	−40°F
'Royal Blue'	Deep blue	14″	−40°F

These varieties are noted for deep green foliage, rich flower color, and early summer bloom. Though they are short, they do tend to topple over.

Veronica gentianoides			
(Gentian Speedwell)			
'Variegata'	Pale blue	24″	−30°F

This is a fine spring-blooming plant quickly forming an attractive mat of green foliage with creamy white markings and spires of wide pale blue flowers. Variegation is strongest on leaves close to the ground.

Veronica longifolia			
(Longleaf Speedwell)	Violet blue	36″	−40°F
'Blue John'*****	Purple blue	30″	−40°F
'Lilac Fantasy'	Bluish lilac	30″	−40°F
'Sonja'	Fuchsia pink	30″	−40°F
'White Jolanda'	Pure white	30″	−40°F

These are excellent upright accent perennials for mid to back sections of the border. Longleaf Speedwells have clean green foliage and bloom for six to eight weeks in mid- to late summer. They require evenly moist soils for best growth.

Veronica pectinata			
(Woolly Creeping Speedwell)	Sky blue	4″	−40°F
'Rubra' ('Rosea')	Rose pink	2″	−40°F

This is a good ground cover or rock garden plant with gray woolly leaves. It spreads into large, dense clumps by rooting wherever the leaf nodes touch soil. This may be the most drought tolerant of the Speedwells.

Veronica prostrata			
(Sprawling Speedwell)	Blue	8″	−30°F
'Aztec Gold'	Sky blue	6″	−30°F
'Heavenly Blue'	Sapphire blue	4″	−30°F
'Mrs. Holt'	Bright lavender pink	4″	−30°F

Another of the creeping Speedwells, these perennials are ideal along the front edge of a border or used as a ground cover for small areas. They bloom in late spring and early summer. 'Aztec Gold' has brilliant gold foliage.

VARIETY	COLOR	HEIGHT	HARDINESS
Veronica repens			
(Creeping Speedwell)	Pale blue	4″	−30°F
'Sunshine'	Light blue	4″	−30°F

This spring-blooming Creeping Speedwell forms a dense mat of medium green moss-like leaves, making it an excellent ground cover. 'Sunshine' has golden yellow foliage.

Veronica rupestris (see *Veronica prostrata*)			

Veronica spicata			
(Spike Speedwell)			
'Blue Fox' ('Blaufuchs')	Lavender blue	15″	−40°F
'Blue Peter'	Purple blue	24″	−40°F
'Erika'	Dark pink	14″	−40°F
'Glory' ('Royal Candles')*****	Deep violet blue	18″	−40°F
'Heidekind'	Rose pink	10″	−40°F
'High Five'	Lavender blue	30″	−40°F
'Icicle'*****	White	24″	−40°F
subsp. *incana*	Purple blue	18″	−40°F
'Minuet'	Rose pink	18″	−40°F
'Nana'	Indigo blue	8″	−40°F
'Red Fox' ('Rotfuchs')	Deep rose red	18″	−40°F
'Ulster Blue Dwarf'*****	Purple blue	12″	−40°F

Varieties of Spike Speedwell are very popular for their wide color range and early to midsummer bloom. 'Glory' is a heavy-blooming cultivar with excellent foliage. 'Icicle' blooms from midsummer into fall and is one of the best white-flowered Speedwells. *Veronica spicata* ssp. *incana* has distinctive, silvery gray foliage. 'Ulster Blue Dwarf' is a choice long-blooming, dwarf selection.

Veronica (Named varieties and hybrids)			
'Baby Doll'*****	Clear pink	14″	−40°F
'Blue Reflection'	Lavender blue	8″	−40°F
'Darwin's Blue'	Dark purple blue	24″	−40°F
'Eveline'*****	Rich rose purple	24″	−40°F
'Fairytale'*****	Silver pink	20″	−40°F
'Giles van Hees'*****	Medium pink	10″	−40°F
'Goodness Grows'	Purple blue	14″	−40°F
'Pink Damask'	Pink	36″	−40°F
'Purpleicious'	Purple	18″	−30°F
'Royal Pink'	Soft pink	20″	−40°F
'Waterperry Blue'*****	Lavender blue	6″	−40°F

'Baby Doll' forms a dense, bushy plant with numerous spikes of showy flowers. Blooming in late spring, 'Blue Reflection' makes a fine ground cover with its dense mat of foliage. 'Darwin's Blue' has attractive dark green foliage and blooms throughout summer. 'Eveline' has a distinct upright appearance, rich flower color, and heavy bloom. The combination of attractive, disease-free foliage and heavy flower production makes 'Fairytale' an excellent choice for the garden. 'Giles Van Hees' is of particular note for its attractive green foliage and long bloom season. A compact selection, 'Goodness Grows' will bloom throughout the summer if regularly deadheaded. A tall upright form, 'Pink Damask' blooms for several weeks in early to midsummer. Though bred primarily for the cut flower market, 'Purple-icious' has also proven to be an excellent garden plant. It has glossy, dark green foliage, and it blooms on sturdy stems over an extended period. 'Royal Pink' has attractive medium green foliage and blooms for the better part of summer if regularly deadheaded. 'Waterperry Blue' forms a mat of foliage with wonderful bronzy tints. Bloom peaks in spring, but, in cooler regions, additional bloom occurs throughout summer into fall.

PART II

The Basics of Growing Perennials

In the chapters that follow, you'll find information that is essential to growing perennials in cold climates. Some of this repeats information given in the individual plant listings in Part I, but some of the more general details on growing perennials is presented here for the first time. Part II will give you a crash course in perennial gardening. Even if you're an experienced gardener, you'll likely pick up more than a few secrets or tips.

CHAPTER 2

UNDERSTANDING PERENNIALS

Perennials have soared in popularity in recent decades. Perhaps it's because gardeners realize that working with perennials is like painting with a full palette of colors. Following are a few tips to help you match plants to your personality.

How Perennials Grow

The perennials in this guide grow in a wide variety of ways. Each section of Part I explains in detail the style of growth for an individual group (genus) of plants.

Perennials generally do not bloom for long periods, but while in bloom, they are quite spectacular. The plants generally die back to the ground at the end of the season and reemerge the following year. Plants that do this are known as *herbaceous.* The life expectancy of each perennial varies. Some last only a few seasons, others for many decades. In this guide, we tell you what to expect and how to achieve the best results and longest life from individual plants.

Buying Perennials

Whenever possible, buy plants from a reputable, local source. This way you have a chance to check stock personally and to return plants that are improperly labeled. However, a number of plants are hard to find in local nurseries and retail outlets. To help you, each section of Part I includes a list of potential mail-order sources for these more unusual plants.

When buying plants either through the mail or at a local nursery, take the following things into consideration:

- **Hardiness:** Most of the perennials listed in this guide are extremely hardy and able to survive even the coldest and windiest winter conditions provided they have adequate snow cover. Some, however, are more prone to die out in extreme winters. You'll find detailed information on hardiness with each variety listed.
- **Winter protection:** Some plants require less effort to protect than others. So, if you want to avoid lots of work in fall, then you might want to avoid certain types of perennials altogether. Information on what is and isn't required for each type of perennial or for a specific variety is given throughout the guide. Once mature, most of the perennials listed do not need winter protection other than snow cover.
- **Overall use:** The value of each perennial to you will vary according to how you want to use it. You may want cut flowers, a bold specimen plant that acts like an isolated shrub, or a climber to cover a

trellis or ramble over a split-rail fence. Or perhaps you have a problem area and want to use a plant to cover banks or large open areas for mass color. Information on the best use for specific perennials is included in each section.

- **Care:** Some perennials require quite a bit of care to grow well. Others require very little maintenance. This is extremely important to gardeners with limited time or patience. The amount of care required by plants is emphasized throughout, so that you can match your plant selection to your personal garden philosophy.

- **Color:** There is an infinite variety of coloration. We have listed so many varieties within individual groups that you will be able to blend colors into a living tapestry. How you choose to do this is strictly a matter of taste.

- **Flower form and size:** Perennial flowers may be dainty or bold, minuscule or immense. They may have only a few petals or be large globes of petals melded together. Part of good garden design is understanding the visual effect of each flower, either from a distance or up close.

- **Bloom time:** In order to make skillful combinations of plants, you need to know when a flower will come into bloom. This varies by season and region, but in general, plants bloom within a week or two of a specific time each year. Gardeners who have grown perennials over a period of years begin to note the times when flowers bloom so that they can arrange lovely combinations. We give suggestions for possible combinations in each section under the heading "Companions." This will help you get off to a good start. So will a notebook for making notations on bloom times.

- **Foliage and stem characteristics:** The scent, shape, color, and texture of foliage and stems can be important in selecting a plant. These qualities make some perennials desirable in arrangements of cut or dried flowers. Foliage varies by group and individual variety. Leaves are soft, smooth, coarse, or ferny. Some are dull, others glossy. Some are green, while others are blue, bronze, gray, red, purplish, or yellow. Some foliage exudes a delightful aroma, especially when touched lightly. Throughout the guide you'll find information on foliage and stem characteristics to help you decide whether a plant may fit a special need.

- **Flower fragrance:** In each section, you'll also find detailed information on fragrance so that you can choose varieties by scent. Scent varies by temperature and humidity. High temperatures and high humidity increase fragrance, whereas during cool to cold periods, many fragrant flowers have little scent. Fragrance also depends on the stage of maturity. Some perennials give off a scent only as they open, while others exude perfume when fully mature. Scents even vary by the time of day, with some flowers exuding perfume only at night. Scents vary greatly and may be subtle to overpowering. People also vary in their ability to detect fragrance; some simply cannot smell scents.

- **Height:** Although perennials generally die back each year, some of them can become extremely high or wide in one season. Knowing the exact height of a plant is extremely important in design. Maximum plant heights under normal growing conditions are given throughout the book.

- **Resistance:** A plant's ability to resist disease and insect infestations is an important consideration for anyone who doesn't like to use sprays. Frankly, in a typical perennial garden you can get by in most seasons without the use of pesticides. If you use intelligent gardening techniques, which are outlined later, you will rarely need to buy chemicals for disease or insect control.

CHAPTER 3

SELECTING AND PREPARING A SITE

This chapter gives you advice on the somewhat complex subject of placing perennials in just the right spot for best results. The most common considerations are correct exposure to sunlight; soil conditions, including moisture; and exposure to drying or potentially damaging winds. The chapter also includes tips on soil preparation—probably the single most neglected or misunderstood aspect of growing perennials properly.

Site and Light

One of the most exciting aspects of perennials is that you can find one to match almost any light condition. The light requirements of each perennial are well defined in each section of Part I so that you'll know exactly where to place a given plant for best results. Some plants are tolerant of a wide variety of light conditions, while others are extremely finicky. The right placement of a plant results in luxuriant foliage, brilliant flower coloration, and resistance to disease and insects. The opposite is also true.

Observe where sun is shining during the day. Watch where shadows fall—not only where, but also when and for how long. Study light carefully, since perennials have specific needs for light. You'll be amply rewarded for this extra effort.

Some plants need full light, while others tolerate or thrive in shade. The most intense light is from the south, with west close behind. An eastern exposure provides less intense light, while northern light is the least intense. Match plants to the light they need to grow properly. Shade-loving plants will generally perform poorly in intense light, and vice versa.

Light is affected by structures as well as by other plantings. For instance, light under eaves is reduced considerably, as is light under a large tree. Fences and hedges may also exclude or filter light, changing its intensity.

As noted, throughout this guide you'll also find information on the hardiness of different groups and named varieties. You'll often read in gardening books or catalogs that you live in a certain climatic zone; this general information is helpful but often somewhat misleading. In reality, your yard has a number of zones, known as *microclimates*. For example, plants on top of hills are in a warmer zone than plants at the bottom of hills or in low-lying areas prone to frost. Plants facing south or west are in warmer zones than plants facing east or north. Plants protected by fences, hedges, and walls are in warmer zones than those exposed to drying or cold winds. Likewise, plants covered by deep snowdrifts are in a warmer zone than plants exposed in open areas, since the snow acts as a protective blanket during deep-winter cold spells.

Bear in mind that some plants really like it hot, while others prefer it cool. How they grow is directly related to where they are planted. Full sun means lots of heat; a shaded area means cooler temperatures.

Some perennials are prone to wind damage. Although they need good air circulation, protection afforded by fences, hedges (not too close), and other barriers may be helpful.

Some perennials do poorly when planted next to hedges and trees. These compete with the plants for nutrients, light, and moisture. Other perennials, however, do quite well under the canopy of trees. Information about ideal placement of each perennial is given throughout Part I under the "Site and Light" heading in each section.

Soil and Moisture

While there are many contributing factors to a plant's health and longevity, the beginning point is always the quality of your soil. Providing perennials with the right kind of soil is the first step to success with these lovely plants. Ideally, you want to provide them with good soil to a depth of 15 to 18 inches (37.5 to 45 cm). Here is some critical information on good soil.

The Purpose of Good Soil

Good soil is firm enough to hold your plants in place, yet loose enough for easy penetration of water and oxygen to a plant's root system. Good soil drains freely. Good drainage, especially in winter, is extremely important to the survival of most perennials. Only a few thrive in boggy or low-lying areas. Good soil, while draining freely, also has the ability to retain moisture during drought and heat waves. It holds essential nutrients and makes them available to the plant over a long period. Good soil is alive, filled with billions of microorganisms. These microscopic creatures benefit the plant by providing and helping the perennial take in nutrients. Good soil attracts worms, which tunnel through the ground to keep it loose and also fill it with nitrogen through their droppings (castings). If weeds or grass are thriving in an area, you know you have some good soil, at least on the surface. Soil contaminated by pollution, herbicides, oil, and salt is often bare, a sign that the soil should be replaced.

What Makes Up Good Soil

Good soil is composed of both inorganic and organic materials. *Inorganic* means that a material does not come from plants or animals. *Organic* means that a material comes from the decomposition of anything that was once alive, whether plant or animal.

INORGANIC MATERIALS

The inorganic materials are clay, silt, and sand. Clay is made up of minuscule particles that cling together when wet. When wet clay dries, it turns almost rock-hard and tends to crack apart. Clay is usually a light tan to grayish tan in color. It sticks to your shovel and is very hard to work. However, nutrients cling to clay. So, some clay in your soil is beneficial because it holds nutrients. Silt is made up of larger particles than clay. When wet, it feels somewhat slippery. Sand is made up of the largest particles. When wet, sand has a grainy feel. Water slides through sand quickly. Having silt and sand in the soil helps keep it loose.

ORGANIC MATERIALS

The organic material found in good soils is the result of the decomposition (rotting) of anything once alive. Everything alive eventually dies, and when it does, it rots. Actually, it is being eaten by billions of different creatures, many of them microscopic. Some are plants, others are animals, and some have characteristics of both plants and animals. Organic material is especially attractive to worms. When worms die, their nitrogen-rich bodies decompose to give plants even more valuable food. The wide variety of unseen creatures digest organic matter into a light brown, fluffy material called *humus*. The benefits of humus to the soil are incredible. It keeps the soil loose and airy, holds moisture during drought, contains essential nutrients, and provides a home for helpful soil microorganisms, many of which help perennials take in food. It is essential to have lots of organic material in the soil.

The pH Value of Soil

Humus also maintains soil at just the right pH, a technical term referring to the activity of hydrogen ions. In simple language, pH is a gauge of how acidic or alkaline soil is. The pH scale runs from 0 (totally acidic) to 14 (totally alkaline). Neutral soil has a pH of 7. Most perennials grow best in a slightly acidic to neutral soil with a pH of 6.5 to 7. The exceptions are noted in Part I. The right pH determines the availability of nutrients to plants. If the pH is too high or too low, many essential plant foods will be locked into the soil and unable to be absorbed by the roots. If you're regularly adding lots of organic matter to the soil, it will often be at the correct pH and nutrients will be available to the plants.

Organic Matter as a Soil Amendment

The organic matter you add to soil is called a *soil amendment.* Leaves are usually readily available and are excellent for this purpose. Let them rot in a pile until they form what is called leaf mold—nothing more than decomposed leaves. Mix this material into the soil when preparing a bed. Add as much leaf mold as possible throughout the growing season as a summer mulch. The term *mold* implies disease, which is not the case. Leaf mold is like gold in the garden.

Peat, sold in most nurseries, is a superb soil amendment. For the average gardener, the most economical way of buying it is in large bales. Peat rarely contains disease organisms or weed seeds. When buying it, ask for acidic peat. The various brands imported from Canada generally are acidic, as are some from the United States.

Another fine soil amendment is rotted horse manure. It may contain some weed seeds and disease organisms. However, if horse manure is available, use it. Horse manure is also a mild fertilizer. If other manures are available, they're also highly recommended. Let them rot before using them.

Composting Made Easy

COMPOST IS NOTHING MORE than rotted organic debris. Many home gardeners build simple structures to produce compost. Here are the basic tips:

- Enclosures should be at least 4 feet (120 cm) square.

- Organic debris breaks down best if material is exposed to air. Use wires or slats for the side of the bin.

- Anything organic will break down in time. However, if you shred it before putting it into the pile, it will break down faster.

- Kitchen scraps are excellent for compost piles, but cover them well if you add them to the pile to avoid attracting animals.

- Keep the pile evenly moist at all times.

- Add a little 10-10-10 fertilizer to the pile every few weeks. The added nitrogen helps break down the organic matter.

- Every few days, turn the pile with a pitchfork or spading fork to speed up decomposition. If you don't have the energy, just let the material decompose slowly.

- Expect the pile to shrink to a small fraction of its original size. If you let the material decompose long enough, it will turn into a light brown, fluffy material called *humus.*

Finally, compost is another option. Composting is more popular in rural than suburban areas, but it can be done discreetly in large containers or attractive bins. However, while compost is a wonderful soil amendment, there is rarely enough of it after the pile breaks down over a period of weeks, months, or years.

Think of soil as living, something that needs to be fed and cared for to be healthy. Every year you must add organic matter to it. The inorganic substances break down very slowly, but the organic matter disappears rapidly, eaten by the billions of living creatures in the soil itself.

Loam

When inorganic and organic materials are mixed together in just the right proportion, the soil is called *loam*. About one-third of the soil should be organic matter. The rest is best in a combination of clay, silt, and sand in nearly equal parts. Very few soils will meet these standards exactly, but when soil gets close to these proportions, you'll know it.

Loam is usually very dark, almost black. This coloration is very good because it attracts sunlight in spring and warms up quickly. It also retains heat in the fall. Loam also usually has a loose feel to it. Superb loam is so loose that you can dig into it with your bare hand. It does not get compacted easily; this means that water drains quickly through it. Water gets to the roots easily but does not pool up around the roots, shutting off oxygen. Excess water drains away, carrying toxic salts with it.

The looseness of the soil induces rapid root growth. Roots spread out in all directions and form an intricate system to support the plant and to provide it with water and nutrients essential to vigorous growth. Often, the root system is much larger than the above-ground portion of the plant.

Loam, when dry, crumbles in your hand. If it gets wet, it is mildly sticky but doesn't form a solid, sticky ball. It will still crumble through your fingers. Loam has all of the good characteristics of the individual components without the negative ones. For example, the small amount of clay retains nutrients in the soil but doesn't make the soil hard or compacted when dry.

Getting Good Soil for Your Garden

You may already have good soil in the area where you intend to plant your perennials. However, most people don't. To find out, the first thing to do is to dig into the ground with a spade. Dig down at least 18 inches (45 cm). Usually, the top portion of the soil will be dark brown or black. This may be 3 inches (7.5 cm), half a foot (15 cm), or even a full foot (30 cm) deep if you're lucky.

In most areas you will find only a thin layer of loam or topsoil. This is because topsoil is expensive. When builders construct homes, they often cover just the surface of the soil with loam. Usually, it's barely enough for a good lawn. Underneath the topsoil you often find clay, sand, rock, and debris.

In most instances, the area where you'll be growing perennials will be covered with lawn or weeds. You must kill or remove these. Roundup® and similar products are effective nonselective herbicides and will kill all green plant tissue. Sometimes, you may have to apply them more than once for tough plants. Ideally, do this in late summer. The vegetation will die and turn brown. Roots should also die.

If you're an organic gardener, you'll have to remove the lawn and dig up the weeds. One of the easiest ways to remove lawn is in stages with a pickax. Shake off all the topsoil; place the sod in a wheelbarrow, and then compost it in another area.

Once you've removed or killed all weeds and lawn, dig up the good topsoil (black dirt or loam) and place it on a tarp to the side of the garden area. Naturally, if your soil is good to a depth of 18 inches (45 cm), just loosen it by digging or rototilling it. Whenever using a rototiller, stir up just the topsoil.

Never work in the soil when it is wet, just when it is damp at most. Working wet soil will cause it to compact.

Dig out the poor soil underneath the topsoil to a depth of 18 inches (45 cm). Cart this poor soil off to another area of your property. This can be back-breaking work. If you're making a large garden in an accessible location, hire a skid steer (commonly referred to as a Bobcat) to do this for you. A skid steer can do this job easily and quickly.

Next, place the topsoil back in the garden. Your problem is now obvious: you haven't filled the hole. You may have to buy soil from a garden center, nursery, or other source. If you've rented a skid steer, have the appropriate amount of soil delivered ahead of time. The operator can dig the hole and fill it with good soil at the same time. Mix in lots of organic matter, so that it makes up about one-third of the soil.

You'll buy garden soil by the cubic yard (cubic meter). The price varies by quality and region. You want mineral-based loam or quality field topsoil. It should come from a source not contaminated by herbicides or other chemicals. Reputable businesses will sell good garden soil, but a few may try to get rid of problem soil by selling it to unsuspecting customers. Check the soil before buying it. It should be black and have a nice, loose feel to it. Ask about its source.

Not everyone has the energy, time, or money to create a garden as just described. If you have a small garden or are just digging a few planting holes, here are a few tips:

- Dig a hole at least 18 inches (45 cm) deep and 24 inches (60 cm) wide for each plant. Remove all grass, weeds, rocks, and debris from the soil. Save only the topsoil. To fill the holes you may have to purchase additional soil in bulk, or potting soil in bags.
- Potting soil contains black dirt, peat, and perlite. Perlite—expanded volcanic material—looks like little white balls mixed into the potting soil. It acts as a spacer in the soil to keep it loose and airy.
- Now fill the hole with a mix of your topsoil and the potting soil or soil purchased in bulk.
- Mix in the appropriate amount of organic matter to get loam.
- In heavy clay or rock, this hole will gather water and may kill plants. If that's a possibility, we suggest building a raised bed instead, as outlined on page 390.

Moisture

Most perennials thrive in soil with good drainage. If surplus water remains around their crowns or roots for long periods, they often die out, especially in winter. A few plants thrive in low-lying or swampy areas. The special requirements for each group of perennials and for individual plants within these groups is covered in detail in each section of Part I.

Spacing

Proper spacing is important to allow for good plant growth and to prevent disease. Perennials vary greatly in their need for space. Some are tiny, while others grow many feet (more than a meter) tall and equally as wide. Proper spacing encourages good air circulation around the plant, which in turn helps prevent disease. Proper spacing also allows each plant to draw essential nutrients and water from the soil without competition from other plants. Proper spacing makes it easier to weed and care for perennials. Some plants that are small when you first plant them end up spreading to take up a great deal of space. Comments on spacing are included in each section of Part I to help you.

Taking advantage of vertical space with *Clematis*

Also remember to take advantage of vertical space. Some of the most memorable and charming effects are those of vining or climbing plants on a fence, wall, pergola, pillar, or trellis.

Companion Planting and Good Design

Companion planting refers to the skillful combi-

Here's a simple combination of *Lilium* (Lily) and *Veronica* (Speedwell). The object of such combinations is to have plants blooming at the same time as a delight to the eye.

nation of plants that bloom at the same time or have complementary forms and foliage. Designing with perennials is more far-reaching than companion planting and can be complex or simple. It depends on the number of perennials you want to grow and how extensive your plantings will be. The important thing is to feel good about your plants. They are meant to give you joy and peace of mind. Simple gardens are often the loveliest. Good design frequently occurs by chance, even by gambling with plants just to see what happens. The combination you enjoy is what counts,

and that varies with personal taste. Experienced gardeners experiment with varied perennials.

The points that follow are tips, nothing more than that, to help you with the varied elements of companion planting and design.

Placement

Light often determines design. Combining shade plants such as *Astilbe* (False Spirea), **Ferns**, and *Hosta* works well, but if you were to place them in direct

Raised-Bed Gardens

IF YOUR SOIL IS solid clay, rock-hard, or literally made of rock, you can still have a garden. The type of garden you'll be constructing is called a *raised-bed garden.* This method of mounding soil or enclosing it with timbers, rot-resistant wood, or rocks works fine for flowers. Growing plants in mounded soil has been done for thousands of years in China and for centuries in France.

Ideally, you'll want 18 inches (45 cm) of soil above the hard surface to work with. Some people get by with less. You'll have to buy the soil and have it placed where you want it. Again, when making a raised-bed garden, mix in lots of organic matter. The big advantage of a raised bed is that it warms up quickly in spring; its major disadvantage is that it tends to dry out faster in hot or windy weather.

Sometimes, if you have bad soil or an unusual situation—in this case, a hill sloping downward—you need to build a raised bed. This bed is 4 feet (120 cm) deep at one end, 2 feet (60 cm) at the other, and has been filled in with good soil.

One year later, the bed begins to show the color of an immature but delightful perennial border.

Borders or beds do not have to be contained by timbers. Some are simply mounds of earth placed on a flat surface and then planted with perennials.

Here's a stunning example of this simple method of making a raised bed in this manner.

Examples of Good Garden Design

This stunning example of good garden design is deceptively simple. What a graceful and haunting combination of color, form, and texture!

Here the skillful gardener achieves a riot of color with a vivid, vibrant variety of perennials blooming all at once.

A combination of Grasses protects a sandy bank from erosion, requires little maintenance, yet provides striking contrasts in color and form.

sun with plants thriving in bright light, the results could be disappointing.

In general, large plants are placed in the back of borders or in the center of island beds (flowers completely surrounded by lawn). This is aesthetically pleasing and allows sunlight to get to the plants. Medium-sized plants would then go in front of the larger ones, with the smallest plants right at the front. By varying the height of plants in the back slightly, you often get an undulating effect pleasing to the eye.

Match plants to the right place. Dainty plants with dainty flowers are meaningless viewed from a distance, delicate and haunting when viewed close up. On the other hand, large, bold plants with vibrant colors make vivid impressions even from far away.

Technique

Decide from the beginning whether you want a formal or informal garden. Formal gardens are symmetrical and often have straight lines, repetitive plantings, and so on. Informal gardens are asymmet-

rical, with curving lines, and a casual feel appropriate to most modern homes.

Use backdrops, such as fences, hedges, and evergreens, to add importance to your flower borders. They define and limit areas, especially on large pieces of property where you may not want to do more than a certain amount of gardening or design work.

Group flowers in masses (drifts) for greatest effect. Dozens of *Narcissus* (Daffodil) or *Tulipa* (Tulip) of a single color make stunning statements. These drifts don't have to be round or oval. Vary their form for added interest. Interweave drifts so that they appear like waves of color splashing against one another.

Plant at least three to five plants of any given variety together for a bold statement. Having several plants also increases the odds that you'll have one or two that are particularly beautiful in full bloom.

Use plants that grow into large clumps as main focal points, and work around them. *Baptisia* (False Indigo) and *Paeonia* (Peony) are good examples of

Imaginative Uses for Perennials

- Attract butterflies with varieties of *Asclepias* (Milkweed), *Aster*, *Coreopsis* (Tickseed), *Echinacea* (Purple Coneflower), *Liatris* (Gayfeather), *Nepeta* (Catmint), *Phlox*, *Rudbeckia* (Coneflower), and *Sedum* (Stonecrop).

- Entice hummingbirds with *Aquilegia* (Columbine), *Delphinium* (Larkspur), *Hemerocallis* (Daylily), *Heuchera* (Coral Bells), *Iris*, *Lilium* (Lily), *Monarda* (Bee Balm), *Nepeta* (Catmint), *Phlox*, and *Salvia* (Sage).

- Let some of your plants go to seed to attract many different species of birds in late summer and fall.

- Place flowers and foliage with a sweet scent along pathways, under windows, or near doors. Some varieties have scent only during a short time, such as *Sedum* 'Autumn Joy' which exudes the aroma of orange blossoms as it just begins to flower.

- Stop erosion on a bank with a ground cover, or by tucking tiny plants into its nooks, making it come alive with color that cascades like water over the steep embankment.

- Plant a cutting garden with perennials grown for different reasons: for fresh floral arrangements, dried flowers, seedpods, vibrant foliage, or exquisite scent.

such perennials. They live for years and never need to be moved. These are known as *accent* or *specimen* plants.

Climbers covered in clusters of blooms soften horizontal lines, such as those of a split-rail fence. They often stand out from a distance.

Color

Designing with perennials is much like painting. The primary colors are blue, red, and yellow. Combining these takes a special touch. Entire books have been written about the way to combine different colors effectively. We suggest you simply try combinations. If you like them, great; if not, try a new combination the following year.

Form

Plants are living architecture. Each is unique with a special shape, form, and height. Some plants almost weep, others are angular and hard, many stand upright in bold clumps, while others are more rounded and sensuous. Some Grasses flow and dance in even the mildest breeze. Paint your landscape with varied textures, just like a skilled artist.

CHAPTER 4

PLANTING PERENNIALS

This chapter will help you select healthy bare root and potted perennials. It also gives you detailed instructions on when and how to plant both. Most perennials are quite easy to plant once you're familiar with the general instructions given here. However, some require special attention as explained in the individual sections in Part I.

Buying Bare Root Plants

A bare root perennial usually is a dormant plant sold without any soil around its roots. Some of the varieties in this book may not be available locally but you can get them from mail-order companies as listed at the end of each section.

Bare root plants ordered through the mail should arrive in good condition if properly packaged and shipped at the right time.

Healthy bare root plants are typically one-year-old field-grown plants. They will often appear dry, but do not assume that they are dead. If you take care of them properly, they will spring to life.

Roots should be firm and healthy. They should not be broken or mashed.

White molds are rarely serious. Wash off the mold, and check the roots; cut off any mushy portions. If most of the root system is firm, the plant will

probably do fine. Dip the entire plant in a solution of 1 cup (about 240 ml) bleach to 5 gallons (19 liters) of water just before planting. Do this for about 30 seconds. This procedure kills many disease-causing organisms.

Blue gray or brownish, fuzzy molds can be extremely serious. These may indicate the presence of a disease over which you have little control. Get a new plant.

Place your order for bare root plants as early in the year as possible. The most popular plants often sell out. Choose them by specific named variety. Use the Latin name when ordering to avoid confusion. We understand that Latin names can be difficult to pronounce and remember, but they are extremely important in ordering. We have included them throughout the guide and list all plants under Latin names when appropriate, since common names often overlap.

Planting Bare Root Perennials

Most perennials are best planted in the spring. Exceptions are noted in the guide. When you order plants by mail, you'll usually get planting instructions in the package. Follow these or the ones given in this book. Adhere to instructions closely for best results.

The Diversity of Root Structures

BARE ROOT AND potted perennials have diverse root structures. Pictured below are examples of the main types. In each section of Part I you'll find explicit instructions on how to plant these varied structures. For example, each of these are planted at different depths from as deep as 6 inches (15 cm) for some bulbs, to just under the soil surface for rhizomes.

Plantlet

Bulb (like onion)

Corm

Bulb (like garlic)

Rhizome

Tuberous root

Planting bare root perennials is similar to planting potted plants, as illustrated later in this chapter. Follow the basic advice given under "Planting Potted Perennials in the Garden" for preparing the soil, planting, fertilizing, and watering.

Buying Potted Perennials

You'll find many of the perennials listed in this guide in local garden centers and nurseries. However, the choice in these stores is limited. As mentioned with bare root stock, you may have to buy a number of less common varieties through the mail. Unfortunately, a few perennials that are not reliably hardy in colder climates are sold in local nurseries and retail outlets. Even with proper winter protection, these will die out. The plants listed in this guide won't. Whenever you buy a potted perennial, check the plant carefully. Foliage should be healthy. Look closely at leaves, stems, and flowers. Look for healthy foliage and no insect infestations on the stems or undersides of leaves.

Also check the soil. If it has moved away from the edge of the pot, this indicates inconsistent watering, which stresses potted plants. If the soil is extremely dry, it also indicates careless handling. If a plant otherwise looks healthy, you can remedy both situations by pushing the soil back against the side of the pot and by watering the plant immediately. However, it would be better if you could find a plant that has been properly cared for from the start.

Most garden centers try to sell plants when they are in flower. For instance, *Chrysanthemum × morifolium* (Garden Mum) are often sold in full bloom in spring, whereas their natural blooming period is in the fall. The reason growers do this is that it is difficult to sell plants that are not in bloom. For any potted perennials you buy, read the appropriate sections in Part I carefully to determine proper planting time and what to do with potted flowers, since forced blooming may not be ideal for the plant's health. You may have to overcome the commercial grower's need to sell with some special attention.

Many garden centers charge more for larger plants. In some instances, larger plants are worth more, since it may take a long time for the plant to mature. However, in other cases it's better to buy smaller plants that cost less. This is particularly true for any perennial that grows quickly or spreads rapidly. Information about a plant's growing habit is included in every section of Part I to help you decide whether to pay more for a larger plant of that group.

Whenever you buy a potted plant, get it home quickly. Avoid leaving it in a hot car while you run errands or do additional shopping. This overheating can stress a plant badly or even kill it. Also, if the plant will be exposed to wind on the way home, have the garden center or nursery wrap paper or plastic around the entire plant. At home, remove the covering from the plant at once, and soak the soil until water runs out the bottom drain holes. Watering the plant a second time is recommended if the soil was somewhat dry to begin with.

If grown in a greenhouse, slowly move the plant from light shade into full sun over a period of 10 to 14 days. This hardening off helps the plant adjust to bright light and varying temperatures. If a plant has been outdoors for a few weeks before you buy it, this process is not necessary. Ask where the plant has been for the last 7 to 10 days at the nursery or garden center when buying it to see whether it has already been exposed to varying light and temperature for the correct period of time.

Naturally, if a plant thrives in shade, you will not move it into full sun. The light requirements of all plants are given throughout the guide. Expose plants only to the correct light.

Planting Potted Perennials in the Garden

Following is a step-by-step planting method to get your plants off to a good start.

Plant a potted perennial only after all danger of frost in spring has passed. Otherwise, keep it in your garage or in a sheltered location until it's safe to plant it out.

Dig a hole much larger than the size of the pot.

Since phosphorus travels poorly through the soil, it's important to get it under the roots of both bare root and potted plants at the time of planting. To do this, sprinkle a little superphosphate into the base of the hole according to the directions on the package. Cover it with 3 inches (7.5 cm) of soil to prevent roots from coming into direct contact with the chemical.

If you're an organic gardener, use bone meal instead. Bone meal is processed differently today than it was in the past, so it is less rich in nutrients than it once was. It also breaks down slowly and is more expensive than superphosphate when comparing relative levels of available phosphorus. However, it is long lasting and a reasonable alternative.

Set the pot in the hole. Check to see if the surface of the soil in the pot is almost level with the surrounding soil. Add soil to the hole until the pot rests just below the surrounding soil.

If there are any roots growing out of the drain holes, slide your finger across these to break them off. If a plant is somewhat root-bound, making it difficult to get it out of the pot, run a knife around the edge of the soil next to the pot. This often loosens the root ball. Support the plant between your fingers as you turn it upside down to tap the side of the pot on a hard surface. The plant should slide out of the pot. Avoid disturbing the root ball as best you can. You should not have to tap the plant very hard to get it out of the pot.

Place the root ball on the soil so that it ends up just a little lower than the surrounding soil to create a shallow basin to collect water.

Fill in the area around the root ball with soil or a soil-less mix. Press the soil firmly into place, making sure the plant remains at the correct level.

Mix ½ cup (about 114 g) of 10-10-10 fertilizer in 1 gallon (about 4 liters) of water, and shake it up. Do this several days in advance. A few granules may not dissolve, but don't worry about this. Then pour ½ cup (about 120 ml) of this starter solution around the planted perennial. Diluted solutions of water-soluble fertilizers are also fine alternatives. Or, use organic fertilizers high in nitrogen and potassium if you prefer, to get the plants growing quickly. Fish emulsion is highly recommended.

Soak the plant thoroughly with a hose, letting the water soak into the ground. The soil may sink slightly. If so, add more soil, and press it lightly into place. Then water again, saturating the soil.

Planting Potted Perennials in Large Pots

Some perennials thrive in large pots. We suggest that you follow the guidelines for planting a perennial directly in the garden when potting up (placing a potted plant in a larger pot). The main points are to get phosphorus into the soil and to use potting soil or soil-less mixes such as Pro-Mix in the pot. Pots should have good drainage holes. If they are placed on a deck,

they should have little feet under the pot to keep it off the wood. Most materials, including ceramic, clay, plastic, and wood, are fine as long as there are drain holes. However, perennials grown in pots require lots of care, especially when it comes to watering. Check the soil every day to make sure it stays moist.

Transplanting

Most perennials should be transplanted in early spring just before growth begins. A few, however, are best transplanted later or even in fall. The correct time is usually identical to that recommended for division in "Propagation" sections of Part I.

Have a planting hole ready before you begin to transplant a perennial. Also have all the appropriate materials at hand, so that you won't have to wait to get the new plant into the ground.

Dig up the plant, getting as much of the root system as possible. Some perennials resent being transplanted and may even die. When this is the case with a plant listed in this book, it is underscored in the appropriate section.

Plant the perennial immediately in its new location. Saturate the soil, then keep it evenly moist until the plant is growing well.

Finally, keep in mind perennial gardens are not as permanent as some people think. Revitalizing beds often means lifting older plants in early spring, cutting off old growth, and then replanting them in soil amended with organic material and fertilizers. This does not mean lifting all plants, but most. Some, as outlined in the individual sections, are essentially permanent and will resent being lifted. But many others respond beautifully to this treatment.

Renewing a Perennial Bed or Border

Here's a group of Bearded Iris being smothered by weeds. If nothing is done, they will die out.

Weed around the plants. Do not weed the main clump, but dig it up.

Once the plant is out of the ground, pull or cut it apart. Do this at the appropriate time of year (in this case, 6 weeks after normal flowering). Remove all weeds.

Remove all dead foliage, and cut off the tips of any leaves spotted with disease. Cutting leaves back also compensates for root disturbance and loss.

Dig up the entire bed. Remove even the tiniest portion of weed roots, as these might resprout. Then add lots of organic matter to the soil.

Place the divisions where you would plant them. Dust the cut ends with a fungicide to protect them from disease. Or, use a chlorine powder if you prefer.

Now plant the rhizomes just under or at the surface of the soil. Water them immediately, saturating the soil to a depth of a foot (30 cm) or more. The rejuvenated plants will grow into a healthy clump by the following year.

CHAPTER 5

CARING FOR PERENNIALS

While a few perennials survive and bloom fairly well with what amounts to benign neglect, most demand consistent and conscientious care. The tips in this chapter will help you get vigorous growth, lush foliage, excellent bloom color and scent, long-lasting or repeat bloom, desired form, better disease and insect resistance, and longer life of individual plants. Furthermore, if you follow the advice provided here, you'll reduce the amount of time and energy needed to take care of your perennial garden.

Water

Each perennial has its own unique water needs. Some require lots of water early in the season, then little later on. Others need lots of water throughout the entire growing season. The exact requirements of each type of perennial are covered in detail throughout Part I.

When to Water

There is no formula for proper watering. You know when to water by actually feeling the soil and looking at the plant; don't just look at the soil. Dig into it with your hand or with a trowel. Water the soil whenever the top 3 inches (7.5 cm) begin to dry out.

Don't be fooled by rain. Some rainfall appears heavy but may be quite light. A light sprinkling is meaningless. Each time you water, saturate the soil.

The basic rule is water, water, water. Most perennials respond to consistent watering with lush growth and abundant bloom. Proper watering also extends the bloom period. If your soil is well-drained and properly prepared, it is almost impossible to overwater perennials.

How to Water

Use overhead watering with a sprinkler or direct watering at the base of the plant from a hose. If you enjoy watering, hold the hose in place to saturate the soil around the base of the plant. If hand watering is a chore, set the hose down at the base of the plant. Let it run until the ground is thoroughly saturated. Some gardeners place the hose on a board to prevent the formation of a hole where the water runs out.

Overhead watering with sprinklers is fine as long as you do it long enough for the ground to get thoroughly saturated. Overhead watering during hot, dry periods is helpful in preventing the formation of aphid and spider mite colonies.

Tips on Watering

Always saturate the soil with water before and after the application of any fertilizer. This protects the plant from possible damage, often referred to as *burn*. Deep watering dissolves nutrients and carries them to the roots where they become available to the plant.

Always saturate the soil around the plant base before spraying with fungicides, insecticides, or miticides to prevent leaf burn.

Water also dissolves carbon dioxide, forming a mildly acidic solution. This reacts with minerals in the soil to form nutrients that can be absorbed easily by the plant.

When to Stop Watering

Continue watering plants until the ground freezes. The soil should be moist until the end of the season.

Mulch (Summer)

Mulch is any material that you put on the surface of the soil around a perennial to keep the soil moist and cool during hot weather. Most perennials thrive in soils kept consistently moist throughout the season. Mulch helps do this and cuts down on the need for watering.

Mulch also inhibits annual weed growth and makes it far easier to pull up the few weeds that do sprout. Many annual weeds need light to germinate. A mulch covers seed deeply enough so that they are shrouded in darkness and cannot sprout. Weeds compete with perennials for moisture and nutrients.

Weeds can get larger than many perennials. They block out available light. They also reduce air circulation around the stems of the perennials, and this can lead to disease. It is common for weaker or less vigorous perennials to die off in a border choked with weeds.

Mulch has an added benefit of stopping soil from splattering against the leaves, a frequent cause of disease. Mulch can actually kill some diseases. It also feeds soil microorganisms and worms, which benefit the plant enormously by keeping the soil loose, allowing oxygen and water to get to the roots. The living creatures in the soil eat the mulch and in the process keep the soil more fertile than it would naturally be. Some of them help roots take in nutrients at the same time.

We suggest that you use organic mulches. These are materials derived from living things. Except in rock gardens, avoid rock or pebble mulches, since they often get too hot during the summer and stunt plant growth.

Placing Mulch

Place organic mulches around the base of plants as soon as the ground warms up in spring or early summer. In most cases, this is when the soil reaches a temperature of approximately 60°F (16°C). The best time to mulch varies a little each season, but this is a good guideline. Too early application of mulch may retard growth in some perennials.

Place mulch around the entire plant, but do not touch the stems, cover crowns, or cover the growth of plants that multiply freely by spreading stems or stolons. If you place mulch over or against growing stems or leaves, you can cause disease or smother the plants. This does not mean that you cannot place mulch under the foliage canopy. You can slide it under spreading foliage without doing any damage. Just keep it away from the main growing stems.

There are a few plants that prefer somewhat hot and dry conditions. These respond well to thin, rather than thick layers of mulch around their crowns. When this is the case, it is indicated in the individual plant listings. It's the exception, definitely not the rule.

Replace mulch when it disappears during the summer as soil microorganisms and worms feed on it. It seems to melt away as the summer progresses.

Removing Mulch

Although perennials will self-sow in mulch, we suggest removing all mulch after the plant forms seedpods. This way seeds drop directly onto the soil. When you remove the mulch, scratch the surface of the soil lightly to create little crevices for the seeds to drop into. If you do not want to remove mulch, be sure not to add additional mulch once seeds are dispersed.

The removal of summer mulch in the fall for sanitary reasons is controversial. One group asserts that

Common Organic Mulches

SOME MATERIALS USED FOR mulch may cause a nitrogen deficiency in the soil. The reason is that soil microorganisms will use up nitrogen in the process of breaking these materials down. Materials high in carbon are ones that cause the most problems. Bark and wood chips fall into this category. Whenever you use these for mulch, sprinkle additional nitrogen around your plants.

Here is a list of the most popular organic mulches:

Bark (shredded): Quite expensive, nice color and texture, and easy to apply. It looks sensational with larger, isolated specimen plants. Fine in beds if you add more nitrogen to the soil than you would otherwise.

Cocoa bean hulls: Quite expensive, nice color and texture, easy to apply. Has noticeable odor of chocolate. Will mildew if applied more than 2 to 3 inches (5 to 7.5 cm) deep at a time. Water penetrates this mulch easily. It does a good job keeping soil moist and cool.

Grass clippings: Costs nothing, readily available in colder climates. Gets hot and will mildew if applied fresh (can cause slight odor). Apply dry to a depth of 2 to 3 inches (5 to 7.5 cm) at a time. Compost it if it has recently been treated with a herbicide. Not particularly attractive, but quite effective.

Leaves: Should be shredded with a shredder or rotary mower before application, since whole leaves stop water from penetrating the soil easily. Apply to a depth of 2 to 3 inches (5 to 7.5 cm) at a time. This is the best and most readily available mulch for gardeners in cold-climate areas. Worms love it, and it has a nice rich color and terrific texture.

Pine needles: Free, drains well, never compacts. Apply to a depth of 2 to 3 inches (5 to 7.5 cm). An excellent alternative to leaves if available. Acidifies the soil slightly. Mild risk of fire if garden is not kept moist. As attractive as leaves, and effective.

Wood chips: Expensive if bought in stores. Often available for free in large quantities from local utility companies. Attractive if properly chipped. May take nitrogen from the soil; apply fertilizer more liberally than normal. Wood chips are best around bold accent plants, not in the border itself. Keep depth at 2 inches (5 cm). Wood chips take a long time to break down.

mulch is a refuge for insect eggs and spores of various disease-causing organisms during the winter. They maintain that the removal of mulch at the end of the season is one of the essential elements of good organic gardening. A second group agrees that mulch should be removed if disease has been a problem during the growing season. Otherwise, they insist on leaving mulch as added winter protection for perennials.

Fertilizing

To create magnificent bloom, fertilize exactly as directed in the individual sections of Part I. Use fertilizers that are either inorganic, organic, or a combination as suggested for best results.

Fertilizer Basics

Plants, like people, need a balanced diet to grow well. Fertilizer is plant food, which consists of a number of chemicals found in the air and soil. Perennials need lots of some elements (macro elements) and very little of other elements (micro or trace elements). Loam with a high amount of organic material contains most of the elements needed by a perennial. However, some of the elements are used up fairly quickly and must be replaced on a regular basis for healthy plant growth.

Fertilize plants as directed throughout the book. This illustration shows the approximate intensity of sprinkling inorganic granules on the ground. Water these immediately to dissolve them and carry nutrients into the root zone.

You will probably need to add three major elements to the soil on a regular basis. These are nitrogen (N), phosphorus (P), and potassium (K). Phosphorus moves extremely slowly through soil. Ideally, place it just below the plant's root system at the time of planting either as bone meal (organic) or superphosphate (inorganic).

Fertilizers are either inorganic (synthetic) or organic (naturally occur-ring from living things). Most perennials grow best using either of these types of fertilizers. A few respond best to organic fertilizers only. Specific information is given throughout the guide. Here are some tips on the two types of fertilizers.

Inorganic Fertilizers

There are several advantages to inorganic fertilizers. They provide essential food to plants quickly. They work early in the season before the ground gets warm enough for organic fertilizers to be effective. They are inexpensive. For example, one 40-pound (18-kg) bag of 10-10-10 inorganic fertilizer contains as much of the three essential elements as 1 ton (about 900 kg) of organic material. Used inappropriately, however, they can damage the environment.

TYPES OF INORGANIC FERTILIZER

Use any 10-10-10 all-purpose garden fertilizer without herbicides (weed killers). You can also use 12-12-12 or 20-20-20, but these are more powerful and not as commonly available. However, if they are the same price as an equal amount of 10-10-10, then they are a better value. Balanced fertilizers are available in granular formulations sold in bags at most nursery and garden centers. The label will indicate whether the fertilizer is quick or slow release. Slow-release fertilizers consist of coated granules. The outer coating breaks down to gradually release the fertilizer over a period of weeks. Scatter granules around the base of the plant. A ballpark quantity would be 1/3 cup (about 80 grams) per square foot (930 square cm) of soil around mature plants, if using 10-10-10, and less if using a more powerful fertilizer.

This is truly an approximation. Each plant responds differently to varying amounts of fertilizer. Giving an exact amount is like trying to tell you how much each person should eat. You'll know whether your feeding is correct by letting the plant tell you. If it's doing well, you'll get a lush plant with lots of foliage, new growth from the base, and plenty of flowers.

Water-soluble fertilizers are also quite effective. Jack's Classic® (20-20-20), Miracle-Gro® (18-24-16), and Rapid-Gro (23-19-17) are among the most commonly available. Dissolve these fertilizers in water before applying them to the ground around the plant. Some growers also spray leaves with water-soluble fertilizers in what is known as *foliar feeding*. Follow the directions on the package.

If you have a large bed, consider using a Siphon Mixer to make fertilizing easier. You dissolve 2 pounds (about 1 kg) of 20-20-20 water-soluble fertilizer in a 5-gallon (19-liter) pail. For fish emulsion, the amount is 1 quart (about a liter) per pail. The Siphon Mixer will automatically mix the solution in the pail with

Essential Elements for Healthy Perennials

Boron (B): Needed in minute quantities. Important in cell division, flower formation, and pollination. Helps transfer food between cells. Ample amount in most soils. Augment by the addition of fish emulsion to the soil. (.005 percent of plant tissue)

Calcium (Ca): Needed in moderate amounts. Important to cell structure and good root growth. Gets plants off to good early growth. Ample amount in most soil. Found in gypsum (calcium sulphate), which is sometimes added to soil to get rid of salt deposits. Augment by adding bonemeal or superphosphate to the planting hole. Also available in lime and wood ash, but use these in tiny amounts, since they raise the pH of the soil. (0.6 percent of plant tissue)

Carbon (C): Needed in large amounts. Ample supply in air. (44 percent of plant tissue)

Chlorine (Cl): Needed in minute quantities. Important in transfer of water and minerals into cells and in photosynthesis. Ample supply in soil or city water. (.015 percent of plant tissue)

Copper (Cu): Needed in minute quantities. Important in stem development and color. Essential in enzyme formation, root growth, and respiration. Ample amount in most soil. Augment by addition of Milorganite to the planting hole. (.001 percent of plant tissue)

Hydrogen (H): Needed in large amounts. Ample supply in water. (6 percent of plant tissue)

Iron (Fe): Needed in minute quantities. Important in chlorophyll formation and for proper plant respiration. Ample amount in most soils. Augment by adding bonemeal to the planting hole. (.02 percent of plant tissue)

Magnesium (Mg): Needed in small amounts. Important in chlorophyll formation and respiration. Essential for healthy foliage and disease resistance. Ample amount in soil, but present in fish emulsion. (0.3 percent of plant tissue)

Manganese (Mn): Needed in minute quantities. Important in chlorophyll formation and the production of food through photosynthesis. An enzyme regulator. Ample amount in most soils. Augment by addition of Milorganite to the planting hole. (.05 percent of plant tissue)

Molybdenum (Mo): Needed in minute quantities. Helps perennials use nitrogen for vigorous growth. Essential for enzyme formation, root growth, and respiration. Ample amount in most soils. Augment by addition of Milorganite to the planting hole. (.0001 percent of plant tissue)

Nitrogen (N): Needed in large amounts. Critical to healthy stem growth, lush foliage, and beautiful bloom. Important in cell growth and plant respiration. Essential food for soil microorganisms. Must be added to soil on a regular basis. (2 percent of plant tissue)

Oxygen (O): Needed in large amounts. Ample supply in both air and water. (45 percent of plant tissue)

Phosphorus (P): Needed in large amounts. Essential to rapid root growth. Important to proper formation of stems, good color, and solidity of petals. Must be added to soil at planting time as bonemeal or superphosphate. (0.5 percent of plant tissue)

Potassium (K): Needed in large amounts. Important to root growth, formation of blossoms, and bloom color. Critical in forming sugar and starches. May need to be added to soil on a regular basis. (1 percent of plant tissue)

Sulfur (S): Needed in small amounts. Keeps soil at the right pH (slightly acidic). Important in formation of plant proteins needed for good health and root growth. Ample amount supplied by rain. (0.4 percent of plant tissue)

Zinc (Zn): Needed in minute quantities. Important in stem and flower bud formation. Essential to enzyme formation, root growth, and respiration. Ample amount in most soils. Augment by adding Milorganite to the planting hole. (.01 percent of plant tissue)

water running through a hose. You'll get roughly 60 gallons (228 liters) of fertilizer mixture per 5-gallon (19-liter) pail.

TIPS ON USING INORGANIC FERTILIZERS

When using inorganic fertilizers, follow directions exactly. Frequent small feedings are better than large doses of fertilizer all at once. When in doubt, reduce the amount given at any one time and feed more often.

Fertilize each type of plant as indicated in the specific section of Part I. Improper fertilization cannot only damage plants but also is a waste of time, money, and energy.

When using inorganic fertilizers, always saturate the soil with water before and after application. This will prevent any damage to the plant's root system.

If you want to grow perennials from seed, never use inorganic fertilizer in the growing medium. It may kill seedlings just as they begin to sprout.

If you use inorganic fertilizer such as 10-10-10 in a planting hole, cover it with 3 inches (7.5 cm) of soil to prevent any contact with the plant's roots.

When using hoses for foliar feeding, you are required by most state building codes to use a backflow preventer. This attachment prevents fertilizers and chemicals from getting into your home water system.

Organic Fertilizers

All perennial beds should contain organic matter. The importance of this was stressed in the section on good soil in Chapter 3. Most organic materials contain relatively low amounts of the three essential elements, but they are excellent as food for soil microorganisms and worms. These creatures help plants take in nutrients and enrich the soil at the same time.

Organic fertilizers are released slowly into the soil. They do not damage seeds or seedlings when applied in small amounts. They also can be added to planting holes in moderation without root damage. As with any other product, read the manufacturer's label.

However, organic fertilizers are expensive and are not effective early in the season when the ground is still too cold for soil microorganisms to be active. A number of them are better considered as soil amendments or conditioners rather than fertilizers.

TYPES OF ORGANIC FERTILIZER

The best and most commonly available organic fertilizers are alfalfa meal, sold as rabbit pellets in farm stores; blood meal (15-2-1); bone meal (0-10-0); compost (4-1-3); cow manure (.6-.2-.3); fish emulsion (10-7-0); horse manure (.7-.3-.5); and Milorganite (6-2-0).

Alfalfa meal contains triacontonal, a substance that appears to encourage lush growth in a number of plants. In a 32-gallon (122-liter) plastic garbage can, place 10 cups (about 1 kilo) of rabbit pellets, 1 cup (about 227 g) Epsom salts (available at pharmacies), and ½ cup (about 114 g) Sprint 330 (a source of iron). Fill the can with water, and cover it firmly with a lid. Stir it every day for 4 to 5 days. Yes, it does stink, so keep the lid on. This is known as alfalfa meal tea. Pour 1 gallon (about 4 liters) around larger plants, and ⅓ this amount around smaller plants each spring.

Blood meal, high in nitrogen, contains a number of valuable trace elements.

Bone meal is high in phosphorus, which moves extremely slowly through soil, so place it close to root systems for good results.

Compost is nothing more than decomposed organic matter.

Cow manure is available in many nurseries in bags. While very low in nutrients, it attracts worms.

Fish emulsion, high in nitrogen, also contains a number of trace elements.

Horse manure is available in a number of areas. Let it decompose fully until it is light brown and fluffy. Strangely, it has a pleasant smell once fully rotted and attracts worms.

Milorganite is treated human sewage. Thoroughly mix it into the soil to avoid odor.

Weeding

Weeds compete with perennials for available moisture and nutrients. They also grow prolifically in good soil and form a canopy that can smother perennials or cut off good air circulation around the plants. This often results in disease. Weeds also act as hosts for insects and disease organisms that can do a great deal of damage to your perennials.

Weeds fall into two main categories. One group of weeds plays out its entire life cycle in a single year. These are *annual* weeds, which you can pull out of the soil or prevent with a preemergent herbicide. Many of them produce seed that needs light to germinate and can be held in check by use of a summer mulch. Most annual weeds have relatively shallow root systems and are easy to pull by hand.

The other group of weeds survive longer than a year and are called *perennial* weeds, and they are a perennial gardener's nightmare. Many have long roots that are difficult to pull up from the ground. If even an infinitesimal portion of the root snaps off, the weed will resprout and eventually go to seed. Some of the more common perennial weeds are dandelions, grass, quack grass, vines, and thistles. So, when preparing a bed, use a nonselective herbicide such as Roundup® to kill them. This chemical is absorbed by the plant in such a way that all roots are killed. Herbicides of this type are called *systemic*. Ideally, kill all weeds in late summer and early fall with a systemic herbicide before making a bed. Then plant the following spring.

If you're an organic gardener opposed to the use of herbicides, dig up all weeds. Dig deep down to the very tips of all roots. Remove every little bit of root, or it may resprout.

To manage the growth of annual weeds, lightly hoe the upper inch (2.5 cm) or so of soil before applying a summer mulch. The best tool for this is a pronged hoe. Just scratch the surface. Avoid hoeing close to the base of any perennial. Hoeing may wound roots or stems, inviting infection by disease and infestation by insects. Loosening the soil keeps it from compacting, kills off germinating weed seeds, and helps oxygen get to the plant's root zone.

Once plants are growing and the soil has warmed up, the use of a summer mulch prevents most annual weed growth, since many weed seeds need light to germinate. The few weeds that do appear are easy to pull up by hand from the moist soil. Hand weed around the base of plants to avoid damaging the shallow root system.

Using a herbicide such as Roundup® on growing weeds requires extreme care if it's sprayed near perennials. If any wind is blowing, some of the herbicide can get on perennial leaves and cause damage or death. One way to avoid damaging valuable plants is to soak a sponge in the herbicide (mixed with water as directed on the label) and rub it on the weeds you want to kill. When doing this, wear rubber gloves, and wash them off in water with detergent after each use. A small paintbrush is equally good and easier for some gardeners to use. Killing perennial weeds in this way takes time but prevents accidental damage.

Grass

Keep turf grass out of your garden. Often beds are surrounded by lawn. Grass thrives in the moist, rich soil provided by appropriate watering. The underground stems (stolons) of grass search out such an area and spread rapidly. Each spring, use an edger to outline your bed. Step on it firmly so that the blade goes down as deeply as possible. Move along the edge, cutting the outline with the edger. Once you've cut the entire edge, go back to pick up the sod. Knock it hard against the ground to get loose soil off the roots. Pick up bits of root that break off. Then toss the grass into a wheelbarrow. Do this along the entire edge, removing all grass and roots. Even the tiniest piece of root may take and grow into grass.

Staking

Staking or supporting specific perennials may be necessary. Staking is best done early in the season. Slide the support into the soil an inch (2.5 cm) away from the outermost part of the stem. The most commonly used supports in perennial beds are bamboo or plastic stakes. They are inexpensive, light, easy to use, and often colored green to be inconspicuous.

The easiest way to attach a stem to a support is with a loose figure-eight knot. Avoid restricting stem growth. Keep tying the plant farther up on the stem

Tying Plants to Stakes

THERE ARE MANY WAYS to support plants with stakes. By far the most common is with green bamboo, metal, or plastic stakes. The photo illustrates the basic principles of staking.

We suggest tying plants to stakes with a figure-eight knot as pictured here. We have used two spade handles to depict the correct manner of tying the knot. The figure-eight knot is recommended because it cushions the stem from the stake, doesn't restrict the stem's growth, and holds the stem firmly in place. We often use soft green fabric for the knots because it is inconspicuous and never digs into the stem as the plant matures. However, many other ties also work well.

Begin tying stems to stakes early in the season. Tie them in several places as they grow. Green stakes are inconspicuous once plants mature. Using green ties also helps disguise the support.

as it grows throughout the season. This stops the plant from toppling over or breaking in gusts of wind. Twine, nylon stocking, thin rags, and any other soft materials make good ties.

Occasionally, we refer to pea stakes as a means of support. Vegetable gardeners get vining pea plants off the ground and easier to pick by placing brush at different angles over emerging seedlings. The vines creep up and over the branches, which act as support throughout the season. The use of pea stakes works well with specific perennials, and we tell you when their use is appropriate.

For certain types of plants, such as *Paeonia* (Peony), special metal rings work well. Always put these in place early in the season. Guide the stems to keep them within the rings.

Deadheading

Removing spent blossoms on perennials is very easy. You can do it with your hands, pruners, grass clippers, or scissors. It doesn't take a lot of time and helps in many ways. Here are some of the reasons to deadhead:

Removing spent blossoms on many perennials forces growth buds lower down on the plant to form branches. These produce flower buds later in the season. This isn't true for all perennials, but it is for many. The little extra time needed to remove spent blossoms results in more color later in the season, often at a time when it is sorely lacking.

An obvious reason to remove spent blossoms is that plants look so much better when this is done. Of course, there are a few perennials whose flowers seem to melt away and really don't need deadheading for their overall appearance. But, for the most part, deadheading makes for a much nicer-looking garden.

Deadheading prevents petals from dropping to the ground or decaying on the foliage. Dead petals can become homes for insects and disease-causing organisms. By removing all dead plant tissue from or around the plant regularly, you keep the garden clean and lessen the chance of outbreaks of disease and infestations by insects.

Deadheading also stops the plant from going to seed. Forming seed takes energy from a plant. In some cases, it exhausts the plant so that it dies out earlier than it would if deadheaded regularly. This certainly is not the case for most perennials, but the individual sections in Part I will indicate when it is an important consideration for a given plant group or variety.

Stopping seed formation is also important to some gardeners who want plantings to remain uniform. The seedlings of specific plants can be different from their parents, and some gardeners do not like the resulting mix in the garden.

However, the seed heads or pods of some peren-

Deadheading

A FEW PERENNIALS, such as *Hemerocallis* (Daylily), look messy unless you remove spent flowers daily.

Other plants need to be deadheaded only once after the flower dies. The brown spikes of *Liatris* (Gayfeather) may be removed for aesthetic reasons and to stop the plant from forming seed. Simply snip off the spikes just above the highest leaf with pruning shears. Preserve as much foliage as possible.

Once deadheaded, the plant displays a lush foliage mound for the rest of the season.

nials are often stunning and make good additions to dried arrangements. Again, individual sections in Part I always tell you when this is the case.

The best method of removing spent blossoms is also covered in each section. No matter how you remove blossoms, always toss them into a bucket to keep the garden clean and to prevent disease.

Pruning

Pruning is a term most commonly used with woody plants, but in recent years a number of gardeners have begun to classify related growing techniques under this term. Following are some of these techniques with explanations of how, why, and when to use them.

Disbudding

Some perennials produce a cluster of buds at the end of a stem. However, certain gardeners prefer one large

bloom to a number of smaller ones. Whether or not to remove buds to create a different effect is a matter of personal choice. To disbud, simply pinch off young buds under the main bud as soon as they appear. The sooner you do this, the better. This subject is covered in detail in individual sections of Part I.

Removing Flowers

When you buy young potted plants, they're often in bloom. As mentioned in Chapter 4, growers have learned that

Some growers like to get single large flowers on certain plants, such as *Paeonia* (Peony). By removing the side buds just as they form, you channel all energy into creating a larger central flower.

it is much easier to sell blooming plants. Many plants are forced to bloom before their natural bloom period just to sell them.

You want to remove all buds and bloom from such plants so that they will grow properly their first growing season, creating a large, healthy plant. They will then form buds in fall or the following season and bloom at the appropriate time.

Pinching and Shearing Back

Pinching off the tips of young shoots early in the growth of some perennials creates bushier plants with more bloom.

Shearing plants back to a lower height or all the way to the ground is yet another technique that can promote bloom or be important to the health of the plant if it's infected by specific diseases.

Both of these techniques are included in individual sections of Part I when appropriate.

Thinning

Some gardeners cut out all but three to five stems from clumps of certain mature perennials. This increases air circulation around the stems and can help prevent disease. It also results in better flowering on the few remaining stems. This is advised in the relevant sections of Part I where it is appropriate for specific plants.

Winter Protection

Ratings for hardiness are given for each variety listed in Part I. Most of the plants in this guide have been chosen because, once mature, they require little or no winter protection other than normal snowfall.

Winter Protection

A severe frost is a warning sign that winter is close behind. When many of your flowers die back and turn brown, it's time to clean up the bed. Remove all dead foliage. Clean up debris and leaves from the bed. Get the garden as clean as possible. If plants remain green, leave them alone. You can always clean them up in spring.

Here's a bed covered with straw and a lovely blanket of snow. The use of whole leaves, marsh hay, or pine needles would have been just as good. We highly recommend the use of winter cover during the first year and in subsequent years for more tender varieties. However, most of the perennials listed in this guide do not need winter protection other than minimal snowfall once they've matured.

As soon as it warms up in spring, remove the winter mulch. This prevents crown rot. However, keep the winter mulch close by in case of a sudden, unexpected cold snap. You can put it back over the plants easily and quickly in such an emergency to protect the young shoots.

If plants do require winter protection, follow these simple steps: Remove all dead foliage and stems in late fall after a killing frost. As soon as the ground freezes permanently, apply winter mulch to the appropriate depth (as outlined in the sections of Part I). Remove the mulch as soon as it warms up in spring to prevent plants from rotting out.

There is considerable debate among growers as to the best winter protection: everyone agrees that lots of snow is the best protection of all, but after that it gets more controversial.

In colder climates the most readily available materials for winter protection are whole leaves, marsh hay, straw, and pine needles. All provide adequate protection if at least 6 inches (15 cm) thick. Whole leaves sometimes mat down and cause rot in early spring, but this is rare if they are removed on time. Oak leaves are your first choice if available, since they rarely mat down. If you apply shredded leaves of any kind, they may mat badly and often will cause rot. Marsh hay, a type of grass, is excellent and rarely contains weed seeds if harvested late in the season. Straw also provides good winter protection. It is expensive, sometimes contains weed seed (especially thistle), and is somewhat messy to work with. Yet it does the job well and is used yearly by many fine gardeners. Pine needles, if available in sufficient quantities, are excellent. Pine needles don't mat down and are fairly easy to remove in spring. Although readily available, avoid the use of grass clippings. These mat quickly and often cause covered plants to rot out.

When applying mulch, let the ground freeze first, as we've already pointed out. Mice and moles like to use mulch as a winter home. If the ground freezes first, this helps protect your plants from these voracious feeders. Some gardeners put poison bait under mulch if they've had problems in the past. Make sure that your pets cannot get into these baits.

CHAPTER 6

SOLVING PERENNIAL-GROWING PROBLEMS

Perennials have survived in the wild for millions of years without any help from us. The purpose of good gardening techniques is to aid nature, not fight it. The results can be spectacular. Perennials, like all other plants, are vulnerable to diseases and insects, which you can prevent or control. Other enemies include deer and an assortment of rodents. One of the worst enemies of perennials, however, is a gardener using chemicals inappropriately.

Diseases and Insects

Diseases and insects are common in any garden. Organic methods are helpful but may not prevent or control all problems. Nevertheless, some growers never use sprays in the garden, not even those derived from organic substances. The reason is that sprays are indiscriminate, often killing good as well as bad living organisms. Organic gardeners let nature take its course, helping it along as best they can in a natural way but allowing some damage to take place.

We rarely use fungicides or insecticides in our home gardens. Yes, we do lose a plant occasionally, but the replacement cost is often less than that of using chemicals on a regular basis.

Chemicals are potentially dangerous and must be handled according to the directions on the label.

Chemicals used on perennials include fungicides (kill fungi), insecticides (kill insects), and miticides (kill mites). Herbicides kill weeds, which often act as hosts for insects and disease.

Organic Disease and Insect Prevention

Whether you use chemicals or not is a personal decision. Either way, preventing and controlling diseases and controlling insects before their populations balloon makes a lot of sense. If you follow basic organic-growing strategies, you'll often reduce or eliminate the need for chemicals.

Buy disease-resistant varieties. Resistance or tolerance is noted in most catalogs. These qualities are being bred into many plants by commercial growers. Inquire locally to learn about varieties that tend to be disease-resistant or -tolerant in your area.

Return packaged or mail-order plants that you can tell are dead. If bare root plants are covered with deadly mold or fungal growth as outlined in Chapter 4, return them. If there is just a little white mold in one spot, rinse it off, and then disinfect the area with a bleach solution as explained in that chapter under "Buying Bare Root Plants." Plant only healthy bare root plants.

Buy potted plants with no signs of disease or insect infestations. Check the plant to make sure that the soil has not moved away from the rim of the pot. This indicates improper watering and potential stress to the plant.

Segregate newly purchased potted plants for several days. Keep them cool and moist. Be sure to check for any disease. Then plant them with your other plants.

Healthy perennials resist disease, whereas weak or poorly cared for plants are most susceptible. So, keep your plants well watered and well fed. Plant them only in appropriate light and soil.

Give plants enough space for good air circulation. This helps reduce the risk of disease. Some perennials take up a large amount of space. Plant according to the perennial's potential size, giving lots of space for future growth.

Water by hand or let water run from a hose at the base of a plant to saturate soil thoroughly. Use a sprinkler only as advised in this guide.

If you're watering with a sprinkler, water early in the day so that the foliage has a chance to dry off by evening. But ignore this advice if the soil around your plants is dry enough to stress them; plants that are wilting in the evening are showing signs of stress and should be watered immediately. Wilting in full sun may be either a reflection of high temperatures and winds or an indication of dry soil.

Remove dead or yellowing parts of plants immediately from the plant or soil. These often get infected by disease or infested by insects.

Get rid of all weeds. Many serve as host plants for insects that feed on plants and also carry deadly diseases.

Mulch encourages healthy root growth and induces a plentiful supply of soil microorganisms, which help provide the plant with valuable nutrients. Mulch also prevents disease organisms from splashing onto foliage during heavy rains.

Mulch is excellent food for worms as well. Worms keep the soil loose and airy by digging through it. They also fertilize the soil with their droppings or castings and with their bodies when they die. Their flesh is high in nitrogen, an essential plant food. One source estimates that worms produce 16 tons (just over 7 metric tons) of castings per acre (0.4 hectare) in healthy, cultivated soil.

Inspect plants frequently and carefully, checking the undersides of leaves closely. Pick off any insects by hand. Shake plants infested with large insects such as Japanese beetles over a white plastic garbage bag. Toss the insects into soapy water or vinegar. Spraying infested plants with water also acts as a partial control.

Invite birds into the garden by providing lots of nesting sites. Have birdhouses nearby and a birdbath right in the garden. Birds eat their full body weight in insects each day. They are voracious feeders and one of your best allies in the garden. Keep cats indoors unless you're trying to reduce the rabbit population in early spring.

Frogs, lizards, salamanders, snakes, spiders, and toads are also good friends to the organic gardener. If you place the birdbath right on the ground with the rim even with the surrounding soil, you will give wildlife a watering hole.

Don't buy predator insects advertised in gardening magazines. They are effective only as long as their

Recommended Products for Organic Control

Product	Use
Bacillus popilliae	Insecticide (grubs)
Bacillus thuringiensis (Bt)	Insecticide (caterpillars)
Baking soda	Fungicide
Copper	Fungicide/insecticide
Diatomaceous earth	Insecticide (slugs)
Horticultural oils	Fungicide/insecticide
Insecticidal soaps	Insecticide
Lime-sulfur (liquid form best)	Fungicide/insecticide
Neem products (Azadirachtin)	Fungicide/insecticide
Pyrethrum (Pyrethrin)	Insecticide
Rotenone (liquid form best)	Insecticide
Soap (flakes or dishwashing)	Insecticide
Sulfur (see Lime-sulfur)	Fungicide/insecticide
Wilt-Pruf® (or similar antitranspirants)	Antifungal properties

prey is present. The predator insects move on or die out quickly in most home gardens. Predator insects are fine for large, commercial growers working with vast fields or large greenhouses. However, protect and attract naturally occurring predator insects such as dragonflies and ladybugs by planting *Achillea* (Yarrow), *Anethum graveolens* (Dill), *Cosmos bipinnatus* (Cosmos), and *Tanacetum vulgare* (Tansy) in or near your garden.

Provide diversity in the garden—lots of different types of plants, including trees, shrubs, and grasses that offer areas for beneficial, predatory insects to survive. These feed on their destructive cousins and often are great allies to organic gardeners.

At the end of the season, when plants have turned brown, cut them back to the ground. Remove any mulch or debris from the bed. Dig the soil around the plants (not too close, to avoid damaging roots) to a depth of 6 to 8 inches (15 to 20 cm). This often exposes insects in various stages of maturation to birds and to winter cold.

Organic Control

Use *Bacillus thuringiensis* (Bt) to kill caterpillars and inchworms. Use Milky Spore Disease over a period of years to control grubs. Although organic, they should be handled with the same care as inorganic products. Follow label directions precisely.

Use organic traps for insects as long as they do not contain any sexual scent (pheromones). The latter often cause more problems than they solve by attracting unwanted insects into the garden. Organic traps are advertised in organic-oriented publications. You can also make inexpensive traps on your own to reduce costs. For example, cut up yellow antifreeze containers into thin strips. Paint them with oil, and hang them from plants attacked by whiteflies. The insects are attracted to the color and get stuck on the strips.

Some organic growers advocate a simple all-purpose spray for perennials that does little harm and lots of good. Every 3 days, they spray their plants with a solution of 1 tablespoon (15 ml) of liquid detergent or dish soap to 1 gallon (about 4 liters) of water.

Since detergents vary in their makeup, you should start with as little soap as possible and work up from there. An alternative is to mix 1 cup (about 240 ml) coconut or palm oil with 1 tablespoon (15 ml) soap, then use a little more than ¼ cup (about 60 ml) of this per gallon (about 4 liters) of water as a spray. The oil helps the soap adhere to foliage.

Organic alternatives exist for synthetic sprays. However, the word *organic* does not necessarily mean "safe." For example, just as some synthetics can kill bees, so can some organics. Organic alternatives vary from relatively nontoxic to highly toxic. In fact, some synthetic sprays are safer than some organic ones. Read and follow labels carefully. A few of the organic alternatives, such as some brands of rotenone, have synthetic compounds (piperonyl butoxide) added to make them more toxic.

Storage of organic materials can be extremely important to prevent deterioration of the substance. Buy fresh products, and store them appropriately.

Finally, wear a mask and appropriate clothing (especially rubber gloves) when working with organic pesticides, some of which can irritate the skin or mucous membranes. As added precaution, follow the tips outlined later in the chapter for using inorganic chemicals for spraying.

Inorganic Disease and Insect Prevention

You can greatly reduce the use of chemicals if you follow the foregoing advice on growing perennials organically. The most important tip of all is that healthy plants have the best chance of resisting both disease and insect infestation.

The second most important tip is that you want to catch the problem early, identify the specific problem, and, if necessary, use the appropriate chemical in response. It does little good to use an insecticide when dealing with spider mites. They are killed only with a miticide. When in doubt, place an infected plant part in a clear plastic bag, and take it to a local garden center or county extension office for advice; don't take the plant out of the bag at a nursery, where it could contaminate other plants.

When dealing with insects or disease, use the least toxic substance possible to take care of the problem. If you begin treatment early, this is usually effective. Once a problem has spread, you often need more potent chemicals.

The number of chemicals that you could use in the perennial garden is staggering. However, each year, some are taken off the market; therefore, we are reluctant to name specific chemicals. Your county extension office or garden center can help you and often has a reference manual for your use.

TIPS ON SPRAYING FOR PLANT PROTECTION

Spraying is the most effective and easiest way to apply chemicals to perennials. It is the only sure way to cover all stems and foliage, especially the undersides of leaves.

If you are going to use chemicals, regular preventive spraying of mild doses is preferred over heavier doses needed to control a problem.

If you prefer to spray only after a problem begins, you must use the appropriate chemical. To do this correctly, you must be able to identify diseases, insects, and spider mites. You may need a magnifying lens. Dealing with a problem should begin as soon as possible. The longer you wait, the more difficult the solution will be.

When dealing with a problem, begin with the least toxic substances. Work your way up to more powerful chemicals only as needed. You may need a variety of chemicals to care for a diverse garden.

Do not mix chemicals unless labels indicate that it is okay. Consider buying a chemical that serves more than one purpose. For instance, some products will kill many fungi, insects, and spider mites with one application.

Read labels carefully and completely, and follow the directions exactly. Using too much of a chemical can cause leaf burn. Formulas vary, and the same chemical may come in a wide variety of strengths. Labels may also indicate that the chemical will harm specific plants. Certain plants do not tolerate specific chemicals well. Keep notes on those that react badly to any particular one.

Saturate the soil with water before using any chemical sprays. Dry soil stresses plants, especially new growth. The latter will be damaged by sprays under dry conditions. Mix only the amount of spray needed. Use it up entirely on the plants. Never pour excess solution down a drain or on the ground.

Use a sprayer, such as Atomist brand, that produces a fine mist. Cover the entire plant with the mist, including the undersides of leaves and the soil at the base of the plant.

Spray early in the morning or evening on a calm day to prevent unwanted drift of the spray. If sprays can kill honeybees, spray in the evening after bee activity has stopped.

If possible, spray during cool and cloudy periods, not during hot and sunny portions of the day, since many chemicals will burn foliage at higher temperatures. During prolonged heat waves, spray in the evening when sun is not shining on foliage.

When a disease persists, maintain a regular schedule of spraying throughout the growing season. Frequency depends on the weather and amount of rain but is normally no less than once every 7 to 10 days. Prevent rather than try to control disease.

Add 3 drops of liquid detergent to every 10 gallons (38 liters) of a complete spray. It helps the spray stick to leaves and stems. Some sprays contain substances (spreader stickers) that make them adhere to leaves. Adding detergent to these is not necessary. Do not add detergent if the label advises against it.

Use systemic fungicides, ones absorbed by plant tissue, several hours before a rain. They will be extremely effective in preventing disease during wet or humid periods.

Spray after a rain to kill insects. They must touch or eat insecticides to be controlled. If it rains again shortly after spraying, reapply the spray, or use a systemic insecticide—one absorbed by the plant—which will then destroy insects that eat foliage or flowers. Systemics are effective, but quite dangerous.

TIPS ON THE SAFE USE OF CHEMICALS

Read labels carefully before using any chemical. The labels tell you which plants the chemical can be used on, how toxic a substance is, what to do in case of a problem, and often whom to call in an emergency. Follow all directions exactly.

Cover all of your skin with clothing. Wear long rubber gloves and goggles that completely protect your eyes from all sides. Use a respirator to prevent inhaling chemicals. The point: don't let chemicals touch your skin, don't breathe them in.

Use equipment that is working properly. Use water for a trial run: bad nozzles or leaky hoses will get your clothing wet. Fix old or buy new equipment.

Mix chemicals outdoors in a well-ventilated area. When mixing liquids be careful not to spill them.

If you accidentally spill a chemical on your skin, wash it off immediately. Use a detergent instead of soap. Read the label for further instructions. If in doubt, get to a doctor, and remember to take the container with you.

If you spill or spray any chemical on your clothing, stop and remove your clothing immediately. Wash it at once by itself using a detergent. Wash yourself off wherever wet clothing came in contact with your skin. Put on dry clothes.

Immediately after spraying, wash your gloves off in water with detergent before removing them. Have a bucket ready ahead of time. Then remove all clothing. Wash your entire body well, especially your hands and face. Also wash your clothing right away. Do not mix it with other clothing. Use plenty of detergent.

Wash your goggles in soapy water. Clean respirators according to directions on the label after each use.

Never eat or smoke while, or immediately after, spraying. First, change clothes and wash well.

Never spray plants whose flowers will be used for food.

Avoid getting chemicals in sandboxes, in pools, or on play equipment by spraying only when there is no wind. If any equipment does get contaminated, wash it off.

Protect pets and wildlife by moving food or water dishes indoors. Cover birdbaths if you'll be spraying near them.

Allow children and pets into a sprayed area only after the appropriate waiting period is over as indicated on the label.

Keep all chemicals in their original containers. They should be in a dry, dark place. The best place to keep chemicals is in a locked cabinet. All chemicals should be out of the reach of children.

Buy only the amount of chemicals needed for one season. This is sometimes hard to judge. If you have any left over, move them indoors (especially if liquids) during the winter. Keep them in a locked storage cabinet.

Get rid of chemical containers without charge at hazardous waste sites now available in most communities. Your local government will tell you where these are, as will the Environmental Protection Agency (EPA).

Marauders

Perennials are vulnerable to many animals. Here are a few tips.

Deer

Deer will eat many perennials and can destroy numerous plants in one night of grazing. They are also very fond of more mature plants of specific groups, such as Hostas.

A tall fence—10 feet (3 meters)—with an electric wire on top will generally keep deer out of an area, but they are capable of jumping even these. You may want to encircle the entire fence with a single strand of wire several feet (about a meter) away. Deer shy away from this double fencing. This is one of the most reliable methods for keeping deer out of a garden, but it is expensive and unsightly. For alternatives, still expensive, check on fencing and other products by contacting Deer-resistant Landscape Nursery, 3200 Sunstone Court, Clare, MI 48617, (989) 386-4955.

Various gardeners claim that the following, used religiously, prevent deer damage. Spread Milorganite (dried sewage) on the soil surface after every rain. It's available in bags at many nurseries as organic fertilizer. Soap flakes, human hair, and bright reflectors (very unsightly) are also recommended. Commercial repellents—Hinder is one example—claim to keep deer away as long as they are applied after every rain. **Tip:** Orchard owners vary the deer deterrent or repellent frequently for best results. Deer get used to the sight and smell of a particular repellent quite quickly.

Field Mice

Cut growth to the ground at season's end, and remove it from the garden. Clean the garden thoroughly.

Let the ground freeze before applying any winter protection. Otherwise, field mice will nest in it and use perennial roots and crowns as food throughout the winter.

Place poisoned baits underneath any form of winter protection for added insurance.

Gophers

Gopher refers to pocket gophers and ground squirrels. Pocket gophers and ground squirrels are most often a problem in developments near open areas or large fields. Pocket gophers feed on the crowns and roots of perennials. Ground squirrels are notorious for climbing stems and nibbling off flower buds.

The only reliable way to get rid of gophers is to shoot, trap, or poison them. We suggest trapping them because pets and wildlife can get into poisoned baits or pick up the bodies of poisoned rodents.

Moles, Shrews, and Voles

Moles and similar animals can be a problem since they eat roots and crowns of plants. The best way to control them is with traps specifically designed to kill them. Use traps in early spring before moles form colonies. Ask local nurseries or agricultural supply stores where to buy traps designed for mole control.

Rabbits

Baby rabbits are born early in the spring and enjoy feeding on the young shoots of many perennials. Stop rabbits from getting into gardens by surrounding the area with chicken wire. Or, if you have a cat, let it run loose at this time.

If you don't want a fence, either live-trap rabbits or grow plants that rabbits don't like: *Achillea* (Yarrow), *Aconitum* (Monkshood), *Aquilegia* (Columbine), *Artemisia* (Wormwood), *Astilbe* (False Spirea), *Baptisia* (False Indigo), *Campanula* (Bellflower—they will eat some of these), *Cimicifuga/ Actaea* (Bugbane), *Filipendula* (Meadowsweet), *Geranium* (Cranesbill), *Hemerocallis* (Daylily), *Iris* (Bearded and Siberian), *Narcissus* (Daffodil), *Nepeta* (Catmint), *Paeonia* (Peony), and *Salvia* (Sage). Rabbits, if hungry enough, will eat almost anything, but these plants are definitely the second choice if other more delectable ones are available.

Woodchucks

These furry creatures have an uncanny ability to nibble off the new growth of some of your finer perennials. They can do lots of damage quickly. You can catch them by baiting a live trap next to their holes. Woodchucks reproduce rapidly. Control them early in the season before they have a chance to reproduce.

CHAPTER 7

PROPAGATING
PERENNIALS

Propagation is the technical term for creating new plants from old ones. **Some of the plants listed in this book have patents or patents pending. It is illegal to propagate them without the permission of the patent holder.** There are two broad categories of propagation: sexual and asexual.

Sexual Propagation

Sexual propagation refers to growing plants from seed, which are created when male and female sex cells unite. This includes hybridization, but also such simple methods as letting mature plants form seed. The seeds drop to the ground and grow. The advantage of sexual propagation is that you can get many plants inexpensively. The disadvantages are that it may take quite a long time to get mature plants of certain perennials, and seed-grown plants do not always have characteristics identical to the parent plants. You'll find references to *mixes* and *strains* included in the varietal sections of Part I; these grow into mature plants with only slight variations from the parents.

Seed

Species (wild) perennials and most named varieties produce seed, which normally develops into plants similar to the parent. You can either collect or buy seed.

Buy seed from a reputable source. Some varieties listed in this guide need to be started from seed. Buy seed far enough in advance to start it well before the growing season. Store it in a dry, cool, and dark place.

Use a sterile growing medium when growing seeds. Your seedlings are likely to die if the medium is contaminated with disease-causing organisms. In general, peat, perlite, and vermiculite are completely sterile. While seeds of different perennials respond differently to these, most seeds grow well in a mix of these three substances.

Seeds may need special treatment to encourage them to germinate. Scratching or nicking the outside of a seed is called *scarification*. By opening the outer coating, you allow moisture into the seed. Some growers use sandpaper, a pin, or a file to make a crack in the outer surface.

Other seeds need to be moist-chilled before they will germinate. This process is called *stratification*. Generally, the home gardener puts the seeds into barely moist peat in a plastic bag or tray to be stored in the crisper of a refrigerator for a certain length of time, which can be several weeks to several months, depending on the plant being grown. In extreme cases, some growers place the tray in the freezer to shock the seed out of dormancy. This entire procedure is an artificial replacement for winter.

Some seeds need light to germinate; others don't.

Follow instructions on the package or in the individual sections of Part I in this regard.

Seeds are generally buried to a depth of two to three times the diameter of an individual seed if they do not require light for germination. If seeds need light to germinate, simply press them into the growing medium.

The growing medium must be kept evenly moist at all times. It should never be soggy. If it is allowed to dry out, the sprouting seeds will often die. When watering the medium, mist it lightly to keep it moist.

Most seeds germinate best in high humidity. The easiest way for the home gardener to provide this is to surround the pot or tray with plastic. Remove this covering regularly to check on the dampness of the growing medium. The plastic will keep moisture in the medium longer than if the pot or tray were exposed to air.

Most seeds benefit from bottom heat during germination. The ideal temperature for germination varies widely by the type of perennial. If high temperatures are necessary, place the pot or tray on heating cables, a heating pad, or a propagation mat. It is remarkable how often this induces germination in certain finicky seeds.

Watch for diseases such as damping off. Seedlings begin to topple over, their bottoms crimped and mushy. If damping off occurs, use a fungicide to control the disease (really several diseases), and cut back on watering. Have some fungicide on hand, since damping off spreads quickly.

Remove the plastic when the first seeds have begun to germinate. Provide light as indicated on the seed package or in the appropriate section of Part I. Keep the soil evenly moist but never soggy. Use appropriate fertilizers in just the right amounts; seedlings are often killed by improper feeding. Generally, low doses of water-soluble fertilizers are best.

Some seedlings produce one leaf (such as Irises), but most produce two. When seedlings have a second set of leaves (*true leaves*), dig them out of the medium, and pot them up in individual pots. This is called *pricking out.* Keep the seedlings under lights, and fertilize lightly with every watering.

Tip: some seedlings are difficult to prick out as individual plants. Sometimes it's much easier to scoop out a small group of seedlings and plant these as if they were one plant. Then let the strongest plant emerge. At that point, snip off the stems of the weaker plants with cuticle scissors.

After all danger of frost has past, move the seedlings outdoors into increasingly brighter light over a period of 14 days. This process of acclimation to light and temperature is called *hardening off.*

If you want plants to self seed in the garden: Allow flowers to form seed, remove all summer mulch and loosen the soil lightly around the plant, and avoid the use of herbicides and inorganic fertilizers in that area. Keep the area free of weeds through the following spring when seedlings will emerge. In spring, do not place mulch or use herbicides or fertilizer in the area where seedlings may sprout.

Asexual or Vegetative Propagation

Asexual propagation refers to the creation of young plants from the tissue of the parent plant. The big advantage of asexual, or vegetative, propagation is that the new plants will be identical to their parents. The main techniques are given here. Throughout Part I you'll find detailed information on this subject, but here are the basic techniques with appropriate steps outlined in a general way.

Basal Stem and Stem Tip Cuttings

Cutting off a portion of stem to create a new plant is successful with many perennials. Which perennials respond well to this method is indicated throughout Part I, as is the correct time to begin the process. The method is relatively straightforward:

With a sharp knife, cut off the tip of the plant above a set of leaves. The tip should have three sets of leaves.

Creating New Plants from Stem Cuttings

Cut a piece of stem containing at least three sets of leaves from the plant. Cut just above a set of leaves. On some plants, there will be just one leaf at a node rather than two, but we refer to both single and double leaves as a "set of leaves" throughout the book.

Cut the stem ¼ inch (6 mm) below a node, the place where leaves join the stem. Make this cut below the lowest set of leaves. Strip off all but the top set of leaves.

Dip the cut end in rooting hormone. Tap off any excess powder. Here are cuttings from three plants showing how different they may end up in length.

Place the cutting in moist rooting medium. Keep the medium consistently moist until the cutting takes root.

Then make a cut ¼ inch (6 mm) below the lowest leaf before stripping off the two lower sets of leaves.

Occasionally, taking a cutting that includes a small portion of the base (crown) of the plant early in the season is recommended for best results. We refer to this as a *basal cutting*.

Dip the end of the cutting in rooting hormone, and tap off any excess powder.

Make a hole in the rooting medium with a pencil (dibble), and place the cutting into the hole. Firm the medium around the cutting and keep it moist at all times.

Most perennials root more successfully in high humidity. Place three cedar or rot-resistant sticks or pieces of wire in the rooting medium around the edge of the pot. Then cover the entire pot with a clear plastic bag, making sure that the plastic doesn't touch the cuttings. Tie a piece of twine or place a large rubber band around the lower portion of the bag to keep it in place. The plastic keeps humidity high and increases the chances of the cuttings taking root. Remove the bag occasionally to check on the soil moisture. Moisten as necessary, never allowing the rooting medium to dry out. Consistently moist soil and high humidity are secrets to success with most cuttings.

Place the pot in indirect sun or under artificial light indoors. Heating cables outdoors or heating pads or propagation mats indoors can be helpful. Maintain soil temperatures between 70°F and 77°F (21°C to 25°C). When the cuttings begin to show new growth, they have begun to take root. Remove the plastic bag for longer periods each day to harden off the young plants. Keep the soil moist at all times. Tug gently on one of the plants. If it pops out of the soil, it has not formed a solid root system. If there is resistance, roots have begun to form. Rooting time varies greatly with the type of plant being propagated.

Root Cuttings

Some perennials have roots that produce new plants when cut into sections. There are two methods of getting roots for the final cuttings. The first is to dig up the entire plant, remove one or more roots, and then replant the mother plant immediately.

The second method is to dig a hole just on the edge of the mother plant's crown. This exposes some of the larger roots attached to the crown. Sever one or more of the roots from the mother plant with a sharp knife.

Whichever method you use to get the roots, cut them into sections. Plant these cuttings immediately in a moist growing medium.

Division

Many perennials form large clumps that are easy to divide into several plants. This is known as crown division. Dig up the entire clump with as many roots as possible. Sever the clump into several divisions with a sharp spade or knife. The easiest way to do this is to step down on the spade with your full weight. You may damage some new growth. Keep at least several eyes or shoots, the new growing tips that become stems, with each division. For most perennials, this procedure is best done in early spring, ideally when new growth is just starting. Plant the divisions

immediately as you would a bare root plant, and keep the soil moist at all times until they are growing vigorously. Some plants are tender enough to cut with a knife, while others are so tough you may need to use an ax instead of a spade.

Another type of division is possible with a perennials that produce plantlets to the side of the mother plant. These plantlets are commonly referred to as offsets, runners, or suckers. Offsets spring up right next to the mother plant. Runners appear at leaf nodes on the soil surface, while suckers grow from underground stems (stolons) off to the side of the mother plant. By cutting off these plantlets, you get an additional plant.

Use a spade to cut straight down next to the mother plant. Dig up the young plant, trying to keep as much soil around its base as possible. Sometimes the soil falls off. This is okay as long as you plant the plantlet immediately and give it lots of water.

The best time to do this is in early spring as soon as the ground can be worked.

Creating New Plants from Root Cuttings

Dig up a plant to expose its roots. Cut off one or more of the main roots, and replant the mother plant immediately.

Cut the root into 2- to 3-inch (5- to 7.5-cm) sections. Make a slanting cut at the bottom of each, and a horizontal cut at the top.

Place the cuttings slanted end down. If you're not sure which end is which, lay the cutting horizontally on the rooting medium. This photo shows the placement of new cuttings into the medium plus cuttings planted earlier already emerging.

Cover the cuttings. Keep them consistently moist until they begin to sprout.

CHAPTER 8

SPECIAL USES
FOR PERENNIALS

A number of perennials last well as cut flowers, can be dried, or can even be eaten. The tips in this chapter will prove helpful.

Cut Flowers and Foliage

Many varieties of perennials produce excellent cut flowers and foliage. Here are some points on using them for ornamental purposes.

Cutting the Flowers and Foliage

Carry a bucket of water into the garden with you.

Avoid picking flowers and foliage in full sun during the peak heat of the day.

The correct stage of maturity at which to cut flowers and foliage varies with each group. Suggestions are given throughout the guide. For instance, *Achillea* (Yarrow) should be almost completely open, while *Phlox* is best picked when about 50 percent of the flowers are open.

Remove only the amount of stem necessary for your arrangement. The more foliage you leave on the plant, the better. Harvest cut flowers and foliage from mature plants only.

Place the stems immediately into the bucket of water. The longer you delay, the greater the chance of air getting into the stem. If you do delay, recut the

Cut stems as indicated throughout the book. As in this photo, cut *Alchemilla* (Lady's Mantle) off at the base.

When cutting flowers, get them into water immediately. Carry a bucket with you for this reason.

stem just a little bit shorter while holding the stem underwater.

If air gets into the stem, it blocks water from going up the stem to the blossom. This will cause the blossom to droop.

Get flowers indoors and conditioned in the proper way as quickly as possible. If you cannot get them indoors right away, at least keep them in shade until you do.

Conditioning Flowers and Foliage

Preparing flowers or foliage for arranging and treating them in the best possible manner to get the longest life from them is called *conditioning*. Over the years, growers have learned tricks or secrets to get flowers and foliage to last longer once they've been cut. Throughout Part I, we mention the best technique for individual plants in the appropriate sections.

Arranging Flowers and Foliage

Creating beautiful floral arrangements is an art. Here are a few quick tips:

Choose containers or vases that will best match the form and colors of the flowers and foliage to be arranged. Containers must be heavy enough to hold up the flowers. Lead, stones, heavy copper pin holders (frogs), oasis (green foam material to hold stems in place), and wire netting with 2-inch (5-cm) holes are recommended to add weight to the bottom and to keep flowers in place.

Fill the container to an appropriate level with fresh water before arranging (generally three-quarters full). Once you have made the arrangement, top off the vase with water so that it is nearly full.

Before placing cut flowers and foliage in an arrangement, cut off an additional inch (2.5 cm) of the lower portion of stem while it's still underwater. Remove any foliage that would end up underwater in your arrangement, to prevent formation of bacteria. Hold your finger over the end of the cut stem as you transfer it to the container and into the oasis, netting, or frog.

Caring for Flowers and Foliage

Good floral preservatives, available at floral shops, will increase the life of cut flowers and foliage. Preservatives contain sugar (gives the flower energy), acidifiers (keeps the solution at the correct pH), respiration inhibitors (reduces food intake), and substances to kill microorganisms, such as fungi and bacteria. If a commercial preparation is not available, nondiet 7-Up soda makes a good substitute. Add 1 drop of liquid bleach to keep it sterile. Other home preservatives: mix 2 tablespoons (30 ml) lemon juice, 1 tablespoon (14 g) sugar, and ½ teaspoon (2.5 ml) bleach, in 1 quart (about a liter) of water. Or try mixing 2 tablespoons (30 ml, 28 g) each of vinegar and sugar per quart (about a liter) of water.

Add water and preservatives as necessary, generally changing the water every day if possible. Recutting stems each time you change water is an excellent idea in theory but totally impractical for many arrangements.

Finally, keep vases and wire netting sterile. Remove all water rings and stains inside vases each time they're used. Boil wire netting regularly. Also place containers and netting in 1 part bleach to 9 parts water for a half-hour to kill off any bacteria.

Dried Flowers, Foliage, and Seed Heads

Many perennials produce flowers, foliage, fronds, or seed heads and pods that are stunning in arrangements for their color, form, or texture.

Cutting the Flowers

Flowers for drying can be cut in many stages, varying from bud to full bloom. Flowers cut in the bud stage often last the best when dried, but there are many exceptions. Cut the stems of each perennial at the right stage of maturity as indicated throughout Part I. Remove all foliage unless that is what you're after. Foliage retards the drying process.

Drying

There are several methods of drying perennial flowers.

Air Drying

There are several ways of air drying plants. One is to hang stems upside down from wire nailed to the ceiling or from rafters in a garage or basement area. Drying flowers in an upright position is also possible and easiest if there is some way of keeping the flowers apart. One method is to tack hardware cloth across a support and then poke stems through it far enough apart so that air circulation is excellent. Hardware cloth is simply pliable galvanized wire with varying sizes of holes. You can find it in most hardware or building stores.

A few tips to remember when air drying: The faster the flowers dry, the better the coloration.

Flowers need lots of space for good air circulation. If mildew begins to develop, remove infected stems immediately to stop its spread.

You can control the shape of flowers by changing their position. For example, you might begin by hanging flowers upside down and then turn them upright to get a more natural look as they begin to dry completely.

Desiccants

A second method popular for drying is the use of silica gel. A good replacement desiccant for gel is Scoop Away cat litter. You can dry stems with flowers attached (remove all foliage) or cut individual flowers off stems.

Place them in gel for approximately 1 week according to instructions on the package. Generally, you place 1 inch (2.5 cm) of gel or cat litter in a box large, deep, and long enough to hold the stems or flowers. If you're drying individual flowers, insert a 4-inch (10-cm) piece of florist wire directly into the stem immediately after cutting it. Shape flowers to your taste by filling in the space with the desiccant. For an individual flower, face it up, and fill in with gel or litter. Form the petals exactly as you would like them to dry. If you've inserted a wire, bend it up to the side of the flower. Cover the stems or individual flowers completely with the desiccant. In most instances, you'll seal the box so that it is airtight. Do not expect to retain the full depth of color of the original flower. When removing the stems or individual flowers, be gentle. Shake out all desiccant. Brush off any drying material left on the petals with a soft brush.

If you inserted a wire into a flower for drying, you'll then connect it to a thicker wire, wrap the base with floral tape, and then insert the wire "stem" into an arrangement.

When working with silica gel or cat litter, always dry out the material when it begins to get moist by baking it in the oven.

Preserving

Whether you dry flowers in air, gel, or kitty litter, always spray them with a sealant when done. The sealant helps them retain their shape, stops the formation of mildew, kills off insect eggs, and makes breakage less of a problem, although dried flowers should always be handled with care. Ask florists about sealants currently on the market or use hairspray in a pinch. When spraying, cover all surfaces of the flower and stem. Gently apply an even coat in a well-ventilated area. Let the spray dry, and then repeat the process. Also, once you have arranged your flowers, spray the entire arrangement as well. It will help it stay in place. These sprays seem to make the flowers tougher, but don't overdo it. A gentle mist on all surfaces, not a soaking, is what's best.

One last method for preserving fronds, leaves, seed heads, and stems is the use of glycerin. When glycerin is called for, it's mentioned in the appropriate sections of Part I. You can purchase it at a drugstore. Mix 1 part glycerin with 3 parts warm water. When you place a stem into this mixture, the plant draws it into its tissue. Get the solution as far up the stem as possible for best absorption. Note that some people simply soak the entire leaf, stem, or frond in this solution. The result is a pliable plant part. Do not spray glycerin-treated parts with a sealant.

Perennials as Food

Some of the perennials listed in this guide are considered delicacies in a number of countries. *Hemerocallis* (Daylily) roots are prized in some Asian cultures. The sprouting heads of specific **Ferns** are now a gourmet's delight in specialty restaurants. *However, it is extremely important to keep in mind that the seeds, leaves, flowers, stem juices, and roots of many perennials are partially to highly toxic.*

CHAPTER 9

TOOLS AND SUPPLIES

Atomist This is the brand name of an excellent and expensive chemical spray applicator. These electric applicators produce a very fine mist. You can find sources for this product online. Less expensive applicators are sold in local nurseries and garden centers.

Bucket (pail) A large plastic bucket is helpful in many ways.

Dandelion digger or **Asparagus knife** Use them to remove weeds from the garden.

Edger This tool is used to cut deeply between lawns and garden beds. The kinds with rounded (crescent) blades work best.

Fencing (see p. 413)

Fertilizer *Inorganic:* 10-10-10, water soluble 20-20-20, and superphosphate. *Organic:* blood meal, bone meal, compost, cow manure, fish emulsion, horse manure (rotted), Milorganite, and rabbit pellets.

Fungicide You may need several fungicides to prevent or control the spread of diseases in the perennial garden.

Glasses (safety) Get the kind of safety glasses that cover your eyes completely. Wear them when mixing or spraying fertilizers and chemicals.

Gloves Get an assortment of cotton, leather, and rubber gloves for varied uses.

Grass clippers Clippers trim grass close to bed edges. They are also excellent for cutting back certain perennials at the end of the season or trimming off old flowers to encourage a second round of bloom.

Hedge trimmers The two-bladed hand type work well to cut down larger perennials at the end of the season. Keep the blades sharp to make work easier.

Herbicide We recommend herbicides only for bed preparation and selective use on perennial weeds. Roundup® and similar systemic herbicides are best because they destroy foliage and roots.

Hoe (pronged) This is the best tool for breaking the top surface of soil after walking on it or just before applying a mulch.

Hose Regular and soaker hoses are indispensable to perennial gardeners. Attach sprinklers to regular hoses to cover a wider area or water by hand to saturate the base of each plant.

Insecticide You may need several insecticides to prevent or control problems.

Knife A regular pocketknife comes in handy.

Mister If you plan to raise perennials from seed, get a mister to gently water the surface of the germination medium. The plastic ones are inexpensive, hold lots of water, and work well.

Miticide A chemical that kills spider mites, which may be a problem in hot, dry weather.

Peat Buy this in bales; the larger ones are the best value. Ask for acidic peat.

Pickax Very helpful in removing roots of small trees, digging up hard soil, and shearing sod off a lawn area being converted into a perennial bed.

Pitchfork This tool is very helpful in removing winter protection in early spring.

Potting table A special place to work is useful.

Pots You may need lots of different-sized pots.

Pro-Mix Many good soil-less mixes are available. This is one of the best. Its availability can be a problem in some areas. For information on this product and where to buy it, contact the following: Premier Horticulture, 127 Fifth Street, Suite 300, Quakertown, PA 18951, or Premier Horticulture, 1 Avenue Premier, Riviere du Loupe, Quebec G5R 6C1 Canada. They can also be reached by phone at (800) 667-5366.

Pruning shears (secateurs) Keep them sharp at all times. The bypass type (two crossing blades) are better than the anvil type.

Rake (garden and leaf) Heavy-duty metal garden rakes are excellent when you're leveling soil. Leaf rakes are essential for cleaning off the soil surface and gathering leaves in the fall.

Rototiller A machine with sharp, rotating blades that dig up and loosen soil easily. The kind with blades in front are less expensive but more difficult to use.

Roundup® (glyphosate) One of the safer herbicides on the market. It is effective on most annual and perennial weeds. For consumer information on Roundup®, call (800) 225-2883.

Scissors Good for cutting twine and removal of spent flowers on certain perennials.

Seeds Order these far in advance to make sure that the supplier doesn't run out before filling your request.

Seed-starting mix (germination medium) You can use peat, perlite, sand (sterile), soil (sterile), vermiculite, or a combination of these to start seeds. Alternatively, you can buy sterile seed-starting mixes such as Pro-Mix PGX and many others from local nurseries.

Sharpeners Most gardeners will have some sort of sharpener for pruning shears and a different type for larger tools. Sharpeners include various files, grindstones, hones, and sharpening stones. Most hardware stores sell sharpeners or have a professional tool sharpener on call to sharpen tools.

Shredder A leaf shredder is extremely helpful in making summer mulch for a perennial garden. If you don't have a shredder, a rotary lawn mower will also pulverize leaves quickly.

Siphon Mixer This gadget allows you to spray fertilizer on many plants at a time. Its use is explained in detail on the package. Check garden centers for it. If unavailable locally, go online, where many brands are advertised.

Spade A pointed spade is necessary for digging holes, dividing plants, and transplanting. A flat-edged spade is even better for dividing plants. Keep it sharp and clean. Some growers mix sand and oil in a box and dip the end of the spade in it after washing the spade off.

Spading fork Some gardeners prefer a spading fork to a spade.

Sprayer Sprayers are useful for killing weeds, insects, and diseases. They are also excellent for foliar feeding. Having several sprayers dedicated to specific purposes is recommended. There are numerous varieties of sprayers, but most gardeners get by with simple and readily available ones. Prices do vary, but reasonably priced ones are available locally or online.

Sprinklers These come in many models, from the oscillating kind, which covers a broad area, to little metal sprinklers with holes in them. The latter are made to cover circular, rectangular, and square areas.

Supports Larger perennials may need some sort of artificial support.

Tarp Either plastic or canvas is fine.

Ties Keep ties loose, and use a figure-eight knot for good, nonrestrictive support.

Traps These come in many types, from those that kill to those that capture animals without doing any harm whatsoever.

Trowel Get a solid one, not a cheap one. You'll be using it for years.

Wheelbarrow Get a good, solid wheelbarrow with a large, inflatable tire.

Wilt-Pruf® Wilt-Pruf® and similar products are antitranspirants, which help prevent cuttings and plants from drying out. You'll find them in most garden centers.

GLOSSARY

Accent plant A plant that stands out, usually because of its color, foliage, form, size, or texture.

Acid soil A soil with a pH less than 7.0. Most plants thrive in slightly acidic soils.

Adventitious Descriptive of vegetative buds that are in an unexpected place, as on roots of certain perennials.

Aeration Lots of oxygen in well-drained and properly composed soil.

Aerial bulb (bulbil) A small bulb produced above ground, often where leaves join stems.

Aerobic bacteria Bacteria that thrive in the presence of oxygen.

Alkaline soil Any soil with a pH above 7.0. Few plants do well in alkaline soil.

Amendment Any material added to the soil to improve its structure.

Anaerobic bacteria Bacteria that thrive without oxygen.

Annual A plant whose life cycle is complete in one year.

Anther (see **Flower**) The upper part of the stamen containing pollen in a flower. Part of the male organ.

Anthracnose A fungus disease that creates dead areas on leaves and stems.

Antitranspirant A spray applied to plants to prevent them from drying out.

Aphids Prevalent garden pest that sucks juices from plants and clusters on leaves and growing tips.

Apical dominance Hormonal influence that causes the terminal bud (top bud on a stem) to start growing before side (lateral) buds.

Asexual propagation Creating a new plant from a plant without seed.

Axil The point or angle at which a leaf joins a stem.

Bacillus thuringiensis (Bt) A biological control of caterpillars that is nontoxic to humans.

Bacteria Microscopic one-celled organisms that can be either beneficial or destructive to plants.

Bare root Plants sold without any soil around the roots.

Basal Refers to the lowest part of a plant.

Basal cutting A short portion of stem cut off close to the crown. Basal cuttings may include a small portion of tissue from the crown itself.

Bearded Having long hairs, as on the falls of Iris.

Bedding plant A flowering plant that is planted for color—usually in large groups in flower beds.

Biennial A plant that plays out its life over a 2-year period.

Blood meal An organic fertilizer with a high concentration of nitrogen (generally from 10 to 14 percent).

Bloom A flower.

Bone meal Bones pulverized into a fine powder used as a slow-release source of phosphorus.

Border plant A perennial placed along the edge of a garden.

Bottom heat Heat applied to the bottom of a bed or container to speed up germination of seeds or encourage root growth from cuttings.

Bract A leaflike plant portion, often colorful, simulating a flower.

Bud A protrusion on a crown or stem turning into a shoot, leaf, or flower.

Bulb A general term applied to the underground storage parts of many plants. Many parts are described as bulbs when they are really corms, rhizomes, tubers, or tuberous roots. True bulbs are made up of overlapping layers of scales similar to those of an onion.

Bulbil A small bulb produced above ground, often where a leaf joins the stem.

Bulblet A small bulb produced off to the side of an underground bulb.

Burning Damage to leaves caused by contact with chemicals at the wrong temperature or placement of immature plants in direct light before hardening off is complete. Leaves scorch and turn pale. Also refers to damage done to plants by placing overly strong fertilizer around seedlings or mature plants. The same effect can occur from salts in the soil.

Callus Healing growth over a plant wound.

Calyx (see **Flower**) The lower or outermost flower parts. Consists of sepals, not petals.

Casting Worm droppings extremely high in nitrogen.

Caterpillars Larvae of butterflies and moths, which feed on plant tissue.

Chlorophyll Green pigment in plant cells necessary for photosynthesis.

Chlorosis Lack of chlorophyll indicated by yellowing between veins of leaves.

Clay Very fine soil particles that adhere in moist conditions, causing poor drainage and compacted soil. It is important in limited quantities in good soil, since nutrients and moisture cling to it.

Climber Any plant that shoots out flexible branches that grow upward. Includes many vines.

Cold frame Any small structure built to protect plants from bad weather.

Cold hardiness The tolerance of a plant to cold.

Companion planting Placing plants together that bloom at the same time in pleasing color combinations. Or, combining plants with interesting form, color, and texture.

Compost Material produced by the collection and decomposition of organic wastes.

Corm A thickened, underground stem from which a plant grows. Corms store food in a single compartment. A new corm generally forms on top or to the sides of the old one each year.

Cotyledon The first leaf or leaves to appear from a seed during germination.

Cross-pollination The transfer of pollen (male sex cell) from one flower to the stigma (female part) of a different flower.

Crown The portion of a plant, usually at ground level, between the stem and roots.

Cultivar (cv.) An abbreviation for the term *cultivated variety.*

Cultivate To loosen soil to get rid of weeds and to make oxygen available to roots.

Cut flower A flower that remains beautiful after being cut from the plant. Used in flower arrangements.

Cutting Any portion of a plant that can be cut off and grown into a new plant.

Damping off Technically, a combination of fungal diseases that causes young seedlings to topple over at the base.

Deadheading Removing dead or spent flowers.

Decomposition The decay of organic material as it is digested by soil microorganisms into humus.

Defoliation Unnatural loss of foliage from improper pesticide use or poor growing conditions.

Desiccant Powdery material used to dry flowers.

Diatomaceous earth White powder consisting of skeletal remains of microscopic marine organisms called diatoms, used to retard or kill insects.

Dibble Any pointed instrument used to make a hole in soil for planting.

Dicot Plants that germinate into two little leaves opposite each other.

Diploid A plant with the normal number of chromosomes.

Direct seeding Planting seeds directly in the garden. Fine for a number of perennials that grow quickly.

Disbudding Removing flower buds around a main bud to increase its size.

Division A way of creating two or more plants from a parent plant whose crown and roots are cut into sections with a spade or knife.

Dormant Plants in an inactive period of growth (as in winter). Some perennials flower and then go dormant for a period in summer as well.

Double A flower with more than the normal number of petals.

Drainage The ability of water to move rapidly through a soil.

Drift A group of identical plants placed together to create a wave of color in the landscape.

Dwarf Any plant that grows much smaller than others of its same kind.

Edging plants Any low-growing plants placed along edges of lawns or borders.

Epigeal Refers to seeds that germinate quickly, especially in dealing with *Lilium* (Lily).

Established plant Any plant that has taken root and is growing well.

Eye A visible bud or growth point, as on a Peony. Also, the center of a bloom with different coloration from the petals.

False A term used in common names to distinguish the plant being described from one with the same Latin name. For example, False Spirea refers to *Astilbe*, not to the shrub with the Latin name *Spiraea*.

Family A grouping of plants by similarities.

Fan The name for a division in certain groups of plants, such as Bearded Iris.

Fertile A flower that can form seed.

Fertilization (1) The moment at which pollen enters the stigma (female organ) of a flower. With fertile plants it results in seeds. (2) The process of supplying plants with nutrients.

Fertilizer Any material that contains plant nutrients.

Fertilizer burn Damage or death to plants from the application of too much fertilizer.

Fibrous roots Root systems with a dense network of fine roots, rather than one single root.

Filament (see **Flower**)

Fish emulsion An organic fertilizer highly recommended for its valuable trace elements.

Flat Any shallow container used for starting seeds.

Flower The often colorful reproductive organ of seed-bearing plants (see illustration below).

Foliage Leaves.

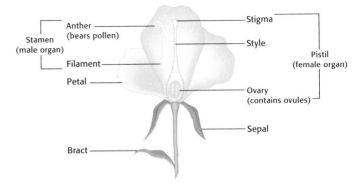

Foliar feeding Application of fertilizer directly to the leaves of plants.

Fragrance The scent or smell of a flower. Typically, it comes from oil evaporating from cells at the base of petals. Many perennials also exude a scent from their foliage.

Frond The stem and leaves of a Fern.

Fungi A group of plants without chlorophyll, which do both good (break down organic matter) and bad (cause disease) in the garden, depending upon the specific fungus involved.

Fungicide A pesticide that kills or controls fungi.

Genus (genera) A group of species with common characteristics. Each section in Part I of this guide covers a specific genus.

Germination Sprouting of seed into active growth.

Granule A particle of fertilizer or pesticide sometimes coated with a substance that breaks down in time.

Ground cover Any plant grown to stop erosion, control weed growth, or cover a wide area.

Habit (growing habit) The general shape or contour of a plant. Often refers to the way the plant appears and grows.

Half-hardy A plant that can tolerate some cold with limited protection.

Hardening off Adjusting plants to outside conditions gradually. Seedlings must be hardened off before setting out in the garden.

Hardiness The ability of a plant to withstand hot or cold temperatures.

Hardy A plant that can withstand cold in winter.

Heaving Lifting of plants from the ground caused by freezing and thawing of soil.

Heel A small portion of the crown taken with a basal cutting to induce faster growth.

Herbaceous plant Any plant that dies back to its crown in winter and regrows in spring.

Herbicide Any substance that kills plants (weeds).

Honeydew A sweet, sticky substance excreted from insects (primarily aphids).

Hormone powder A powder or liquid containing root-inducing chemicals.

Humus The end product of the breakdown of organic material in nature.

Hybrid Plants created by crossing plants with different genetic makeups.

Hypogeal Refers to seeds that are slow to germinate, especially when dealing with *Lilium* (Lily).

Inorganic Any chemical not made from animal or vegetable products.

Insecticidal soap Popular control for insects. Soaps can be either inorganic or organic, depending on active ingredients.

Insecticide A pesticide that kills insects.

Invasive A perennial that spreads so rapidly that it becomes a nuisance in the garden.

Landscape The surrounding terrain and its features.

Lanky Describes a plant that appears spindly or weak. Generally, caused by improper light exposure or over-feeding with nitrogen-rich fertilizer.

Larva (larvae) An immature insect, usually a caterpillar, grub, or worm of some sort, which damages plants badly by eating roots or foliage.

Leaf axil The point at which a leaf joins the stem. Buds that produce side branches are often located just above these.

Leaf burn Spotting on a leaf from high temperature or careless application of fertilizer.

Leaflet A small, divided part of an overall leaf.

Leaf mold Partially decayed leaves used as a soil amendment or mulch.

Leggy Excessively tall and weak stems, with few lower leaves—usually caused by poor light conditions or overcrowding in the garden. May also be caused by excessive fertilization with nitrogen-rich fertilizers.

Loam An ideal soil consisting of just the right amount of clay, sand, and silt with a high content of organic matter.

Macronutrient One of the essential nutrients for good plant growth, needed in large amounts.

Manure Animal waste used to improve soil structure and fertility. Not as fertile as most people think.

Mass Lots of the same plant, usually in the same color, planted together for a bold impression.

Microclimate Any area in your yard that is somewhat different in temperature, wind protection, soil, or water moisture.

Micronutrient (trace element) Plants need sixteen chemicals to do well. The ones needed in minute quantities are called micronutrients or trace elements.

Microorganisms Microscopic living creatures found by the billions in healthy soil. Essential for the breakdown of organic matter and the intake of nutrients by perennials.

Mildew A fungus that often produces a powdery substance on plants.

Milorganite Treated human sewage, which provides valuable nutrients to plants.

Miniature A plant selected for its small size.

Mist To shower plants with a fine and delicate spray of water. Essential for germinating seeds and starting plants from cuttings.

Mites Spiderlike creatures (not insects), which do both good and bad in the garden.

Miticide A pesticide that kills mites.

Mold Visible fungal growth on the surface of plant tissue. Color often indicates potential for damage.

Molluscide A pesticide that kills slugs and snails.

Monocot A plant that forms a single pointed leaf as it germinates.

Mosaic A viral disease that causes mottled leaves.

Mulch Any material used to cover the soil surface.

Naturalized A plant introduced from another area but thriving in its present home.

Nematode Microscopic worms. They can be either beneficial or destructive.

Nitrogen One of the essential plant foods. It must be supplied to perennials in appropriate amounts.

Node The bud on a stem from which a branch or leaf will emerge.

Nonselective herbicide A chemical that will kill all plants.

Offset Young bulb or plantlet that forms to the side of a mother bulb or plant.

Organic Of plant or animal origin.

Organic fertilizer Any fertilizer derived from a living or once-living organism. If an organic fertilizer is processed and concentrated, it becomes synthetic (urea is the best example).

Organic gardening A system of gardening using only natural or organic materials for fertilizing and pest control.

Organic matter Anything once living that is now dead and decomposing or decomposed.

Ovary (see **Flower**)

Ovule (see **Flower**) The portion of the ovary that becomes a seed when fertilized.

Parasite Any organism living off a host plant and causing damage.

Pathogen Something that causes a disease on a plant.

Pea stakes Thin branches placed in the ground around a plant to give it support.

Peat Partially decomposed organic matter from wetland areas used as a soil amendment.

Perennial A plant that lives 3 years or longer. Herbaceous perennials die back to the ground each fall, only to spring back to life the following year.

Perlite Light, fluffy expanded volcanic material used to aerate soil mixtures.

Pesticide Any poison that kills pests or diseases.

Petal A modified leaf that makes up part of the flower.

pH (potential Hydrogen) A scale measuring acidity–alkalinity on a range from 0 to 14. A pH of 7 is neutral. Most perennials thrive in soils with a pH running from 6 to 7.

Pheromone Sex attractant used to lure insects into traps.

Phosphorus A major nutrient required for good plant growth. Best placed in the soil at planting time directly below the plant's roots as it moves slowly through soil. Commonly provided by adding bone meal (organic) or superphosphate (inorganic) fertilizers to the planting hole.

Photosynthesis The process of using chlorophyll to produce food in plants.

Pinching (pinching back) Nipping off the end of growing tips or branches to increase bushiness and flower production.

Pinnae The leaves that make up a fern frond.

Pistil (see **Flower**) The female organ in a flower. It consists of the portion that receives the pollen (stigma), and a slender tube (style) running down to the ovary, which contains ovules that form seed when fertilized.

Ploidy A term describing the number of chromosomes found in a plant.

Pollen Fine grains in a seed plant containing male sex cells.

Pollination The transfer of male sex cells to the female organ of flowers to create seeds.

Postemergent herbicide A herbicide applied on growing plants.

Potassium An essential nutrient for perennials.

Predator An insect or mite that kills other insects or mites.

Preemergent herbicide A herbicide that stops seeds from sprouting.

Pricking out Carefully lifting out a seedling from the medium in which it was germinated and planting it in a different container.

Propagation Reproduction of plants from seed (sexual) or plant parts (asexual).

Pruning Cutting plants back to create more attractive, healthy, or productive plants.

Pubescent Downy, or covered with soft, hairlike growth.

Raceme An elongated cluster of flowers that normally begin blooming from the bottom up.

Recurved Petals bending backward. Describes a flower form.

Reflexed Petals bent backward or downward. Describes a flower form.

Respiration The ability of cells to produce energy using chemical processes.

Rhizome An underground stem that stores food while also producing buds forming new plants (as with Iris).

Root ball Roots and surrounding soil. Best kept intact when planting.

Root-bound The condition in which plants have outgrown their root space in a pot, creating a mass of roots in the shape of the container.

Rooting hormone A powder dusted on cuttings to stimulate root growth. May also be in liquid form.

Rooting medium Any material in which cuttings are placed to take root.

Roots The portion of the plant that extends underground from the crown.

Rosette A clump of leaves forming close to the ground.

Rossizing A method for inducing the formation of more plants from a single crown by making deep cuts into its tissue. The process is named after Henry Ross, who used the technique on Hostas.

Rototiller A machine that digs up soil with sharp, revolving blades.

Runner A plantlet emerging from the spot where a leaf node touches the soil surface.

Sand Large soil particles that cannot retain water or nutrients easily.

Scape Same as a flower stalk. Generally leafless.

Scarification Scratching or sanding tough seeds to break through their outer protective coating to make them germinate faster.

Seed An embryonic plant protected by a thin cover.

Seed leaves The first two leaves that appear as a seed sprouts. These are not true leaves.

Seedling A young plant just started from seed. Plants are very vulnerable at this stage.

Self-pollination The transfer of pollen (male sex cell) to the stigma (female part) in the same flower.

Sepal One portion of a calyx, the outer protective covering of the flower. It is usually green in most perennials but occasionally is colored to mimic petals.

Shade plant A plant that prefers or tolerates shade.

Shoot New growth emerging from the crown in spring. Shoots become stems.

Shrub Any woody plant with numerous stems coming up from its base. A few perennials, such as *Baptisia australis* (Blue Indigo) resemble shrubs.

Silt Soil particles larger than clay but smaller than sand.

Soil A mixture of chemicals, inorganic particles, water, air, organic matter, and millions of living plants and animals. It is best to think of soil as a living creature, not an inanimate object.

Soil amendment Anything added to the soil to create better tilth or texture. May also enrich the soil with mild amounts of nutrients.

Soil test An analysis of the soil pH, structure, and nutrient levels.

Species Plants occurring naturally in the wild and capable of interbreeding. A species is a subdivision of a genus.

Sphagnum moss A bog moss used for starting seeds (if screened) and to propagate perennials by air layering. Sphagnum moss has been associated with a rare fungal disease, so wear gloves and a mask when working with it. It is *not* sphagnum peat moss.

Spore A minute cell that acts as a reproductive body for Ferns and fungi.

Sporophytes Ferns in the very early stage of development.

Stalk The part of the plant that supports leaves and flowers.

Staking Artificially supporting a plant for better growth.

Stamen (see **Flower**) The male part of a flower, consisting of a slender, stemlike growth (filament) with a pollen sac (anther) at the tip.

Starter solution Fertilizer in highly diluted form used to boost the growth of young plants.

Stem The main aboveground portion of a plant.

Stem cutting A piece of stem rooted in an appropriate medium to create a new plant.

Sterile (1) Not capable of producing seed. (2) Condition of a pot or tool that has been treated so that it is free of any disease-causing organisms (usually cleaned, then soaked in 1 part bleach to 9 parts water).

Sterile soil Soil treated with high heat or chemicals to kill off pathogens and weed seeds.

Stigma (see **Flower**)

Stolon A branch growing on or below the soil surface. It often forms one or more plantlets from its leaf nodes.

Stoloniferous A plant that shoots out many branches on or below the soil surface to form a colony of plants.

Strain Seed produced plants very similar, but not necessarily identical, to their parents.

Stratification Storing seeds in cool temperatures to fool them into believing that they've passed through a winter. This overcomes their dormancy.

Style (see **Flower**) The tubelike structure that connects the top portion of the female flower (stigma) to the lower area (ovary). The male sex cells (pollen) grow down this tube to fertilize the flower.

Subspecies (ssp.) Naturally occurring variant of a species from a specific geographic area.

Sucker Plantlet that forms off to the side of a mother plant from an underground branch (stolon).

Sun scorch Burning of leaves caused by moving young plants too quickly into the sun or by placing shade-loving plants in full sun.

Superphosphate An inorganic fertilizer that is high in phosphorus.

Synthetic Man-made, as opposed to organic.

Systemic A type of herbicide or pesticide absorbed by a plant (it can't get washed off by rain, since it becomes a part of the living organism).

Taproot The main root descending downward in the soil. A taproot often has other roots shooting off to the side. Not all plants have a main root.

Tender plant Any plant killed off or harmed by cold weather.

Tendril A slender part of a vining plant that winds itself around supports, as with *Clematis.*

Terminal The end point of a stem or branch.

Tetraploid A plant with double the number of chromosomes. Some plants occur naturally as tetraploids. Tetraploids can also be created by the controlled use of chemicals.

Topsoil The fertile upper portion of soil. The critical area for plant growth.

Trace element (micronutrient) A chemical used by plants in minute quantities.

Transpiration Water movement from leaves to the air. Plants cool themselves in this process.

Transplant To move a growing plant from one area to another.

Transplant solution Mild liquid fertilizer used on seedlings to help them survive the ordeal of transplanting. Synonymous with starter solution.

True from seed Plants that when started from seed are identical to their parent plants.

True leaves The second set of leaves produced after the seed leaves appear. Once true leaves develop, a plant can be transplanted.

True to type (see **True from seed**)

Tuber Fleshy underground stem that produces shoots from eyes. Tubers multiply and can be divided regularly to produce new plants as long as each cut portion of tuber has an eye for new growth.

Turgid Firm versus limp.

Variegated Varied colors in foliage. May appear as bands, blotches, spots, stripes, and other forms.

Variety (var.) Technically, any plant that occurs naturally in the wild as a variation from the original parent plant (species).

Vegetative propagation Propagating plants using any part of a plant except seeds.

Vein Portions of a leaf that define its structure and carry food and water.

Vermiculite Mica heated until it pops. Used for starting seed and cuttings.

Verticillium wilt A fungal disease that causes plants to droop over and die. Affected plants must be dug up and destroyed. The soil often is contaminated as well.

Viable Refers to seed that will germinate. Seed viability varies by plant, age, and how the seed is stored (best kept dry, cool, and dark).

Vine A plant requiring a support to grow upward.

Virus A disease-causing organism that can be seen only with an electron microscope.

Weed Any plant growing where you don't want it to.

Wilting Hanging limply, from water loss or disease. Wilting is usually a sign of trouble.

Windbreak Anything that provides protection from the wind.

ABOUT THE AUTHORS

Mike Heger, co-owner of Ambergate Gardens with his wife Jean for the past 25 years, is one of the country's leading experts on growing perennials in cold climates. Each year, he grows and sells more than two thousand varieties of perennials. He was hired as a young man by the late Leon Snyder to work at the Minnesota Landscape Arboretum, where he spent fifteen years learning about every aspect of growing perennials. Snyder and Francis de Vos were his mentors, teaching him much of what he knows about the selection, care, and propagation of perennials. Heger has served on the board of the American Daffodil Society, the American Hosta Society, the North American Lily Society, and the Perennial Plant Association. He presently serves on several committees of the Minnesota Nursery and Landscape Association. He is also a lecturer and award-winning writer. He wrote a series of articles for what is now the *Northern Gardener* magazine and has written for the *American Daffodil Journal*, the *Quarterly Bulletin of the North American Lily Society*, the *Journal of the American Hosta Society*, and the *Daylily Journal of the American Hemerocallis Society*. He has been honored with the Award of Merit from the Minnesota State Horticultural Society. He has learned what he knows from hands-on experience with plants.

Debbie Lonnee has worked in the nursery industry for more than 30 years, after receiving a B.S. in Horticulture from the University of Minnesota. She works in the wholesale nursery industry at Bailey Nurseries, Inc., in Newport, Minnesota. She is currently the manager of the Planning and Administrative department. Among her many responsibilities, she oversees new plant acquisitions and field trials and is expert on which plants are superior and do well in cold climates. She travels the United States and Europe seeking new plants to sell. She is a prolific garden writer and the horticultural editor for *Northern Gardener* magazine (the magazine of the Minnesota State Horticultural Society). She writes a 'Plant to Pick' article for each edition. She also lectures extensively in Minnesota and across the country to professional nursery groups, master gardener groups, and garden clubs. She is currently serving on the Board of Directors of the Minnesota Nursery and Landscape Association and chairs its Publications committee. Gardening is her passion and she has a collector's garden full of new varieties and plants undergoing field testing.

John Whitman has been writing nonfiction books for more than 45 years. He is an avid gardener with more than fifty years of gardening experience. Early in his career he was a grower at Bachman's, the largest retail florist and nursery in the United States. As with Mike Heger, all of his gardening knowledge comes from hands-on experience. His book *Starting From Scratch: A Guide to Indoor Gardening* was chosen as a main selection of the Organic Gardening Book Club and an alternate selection of the Book-of-the-Month Club. He was one of seven contributing writers to the *Better Homes and Gardens New Garden Book* and the sole writer of the *Better Homes and Gardens New Houseplants Book.* He is co-author of the award-winning *Growing Roses in Cold Climates* and the well-known *Growing Shrubs and Small Trees in Cold Climates.* For the past twenty-five years he and his wife, Donna, have been growing and field-testing many of the perennials listed in this guide.